INSTRUCTIONAL STRATEGIES

FOR SECONDARY SCHOOL PHYSICAL EDUCATION

SECOND EDITION

INSTRUCTIONAL STRATEGIES

FOR SECONDARY SCHOOL PHYSICAL EDUCATION

JOYCE M. HARRISON
Brigham Young University

CONNIE L. BLAKEMORE
Brigham Young University

Wm. C. Brown Publishers
Dubuque, Iowa

Consulting Editor Aileene Lockhart

Cover design by Jeanne Marie Regan.

The credits section for this book begins on page 582, and is considered an extension of the copyright page.

Library of Congress Catalog Card Number: 87-072271

ISBN 0-697-07285-1

Printed in the United States of America by Wm. C. Brown Publishers 2460 Kerper Boulevard, Dubuque, IA 52001

10 9 8 7 6 5 4 3 2 1

contents

preface

The purpose of this book is to help teachers and prospective teachers acquire the skills necessary to design and implement effective instructional programs in secondary school physical education, including middle schools and junior and senior high schools. Effective programs require both effective instruction and a balanced curriculum. Either one without the other results in failure to educate students physically. Therefore, prospective teachers need to be instructed in both aspects of the physical education program included in this book—curriculum and instruction.

In the past, curriculum theory and design have been delayed until graduate school. However, since many beginning teachers are involved in curriculum development, an attempt has been made in the text to integrate the process of curriculum design with that of designing instruction. The curriculum chapters relate specifically to the entry-level teacher and can be taught most effectively by forming curriculum committees of three to five students and actually designing a curriculum.

This second edition is more closely tied to current research in education and physical education, with more references given for further study if desired. It has also been reorganized into a more cohesive format. Units 1 and 2 have been completely rewritten to incorporate research on education, the teacher, the learner, and learning. New information has been added to unit 3, incorporating suggestions for learning activities in each of the three domains. The remainder of the text has been extensively updated.

Unit 1 provides an introduction to the educational and teaching environment. Unit 2 presents the theory essential to understanding the learning process and the characteristics of the learners, with implications for teaching physical education. This is followed in unit 3 by a presentation of the decisions that occur prior to instruction. Procedures for planning, implementing, and evaluating instruction are presented in unit 4. Unit 5 takes the prospective teacher through the process of curriculum design and evaluation of the instructional program.

This book follows the progression usually followed in teaching undergraduate physical education majors. That is, it assumes that lesson and unit planning and basic instructional skills are prerequisite to understanding the curriculum. Students should apply the principles taught by actually writing lessons and units and designing a curriculum as suggested in the various units of the text. In this way the entire process will be more meaningful to the learner.

The book is divided in such a way that portions of it can be used in several classes. For example, unit 1 can be used in an introductory class; units 2, 3, and 4 in a class on methods of teaching physical education; and units 1, 2, and 5 to teach a separate unit on the curriculum. The entire text can also be used in one traditional methods course.

This text is different in its approach in that it ties together all three of the learning domains—cognitive, psychomotor, and affective—as a basis for the design and implementation of instructional strategies. In addition to the background theory, a large number of practical applications and examples are provided. The recent emphasis by the American Alliance for Health, Physical Education, Recreation and Dance on teaching students the conceptual background of physical education requires that prospective teachers understand the cognitive domain and strategies for teaching intellectual skills. The development of positive student feelings toward physical education is the key to continued participation by students in physical activities outside of the school. Teaching traits such as fair play and teamwork are also essential. Therefore, the affective domain should also be studied.

The text includes a number of learning aids to help students focus on the concepts presented. Study stimulators at the beginning of each chapter introduce the main ideas of the chapter in a question format. A step-by-step approach helps students apply what is learned to actual school situations. Questions and suggested activities provide further review and expansion of learning. For more in-depth study of a topic, the student is directed to a number of suggested readings.

The book includes numerous practical examples in the areas of performance objectives, evaluation, preassessment, learning strategies, motivation, discipline, and classroom management.

Although the text is written on an undergraduate level, it can be used at the graduate level as well by supplementing the text with the suggested activities and readings at the end of each chapter. Graduate students can actually form committees and design a resource unit and a school curriculum.

Acknowledgments

This text became a reality only through the encouragement and cooperation of many individuals, including students, colleagues, and friends. We wish to thank Elmo Roundy, associate dean of the Brigham Young University College of Physical Education; Boyd Jarman, department chair of the Department of Physical Education—Sports; Dwayne Belt, of the BYU Department of Secondary Education; Marilyn Harding, Springville Junior High School, Springville, Utah; and many other colleagues for their support and encouragement throughout the development of the text. A special thanks goes to Berne and Miriam Broadbent for the many hours of borrowed time on the word processor and to Cheryl Skousen and Lisa Boyack for typing many of the figures and tables. We also wish to thank those authors and publishers who generously consented to have their work reproduced or quoted, and the reviewers who offered such valuable feedback (they include: Tom Evaul, Temple University; P. J. Powers, University of Montana; Cecilia Martin, Colorado State University; Sue Whiddon, University of Florida; Nancy Rickert Colton, Montana State University; and Thomas W. Steele, SUNY–Cortland.

INSTRUCTIONAL STRATEGIES

FOR SECONDARY SCHOOL PHYSICAL EDUCATION

Viewing the World of Teaching

The educational system in which teachers of physical education operate is three-sided. The system can be envisioned as an equilateral triangle as shown in unit figure 1.1. Its apexes represent: (1) the teacher, (2) the subject, and (3) the environment. The triangle would be incomplete without any one of the sides. Any two sides are dependent on the third to form a perfect and complete triangular shape. Any of the sides could be interchanged. Packed within these walls are the essentials of education. Included therein, would be the ability to

1. Use language, to think, and to communicate effectively.
2. Use mathematical knowledge and methods to solve problems.
3. Reason logically.
4. Use abstractions and symbols with power and ease.
5. Apply and to understand scientific knowledge and methods.
6. Make use of technology and to understand its limitations.
7. Express oneself through the arts and to understand the artistic expressions of others.
8. Understand other languages and cultures.
9. Understand spatial relationships.
10. Apply knowledge about health, nutrition, and physical activity.
11. Acquire the capacity to meet unexpected challenges.
12. Make informed value judgments.
13. Recognize and to use one's full learning potential.
14. Prepare to go on learning for a lifetime.[1]

Unit 1 introduces you to the components of the educational system in which teachers function. Since physical education is a means toward the total education of the student, physical educators must be educators first and physical educators second.

The role and status of education in a democratic society is the focus of chapter 1. Past and present purposes, as well as the future direction of education, are reviewed.

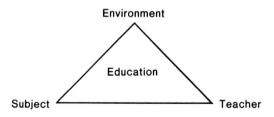

Unit Figure 1.1 The educational system.

Chapter 2 stresses the importance of physical education in the curriculum of the school. The purposes of physical education are presented looking at the past, present, and future with the intent of structuring a foundation for building a philosophy.

In chapter 3 the guidelines for becoming an effective teacher are introduced. The realities of the day-to-day existence within the school are presented, along with coping strategies for the teacher.

References

1. Organizations for the Essentials of Education, "The Essentials of Education: A Call for Dialogue and Action" (Urbana, Illinois: Organizations for the Essentials of Education, n.d.).

Understanding the Role of Education

Study Stimulators

1. Is education synonymous with schooling?
2. What similarities exist among the various sets of educational goals? Why might goals be different in the future?
3. Have the purposes of education expressed in the past, present, and for the future remained the same?
4. Does the crisis in education predict its death or its rebirth?
5. How should education be different in the future?
6. What has been the impact of educational reform?

> Nothing matters more—nothing. Education is the public enterprise in our country that is closest to people's hearts and most important to their lives. And education is the enterprise that is crucial to success in everything we attempt as a nation.
>
> Governor James B. Hunt, Jr.
> to the Task Force on Education for
> Economic Growth[1]

Have you ever stopped to ponder the question what is education? As a high-school or college graduate, do you feel "educated"? Do you think you will ever be truly educated?

Webster's New Collegiate Dictionary defines *educate* as "to provide schooling for."[2] How does this definition compare with your own definition of education? Do you think that education always results from, or even develops most efficiently, through formal schooling?

Someone once said, "Don't let your schooling interfere with your education." Consider the classroom in which the students were interested in an exhibit of frogs, only to be told, "Come and sit down. We're going to have science now!" A student might listen to the driver education teacher talk about how to change a tire when the previous weekend she had rotated all five tires on the family car or be asked to jog two laps of the track during physical education class when the night before he had run five miles preparing for an upcoming race.

Aristotle said, "All men by nature desire to know." Coming to "know" might take place in the formal classroom, but just as likely it will transpire in the natural setting. Historically, education occurred in the home, on the farm, or in the artisan's shop. Even today, much learning occurs on the job, in the home, or by way of the media. *Education is a process of learning, not a place.*

Today's advanced technological society demands continuous learning for effective living and working. Before the turn of the twentieth century, Spencer declared that the function of education is to prepare for complete living.[3] The educational process and its purposes must adapt to changes in society in order to prepare citizens to function in an effective way.

The educational process must adapt to the
changes in society.

Krajewski illustrated how education must adapt its purposes to changes in society with
the following story:

> This is a story of civilization of some thousands of years ago. The people lived in the
> warm lands, covered by streams fed by glaciers far to the north. They supported
> themselves by spearing fish and by trapping tigers.
>   The glaciers moved south. The lands became cold. The tigers left and sediment
> from the glaciers choked the rivers. Still, the people remained.
>   Before the advent of the cold weather the people had prospered and in their
> prosperity they felt that they should embellish their society and they set up a school
> system. In that school system, quite logically, they taught the spearing of fish and the
> trapping of tigers. Then the cold came and the fish left and the tigers left. The people
> of this area now survived by snaring eel and hunting bear. And they prospered again.
> They went back to examine their school system. They asked the headmaster what he
> taught. And he said, 'I teach spearing fish and trapping tigers.' And they said, 'Well, do
> you not teach snaring eels and hunting bears?' He said, 'Well, of course, if you want a
> technological education; but for a well-rounded education I prefer the classics.'[4]

The Purposes of Education

The educational process should reflect what the people in a given society think, feel, believe,
and do. In general, the purposes of education in any society include one or more of the following:

1. To preserve and maintain the desirable aspects of the society or culture by
   transmitting them to the young.

2. To teach the skills and competencies needed to function effectively as an adult member of society, both socially and vocationally.
3. To help the individual function within society to the fullest extent possible, both currently and in the future, through intelligent self-direction, group deliberation, and action.
4. To teach the individual to constructively evaluate societal issues and to influence the social order by contributing to ordered, purposeful change.

The purposes of education remain constant even though society, in which the educational structure operates, is an institution of change. As change occurs, the educational process adapts to meet the needs of society. Historically, the American society has been a role model for the rest of the world and its purposes of education have been unique.

A Historical Perspective of the Purposes of Education in America

Horace Mann, accorded the title of Father of American Education, wrote, "The public school system that evolved in Massachusetts had no precedent in world history."[5] As Vayhinger[6] pointed out, education in America has been built on the foundation of universal education for all. Such roots go back to Puritan beliefs and practices in early New England settlements. Compulsory, yet free, comprehensive education for twelve years is extended to all students. Over sixteen thousand school districts operate without centralized federal direction or control. Even though today the federal government contributes 8 percent of the current operating budgets of schools across the nation, the individual states retain control of their systems.

In 1751, Benjamin Franklin proposed the creation of academies designed to provide for teaching not only the basics, but significantly widening the program. He proposed the inclusion of "Those things useful as well as those ornamental."[7] This expanded view of education never excluded the premise that learning is power. Indeed, America has become a powerful republic, and as Vayhinger stated, "Our education system has been a prime factor in the development of whatever greatness our society has, especially in terms of the freedom and the value of the individual."[8]

The schools have been a part of virtually every social change in recent American history.[9] During the 1930s, America adjusted to the depression. During the fifties, society and its schools adapted to the population explosion, and as the "baby boomers" and their children moved through the schools, the effects were felt into the eighties. The fifties also felt the reverberation of the Soviet Union's launching of Sputnik, and the schools responded by shaping a scientific and technological curriculum. In the sixties, the schools echoed society's cry to solve the problems of racism, poverty, and other issues. The seventies found schools making further adjustments as enrollment declined and birth control became an issue. The women's movement had an impact on education as many bright women, previously trained in education, prepared for employment in other fields. The 1980s brought renewed cries of "crisis in education."

As the American educational system has attempted to adjust to the social changes throughout history, a number of specific educational goals for secondary education have emerged. These are summarized in table 1.1.

Table 1.1 A perspective of the national goals of education

Cardinal Principles [1918]	Educational Policies Commission [1938–44]	Imperatives of Education [1964]
	Aims	
	Self-realization	
	Human relationship	
	Economic efficiency	
	Civic responsibility	
	Eleven imperative needs of youth	
Health (physical fitness)	Good health and physical fitness.	Deal constructively with psychological tensions.
Command of fundamental processes	Think rationally, express thoughts clearly, read and listen with understanding.	
Vocation	Develop salable skills.	Prepare for world of work.
Civic education	Understand the rights and duties of a citizen.	Keep democracy working.
	Develop respect for others, live and work cooperatively with others.	Work with other peoples of the world for human betterment.
Worthy home membership	Understand the significance of the family.	
Worthy use of leisure	Use leisure time well.	Make the best use of leisure time.
Ethical character	Develop ethical values and principles.	Strengthen the moral fabric of society.
	Know how to purchase and use goods and services intelligently.	Make intelligent use of natural resources.
	Develop capacities and appreciate beauty in literature, art, music, and nature.	
	Understand the influences of science on human life.	Discover and nurture creative talent.
		Make urban life rewarding and satisfying.

Table 1.1 (Continued)

National Goals [1973]	Seven New Cardinal Principles [1978]	Four Essential Goals for High Schools [1983]
Adjustment to change (mental health.)	Personal competence and development.	Develop critical thinking.
Communication skills.	Skilled decision making	Prepare students for further education.
Computation skills.		
Critical thinking.		Increase students' career options.
Occupational competence.		
Responsibility for citizenship.	Civic interest and participation.	Build a spirit of community service.
*Respect for law and authority.	Global human concern.	
*Appreciation of others.	Family cohesiveness.	
*Clarification of values.	Moral responsibility and ethical action.	
Clear perception of nature and environment.	Respect for the environment.	
Economic understanding.		
*Appreciation of the achievements of individuals.		
*Knowledge of self.		

* = Process goals

In 1913, the National Education Association (NEA) appointed a committee known as the Commission on the Reorganization of Secondary Education to develop fundamental principles through which the responsibilities of education for democracy could be met. After five years of work, one of the most influential documents in education emerged. It was based on the philosophy that the purposes of secondary education should be determined by the needs of society, the characteristics of adolescents, and a knowledge of the best available educational theory and practice. The worth of each subject area was to be evaluated on the basis of its ability to contribute to the attainment of the seven "cardinal principles" of education shown in table 1.1.[10]

In 1935, the NEA created an Educational Policies Commission to resolve the problems created in education by the Great Depression. The commission produced two reports. The first, in 1938, resulted in a set of four comprehensive educational aims as follows: (1) self-realization, (2) human relationship, (3) economic efficiency, and (4) civic responsibility.[11] The second, in 1944, listed the eleven "imperative needs of youth" that further clarified these aims[12] (refer to table 1.1). Following World War II, the commission reacted to an obvious lack of implementation of these aims in the schools by producing a set of three volumes describing an ideal educational system in each of two supposedly typical settings—Farmville and American City.

In 1964, the American Association of School Administrators appointed its own commission to identify the imperatives of education. This commission identified the nine imperatives shown in table 1.1.[13] These two lists were later combined into one list of fifteen needs of youth for the eighties by the Institute for Educational Management at United States International University at San Diego, California.[14]

In 1973, the Commission on the Reform of Secondary Education drew up a new set of goals for secondary education. It consisted of seven content goals and six process goals (specific outcomes for the individual).[15] In 1978, Gross proposed seven new cardinal principles of education to make the original list more relevant to today's world.[16]

A deterioration in the quality of education in America was documented by several reports released in the eighties beginning with *A Nation at Risk,* in 1983.[17] From this atmosphere emerged the Carnegie report on secondary education in America and "Four Essential Goals" for high schools.[18]

A quick glance at table 1.1 shows many similarities in the goals of education from 1918 to 1983. All of the original seven cardinal principles have been reemphasized in at least two of the other five sets of goals. The major additions have been in the areas of respect for the environment, appreciation of beauty and achievement, economic understanding, and the personal responsibility of the individual.

The Current Purposes of Education

Currently, the educational system in America is under attack, and the purposes of education are being critically examined to determine outcomes. At the present time, the schools are attempting to hear the cries of "crisis in education" and effect changes to strengthen the foundations of the educational system. "Reports of dissatisfaction with the public educational system have been common throughout United States history. . .and claims about the nature and severity of deficits throughout history parallel those being made today."[19] However, between 1983 and 1985 more than a dozen reports critical of current education practices found their way into print. As Boyer pointed out, "Education is in the headlines once again. After years of shameful neglect, educators and politicians have taken the pulse of the public school and found it faint."[20]

The National Commission on Excellence in Education issued its report, *A Nation at Risk,* in April of 1983.[21] Soon to follow were the most influential reports including, *Action for Excellence* produced by the Task Force on Education for Economic Growth,[22] *The Paideia Program*[23] from Mortimer J. Adler and his colleagues, *High School*[24] written by Ernest Boyer but coming from the Carnegie Foundation, and *A Place Called School*[25] by John Goodlad. The Committee for Economic Development published a report in 1985, *Investing in Our Children.*[26] From *A Nation at Risk* came the spine-tingling declaration that "the educational foundations of our society are presently being eroded by a rising tide of mediocrity that threatens our very future as a nation and a people."[27] Boyer and Goodlad were, in general, less harsh on the schools. Even though the Twentieth Century Fund Task Force[28] reported that "the crisis in American education is greatly exaggerated," it also proclaimed that American education had problems. All of the reports made recommendations to correct the shortcomings of the schools. Some of the more important recommendations of the reports included the following:

1. The schools must stress science and math and move away from the "frills."
2. The teaching profession must be strengthened. The quality, pay, and autonomy of teachers needs to be improved, and teacher education programs must be bolstered.
3. The school curriculum should be more related to the job market and to perceived needs of industry (including computer literacy).

4. Foreign-language instruction should be started in the elementary schools and should generally receive a high priority.
5. Students should spend more time in school, and their time should be used more effectively for instructional purposes.[29]

The concern about American schools, as evidenced by these reports, has resulted in an education reform movement and many changes in public education. The Carnegie report stated, "There is an eagerness to move beyond the alarming headlines; to begin to rebuild, with confidence, the public schools."[30] The rebuilding process leaves evidence of positive results. Expectancies and standards for both students and teachers, as well as teachers' salaries, have risen. Problems in the schools still exist, but the public is more optimistic about their solution, and public support for the schools has increased. Ratings given the public schools by the 18th Annual Gallup Poll[31] indicated that 41 percent of Americans rated the public schools locally as either an A or B grade. This rating compares favorably with the 48 percent of 1974 (the all-time high) and is up considerably from 1983 (the all-time low) when only 31 percent rated the schools as either A or B. Interestingly enough, as shown in figure 1.1, this same poll identified the "use of drugs" to be the biggest problem confronting the public schools. Lack of discipline dropped to second place after being rated the most important problem for sixteen of the preceding seventeen years.

Although reports of dissatisfaction with the public educational system in the United States and the severity of the problems are not unique to the 1980s, the outpouring of concern during this time, as evidenced by the reports, is not equaled in the pages of history. The impact of the eighties on education will be felt in the future.

The Future Purposes of Education

To understand the purposes of education in the future, their present relevance and application must be examined and future events predicted as they might affect educational needs. Haas indicated that Americans are faced with "a crisis of purpose such as we never faced in the past."[32] Shane identified a possible reason for that crisis as follows:

> To put it simply, change has confronted us so rapidly that we have been wrenched from *yesterday* and thrust into *tomorrow* without having been given an opportunity to adjust ourselves to *today*. As Alvin Toffler phrased it years before he published *Future Shock,* we are suffering from '. . . the dizzying disorientation brought on by the premature arrival of the future.'
>
> In effect, the crisis of transition has subjected us to new customs, changed behaviors, and strange mores and morals *in our own land and in our own time.* The transition has left us feeling alien—as if we were in a different land—with one big difference! We never left home! Nor is there any place to which we can return. . . . Small wonder that our life and the times have sometimes failed to make sense to us.[33]

Haas outlined the specific problems that accompany contemporary change, "like so many planes on a runway," as "environment, the energy crisis, changing values and morality, the family, urban and suburban crises, equal rights, and other social problems."[34] The schools will need to adjust to these many, rapid changes. Based on what has happened in the past and what is happening at the present time, predictions for the future can be made and the schools can begin to prepare for the twenty-first century now.

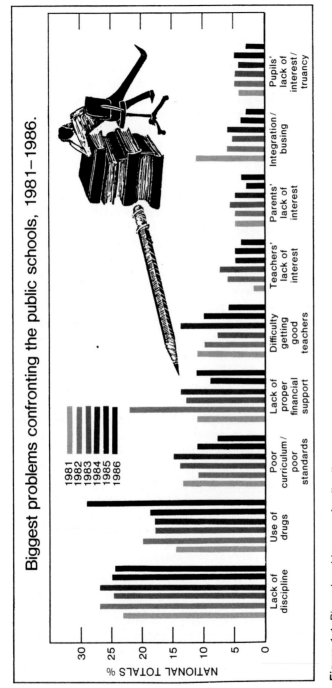

Figure 1.1 Biggest problems confronting the public schools, 1981–1986.
Gallup, Alec M., "The 18th Annual Gallup Poll of the Public's Attitudes Toward the Public Schools," *Phi Delta Kappan* 68 (September 1986):45.

John Naisbitt, in his book *Megatrends*,[35] identified the following ten major trends that will be the social forces of tomorrow. Educators need to be aware of these trends and how they will have an impact on the operation of schools.

1. *Society has moved from industrial to information processing.* The telephone, computer, and television have merged into an integrated communication system that will have a great impact on society and the schools. By 1990 Naisbitt estimated computer skills will be needed in up to 75 percent of all jobs. This high-tech communication system will affect the schools in several ways. First, the schools must implement sweeping changes to prepare their students to qualify for employment opportunities. Second, potential advantages to instruction will emerge with the use of cable television, videodisc and videotape recording, home computers, and other media and electronic devices.

The shift to the high-tech, information society has had a further impact on public education. The schools have become the center for retraining and recycling employees in the workplace. Between 1979 and 1984, an estimated 11.5 million people lost their jobs through plant closings, relocations, or technological innovations. An estimated 20 percent of those people need to improve their basic skills in reading, writing, mathematics, and communication if they are to find jobs. About 13 percent of U.S. adults are illiterate in English, making job relocation much more difficult.[36]

The shift of society to high tech will further affect the curriculum in the schools. Since 1956, white-collar workers have outnumbered blue-collar workers, and in 1981, the job ratio was three to two.[37] In the next decade, about six million more white-collar jobs are projected.[38] Such a prediction affects curriculum taught in the schools as more students will need to be prepared to move into higher education. In 1982, of the almost three million public high-school graduates who were handed diplomas, nearly 60 percent went on to higher education.[39]

As part of the process of training workers for this high-tech, information-processing society, schools must do a better job of educating minority students. Boyer emphasized that the youth population among black and Hispanic Americans remains large and is proportionately increasing.[40] Also, an estimated 29 percent of the net growth in the work force during the next fifteen years will be in minority groups. However, high-school dropout rates, which run nearly 30 percent nationally, are 40 to 50 percent in some inner-city areas with large minority populations.[41] So, while minority students are the most available candidates for white-collar jobs, they are dropping out of school at the highest rate. In 1980, 78 percent of white nineteen-year-olds were high-school graduates; 61 percent black; and 56 percent Hispanic.

Women will ease some of the demand for workers to fill high-tech jobs as they will account for about 63 percent of the new entrants into the labor force between 1985 and 2000.[42]

2. *As society becomes more high tech, more high touch is needed.* The more technology that is introduced into society, the more will be the need for the human touch and the more people will want to be with other people. Couple this need with the fact that family patterns have changed dramatically in the past twenty years and the role of the school as a socializing institution becomes even more vital. The school must often assume some of the functions that formerly belonged to the family. Figures show that the number of children in America who are affected by divorce has more than doubled since 1960. At

least 50 percent of the nation's schoolchildren have no parent at home during the day.[43] Single-parent families increased 27 percent between 1980 and 1985. Single parents— mostly women—now head more than one out of every four families with children.[44] About half the children currently in first grade will have lived in one-parent homes by the time they graduate from high school.[45]

With a shift in the family structure, who then teaches values and ethics to America's schoolchildren? The 1981 Gallup Poll indicated that 70 percent of those polled favored instruction in values and ethical behavior as part of the public school curriculum.[46] Naisbitt suggested that the schools of the future will take more of the responsibility for teaching values.

Schools must do more than teach reading, 'riting, and 'rithmetic. They must add to the general quality of life. To do this effectively, the schools of the future must create an atmosphere of trust. The schools of the past have not always been a safe place to be. In 1982, more than 35 percent of the nation's teachers said they have felt unsafe in school, and 4 percent of them have been physically abused or threatened.[47]

3. *Society has moved from a national to a world economy.* In 1979, the U.S. share of world manufacturing slipped to just over 17 percent.[48] As Naisbitt declared, "We must move toward the new enterprises of the future."[49] The American economy is no longer based primarily on industry. New technologies such as electronics, biotechnology, and alternative energy sources must be explored. The schools must prepare their graduates with the skills needed to compete in new and expanding economic territories in a worldwide market. Successful graduates of the future will have to be fluent in English, Spanish, and computer languages.

4. *Perspective has shifted from the short term to the long term.* Where formerly schools prepared specialists, they must now train generalists. In 1982, about 4 percent of public high schools were "specialized." Most were "comprehensive," while a few were "alternative."[50] The emphasis in the schools will be that of lifelong education. Graduates will be discouraged from specializing too much, as they might find a specialty becoming obsolete in the long run. Schools will need to stress critical and creative thinking.

5. *Structure has moved from centralization to decentralization.* As much of the population moves to the suburbs and the country, large metropolitan school districts are closing schools. Minorities occupy the majority of inner-city classrooms. Such a shift in ethnic and cultural composition dictates changes in classroom direction. In 1982, about 2.9 million students were enrolled in city schools (10 percent), while 54 percent were in rural schools and 34 percent were in the suburbs.[51]

6. *Individuals have moved from institutional help to self help.* More parents are teaching their children at home, and parental activism has increased in the schools. The fitness and wellness craze is evidenced by the walkers, joggers, and cyclists on the streets. The schools must play an active role in providing students with the skills they will need to be self-reliant and to confidently function in the decision-making process.

7. *Society has shifted from a representative democracy to a participatory democracy.* More people are taking part in the political decision-making process. Schools have a responsibility to prepare students to act in a responsible way. That fewer and fewer school bonds are being passed throughout the country indicates that as today's public school students become adults they will make decisions that have an impact on society.

8. *Persons in society are moving from hierarchies to networking.* Communication will be lateral, diagonal, and bottom up. Young people will need to be trained to make responsible decisions, as many more decisions will be made at the grass-roots level.

9. *Population will shift from the North to the South.* This shift will actually be a shift to the West, the Southwest, and Florida. Some schools in these areas can then expect a growth in population and need to prepare for this influx of students.

10. *Decisions will shift from the either/or to multiple options.* Everyone is now liberated, and everything comes in thirty-one flavors. Cultural, ethnic, and racial diversity are now celebrated in America. The school curriculum must capitalize on this diversity. Further, the school of the future must be much more flexible in meeting the needs of society. In 1982, the typical school year was 178 days long with the average school day convening for over five hours. Today, many more options are being tried by local schools. Year-round schools, work-study programs, and other nontraditional programs are replacing traditional practices.

Implications for Education in the Future

Although the public education system has been severely criticized in the past, it has always struggled to right itself. Based on past performance, the American educational system should continue to be the backbone of the nation. In the future, America will persist in its pursuit of excellence and continue to attack the problems it faces in education. Schools will have to adjust to the changes in society if they are to make progress. By 1990, the school-age population will have declined 14 percent from its peak in 1970, and by the year 2000, only 34 percent (down from 41 percent in 1981) of all Americans will be under age twenty-five, while about 28 percent (up from 26 percent) will be fifty or over.[52]

Hawley predicted a severe shortage of qualified teachers in the years ahead and stressed that school administrators must find solutions to this problem.[53] Justification for such a prediction is based on the fact that math and science teachers are already in short supply. Only 6 percent of college freshmen in 1985 indicated that they would like to make teaching a career. This was down from 24 percent in 1968.[54]

The costs of education continue to rise. In 1982, 126.7 billion tax dollars were spent to finance public education.[55] Other acceptable ways must be found to finance education in the future. The 1986 Gallup Poll revealed that "Despite the public's professed desire for better schools, resistance to increased local taxes for improving public education persists. Only about one-third (37 percent) of Americans would be willing to pay more taxes should local school authorities say they are needed. This percentage has stayed about the same over the past fifteen years."[56]

The widely circulating reports on education in the eighties have given rise to many solutions to the problems and predictions by futurists. Finn looked ten years into the future, citing nine probabilities that should logically restore health to the teaching profession:[57]

1. Teachers will be markedly better paid because schools will operate year-round.
2. Teaching will have a "career ladder" built in so teachers do not have to move into administration to gain status and financial benefits.
3. The teaching profession will include many part-time, short-term professionals who only want to teach temporarily.
4. High standards will determine who is a teaching professional. These standards will be based on intellectual acumen and mastery of content.
5. Ability, knowledge, and performance of teachers will be appraised by examinations and sophisticated indicators of intellect, knowledge, and analytical skills.
6. Most professional training programs will move out of the colleges. Programs will be provided by internships, apprenticeships, on-the-job training, in-service, and postgraduate higher education programs.
7. Educators will do more than teach children. They will engage in training, supervision, curriculum planning, and leadership.
8. Working conditions will become significantly more pleasant.
9. The status of teaching in the American society will be elevated.

Toffler cited three goals for the education of the future that if incorporated will better prepare students to meet the demands of a changing society.[58] They are

1. to learn how to learn;
2. to learn how to relate with others—to make and maintain rewarding human ties; and
3. to learn how to choose—to make decisions in an environment of overchoice.

To Learn How to Learn
Students starting school now will be entering the labor force in about the year 2000. As Silberman expressed

> To be 'practical,' an education should prepare them for work that does not yet exist and whose nature cannot even be imagined. This can only be done by teaching them how to learn, by giving them the kind of intellectual discipline that will enable them to apply man's accumulated wisdom to new problems as they arise. . . .[59]

Education must turn out men and women who are capable of educating themselves and their families as circumstances change. Silberman continued

> 'Merely to let children live free, natural, childlike lives,' as Carleton Washburne, one of the giants of American progressivism, warned in 1925, 'may be to fail to give them the training they need to meet the problems of later life.' Thus Washburne insisted on a dual focus. 'Every child has the right to live fully and naturally as a child,' he wrote. 'Every child has the right also to be prepared adequately for later effective living as an adult.'[60]

The Back-to-the-Basics and the accountability movements are an attempt to ensure that every student has the opportunity to learn the skills needed for effective living in the world of the future. The Council for Basic Education advanced three propositions: (1) the primary purpose of education is academic, not social; (2) basic subjects are inherently more worthwhile than other subjects; and (3) all children can learn.[61] Basic subjects are identified as those that enable people to go on and learn whatever they need or want to in later life.

Students themselves want the schools to help them learn how to learn. In a survey by Doll, which asked students how schools should educate them in ways no other agencies could, the student responses could be summarized as follows:

1. Put what we learn in school into a framework or system that will help us understand it better. . . .
2. Teach us "fundamentals." Nowhere except in school are we likely to gain the tools we need for thinking and serving.
3. Give us opportunities and materials in school to help us inquire, discover, and probe meaning. Getting meaning is perhaps the most important thing schools can help us do.
4. Stop attempting to compete with and to destroy what we learn elsewhere. Instead, seek to coordinate what we are taught in school with what we learn outside school.[62]

Finally, in *Teaching as a Subversive Activity,* Postman and Weingartner suggested that education should equip students with skills that would enable them to process the vast amounts of material thrust at them by the media. This would require instruction in the techniques of inquiry, such as questioning and examining alternatives to arrive at truth.[63]

To Learn How to Relate to Others
One of the goals of American education is to facilitate the fullest possible growth and development of each individual regardless of race, religion, sex, or ability. As this goal is realized, each individual feels worthwhile and is confident in interacting with others in society. If any person fails to develop his or her potential and to use it for worthy purposes, the educational system has fallen short of achieving its purposes.

To design educational programs that serve all students in ways adapted to their different capabilities and needs is a challenge to those who plan and conduct educational programs. The future success of America as a nation depends increasingly on the abilities of teachers to promote common concerns through cooperative problem solving that is based on fact, reason, and brotherly and sisterly love rather than authority or force. Mutual understanding and empathy for others are becoming essential in today's "pressure-cooker" society. For this reason, skills in cooperation should be emphasized in classes such as physical education.

Another value traditionally held by American society is the freedom to interact with others while, at the same time, being responsible for one's own actions. Respect for the rights and feelings of others and sensitivity to one's actions on others are essential components of an individual's moral responsibility in society. Classroom management should be based on the principles of individual responsibility for one's own behavior. Chapter 12 describes how this can be done.

To Learn How to Choose
"Security is the best preparation for an insecure future," said Shane.[64] One key to learning security is discovering how to make choices. Coping with change demands that students explore possible alternatives for the future. Teachers can assist students in acquiring these skills by helping them look at ideas and skills that have helped people adjust in the past.

They can also encourage students to search for generalizations or concepts that organize learning into meaningful wholes. Course subject matter should have wide application to everyday life, both now and in the future. Students need to be taught to think seriously about why they are doing what they are doing and to learn the consequences for the decisions they make.[65] Thus, critical thinking and problem-solving skills need to become important components of the educational program. The development of these skills is discussed in chapter 6.

Characteristics of Successful Schools

Schools of the future that are successful in carrying out the purposes and goals of education will need to incorporate certain characteristics into their operational procedures. In a study of successful schools across the United States, Benjamin zeroed in on the following characteristics (italics added):

1. Strong instructional *leadership* marshalling the school's resources toward common purposes.
2. A climate of *high expectations* in which no children are allowed to fall below minimum standards of achievement.
3. An orderly, but not rigid, *school atmosphere* conducive to instruction.
4. A clear, shared emphasis on the *basic skills* which takes precedence over all other school activities.
5. Frequent, careful *monitoring of pupil progress.*[66]

Leadership

Leadership in schools depends on two very important groups—administrators and teachers. Benjamin emphasized and reemphasized the critical relationship between the principal's leadership and the quality of the school. Studies show that effective principals take the initiative in defining instructional goals and objectives. They serve as instructional leaders, spending a large amount of time in classrooms and halls. They employ teachers who set high expectations for students and put pressure on incompetent teachers to leave.[67] Silberman emphasized that successful schools also have "unusually able and dedicated teachers."[68]

High Expectations

The second prerequisite for a successful school is, as Silberman indicated, "the teachers' unshakable conviction that their students *can* learn. . . . In every successful program, in fact, a major reason for success is the fact that project directors and teachers expect their students to succeed, and that they hold *themselves*—not only their students—accountable if the latter should fail."[69] Chapter 10 presents instructional strategies addressing this issue.

School Atmosphere

Directly related to academic standards are standards for behavior. Enochs stated, "Kids want adults to act like adults. They want to know who's in charge. They want to know what's expected of them. They want to know what's right and wrong today will be right and wrong tomorrow."[70]

In his Modesto, California, schools, Enochs established written conduct codes for students from kindergarten through grade twelve (The Modesto Plan). The codes specify the rights and responsibilities of students and the consequences for infractions. A handbook outlining the codes is distributed to parents, who sign a receipt verifying they received it. Character and citizenship education programs complement the behavior codes, and students receive a grade for punctuality, preparedness, and other appropriate behavior. Various school privileges can be earned or lost on the basis of these grades. The entire Modesto plan is based on a system of mutual accountability between the schools and the community. The public schools hold the parents and community responsible for the behavior of their young people, and the community holds the schools responsible for the academic achievements of the students.[71]

Instruction in Basic Skills

In a review of research on classroom instruction and student achievement, Rosenshine concluded that "effective classroom teaching of basic skills takes place in an environment characterized by an emphasis on academic achievement. . . . Teachers who make a difference in students' achievement are those who put students in contact with curriculum materials and who find ways to keep them in contact."[72]

Academic Learning Time (ALT), discussed in more detail in chapter 6, is time engaged directly in tasks to be learned at an appropriate level of difficulty for the learner. ALT correlates significantly with student achievement. Frequent, careful monitoring of student progress, with specific feedback to students, is also an essential component of effective learning. Enochs reminded us in *The Restoration of Standards* that "it [is] easier to make students feel good than to hold them accountable to the rigors of learning." Further, Enochs stated that teachers should not feel guilty for required courses, demanding courses, required homework, honest grading, and earned promotion.[73]

Monitoring of Pupil Progress

In addition to monitoring progress and providing continuous feedback during instruction, several states and districts are requiring minimum competencies for promotion and graduation. Such reform has been spurred on by lawsuits claiming inadequate education for students and the cries of crisis in education. The 1983 outcry of problems in the schools resulted in Florida, Arkansas, Texas, South Carolina, Georgia, and Missouri being the first states to impose required testing programs upon students, holding them accountable for basic competencies. Between 1980 and 1986, forty-five states and the District of Columbia altered their reported requirements for earning a standard high-school diploma. During this time, mathematics requirements were increased in forty-two states, thirty-four states changed their science requirements, eighteen states modified their language arts requirements, twenty-six states changed social studies requirements, and physical education and health requirements changed in fourteen states. Computer literacy was a requirement in six states.[74]

Educational reform was the cry of the eighties with results being less evident toward the end of the decade as the movement tapered off. The impact of the movement is permanent, however, and the results will be felt by future generations. More than thirty states have taken action on career ladders, more than forty states have changed high-school graduation requirements, testing programs for students have increased everywhere, and changes in teacher training programs and teacher certification procedures are evident in nearly every state.[75] Future emphasis will be turned to implementation of new and revised policies and programs.

Further implications for reform will be scaled down but will still include the following issues:

1. Society concerns such as the slow economy, poverty, divorce, teenage pregnancy, drugs and alcohol, crime, teenage suicide.[76]
2. Control by local school districts.
3. Competency testing for practicing teachers.
4. Higher academic standards for participation in extracurricular activities.
5. Incentives for districts perpetuated by legislative action.
6. Public interest in choice and voucher programs.
7. Curriculum and testing plans.[77]

Future attention in the schools will be turned to the practicality of what the schools can actually accomplish. Rittenmeyer reminded us that the schools cannot do it all.

> Our teachers should be capable and dedicated professionals, and our facilities and resources should be adequate for the educational tasks we wish to accomplish. However, we must understand that our schools can't do it all. . . . Our teachers and principals should be required to address educational issues, not unmet social needs. . . . If we wish to improve the educational performance of our schools, we must first improve the quality of life for our youth. Only then can we fairly evaluate the degree to which our schools are fulfilling their educational objectives.[78]

Education in the future should do two things claimed Adler.[79] It should improve the quality of basic schooling in this county while making that quality accessible to all children. Such is the challenge of existing and future educators.

Questions and Suggested Activities

1. Formulate your own definition of education.
2. Interview several community leaders to determine what they think the purposes of education should be. Compare their ideas with those presented in this chapter.
3. As a group of parents, teachers, and concerned citizens (or other selected roles), list the things that a graduate of a high school in your city should be able to do to receive a diploma from your district.
4. If you were a principal in a school today, describe how that school would operate. Identify factors that might hinder a student from achieving his or her potential. List the things that would be different if you were principal in that same school in the future.
5. Study lists of educational goals published by state and/or district boards of education. Compare them with each other and with the goals listed in this chapter.
6. As a reporter for the local newspaper, you are doing a feature article on "Educating Our Youth." Include the factors that have had an impact on education in the twentieth century. Discuss the results of these factors as they relate to the past and present. Present a theory of future educational directions based on past outcomes, present trends, and predictions by futurists.

Suggested Readings

Adler, Jerry, and Pamela Abramson. "The School That Flunked." *Newsweek,* October 6, 1980, p. 86.

Adler, Mortimer J. *The Paideia Proposal.* New York: Macmillan Publishing Company, 1982.

Boyer, Ernest L. *High School: A Report on Secondary Education in America.* The Carnegie Foundation for the Advancement of Teaching. New York: Harper & Row, Publishers, 1983.

Boyer, Ernest L. "Critical Thoughts on Education." *Phi Kappa Phi Journal* (Winter 1985):33–34.

Cohen, Michael. "Effective Schools: What the Research Says." *Today's Education* (April–May 1981):58GS–60GS.

Committee for Economic Development. *Investing in Our Children: Business and the Public Schools.* New York: Committee for Economic Development, 1985.

Goodlad, John I. *A Place Called School: Prospects for the Future.* New York: McGraw-Hill Book Company, 1984.

Naisbitt, J. *Megatrends: Ten New Directions Transforming Our Lives.* New York: Warner Books, 1982.

National Commission on Excellence in Education. *A Nation at Risk: The Imperative for Educational Reform.* Washington, D.C.: U.S. Government Printing Office, 1983.

Natthan, Joe. *Free to Teach: Achieving Equity and Excellence in Schools.* New York: The Pilgrim Press, 1983.

Nivens, Maryruth K. "Is Yours a Thumbs-Up or a Thumbs-Down School?" *Phi Delta Kappan* (February 1985):427–429.

Pierce, Kenneth M. "Trying the Old-Fashioned Way." *Time* 9 (March 1981):65.

Pipho, Chris. "States Move Reform Closer to Reality." *Phi Delta Kappan* (December 1986):K1-K8.

Rittenmeyer, Dennis C. "Social Problems and America's Youth: Why School Reform Won't Work." *National Forum* (Winter 1987):34–37.

Task Force on Education for Economic Growth. *Action for Excellence: A Comprehensive Plan to Improve Our Nation's Schools.* Washington, D.C.: Education Commission of the States, 1983.

Toffler, Alvin. *Future Shock.* New York: Random House, 1970.

Tomlinson, Tommy. "Effective Schools: Mirror or Mirage?" *Today's Education* 70 (April–May 1981):60GS.

Twentieth Century Fund Task Force on Federal Elementary and Secondary Education Policy. *Making the Grade.* New York: The Twentieth Century Fund, 1983.

References

1. Task Force on Education for Economic Growth, *Action for Excellence: A Comprehensive Plan to Improve Our Nation's Schools* (Washington, D.C.: Education Commission of the States, 1983).
2. By permission. From *Webster's New Collegiate Dictionary,* © 1981 by G. & C. Merriam Co., Publishers of the Merriam-Webster® Dictionaries.
3. Herbert Spencer, *Education: Intellectual, Moral, and Physical* (New York: D. Appleton, 1860), p. 31.
4. Frank R. Krajewski and Gary L. Pettier, eds., *Education: Where It's Been, Where It's At, Where It's Going* (Columbus, Ohio: Charles E. Merrill, 1973), p. 134; J. Abner Peddiwell, *The Saber Tooth Curriculum* (New York: McGraw-Hill Book Company, 1939).
5. Harold P. Vayhinger, "The Great Experiment: The American System of Education," *Phi Kappa Phi Journal* (Winter 1977), pp. 29–36.
6. Ibid.
7. Ibid., p. 32.
8. Ibid., p. 39.
9. Philip G. Altbach, "The Great Education 'Crisis'," in *Excellence in Education: Perspectives on Policy and Practice.* Paul G. Altbach, Gail P. Kelly, Lois Weis (eds.) (Buffalo: Prometheus Books, 1985), p. 15.

10. Commission on Reorganization of Secondary Education, *Cardinal Principles of Secondary Education* (Washington, D.C.: U.S. Government Printing Office, 1918), pp. 7–15.
11. Educational Policies Commission, *The Purposes of Education in American Democracy* (Washington, D.C.: National Education Association, 1938), pp. 50–123.
12. Educational Policies Commission, *Education for ALL American Youth* (Washington, D.C.: National Education Association, 1944), pp. 225–26.
13. American Association of School Administrators, *Imperatives in Education* (Washington, D.C.: American Association of School Administrators, 1966).
14. As developed by the Institute for Educational Management for the Northwest Regional Educational Laboratory in preparation for the Employer Based Career Education program.
15. B. Frank Brown, *The Reform of Secondary Education* (New York: McGraw-Hill Book Company, 1973), pp. 32–35.
16. Richard E. Gross, "Seven New Cardinal Principles," *Phi Delta Kappan* 60 (December 1978), pp. 291–93.
17. National Commission on Excellence in Education, *A Nation at Risk* (Washington, D.C.: United States Department of Education, 1983).
18. Ernest L. Boyer, *High School: A Report on Secondary Education in America* (New York: Harper & Row, Publishers, 1983). [The Carnegie Report]
19. Larry Harris, Thomas Hunt, Rosary Lalik, "Are Public Schools Failing?" *Clearing House* (February 1986), p. 281.
20. Boyer, *High School*, p. 1.
21. National Commission on Excellence in Education, *A Nation at Risk*.
22. Task Force on Education for Economic Growth, *Action for Excellence*.
23. Mortimer J. Adler, *The Paideia Program: An Educational Syllabus* (New York: Macmillan Publishing Company, 1984).
24. Boyer, *High School*.
25. John I. Goodlad, *A Place Called School: Prospects for the Future* (New York: McGraw-Hill Book Company, 1984).
26. Committee for Economic Development, *Investing in Our Children: Business and the Public Schools* (New York: Committee for Economic Development, 1985).
27. National Commission on Excellence in Education, *A Nation at Risk*, p. 5.
28. Twentieth Century Fund Task Force on Federal Elementary and Secondary Education Policy, *Making the Grade* (New York: The Twentieth Century Fund, 1983).
29. Altbach, "The Great Education 'Crisis'," pp. 19–20.
30. Boyer, *High School*, p. 1.
31. Alec M. Gallup, "The 18th Annual Gallup Poll of the Public's Attitudes Toward the Public Schools," *Phi Delta Kappan* 68 (September 1986), pp. 43–59.
32. Glen Hass, *Curriculum Planning: A New Approach*, 2d ed. (Boston: Allyn & Bacon, Inc., 1977), p. 27.
33. Harold G. Shane, *The Educational Significance of the Future* (Bloomington, Indiana: Phi Delta Kappa, Inc., 1973), pp. 40–41.
34. Hass, *Curriculum Planning*, p. 27.
35. John Naisbitt, *Megatrends* (New York: Warner Books, 1982).
36. Boyer, *High School*, p. 1.
37. Ibid., p. 4.
38. "Chronicle of Higher Education" (September 17, 1986), p. 1.
39. Boyer, *High School*, p. 119.
40. Boyer, *High School*, p. 4.
41. "Chronicle of Higher Education," p. 1.
42. Ibid.
43. Dennis A. Williams, et al., "Why Public Schools Fail," *Newsweek* (April 20, 1981), pp. 62–65.
44. *Deseret News*, (November 5, 1986), p. 4A.
45. Boyer, *High School*, p. 37.

46. George H. Gallup, "The 13th Annual Gallup Poll of the Public's Attitudes Toward the Public Schools," *Phi Delta Kappan* 63 (September 1981), pp. 33–47.
47. Boyer, *High School,* p. 21.
48. Ibid., p. 4.
49. Naisbitt, *Megatrends,* p. 56.
50. Boyer, *High School,* p. 20.
51. Ibid.
52. Ibid., pp. 4–5.
53. Willis D. Hawley, "Toward a Comprehensive Strategy for Addressing the Teacher Shortage," *Phi Delta Kappan* 67 (June 1986), pp. 712–18.
54. "Chronicle of Higher Education," (November 5, 1986), pp. 32–35.
55. Boyer, *High School,* p. 20.
56. Gallup, "The 18th Annual Gallup Poll of the Public's Attitudes Toward the Public Schools," p. 50.
57. Chester Finn, "Nine Big Ideas for the Next Ten Years," *Instructor* (November/December 1985), pp. 90–94.
58. Alvin Toffler, *The Schoolhouse in the City* (New York: Frederick A. Praeger, in cooperation with Educational Facilities Laboratories, 1968), pp. 367–69.
59. Charles E. Silberman, *Crisis in the Classroom: The Remaking of American Education* (New York: Random House, 1970), p. 114.
60. Ibid., p. 116.
61. Robert Benjamin, *Making Schools Work: A Reporter's Journey Through Some of America's Most Remarkable Classrooms* (New York: The Continuum Publishing Corporation, 1981), p. 36.
62. Ronald C. Doll, "Alternative Forms of Schooling," *Educational Leadership* 29 (February 1972), pp. 391–93.
63. Neil Postman and Charles Weingartner, *Teaching as a Subversive Activity* (New York: Dell Publishing Company, 1969).
64. Shane, *The Educational Significance of the Future,* p. 33.
65. Silberman, *Crisis in the Classroom,* p. 36.
66. Benjamin, *Making Schools Work,* pp. 118 and 140.
67. Ibid., p. 113.
68. Silberman, *Crisis in the Classroom,* p. 97.
69. Ibid., p. 98.
70. Enochs, cited in Benjamin, *Making Schools Work,* p. 173.
71. Ibid., pp. 174–79.
72. Barak V. Rosenshine, "Academic Engaged Time, Content Covered and Direct Instruction," *Journal of Education* 160 (August 1978), pp. 38–66.
73. James C. Enochs, *The Restoration of Standards: The Modesto Plan* (Bloomington, Indiana: Phi Delta Kappa Educational Foundation, 1979), pp. 7–8.
74. Chris Pipho, "States Move Reform Closer to Reality," *Phi Delta Kappan* (December 1986), pp. K1–K8.
75. Ibid., p. K7.
76. Dennis C. Rittenmeyer, "Social Problems and America's Youth: Why School Reform Won't Work," *National Forum* (Winter 1987), pp. 34–37.
77. Pipho, "States Move Reform Closer to Reality," p. K8.
78. Rittenmeyer, "Social Problems and America's Youth," p. 37.
79. Adler, *The Paideia Program,* p. 1.

Determining the Role of Physical Education

Study Stimulators

1. What are the goals of physical education?
2. How do the goals of physical education fit with the national goals of education in chapter 1, table 1.1?
3. What are the values of physical education?
4. What is a philosophy? How does one develop a philosophy of physical education?
5. What major philosophies have developed in physical education since 1900?
6. What is the current status of physical education in the United States?
7. Describe the physical education program of the future.

Physical education is the study, practice, and appreciation of the art and science of human movement. It is a part of the total process of education. Movement is natural and basic to existence for most human beings. "Children . . . are prewired for movement at birth."[1] While movement itself is spontaneous, the refinement and perfection of movement is a process of education that is often the charge of the physical educator. This charge must not be taken lightly. The body, that machine that enacts movement, should be highly esteemed.

> The human body is sacred . . . it is a solemn duty of humankind to protect and preserve it from pollutions and unnecessary wastage and weakness. . . .[2]

The National Association of Secondary School Principals emphasized the worth of the human body in stressing the importance of physical education programs as follows:

> Today's physical education programs are aimed at helping students acquire constructive concepts and desirable habits regarding the preservation of our environment's most prized natural resource: the well-tuned, efficiently functional human body and all its healthy competitive components. . . .
> Furthermore, physical education has earned a role as one of the essential elements in any curriculum designed to educate the whole person. . . .[3]

Physical educators striving to impart the worth of the human body to students must realize that many Americans are dissatisfied with their bodies. A 1986 survey indicated that 38 percent of women and 34 percent of men are dissatisfied with their appearance and body dimensions. Dissatisfaction has increased since 1972 when 32 percent of women and 15 percent of men expressed dissatisfaction with their overall appearance. This same survey also revealed that 55 percent of women and 41 percent of men were dissatisfied with their current weight.[4] The worth of the body and of human movement are the prime considerations when the purposes of physical education are formulated. Such considerations result in purposes that stress meaningful outcomes of programs.

The Purposes of Physical Education

An *aim* or *purpose* of a program is an ideal that acts as a compass by giving direction to the total program. It also provides a basis for designing and evaluating curricular offerings. The following statement is an aim for physical education:

> Physical education is that integral part of total education which contributes to the development of the individual through the natural medium of physical activity—human movement. It is a carefully planned sequence of learning experiences designed to fulfill the growth, development, and behavior needs of each student.[5]

Since an aim is something that is usually distant (in the future) or ideal, it must be broken down into a number of *goals* that, when achieved, give direction toward the aim. These instructional goals are statements of more immediate outcomes to be expected of students in the school. The following statements are instructional goals for physical education (italics added):

1. To develop *physical skills* which will enable participation in a wide variety of activities.
2. To develop *physical fitness* and soundly functioning body systems for an active life in his/her environment.
3. To develop *knowledge and understanding* of physical and social skills, physical fitness, scientific principles of movement, and the relationship of exercise to personal well-being.
4. To develop *social skills* which promote acceptable standards of behavior and positive relationships with others.
5. To develop *attitudes and appreciations* that will encourage participation in and enjoyment of physical activity, fitness, quality performance, a positive self concept, and respect for others.[6]

These goals have generally been accepted by leaders in the profession as the basic goals of physical education.

Physical Skills

The development and refinement of neuromuscular skill essential for efficient everyday movement (posture and body mechanics), and for efficient movement in a variety of activities, lead to less energy wasted in skill performance and more enjoyment in activity. Basic movement (fundamental) skills, sport skills, and skills in rhythmic activities are all important components of this aim.

Physical Fitness

President John F. Kennedy once said, "Fitness is the basis for all other forms of excellence."[7] The development of physical fitness and health contributes to effective living and enjoyment of life, and its components should be taught with two goals in mind. First, students should be expected to achieve fitness, and second, they should acquire the knowledge and desire to make it a lifelong pursuit. One aspect of physical fitness is health-related fitness, including such components as strength, flexibility, endurance, and body composition. Motor fitness expands the definition to include such areas as balance, agility, coordination, and speed.

The physical education program should develop physical skills, fitness, knowledge, social skills, and positive attitudes.

Knowledge and Understanding

An understanding of the importance of physical activity and how it relates to one's health and well-being is essential. Knowledge of scientific principles related to physical activity, exercise, and health should be included in the physical education instructional program.[8] Dr. Ernest Wynder of the American Health Foundation said, "It's as important to teach kids about the body as about math and science."[9] Such an understanding must include skills in designing and implementing a fitness or weight-control program, evaluating fitness, and participating safely in activity. Knowledge about game rules, strategies, and techniques enhance participation in a variety of physical activities. Game play can also increase one's ability to solve problems in highly emotional situations. Students should also learn the processes for acquiring physical skills and the basic principles of movement (e.g., equilibrium, absorption of force) that are common to all activities.

Social Skills

Desirable social values—such as cooperation, commitment, leadership, followership, fair play, and courtesy—should be taught through participation in physical education activities. The traditional physical education program offerings are geared to instill social values, with more recent programs likely to include adventure and cooperative activities as described in chapter 9.

Attitudes and Appreciations

Students should have experiences that help them understand the role of physical activity and sport in society.[10] The attitudes a student has toward physical activity and toward his or her feelings of successful accomplishment in activity influence future participation. Care should be taken to ensure that only positive attitudes and appreciations result from physical education classes. Students should see value in what they are doing, and they should derive joy and pleasure while doing it.

Physical activity also provides an opportunity for releasing emotional tension through appropriate channels. When participation occurs in a supportive environment, students can increase their feelings of self-esteem, release tension, and develop initiative, self-direction, and creativity. Hellison suggested that "our profession needs to achieve some balance between helping people and developing and promulgating the subject matter (skills, fitness, strategies, etc.)."[11]

Goals can be further broken down into *objectives,* which specify short-term expectations. Objectives can more easily be adjusted to meet the needs of individual students. The writing of objectives will be further discussed in chapter 7. Examples of objectives that further clarify and give direction to goals and aims might be:

1. The student will make three out of five legal foul shots.
2. The student will participate in fitness activities for thirty minutes twice a week outside of class.

The overall aims and purposes of physical education remain constant, but the more immediate goals and objectives are continually changing to meet the needs of a changing society.

How Are Purposes, Goals, and Objectives Developed?

The stated purposes, goals, and objectives of physical education programs are a result of a step-by-step process of thought that considers (1) the relationship of physical education to the purposes of education, (2) the values of physical education, (3) the needs and interests of students, (4) the nature of the school and its community, and (5) the personal philosophies of the faculty.

Physical Education and the Purposes of Education

Since physical education is a part of the total education of a student, the curriculum in physical education must be based on a sound philosophy that, in turn, is consistent with the social and educational philosophies of the time and place in which it functions. The goals of physical education should be integrated with the national goals of education listed in table 1.1. An evaluation of these lists reveals that approximately one-fourth of the goals relate directly to outcomes attained in physical education programs. Most of the remaining goals relate indirectly to outcomes of such programs. For example, physical education contributes to health and physical fitness through the development of organic vigor; to the worthy use of leisure through the development of skills for use in leisure-time activity; to ethical character as one develops the ideals of fair play, decision-making ability, and appreciation for both winning and losing; to respect for others and appreciation of achievement as one participates on a team; to appreciation of the arts as creativity is developed in such areas as dance; to an understanding of science as the workings of the human body are demonstrated; to personal competence through the enhancement of psychomotor skills; and to respect for the environment through participation in outdoor and challenge activities. Other more indirect correlations relate to such outcomes as critical thinking, career options, making life more satisfying, dealing with psychological tensions, and knowledge of self.

The specific values of physical education are not always reflected in national goals of education and should be explicitly defined.

The Values of Physical Education

Seefeldt and Vogel[12] listed twenty values of physical education (activity) deemed important by the National Association for Sport and Physical Education. They are summarized into the ten statements below:

1. Promotes and assists the early growth, development, and function of the nervous system such as changes in brain structure and refinement of perceptual abilities involving vision, balance, and tactile sensations.
2. Promotes cognitive function through imitation, symbolic play, the development of language, and the use of symbols in the early years and aids in developing learning strategies; making decisions; acquiring, retrieving, and integrating information; and solving problems in the later years.
3. Fortifies the mineralization of the skeleton and promotes the maintenance of lean body tissue, while simultaneously reducing the deposition of fat. Obesity is regulated because energy expenditure is increased, appetite suppressed, metabolic rate increased, and lean body mass increased.
4. Leads to proficiency in the neuromuscular skills that are the basis for successful participation in games, dances, sports, and leisure activities.
5. Improves aerobic fitness, muscle endurance, muscle power, and muscle strength while improving cardiac function as indicated by an increased stroke volume, cardiac output, blood volume, and total hemoglobin.
6. Prevents the onset of some diseases and postpones the debilitating effects of old age. It is an effective deterrent to coronary heart disease due to its effects on blood lipids, blood pressure, obesity, and capacity for physical work, and is associated with a reduction in atherosclerotic diseases.
7. Provides an avenue for developing social competence, moral reasoning, problem solving, and creativity while enhancing self-concept and self-esteem as indicated by increased confidence, assertiveness, emotional stability, independence, and self-control.
8. Promotes a more positive attitude toward physical activity that leads to a more active life-style during unscheduled leisure time.
9. Provides an effective deterrent to mental illness and the alleviation of mental stress.
10. Improves the psychosocial and physiological functions of mentally and physically handicapped individuals.

In a study conducted with prospective physical education teachers to determine the values of physical education they considered to be most important, health and fitness, and general well-being were ranked as excellent. These same students ranked the values of social experience, recreational-relaxational, and emotional release (relaxation and getting away from the tensions of the day) as good. Females tended to view physical education more as a social experience than did males.[13]

The Needs and Interests of Students

All teachers must be concerned about the needs and interests of students, but teachers in physical education should be particularly sensitive to the physical fitness and motor development needs of students and the intellectual, personal, and social needs that revolve around these important goals.

Well-planned and implemented physical education programs should provide opportunities for all students to experience success in physical activity and improve existing skills. Achievement must be measured and demonstrated. Units 2, 3, and 4 suggest some ways to study student needs and interests and provide some principles for planning appropriate educational programs, including various ways to evaluate and track student progress and achievement.

The Nature of the School and Community

A number of local factors must be considered when selecting the goals of physical education. These include the economic and cultural background of the community surrounding the school. Programs must be adapted to the needs, interests, and limitations of both the students and community. Chapter 15 outlines guidelines for incorporating these factors into the goals that determine curriculum planning.

Personal Philosophies of the Faculty

A philosophy is a composite of the knowledge, attitudes, beliefs, and values that forms the basis for a person's actions and provides central direction or purpose to his or her activities. Oberteuffer and Ulrich indicated that

> To understand anything one must relate all of the parts, episodes, or individual actions to the "grand plan," the overall purpose. This is sometimes called the point of view—or the philosophy underlying the effort. Without an overall plan, direction, or philosophy, a physical education program, or anything else, becomes nothing more than a series of disconnected and unrelated activities, having no unifying purpose.[14]

A sound philosophy is the basis for a sound program. The personal philosophies of the faculty have an important effect on the selection of goals and content for the physical education program. Teachers not only help to formulate these goals and aims, but they are the facilitators in making them a reality. In essence, philosophy dictates what is taught, how it is taught, and how the work is graded. A teacher whose philosophy stresses physical fitness will have a strong school physical fitness program. Another who believes strongly in student responsibility for learning will use many individualized learning methods. Because of a philosophy that emphasizes the totality of learning, a third instructor stops activity on a beautiful spring day to point out the awe-inspiring mountains capped with snow.

Every educational institution should have a written statement of its philosophy that can serve to guide the development of the curriculum. The following was a statement of philosophy published by the American Alliance for Health, Physical Education, Recreation and Dance:

> Physical education is the study and practice of the science and art of human movement. It is concerned with why man moves; how he moves; the physiological, sociological, and psychological consequences of his movement; and the skills and motor patterns which comprise his movement repertoire. Through physical education, an individual has the opportunity to learn to perform efficiently the motor skills he needs in everyday living and in recreational activities. He can develop and maintain sound physiological functions through vigorous muscular activity. He may increase the awareness of his physical self. Through expressive and creative activities, he may enhance his aesthetic appreciations. Physical education provides situations for learning to compete as well as to cooperate with others in striving for achievement of common goals. Within the media of physical activity, concepts underlying effective human movement can be demonstrated and the influences these have on the individual can be better understood. Satisfying and successful experiences in physical education should develop in the individual a desire to regularly participate in activity throughout life. Only through enjoyable and persistent participation will the optimum benefits of physical activity be derived.[15]

Parents, school boards, administrators, teachers, and students all want to know where physical education programs are headed. Leland Stanford used to say, "The world stands aside for the man who knows where he is going."[16] Stanford was right. If a physical educator knows where he or she is going, people will pay attention.

Daughtrey suggested that prospective teachers defining a philosophy ask themselves the following questions:

1. Do I know where I am headed? What is my aim?
2. Can I scientifically justify the activities I wish to teach?
3. Am I willing to abandon the teaching of certain activities if they are shown to be educationally unsound?
4. Is my program self-centered or pupil-centered?
5. Are the activities safe?
6. Is my program a play program or is it a teaching program?[17]

A philosophy is the result of continuously changing knowledge and experience. It is dynamic, always evolving, never static. The development of a philosophy of physical education involves the following steps:

Step 1. Study the philosophies of various leaders.

Step 2. Analyze your own feelings and experiences.

Step 3. Obtain feedback from others.

Although general agreement exists among the leaders of physical education on the goals to be achieved, there are differences in the priorities (or ranking) of these goals. To be effective, both aims and goals must be worthwhile, be in harmony with educational and physical educational philosophy, be attainable, and be incorporated in the classroom. The question that remains to be answered is whether the goals deemed important for physical educators are being realized in actual practice. The priority given to each goal by individual teachers determines whether they are planned for and incorporated. Placek did a study to discover what influences determine planning by physical education teachers. She concluded that teachers did not view student learning or achievement to be as important as classroom environment. Teachers seemed to equate success in the classroom with keeping students busy, happy, and good.[18] One must then ask if physical educators have their priorities straight.

Physical Education in a Historical Perspective

The Greeks appear to have been the first people who made sport and athletics an integral part of their daily lives.[19] From the inception of the Olympics in 776 B.C., sports and games have played an important role in the lives of people throughout the world. The early Romans popularized spectator sports through the Greco-Roman shows and gladiator exhibitions. At first, such events had religious significance and were designed to honor the Greek gods. They later evolved into spectacular exhibitions. As the Middle Ages evolved, physical education centered around the physical prowess of the knights. The Renaissance period stressed humanistic education, and Greek gymnastics found their way into educational programs.[20]

Physical education took on a new identity in both the eighteenth and nineteenth centuries. The eighteenth century became known as the "era of enlightenment," and the child's natural inclination to play was stressed.[21] A most significant event of the 1800s was the reestablishment of the Olympic Games. De Coubertin almost single-handedly reestablished the Games in 1896.[22] The many military campaigns of the nineteenth century resulted in a pressure to physically condition the soldiers. It was at this time that the German system of formal gymnastics, directed by Friedrich Ludwig Jahn ("Father of Gymnastics"); "free exercises" from Adolph Spiess; and Swedish Gymnastics, introduced by Pehr Henrik Ling, came into being. England did not adopt the gymnastics movement during the nineteenth century, as it favored games, sports, and recreation. The British led the way in the development of amateur sports. Herbert Spencer, an Englishman, stressed the importance of diet and exercise to the well-being of youth and lamented the fact that girls were neglected in this regard.[23]

In the United States, after what is now the American Alliance for Health, Physical Education, Recreation and Dance was founded in 1885, physical education was considered a subject that should be included in the school curriculum. Many states passed laws requiring physical education in the schools in the early 1920s. However, the brunt of the implementation of programs was left to the colleges and universities.[24] Edward Hitchcock, Dudley Sargent, H. J. Kohler, Edward Hartwell, and Delphine Hanna were particularly instrumental in promoting physical education at the post-high-school level.[25] In Europe physical education was required in educational systems after 1919.[26]

After the initial introduction of physical education as a school subject, its direction in American schools took different paths. At the outbreak of World Wars I and II, physical fitness was the motivating force for program direction. One-third of all men drafted for military service during World War II were rejected as unfit to serve, and most of those admitted were described as soft and flabby.[27] These facts shocked America into doing something to increase the physical well-being of its citizens.

In the 1960s physical education programs emphasized sports and competition and typically fed into intramural and varsity sports programs. By the 1970s physical education programs again made a shift in direction and began to emphasize lifetime skills.[28]

During the twentieth century, three philosophies emerged to influence the direction of physical education in the United States. They were (1) education of the physical, (2) education through the physical, and (3) education for leisure time and recreation.[29]

Education of the Physical

In the early history of physical education in the United States, the emphasis was predominantly on health and physical fitness—the development of the body as an end in itself. Programs consisted primarily of gymnastics and calisthenics. This philosophy was later dubbed "education of the physical."

The emphasis on physical fitness was resurrected during World Wars I and II and the Korean War. It was also emphasized following the report of the Kraus-Weber Tests in 1953. These tests showed that American children were inferior in strength and flexibility to European children. This report sparked a national interest in physical fitness and a number of conferences on youth fitness. It finally resulted in the formation of a National Council on Youth Fitness and various other efforts to support physical education in the schools.

The emphasis on physical fitness was championed by Arthur H. Steinhaus and Charles H. McCloy. McCloy stated, "For a profession that has glorified the physical side of man from before 500 B.C. until, shall we say, A.D. 1915, the physical education literature of today is strangely silent about the more purely body-building type of objectives."[30] Steinhaus emphasized that "all forms of education may develop the mind and spirit of man but only physical education can develop his body."[31]

Education through the Physical

Jesse Feiring Williams defined physical education as "education *through* the physical rather than *of* the physical."[32] As early as 1893, Thomas Wood emphasized the need to replace physical training with physical education. Wood later wrote:

> Physical education must have an aim as broad as education itself, and as noble and
> inspiring as human life. The great thought in physical education is not the education of
> the physical nature, but the relation of physical training to complete education, and
> then the effort to make the physical contribute its full share to the life of the individual,
> in environment, training, and culture.[33]

Wood was accompanied in his effort by Luther Halsey Gulick and Clark W. Hetherington. Together they emphasized a "new physical education," consisting of sports and games, outdoor recreation, and educational gymnastics. This new emphasis was a break from formal gymnastics and was important in the move for physical education to become an accepted part of the educational curriculum.

Gulick, a prominent leader in the recreation and outdoor education movement, emphasized the social and play needs of youth. He stated:

> The first necessity . . . is to provide for the development and fashioning of out of school
> play and games that shall engage large numbers of children. . . . Gymnastics can
> never take the place of play, and upon play we must depend in the future, as we have in
> the past, for the fundamental conditions for the development of organic life and
> power.[34]

Hetherington emphasized the importance of educating the total person—physically, mentally, emotionally, and socially—by meeting the specific needs and interests of each age group. He attempted to "describe the function and place of general neuromuscular activities, primarily general play activities, in the educational process." He said:

> We use the term *general play* to include play, games, athletics, dancing, the play side of gymnastics, and all play activities in which large muscles are used more or less vigorously.
> The interpretation given might be called the new physical education, with the emphasis on education, and the understanding that it is "physical" only in the sense that the activity of the whole organism is the educational agent and not the mind alone.[35]

It was Hetherington who presented the four basic processes, or objectives, of physical education that have continued for more than half a century. They are: organic education, psychomotor education, character education, and intellectual education.[36]

It was some time before "education through the physical" became the dominant philosophy of physical education. This philosophy was a natural outgrowth of the broadening of the curriculum to reflect the life of the community as advocated by John Dewey. Jesse Feiring Williams defined once and for all the distinction between the two theories in his 1930 article "Education Through the Physical":

> No one can examine earnestly the implications of physical education without facing two questions. These are: Is physical education an education *of* the physical? Is physical education an education *through* the physical? . . .
> Education of the physical is a familiar view. Its supporters are those who regard strong muscles and firm ligaments as the main outcomes. . . .
> Modern physical education with its emphasis upon education through the physical is based upon the biologic unity of mind and body. This view sees life as a totality. . . . It sees physical education primarily as a way of living.[37]

Education *through* the physical included the human movement, or movement education, philosophy developed by Rudolph Laban in England in the late 1930s. This philosophy attempts to help students understand the principles of efficient movement through participation in movement experiences. A combination of kinesiological and biomechanical concepts are combined with the four concepts of movement proposed by Laban—body, effort, space, and relationships. It also encourages self-expression and social interaction. One of the earlier advocates of the philosophy in the United States was Eleanor Metheny. She wrote:

> If we may define the totally educated person as one who has fully developed his ability to utilize constructively all of his potential capacities as a person in relation to the world in which he lives, then we may define the physically educated person as one who has fully developed the ability to utilize constructively all of his potential capacities for movement as a way of expressing, exploring, developing, and interpreting himself and his relationship to the world he lives in. This is the part of education we have chosen as our peculiar task. Our job is to help him learn to move his body.[38]

Programs with a human movement emphasis are usually found in elementary schools with some influence in secondary and college courses.[39] The human movement philosophy was adopted and promoted by Camille Brown and Rosalind Cassidy.

No prominent physical educator in the past thirty years has deviated significantly from the philosophy of "education through the physical."

Human movement is an expression of the
individual interacting with the environment.

Education for Leisure Time and Recreation

Jay B. Nash taught "that children should be educated for their leisure-time activities as well
as for a vocation." He defined recreation as the "re-creation" of the person through a change
in the pattern of his or her activities.[40] Nash also believed that physical education was "all
the experiences children have in neuromuscular activities which are directed to the desired
outcomes."[41] Joining with Williams to promote the social and moral aspects of physical education, Nash emphasized that "character is one of the desirable outcomes of education and
hence is one of the desirable outcomes of physical education."[42]

The depression accentuated recreation in the lives of Americans as they sought relaxation in less expensive community recreation programs. Educators were encouraged to include activities in physical education programs with carryover value that prepared youth for leisure-time pursuits. "Progressive educators experimented with coeducational classes in swimming, folk and social dancing, mixed doubles in sports and mixed volleyball, bowling, and outing activities."[43]

Today physical educators and recreational specialists work closely together to bring a greater variety of opportunities to those seeking physical activity.

Physical Education Today

The cries of "crisis in education" heard in the 1980s, and discussed in chapter 1, had a resounding and deep-felt effect on physical education programs in the schools. The *Nation at Risk*[44] report questioned the inclusion of physical education courses in the school curriculum and recommended that school boards include more "academic" subjects in course requirements at the expense of physical education and certain other subjects. Jewett acknowledged at this time that "education is receiving a great deal of attention but, unfortunately, most of this attention is not supportive of physical education."[45] Moreover, Hutslar emphasized that "physical education appears to be in a struggle for its existence as a credible subject in the curriculum."[46] As a result of the attacks on physical education, fewer teachers are needed. In the 1985–86 teaching year, placement officials expected a surplus of teachers in only one field—physical education.[47]

Teacher morale is low at this time. Griffin outlined the following eight obstacles to excellence that face teachers of physical education:

1. Lack of teacher or program evaluation.
2. Lack of formal incentive or reward.
3. Lack of professional support and development.
4. Inadequate facilities, equipment, and scheduling.
5. Failure to include teachers in decision making.
6. Compliance and smooth operations valued over teaching competence.
7. Acceptance of mediocrity.
8. Isolation (for the most part, working alone).[48]

Although physical educators face a struggle in the eighties, a hopeless attitude is not warranted. Lambert emphasized that "there are problems in secondary physical education, but none that cannot be addressed optimistically."[49] Many physical educators suggest the following guidelines to help teachers achieve excellence amidst struggle: (1) prepare for and adjust to workplace realities, (2) align goals and practices so that students master meaningful skills, (3) avoid professional isolation, (4) take full membership in the school community and involve citizens in the program, and (5) educate administrators so they can give effective support.[50]

The added attention to the profession gives educators an opportunity to proclaim the worth of what they do. On the heels of the *Nation at Risk* report, Secretary of Education William J. Bennett published *First Lessons: A Report on Elementary Education in America*.[51] This report gave a real boost to the necessity of including physical education programs in the elementary school curriculum. The report pointed out that "American children are in remarkably bad shape"[52] and presented facts from the National Children and Youth Fitness

Table 2.1 Rank order of students' attitudes toward subjects: By level of schooling

Liking

Upper Elementary			Junior High			Senior High		
Subject	% Like	N	Subject	% Like	N	Subject	% Like	N
Arts	93.2	1621	Arts	85.9	5130	Arts	83.6	6903
Physical ed.	86.9	1615	Voc./Career ed.	81.0	4912	Voc./Career ed.	80.8	6884
Math	81.5	1609	Physical ed.	80.1	5177	Physical ed.	79.8	6969
Reading/English	81.3	1622	Math	74.8	5160	English	72.1	7046
Science	80.9	1604	English	69.3	5231	Math	65.0	6966
Social studies	65.6	1617	Social studies	66.0	5184	Social studies	65.0	6958
			Science	66.1	5068	Science	64.1	6908
			Foreign lang.	62.0	4734	Foreign lang.	52.8	6825

Importance

Upper Elementary			Junior High			Senior High		
Subject	% Imp.	N	Subject	% Imp.	N	Subject	% Imp.	N
Math	93.9	1618	Math	95.0	5154	Math	94.3	6988
Reading/English	93.5	1617	English	91.5	5220	English	93.6	7043
Science	89.4	1593	Voc./Career ed.	85.1	4972	Voc./Career ed.	85.9	6899
Social studies	88.9	1614	Social studies	83.1	5146	Science	79.2	6863
Physical ed.	87.2	1621	Science	78.8	5045	Social studies	77.8	6961
Arts	80.2	1610	Physical ed.	75.3	5174	Physical ed.	67.4	6998
			Foreign lang.	73.5	4842	Arts	65.3	6929
			Arts	70.4	5103	Foreign lang.	65.1	6784

Difficulty*

	Upper Elementary					Junior High					Senior High			
Subject	% Hard	% Easy	% Just Right	N	Subject	% Hard	% Easy	% Just Right	N	Subject	% Hard	% Easy	% Just Right	N
Social studies	19.9	47.1	33.0	1602	Foreign lang.	23.3	29.2	47.5	219	Science	27.8	25.2	47.0	1313
Math	17.7	55.0	27.3	1610	Social studies	17.9	27.5	54.6	1420	Math	26.0	28.3	45.7	1587
Science	14.5	54.5	31.0	1594	Science	17.1	29.0	53.9	1056	Foreign lang.	24.2	29.8	46.0	526
Reading/English	10.7	46.3	43.0	1613	Math	14.0	32.2	53.8	1670	English	16.1	32.3	51.6	1793
Physical ed.	10.3	67.1	22.6	1609	English	12.5	31.6	55.9	1644	Social studies	15.9	35.2	48.9	1749
Arts	3.4	78.6	18.0	1608	Voc./Career ed.	8.2	42.0	49.8	1023	Arts	9.3	45.4	45.3	1474
					Arts	7.6	45.7	46.7	1176	Voc./Career ed.	9.1	42.5	48.4	1726
					Physical ed.	5.0	45.8	49.2	754	Physical ed.	7.8	54.0	38.2	768

*As perceived only by students who were currently enrolled in each subject.

Goodlad, John I. A Place Called School: Prospects for the Future. New York: McGraw-Hill Book Company, 1984, pp. 116–17.

Study published in 1985.[53] It revealed that 40 percent of boys six to eleven could do only one pullup; 25 percent could not do any. Fifty-five percent of all girls could not do any pul-lups. Fifty percent of girls six to seventeen and 30 percent of boys six to twelve could not run a mile in less than ten minutes. When considering that children spend an average of seven and three-fourths hours a day watching television, usually eating junk food at the same time, these results are not surprising.[54] The National Children and Youth Fitness Study also pointed out that American young people have become fatter since the 1960s.[55] *First Lessons* emphasized that physical education programs belong in the elementary schools "not only because they promote health and well-being, but because they contribute tangibly to aca-demic achievement." It was emphasized that today's children do not get a test of fitness when they are young because programs have been dropped.[56] George Allen, chairman of the Pres-ident's Council on Physical Fitness and Sports, stated that physical education used to be a required subject in schools, just like English and math and history and economics. He pointed out that in many states it has been almost eliminated from the curriculum.[57]

Figures released in 1985 showed that nationally, 80.3 percent of students in grades five through twelve were enrolled in physical education. A slightly higher percentage of boys (81.66 percent) than girls (78.88 percent) took physical education. These rates declined from 97 percent for both boys and girls in the fifth grade to 55.73 percent for males and 48.47 percent for females in the twelfth grade.[58] Such figures can be misleading because enroll-ment does *not* mean that students are being taught by specialists or that they are exposed to a physical education program on a regular basis. Goodlad pointed out that the kinds of programs offered in elementary schools vary greatly and that the gap between the ideal cur-riculum and the practices observed at all levels appears to be substantial.[59]

Although physical education programs and student outcomes were being scrutinized and criticized at this time, the popularity of the classes remained high. Goodlad emphasized that students like physical education. Table 2.1 shows that students ranked physical edu-cation high for "liking" but relatively low for "importance" and "difficulty."[60]

As a result of the Youth Fitness Hearings, the following recommendations were made by the President's Council.

All children K–12 should

1. Participate in *daily* physical education which emphasizes both fitness and skills,
2. Be tested twice a year in fitness,
3. Understand and be able to apply exercise science principles,
4. Have posture checks, routine health screenings, and appropriate follow-ups,
5. Have remedial attention as needed, and
6. If they are disabled, be identified and provided with appropriate programs.[61]

The first recommendation got support from the federal government in the fall of 1986 when Senate Concurrent Resolution 145 was passed. As shown in figure 2.1, this resolution stated that daily physical education programs should be required for all children K–12.

Title IX has had a significant impact on physical education programs today. This gov-ernment mandate of the Education Amendments Act of 1972 provides that "no person in the United States shall on the basis of sex be excluded from participation in, be denied the benefits of, or be subjected to discrimination under any education program or activity re-ceiving Federal financial assistance."[62] The law requires that all schools avoid discrimination

Senate Concurrent Resolution 145—Relating to Daily Physical Education Programs for All Children

S. Con. Res. 145

Whereas physical education is essential to the physical development of the growing child;

Whereas physical education helps improve the overall health of children by increasing cardiovascular endurance, muscular strength and power, flexibility, weight regulation, improved bone development, improved posture, skillful moving, increased mental alertness, active lifestyle habits, and constructive use of leisure time;

Whereas physical education helps improve the mental alertness, academic performance, readiness to learn, and enthusiasm for learning of children;

Whereas physical education helps improve the self-esteem, interpersonal relationships, responsible behavior and independence of children;

Whereas children who participate in quality daily physical education programs tend to be more healthy and physically fit;

Whereas physically fit adults have significantly reduced risk factors for heart attacks and strokes;

Whereas the Surgeon General, in "Objectives for the Nation," recommends increasing the numer of school mandated physical education programs that focus on health-related physical fitness; and

Whereas a quality daily physical education program for all children from kindergarten through grade 12 is an essential part of a comprehensive education: Now, therefore, be it

Resolved by the Senate (the House of Representatives concurring), that the Congress encourages state and local governments and local educational agencies to require quality daily physical education programs for all children from kindergarten through grade 12.

Figure 2.1 Resolution 145.

on the basis of sex in such areas as course offerings, extracurricular activities, behavior, appearance, and student services. It also requires equal employment opportunities and compensation of faculty.

Title IX has been the impetus to implement coeducational instructional classes. It has given females the opportunity to participate in greater numbers on sports teams, but it has also brought about the decline of female coaches and administrators in sports programs.

After the implementation of Title IX, participation in interscholastic athletics by women at the high-school level grew by almost 700 percent. A similar increase was evidenced at the collegiate level. The number of female participants grew from 15,000 participants in 1966–67 to over 64,000 a decade later (concurrent figures for men were 154,000 and 170,000).[63]

Historically physical education movements and programs have undergone significant changes in direction. At the present time the schools are dictating these changes. "Our nation's schools are currently undergoing the most far-reaching reforms and renewal processes since the turn of the century."[64] As a result of this reform movement, citizens are asking if physical education is a viable subject in the school curriculum. If the profession is to survive in the future, physical educators must answer the critics by proving its worth and expanding its base of existence from the schools to all citizens of the community who incorporate similar purposes as a way of life.

Physical Education in the Future

The physical educator of the future will have to offer programs that meet the needs of a changing American society. Health and fitness levels are predicted to be higher than ever in the twenty-first century. Medical technology, although costly, will enable people to maintain life almost indefinitely.[65] While people will live longer, they will also assume more of the responsibility for their own health. As Naisbitt pointed out, at least one hundred million Americans, almost half the population, are now exercising in some way—up from only about one-quarter of the population in 1960. One in seven Americans now jogs on a regular basis. As the United States ceased to be a nation of farmers and factory workers, it became a country of joggers, bicyclists, and weight lifters. Americans have also reduced their fat intake, cut down on smoking, switched from hard liquor to wine, and increased health food consumption. The corporate world has increased the number of fitness programs available to employees.[66] These trends show no indication of changing in the future. Physical educators need to capitalize on them and guide both the young and the old in their pursuit of a healthy life-style. Freeman pointed out that twentieth-century physical educators

> have not been very successful in communicating either the values of physical education or the need for physical education to the public. . . . The new physical educator needs to be very skill-oriented—capable of demonstrating as well as teaching the skills used in any class—and, at the same time, he or she must be broadly educated in the liberal arts and sciences in order to be able to converse meaningfully with people in all academic fields. For too long the physical educator has been cut off in the gym, with a reputation of having few interests beyond the sports pages. That type of physical educator cannot survive in the modern world, much less the future, because that type has become an educational dinosaur.[67]

Present trends and future predictions are helpful in formulating principles to be followed in future programs. The following list suggests future program direction:

1. Strong leadership will be the key to a successful physical education program.
2. The need for physical activity will be even more important than it has been in the past.
3. Programs must be designed to meet the needs of all people regardless of age, sex, race, or ability. This may necessitate the expansion of programs outside the traditional walls of the school.
4. Programs must stress a health-maintenance life-style and ways in which students can evaluate and design their own fitness programs.
5. Students must be taught how to learn new skills and be gradually exposed to programs in which they can learn to be self-directing rather than dependent on teacher instruction.[68]
6. Research findings about the effects of exercise on individuals must be used to enhance personal development and improve society.[69]

7. General practitioners must be trained. Even though physical educators have become more specialized within the profession—training sport psychologists, exercise physiologists, sports trainers, education practitioners, and other specialists—the public schools will demand a practitioner who can teach a wide variety of activities.

8. Teachers must become much more sensitive to the uniqueness of each person. They will need to be more specialized in exercise evaluation and prescription for each individual.

9. Athletic competition must be adapted to the electronic age. Expensive travel schedules will have to be modified, maybe by adapting to competition over communications satellites. For example, swimmers in different parts of the world will appear to be swimming side by side due to modern media technology. Judges of such sports as gymnastics can watch performers from far-reaching world sites by the same media wizardry.

10. Movement possibilities in a relatively weightless medium must be discovered.[70]

The future holds exciting possibilities for the physical educator. The time is right to revitalize and nourish the roots of the past while soaring on widespread wings of the present into the wonderment of the future.

Questions and Suggested Activities

1. Observe several students in physical education classes for at least a week and record your findings in a journal. Be prepared to serve as a witness in a pretrial hearing in which the following complaint is expressed: School physical education classes fail to make a significant contribution to all students enrolled; therefore, (1) the required physical education program should be rescinded and (2) tax funds expended for physical education should be used for some other educational program. Document your findings of both the values and weaknesses of the physical education program and be prepared to be questioned by both the defense and prosecution lawyers.

2. Write your philosophy of physical education. Try to keep this philosophy in harmony with your philosophy of education. Keep it short, concise, and written so that the average parent can understand it. Include such areas as how you feel about students, how physical education can help them meet the goals of education, and the values of physical education for students and others in out-of-school situations.

3. As parents, concerned citizens, administrators, teachers, medical doctors (or other selected groups), list the things that a graduate of a successful physical education program should be able to do to receive a high-school diploma.

4. What kinds of experiences might be needed to do the things listed in activity 3? Can "throw out the ball" programs be justified?

5. In considering students' needs on the high school level, if you had a choice of either having an elective program or a required program, which would you choose and why?

6. You are a physical education department head in a large, middle-class high school in the year 1995. Outline the physical education program that you would administer in the school.

Suggested Readings

Acosta, R. Vivian, and Linda Jean Carpenter. "Women in Athletics—A Status Report." *Journal of Physical Education, Recreation and Dance* 56 (August 1985):30–34.

Annarino, Anthony A. "Changing Times: Keeping abreast professionally." *Journal of Physical Education, Recreation and Dance* 55 (May/June 1984):32–34, 52.

Austin, Dean A. "Economic Impact on Physical Education." *Journal of Physical Education, Recreation and Dance* 55 (May/June 1984):35–37.

Broten, G. Arthur. "A Look to the Future." *Journal of Physical Education, Recreation and Dance* 56 (April 1985):125–26.

Corbin, Charles B. "The Importance of Physical Education." *Physical Educator* 41 (May 1984):58–59.

Ennis, Catherine D. "A Future Scenario for Physical Education: The Movement for Life Curriculum, 2017–2035." *Journal of Physical Education, Recreation and Dance* 55 (September 1984):4–5.

Gillam, G. McKenzie. "Physical Education Report Card: Public Attitudes in Alabama." *Journal of Physical Education, Recreation and Dance* 57 (November/December 1986):57–60.

Heitmann, Helen M. "Physical Education for Survival: Back to Basics." *Journal of Physical Education, Recreation and Dance* 55 (August 1984):25–26.

Hutslar, Jack. "Fizz Ed: Problems and Solutions." *Journal of Physical Education, Recreation and Dance* 57 (February 1986):70–75.

Jewett, Ann E. "Excellence or Obsolescence: Goals for Physical Education in Higher Education." *Journal of Physical Education, Recreation and Dance* 56 (September 1985):39–43.

Johnson, Martin W. "Physical Education—Fitness or Fraud?" *Journal of Physical Education, Recreation and Dance* 56 (January 1985):33–35.

Kneer, Marian E. "Exit Competencies in Physical Education for the Secondary School Student." *Journal of Physical Education and Recreation* 49 (January 1978):46.

Leonard, George. *The Ultimate Athlete.* New York: Viking Press, 1975.

Locke, Larry, Pat Griffin, Thomas Templin, eds. "Profiles of Struggle." *Journal of Physical Education, Recreation and Dance* 57 (April 1986):32–63.

Melograno, Vincent. "Physical Education Curriculum for the 1980s." *Journal of Physical Education and Recreation* 51 (September 1980):39.

Mitchner, James Albert. *Sports in America.* New York: Random House, 1976.

Norton, Candace J., ed., "High School Physical Education: Problems and Possibilities." *Journal of Physical Education, Recreation and Dance* 58 (February 1987):19–32.

Ojeme, Emmanuel O. "Teaching Physical Education: A Conceptual Analysis with Implications for Teachers." *Journal of Teaching in Physical Education* 5 (July 1986):221–29.

Pearson, Kathleen. "Applied Futurism: How to Avoid Professional Obsolescence." *Physical Educator* 39 (December 1982):170–75.

Powell, Kenneth E., Gregory M. Christenson, and Marshall W. Kreuter. "Objectives for the Nation: Assessing the Role Physical Education Must Play." *Journal of Physical Education, Recreation and Dance* 55 (August 1984):18–20.

Razor, Jack E. "Elective PE Programs: Expansion vs. Limitation." *Journal of Physical Education and Recreation* 46 (June 1975):23–24.

Ross, James G., and Glen G. Gilbert. "Summary of Findings from National Children and Youth Fitness Study." *Journal of Physical Education, Recreation and Dance* 56 (January 1985):43–90.

Sherrill, Claudine. "The Future is Ours to Shape." *Physical Educator* 40 (March 1983):44–50.

Stier, William F. "Challenges Facing Physical Education: Alternative Career Options." *Journal of Physical Education, Recreation and Dance* 57 (October 1986):26–27.

Taylor, John L. "Surviving the Challenge." *Journal of Physical Education, Recreation and Dance* 57 (January 1986):69–72.

References

1. Robert M. W. Travers, ed., *Second Handbook of Research on Teaching* (Chicago: Rand McNally College Publishing Company, 1973), p. 1210.
2. Stephen L. Richards, *Where Is Wisdom?* (Deseret Book Company, 1955), p. 208.
3. Roberta Mesenbrink, et al., National Association of Secondary School Principals, *Curriculum Report,* vol. 4 (December 1974).
4. Research Works, "How Satisfied Are Americans with the Way They Look?" *Journal of Physical Education, Recreation and Dance* 57 (May/June 1986), p. 7.
5. American Association of Health, Physical Education and Recreation, *Guidelines for Secondary School Physical Education* (Washington, D.C.: AAHPER, 1970).
6. Curriculum Action Project, Physical Education Department, Calgary Board of Education (Calgary, Canada: 1978).
7. *USA Today,* May 16, 1986, p. 14A.
8. National Association for Sport and Physical Education, *Guidelines for Secondary School Physical Education: A Position Paper* (Reston, Virginia: AAHPERD, 1986).
9. *USA Today,* May 16, 1986, p. 14A.
10. National Association for Sport and Physical Education, Guidelines.
11. Don Hellison, *Beyond Balls and Bats: Alienated Youth in the Gym* (Washington, D.C.: AAHPERD, 1978), p. 1.
12. Vern Seefeldt and Paul Vogel. *The Value of Physical Activity* (Reston, Virginia: AAHPERD, 1986), pp. 1–2.
13. Suzanne Glair, "Values of Physical Activity as Expressed by Physical Education Majors," *Physical Educator* 41 (December 1984): pp. 186–89.
14. Delbert Oberteuffer and Celeste Ulrich, *Physical Education: A Textbook of Principles for Professional Students,* 4th ed. (New York: Harper & Row, Publishers, 1970), p. 6.
15. American Alliance for Health, Physical Education, and Recreation, *Guide to Excellence for Physical Education in Colleges and Universities* (Washington, D.C.: AAHPER, 1970).
16. Leland Stanford, in Carl E. Willgoose, *The Curriculum in Physical Education,* 4th ed. (Englewood Cliffs, New Jersey: Prentice-Hall, 1974), p. 189.
17. Greyson Daughtrey, *Effective Teaching in Physical Education for Secondary Schools,* 2d ed. (Philadelphia: W. B. Saunders, 1973).
18. Judith H. Placek, "Conceptions of Success in Teaching: Busy, Happy and Good?" in Thomas J. Templin and Janice K. Olson, eds., *Teaching in Physical Education* (Champaign: Human Kinetics Publishers, 1983), p. 49.
19. Betty Spears and Richard A. Swanson, *History of Sport and Physical Activity in the United States* (Dubuque, Iowa: Wm. C. Brown Company Publishers, 1983), p. 317.
20. C. W. Hackensmith, *History of Physical Education* (New York: Harper & Row, Publishers, 1966).
21. Ibid., p. 114.
22. Mary H. Leigh, "The Renaissance of the Olympic Games," *Journal of Physical Education, Recreation and Dance* 55 (February 1984), p. 20.
23. Hackensmith, *History of Physical Education,* pp. 158–59.
24. Spears, *History of Sport and Physical Activity in the United States,* p. 237.
25. Joseph B. Oxendine, "100 Years of Basic Instruction," *Journal of Physical Education, Recreation and Dance* 56 (September 1985), pp. 32–36.
26. Hackensmith, *History of Physical Education,* p. 205.
27. Oxendine, "100 Years of Basic Instruction," p. 32.
28. Daryl Siedentop, Charles Mand, and Andrew Taggart, *Physical Education: Teaching and Curriculum Strategies for Grades 5–12* (Palo Alto: Mayfield Publishing Company, 1986), p. 148.
29. Spears, *History of Sport and Physical Activity in the United States,* p. 223.

30. Charles H. McCloy, "How About Some Muscle?" *Journal of Health and Physical Education* 7 (May 1936), pp. 302–3, 355.
31. Arthur Steinhaus, cited in "Physical Education for Physical Fitness," Chapter 4 in Daryl Siedentop, *Physical Education: Introductory Analysis* (Dubuque, Iowa: Wm. C. Brown Company Publishers, 1972), p. 63.
32. Spears, *History of Sport and Physical Activity in the United States*, p. 223.
33. Thomas D. Wood, "The Scientific Approach in Physical Education," in *The Making of American Physical Education*, Arthur Weston, ed. (New York: Appleton-Century-Crofts, 1962), p. 151.
34. Luther Halsey Gulick, "Physical Training in the Modern City," in *The Making of American Physical Education*, Arthur Weston, ed. (New York: Appleton-Century-Crofts, 1962), p. 169.
35. Clark W. Hetherington, "Fundamental Education," in *The Making of American Physical Education*, Arthur Weston, ed. (New York: Appleton-Century-Crofts, 1962), p. 160.
36. Ibid.
37. Jesse Feiring Williams, "Education Through the Physical," in *The Making of American Physical Education*, Arthur Weston, ed. (New York: Appleton-Century-Crofts, 1962), p. 219.
38. Eleanor Metheny, "The Third Dimension in Physical Education," in *The Making of American Physical Education*, Arthur Weston, ed. (New York: Appleton-Century-Crofts, 1962), p. 238.
39. Spears, *History of Sport and Physical Activity in the United States*, p. 305.
40. William H. Freeman, *Physical Education and Sport in a Changing Society* (Minneapolis: Burgess Publishing Company, 1982), p. 42.
41. Spears, *History of Sport and Physical Activity in the United States*, p. 223.
42. Jay B. Nash, "Character Education As an Objective," in *The Making of American Physical Education*, Arthur Weston, ed. (New York: Appleton-Century-Crofts, 1962), p. 256.
43. Hackensmith, *History of Physical Education*, pp. 440–43.
44. National Commission on Excellence in Education, *A Nation at Risk* (Washington, D.C.: United States Department of Education, 1983).
45. Ann E. Jewett, "Excellence or Obsolescence: Goals for Physical Education in Higher Education," *Journal of Physical Education, Recreation and Dance* 56 (September 1985), pp. 39–43.
46. Jack Hutslar, "Fizz Ed: Problems and Solutions," *Journal of Physical Education, Recreation and Dance* 57 (February 1986), pp. 70–75.
47. Association for School, College, and University Staffing, *Annual Survey of Placement Officials* (Box 4411, Madison, Wisconsin).
48. Pat Griffin, "What Have We Learned," *Journal of Physical Education, Recreation and Dance* 57 (April 1986), pp. 57–59.
49. Leslie T. Lambert, "Secondary School Physical Education Problems: What Can We Do About Them?" *Journal of Physical Education, Recreation and Dance* 58 (February 1987), p. 30.
50. Larry Locke, "What Can We Do?" *Journal of Physical Education, Recreation and Dance* 57 (April 1986), pp. 60–63; and Candace J. Norton, ed., "High School Physical Education: Problems and Possibilities," *Journal of Physical Education, Recreation and Dance* 58 (February 1987), pp. 19–32.
51. William J. Bennett, *First Lessons: A Report on Elementary Education in America* (Washington, D.C.: United States Department of Education, 1986).
52. Ibid., p. 37.
53. Ross, James G., Glen G. Gilbert, eds. "Summary of Findings from National Children and Youth Fitness Study," *Journal of Physical Education, Recreation and Dance* 56 (January 1985), pp. 43–90.
54. *USA Today*, May 16, 1986, p. 14A.
55. "Summary of Findings from National Children and Youth Fitness Study," *Journal of Physical Education, Recreation and Dance*, p. 48.
56. Bennett, *First Lessons*, p. 37.
57. *USA Today*, August 14, 1986, p. 9A.
58. "Summary of Findings from National Children and Youth Fitness Study," *Journal of Physical Education, Recreation and Dance*, p. 32.

59. John I. Goodlad, *A Place Called School: Prospects for the Future* (New York: McGraw-Hill Book Company, 1984), pp. 222, 224.
60. Ibid., p. 224.
61. Ash Hayes, "Youth Physical Fitness Hearings: An Interim Report from the President's Council on Physical Fitness and Sports" *Journal of Physical Education, Recreation and Dance* 55 (November/December 1984), p. 32.
62. *Federal Register,* vol. 42, May 4, 1977, p. 22676.
63. R. Vivian Acosta and Linda Jean Carpenter, "Women in Athletics—A Status Report," *Journal of Physical Education, Recreation and Dance* 56 (August 1985), p. 30.
64. Janet A. Wessel and Luke Kelly, *Achievement-Based Curriculum Development in Physical Education* (Philadelphia: Lea & Febiger, 1986), p. 282.
65. Claudine Sherrill, "The Future is Ours to Shape," *Physical Educator* 40 (March 1983), p. 45.
66. John Naisbitt, *Megatrends* (New York: Warner Books, 1982), pp. 146–49.
67. Freeman, *Physical Education and Sport in a Changing Society,* p. 288.
68. Richard L. Marsh, "Physically Educated—What It Will Mean for Tomorrow's High School Student," *Journal of Physical Education and Recreation* 49 (January 1978), p. 50.
69. Tom Evaul, "Organizing Centers for the 1980's," *Journal of Physical Education and Recreation* 51 (September 1980), pp. 51–54.
70. Kathleen Pearson, "Applied Futurism: How to Avoid Professional Obsolescence," *Physical Educator* 39 (December 1982), pp. 170–75.

Understanding the Role of the Teacher

Study Stimulators

1. Would you advise someone to enter the teaching profession today? Why or why not? What job placement tips would you give them?
2. What teaching characteristics do effective teachers possess?
3. How do you stack up as a potential teacher?
4. Is it possible to be an effective teacher of physical education and at the same time succeed as an interscholastic coach?
5. What is a code of ethics? Of what value is it to a physical educator?
6. What responsibilities to the profession of education do physical educators have?
7. What causes teacher stress, and how does one deal with it?

What is a teacher? In response to that question, a fourth-grade student replied, "A teacher is someone who knows that you can do what you never did before."[1] A good teacher has the vision to see what the student is capable of doing or becoming and the ability to help the student achieve that goal. Those working with students should keep in mind that the mediocre teacher *tells,* the good teacher *explains,* the superior teacher *demonstrates,* and the great teacher *inspires.* Someone once said, "Your students deserve more than your knowledge. They deserve and hunger for your inspiration."

What is teaching? In one sense it is the business or occupation of teachers. In another sense it is the act of helping (inspiring) students to do that which they never did before. If teaching is an occupation, those entering the profession must make a decision to become teachers and go through the training process necessary to become qualified.

Deciding to Become a Qualified Teacher

Now is an exciting time to enter the field of teaching. The world is always ready for a creative, enthusiastic, dedicated, and capable teacher. Those desiring to teach in today's society have the opportunity to make things better and be part of a new era in public education. Because public attention and support have been drawn to the schools, proposals have been made to remedy the problems facing the schools today. Educators, parents, and legislators are committed to improving public education. Much has already changed as a result of the education reform movement. "States and local school boards have raised standards for students and teachers alike, substantially raised teacher salaries in many locales, created career ladders, and instituted merit pay plans."[2]

Unique challenges do face the prospective teacher of today, however. Chapter 1 discussed the crisis in education, and chapter 2 reported a lack of support for physical education programs. The many reports on education that surfaced during the 1980s included two that stressed the need to improve teaching. In April of 1986 the Holmes Group released its controversial report, *Tomorrow's Teachers.*[3] The Carnegie Forum published *A Nation Prepared: Teachers for the Twenty-First Century* in May of the same year.[4] Both documents outlined proposals to produce teachers who have competency, prestige, high earnings, role differentiation, and an improved workplace. A summary of both reports includes the following recommendations:

1. Establish high standards of academic excellence for teachers. Require a bachelor's degree in a specialized subject area as a prerequisite for the professional study of teaching, which would come at the graduate level.
2. Incorporate teacher certification requirements to establish levels of competency and differentiation of roles.
3. Establish certain universities as research and training centers to certify professional teachers.
4. Upgrade the working place by providing increased salaries and better working conditions.

Teachers themselves express concern about their chosen profession. Harris reported in the second annual *Metropolitan Life Survey of the American Teacher* that 36 percent of public school teachers said they experience "great stress" on the job, compared with only 27 percent of all American adults who say they feel that way. In addition, 27 percent of teachers said they were "very likely" or "somewhat likely" to leave the profession in five years.[5]

Such problems were compounded by the fact that the pool of new teachers got smaller each year. Not only were fewer prospective teachers enrolling in college courses, but many of the more capable students were not entering the teaching profession. The Carnegie Foundation reported that in 1982 high-school seniors intending to major in education scored eighty points below the national average on combined scores of the verbal and math sections of the SAT.[6] Poor salaries and low prestige were blamed for this state of affairs.

Much has changed since the cries for educational reform were first heard in the early 1980s. "Neither the individuals responsible for writing the reform reports nor the education establishment were able to judge accurately the depth and breadth of public support for education reform."[7]

Most states have taken active measures to assess the teaching profession and are striving to upgrade working conditions and provide adequate compensation for good teaching. The present prospects for teachers are good. Effective teachers will always be in demand in the public schools, and optimism is the key for those preparing to enter the educational workplace.

The decision to become a teacher must take into consideration the pros and cons of the profession as well as personal aptitude. Mark A, B, or C on the following questions to see how you stack up as a prospective teacher:

_____ 1. I like myself.
_____ 2. I enjoy working with people regardless of race, gender, socioeconomic status, or occupation.
_____ 3. I am sensitive to the needs and feelings of others.
_____ 4. I have a sense of humor.
_____ 5. I am aware of my strengths and weaknesses as a teacher and am working to improve my present skills and abilities.

_____ 6. I am a positive example of personal appearance and hygiene.

_____ 7. I am physically fit.

_____ 8. I can use a variety of teaching methodologies and demonstrate a wide variety of physical skills.

_____ 9. I can explain the basic concepts of physical education (e.g., exercise physiology, mechanical analysis, strategies).

_____ 10. I am skilled in a variety of classroom management skills.

_____ 11. I am a member of a professional organization, and I attend professional meetings.

If you rated yourself mostly As and Bs and are actively engaged in upgrading the Cs, you should consider becoming a teacher.

Characteristics of Effective Teachers

What makes some individuals effective teachers? Four essentials of good teaching have been identified: (1) know the subject, (2) show interest in the subject, (3) know and like the students, and (4) possess a sense of humor. More recently, the characteristics of caring and flexibility in adapting to changing needs have been found to be qualities of successful teachers.[8]

In the past, research on teaching has not produced answers to such questions as to what makes some individuals effective teachers. As Siedentop pointed out, "Research on teaching doesn't have a good reputation. It has suffered through a long history of inconclusive results, inappropriately asked questions, and less-than-useful techniques."[9] Research done on the effectiveness of teachers substantiates these claims. The first researchers isolated certain personality _characteristics_ of teachers as the criteria for judging teacher effectiveness.[10] Some writers continue to update lists of such characteristics. In a recent survey of undergraduate students enrolled in teacher education programs, the students were asked to recall their best elementary school teacher and identify the qualities and strategies of that teacher that made a significant impact on them.[11] Table 3.1 identifies their common descriptors of memorable teachers. Studies, however, fail to confirm any personal qualities possessed in common by effective teachers.[12]

The later evolution of thought by researchers on teacher effectiveness focused on _methods_ of teaching. This kind of research was very value-laden, and it proved to be no more credible than centering on personality characteristics.[13] No common method used by successful teachers could be isolated, since each situation may call for a different method.

Researchers then determined that effective teachers created and maintained a certain _climate_ in the classroom based on teacher-student interaction. With the use of teacher observation (process-product) tools, patterns such as clarity, time-on-task, and enthusiasm could be evaluated and later modified by appropriate training. Process-product techniques tallied both teacher and student behavior enabling researchers to describe, analyze, and explain what was actually happening in the classroom rather than portray romantic visions of how things should be. Patterns of achievement for high-achieving and low-achieving classrooms then emerged.[14] Although researchers have gained much credibility through this line of investigation, the scope of experiences that can be tallied is still limited.

Researchers next developed a model that determined that effective teachers had a large repertoire of _competencies_ (such as methods of teaching, providing feedback, directing motivation, and managing the classroom) from which to draw. The evaluation of teacher effectiveness was based on the ability to deploy these competencies appropriately to affect student

Table 3.1 Descriptors of good teachers

Classroom Management	Personality	Strategies Techniques	Appearance
Flexibility	Loving	Variety	Young
Organization	Caring	New ideas	Pretty
Equal	Helpful	Clarity	Well-dressed
Fair	Enthusiastic	Interesting	Jolly
Respect	Encouraging	Inductive	Happy
Firm	Perceptive	Concrete	Attractive
Even-tempered	Warm	Visual aids	
Diplomatic	Vivacious	Centers	
Disciplinarian	Positive	Participation	
	Patient	Individualized	
	Compassionate	Read aloud	
	Cheerful	Involved	
	Understanding	Parents	
	Sensitive	Discussion	
	Honest	Supplements	
	Tactful		
	Genuine		
	Attentive		
	Open-minded		

Lester L. Laminack and Betty M. Long, "What Makes a Teacher Effective: Insight from Preservice Teachers," *Clearing House,* 58 (February 1985): 168. Reprinted with permission of the Helen Dwight Reid Educational Foundation. Published by Heldref Publications, 4000 Albemarle St., N.W., Washington, D.C. 20016. Copyright © 1985.

achievement. In this respect, teacher effectiveness refers to the ability of a classroom teacher to produce higher-than-predicted gains on standardized achievement tests.[15] Studies have shown that student achievement is significantly related to teacher attributes such as experience and educational attainment.[16]

Investigators have concluded from all the available research that most teacher behaviors are situation-specific; that is, they are directly related to the subject matter, environment, and characteristics of students. Some factors associated with effective teaching can be identified, however. The third edition of the *Handbook of Research on Teaching* emphasized the role of the individual teacher as a decision maker in producing effectiveness in the classroom. It pointed out that the social organization of the classroom determines teacher effectiveness, and such organization is largely the responsibility of, and determined by, the

Effective teachers provide feedback.

teacher. Research findings showed that successful teachers had the following cognitive skills: (1) rapid judgment, (2) chunking (ability to group discrete events into large units), and (3) differentiation (separating out important information).[17] Researchers are unable to answer with confidence other influences a teacher has on student performance or behavior because too many variables are involved.[18]

In Thomas's point of view, good teaching is an art rather than a science and, as such, cannot be quantified, qualified, or conveniently duplicated:

Teaching is an art. One becomes a good teacher in the same way one becomes a good actor, a good poet, a good musician, a good painter. One develops a unique style, a personalized method, a way of teaching that cannot be mass produced or even replicated. . . . Some teachers are great; some, average; some, poor. No one has yet been able to identify what makes one person a better teacher than another. We can recognize the art, but we cannot identify its separate common components. . . . A good teacher is one that teaches well, much as a good surgeon operates with skill. What makes a good teacher or a good poet or a good surgeon only the stars know; and they are not, as yet, willing to tell us the secret.[19]

One characteristic of effective teachers that appears time and time again in the literature is teacher warmth. Earls demonstrated that distinctive physical education teachers love children, suggesting that the key difference between effective and ineffective teachers may be the intention and commitment to helping these students, whom they care about, to learn. The greatest dissatisfaction of the teachers studied was not being able to reach every child. Such teachers were characterized by: (1) authenticity, (2) empathy, (3) impartiality, (4) individuality, and (5) openness. The absence of discipline and motivation problems was conspicuous in their classes.[20] A study by Williams revealed that woman teachers, as compared with men, perceived themselves as being warmer, more friendly, and more comforting. Student teachers for primary schools, as compared with those for the secondary level, perceived themselves as more warm and supportive.[21] Postman emphasized these qualities, stating:

> When a student perceives a teacher to be an authentic, warm, and curious person, the student learns. When the student does not perceive the teacher as such a person, the student does not learn. There is almost no way to get around this fact.[22]

Teacher warmth and genuine concern for the student is one of the most important qualities of a good teacher. This concern is demonstrated through learning the students' names, getting to know students as individuals, sharing experiences with students, and inviting students' responses. Students do not care how much teachers know until they know how much they care, or as Pullias said, "For teaching to be great, it has to be something like a love affair."[23]

The teacher who can communicate an interest and concern to each student creates a feeling of mutual respect encouraging students to want to learn and achieve in school. Such feelings are engendered by showing courtesy and avoiding criticism, ridicule, or embarrassment. Acceptance of individual differences in backgrounds, abilities, and personalities tells students that the teacher is interested in them as human beings and that they are essential to the success of the class. A willingness to listen to students and incorporate student ideas into the curriculum, when appropriate, are important factors in establishing student-teacher rapport.

Without adequate data to formulate a teacher effectiveness model, prospective teachers would do well to determine their love for children. Once such caring is substantiated, then the teacher can help the child reach his or her full potential. As Calisch stated:

> Most books I've read about teaching indicate that the prime perquisite for a teacher is a "love of children." Hogwash! . . . What you must love is the vision of the well-informed, responsible adult you can help the child become.
>
> Your job as a teacher is to help the child realize who he is, what his potential is, what his strengths are. You can help him learn to love himself—or the man he soon will be. With that kind of understanding self-love, the student doesn't need any of your sentimentality. What he needs is your brains, and enabling him to profit from them calls for decisive firmness.[24]

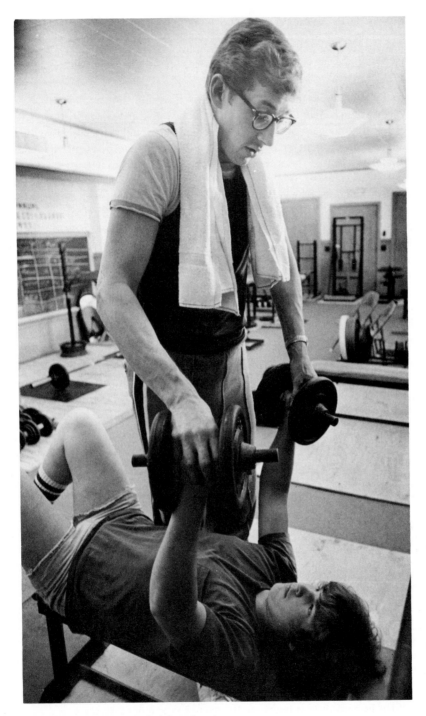

Teachers who communicate interest and
concern for students encourage student
learning.

Teachers who expect a lot from their students tend to spend more time working with students on on-task behavior and push students to work to their full capacities. These teachers can expect that their beliefs will be rewarded. They seldom say things they can get learners to say for them. "But when they do say things, they say them loudly enough to be heard and clearly enough to be understood."[25]

The Role of Teacher/Coach

Anyone engaged in teaching physical education and coaching needs to be aware of the role conflicts that may be involved. One might ask if it is possible to be an effective teacher while coaching an athletic team. Both roles are vitally important; but their aims, goals, and objectives are often in conflict, and a person playing both roles may tend to favor one over the other. Typically the coach deals with relatively small numbers of students with comparable advanced ability who are highly motivated and participating on a volunteer basis. The teacher, however, usually transmits knowledge to large numbers of students with a wide range of abilities who are required to be in class and are sometimes unmotivated or hostile.[26] It is not surprising that the role of coach is not always preferred to that of teacher. The coach could neglect physical education classes and place more importance on coaching if allowed to accentuate the teacher/coach role conflict, the pressure to produce a winning team, the added financial gain, and the higher public credibility attributed to the coach. Begly viewed this role conflict as the rule rather than the exception and stated:

> The crux of the teacher/coach role conflict is not that educators occupying both roles concurrently perceive them as totally different, and therefore choose the one they prefer as the dominant role. Rather . . . the core of the difficulty is mostly a matter of time. . . . The impossibility of meeting the demands of both roles simultaneously is often compounded by powerful social and personal incentives to make the coaching role preeminent.[27]

In a 1983 study of undergraduate physical education majors, the majority of the students did not anticipate a role conflict between their teaching and coaching duties. Fifty-eight percent of the females and 45 percent of the males were equally committed to teaching and coaching. They viewed the abilities needed for each of the roles as similar.[28] Experienced teachers, however, are very much aware of this conflict of roles. Earls reported that distinctive physical educators expressed concern for the interference of athletics with physical education, being intensely aware of the detrimental effects that coaching can have on physical education instruction.[29] Gender, years of experience, coaching or noncoaching assignment, undergraduate major, school socioeconomic status, and level of career aspiration were significant determiners of perceived and experienced conflict between the teaching and coaching roles.[30]

Locke and Massengale[31] found that females perceived more, and often experienced as much, role-related conflict as their male counterparts. Women may be feeling an added pressure to perform successfully as coaches because their numbers have declined. Between 1973 and 1983, since the inception of Title IX, the percentage of women coaches at the high-school level had dropped from 89 percent to 38 percent.[32]

Many professionals believe that physical education and athletics can and must continue to coexist. Administrators, such as athletic directors or principals, can be instrumental in solving the teacher/coach role conflict. They must take the initiative to schedule classes, practices, and competition to aid the coach in fulfilling commitments while providing an atmosphere of support. Both teaching and coaching programs are needed, and while physical educators are better trained to wear both hats, they must not allow their role as coaches to overpower their role as educators.[33] Some feel this conflict of roles will lead to the demise of the teaching program and what is needed is a separation of coaching and teaching. Kneer went so far as to say that secondary physical education cannot survive under the present conditions, and "the profession of physical education and coaching should and must begin the divorce proceedings immediately."[34]

Physical educators need to answer the question "Do I want to be a teacher, or a coach, or both?" Once the decision is made, they must then perform with excellence.

Physical educators will often be addressed as "coach" whether that is an official title or not. Both teachers and coaches can identify with the following poem.

The Coach

She's the first one there in the morning
The last to leave at night
She's also the first one who catches it
When things don't go just right.
A coach is someone who wears a whistle around her neck,
Someone who teaches kids to run and jump and throw and
Kick and catch.
A job that's seldom noticed, "Oh, it's just P.E.," they say.
But I wonder? Do they really know
The things we teach each day?
Things like how to keep on trying—even though you know you
Can't win,
And how to get up when you fall and try again and again
And again.
And when the game is over and your team lost fifty to two,
To be proud because you know deep down that you did the
Best you could do.
How to give one hundred percent each and every day.
And to do the things that you know are right,
As you travel along life's way.
You see, my friend, the things we teach aren't exactly as
They seem.
For we teach kids how to set a goal and how to reach their
Dream.
And even if they try and fail, to be proud of what they've done.
Because in the end it's not the score—it's the game of life
They've won.[35]

(Reprinted by permission of the American Alliance for Health, Physical Education, Recreation and Dance, 1900 Association Drive, Reston, VA 22091.)

Ethical conduct on the part of the teacher/coach often solves the problem of role conflict.

A Professional Code of Ethics

A code of ethics is a statement of conduct that governs individuals within a profession. It refers to all of the relationships that occur among people and between people and institutions in the educational environment. It deals with what is right and wrong or good and bad in human conduct. Ethics deals with values as it attempts to answer the question "Why?" For the physical educator, it includes such ideals as good conduct, tolerance, understanding others, loyalty toward group welfare, fair play, cooperation, support of others, and sacrifice of self for the welfare of others. Because ethics involves conduct, it is not complete without the decision-making process of *what ought to be*.[36]

Physical educators will be confronted with ethical decisions on and off the playing field, and they must be prepared to take a stand and be an example for students forming their own set of values. They must also be willing to accept responsibilities that might include belonging to professional organizations; attending conventions, workshops, clinics, and in-service meetings; acquiring and reading appropriate books and periodicals; and continuing their education. The American Alliance for Health, Physical Education, Recreation and Dance endorses the code of ethics of the National Education Association. This code consists of the expected commitment of the teacher to the student, the public, the profession, and the employer.

Commitment to the Student

The teacher must be committed to the optimum development of every student, regardless of skill level, gender, race, or handicap. "Physical education should be adapted for those students who have special needs."[37]

A friendly but professional relationship should be established with students. When a student and teacher become too familiar, the teacher-student link is weakened and the nature of the educational relationship is impaired. Information of a personal nature should be kept in strictest confidence, and all students should be protected from unnecessary embarrassment.

Meaningful instructional opportunities should be available to all students. Elementary school students should have a *daily* instructional period of at least thirty minutes. The minimum instructional period for students in secondary schools should be a *daily* standard class period.[38]

Commitment to the Public

Everyone in the profession should assume the role of promoting a positive image in the eyes of the public. There is a need to do an exemplary job of teaching to sell physical education programs to the taxpayers. Those involved in athletics must work tirelessly to be sure practices are completely ethical. Crawford stressed the ethical commitment that physical educators must demonstrate:

> Physical educators have a moral responsibility to speak up, speak out, and speak at young people to stress that difficult "right" and "wrong" decisions have to be made if sport is to remain as an expressive and dramatic facet of human experience dependent on ethical behavior.[39]

Each teacher should participate in community affairs, promote good community-school relationships, and refrain from using school affiliation for personal gain.

Commitment to the Profession

A professional person is one who is dedicated to providing a service to other people. Educators should strive to provide a service that is highly esteemed. In the professions of medicine, law, and social work, the clients choose whom to ask for service. An incompetent person in these areas is quickly weeded out. Educators are often shielded from this process, and they must take their professional commitment even more seriously. In education, more often than not, the students have no choice of which teacher to take. Moreover, tenure laws, which originated to protect teachers, now protect incompetent teachers from being terminated.

Teachers should make every effort to maintain relationships with other members of the profession based on mutual respect for one another. Teachers have an obligation to be objective, honest, and fair; to respect and defend the rights of their associates; and to hold in confidence information shared by colleagues. However, professionals also have a responsibility to confront associates who are acting unethically or are incompetent. Moreover, they also have the responsibility to follow proper administrative channels and to be willing to listen to the other person's point of view.

Physical educators should never forget that they are educators and that the purposes of all programs in the school are to educate students. As such, physical education teachers and coaches should share the concerns of other teachers in the school and work together with them to promote total school unity. They can show their concern by attending general faculty meetings; serving on faculty committees; upholding school policies; and taking turns with hall, cafeteria, or bus duty. Cooperation with the school custodial staff is also essential because of the many and varied facilities necessary for physical education programs.

Far too often, physical education teachers divorce themselves from the total school environment. Effective teachers will make the effort to emerge from the gymnasium to share experiences with the rest of the faculty. Time should be taken each year to discuss the physical education program with the principal, including an overview of the program, goals for the year, changes that have been implemented, achievements, and new trends or ideas. Good public relations can be enhanced by teachers as they volunteer to serve on faculty committees, let others know about the program, and integrate physical education concepts with other subject areas in the curriculum. Additional good will can be initiated as administrators, faculty, and staff are invited to participate in faculty fitness programs, clinics to learn new skills, tournaments, and free-play activities. Further, teachers should make every effort to sell themselves and the program by personal appearance, manner of speech, and enthusiasm about the program and the entire school.

Professional Organizations

Professional organizations exist to help members of a given profession work together to achieve common goals. The American Alliance for Health, Physical Education, Recreation and Dance (AAHPERD) is the national affiliate for the profession. Physical educators should make every effort to join this organization at the state, regional, or national level.

Larger education associations operate at the local, state, and national levels. The National Education Association (NEA) and the American Federation of Teachers (AFT) bring together teachers of all disciplines to capitalize on collective-bargaining opportunities and to promote common aims and goals and enhance communication among individuals. It is at the national level that unions, such as the AFT, provide beneficial resources for teachers.

Unions supposedly increase productivity by reducing worker turnover, expanding worker training programs, and facilitating communication between workers and management. Evidence provides overwhelming support for the claim that union workers are paid more than nonunion workers.[40]

Professional organizations catering to specialized groups such as athletic trainers, administrators, and coaches afford numerous opportunities for group affiliation. Members of professional organizations can share ideas with each other by speaking at conventions, writing articles in professional journals, serving on committees, holding an office; or by just attending, listening, reading, or helping. In any case, the growth from such professional involvement is passed on to both students and colleagues. Professional organizations also help with employment needs by publishing job openings and providing opportunities at conventions for potential employers and employees to get acquainted.

A study to determine the commitment of elementary and secondary physical educators to professional organizations revealed that state conventions had the best support. One-third of the teachers polled attended a state HPERD conference during a two-year period. Elementary and junior high physical education teachers were twice as likely as senior high teachers to attend these state conferences. Women teachers were also more likely than men (41 percent and 26 percent) to be in attendance. Attendance by these professionals at regional conferences dropped to 6 percent, and at national conventions, attendance by these teachers was 2 percent. Teachers in this survey were more likely to attend clinics and workshops sponsored by local school districts or organizations (56 percent). The lowest attenders at local meetings were the least-experienced teachers.[41]

Professional Development

Every teacher should develop a personal plan for professional development. Although some states or districts require attendance at in-service workshops or college classes for recertification or salary increases, the need for continuous updating of skills by each teacher should be a matter of professional pride, whether required or not. In addition to in-service workshops and college classes, other options include (1) reading professional books and journals; (2) participating in professional organizations; (3) doing research or writing books or articles; (4) traveling to observe programs, meet other professionals, and view facilities; (5) pursuing a graduate degree; (6) speaking at clinics or professional meetings; and (7) participating on professional committees.

Commitment to Professional Employment Practices

Once a contract has been signed with a school district, the teacher is legally and ethically committed to complete the term of service specified with high-quality work and integrity in employment practices. If the contract must be terminated because of reasons beyond control, then the teacher and the district should arrive at a mutually agreed upon solution to the situation.

Adherence to ethical policies and practices of the employer should always be standard procedure for teachers. Likewise, employers should be expected to act in the same manner. Professional organizations can often assist members experiencing unethical behavior by employers.

Seeking Employment

While competition for positions in physical education may be keen, an ambitious person can enhance his or her opportunities by incorporating definite strategies in securing a position. Lambert outlined the following systematic planning techniques for seeking employment:

1. Explore job possibilities early. Find a job, or volunteer, working at as many different jobs as you can.
2. Stay current about job opportunities. Consult the school placement office regularly. Check library resources.
3. Maintain a 3.0 GPA.
4. Prepare a resumé.
   a. List all previous jobs by year.
   b. List educational background.
   c. List activities you have done that enhance credibility (e.g., Sunday school teacher, camp counselor, recreation leader)
   d. Collect letters of recommendation.
   f. Write personal philosophy.
5. Inform relatives, friends, acquaintances, and former employers you are job hunting.
6. Follow up on all leads and advice.
7. Keep names of important contacts.
8. Start interviewing.
   a. Be positive.
   b. Find out all you can about the organization before going.[42]

The Beginning Teacher

Beginning teachers in all fields have similar concerns about teaching. If these concerns are known, steps can be taken to diminish or alleviate first-day and first-year jitters. Houston and Felder[43] listed the following concerns of new teachers:

1. Expectations about them by their principal and fellow teachers.
2. Classroom management and discipline.
3. Planning and preparing for the day.

When beginning teachers believed in themselves, however, they looked forward to working with students and entered the classroom with enthusiasm. Beginning teachers must be well prepared before school starts. Textbooks should be read, materials collected, policies formulated, and caring people to talk to brought into the picture. Teachers need to also recognize that once teaching has begun they will be more fatigued, may develop other somatic symptoms, may become emotionally drained, or may feel that they are just surviving. These symptoms will usually dissipate after three to four months. New teachers can cushion this process by knowing that it will happen and by surrounding themselves with a support system. Experiences should be talked about, and fellow teachers should be part of one's social experiences. More and more school districts realize the trauma of first-year teachers and are surrounding them with a support system and easing them into full-time teaching more gradually.

Teacher Stress

In most industrialized countries throughout the world, stress has become the main health concern of teachers.[44] Common symptoms include fatigue, nervousness, frustration, and sleeplessness. These can lead to many more serious illnesses, as well as to many psychological disorders.

To prevent stress, teachers need to plan, early in their careers, a personal life-style that can dissipate the stresses of teaching. Proper nutrition, exercise, and sleep are essential. Developing hobbies and interests totally separate from physical education is also important. Attending cultural events, engaging in interior decorating, woodworking, and many other activities can provide a release of built-up tension. Involvement with people from many other walks of life is also valuable.

Within the school environment, teachers should learn to use time efficiently so that they do not need to work longer than necessary. Careful planning and organizing saves last-minute wear and tear on the nerves. Knowing school policies and procedures in advance of an emergency helps one to be calm in the face of adversity. Allowing students and para-professionals to help also saves time and effort.

Time-management techniques are a must for busy teachers who desire to avoid stress. The following time-management techniques should increase efficiency and allow time to pursue high-priority goals:

1. *Plan.* Use a large yearly calendar for school and personal activities. Make a list of daily tasks in order of importance and try to complete the high-priority items. Plan lessons efficiently.
2. *Put an end to putting it off.* Reduce procrastination.
3. *Get organized.* Organize and simplify your work space, filing system, materials, etc. Develop specific class procedures that students know and follow.
4. *Consider time constraints.* Remember that it is okay to say no. Avoid the paper avalanche by setting aside time to go through correspondence saving only vital items.
5. *Modify teaching routine.* Team teach by planning together and sharing facilities and equipment. Organize a physical education club training students to assist. Maintain a lesson plan for substitutes taking over the class.
6. *Exercise with class.* Time to do this outside of school may not materialize.
7. *Guard against interruptions.* Shut the door or find a hideout to unwind. Play the ball; do not let the ball play you.
8. *Take time to be yourself.* Engage in recreational or social activities that are enjoyable.
9. *Develop a support system.* Ask yourself, "Who can help? How can they help?"[45]

Many of the suggestions listed above will help a teacher avoid *"burnout."* Teacher burnout has been described as a response to a circuit overload—a result of unchecked stress on the physical, emotional, or intellectual system of the teacher.[46] With the problems facing educators today, it is no wonder that they are faced with burnout. Solutions for this widely recognized malady fall into two categories, those solvable by

1. Administrators, teacher educators, supervisors, curriculum planners, and society itself, and solved by
   a. Expanding options for teacher behavior.
   b. Organizing support systems.

c. Providing adequate techniques in the survival skills of
   —classroom management
   —public relations
2. Teachers themselves and solved by
   a. Social contacts that revitalize
   b. Physical renewal including
      —Appropriate rest, nutrition, drug use
      —Exercise[47]

Teacher burnout has neither a single cause nor a single solution. Physical education teachers must be alert to the reality that the dual roles of teacher/coach may lead to burnout. "Teachers must recognize the problem, look to its sources, and plan for correction."[48] Teachers may wonder if they are "burning out." Look back over the past six months. Answer the following questions by assigning a number from one (for no or little change) to five (for a great deal of change):

_____ 1. Do you tire easily? Feel fatigued rather than energetic?

_____ 2. Are people annoying you by telling you, "You don't look so good lately"?

_____ 3. Are you working harder and accomplishing less?

_____ 4. Are you increasingly cynical and disenchanted?

_____ 5. Have you lost your enthusiasm for the job and concern for your students?

_____ 6. Are you lacking desire and motivation to seek new ideas for your teaching or remain current with teaching techniques?

_____ 7. Are you often invaded by a sadness you cannot explain?

_____ 8. Are you forgetting (appointments, deadlines, possessions)?

_____ 9. Are you increasingly irritable? More short-tempered?

_____ 10. Are you seeing close friends and family less frequently?

_____ 11. Are you too busy to do even routine things such as make phone calls or read reports?

_____ 12. Are you suffering from physical complaints (aches, pains, headaches, a lingering cold)?

_____ 13. Do you feel disoriented when the activity of the day comes to a halt?

_____ 14. Is joy elusive?

_____ 15. Are you unable to laugh at a joke about yourself?

_____ 16. Does sex seem like more trouble than it is worth?

_____ 17. Do you have very little to say to people?[49]

_____ TOTAL SCORE (80=burnout high; 15=low)

Burnout is real. Prospective teachers should understand thoroughly the demands of the profession so that they can avoid it. Other strategies to minimize burnout include getting involved in other activities, focusing on the positive aspects of the job, allowing fellow workers to complete their share of the responsibilities, and incorporating time-management techniques into the daily routine.[50]

The teaching profession today offers many challenges, yet many exciting and creative opportunities. The prospective teacher should be optimistic about a future that is bright.

Questions and Suggested Activities

1. List five teachers whom you have admired very much. What personal and/or professional qualities did they have that set them apart from other teachers? List the qualities you would like to concentrate on to help you become like these great teachers.

2. List the special talents, attitudes, abilities, or knowledge you now possess that you could offer to public school students. List the abilities you feel you need to acquire to aid you in working in the schools. What experiences might you need to help you acquire the qualities you desire?

3. Create a self-development plan to help you become a better teacher. Include each of the areas discussed in "A professional code of ethics" in this chapter.

4. React to this statement: "A good teacher is born, not made."

5. You are teaching four physical education classes and coaching two major sports in a large metropolitan high school. You realize that you are devoting much more time to your coaching assignments although you have many more students in your physical education classes. What will you do to solve the teacher/coach role conflict so your regular classes are getting their fair share of your time and efforts?

6. In May, afraid of not getting a job, you signed a contract to teach at Podunk High School. In August, an offer comes from Centerville Junior High School where you prefer to teach and live. What will you do?

7. Read "What Ever Happened to Steve?" in the *Journal of Physical Education, Recreation and Dance* 55 (August 1984): 12–15. Write your reactions to this article.

8. Explore the many career options in physical education. List the pros and cons of each. Group options together that you think might be performed by the same person. Using these options, define the professional person you are or hope to become.

9. List the things you will do in your own life to avoid stress and burnout connected with your job as a teacher/coach.

Suggested Readings

Austin, Dean A. "The Teacher Burnout Issue." *Journal of Physical Education, Recreation and Dance* 52 (November/December 1981):35–36.

Bach, Richard. *Jonathan Livingston Seagull.* New York: Macmillan Publishing Company, 1970.

Bianco, Albert and Paul C. Paese. "So You Want to Be a Teacher/Coach." *Journal of Physical Education, Recreation and Dance* 55 (January 1984):55.

Check, John F. "Wanted! A Humorous Teacher." *The Physical Educator* 36 (October 1979):119–22.

Figone, Albert J. "Teacher-Coach Burnout: Avoidance Strategies." *Journal of Physical Education, Recreation and Dance* 57 (October 1986):58–61.

Gallague, David L. "Excellence in Teaching: The Students' Point of View." *The Physical Educator* 31 (May 1974):59–60.

Ingram, Ann. "A Teacher of Physical Education Should Have These Attributes." *The Physical Educator* 34 (March 1977):34.

Kneer, Marian E. "Solutions to Teacher/Coach Problems in Secondary Schools." *Journal of Physical Education, Recreation and Dance* 58 (February 1987):28–29.

Lambert, Charlotte. "Career Directions." *Journal of Physical Education, Recreation and Dance* 55 (May/June 1984):40–43, 53.

Landsmann, Leonna. "Is Teaching Hazardous to Your Health?" *Today's Education* (April/May 1978):48–50.

Miller, David K. "The Effective Teacher." *The Physical Educator* 35 (October 1978):147–48.

NASPE News. "The Role of the Teacher/Coach." *NASPE News* 17 (Winter 1987):6–8.

Shea, Edward J. *Ethical Decisions in Physical Education and Sport.* Springfield, Ill.: Charles C. Thomas, 1978.

Templin, Thomas J., ed. "Profiles of Excellence: Fourteen Outstanding Secondary School Physical Educators." *Journal of Physical Education, Recreation and Dance* 54 (September 1983):15–34.

Williams, Dennis A., Vincent Coppola, Lucy Howard, Janet Huck, Patricia King, and Sylvester Monroe. "Teachers Are in Trouble." *Newsweek* (April 27, 1981):78–84.

References

1. Eleanor Fisher, "What Is a Teacher?" *Instructor* (May 1970), p. 23.
2. Marc Tucker and David Mandel, "The Carnegie Report: A Call for Redesigning the Schools," *Phi Delta Kappan* 68 (September 1986), p. 24.
3. Holmes Group, *Tomorrow's Teachers: A Report of the Holmes Group* (East Lansing: The Holmes Group, Inc., 1986).
4. Task Force on Teaching as a Profession, *A Nation Prepared: Teachers for the 21st Century* (New York: Carnegie Forum on Education and the Economy, 1986).
5. *Daily Universe,* September 13, 1985.
6. *Philadelphia Inquirer,* August 29, 1983, p. 6A.
7. Chris Pipho, "States Move Reform Closer to Reality," *Phi Delta Kappan* 68 (December 1986), p. K2.
8. Lester L. Laminack and Betty M. Long, "What Makes a Teacher Effective: Insight from Preservice Teachers," *Clearing House* 58 (February 1985), p. 268.
9. Daryl Siedentop, *Developing Teaching Skills in Physical Education,* 2d ed. (Palo Alto: Mayfield Publishing Company, 1983), p. 37.
10. Donald M. Medley, "The Effectiveness of Teachers," in Penelope L. Peterson and Herbert J. Walberg, eds., *Research on Teaching: Concepts, Findings, and Implications* (Berkeley: McCutchan Publishing Corporation, 1979), p. 12.
11. Laminack and Long, "What Makes a Teacher Effective," p. 268.
12. George Graham and Elsa Heimerer, "Research on Teacher Effectiveness: A Summary with Implications for Teaching," *Quest* 33, no. 1 (1981), pp. 14–25.
13. Siedentop, *Developing Teaching Skills in Physical Education,* p. 39.
14. Ibid., pp. 39–40.
15. Merlin C. Wittrock, ed., *Handbook of Research on Teaching,* 3d ed. (New York: Macmillan Publishing Company, 1986), p. 52.
16. Randall W. Eberts, "Union Effects on Teacher Productivity," *Industrial and Labor Relations Review* 37 (April 1984), p. 347.
17. Wittrock, *Handbook of Research on Teaching,* pp. 133, 279.
18. Allan C. Ornstein, "Considering Teacher Effectiveness," *Clearing House* 58 (May 1985), pp. 399–402.
19. Donald Thomas in Leonard O. Pellicer, "Effective Teaching: Science or Magic?" *Clearing House* 58 (October 1984), p. 53.
20. Neal F. Earls, "Distinctive Teachers' Personal Qualities, Perceptions of Teacher Education and the Realities of Teaching," *Journal of Teaching Physical Education* (Fall 1981), pp. 59–70.
21. L. R. T. Williams, "Professional Self-Perception of Physical Education Teachers," *Journal of Teaching Physical Education* 2 (Winter 1982), pp. 77–87.
22. Neil Postman, in an article that first appeared in *Sensorsheet,* a publication of the Earth Science Educational Program (Boulder, Colorado), and later in *Media Ecology Review,* published by the New York University School of Education.
23. Earl V. Pullias and James D. Young, *A Teacher Is Many Things* (Bloomington: Indiana University Press, 1968).
24. Richard W. Calisch, "So You Want to Be a Real Teacher?" *Today's Education* 58 (November 1969), pp. 49–51.
25. Dugan Laird and Forrest Belcher, "How Master Trainers Get That Way," *Training and Development Journal* (May 1984), p. 74.

26. Thomas J. Templin and Joseph L. Anthrop, "A Dialogue of Teacher/Coach Role Conflict," *Physical Educator* 38 (December 1981), p. 183.

27. Glen Begly, "The Role of the Teacher/Coach," *NASPE News* 17 (Winter 1987), p. 6.

28. Linda L. Bain and Janice C. Wendt, "Undergraduate Physical Education Majors' Perceptions of the Roles of Teacher and Coach," *Research Quarterly for Exercise and Sport* 54 (June 1983), pp. 112–18.

29. Earls, "Distinctive Teachers' Personal Qualities, Perceptions of Teacher Education and the Realities of Teaching."

30. Lawrence F. Locke and John D. Massengale, "Role Conflict in Teacher/Coaches," *The Research Quarterly* 49 (2), pp. 162–74.

31. Ibid.

32. Carol Potera and Michele Kort, "Are Women Coaches an Endangered Species?" *Women's Sports & Fitness* 8 (September 1986), pp. 34–35.

33. Constance M. Trifletti, "Issues," *Journal of Physical Education, Recreation and Dance* 56 (August 1985), pp. 8–9.

34. Marian E. Kneer, "Physical Education and Athletics Need a Divorce," *Journal of Physical Education, Recreation and Dance* 57 (March 1986), p. 7.

35. *Alliance Update* (May 1984).

36. Edward J. Shea, *Ethical Decisions in Physical Education and Sport* (Springfield: Charles C. Thomas, 1978), pp. 4–8.

37. The Society of State Directors of Health, Physical Education and Recreation, *The School Programs of Health, Physical Education, and Recreation: A Statement of Basic Beliefs* (Kensington, Maryland: Society of State Directors of Health, Physical Education, and Recreation, 1985), p. 8.

38. Ibid.

39. Scott A. G. M. Crawford, "Values in Disarray: The Crisis of Sport's Integrity," *Journal of Physical Education, Recreation and Dance* 57 (November/December 1986), p. 42.

40. Eberts, "Union Effects on Teacher Productivity," p. 346.

41. Dorothy Zakrajsek and Janet L. Woods, "A Survey of Professional Practices—Elementary and Secondary Physical Educators," *Journal of Physical Education, Recreation and Dance* 54 (November/December 1983), pp. 65–67.

42. Charlotte Lambert, "Career Directions," *Journal of Physical Education, Recreation and Dance* 55 (May/June 1984), pp. 40–43, 53.

43. W. Robert Houston and B. Dell Felder, "Break Horses, Not Teachers," *Phi Delta Kappan* 63 (March 1982), pp. 457–60.

44. "Trends: Teachers Suffer Stress Around the World," *Today's Education* 70 (November/December 1981), p. 6.

45. Stephen J. Virgilio and Paul S. Krebs, "Effective Time Management Techniques," *Journal of Physical Education, Recreation and Dance* 55 (April 1984), pp. 68, 73.

46. Lowell Horton, "What Do We Know About Teacher Burnout?" *Journal of Physical Education, Recreation and Dance* 55 (March 1984), p. 69.

47. Ibid., pp. 69–71.

48. Ibid., p. 71.

49. H. J. Freudenberger and G. Richelson, *Burn-out* (New York: Bantam Books, 1980), p. 17.

50. Albert J. Figone, "Teacher-Coach Burnout: Avoidance Strategies," *Journal of Physical Education, Recreation and Dance* 57 (October 1986), p. 60.

Understanding the Learner and Learning

Study Stimulators

1. Define learning.
2. What is cognitive learning? Affective learning? Psychomotor learning?
3. What is a taxonomy? Of what advantage is it to physical educators?

Learning is a persistent change in behavior because of practice or experience. According to Woodruff, learning depends on (1) the capacity of the learner, (2) the degree of motivation, and (3) the nature of the task. He perceived the process as follows:[1]

1. Internal motivation makes the learner receptive.
2. A goal is perceived as a solution to the need.
3. Inability to immediately reach the goal increases tension within the learner.
4. The learner seeks an appropriate solution to the problem.
5. Progress resulting from the selected solution results in a decrease in tension.
6. Inappropriate behaviors are discarded.

The Three Learning Domains

Bloom and his associates are well known for dividing learning into three categories or *domains*—cognitive, psychomotor, and affective.[2] The *cognitive domain* includes the learning and application of knowledge. The *psychomotor domain* incorporates the development of the physical body and neuromuscular skills. The *affective domain* involves the acquisition of attitudes, appreciations, and values. To influence any one of these areas will almost invariably affect the other two. Therefore, all three areas should be considered when planning the learning outcomes of instruction. To achieve the goals of physical education, the various domains or areas of learning must be integrated into every aspect of instruction and curriculum planning in physical education. The learner then becomes the focus of the teaching-learning process as shown in unit figure 2.1.

The learning outcomes in each area were arranged by Bloom and his colleagues into levels that they thought to be hierarchical in nature. That means that the performance of behaviors at each level would be prerequisite to the performance of behaviors at a higher level.

A taxonomy is a system for classifying something. An educational taxonomy classifies the behaviors that students can be expected to demonstrate after learning. Perhaps the most commonly known taxonomy is the cognitive taxonomy of Bloom and his associates shown in unit table 2.1. Their taxonomy for the affective domain, which is shown in unit table 2.2, was developed later and has also been widely accepted, although rarely implemented in physical education.[3] Bloom also constructed a taxonomy in the psychomotor domain, although he preferred to omit it in later editions of his work.[4] Several other efforts have been made to develop taxonomies in the psychomotor domain.[5] The one proposed by Jewett and her associates is shown in unit table 2.3.[6] Corbin has outlined a separate taxonomy for physical fitness,[7] and Singer and

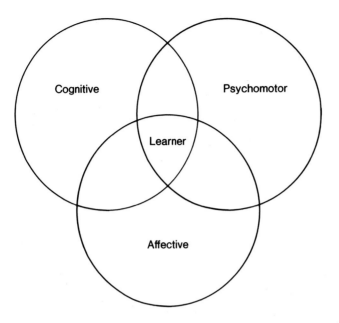

Unit Figure 2.1 Integration of the cognitive, psychomotor, and affective domains.

Dick proposed one for the personal-social area of physical education.[8] Annarino proposed an operational taxonomy for all areas of physical education—physical, psychomotor, cognitive, and affective.[9]

The Cognitive Domain

The cognitive domain includes knowledge, comprehension, application, analysis, synthesis, and evaluation, as shown in unit table 2.1. Each category on the taxonomy contains some elements of the previous categories. Attempts to validate the hierarchical nature of the cognitive taxonomy have not been successful past the application level, at which point the taxonomy may split into a Y-shape, with synthesis and evaluation on one side and analysis on the other.[10] However, the taxonomy has been useful for curriculum design and test construction.

Knowledge
The first level on the taxonomy is knowledge or the ability to recognize or recall specific facts, methods of organizing information, or the theories that dominate a particular subject. This level is often referred to as memorization or rote learning. Some examples of physical education content that fit into the knowledge level of the taxonomy include the learning of

1. game rules and strategies
2. terminology
3. history and current events
4. body systems

Unit Table 2.1 Bloom's cognitive taxonomy

Levels of Behavior

1. *Knowledge*—Involves recognition and *recall* of:
   —specific facts, terms, definitions, symbols, dates, places, etc.
   —rules, trends, categories, methods, etc.
   —principles, theories, ways of organizing ideas

2. *Comprehension*—Involves ability to use learning:
   —translating, paraphrasing
   —interpreting, summarizing
   —extrapolating, predicting effects or consequences

3. *Application*—Involves ability to use learning in a variety of situations:
   —using principles and theories
   —using abstractions

4. *Analysis*—Involves breaking down the whole hierarchy of parts:
   —identifying or distinguishing parts or elements
   —discovering interactions or relationships between parts
   —relating organizational principles (parts to whole or whole to parts)

5. *Synthesis*—Involves combining elements into a new whole:
   —identifying and relating elements in new ways
   —arranging and combining parts
   —constructing a new whole

6. *Evaluation*—Involves judgments of value of material and methods for a given purpose:
   —judgments in terms of internal standards
   —judgments in terms of external criteria

Source: Concepts taken from Bloom, Benjamin S., ed. *Taxonomy of Educational Objectives, Handbook I: Cognitive Domain.* New York: McKay Co., 1956.

Comprehension

Most meaningful learning consists of more than just facts. Students must understand what they have learned. Comprehension is evidenced by the ability to translate or paraphrase information, to interpret or explain why something is occurring, or to summarize, extrapolate, or use facts to determine consequences and implications. In physical education, examples of items that students must comprehend include

1. game rules and strategies in specific game situations
2. the effects of exercise on the body
3. the benefits of exercise
4. factors affecting exercise
5. social and psychological factors affecting sports participation

Application

Once students have a good comprehension of verbal information, they are ready to use or apply the information in new problems and situations. Students use formulas, principles, theories, ideas, rules, procedures, and methods in particular situations to solve problems. For example, in physical education, students must apply

1. game rules and strategies
2. biomechanical principles to produce effective body movement
3. processes for learning new skills
4. techniques for relaxation and stress management
5. principles of safety
6. game etiquette

Analysis

The ability to break down information into its components or parts to see their relationships is called analysis. Students learn to organize, classify, distinguish, discriminate, and clarify information by demonstrating or making explicit the relationships between ideas. Knowledge, comprehension, and application are all involved in analyzing information. Examples of analysis include relating hypotheses to evidence, assumptions to arguments, or creating systematic arrangements of structures and organizations. In physical education, students analyze

1. game strategies for effectiveness in specific situations
2. commercial physical fitness and recreation programs for effectiveness and accuracy of information distributed

Synthesis

Another cognitive process based on knowledge, comprehension, and application is synthesis. It involves creating something by arranging or combining elements into patterns to form a whole, a structure or pattern not clearly there before. In synthesis, there is no "right answer." Students use their creativity to

1. create exercise programs to attain physical fitness
2. invent new games or game strategies
3. choreograph dance and gymnastics routines

Evaluation

Evaluation includes both quantitative measurements and qualitative judgments about the value of ideas, works, solutions, methods, or materials. It is used to determine if methods or materials satisfy the criteria or standards specified for appraisal. Either internal or external evidence may be used to evaluate such things as policies and situations for their accuracy, precision, or conclusions. Evaluation appears to involve synthesis as one of its components. Students in physical education evaluate

1. the quality of sports-related consumer goods
2. exercise programs
3. rules and strategies and their effects on game play
4. how equipment affects game play

The Affective Domain

Affective learning refers to the emotional aspects of learning. It deals with how students feel about the learning experience, how they feel about the subject, and how they feel about themselves. It considers their interests, appreciations, attitudes, values, and character.

Since attitudes and appreciations cannot be measured directly, they are inferred from the tendencies of persons to engage in certain behaviors when they have positive attitudes and in certain other behaviors when they have negative attitudes toward some subject. For example, Greta has a positive attitude toward sports events. She demonstrates this attitude by talking about sports, attending every sporting event she possibly can, and learning the names and characteristics of each of the players. Once she even took her radio to a club meeting so she could listen to a championship game.

In general, people who like something keep going back for more experiences with the subject. They seek opportunities to be involved with the subject in preference to other activities. The stronger their attraction, the more obstacles they will overcome to get involved and stay involved. People who do not like something choose to engage in other activities. They go to great lengths to avoid it by changing the subject, inventing excuses, or walking away from it. When forced to become involved in instructional situations that they dislike, they threaten never to have anything to do with the subject in the future. Once such an attitude has developed, the chances are slim that it will be reversed, since the opportunities to influence students become fewer and fewer as time goes by.

The taxonomy of affective behaviors developed by Krathwohl, Bloom, and Masia describes levels on a continuum of internalization of behaviors as shown in unit table 2.2.[11] It will be illustrated with an example from physical education.

Receiving

Receiving involves passive attention to the activity or event. Adam first becomes aware of what physical fitness is, begins to listen to material concerning fitness activities, and even selects and reads articles about fitness to the exclusion of other reading materials.

Responding

When a person does something about the activity, it is called responding. Adam responds to his information by forming an opinion about physical fitness, initially only by complying with a teacher-initiated fitness program. He participates voluntarily in a school-sponsored fitness program and begins to feel some satisfaction in doing so.

Valuing

When Adam can be seen trying to convince his friends of the importance of a fitness program, he is beginning to place worth on the activity, or he is valuing it.

Organization

Adam internalizes his conviction of the importance of physical fitness and incorporates it into his hierarchy of values. His own beliefs, rather than the opinions of others, now guide his actions. This step involves seeing how the values relate to other values held by the individual and weighing these values to determine which ones are more important.

Levels of Behavior

1. *Receiving*—Involves passive attention to stimuli:
   —awareness of a fact, occurrence, event, or incident
   —willingness to notice or attend to a task
   —selecting stimuli

2. *Responding*—Involves doing something about stimuli:
   —complying, following directions
   —voluntarily involves self
   —satisfaction or enjoyment

3. *Valuing*—Places worth on something; involves display of behavior consistent with values:
   —expressing strong belief in something
   —expressing preference for something
   —seeking activity to further something and convert others to own way of thinking

4. *Organization*—Organizes values into a system:
   —seeing how the value relates to other values held
   —establishing interrelationships and dominance of values

5. *Characterization*—Acts consistently with internalized value system:
   —acting consistently in a certain way and can be described by others in terms of actions or values
   —developing a total *consistent* philosophy of life, integrating beliefs, ideas, and attitudes

Source: Concepts taken from Krathwohl, David R.; Bloom, Benjamin S.; and Masia, Bertram B. *Taxonomy of Educational Objectives, Handbook II: Affective Domain.* New York: David McKay Co., 1964.

Characterization

When a person acts consistently with an internalized value system, the particular behavior is said to be characteristic of that person. Adam becomes so committed to the importance of physical fitness that he may even decide on a career in the fitness area or do volunteer work instructing others about the importance of physical fitness.

A close relationship exists between the affective domain and the other two. By learning about something (cognitive) or doing some skill (psychomotor), instructors can produce attitudinal changes in students. By increasing positive attitudes toward physical education, students can be motivated to learn cognitive or psychomotor skills.

The Social Domain

The social domain is closely related to the affective domain and is concerned with personal adjustment and social interaction skills. Singer and Dick included the following areas in the social domain:

1. Conduct (sportsmanship, honesty, respect for authority)
2. Emotional stability (control, maturity)
3. Interpersonal relations (cooperation, competition)
4. Self-fulfillment (confidence, self-actualization, self-image)[12]

Teachers must ensure that positive, rather than negative, social skills are outcomes of physical education classes.

Unit Table 2.3 A psychomotor taxonomy

Learning Behavior	Definition
1.0 Generic movement	Movement operations or processes, which facilitate the development of human movement patterns.
1.1 Perceiving	Recognition of movement positions, postures, patterns and skills by means of the sense organs.
1.2 Imitating	Duplication of a movement pattern or skill as a result of perceiving.
1.3 Patterning	Arrangement and use of body parts in successive and harmonious ways to achieve a movement pattern or skill.
2.0 Ordinative movement	Meeting the requirements of specific movement tasks through processes of organizing, performing and refining movement patterns and skills.
2.1 Adapting	Modification of a patterned movement or skill to meet specific task demands.
2.2 Refining	Acquisition of smooth, efficient control in performing a movement pattern or skill as a result of an improvement process, e.g., a. elimination of extraneous movements. b. mastery of spatial and temporal relations. c. habitual performance under more complex conditions.
3.0 Creative movement	Processes of inventing or creating skillful movements which will serve the unique purposes of the learner.
3.1 Varying	Invention or construction of unique or novel options in performing a movement pattern or skill.
3.2 Improvising	Extemporaneous origination or initiation of novel movements or combinations of movements.
3.3 Composing	Creation of unique movement designs or patterns.

Source: Jewett, Ann E., L. Sue Jones, Sheryl M. Luneke, and Sarah M. Robinson. "Educational Change Through a Taxonomy for Writing Physical Education Objectives," *Quest*, XV (January 1971): 35–36.

The Psychomotor Domain

The psychomotor domain deals with learning physical or neuromuscular skills. By watching a baby learn to walk, an idea of how humans learn motor skills is obtained. Once the child gets an idea of what is required and has the prerequisite skills—strength, maturity, and so forth—the child makes crude attempts that are gradually refined through constant feedback from the environment—door sills, falls, carpet textures, and parents "ohing and ahing." Finally, a skilled performance emerges that is unique to that particular toddler.

The taxonomy for the psychomotor domain shown in unit table 2.3 follows the normal learning process just described. When learning psychomotor skills, people progress through three stages of development: (1) generic movement, (2) ordinative movement, and (3) creative movement. Examples of some of the processes involved in this progression are presented in unit table 2.4. An understanding of these stages of development is essential when planning the instructional sequence in physical education. Unless the teacher understands the higher levels of the taxonomy, the tendency is to stop too soon and omit several of the most important aspects of the learning process.[13]

Unit Table 2.4 Two examples of the movement behaviors described in the taxonomy

Movement Process	Balance Beam	Soccer
Perceiving	The child walks on the balance beam hesitantly, stops frequently to maintain balance; may hang onto partner or teacher. Experiments with body and arm positions. Child may use a shuffle step or slide step.	After a demonstration, the student replicates a kicking pattern. A fundamental striking pattern (swing) with the foot is the goal of performance. Neither accuracy nor distance is brought into focus.
Patterning	Child walks on the balance beam using an alternating step pattern with a well balanced body position. Some hesitancy or slowness in performance may still exist.	The student executes a kicking pattern. The force, point of contact, and follow through is the focus.
Adapting	Child walks on a balance beam with an alternating step pattern. He/she walks over a wand and through a hula hoop. May lack smoothness in performance.	The student adjusts his/her kicking pattern to perform an instep kick.
Refining	Each time the child walks on the balance beam, he/she performs the task smoothly with an alternating step pattern and good body position. He/she is able to move over the wand and through the hula hoop with no hesitation or loss of body control.	The student performs efficiently the instep kick in soccer. The pattern of the kick is performed smoothly with the same force and accuracy each time.
Varying	The child while walking on the balance beam varies the walk by adding a hop. The child is trying to perform a movement in a different way.	The student alters his/her kicking pattern to perform several variations. The student tries to perform the soccer kick from varying distances and positions from the goal.
Improvising	The child while walking on the beam uses a leap to go over the wand instead of a step.	The student in a game of soccer modifies the pass pattern to take advantage of his/her opponent's being pulled out of position.
Composing	The child designs and performs a series of moves on the balance beam.	The student will be able to design an offensive strategy (kick at goal), responding to a set pattern of play developed with teammates.

Source: Gotts, Sheryl L., unpublished paper, Purdue University, 1972, 1976. Cited in Jewett, Ann E. and Marie R. Mullan. *Curriculum Design, Purposes and Processes in Physical Education Teaching-Learning,* Washington, D.C: American Association of Health, Physical Education and Recreation, 1977.

Generic Movement

Generic movement includes the initial processes of receiving information and transforming it into a motor pattern. These processes are perceiving, imitating, and patterning. *Perception* is the basis for all learning. The student must be helped to perceive, or focus on, the important aspects of the skill to be learned. For example, the swimmer senses the feel of the water on the hands and arms as they pull through the water. *Imitating* involves "trying out" a movement pattern or skill such as imitating the S-pull of the freestyle by "mirror imaging" the instructor's movement. *Patterning* is the process of acquiring a specific movement pattern such as throwing, catching, leaping, galloping, or swimming. Guided practice is essential in helping the learner achieve the desired psychomotor objective.

Ordinative Movement

Ordinative movement involves the processes of organizing and refining generic movement patterns into skillful movement. *Adapting* consists of modifying a skill to meet the needs of a variety of conditions, such as shooting from different distances at archery targets or adapting to an opponent's movements on a basketball court. *Refining* a skill involves a process of practicing the skill until it becomes smooth, efficient, accurate, and automatic, so that the learner can concentrate on game strategy rather than on the skills themselves.

Creative Movement

Creative movement includes the processes of creating or changing movement patterns to serve the unique needs of the individual performer. To be completely at home in an activity, students need the experience of developing their creative skills in movement activities.

Varying occurs when the performer changes force, speed, effort, shape, or other variables to make the movement unique to the learner. Advanced players create their own grip on the racquet or club, their own free-throw variation, or even a Fosbury flop (a creative high-jump technique). *Improvising* uses spontaneous movements to create new or previously untried movements or combinations of movement, such as when a student must recover from an error in a gymnastics routine or when the ball must be saved from traveling out-of-bounds. *Composing* makes use of consciously planned movements to create a new movement or a movement unique to the individual performer. This occurs when a learner choreographs a dance or synchronized swimming routine, or creates a new game or movement skill.

Two examples of each of the processes just identified are presented in unit table 2.4.

The physical fitness domain specified by Corbin includes the following components:

1. Fitness vocabulary
2. Exercising
3. Achieving fitness
4. Establishing regular exercise patterns
5. Fitness evaluation
6. Fitness problem solving[14]

Importance of the Taxonomies

Despite the classifications determined by learning theorists, dividing outcomes of learning into psychomotor, cognitive, or affective learning is difficult. For example, driving a car may involve mental and physical skills, and attitudes and values such as courtesy and respect for the rights of others. Skills can be classified on various continuums by their cognitive, psychomotor, or affective involvement.[15]

The importance of each taxonomy is to encourage physical educators to include in their instruction a progression of learning outcomes from those lower on the taxonomy through the higher-order objectives listed at the top of each taxonomy. In this way, the taxonomy also can be used as a checklist by teachers to make sure the entire range of behaviors is included in the curriculum or learning situation.

Corbin listed three common errors that result in failure to include the entire range of behaviors in the taxonomies. They are (1) trying to teach advanced skills and information without teaching essential prerequisites, (2) overemphasizing lower-order objectives, and (3) sacrificing higher-order objectives in the process of achieving lower-order objectives.[16] The higher-order, problem-solving skills must be taught, so that students can learn to apply their knowledge and skills to real-life problems. The challenge, then, is to help students develop the capabilities to meet a full range of learning outcomes in each of the learning areas—cognitive, psychomotor, and affective.

The study of learning generally includes research on the learning process, the conditions that affect learning, and the learner.[17] Chapter 4 will review the various theories and models that form the basis for studying learning, along with an analysis of the various factors that influence learning in all of the domains. Chapter 5 will discuss the learner and ways to meet the needs of all students. In chapter 6, learning strategies for each of the domains will be presented.

Suggested Reading

Annarino, Anthony A. "Operational Taxonomy for Physical Education Objectives." *Journal of Physical Education and Recreation* 49 (January 1978):54–55.

References

1. Asahel D. Woodruff, *The Psychology of Teaching* (New York: Longmans, Green & Co., 1951), p. 241.
2. Benjamin S. Bloom, ed., *Taxonomy of Educational Objectives, Handbook I: Cognitive Domain* (New York: David McKay Co., 1956).
3. David R. Krathwohl, Benjamin S. Bloom, and Bertram B. Masia, *Taxonomy of Educational Objectives, Handbook II: Affective Domain* (New York: David McKay Co., 1964).
4. Benjamin S. Bloom, personal communication.
5. E. J. Simpson, "The Classification of Objectives, Psychomotor Domain," *Illinois Teacher of Home Economics* 10 (1966/1967), pp. 110–44; Anita J. Harrow, *A Taxonomy of the Psychomotor Domain: A Guide for Developing Behavioral Objectives* (New York: David McKay Co., 1972); Charles B. Corbin, *Becoming Physically Educated in the Elementary School,* 2d ed. (Philadelphia: Lea & Febiger, 1976), pp. 52–66; and Margaret M. Thompson and Barbara A. Mann, *An Holistic Approach to Physical Education Curricula: Objectives Classification System for Elementary Schools* (Champaign, Illinois: Stipes Publishing Company, 1977).

6. Ann E. Jewett, L. Sue Jones, Sheryl M. Luneke, and Sarah M. Robinson, "Educational Change Through a Taxonomy for Writing Physical Education Objectives," *Quest* 15 (January 1971), pp. 35–36.
7. Corbin, *Becoming Physically Educated in the Elementary School,* pp. 52–56.
8. Robert N. Singer and Walter Dick, *Teaching Physical Education: A Systems Approach* (Boston: Houghton Mifflin Company, 1974), pp. 105–7.
9. Anthony A. Annarino, "Operational Taxonomy for Physical Education Objectives," *Journal of Physical Education and Recreation* 49 (January 1978), pp. 54–55.
10. William G. Miller, Jack Snowman, and Takeshi O'Hara, "Application of Alternative Statistical Techniques to Examine the Hierarchical Ordering in Bloom's Taxonomy," *American Educational Research Journal* 16 (Summer 1979), pp. 241–48; and G. M. Seddon, "The Properties of Bloom's Taxonomy of Educational Objectives for the Cognitive Domain," *Review of Educational Research* 48 (Spring 1978), pp. 303–23.
11. Krathwohl, Bloom, and Masia, *Taxonomy of Educational Objectives, Handbook II: Affective Domain.*
12. Singer and Dick, *Teaching Physical Education: A Systems Approach,* p. 105.
13. Ann E. Jewett and Marie R. Mullan, *Curriculum Design: Purposes and Processes in Physical Education Teaching-Learning* (Washington, D.C.: American Association of Health, Physical Education and Recreation, 1977).
14. Corbin, *Becoming Physically Educated in the Elementary School,* pp. 52–56.
15. Joseph B. Oxendine, *Psychology of Motor Learning* (Englewood Cliffs, NJ: Prentice-Hall, Inc., 1984), pp. 14–15.
16. Charles B. Corbin, "First Things First, But, Don't Stop There," *Journal of Physical Education, Recreation and Dance* 52 (June 1981), pp. 12–13.
17. Oxendine, *Psychology of Motor Learning.*

4

Understanding Learning

Study Stimulators

1. Compare and contrast the behaviorist and cognitive theories of learning.
2. What implications do the factors that affect learning have for instruction in physical education?
   a. Readiness
   b. Motivation
   c. Anxiety and arousal
   d. Teacher expectations (the self-fulfilling prophecy)
   e. Praise
   f. Perception and attention
   g. Information feedback
   h. Practice
   i. Transfer
   j. Retention

A study of learning results in specific principles that determine teaching methods. Without a knowledge of learning, teaching would be, at best, a trial-and-error situation. Only a brief review is presented here. For an in-depth study of each area, the reader is referred to the many excellent texts on learning that are available. This chapter is divided into two sections. The first part is a review of learning theories and models; the second part is an analysis of the various factors that influence learning in all of the domains.

Learning Theories and Models

Whether it is obvious or not, every teacher has a theory that guides the teaching-learning process. To be effective, that theory must be based on accurate information about the learning process. Theories begin as hypotheses and evolve into theories only after substantial research has been done to prove or disprove them. Theories help to organize facts, provide explanations, ask the right questions, make predictions, and form the basis for action.[1]

Theories are "sets of expectations about how our world works," or, in this case, about how and why learning occurs. They are based on prior experience and data and help people relate various phenomena to one another. "A good theory must be the simplest formulation possible that takes into consideration all the data while still maintaining appropriate precision."[2]

Models are similar to theories, but are less abstract and more flexible. They serve as more practical approaches to the study of behavior and are often expressed as flowcharts or diagrams to illustrate the relationships among events in the system. This makes them easier to visualize and investigate than theories. Like theories, models can help people formulate their own hypotheses about learning. When teachers develop their own theories, they can formulate a more consistent approach to teaching.[3]

Until recently, educational psychologists have searched for one theory to explain all aspects of human learning. However, of the many theories proposed, none has been successful in predicting how individuals learn in all situations and for all outcomes. Two general approaches that have emerged are the behaviorist and the cognitive traditions, although the distinctions between the two are not always clear. Some points are agreed upon by both approaches; other points are controversial among proponents of the same approach. The names most often associated with the behaviorist tradition are Pavlov, Thorndike, Guthrie, Skinner, and Hull. Names usually associated with the cognitive tradition include Wertheimer, Koffka, Tolman, Lewin, Piaget, Bruner, and Ausubel.

Behaviorist Theories

The behaviorists emphasize behavior changes in the learner that can be observed through scientific research. To them, learning consists of relatively permanent changes in behavior brought about by an environment that controls perception and feedback for the learner. Important concepts stressed in different ways by the different theories include contiguity—the occurrence of two events at the same time and place, and reinforcement—an event that increases the chances of recurrence of a behavior.[4]

During his studies on digestion, the Russian physiologist Pavlov discovered that the dogs salivated not only to food, but also to a bell sounded just prior to receiving food. The salivation to food was a response (R) to a stimulus (S), thus forming an S-R bond, an unlearned response. However, salivation in response to the bell was a learned or conditioned response. In this way, reward serves to condition a certain response, while punishment, or the lack of reward, helps to extinguish the response. Behaviors that are overlearned are difficult to extinguish. Pavlov's theory was called *classical conditioning* or association theory. In the United States, Watson, commonly considered the founder of American behaviorism, amplified Pavlov's ideas and urged a more scientific approach to the study of learning.[5]

Thorndike's *connectionist theory* specified that learning occurs through a trial-and-error process in which associations between stimuli or between stimuli and responses (S-R bonds) are strengthened and the connections made in the nervous system. Thorndike created three laws of learning—readiness, exercise, and effect. The law of readiness stated that when the learner is ready to do something, to do it is satisfying and to be prevented from doing it is annoying. On the other hand, if a learner is not ready, to be forced to respond is annoying. The law of exercise indicated that an S-R bond becomes stronger with use and weaker with disuse. The law of effect stated that S-R bonds are strengthened by the presence of a reward or weakened by punishment or lack of reward. He later indicated that punishment had little or no effect on the bond. Instruction based on drill and practice is an example of Thorndike's method of instruction. Current knowledge about the specificity of transfer, the transfer of identical elements, also comes from Thorndike.[6]

Guthrie's *contiguity theory* had only one law of learning. It stipulated that any response that occurred in the presence of a stimulus was established as a bond and would be repeated whenever the stimulus recurred. This "one-trial learning" occurred for each variation of the stimulus and therefore many practice trials were still needed. Rewards were useful only to keep the learner actively engaged in the learning process. Forgetting was not caused by disuse, but rather from interference resulting from subsequent learning. Guthrie's theory has never been tested due to the impossibility of recreating the mini S-R combinations inherent in each trial.[7]

Skinner is probably the most well known of the behaviorists. He emphasized the importance of *operant conditioning*—errorless learning through the use of rewards or reinforcements to shape behavior in progressive approximations toward the desired goal. His theory stressed reinforcement to increase the probability of a given response. Skinner felt that through controlling the environment, the behavior of animals and people could be predicted because they will attempt to reduce aversive or negative stimuli and increase positive reinforcement. Skinner and his followers also studied the effects of reinforcement schedules and found that variable (random) schedules led to more consistent behaviors than fixed schedules. Individuals also responded more favorably to reinforcements based on work done than to reinforcements at specified intervals. In an attempt to increase the number of reinforcers in the classroom, Skinner developed teaching machines, which used programmed learning to teach subjects such as arithmetic. Other educational procedures resulting from his views are task analysis, learning hierarchies, programmed instruction, and performance objectives.[8]

Hull emphasized drive reduction as a component of learning in his *reinforcement theory*. He proposed that physiological or psychological needs result in drives that provoke responses. Any response that reduces the drive results in learning. The strength of the need (stimulus) and prior experience in the effort (work) required to obtain drive reduction and the strength of the reward determine motivation.[9]

Cognitive Theories

Cognitive theories are based on the assumption that individuals give meaning to their experiences and act upon and interact with their environments rather than being acted upon. All environments consist of infinite stimuli. Individuals perceive these groups of stimuli through the senses and then interpret their perceptions in terms of past experiences. Learning occurs when new interpretations replace or are integrated with the psychological "structure" of the learner. Learning is specific and is determined by the biological and genetic makeup of the learner.[10]

Gestalt Theory

The classical *gestalt theory* was advocated by Wertheimer and his colleagues, Koffka, Köhler, and Lewin. Two concepts form the basis for the gestalt tradition. First, sensations occur in a simultaneous field that includes a *figure* against its *background;* second, the individual's perception is influenced by the events or stimuli surrounding the object or event, such as the presence of music or spectators. Oxendine effectively portrayed the figure and background of basketball hoops and backboards of various materials and shapes, with or without nets or painted squares, from the viewpoint of a free-throw shooter.[11] When an unfamiliar stimulus creates a disequilibrium in the learner, a mental trial-and-error process occurs until the individual forms a solution to the problem, an *insight.* In Köhler's studies, apes who were provided with various lengths of poles connected them to obtain bananas placed just out of reach. This "aha!" phenomenon emerges fully learned, with no visible practice. The gestaltists believed that the *whole is greater than the sum of its parts* and, therefore, the learner integrates stimuli into patterns. This integration constitutes learning. In contrast to the behaviorists, the Gestalt psychologists emphasized the need to seek meaningful, rather than rote, learning. In this sense, they represent an early aspect of cognitive theory. Their work led to an interest in discovery learning and to the presentation of the structural relationships among information to be presented.[12]

Koffka defined four laws of perception that have implications for learning. The laws of *proximity* and *similarity* indicated that the learner tends to group objects that are close together in time or space or similar in size, color, or shape. The laws of *closure* and *continuation* imply that the learner will tend to complete a pattern, such as a figure made with broken lines or a portion of a musical tune.

Tolman emphasized the use of thinking to form cues or "signs" to meaningfully direct learning toward goals. The organization of stimuli into patterns or signs was called the *sign-gestalt* concept. Insight was extremely important in arriving at solutions. Motivation was important to keep the learner involved in the learning process.[13]

In Lewin's topological psychology or *field theory,* internal (physiological and psychological) stimuli interact to determine individual behavior. His approach explained why individuals react in different ways to similar treatments on different occasions. He stressed that motivation is related to personal goals and not to general incentives. This explains why rewards may work for some students and not for others.[14]

Information-Processing Theory

The *information-processing theory* helps people make sense out of their environment. It is based on the communication of a message from a sender to a receiver, as in a telephone call. The clarity of the message is based on the reduction of uncertainties, such as unknown vocabulary, noise or distractions in the channel, and anxiety on the part of the receiver. Questions and resulting feedback can help to alleviate transmission problems. Information theory grew out of the theories related to information processing, storage, and retrieval, similar to those used in designing computers. In contrast to the human brain, the computer allowed psychologists to probe its workings for the steps involved in simulated intelligence. New data are constantly evaluated by previously entered data and revised as needed in both content and programming efficiency.

Several information-processing models have been proposed in motor learning. All models have input, central processing, and output functions. Most models are closed loop systems, which use feedback to modify future input, thus closing the cycle in the model. Some models have open loops with no feedback. An example of Stallings's model, a closed loop system, is shown in figure 4.1. Information from the environment is received by the senses and screened by the perceptual filter on the basis of past experience. It then passes into a short-term memory storage where it must be attended to within a few seconds or it will be lost. The amount of information that can be held in short-term storage is limited. In the limited concentration channel, the information is integrated with previous data and encoded into long-term memory. A person can only concentrate on one item at a time without becoming overloaded. The motor control area accepts the action plan formulated in the limited concentration channel and sends messages to the muscles.

Transfer Theory

Another cognitive theory is *transfer theory,* which states that learning is transferred and depends on the knowledge the individual brings to the learning situation and the degree to which input relates to that knowledge.[15] The more knowledge students have, the better able they are to use context cues to relate new information to known information. Research is still needed to verify this theory.

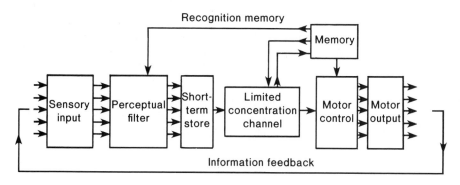

Figure 4.1 An information-processing model of learning.

L. M. Stallings. *Motor Learning: From Theory to Practice* (St. Louis: C. V. Mosby Company, 1982): 94–95.

Wittrock's *generative theory* hypothesized that learners generate associations between or among the parts or ideas of new material and between the new learning and previous knowledge.[16] He suggested that research on aptitude treatment interactions (ATI) will help answer questions about the interaction of characteristics of the learning stimulus and specific learner characteristics such as age, gender, and previous experience, as they relate to achievement. However, since learning is controlled within the learner, these processes are difficult to examine.

Since the identical elements proposed by Thorndike rarely appear in two situations, Royer proposed the *schema theory of transfer*. He hypothesized that transfer occurs in literal situations in which specific prior knowledge facilitates learning, or in figural situations, in which similar previously interconnected bits of information (schemata) are retrieved and analyzed. He suggested two kinds of schemata—hierarchical information and procedural information. Schemata allow perception, which results in new schemata that then permit expanded perception. Schemata provide a plan for obtaining information, guide the search for information, and assimilate the new information.[17]

Schema Theory

A schema is a framework used to relate bits of information into a conceptual unit.[18] Various descriptions of a possible schema structure have been written, but since no one can see a schema, its structure is left to the imagination. It can, however, be inferred from the way in which it is used. Schemata direct perception by selectively influencing the elements attended to by the individual and then provide information to assist in their assimilation. They also limit the amount of learning that can occur, because schemata must be present for the perception and assimilation of information.[19] The schemata developed by different individuals depend on the environment or culture in which the child or youth matures and the genetic makeup of the species. In addition, each person has the cognitive ability to construct his or her own schemata.

According to Rumelhart, schemata are the building blocks of cognition, the elements on which all information processing depends. Schemata are like computer programs. They are networks or trees of subschemata, each of which attempts to find a "goodness of fit" to the available data. For example, if a person had a schema for "face," the subschemata would evaluate the mouth, nose, ear, eye, and so forth to determine if the thing looked at was, indeed, a face. All generic knowledge is embedded in schemata. When the sense organs convey information to the brain, only the most promising schemata are activated. Schemata not only direct incoming information, but they also direct the search process for acquiring information from schemata in the brain and events in the environment to integrate new information with existing information. The search process for remembered data is much like going directly to the room where the dictionary is, then to the correct shelf, and finally to the correct page and entry for a specific piece of information.[20]

Piaget, considered to be the father of the current *cognitive psychology,* proposed a number of stages of intellectual development through which infants and youth pass. He specified that humans learn by assimilating and accommodating new information or responses with prior motor and representational schemata. Learning occurs as a result of disequilibrium when children find that old solutions no longer satisfy them. In contrast to homeostasis, in which normalization occurs to the original state, a state of disequilibrium leads to a higher level of intellectual capability.[21]

Bruner spent some time studying with Piaget and later initiated Piagetian research in America. Bruner emphasized infant acquisition of "programs" of behavior modules similar to computer programs. Complex behaviors consist of many smaller modules similar to Piaget's schemata. Bruner also emphasized the importance of adult modeling in the acquisition of behavior.[22] Bruner went on to develop what he called the "spiral curriculum," in which children first learn basic information about the structure of learning (i.e., how things are related) and then build on that information at each successive confrontation with the subject. By emphasizing the structure of the subject, students can be taught "the foundations of any subject . . . at any age in some form," according to Bruner, and then the principles and attitudes learned could be transferred to subsequent learning problems.[23] He also emphasized intuitive thinking and discovery as essential methods of learning. These principles and attitudes and the placing of detail into a structured pattern increased retention.

For learning motor skills, a schema is a rule that guides motor responses to ensure success under unencountered environmental conditions. The rule is discovered by the learner through practicing in a variety of environmental conditions representative of those encountered in game situations. Feedback about the relationship between the learner and the various outcomes is integrated to form a schema. For example, by practicing archery at different distances, the learner soon discovers that aiming consists of moving the bowsight down for a longer distance and up for a shorter distance. Students should be helped to relate the feedback obtained to correct movement errors and to generalize the principles learned to other situations.[24]

Cybernetic Theory

Cybernetic theory is a type of information theory based on the concept that information provided during skill performance, especially feedback inherent in the task (such as the way the body *feels*), guides learning. Just as some machines (such as guided missiles) are self-directing, kinesthetic feedback allows the learner to be self-correcting during the performance of motor skills. In the cybernetic theory, the human brain processes learned motor behaviors into a subconscious level from which they are automatically retrieved at the appropriate time and controlled by the central nervous system. In the meantime, new information can be processed and stored. Higher-level behaviors can program the use of these lower-order skills.[25]

Factors Affecting Learning

Much recent research has focused on student thought processes as the link between teaching and achievement. Because each student approaches learning with a different internal makeup, a preassessment of existing knowledge, skills, and strategies is essential. Some of the factors that affect learning include: (1) readiness to learn, (2) motivation, (3) anxiety and arousal, (4) the self-fulfilling prophecy, (5) praise, (6) perception and attention, (7) information feedback, (8) practice, (9) transfer, and (10) retention.

Readiness

Readiness to learn asks the questions "Are students physically and emotionally ready for the material to be taught?" and "Do students have the facts, intellectual skills, and strategies that are prerequisite to the material to be taught?" Readiness was based originally on Thorndike's studies and enlarged by Piaget, Bruner, Havighurst, and others. Certain stages in life are formative periods during which learners possess a readiness for certain kinds of activities. Introducing skills before a child is ready may result in failure and can have negative consequences on the child's self-image. Therefore, readiness has implications regarding the sequencing of skills to be taught within the curriculum.

Readiness for physical education activities depends on physical, mental, and emotional maturation; motivation; previous experience; and attitudes toward the subject. Readiness for a given activity differs among students and in the same student from time to time. Physical readiness depends on maturation; general motor development including strength, coordination, endurance, balance, speed and agility; and prerequisite skills. Prerequisite skills are the skills necessary to teach sport and dance skills and include basic locomotor skills such as running and jumping and fundamental skills such as throwing, catching, and striking. Teachers can help students increase their readiness for future learning by providing a background in a wide variety of activities.[26]

Motivation

Motivation is the process of initiating, sustaining, and directing activity toward a specific goal.[27] It involves both intensity of activity and direction toward the goal. Students who are motivated engage in approach behaviors toward the activity or subject involved. Unmotivated students engage in avoidance behaviors, do not perform the desired responses, and do not learn. The process of learning is more rapid when students are motivated. It works somewhat like a mathematical equation in which skill = performance $\times$ motivation. Learning increases geometrically as motivation increases.

Motivation is an inner urge to do one's best, to surpass one's previous performance, or to exceed the performance of another. It is part of the desire of humankind to improve and excel. Achieving one's best under trying or even disappointing circumstances is a part of living one's life to the fullest. Great moments in sport, as with great moments in life, are not so much those of winning or losing but of doing one's best. Research on motivation has focused on (1) reinforcement, (2) intrinsic and extrinsic motivation, (3) need for achievement, (4) self-efficacy, and (5) attribution and locus of control.

Reinforcement Theory

In reinforcement theory, motivation is associated with rewards for appropriate behavior. The problem with reinforcement theory, as Wittrock paraphrased from Hutchins, is "not that it is wrong, but that it might become true; that is, that learners might start to believe that the world controls them rather than that they can control it."[28]

Extrinsic and Intrinsic Motivation

Extrinsic and intrinsic motivation are based on reinforcement theory. Extrinsic motivation is external to the learner and is result-oriented—a good grade, peer recognition, or teacher approval. Intrinsic motivation is internally perceived and controlled by the learner. It includes the pleasure derived from participation in the activity itself, self-confidence, self-discovery, pride, or a knowledge of personal progress.

Studies have demonstrated that when intrinsic motivation is present, the use of extrinsic rewards can actually decrease satisfaction in the activity.[29] Deci, however, isolated two kinds of rewards, only one of which results in a deterioration of intrinsic motivation. Rewards that intend to make students do what the teacher wants, when and where the teacher wants it done, are called *controlling* rewards. *Informative* rewards are those that provide students with feedback about their competence and self-determination. They include comments such as "good work" written on a student's paper. Deci's results showed that when teachers stressed the informative nature of rewards rather than the controlling nature, students were more intrinsically motivated, had more positive attitudes toward themselves, and were more self-directing. He concluded that "rewards, communications, and other external events can be expected to decrease intrinsic motivation only when the controlling aspect is salient for the recipient."[30]

Harter described two general functions of rewards, motivational and informative. *Motivational* rewards, used as incentives, increase the chances of a child's engaging in certain activities. The degree of pleasure or satisfaction experienced by the child also influences the child's developing self-reward system. The *informative* function tells the child what goals are worthy and appropriate and provides feedback on the child's success in achieving those goals. When deciding how to behave in complex situations, younger children appear to be more responsive to adult feedback, while older children consider social (adult and/or peer) feedback and the objective consequences of their behavior as compared with their internalized standards of success and failure. As children develop, they acquire a set of standards for themselves and a self-reward system, therefore needing less extrinsic motivation. Intrinsically motivated students are capable of operating on a "relatively thin schedule of reinforcement."[31]

Harter also found that for older children, boys had significantly more intrinsic motivation, while girls relied more heavily on adult approval. However, tremendous variability existed within gender groups, as well as considerable overlap between boys and girls. When girls have been found to be equally or more competent than boys on skills, no differences in intrinsic motivation have been found. Teachers should be careful to help students of both genders acquire proficiency in activities and develop strong feelings of self-efficacy in movement patterns.[32]

Many educators question the use of extrinsic motivators in the classroom. However, for those students who have a relatively low level of intrinsic motivation, the use of rewards can be especially significant, just as a paycheck is occasionally motivating to an adult who is working on a particularly nonsatisfying task. In any case, the use of extrinsic motivation is certainly better than having to rely on disciplinary techniques to achieve the same goal. Intrinsic motivation is increased by the selection and implementation of appropriate learning experiences. Classroom management, on the other hand, often makes use of extrinsic motivational techniques.

Need for Achievement

Maslow identified a hierarchy of needs as the basis for all human motivation.[33] These needs include (1) physiological needs, (2) safety (and security) needs, (3) love (or social needs), (4) esteem needs, and (5) the need for self-actualization. He proposed, in general, that lower-order needs must be satisfied before the next higher need can be activated. Thus, when the physiological needs have been met, the individual is concerned with safety and so on up the hierarchy until another physiological need must be attended to. For some persons, minimal satisfaction of a need is enough to progress upward to the satisfaction of another need. For others, the satisfaction must be at a higher level before continuing. Occasionally, a certain need can take precedence over all other needs regardless of its position in the hierarchy. Such is the case when a mother risks her life for her child.

Certain *physiological needs* such as food, water, sleep, exercise, and bodily elimination are essential for survival. When these needs are not met, students cannot learn effectively. Teachers can see evidence of this effect on classes that meet right before lunch, on students after a morning of taking achievement tests, or on a student who is ill.

Both physical and psychological *safety and security* are essential within the school environment. The threat of physical violence in some schools prevents effective learning, as does discrimination on the basis of race, gender, or ability. In physical education, students who are afraid of learning a new skill due to possible failure or ridicule will be concerned about security. Some students have a high level of tolerance for mental or emotional stress or physical risk while others have a low level of tolerance and react strongly to situations in which their security is threatened.

Once the need for safety and security is met, the student seeks to fulfill the need for *love*. This need can be met in part through social approval. Approval may come from adults or peers in varying degrees, but it must come for students to be successful in school. Most dropouts are students who lack acceptance from one of these sources.

Everyone needs to feel capable as an individual; therefore, each student must have some activities in which he or she feels success. Gagné emphasized the need for teachers to arrange the learning environment in such a way that students experience success and thereby develop *self-esteem*. He said:

> Achievement, successful interaction within the learning environment, and mastery of the objectives of an educational program can themselves lead to persisting satisfaction on the part of the learner and can therefore become a most dependable source of continuing motivation. Something like this conception must evidently be a strong component in the development of a "continuing self-learner"; and such development is often stated as one of the most important goals of education.[34]

This fact underscores the value of adapting activities to meet the needs of students with a wide range of abilities so that each student experiences success and enjoyment.

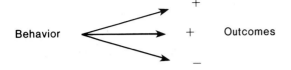

Once the other four categories of needs have been satisfied, the individual can move on to *self-actualization*. Self-actualizing persons are motivated from within and have an intense desire to explore, discover, and create. They are aware of their own strengths and weaknesses and those of the environment that surrounds them and resolve to improve themselves and their environment in a consistent, orderly manner. Maslow felt that only a small percentage of the population would become self-actualized. The school should create an environment in which students can strive to satisfy their basic needs so that they will be free to move on to self-actualization.

Self-efficacy

Bandura described motivation as expectations rather than needs. In his social learning theory, behavior is determined by expectations of personal efficacy and estimates of behavioral outcomes.[35] For example, a person is more likely to behave in a certain way if the resulting outcome is seen as positive and less likely to behave in that way if the result is perceived to be negative. Since most behaviors result in both positive and negative outcomes, the person weighs the perceived outcomes and decides whether or not to engage in the behavior.

The decision involves (1) the importance or value of the outcomes and (2) the probability that the outcomes will occur. An *outcome expectancy* is defined by Bandura as "a person's estimate that a given behavior will lead to certain outcomes."[36] Even if the outcome is considered to be desirable, the individual may feel unable to perform the behavior needed to achieve the outcome and so the behavior may be avoided. An *efficacy expectation* is defined as "the conviction that one can successfully execute the behavior required to produce the outcomes."[37] Students with high expectations will try new activities and expend more effort over a longer period of time than those with low expectations. Efficacy expectations differ in (1) the magnitude or level of the task that can be seen as possible, (2) the generalizability of past successes to similar situations, and (3) the strength in the presence of disconfirming experiences. The model for the theory is shown in figure 4.2.

Bandura proposed four methods for inducing or altering efficacy expectations. The most effective of these is *personal performance accomplishments*. Success experiences may or may not result in stronger expectations of self-efficacy depending on whether individuals credit their achievement to external factors or to their own effort and abilities. Success with minimal effort yields a strong sense of ability, while overcoming challenging tasks through persistence yields a strong sense of self-efficacy.

The second method is *vicarious experience*. Much human behavior occurs through imitating models. Modeling provides a concept of how to perform skills, which is later refined through self-correction based on the consequence of the performance itself and feedback from others. Seeing others overcome obstacles through determined effort is more effective than viewing skilled performers who make the skill look easy. Modeling alone is a less-dependable source of increased self-efficacy because it does not increase students' awareness of their own capabilities, so the expectations are more vulnerable to change.

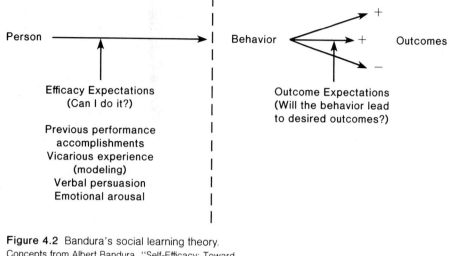

Figure 4.2 Bandura's social learning theory. Concepts from Albert Bandura. "Self-Efficacy: Toward a Unifying Theory of Behavioral Change." *Psychological Review* 84 (1977):191–215; and *Social Learning Theory* (Englewood Cliffs, New Jersey: Prentice-Hall, 1977).

Verbal persuasion can help students try new activities. However, its effectiveness depends on the credibility of the persuader. Prestige, expertise, self-assurance, and trustworthiness in the eyes of the learner affect credibility. If teachers raise expectations without arranging conditions for successful learning, the resulting failure will discredit the influence of the teacher and further undermine the student's self-efficacy.

Emotional arousal can reduce perceived chances of success. Emotional anxiety, increased by fear-provoking thoughts, can exceed the fear experienced in actual situations. Anxiety is best extinguished by teaching effective coping skills.

Perceived competence or self-efficacy can differ in the cognitive, social, or psychomotor domains. One student may have a high level of self-efficacy in the psychomotor and social areas and a very low level in the cognitive area, while another may have a high level of perceived competence in the cognitive and psychomotor domains and feel ill at ease in social situations.

According to Bandura, motivation results from personal goal-setting and evaluation.[38] Individuals prescribe self-rewards for achieving self-prescribed standards and persist in their efforts until their performance matches the standards. After accomplishing these standards, they often make self-reward contingent upon the attainment of even higher achievements. To be most effective, goals should be set at *challenging, but attainable,* levels. Goals that are too easy result in little effort and little satisfaction. Goals that are too difficult yield disappointing results. Frequent failure weakens efficacy expectations and therefore motivation.

Harter emphasized the importance of matching the task to the capabilities of the performer. These *optimum challenges* should reflect a degree of difficulty that is challenging, yet becomes manageable through practice. Students with high persistence levels will sustain effort over longer periods of time, while their low-persistence classmates need skills that can be achieved with minimal practice. Goals should also be *specific*. Clear expectations define the type of performance and effort required to achieve them and facilitate evaluation of how one is doing. Motivation is increased by focusing on *short-term* subgoals that yield self-satisfaction, which "sustains one's efforts along the way."[39]

Since performance accomplishments are the best predictors of self-efficacy, the implication for teachers is to ensure performance success through appropriate instructional strategies. Teachers must structure the environment so that students can perform successfully regardless of their inabilities by modeling skills, working *with* students to perform skills, using graduated tasks, using protective aids (withdrawn as instruction progresses), and varying the severity of the threat. For example, students who are afraid of the water must be gradually introduced to feeling the water on their bodies, putting their faces in the water, opening their eyes underwater, and experiencing buoyancy, perhaps initially through the use of flotation devices. The instructor usually begins by standing nearby to provide assistance and then helps the students to rely successively on peer tutors, performance aids, and finally on their own abilities. By defining realistic performance standards for students, teachers gradually increase students' abilities to achieve and, in turn, their self-efficacy increases. Students are, therefore, more willing to try new skills and to persist until they have learned them.

Attribution Theory and Locus of Control

From the research on *attribution,* the study of student perceptions of the causes of success and failure, new information about motivation is available. At approximately age eleven, children begin to realize that effort and ability are independent of each other and that both cause achievement. Children also develop an understanding of *locus of control,* the belief that events are under one's own or internal control, rather than under control by other people or forces. Four factors generally enter into motivation: ability, effort, luck, and task difficulty. When students attribute success or failure to effort or lack of effort, rather than to forces that they cannot control (such as ability, luck, or the behavior of others), motivation increases. Attribution theory explains that success alone is not enough for motivation. For example, the reinforcement of success attributed to factors over which students have no control, such as the teacher's behavior or easy tasks, does not increase motivation. Effort alone is also insufficient to produce motivation. Students must perceive that the effort results in success. Retraining programs have been used to teach students to take responsibility for their own learning by using cognitive learning strategies.[40]

An important outcome of research on motivation is the emphasis on student responsibility for learning, which parallels the responsibility of the teacher to teach effectively. Cognitive studies have resulted in a move from reinforcement to the old-fashioned values of hard work and effort and student responsibility for learning.[41]

Teachers with high expectations for students
can direct positive learning.

Anxiety and Arousal

Anxiety and arousal are directly related to motivation. Anxiety has to do with stress, while arousal refers to the student's level of alertness. Anxiety and arousal can increase or decrease learning depending on their intensity.[42] The Yerkes-Dodson model predicted that anxiety facilitates performance up to an optimal point and then decreases it. The Taylor-Spence model predicted that people with low anxiety do better on difficult tasks than those with high anxiety, but perform worse on easy tasks.[43] Sieber, O'Neil, and Tobias pointed out that in classroom research, a fairly consistent theme appeared in which high-anxiety learners achieve more with highly structured teaching or instruction that can be repeated as desired.[44] Peterson found that high-anxious, high-ability students learned best with highly structured instruction, while high-anxious, low-ability students performed better with low structure.[45] Apparently anxiety narrows attention and interferes with encoding and memory. Mild arousal appears to be best for learning most skills.

Teacher Expectations or the Self-fulfilling Prophecy

Goethe is thought to have said, "If you treat an individual as he is, he will stay as he is. But if you treat him as if he were what he could and ought to be, he will become what he ought to be." The Pygmalion effect, so dramatically portrayed in George Bernard Shaw's *Pygmalion,* was demonstrated to occur in the classroom in studies by Rosenthal and Jacobson[46] and many others, as reviewed by Brophy and Good.[47] The studies discovered that students perform in agreement with the perceived expectations of their teachers. This was generally found to be more likely when the students were children and especially true of disadvantaged children in urban schools. Brophy concluded that effective teachers perceive their students as being capable of learning and themselves as being capable of teaching effectively. They expect their students to learn and act accordingly.[48]

Studies of the self-fulfilling prophecy in physical education classes confirm that teacher expectations influence student performance.[49] They show that physical education teachers form expectations of students based on such factors as age or grade level, motor ability, physical attractiveness, perceived effort, and the presence or absence of a handicap. For example, younger students tended to receive more nonverbal praise and encouragement (smiles, hugs, pats, and nods) than older students. However, teachers more readily accepted ideas from older students. Students with high skill levels received more praise, contact time with teachers, and criticism, perhaps because teachers felt they were more capable of capitalizing on the feedback than lower-skilled learners. Teachers also had higher expectations for attractive students and students who "tried hard" or were most often on-task.

Student responses to the same teacher expectations may differ from learner to learner, thereby having different effects on achievement.[50]

Hutslar pointed out that to have expectations of students is not necessarily bad. High expectations are positively correlated with achievement. Even having different expectations for different students is not bad. Teacher expectations are bad only when they negatively influence student performance or affect. She listed a number of questions teachers can ask themselves to evaluate their expectations:

1. Do I expect enough from my "low" ability students?
2. Do I present new and challenging material to my "low" as well as my "high" ability students?
3. Do I smile as frequently at my poorest students as I do at my best students, at my least favorite as my favorite student?
4. Do my nonverbal responses convey negative feelings to my "low" students (frowns, shrugs, rolling eyes)?
5. By creating a friendly environment, do I encourage all students to feel free to initiate a conversation with me?
6. Do I give as much corrective feedback on skill performance to my "low" ability students as my "high" ability students?
7. Do I praise and respond positively to appropriate behavior and good performance of my "low" students, or do I allow it to pass unnoticed?
8. Am I less tolerant of incorrect answers and inappropriate behavior of my "low" ability students?
9. Do I give my "low" ability students as much time to answer questions as my "high" ability students?[51]

She then suggested that teachers select several students and behavior categories and tally each interaction, and then set new interaction goals based on the findings. In this way teachers can make the Pygmalion effect work in a positive direction by setting realistic and challenging expectations for all students.

Rink indicated that "a lack of teacher expectation for learning is a critical disease in the physical education field."[52] She suggested three ways for teachers to communicate their expectations to students:[53]

1. Present tasks holistically, concretely, and briefly using concrete examples, brief explanations, and cues.
2. Help students refine, extend, and apply tasks (rather than jumping from one skill to another).
3. Provide specific task-related feedback to students and modify tasks as needed to ensure student success.

Turner and Purkey also emphasized the importance of teacher expectations. They noted that "people respond best when they are invited to feel valuable, able, and responsible . . . and that student potential is best realized in an environment that *intentionally* invites such development" (italics in original).[54] They suggested that teachers evaluate their teaching to determine whether intentional or unintentional *disinvitations* are exhibited and attempt to change them to *invitations*.

The implication for teaching is clear. Effective teachers believe that *all* of their students are capable of success and communicate that belief to their pupils. Teachers should carefully evaluate the ways they interact with students of all ability levels, races, and gender.

Praise

Praise has been used extensively in physical education. However, research shows that it is often ineffective and can be detrimental to learning. Brophy summarized the research on praise and found that it correlates positively with academic achievement for students of low socioeconomic status, especially in the early grades. Praise may be of value to encourage students who are having trouble learning. To be effective, however, it should be contingent on correct performance, specific to the performance, and sincere. General, nonspecific praise is not usually accepted by students as credible. Privately given praise is more effective.[55]

Brophy stated that boys get more praise and criticism simply because they are more active; they get more of all kinds of teacher interaction. Boys tend to be praised more for achievement and girls for such traits as neatness and following directions. On the other hand, girls are more often criticized for unacceptable achievement, while boys are criticized for speaking out of turn and sloppy work. These factors have serious implications for self-concept, especially for girls, who apparently overlook praise and zero in on teacher criticism. They internalize the criticism as a deficiency in their abilities, since they have been praised for their effort and obedience. Boys, on the other hand, generally blame their failures on external circumstances and their successes on their own abilities and, therefore, maintain positive self-concepts.[56]

Introverts, low-ability students, minority group students, and those with an external locus of control tend to respond to praise more than their counterparts. Students with the opposite traits are generally intrinsically motivated and may respond negatively to praise, resulting in a decrease in motivation. Adults and high-school students tend to perceive individuals who are praised for their successes, but given neutral feedback on their failures, as having lower ability levels, in contrast to those who received criticism for their failures and neutral feedback for their successes. Praise, then, appears to convey to learners information about teacher goals and desires and correct answers rather than serving as a reinforcer to student learning.[57]

Teachers should praise correctly rather than often. Verbal praise can be effectively supplemented by written praise on student work and by teaching students to set realistic goals, evaluate their own performance, and provide self-reinforcement. Students also need to be taught to attribute success to their own abilities and effort rather than to external causes. As with the self-fulfilling prophecy, individual students react differently to praise.[58]

Perception and Attention

Perception is the process of entering information into the human brain.[59] A complex system of sense organs receives information from the environment that is processed by its relationship with previously learned data. Only a small part of the information received by the senses is processed. The gestaltists labeled the part attended to as the figure and the undifferentiated part as the background. The recognition of an object as a figure in the perceptual field is called a *percept*.[60] A person's expectations influence perception. Thus, a child hearing "Up, up in the sky" may hear "A pup in the sky," while adults, with many more experiences with the law of gravity would hear the correct version. Adults also tend to check unusual perceptions for authenticity. With common situations the adult easily supplies missing details from past experience. This can be especially advantageous in sports when only part of the information may be available. Ideas and skills may be omitted, distorted, or only partially remembered because of the different perceptions of the learners.

"Perception is goal-directed. . . . We actively seek information relevant to our current needs and goals." Schemata help people interpret information; they guide the information-seeking process and help people relate perceptions to possible actions.[61]

Information processing of visual information occurs in less than one-hundredth of a second. However, one may have to wait for an entire sentence to process verbal material. This has implications for physical education in that a model of a skill will be perceived more quickly than a verbal description. Also, the more senses used to teach something, the better the learner perceives the subject. Children process information relatively slowly, but the rate increases steadily during the growing period. The reception of too much information at once may disorient the learner so that no information is processed.[62]

Gibson noted that perceptual learning involves[63]

1. Discovering the difference between the sets of stimuli (such as the differences in how people look)
2. Emphasizing the distinctive features (Mary wears glasses; John has black hair)
3. Using marked contrasts for the first examples (such as learning the names of the best and the worst students in the class)

Cognitive style influences perception and motivation. *Field-dependent* individuals are those who are much more aware of and responsive to external stimuli, while *field-independent* people are those who are sensitive to cues derived from within themselves. Field-dependent people are socially oriented and have a high level of self-esteem. They pay more attention to faces and social cues, and choose people-oriented professions. They like to be physically close to people. Field-independent people tend toward a more impersonal orientation, have less self-esteem, and choose abstract-oriented fields.[64] Field-independent students learn better with self-definition of goals, intrinsic motivation, and self-reinforcement, while field-dependent learners prefer externally defined goals, reinforcement from others, clearly defined structure, and a minimum of criticism.[65]

Another method for classifying cognitive style uses methods of reasoning. Children who group a table and chairs together because they both have four legs are using an *analytic* style, while those who group them together because both are used for dining demonstrate a *global or relational* cognitive style. Cohen hypothesized that children in an industrialized society would tend toward an analytic style, whereas many low-socioeconomic level children function with a relational style, thereby creating a cultural mismatch in the schools.[66] Standardized intelligence tests measure the students' analytic styles.

Brain hemisphericity studies also relate to cognitive style. Students who are right-handed and most left-handers generally use the left hemisphere and employ an analytic style. Some left-handers, however, use a global style reflective of the right hemisphere. Other research has shown that impulsive children tend to use a global style, while reflective learners tend toward an analytic style. When a global strategy results in the correct answers, global children perform equally with their peers. However, when analytic processing is required, these children have difficulty.[67]

Attention refers to information solicited from a particular aspect of the environment. Normal students show an increasing ability to focus on and recall relevant information and to ignore irrelevant information. A large jump in ability occurs at ages twelve and thirteen. Mentally retarded and hyperkinetic children are unable to disregard irrelevant information. Recent research has focused on the use of strategies to direct attention. The use of questions or performance objectives in textbooks facilitates learning differently when they are placed prior to or following textual material. Prequestions and objectives facilitate factual learning, while postquestions and objectives tend to facilitate conceptual learning. Both influence the selective attention of the learner.[68] Cognitive style also influences the manner in which students attend to the various elements of instruction as indicated in the previous section. For motor learning, attention must be focused on aspects within the environment, such as the speed and direction of the ball.

Information Feedback

Feedback is information about performance or results available during or immediately following performance. Feedback may be verbal, such as "Good serve" or "Your spike is getting better," or it may be nonverbal, such as a nod, smile, glance, or merely continuing on to the next part of the lesson. Visual and verbal feedback can be used simultaneously.

Feedback helps the learner decide what to do differently on the next practice trial.[69] It can also help students determine how well they are progressing toward a course objective. Information provided to the learner that tells about the quality of a performance, such as the contact position with the ball or correct arm action, is called *knowledge of performance*. Information about the outcome of the performance, such as where the ball lands on a tennis court, is called *knowledge of results*. Studies show that little or no learning occurs without feedback or knowledge of results. Bilodeau and Bilodeau stated, "Studies of feedback or knowledge of results show it to be the strongest, most important variable controlling performance and learning."[70]

Because retention improves when behavior is reinforced only 50 percent of the time, various reinforcement schedules have been tried. More-frequent reinforcement results in faster learning. However, less-frequent reinforcement produces higher retention. The best sequence of reinforcement for both learning and retention would be to reinforce frequently at first, tapering off reinforcement as learning occurs.[71] Reinforcement schedules can be arranged in many ways. *Fixed-ratio* reinforcement occurs when a reward is given on every third (or any other numbered) response. Payment for piece work in industry is based on this method of reinforcement. *Variable-ratio* schedules rely on a random reinforcement of responses. *Fixed-interval* reinforcement occurs after every specified period of time. When unpredictable time intervals are used, it is a *variable-interval* schedule.[72]

Feedback can occur from the performance itself, from the performer's kinesthetic awareness of body position, or from visual or verbal cues from the teacher. Feedback directly from the task is called *intrinsic* feedback. It can be produced internally by proprioceptors in the muscles, joints, and tendons, or by the effects of the performance on the environment, such as a strike in bowling or a bull's-eye in archery. Cybernetic theorists rely on intrinsic feedback, especially that within, such as how the learner feels when a certain action is performed.[73] *Extrinsic or augmented* feedback is provided by an outside source such as a teacher, coach, other student, or videotape. Extrinsic feedback may be verbal or nonverbal. *Concurrent* feedback occurs simultaneously with the performance and may be intrinsic or extrinsic. *Terminal* feedback occurs after the performance and may result from the results of the performance (a made basketball shot) or from an external source.

Feedback is most helpful when it is specific and meaningful and provided before the next response. Feedback should be delayed briefly until the learners have had time to analyze their own performances. It should be matched to the individual learner's comprehension and ability to make use of it in subsequent practice. Too much feedback can cause an information overload and confuse the learner. Information that occurs after the next response loses its meaningfulness. Teachers can speed up the knowledge of results by cuing during the performance using verbal, kinesthetic, or visual assistance. For example, having bowlers aim at a spot on the lane rather than at the pins provides feedback much sooner. Placing a hand just behind the wrist of the archer's shooting hand can keep the student from jerking the hand away from the face. Even though many teachers and coaches use this type of feedback, extrinsic concurrent feedback usually has a relatively small effect on learning because gains made are lost when the feedback is terminated unless the learner has transferred the control to an intrinsic cue.[74]

Lawther summarized the research on knowledge of results as follows:

1. Learning is proportionally greater as the quality, exactness, and precision of this playback of knowledge of results increases.
2. When knowledge of results is not available, learners often can improve to some extent by setting up their own criteria from past experience to help them subjectively approximate their results.
3. With a delay of knowledge of results, performance declines.
4. Performance deteriorates when knowledge of results is withdrawn.
5. Continuous and complete knowledge of results fosters much greater learning than discontinuous and incomplete knowledge of results.
6. Precise supplemental aids (graphs, films of action, etc.), which provide more precise knowledge or make apparent the differences between the learner's performance and those of better performers, seem to increase learning.
7. Feedback of incorrect information retards learning in direct proportion to the amount of misinformation.[75]

Evaluation techniques, including preassessment and diagnostic techniques, should be designed to give immediate feedback to students on where they stand in relation to the instructional objectives and to help students recognize when they have achieved the objectives. Students who know where they stand at all times in the learning experience are more secure and can work longer on their own without difficulty. Evaluation techniques also help the teacher adjust to individual differences in rate of learning and/or previous experience.

Practice

Practice variations include massed versus distributed practice, whole versus part learning, and mental practice. Selection of the appropriate practice method depends on the learner, the skill, and the situation.

Massed Versus Distributed Practice

Massed practice is a practice or a series of practice sessions with little or no rest time allotted between. An example is teaching one skill for the entire physical education period. *Distributed practice* is practice interspersed with rest or alternative activities. This can be done by practicing several skills for a brief period of time during each class session.

Research findings about the advantages of each type of practice are contradictory because of the inconsistency in terminology used. However, with verbal skills, a majority of the research concludes that distributed practice is best except when the material is simple or can be learned in its entirety in one session.[76] Research on motor skills shows that, while performance improves with distributed practice, there appears to be no significant difference in the learning of gross motor (sports) skills between the two methods.[77] This is shown by the fact that the wide differences in performance at the end of practice sessions fail to remain on tests of retention given later to determine if students can still perform at the same levels.[78]

When boredom and fatigue are not factors, massed practice is equally effective with distributed practice, assuming that the number of practice trials is the same. Massed practice has the advantage of reaching the goal sooner under these conditions (e.g., three hours on Monday versus one hour on Monday, Wednesday, Friday).[79]

Lawther listed several factors to consider when planning the frequency and length of practice sessions. They include (1) the learner's age, skill level, and experience; (2) the type of skill to be learned; (3) the purpose of the practice; and (4) the circumstances in the learning environment.[80] These factors are presented in table 4.1. Distributed practice is defined in the table as shorter and more frequent, while massed practice is longer and less frequent.

Younger students and students with low ability levels fatigue easily and have shorter attention, or concentration spans, and lower interest levels. Distributed practice sessions in which several skills are practiced during a class period are usually preferred for these students. This results in less chance of boredom, fatigue, and frustration with learning new skills. When students take turns practicing, a built-in rest interval also occurs. Older, more highly skilled students possess higher levels of concentration and motivation and, therefore, can tolerate longer practices with less fatigue.

Strenuous activities often must be scheduled for shorter periods of time due to the effects of fatigue. An overview of an activity may require a different scheduling pattern than intense practice for competition or performance.

Table 4.1 Factors which may influence your choice of massed or distributed practice
organizations

	Shorter and More Frequent	Longer and Less Frequent
If the task:	Is simple, repetitive, boring	Is complex
	Demands intense concentration	Has many elements
		Requires warm-up
	Is fatiguing	Is a new one for the performer
	Demands close attention to detail	
If the learner:	Is young or immature (unable to sustain activity)	Is older or more mature
	Has a short attention span	Is able to concentrate for long periods of time
	Has poor concentration skills	Has good ability to focus attention
	Fatigues easily	Tires quickly

Anne Rothstein, Linda Catelli, Patt Dodds, and Joan Manahan. *Basic Stuff Series I: Motor Learning* (Reston, Virginia:
American Alliance for Health, Physical Education, Recreation and Dance, 1981), p. 40.

Weather conditions, such as heat, cold, smog, or rain, and school activities, such as
assemblies, may interfere with a practice session. With distributed practice, less time is lost
when one practice must be canceled or interrupted than when a massed practice is canceled.

When scheduling practice sessions, one should remember that the time scheduled is
not nearly as important as the amount of time spent in actual activity or the number of trials
the learner attempts. Too often, instructors expect a beginner to learn an entirely new activity in a two-week unit (ten days with thirty minutes of instruction per day equals three
hundred minutes) while they spend two hours every day for months coaching talented students in the same basic skills.

Whole Versus Part Practice

Whole practice is practice of a whole task, such as learning an entire poem, as opposed to
practice of its parts, such as learning individual stanzas. For example, in the breast stroke
in swimming, the whole method is to demonstrate the stroke and have the students imitate
and practice it. In *part practice,* the whole is broken down into parts, each of which is mastered separately before putting them all together into the whole. For example, the kick might
be taught first until it has been mastered. Then, the arms and breathing are taught and
practiced. Finally, the coordination of the entire stroke is demonstrated and practiced.

To overcome the difficulty experienced by the student when putting the parts together,
the *progressive part* method was developed. It consists of learning part one, then learning
and adding part two, then part three, and so on until the whole is completed. When learning
the breast stroke, for example, the student begins with a glide, then adds the arm stroke,
then breathing, and finally the kick.

In a review of thirty studies by Nixon and Locke, the majority found some variation
of the whole method to be superior.[81] This is in agreement with the cognitive theory of learning

Table 4.2 Factors which influence choice of whole or part practice

Practice Should/Can Emphasize:

	Wholes	**Parts**
If the task:	Has highly dependent (integrated) parts	Has highly independent parts
	Is simple	Is made up of individual skills
	Is not meaningful in parts	Is very complex
	Is made up of simultaneously performed parts	If limited work on parts or different segments is necessary
If the learner:	Is able to remember long sequences	Has a limited memory span
	Has a long attention span	Is not able to concentrate for a long period of time
	Is highly skilled	Is having difficulty with a particular part
		Cannot succeed with the whole method

Anne Rothstein, Linda Catelli, Patt Dodds, and Joan Manahan. *Basic Stuff Series I: Motor Learning* (Reston, Virginia: American Alliance for Health, Physical Education, Recreation and Dance, 1981), p. 38.

in unitary wholes. The basic problem seems to be in the definition of the *whole*. In practical teaching situations, an instructor would rarely present the whole game of basketball at once. Instead combinations of skills, such as throwing, catching, dribbling, passing, and shooting, are combined to form play patterns. In sports that require no interaction with others, such as in archery or bowling, the sport itself may be considered to be a whole for the purposes of instruction.[82]

Seagoe described the characteristics of a whole as follows:

1. It should be isolated and autonomous, an integrated entity.
2. It must have "form" quality, a functional, coherent unit.
3. It must be more than the sum of the parts; it must be a rational structure in itself.[83]

Even though use of the whole has been shown to be advantageous, Oxendine cautioned that the evidence does not mean that the whole method should be used exclusively. Rather, the selection of a method should be based on the characteristics of the learner and the task and the instructional style of the teacher. Table 4.2 shows how the first two factors influence the choice of whole or part practice. Older and more mature learners can comprehend larger units of instruction than younger or less-skilled students. Intelligence and cognitive style also influence the learner's ability to handle relationships in complex tasks. Several researchers have found that students with a global cognitive style learn better with whole learning, while students with an analytical cognitive style learn better with the part method.[84] Meaningful, connected activities are best taught with the whole method, while complex, independent tasks can be taught with part practice. When practices are distributed, the whole method appears to work better.[85]

Implications for teaching are that the learner should begin with a whole that is large enough to be meaningful and challenging but simple enough for success to occur. This may involve getting a concept of the whole skill or game and the relationship of the parts to the whole. As skills are practiced, the student should understand how the skills fit into the total activity. Lead-up games are "small wholes" that help learners join parts into meaningful wholes without becoming overwhelmed.[86] Meaningfulness is increased when the skill approximates the final objective sought. Work to improve portions of the performance can occur readily during practice of the whole movement. When the complete action is too complex for the beginner to handle, such as in activities in which there is a chance of injury or the learner is afraid, or the amount of information overloads the processing capability of the learner, it should then be broken into the largest subwhole that the learner can handle.

A combination of wholes and parts, including alternating from one to another, is often the best approach. Variations include *whole-part* and *part-whole* methods and the *whole-part-whole* method in which students learn the whole, then practice the parts, and then put them back together into the whole.[87] In the breast stroke, the whole-part method involves practicing the whole stroke and then working on the arms, legs, and breathing. The part-whole method, in contrast, requires teaching the arms, legs, and breathing separately until they are learned and then combining them into the whole stroke. The whole-part-whole method consists of teaching the entire stroke, then working on each part, and then again practicing the whole stroke.

Mental Practice

Mental practice is sedentary practice in which the learner imagines performing a skill and the muscles receive stimulation, but no overt movement occurs. It is based on the work of Köhler, in which insight plays an important role in learning. Since studies have shown that mental rehearsal increases skill performance, instruction might well include mental practice in addition to physical practice to efficiently use the crowded facilities and inadequate equipment in many schools. A good time for mental practice is when a student is waiting for a turn or a piece of equipment. Mental rehearsal can also be used advantageously to practice perfectly after an error and before the next response, to warm up, to increase concentration during the performance, or to practice while watching a film or videotape of a skill. Mentally rehearsing what to do in certain game situations can be helpful in developing appropriate reactions during game play. For example, in softball, students can imagine that the bases are loaded and the ball goes to third base and determine what should be done. *Reminiscence,* improvement between practice periods, may be the result of mental practice.[88]

To be effective, students must understand the skill and have practiced it overtly prior to mental practice. Encourage students to *feel* the movement during practice and then during mental rehearsal.

Transfer

Transfer is the effect that learning one skill has on the learning or performance of another skill. Transfer can be positive or negative. Positive transfer occurs when previous learning has a favorable effect on the new learning. With negative transfer, prior learning interferes with the learning of new information or skills (proactive transfer) or the new skills interfere with previously learned tasks (retroactive transfer). The behaviorists believe that transfer occurs by manipulating the environment so the learner will see the similarities between the old and the new tasks.[89] The cognitivists emphasize the importance of helping the learner retrieve stored information to use in the new situation.

Transfer theories include (1) the theory that general elements such as balance, kinesthesis, or coordination carry over from one activity to another; (2) the theory that only identical elements (i.e., specific elements common to both tasks) transfer; and (3) the theory that transfer occurs as a result of the ability to apply previously learned principles and insights or problem-solving strategies to new situations; and (4) combinations of the general and specific theories.[90]

Laboratory research shows that very little transfer is seen from one task to another, which tends to support the identical elements theory. However, the transfer of general problem-solving and learning strategies is supported when more complex tasks are studied. Transfer is probably a result of several factors, including those specific to the task and those inherent in the learning environment.[91]

An understanding of the conditions affecting transfer is essential for planning instruction. Singer listed five conditions that affect transfer. They include (1) the similarity between the tasks, (2) the amount of practice on the first task, (3) the motivation to transfer, (4) the method of training, and (5) the intent of transfer.[92] Cratty added a sixth condition—the amount of time between tasks.[93] The amount of transfer depends on the complexity of the task and the capacity of the learner.[94]

Similarity between Tasks

The most important of the six conditions is the similarity between the tasks. The greater the similarity between the tasks, the greater the transfer. If no elements were similar, no transfer would occur (either positively or negatively). In many tasks, however, some elements will yield positive transfer and others will elicit negative transfer. Thus, Cratty indicated that "the degree to which negative or positive transfer is measured depends on whether the *summation* of the negative transfer elements equals, exceeds, or fails to exceed the total of the common elements likely to produce positive transfer."[95]

Similar or identical elements can be found in the student's perception of the stimulus or in the response. Negative transfer occurs when the students are asked to respond to the same verbal or visual perception with a different response. For example, if students have practiced rebounding by batting the ball continuously against the backboard during practice, and then are expected to rebound the ball into the basket during a game, negative transfer will occur. Negative transfer may also result when the weight of an object changes, such as when changing from tennis to badminton, or when the speed of the object differs, such as in rallying a tennis ball off a backboard rather than over a net. Similar movements, such as the overarm softball throw and the overhead volleyball serve, differ in that one is a striking skill and the other a throwing pattern.

Positive transfer occurs when a number of identical elements exist between the two tasks, such as the names of the players in softball and baseball. Some positive transfer occurs when the same response is expected to a number of related situations. Examples include shooting at different sizes of targets or different distances in archery, or throwing a ball fielded from many different directions to first base.

When two tasks have many elements that are similar, but not identical, negative transfer results. An example is in the rules and scoring of soccer, speedball, speed-a-way, and field hockey. Tennis, badminton, and racquetball have similarities in eye-hand coordination and agility. However, differences in wrist action and the weight of the object struck can cause negative transfer.

Amount of Practice on the First Task
Greater positive transfer occurs when the first task is well learned. Less practice on the first task may result in negative transfer. Skills involving similar movement patterns, such as tennis and racquetball, should not be taught at the same time if the learner is a beginner in both activities.

Motivation to Transfer
When motivation toward the transfer of skill or knowledge to a new task is high, greater positive transfer occurs. Increasing the motivation of students should also increase the effects of positive transfer.

Method of Training
The highest positive transfer seems to occur when the whole task is practiced rather than when the parts are practiced separately. For this reason, many current writers discourage the use of drills and progressions to teach skills. Nixon and Locke stated:

> Progression is a near sacred principle in physical education, and is taken most seriously in teacher education. Evidence indicates that the faith . . . may be misplaced. . . . Progressions generally appear not to be significant factors in learning many motor skills.[96]

Progressions, however, are valuable when fear, danger, or lack of self-confidence are present. Unless well planned, drills may introduce elements that do not transfer to the game situation. Therefore, drills should be planned so that the environment and movement relationships are as gamelike as possible. Evaluation should also be in as gamelike settings as possible. No objective test, such as a skills test, has yet been able to replace the subjective opinion of the experts.

Intent of Transfer
When the teacher points out the common elements in the two tasks, the learner will probably make greater transfer to the second task of principles and skills learned in the first task. Often, general problem-solving and learning strategies will transfer to the new situation. Understanding the principles of biomechanics should transfer to new situations, as should principles of learning.[97]

Amount of Time between Tasks
As the amount of time increases between the learning of two tasks, both negative and positive transfer decline until negative transfer disappears entirely. Since negative transfer decreases faster, there is a point at which positive transfer is at its optimum, before it too disappears. For this reason, skills may be best learned during distributed practice sessions.

Retention

Retention, often called memory, is the persistence of knowledge. Forgetting is the opposite of retention. According to the behaviorists, memory is affected by the original association of two events with each other and by the association of an event with a reward. Forgetting may be caused by lack of use over a period of time, by unlearning due to lack of reinforcement, or by interference from other learned events, such as the learning of Spanish after French.

Information-processing research differentiates between short-term memory and long-term memory. Events are only held for a short period of time unless they are rehearsed and transferred to long-term storage. Short-term memory is limited to about seven digits, as in the ordinary telephone number. By "chunking," more information can be attended to, as when phone numbers are changed to letters to form words such as "car-loan."[98] Using cues to chunk information can help learners avoid an information overload. Once the information is encoded into long-term memory, it can be very persistent, as in some motor skills, which have been known to last for many years.

Factors influencing retention include (1) the nature of the task, (2) the meaningfulness of the task, and (3) the amount of overlearning that has occurred. Tasks differ in their outcomes—cognitive, psychomotor, or affective; their complexity—simple to difficult; and their effect on the learner—pleasant versus disagreeable. Fundamental skills, such as walking and bicycling, and higher-order, mental-processing skills are relatively permanent, while facts are difficult to remember.[99] Pleasant tasks are more easily learned, as when an exercise series is done to music. The complexity of some learning tasks can be reduced by chaining concepts to each other, as in learning a poem, a dance, or a musical composition, or in organizing concepts into "chunks" of information, such as a grapevine step, which consists of a number of side and crossover steps.

Meaningful, well-organized material is remembered longer than unorganized facts. Teachers can enhance long-term memory by teaching students mental imagery of concepts or associated objects, chaining concepts, problem-solving and information-processing skills, and teaching the principles underlying performance, such as the effects of ball spin and air resistance or the principles for applying and receiving force. When students know they will be held accountable for certain material, retention is also increased.[100]

That motor skills seem to be retained for longer periods of time than verbal skills may be due to the overlearning that occurs with motor skills. The implication for teaching is that teachers probably spend too much time reviewing skills that have already been learned.[101]

A brief sketch of the traditional theories of learning and the factors that affect learning have been presented in this chapter. A more complete description can be obtained in textbooks on motor learning, educational psychology, or learning theory. An excellent summary of the various theories of learning is included in Oxendine's book, *Psychology of Motor Learning,* and in Grippin and Peters, *Learning Theory and Learning Outcomes.* Strategies for teaching in each of the three domains will be presented in chapter 6.

Questions and Suggested Activities

1. What do behaviorist learning theories have in common?
2. What does "figure-ground" mean? With what group is the concept associated?
3. Compare the information-processing theory of learning with your knowledge about how a computer works.

4. What is a schema? How can it help the learner learn motor skills?
5. What is the basic premise of cybernetic theory?
6. How can one tell if a learner is ready to learn a specific motor skill?
7. Define extrinsic and intrinsic motivation. When is each usually used?
8. Explain Maslow's motivational hierarchy.
9. How does Bandura's social learning theory explain motivation?
10. What is the most effective level of arousal for learning most skills?
11. What is the Pygmalion effect? What does it have to do with teaching?
12. Why are teacher expectations important? How can these expectations be communicated to students?
13. Is praise effective? With whom? When?
14. Why is perception important in all kinds of learning?
15. Summarize the various kinds of feedback and their effects on learning.
16. What kind of practice is best for beginners? For advanced players?
17. What conditions are necessary for positive transfer?
18. What can a teacher do to promote retention?

Suggested Readings

Grippin, Pauline, and Sean Peters. *Learning Theory and Learning Outcomes: The Connection.* New York: University Press of America,® Inc., 1984.

Hutslar, Sally. "The Expectancy Phenomenon." *Journal of Physical Education, Recreation and Dance* 52 (September 1981):88–89.

Martinek, Thomas J. "Pygmalion in the Gym: A Model for the Communication of Teacher Expectations in Physical Education." *Research Quarterly for Exercise and Sport* 52 (March 1981):58–67.

Martinek, Thomas J., and William B. Karper. "A Research Model for Determining Causal Effects of Teacher Expectations in Physical Education Instruction." *Quest* 35 (1983):155–68.

Oxendine, Joseph B. *Psychology of Motor Learning,* 2nd ed. Englewood Cliffs, New Jersey: Prentice-Hall, 1984.

Rothstein, Anne, Linda Catelli, Patt Dodds, and Joan Manahan. *Basic Stuff Series I: Motor Learning.* Reston, Virginia: AAHPERD, 1981.

References

1. Pauline Grippin and Sean Peters, *Learning Theory and Learning Outcomes: The Connection* (New York: University Press of America,® Inc., 1984), pp. 3–8, 11.
2. Ibid., p. 8.
3. Joseph B. Oxendine, *Psychology of Motor Learning* 2nd ed. (Englewood Cliffs, New Jersey: Prentice-Hall, 1984), p. 73.
4. Grippin and Peters, *Learning Theory and Learning Outcomes,* pp. 56–57.
5. Robert M. W. Travers, *Essentials of Learning: The New Cognitive Learning for Students of Education* (New York: Macmillan Publishing Company, 1982), p. 18.
6. Lauren B. Resnick, "Toward a Cognitive Theory of Instruction," in Scott G. Paris, Gary M. Olson, and Harold W. Stevenson, eds., *Learning and Motivation in the Classroom* (Hillsdale, New Jersey: Lawrence Erlbaum Associates, Publishers, 1983), pp. 5–38; and Travers, *Essentials of Learning,* pp. 7–8.
7. Grippin and Peters, *Learning Theory and Learning Outcomes,* p. 61.
8. Resnick, "Toward a Cognitive Theory of Instruction," pp. 7–8; and Grippin and Peters, *Learning Theory and Learning Outcomes,* p. 65.
9. Grippin and Peters, *Learning Theory and Learning Outcomes,* pp. 68–69.
10. Ibid, pp. 96–97.

11. Oxendine, *Psychology of Motor Learning,* pp. 342–43.
12. Ibid., pp. 83–87.
13. Ibid.
14. Ibid.
15. James F. Voss, "Cognition and Instruction: Towards a Cognitive Theory of Learning," in Alan M. Lesgold, James W. Pellegrino, Spike D. Fokkema, and Robert Glaser, eds., *Cognitive Psychology and Instruction* (New York: Plenum Press, 1978), pp. 13–26.
16. Merlin C. Wittrock, "Students' Thought Processes," in Merlin C. Wittrock, ed., *Handbook of Research on Teaching,* 3d ed. (New York: Macmillan Publishing Company, 1986), pp. 297–311 (pp. 306–7).
17. James M. Royer, "Theories of the Transfer of Learning," *Educational Psychologist* 14 (1979), pp. 53–69.
18. Donald A. Norman, Donald R. Gentner, and Albert L. Stevens, "Comments on Learning Schemata and Memory Representation," in David Klahr, ed., *Cognition and Instruction* (New York: John Wiley & Sons, 1976), pp. 177–96 (p. 183).
19. Grippin and Peters, *Learning Theory and Learning Outcomes,* p. 93.
20. David E. Rumelhart, "Schemata: The Building Blocks of Cognition," in Rand J. Spiro, Bertram C. Bruce, and William F. Brewer, eds., *Theoretical Issues in Reading Comprehension* (Hillsdale, New Jersey: Lawrence Erlbaum Associates, Publishers, 1980), pp. 33–58.
21. Travers, *Essentials of Learning,* pp. 164–70.
22. Ibid., pp. 184–87.
23. Jerome Bruner, *The Process of Education* (Cambridge, Massachusetts: Harvard University Press, 1977), p. 12.
24. Anne Rothstein, Linda Catelli, Patt Dodds, and Joan Manahan, *Basic Stuff Series I: Motor Learning* (Reston, Virginia: AAHPERD, 1981), pp. 103–5.
25. Oxendine, *Psychology of Motor Learning,* pp. 90–91.
26. Ibid., pp. 189–95.
27. Wittrock, "Students' Thought Processes," p. 304.
28. M. C. Wittrock, "The Cognitive Movement in Instruction," *Educational Psychologist* 13 (1978), pp. 15–29 (p. 20).
29. Edward L. Deci, et al., "Rewards, Motivation, and Self-Esteem," *The Educational Forum* 44 (May 1980), p. 430.
30. Ibid., pp. 429–33; and Edward L. Deci, et al., "An Instrument to Assess Adults' Orientations Toward Control Versus Autonomy with Children: Reflections on Intrinsic Motivation and Perceived Competence," *Journal of Educational Psychology* 73 (October 1981), pp. 642–50.
31. Susan Harter, "Effectance Motivation Reconsidered: Toward a Developmental Model," *Human Development* 21 (1978), pp. 34–64 (p. 52).
32. Ibid.
33. Abraham H. Maslow, "A Theory of Human Personality," *Psychological Review* 50 (1943), pp. 370–96.
34. Robert M. Gagné, *The Conditions of Learning,* 2d ed. (New York: Holt, Rinehart and Winston, 1970), p. 288.
35. Albert Bandura, "Self-efficacy: Toward a Unifying Theory of Behavioral Change," *Psychological Review* 84 (1977), pp. 191–215.
36. Ibid, p. 193.
37. Ibid.
38. Albert Bandura, *Social Learning Theory* (Englewood Cliffs, New Jersey: Prentice-Hall, 1977), pp. 160–63.
39. Harter, "Effectance Motivation Reconsidered."
40. Wittrock, "Students' Thought Processes," pp. 304–5.
41. Wittrock, "The Cognitive Movement in Instruction," p. 19.
42. Oxendine, *Psychology of Motor Learning,* p. 223.
43. Wittrock, "The Cognitive Movement in Instruction," p. 20.
44. Joan E. Sieber, Harold F. O'Neil, Jr., and Sigmund Tobias, *Anxiety, Learning, and Instruction* (Hillsdale, New Jersey: Lawrence Erlbaum Associates, Publishers, 1977), pp. 115–16.

45. Penelope L. Peterson, "Interactive Effects of Student Anxiety, Achievement Orientation, and Teacher Behavior on Student Achievement and Attitude," *Journal of Educational Psychology* 69 (1977), pp. 779–92.

46. Robert Rosenthal and Lenore Jacobson, *Pygmalion in the Classroom: Teacher Expectation and Pupils' Intellectual Development* (New York: Holt, Rinehart and Winston, 1968).

47. Jere E. Brophy and Thomas L. Good, *Teacher-Student Relationships: Causes and Consequences* (New York: Holt, Rinehart and Winston, 1974).

48. Jere Brophy, "Successful Teaching Strategies for the Inner-City Child," *Phi Delta Kappan* 63 (1982), pp. 527–30.

49. Thomas J. Martinek, "Pygmalion in the Gym: A Model for the Communication of Teacher Expectations in Physical Education," *Research Quarterly for Exercise and Sport* 52 (March 1981), pp. 58–67; Thomas J. Martinek, "Creating Golem and Galatea Effects During Physical Education Instruction: A Social Psychological Perspective," in Thomas J. Templin and Janice K. Olson, eds., *Teaching in Physical Education* (Champaign, Illinois: Human Kinetics Publishers, 1983), pp. 59–70; Thomas J. Martinek and William B. Karper, "Canonical Relationships among Motor Ability, Expression of Effort, Teacher Expectations, and Dyadic Interactions in Elementary Age Children," *Journal of Teaching in Physical Education* 1 (1982), pp. 26–39; and Thomas J. Martinek and William B. Karper, "A Research Model for Determining Causal Effects of Teacher Expectations in Physical Education Instruction," *Quest* 35 (1983), pp. 155–68.

50. Wittrock, "Students' Thought Processes," pp. 297–98.

51. Sally Hutslar, "The Expectancy Phenomenon," *Journal of Physical Education, Recreation and Dance* 52 (September 1981), pp. 88–89 (p. 68).

52. Judith E. Rink, *Teaching Physical Education for Learning* (St. Louis, Missouri: C. V. Mosby Company, 1985), p. 274.

53. Judith E. Rink, "The Teacher Wants Us to Learn," *Journal of Physical Education and Recreation* 52 (1981), pp. 17–18.

54. Robert B. Turner and William W. Purkey, "Teaching Physical Education: An Invitational Approach," *Journal of Physical Education, Recreation and Dance* 54 (September 1983), pp. 13–14, 64.

55. Jere Brophy, "Teacher Praise: A Functional Analysis," *Review of Educational Research* 51 (1981), pp. 5–32.

56. Ibid.

57. Wittrock, "Students' Thought Processes," p. 300.

58. Brophy, "Teacher Praise: A Functional Analysis."

59. Travers, *Essentials of Learning,* p. 25.

60. Ibid., p. 31.

61. Rumelhart, "Schemata: The Building Blocks of Cognition," p. 51.

62. Travers, *Essentials of Learning,* p. 38.

63. Eleanor Jack Gibson, *Principles of Perceptual Development and Learning* (New York: Appleton-Century-Crofts, 1969), cited in Travers, *Essentials of Learning,* p. 60.

64. Grippin and Peters, *Learning Theory and Learning Outcomes,* pp. 125–26.

65. H. A. Witkin, C. A. Moore, D. R. Goodenough, and P. W. Cox, "Field-dependent and Field-independent Cognitive Styles and Their Educational Implications," *Review of Educational Research* 47 (1977), pp. 1–64.

66. R. Cohen, "Conceptual Styles, Culture Conflict, and Nonverbal Tests of Intelligence," *American Anthropologist* 71 (1969), pp. 828–56.

67. Tamar Zelniker and Wendell E. Jeffrey, "Reflective and Impulsive Children: Strategies of Information Processing Underlying Differences in Problem Solving," *Monographs of the Society for Research in Child Development* 41 (5) (1976), Serial Number 168.

68. Wittrock, "Students' Thought Processes," p. 300.

69. Rothstein, Catelli, Dodds, and Manahan, p. 79.

70. Edward A. Bilodeau and Ina McD. Bilodeau, "Motor-Skills Learning," *Annual Review of Psychology* 12 (1961), pp. 243–80.
71. Oxendine, *Psychology of Motor Learning,* p. 107.
72. Travers, *Essentials of Learning,* pp. 481–82.
73. Grippin and Peters, *Learning Theory and Learning Outcomes,* p. 108.
74. Oxendine, *Psychology of Motor Learning,* pp. 117–24.
75. John D. Lawther, *The Learning and Performance of Physical Skills,* 2d ed. (Englewood Cliffs, New Jersey: Prentice-Hall, 1977), p. 55.
76. Robert M. Travers, *Essentials of Learning,* 4th ed. (New York: Macmillan Publishing Company, 1977).
77. Bryant J. Cratty, *Movement Behavior and Motor Learning,* 3d ed. (Philadelphia: Lea & Febiger, 1975), p. 364.
78. Robert N. Singer, *Motor Learning and Human Performance: An Application to Motor Skills and Movement Behaviors,* 3d ed. (New York: Macmillan Publishing Company, 1980), p. 421.
79. Lawther, *The Learning and Performance of Physical Skills,* p. 144.
80. Ibid., p. 139.
81. John E. Nixon and Lawrence F. Locke, "Research on Teaching Physical Education," in R. Travers, ed. *Second Handbook of Research on Teaching* (Chicago: Rand McNally & Company, 1973).
82. Oxendine, *Psychology of Motor Learning,* pp. 304–5.
83. May V. Seagoe, "Qualitative Wholes: A Re-valuation of the Whole-part Problem," *Journal of Educational Psychology* 27 (1936), pp. 537–45 (p. 542).
84. Oxendine, *Psychology of Motor Learning,* pp. 304–6.
85. Ibid., p. 312.
86. Ibid., p. 310.
87. Ibid., p. 313.
88. Ibid., pp. 280–99.
89. Grippin and Peters, *Learning Theory and Learning Outcomes,* p. 46.
90. Cratty, *Movement Behavior and Motor Learning,* p. 387.
91. Ibid., pp. 387, 396–97.
92. Singer, *Motor Learning and Human Performance,* p. 471.
93. Cratty, *Movement Behavior and Motor Learning,* p. 398.
94. Oxendine, *Psychology of Motor Learning,* p. 154.
95. Cratty, *Movement Behavior and Motor Learning,* p. 389.
96. Nixon and Locke, "Research on Teaching Physical Education," p. 1217.
97. Oxendine, *Psychology of Motor Learning,* p. 154.
98. Ibid., p. 164.
99. Ibid., pp. 176–77.
100. Ibid., p. 176.
101. Ibid., pp. 179, 185.

5

Understanding the Learner

Study Stimulators

1. What common characteristics do adolescents of various ages have? What differences do they exhibit?
2. What effect do student similarities and differences have on learning and teaching?
3. How can a teacher best meet the needs of all students?

Ralph Waldo Emerson once said, "The secret of education lies in respecting the pupil." Respect comes from getting to know one another and appreciating the worth of the other person. By getting to know students, teachers can design instructional programs to help them become successful, contributing members of society. "Teachers who become familiar with the background characteristics of their students have a considerable advantage in planning their teaching. Just as the investment of time in coming to know students as individuals reaps a generous return in the classroom, so time invested in ascertaining the expected characteristics of a learner population will benefit the [teacher]."[1] In learning about students, teachers need to consider three areas: (1) common characteristics of children and youth, (2) significant differences among students, and (3) social forces that affect students. Educational programs must then be planned that meet the needs identified in these three areas.

Common Characteristics of Children and Youth

Workman described the typical adolescent of today as

> a youngster born about 1967 (the "Year of the Hippie"), who entered elementary school just as the war in Vietnam was ending and Watergate was beginning, who left junior high school while Iran held America hostage, and who graduated from high school in the Age of the Yuppie, the VCR, the Macintosh, and Star Wars.[2]

Much research has been conducted in child and adolescent growth and development and is available in textbooks of educational and developmental psychology. A summary chart of the characteristics of children is shown in table 5.1, with a corresponding chart for adolescent characteristics in table 5.2. The secondary school years consist of a constantly evolving period of growth and development in which the characteristics are the same. They change only in degree.[3] Caution should be exercised in defining all students by these norms. Since students are continuously growing and developing, all students do not fit the norm for a particular grade level. Students in one grade level may be as much as eleven months different in age, not counting older students who have been held back. Even students of the same age mature at different rates; therefore, there is seldom a time when all children or youth of a given group will be at exactly the same stage of growth and development.

Obviously there cannot be a different school for each student. Therefore, common characteristics of children and youth serve as a general guide for making curriculum decisions for the school.

Table 5.1 Characteristics and interests of children

Kindergarten and First Grade

Characteristics and Interests	*Program Guidelines*
Psychomotor Domain	
Noisy, constantly active, egocentric, exhibitionistic. Imitative and imaginative. Want attention.	Include vigorous games and stunts, games with individual roles (hunting, dramatic activities, story plays), and a few team games or relays.
Large muscles more developed, game skills not developed.	Challenge with varied movement. Develop specialized skills of throwing, catching, and bouncing balls.
Naturally rhythmic.	Use music and rhythm with skills. Provide creative rhythms, folk dances, and singing movement songs.
May become suddenly tired but soon recovers.	Use activities of brief duration. Provide short rest periods or intersperse physically demanding activities with less vigorous ones.
Hand-eye coordination developing.	Give opportunity to handle different objects such as balls, beanbags, and hoops.
Perceptual abilities maturing.	Give practice in balance—unilateral, bilateral, and cross-lateral movements.
Pelvic tilt can be pronounced.	Give attention to posture problems. Provide abdominal strengthening activities.
Cognitive Domain	
Short attention span.	Change activity often. Give short explanations.
Interested in what the body can do. Curious.	Provide movement experiences. Pay attention to educational movement.
Want to know. Often ask *why* about movement.	Explain reasons for various activities and the basis of movement.
Express individual views and ideas.	Allow children time to be creative. Expect problems when children are lined up and asked to perform the same task.
Begin to understand the idea of teamwork.	Plan situations that require group cooperation. Discuss the importance of such.
Sense of humor expands.	Insert some humor in the teaching process.
Highly creative.	Allow students to try new and different ways of performing activities; sharing ideas with friends encourages creativity.

Table 5.1 (Continued)

Kindergarten and First Grade

Characteristics and Interests	Program Guidelines
Affective Domain	
No sex differences in interests.	Set up same activities for boys and girls.
Sensitive and individualistic, self-concept very important. Accept defeat poorly.	Teach taking turns, sharing, and learning to win, lose, or be caught gracefully.
Like small-group activity.	Use entire class group sparingly. Break into smaller groups.
Sensitive to feelings of adults. Like to please teacher.	Give frequent praise and encouragement.
Can be reckless.	Stress safe approaches.
Enjoy rough-and-tumble activity.	Include rolling, dropping to the floor, and so on, in both introductory and program activities. Stress simple stunts and tumbling.
Seek personal attention.	Recognize individuals through both verbal and nonverbal means. See that all have a chance to be the center of attention.
Love to climb and explore play environments.	Provide play materials, games, and apparatus for strengthening large muscles (e.g., climbing towers, climbing ropes, jump ropes, miniature Challenge Courses, and turning bars).

Second and Third Grade

Characteristics and Interests	Program Guidelines
Psychomotor Domain	
Capable of rhythmic movement	Continue creative rhythms, singing movement songs, and folk dancing.
Improved hand-eye and perceptual-motor coordination.	Give opportunity for manipulating hand apparatus. Provide movement experience and practice in perceptual-motor skills (right and left, unilateral, bilateral, and cross-lateral movements).
More interest in sports.	Begin introductory sports and related skills and simple lead-up activities.
Sport-related skill patterns mature in some cases.	Emphasize practice in these skill areas through simple ball games, stunts, and rhythmic patterns.
Developing interest in fitness.	Introduce some of the specialized fitness activities to 3rd grade.
Reaction time slow.	Avoid highly organized ball games that require and place a premium on quickness and accuracy.

Table 5.1 (Continued)

Second and Third Grade

Characteristics and Interests	Program Guidelines

Cognitive Domain

Still active but attention span longer. More interest in group play.	Include active big-muscle program and more group activity. Begin team concept in activity and relays.
Curious to see what they can do. Love to be challenged and will try anything.	Offer challenges involving movement problems and more critical demands in stunts, tumbling, and apparatus work. Emphasize safety and good judgment.
Interest in group activities; ability to plan with others developing.	Offer group activities and simple dances that involve cooperation with a partner or a team.

Affective Domain

Like physical contact and belligerent games.	Include dodgeball games and other active games, as well as rolling stunts.
Developing more interest in skills. Want to excel.	Organize practice in a variety of throwing, catching, and moving skills, as well as others.
Becoming more conscious socially.	Teach need to abide by rules and play fairly. Teach social customs and courtesy in rhythmic areas.
Like to perform well and to be admired for accomplishments.	Begin to stress quality. Provide opportunity to achieve.
Essentially honest and truthful.	Accept children's word. Give opportunity for trust in game and relay situations.
Do not lose willingly.	Provide opportunity for children to learn to accept defeat gracefully and to win with humility.
Sex difference still of little importance.	Avoid separation of sexes in any activity.

Fourth, Fifth, and Sixth Grades

Characteristics and Interests	Program Guidelines

Psychomotor Domain

Steady growth. Girls often grow more rapidly than boys.	Continue vigorous program to enhance physical development.
Muscular coordination and skills improving. Interested in learning detailed techniques.	Continue emphasis on teaching skills through drills, lead-up games, and free practice periods. Emphasize correct form.
Differences in physical capacity and skill development.	Offer flexible standards so all find success. In team activities, match teams evenly so individual skill levels are less apparent.
Posture problems may appear.	Include posture correction and special posture instruction; emphasize effect of body carriage on self-concept.

Table 5.1 (Continued)

Fourth, Fifth, and Sixth Grades

Characteristics and Interests	Program Guidelines
Sixth-grade girls may show signs of maturity. May not wish to participate in all activities.	Have consideration for their problems. Encourage participation on a limited basis, if necessary.
Sixth-grade boys are rougher and stronger.	Keep sexes together for skill development but separate for competition in certain rougher activities.

Cognitive Domain

Want to know rules of games.	Include instruction on rules, regulations, and traditions.
Knowledgeable about and interested in sport and game strategy.	Emphasize strategy, as opposed to merely performing a skill without thought.
Question the relevance and importance of various activities	Explain regularly the reasons for performing activities and learning various skills.
Desire information about the importance of physical fitness and health-related topics.	Include in lesson plans brief explanations of how various activities enhance growth and development.

Affective Domain

Enjoy team and group activity. Competitive urge strong.	Include many team games, relays, and combatives.
Much interest in sports and sport-related activities.	Offer a variety of sports in season, with emphasis on lead-up games.
Little interest in the opposite sex. Some antagonism may arise.	Offer coeducational activities with emphasis on individual differences of all participants, regardless of sex.
Acceptance of self-responsibility. Strong increase in drive toward independence.	Provide leadership and followership opportunities on a regular basis. Involve students in evaluation procedures.
Intense desire to excel both in skill and physical capacity.	Stress physical fitness. Include fitness and skill surveys both to motivate and to check progress.
Sportsmanship a concern for both teachers and students.	Establish and enforce fair rules. With enforcement include an explanation of the need for rules and cooperation if games are to exist.
Peer group important. Want to be part of the gang.	Stress group cooperation in play and among teams. Rotate team positions as well as squad makeup.

Source: Victor P. Dauer and Robert P. Pangrazi. *Dynamic Physical Education for Elementary School Children* (New York: Macmillan Publishing Company, 1986).

Table 5.2 Characteristics and interests of adolescents

Junior High School

Characteristics and Interests	*Implications for Programs*
Cognitive Domain	
Increased attention span and ability to handle complex concepts and abstract thinking.	Teach the *why* of concepts regarding biomechanics, motor learning, exercise physiology, etc. Promote creative thinking and problem solving.
Increased interest in possible career options.	Teach the importance of physical activity throughout life.
Increased interest in societal problems.	Promote leadership and followership through cooperative, democratic living.
Wide range of experiences due to travel, TV, and family mobility.	Avoid talking down to students.
Affective Domain	
Desire for independence from adults. Often critical of adults.	Help students learn responsibility, leadership and decision-making strategies, and the value of rules in their lives. Help students develop self-confidence and feelings of personal worth.
Vacillation between adult and peer-group values.	Provide approval from both peers and adults. Emphasize high ethical standards.
Interest in impressing the peer group and opposite sex.	Provide social interaction in classes and extracurricular activities to help students develop social and leadership skills. Provide success experiences in basic skills.
Interest in and self-consciouness about own bodies, appearance, and abilities.	Help students understand physiological changes, capacities, and limitations and provide help with grooming, clothes, appearance, weight control, physical fitness, weight training, and nutrition. Be aware of student self-consciousness and embarrassment dressing in front of peers.
Moody and easily angered or upset.	Help students learn strategies for emotional control and stress reduction.
Eager to try new things.	Introduce new activities. Satisfy need for adventure in socially acceptable ways.
Competitive.	Provide a balance between cooperative and competitive activities.

Table 5.2 (Continued)

Junior High School

Characteristics and Interests	*Implications for Programs*
Psychomotor Domain	
Widely differing maturation levels among students:	Adjust activities for dramatic differences in sizes and skill levels of students.
Maturation of girls about 1.5 years before boys.	Distribute players to teams based on size or height.
Emergence of secondary sex characteristics.	Be aware of self-consciousness of students. Avoid awkward situations.
First girls and then boys are taller and heavier.	Consider differences in boys and girls when evaluating progress.
Differences in strength, flexibility, balance, and endurance between boys and girls.	Students must be helped to accept the dramatic differences in physical maturation they possess and understand that they are normal. Provide activities to develop health-related fitness.
Poor coordination, low strength and endurance, a greater need for sleep, and increased appetite as a result of growth spurts.	Provide opportunities for developing coordination and skill in a variety of activities. Avoid calling attention to awkwardness.
Bone ossification not yet complete.	Provide supervision to avoid injuries.
Posture affected by peer pressure.	Teach correct posture and body mechanics. Guard against fatigue.
Growth rapid and uneven. Energy absorbed in growth process.	Test for structural deviations such as kyphosis and scoliosis.

High School

Characteristics and Interests	*Implications for Programs*
Cognitive Domain	
Reaching full intellectual potential. Increased knowledge and experience base.	Teach concepts regarding the *why* of biomechanics, motor learning, exercise physiology, etc. Promote creative thinking and problem solving.
Continued interest in societal problems.	Promote leadership and followership through cooperative, democratic living.
Narrowing of career options and lifetime choices.	Teach the importance of physical activity throughout life. Provide opportunities to develop increased specialization in activities of their own choosing.

Table 5.2 (Continued)

High School

Characteristics and Interests	*Implications for Programs*
Affective Domain	
Peer-group and dating activities dominate social lives of students.	Provide appropriate social activities with opportunities to learn leadership and social-interaction skills.
Continued conflict between youth and adult values; highly critical of adults and peers.	Provide both peer and adult approval. Help students develop a personal value system.
Interest in personal appearance and social skills.	Help students with ways to improve themselves and to impress others.
Interest in new activities, adventure, and excitement.	Help students choose appropriate risk activities; avoid drugs, etc.
Emotional conflicts continue.	Help students learn stress-reduction techniques.
Increased competitiveness in dating, grades, and athletics.	Provide activities that involve a balance between cooperation and competition.
Psychomotor Domain	
Physical maturity results in higher levels of motor ability and fitness, with boys ending up bigger, faster, and stronger than girls.	Use different evaluation standards for boys and girls.
Large appetites continue, but some girls restrict intake.	Be aware of incidence of anorexia nervosa and bulimia among girls.
Coordination improves. Interest in personal development continues.	Develop increased specialization in lifetime activities.

Significant Differences among Students

Considerable differences exist among students both within and across age and grade levels in (1) physical growth and development, (2) intellectual development, (3) social development, and (4) emotional development. At the elementary school level, a span of four to five years can exist in student achievement in a single class. Greater variability exists at the secondary school level.[4] A knowledge of individual differences is essential to teachers planning to individualize instruction in their classes.

Physical Growth and Development

Growth and development depend on both heredity and environment. Because of improved nutrition and better health care, today's children grow up faster. Both boys and girls are taller, heavier, and mature earlier than children of previous generations. They can expect the longest life expectancy ever known.

Chamberlin and Girona describe adolescence as a "clash between culture and biology," in which "adults try to cling to and pass on the values and mores of our culture to our children while they struggle with maturing bodies and childlike emotions."[5] Although adolescence

Students differ significantly in physical and
intellectual growth and development, social
experiences, personality, attitudes, and interests.

begins earlier, the economic and educational requirements of a technological society force
it to end later. As a result, curriculum activities that used to be reserved for older students
are now handed down to younger students. This leaves older students frustrated because
nothing new is left for them to try, and yet they are not allowed to assume the privileges and
responsibilities of adulthood. Teachers face the challenge of trying to help students cope with
the physical and emotional changes that challenge them.

One outcome of growing up too fast may be the recent incidence of anorexia nervosa
and other eating disorders among young women ages fifteen to twenty-five. The major sign
of anorexia nervosa is an extreme loss of weight, which is accompanied by amenorrhea. The
symptoms appear at the onset of puberty and the development of the secondary sex characteristics. Anorexia nervosa is found in adolescent girls of all socioeconomic classes. The
young women have a constant preoccupation with diet and exercise and a distorted body
image in which they see themselves as obese, even when malnourished. They desperately
resist help of any kind, although many can be helped through personal and family therapy.

Adolescents differ widely in physical growth and capacity. Some children are early
bloomers and others mature much later. They vary widely in body build and physical capacity. While no significant physiological differences exist between boys and girls at the elementary school level, great variability exists between the genders and within each gender
during the middle and junior high school years. Griffin and Placek summarize these differences as follows:

> Girls have begun or are completing puberty and are growing and maturing rapidly.
> Most boys have not begun their growth spurt and in the early junior high years most
> still possess late childhood characteristics. Thus, in all the physical categories described
> for 7–9 graders, teachers will see a wide range of characteristics in their students.

Height and weight, aerobic capacity, and body proportions will vary depending upon each individual student. With the onset of puberty girls will gain additional body fat. Hip width will also increase in girls, while boys' shoulder width will increase. In effect, boys end up with wider shoulders and narrower hips than girls, whose proportions are the reverse, with wider hips and narrower shoulders. Boys will begin to attain additional muscle mass toward the latter part of junior high.[6]

Because of the variability among students, they should not be automatically grouped by gender for physical education activities. Griffin and Placek summarize the data about students at the high-school level as follows:

At this age level (14 to 18 years) most girls are physically mature and boys are rapidly growing toward adult size. Therefore, most boys will be taller and heavier and have more muscle mass. Boys' heart and lung sizes are larger than the girls', thus increasing their aerobic capacity. Most girls again have a greater percentage of body fat, wider hips, and narrower shoulders in relation to boys. Boys have longer leg length in proportion to trunk length. As adults, the average female has about 2/3 the strength of the average male. . . .

This information gives teachers guidelines about what to expect of students at different developmental levels. However, these studies also show that there is great variation within each sex from the average for each sex. Moreover, there is overlap between the comparisons of girls and boys. This means that even though there may be *average* differences between the sexes on physical characteristics, in any physical education class there will also be full range of variation and overlap in physical characteristics. There will be tall girls, short boys, strong girls, weak boys, strong boys, heavy girls and thin girls. It is important for teachers concerned with equity to teach *individual* students regardless of sex, not average boys or girls.[7]

Motor ability factors—such as agility, balance, coordination, flexibility, strength, and speed—predispose some students to success in some motor activities and others to success in other activities. Body build, muscle composition, and respiratory capacity help some students to be better long-distance runners and others to be better sprinters or jumpers. Other factors that vary include visual and auditory acuity, perception, and reaction time. Physical handicaps enlarge the differences among students.

Because of the wide variety of individual differences among students, physical education programs should include a variety of activities so that students will find some commensurate with their individual abilities. Different levels of activity should be provided so that students will be challenged to extend their abilities, yet experience success during the learning process.

Intellectual Development

The youth of today are better informed than their counterparts of yesteryear. Nursery schools; television and other media, scores of books, newspapers, and magazines; and widespread travel have increased the information available to today's adolescents. As a result of these experiences, children and adolescents are not easily impressed. They have seen it all. However, the abundance of information causes what Chamberlin and Girona call "over choice."[8] Young people have so much information and so many choices provided in dress, life-style, courses, occupations, and values that they are confused as to what information to process and how to make the decisions that confront them. They must be helped to deal with problem-solving behaviors if the school is going to be of value to them.

Intellectual development can be impaired by the failure of some students to take advantage of instruction. For a few students, physical or emotional disabilities disturb learning. However, even as the number of handicapped students is decreasing, the number of so-called learning-disabled students has nearly doubled since 1977.[9] Many of these learning-disabled students may suffer from a late start, after which the self-fulfilling prophecy takes effect, in which students who are labeled as slow learners gradually begin to see themselves as such. Bereiter concluded that

> For any sort of learning, from swimming to reading, some children learn with almost no help and other children need a great deal of help. Children whom we have been labeling as educationally disadvantaged are typically children who need more than ordinary amounts of help with academic learning. . . . From this point of view, a successful compensatory education program is one that gives students plenty of help in learning.[10]

Recent studies on the brain and learning demonstrate that students learn in different ways. While more than one-half of students are right-brained and learn better through visual, holistic means, the majority of teachers teach in a left-brain or verbal mode. The implication is that all students can succeed if helped to use their own natural processes for learning.[11]

Social Development

Adolescence is characterized by a change in social-interaction patterns and a challenging of parental and authority roles. Early adolescents are predominantly interested in groups of friends of the same gender. They are in a process of relinquishing old ties and establishing new ones in an attempt to gain independence and a new identity. Peer approval at this stage is more important than parental approval. Peers become a sounding board for ideas and controversial topics. However, adults are still important for helping adolescents test their newly formed theories. Adolescents who transfer their dependence on their parents to dependence on the group fail to develop the independence needed for mature behavior and personal self-worth. Gangs can be detrimental due to the artificial interaction patterns of the youth involved, both the leaders and the followers, and the failure to learn appropriate procedures for conflict resolution.

During the middle phase of adolescence, same-gender peer groups decrease in size and become cliques, which emphasize certain modes of dress and behavior. Popularity and conformity to group norms is important. In the normal development process, youth gradually discard group choices for individual selection. During this phase, teenagers often identify with the parent of the opposite gender and develop friends of the opposite gender. Problems arise between boys and girls of the same ages because of the different rates of maturation.

During late adolescence, young adults limit friends of the same gender to a few "best" friends. They continue to develop romantic relationships with friends of the opposite gender. In addition, they become more friendly with adults on a new level. They learn to accept the flaws of friends and adults and to understand that "nobody is perfect."

The influence of the peer group, coupled with a desire for adventure, often leads adolescents into situations incompatible with their level of judgment. A lack of judgment often results in an increase in the number of accidents among this age group.[12]

Youth who are economically disadvantaged and affluent youth whose parents lavish them with material goods rather than with personal attention and love often have more difficulty adapting to appropriate interaction patterns.

Emotional Development

A critical factor in adolescent development is the ability to build and maintain feelings of personal worth and belonging. Self-esteem and self-confidence have to do with a belief in one's own worth and positive attitudes toward one's own abilities. To understand and accept other people, individuals must first learn to understand and accept themselves. The foundation for self-esteem and self-confidence is laid in infancy. Love leads to trust and a sense of being acceptable and worthwhile.

One of the tasks of adolescence is a search for a new self. Adolescents struggle with changes in physical appearance, such as being too tall, too short, too fat, too skinny, having acne, or anything else that makes them feel different or unacceptable. Hormonal changes bring on personality and mood changes. Responses vary from excitement to depression. Students fluctuate between childlike and adult emotions and behavior in an attempt to establish a new state of independence from parents, while maintaining their needs for adult approval and affection. Youth spend a lot of energy "trying on" different personalities in an attempt to find the one that suits them.[13] They lose or add nicknames or change from a first to a middle name. They experiment with new styles of penmanship, dress, and behavior. When they do not match up with the ideal self they envision, they become unhappy. All of these adjustments lead to emotional stress. Adolescents need time alone to reflect on and examine themselves. When a young adult learns to accept his or her physical body, public personality, and inner self, a mature personality emerges.

Once the self-concept is formed and internalized, the person tends to nurture it by seeking experiences to validate it. For example, if John feels he is a failure, he will continue to fail, since that supports his image of himself. To change a student's self-concept, significant people in the student's life, such as family, friends, neighbors, and teachers, need to provide encouragement and acceptance over a long period of time. Because the self-concept is an enduring one, even minor changes for the better should be applauded.

Combs stated:

> The student takes his self-concept with him wherever he goes. He takes it to Latin class, to arithmetic class, to gym class, and he takes it home with him. Wherever he goes, his self-concept goes, too. Everything that happens to him has an effect on his self-concept.
>
> Are we influencing that self-concept in positive or negative ways? We need to ask ourselves these kinds of questions. How can a person feel liked unless somebody likes him? How can a person feel wanted unless somebody wants him? How can a person feel acceptable unless somebody accepts him? How can a person feel he's a person with dignity and integrity unless somebody treats him so? And how can a person feel that he is capable unless he has some success? In the answers to those questions, we'll find the answers to the human side of learning.[14]

Adolescents are extremely concerned about social injustices. Unless knowledge and skills are related to students' attitudes, feelings, and beliefs about themselves and their fears and concerns about the community that surrounds them, the likelihood is that education will have a limited influence on their behavior. Instruction then becomes a matter of linking the cognitive and psychomotor aspects of the curriculum to the intrinsic feelings and concerns of the students. When these feelings and experiences are validated for students, students believe they are worthwhile.

Various personality characteristics cause students to feel more comfortable in one activity than another. The aggressive, competitive, social student might prefer participation in a team sport, whereas the cooperative, passive loner might prefer engaging in a jogging or cycling program. Active, assertive people learn better from live instruction, while their less-assertive schoolmates learn better from films.[15] Introverts prefer learning from self-instructional materials, while extroverts prefer interacting with the instructor.[16] Closed-minded students may suffer from anxiety that limits their capacity for self-fulfillment and need activities to build up their confidence and help them become self-directing.[17]

Another basic adolescent need is to learn to accept responsibility for their actions and to demonstrate self-discipline before asking for greater freedom.[18]

Social Forces that Affect Students

Rapid changes in society can have a detrimental effect on youth. Increased mobility has taken families away from relatives and friends. Dramatic role changes for men and women have confused some young people as to what is expected of them. Values and morals change constantly and are no longer a stabilizing force in American society. The influence of the family has steadily deteriorated, with 22 percent of children under age eighteen today living with only one parent, and the U.S. Census Bureau reports that nearly half of the children born in 1980 will live in single-parent families before they reach age eighteen.[19] Divorce, death, and births to unwed mothers lead to many mother-only households with significantly lower incomes.[20] According to a study by Dornbusch and his colleagues, adolescents in these households have a significantly higher level of deviant behavior than those in families with two natural parents.[21]

In many other homes, both parents work outside the home, leaving the children to fend for themselves. A Special Labor Force Report of the U.S. Department of Labor indicated 31.8 million youth under age eighteen (54 percent of the nation's youth) had mothers working outside the home in 1981.[22] According to the 1984 statistics of the U.S. Department of Labor, 65 percent of the mothers of school-age children were employed.[23] Latchkey children (a term describing the housekeys they have often worn hanging around their necks), leave home after their parents have gone to work or come home to an empty house or both. Estimates of the number of latchkey children range from 1.8 to 15 million.[24] Although the majority of these children are from low-income families, they come from all socioeconomic levels.

Social consequences arising from unsupervised youth include crime (especially shoplifting) and drug abuse.[25] Individual consequences include fear, loneliness, boredom,[26] accidents, child molestation, rape,[27] or even teen suicide,[28] not to mention the fear and guilt experienced by parents.[29] Academic achievement may or may not be affected.

Some solutions to the problem include programs offered by community organizations, parent groups, social service agencies, youth groups, private industry, schools, churches, private day-care centers, and worksite centers. Flexible work times have been offered by some employers. Volunteer tutors after school hours, after-school playground programs, and phone-a-friend or tutor hot lines have all proven helpful. Legal liability, money, and a lack of policies regarding these programs have affected their availability for all children.

Implications for teachers include the need to structure homework more carefully, to provide homework hot lines, and to take time to listen to the concerns of youth. Schools need to establish emergency procedures for contacting working parents and to establish or support extended-care programs.[30]

With regard to the incidence of drug abuse, two U.S. government reports indicated:

> If you teach high school, the chances are that about one-fourth of the students in your classes regularly smoke marijuana, more than two-thirds regularly use alcohol, and approximately one-fifth drink on a daily basis. . . . Nor are younger children immune: the beginning average ages of marijuana use and alcohol drinking have now dropped to 11 and 12 years of age respectively.[31]

"Teenagers in the United States have the highest rate of drug abuse of any industrialized country in the world."[32] Towers defined drug abuse as follows:

> I believe that any nonmedically prescribed use of a chemical substance to produce an artificially pleasurable experience by a child or adolescent constitutes drug abuse and has the potential to seriously harm and adversely affect that youngster's life.[33]

Commonly abused drugs include tobacco, alcohol, narcotics, depressants, stimulants, hallucinogens, and marijuana. While adults have been smoking less, teenagers (especially girls) have been smoking more. Other harmful practices include inhaling glue, gasoline, paint, and aerosol fumes and the use of chewing tobacco or snuff. Synthetic drugs or analogs of controlled or illegal drugs can have potencies thousands of times those of their natural counterparts and often result in brain damage or death. Increasingly, youth are indiscriminately mixing drugs such as alcohol and barbiturates that can result in respiratory and heart failure or violent behavior.[34] Three drugs have been singled out as those most frequently used and the "gateway" to the use of all other drugs. They are alcohol, marijuana, and cocaine.[35]

Drugs cripple, kill, or ruin young lives, physically and emotionally. In addition to the personal harm resulting from drug use, drug addicts steal, assault, prostitute, and sell drugs to others to support their habits. Drugged and drunken drivers maim or kill tens of thousands of people each year. Drug use can precipitate violent, senseless crimes.[36]

Experts cite four steps to drug dependence:[37]

1. Experimentation
2. Occasional social use in group settings
3. Regular use, once or twice a week, of one or more chosen drugs
4. Dependence or addiction (daily use)

Precipitators of drug abuse are similar to those for other dysfunctional behaviors and include (1) stress, (2) skill deficiencies, (3) situational constraints, (4) and changes in the nuclear family. All of these factors interact with one another and can contribute separately or together to problem behavior.[38]

Adolescents today experience a great deal of stress, isolation, and alienation. Adolescence is a painful period, in which the body, mind, and emotions change drastically. New roles and increased expectations by teachers and parents create feelings of inadequacy.

Postman and Elkind focused attention on the disappearance of childhood from the life cycle.[39] Norwood added:

> Caught in this frustrated age of development, today's children experiment with behaviors thought to be adultlike with little ability to ascertain the good and bad of such behavior. . . . Thus, the role-modeling of adult behavior encouraged in today's society pressures children to engage in alcohol consumption, smoking, illicit drug use, sexual intercourse, and other roles they perceive to be adult. "Sooner is better" is a message received by our children. . . . The rational behind pressuring children to achieve beyond their age and normal expectations must be re-examined.[40]

Youth have been superficially exposed to so many adult activities and privileges that by the time they are in their mid-teens they are already bored and have nothing to look forward to. Many respond by escaping to drugs, delinquency, or religious cults.

In addition to the factors mentioned above, stress may come from the loss of a parent or friend, rejection or failure, family conflict, or abuse.[41] People vary greatly in their abilities to cope with stress. The more stress they can tolerate, the less likely they are to turn to drugs.[42]

Youth who have the ability to face problems realistically and attack them systematically are not likely to get involved with drugs, while those who deny or blame others for their problems, run away from their problems, or expect others to solve them are especially vulnerable. Skills needed include problem solving, realistic self-assessment, and communication skills. Persons suffering from feelings of inferiority or powerlessness may turn to drugs for the false sense of confidence or power those drugs create.[43]

A major situational constraint is the influence of the peer group. Initial drug use usually occurs between the ages of twelve and eighteen.[44] Association with drug-using friends is one of the strongest predictors of drug use among adolescents.[45] The medical revolution has led to the acceptance of drugs as chemical "miracles" and the widespread availability of prescription drugs to cure the ills of society. People encounter drugs everywhere they look—television, movies, newspapers, sports, and music. Television commercials and programming sell youth on drugs and alcohol and the need to look better, feel better, or escape from their humdrum life-style. The "me"-oriented generation focuses on pleasure, leisure activities, and winning. The need to be first in everything can result in the use of drugs to stay awake, lose weight, or ward off stress.[46] The widespread availability and the casual acceptance of drugs place people in situations in which drug use is desirable.[47] At-risk youth find themselves in many situations in which drug use is expected and supported.[48]

Children who grow up in well-adjusted, happy homes are less prone to use drugs than those who come from troubled environments. Parents who use alcohol and other drugs are poor role models for their children. Changes in the family unit have forced youth into early independence and precipitated feelings of loneliness. American youth passively accept a way of life they see as meaningless with a constricted expression of emotion, a low threshold of boredom, and an apparent absence of joy in anything not immediately consumable such as music, sex, drugs, and possessions. Youth who find no purpose in life and believe that life is dull, uneventful, or boring may turn to drugs for the thrill it affords them.[49] The quality of parent-child interactions has been shown to relate to drug use or nonuse.[50] Another factor in whether children use drugs is the religiosity of the parents. "It may very well be impossible, or next to impossible, to rear a child in these days with real assurance about his future unless there is some religion."[51]

Hafen and Frandsen indicated that:

> In general, people turn to drugs to fill a need—a need to relieve anxiety, a need to grow,
> a need to experience adventure, a need to relieve boredom, a need to cope with stress, a
> need to escape from problems. When drugs begin to satisfy those needs—or when a
> person is simply convinced that they do—the drug behavior is reinforced.[52]

Just because a person matches the above description does not mean that drug abuse is inevitable; however, it does indicate a need to learn to overcome those characteristics by examining alternatives to meet those needs and turning weaknesses into strengths.[53]

Although adolescents can exhibit strange behaviors without being on drugs, some signs of drug use might include a sudden unwillingness to follow parental rules, a decline in academic achievement, increased truancy and class cutting, an endless need for money, evidence of drugs or drug paraphernalia, terrific changes in interpersonal relationships, inappropriate clothing habits for the weather conditions, aggressive behavior, loss of interest in former activities or friends, failure to fulfill responsibilities, and physical or mental deterioration, in short, any sudden and unexplained change in behavior, appearance, or personality.[54] Evidence of drug use could include redness of the skin and eyes; burns on the thumb and fingertips; drug particles on teeth or clothing or protruding from pockets; large numbers of matches; use of excessive deodorant, after-shave lotion, gargles, and breath fresheners to disguise telltale odors; increased illness; or emotional outburst.[55]

When teachers suspect drug use, they are obligated, if not legally, then ethically and professionally, to do something about it. When school personnel act in good faith and show reasonable cause for concern, they are usually protected in a law suit.[56] Towers suggested five steps that teachers should take when they suspect a student is abusing drugs:

> (1) express concern about the youngster's failing grades, moodiness, or other observed behavior; (2) encourage the youngster to seek help and offer to assist in getting that help; (3) if the behavior is extreme or if it persists, notify the parent and similarly express concern over the observed behavior; (4) consult with colleagues about the student and refer the youngster to appropriate staff; and (5) participate in the intervention program if appropriate.[57]

However, he cautioned, if the student is currently under the influence of drugs or alcohol—glazed eyes, extreme lethargy, sleepiness, or mood swings—teachers should avoid confrontation and send the youth to the health room or office.[58]

Students on some drugs may feel invulnerable to pain or injury, have delusions of great strength, or feel threatened by teachers and classmates, who may appear as monsters. In these situations, they can be dangerous to themselves and others. In emergencies such as these, Towers suggested that teachers stay calm; avoid threatening the student; immediately notify the office to call for emergency help; try to keep the class quiet or remove the student to a nonstimulating environment; and speak calmly and try to reassure the student that no one intends any harm.[59]

Prevention efforts should begin in the elementary school. Swett and Towers listed three strategies for preventing drug and alcohol abuse. (1) Education should provide clear and accurate information about drugs and their effects on the individual and help students develop the skills needed to make responsible decisions; cope with stress, responsibility, and peer pressure; and improve their self-esteem. (2) Students must be assisted in finding alternative ways to derive pleasure in natural, more socially acceptable, and less harmful ways by engaging in adventure activities, yoga, religion, political action groups, the arts, music, or dancing. (3) School officials can deter drug use by limiting the availability of drugs and imposing stiff, consistent penalties for use, possession, and distribution. Enforcement of school policies and the law can help students accept the consequences of drug-taking activities, rather than having them absolved by caring parents or professionals.[60]

Coalitions of school personnel, parents, students, business persons, and community agencies can work together to fight drug abuse. The National Education Association publication *How Schools Can Help Combat Student Drug and Alcohol Abuse* has numerous strategies and resources that can be used by these groups to prevent drug abuse in schools.[61]

Once students are dependent on drugs, professional treatment is needed, either on a residential or outpatient basis. The sooner the treatment begins, the better the chances for success; therefore, early identification is critical.[62]

Suicides and suicide attempts have become a major concern of parents and educators in the last few years. The number of reported adolescent suicides has jumped 200 percent for girls and 300 percent for boys in the last twenty-five years.[63] Reported suicides are now second only to accidents as the leading cause of death in youths fifteen to nineteen years of age.[64] Every ninety seconds a teenager attempts suicide, with one succeeding every ninety minutes. In addition, many suicides are not reported due to social stigma or lack of evidence. Adolescents who commit suicide tend to be highly intelligent, physically precocious, and between the ages of fifteen and twenty-four. Some are quiet and uncommunicative. Others are impulsive and delinquent. Many are driven by perfectionism.[65]

Rates of life-threatening behavior (potentially lethal behaviors of all types) were reported by Deykin and her associates to be similar for boys and girls, although suicide attempts were nearly three times more prevalent among females.[66] However, males are three times more likely than females to actually kill themselves because they choose more lethal methods.[67]

Jacobs proposed a five-stage model for adolescent suicidal behavior as follows:[68] (1) a history of problems beginning in early childhood, (2) an escalation of the problems with the onset of adolescence, (3) less and less ability to cope with stress and increasing isolation from others, (4) a "last straw" event (such as breaking up with a boyfriend or girlfriend or the loss of a family member or friend) that leaves little remaining social relationships or hope for resolving the problems, and (5) a justification of the suicide by the adolescent to himself or herself.

Many suicide attempters verbalize their intent to commit suicide before attempting it. Others give behavioral clues to their intent such as changes in dress and grooming, changes in eating and sleeping habits, physical complaints or illnesses, personality changes, school failure, depression, social isolation, acting out behaviors, loss of interest in previous activities or friends, alcohol or drug abuse, running away, sexual promiscuity, or belligerence. Many experiment with death through suicidal gestures such as supposed "accidents," wrist slashing, or overdosing on medication. Verbal remarks about death, giving away personal belongings, or a suicide note may precede or accompany the gesture. Before death is finally attempted, the adolescent is silent. Outside interference at this point is no longer desired.[69]

Dr. Jerome Motto, professor of psychiatry at the University of California at San Francisco School of Medicine, suggested several factors for assessing suicidal risk:[70]

1. A prior suicidal attempt
2. The degree of detail in the current suicidal plan
3. The extent of feelings of hopelessness
4. The presence of a lethal weapon
5. The presence or threat of a progressively disabling physical illness
6. The presence of a psychotic disorder (including temporary disorders induced by alcohol or drugs)
7. Clues related to termination behavior such as giving away valued objects or dropping verbal hints about not being present

Hafen and Frandsen reminded teachers, parents, and friends to never ignore a suicide threat. Confront the individual immediately. Listen calmly and evaluate the seriousness of the situation. Help the adolescent realize that the feelings are temporary and will clear up with time, and that death is a permanent decision that cannot be reversed. Stay with the youth, eliminate possible resources for committing suicide, and get professional help immediately from a suicide prevention center or hospital. Let the youth know that you care.[71]

Another problem of epidemic proportions is child abuse. Although the true incidence of child abuse is unknown, estimates of abuse range into millions of cases per year.[72] Cases involving adolescents are less likely to be reported.[73] Child abuse occurs among persons of all races, social classes, and religious beliefs. Most abusive parents were abused as children, thus perpetuating a cycle of abuse.

In all fifty states, the law requires educators to report suspected child abuse.[74] Educators who report suspected child abuse in good faith (i.e., based on reasonable information) are immune from civil or criminal liability.[75]

Signs of abuse include bruises or other physical injuries not related to normal childhood activities; pain, especially in the genital area; nervous or fearful behavior or fear of going home; inappropriate clothing for weather conditions; malnutrition; untreated sores or cuts; and lack of normal hygiene.[76] Behavioral symptoms may include a decline in academic achievement, increased absence from school, explicit artwork, anger and hostility, and changes in social-interaction patterns. Low self-esteem, depression, and pseudomature sexual behaviors are often seen in adolescents experiencing sexual abuse. Substance abuse and running away from home are common among abused children.[77] Most children are afraid to tell others of their experiences due to embarrassment, fear of repercussions, or fear of not being believed.[78] Victims of sexual abuse are usually girls under the age of seventeen. However, Harrison estimated that one out of four girls and one out of ten boys have been sexually abused before the age of eighteen.[79] Perpetrators are generally males known to the victim.

Teachers should not act surprised or horrified when confronted with the evidence of child abuse. They should provide support, express concern, and praise the child for displaying the courage to tell about it.[80] Educators can follow the guidelines listed by Roscoe:

1. Show feelings of genuine concern for the students.
2. Make oneself available and provide opportunities to allow the student to talk freely about feelings, fears, etc.
3. Maintain the student's normal status within the class.
4. Reassure the student that he or she is not responsible for the assault which occurred.
5. Present learning activities which enhance the student's self-concept and self-esteem.
6. Provide experiences which allow students self-expression and facilitate the constructive venting of emotion.
7. Respect and maintain the student's privacy.
8. Present oneself as a model for appropriate adult-child relationships.
9. Help the student keep fears and anxieties from growing out of proportion.
10. Interact closely and cooperatively with professionals who have been trained to work with sexually abused children (e.g., social workers, police, school psychologists).[81]

Educators must also notify the local Department of Social Services.

Workman summarized a study of youth culture, including student essays about themselves, in four themes. First, students search for *family stability and communication*. Students named parents as the major influence in their lives. Even grandparents outranked the influence of idols in sports and music. Although television ranked third in influence, preferred shows dealt with family life. The second theme involved *identity problems and loneliness*. Teenagers look for connections and guidance. Third, youth live in a culture that moves at a disturbing pace. Therefore, *living with rapid change* is essential. They look forward to some stability in a changing world. The fourth theme was a *fear of failure*. With the increasing knowledge demands for employment, competition is stiff.[82]

The effects of social forces on individual students differ in terms of their various backgrounds and experiences. Ethnic groups have different expectations regarding the value of education. Families differ in the cultural experiences they provide their members, as well as in their goals and interests. Friends, neighbors, and other social groups influence values and attitudes. Experiences of individual students can be so different that generalities are no longer of use in planning some educational programs.

A new program has been developed by the Quest National Center in Columbus, Ohio, to help sixth through eighth graders learn about the challenges of adolescence and how to develop the skills necessary to cope with them. Called "Skills for Adolescence," the program has been adopted by over five hundred school districts. It includes units on entering the teen years, building self-confidence, learning about emotions, improving peer and family relationships, developing decision-making skills, setting goals, and developing one's potential.[83]

Educational Programs that Meet Student Needs

Physical growth and development, intellectual and emotional development, social forces, and personality factors all affect the ways in which students learn. Therefore, various styles of learning should be provided for in the instructional program. Some principles that must be considered when planning educational programs include the following:

1. Each student is unique, a result of both heredity and environment.
2. Each student learns at his or her own rate regardless of how the teacher paces the instruction.
3. Students learn many things simultaneously.
4. Students learn different things from identical experiences.
5. Learning does not take place in a smooth, continuous process. It involves intermittent periods of growth followed by plateaus.
6. Students must learn for themselves. The teacher cannot learn for them.
7. Students learn best when
   a. Learning is positively and immediately reinforced by praise or success.
   b. The learning process involves experiencing and doing.
   c. A wide variety of meaningful learning experiences are provided at the appropriate level for the maturity of the student.
   d. Goals and objectives are set or accepted by the students and provide realistic standards for each student.
   e. Students can see the results of how well they are doing.

f. Students experience many more successful experiences than failures.
g. Learning is directed to the whole student.
h. The learning experience and evaluation are adapted to the individual differences of the student.
i. The learning environment is a comfortable place to make (and learn from) a mistake.

Each of these principles will be discussed in more detail in the following chapters. Doll suggested that "the challenge to education in a democracy appears much more prominently in the differences among children and youth than in their similarities."[84]

Meeting the Needs of All Students

The goal of education is to provide a quality educational experience for every student. There are boys and girls, low-skilled and highly skilled, slow learners and gifted students, normal and handicapped, and a large number of different cultural and ethnic backgrounds, including many non-English-speaking students. Not only must opportunities be provided, but programs must increasingly demonstrate that students achieve the goals of instruction. To meet these needs, programs should include a broad spectrum of activities, with occasional opportunities for students to select their own preferences. Zakrajsek and Carnes noted that

> Too many physical education classrooms foster and perpetuate a method of teaching that supports a singular learning concept for all students based on one kind of motivation, one style of learning, and one set of learning needs.[85]

In the past, some teachers have maintained stereotypes concerning certain groups of students. Because students have performed in a certain way in the past does not mean they will perform in the same way in the future.[86] Lack of opportunities for girls and for students of some racial or ethnic groups may have hindered their performance. Programs that equalize opportunities for all students should find a decrease in performance differences. Teachers should get to know each student as a person of worth and dignity.

Programs designed to meet the needs of all students should consider six steps advocated by Mizen and Linton.[87] Guidelines for specific populations will be presented at the end of this section.

1. *Prepare an environment in which individual differences are respected and valued.* This is achieved by acknowledging differences among students through class discussions and experiences working with people who are different from each other. Students should understand that teasing is often caused by anxious or insecure behavior around those who are different. Wearing blindfolds or ear plugs or playing with Vaseline smeared on the glasses, or with the nondominant hand or foot can also help students understand the challenges others face. Focus on what the students can do rather than on what they cannot do.

2. *Eliminate established practices that unwittingly contribute to embarrassment and failure.* By adapting activities to meet the needs of all students, they will learn faster and experience positive attitudes toward physical activity. Beware of practices that contribute to the failure or embarrassment of some students, such as elimination games, in which the

unskilled children who need the most practice sit on the sidelines, or activities in which obese or handicapped students cannot compete on equal terms with other students. Avoid choosing teams in front of the class. Post most-improved scores, rather than just the top scores, so low-skilled students have an equal opportunity for recognition. Change grading policies to meet the needs of the students. "Learn three new skills" would challenge all students in gymnastics, while "perform a somersault dismount off the balance beam" might discourage all but a few. Consider a combination of factors rather than just skill alone. All students can improve their physical fitness.

3. *Build ego strength*. Help students develop self-esteem and self-confidence by providing success experiences, helping students set realistic expectations, and allowing students to participate at appropriate levels for their abilities. Help students to develop an awareness of their personal strengths.

Teachers can demonstrate their interest in students as individuals through communicating not just by words, but also through feelings. Within every student lies an inner self that can be reached only through invitation from the student. This occurs when the student feels the sincere, unselfish concern of a caring teacher. A teacher who listens to a student sends the student a message, "I love you. Your feelings are important to me." Listening is different from hearing. It involves putting oneself into the other person's shoes and listening with the heart. Stephens wrote, "I have learned . . . that the head does not hear anything until the heart has listened, and that what the heart knows to-day the head will understand tomorrow."[88] It involves patience and compassion. Hanks added:

> The time to listen is when someone needs to be heard. The time to deal with a person with a problem is when he has the problem. . . .
> Every human being is trying to say something to others, trying to cry out, "I am alive. Notice me! Speak to me! Listen to me! Confirm for me that I am important, that I matter."[89]

A teacher can be the one who confirms that the student matters. When talking to a student, encourage the student to express feelings. Then listen with understanding, note the student's facial expressions, posture, and tone of voice as well as what is said.

Other ways to demonstrate an interest in students include calling them by name and recognizing each student in some way each day. A snapshot or photo can be helpful in learning names. Let the students know you want to learn their names and you want them to help you learn them. Jot down identifying characteristics in your roll book. Use games to help learn names. For example, in the name game, students introduce themselves using an adjective that begins with the letter of their name. Each student repeats the names of the previous persons and adds his or her own. For example, "Jumping Miss Jones, Singing Sally, Typing Terry, and I'm Caroling Carolyn." Another way to get acquainted is to have students create name tags. Some ideas include a collage, a personal coat of arms, or a self-commercial, such as a guitar for a student who plays the guitar or a basketball for a member of the team. When all else fails, assign students to a given court or team and learn the names of one group each day. Many other ideas can be created by both teachers and students to help class members get acquainted with one another.

Learn something about each student—interests, achievements, hobbies, favorite subject, favorite sport, or family life. Get feedback from students on how they would like their class to be run. A file card or dittoed form handed out at the beginning of the year or unit could solicit answers to such questions as:

Most of all, what do you like to do?
What is your favorite game, sport, or hobby?
What are your expectations of the class? The teacher? Yourself?
How would you like the class to be run? How will you help?
What would you like me to know about you?

Students might be asked to share their names and something they like to do, such as a hobby, skill, or special interest. Another technique is to ask students to pair up with a student they do not know and interview their partners for a specified period of time, then take one minute or less to tell something that impressed them about their partners.

Make it your business to be in strategic places at strategic times—such as the school play or a band concert when a student of yours is participating. Seek opportunities to say hello when you see students in the hall or on the street. Compliment students when deserved and appropriate. Emphasize their positive qualities. Sit with them at football games or in the cafeteria. Notice their achievements in other curricular areas such as the school newspaper, home economics, wood shop, or in out-of-school service to the community. Share student successes with other teachers and administrators.

When teaching lessons, seek to adjust the content in the light of student needs and interests. Encourage student involvement and sharing. Make it easy for students to ask questions and make comments. Counsel individuals about fitness and skill test scores so students know where they stand on class goals. Focus your attention on both the skilled and the unskilled. All of them deserve equal time and attention.

Give students an opportunity to accept leadership positions and rotate positions often. Do not do for students what they can do for themselves. Students can be assigned to greet visitors, demonstrate skills, lead exercises, and issue and set up equipment. Know the current needs and interests of your students. Provide each student with the opportunity for success and recognition.

Sigmund Freud's niece once recalled a mushroom hunt her uncle had during a family outing. By the end of the activity each child had a prize—for the biggest, oddest, smallest, first, last, or other mushroom. Similar awards or recognition could be given to students in physical education or intramural programs. Possibilities include participant of the month, best equipment monitor, best sport, best official, most-improved player or official, or best scorer. Recognition before the class may carry more weight than individual recognition because of the need for peer approval.

Gustafson suggested that teachers construct a checklist of their strategies for enhancing self-esteem.[90] Teachers could use these checklists to see how well they are doing in incorporating these items into their teaching routine.

Since self-esteem is linked to body image and skill in physical activities, a program that helps students develop physical fitness and proficiency in activity skills can increase self-esteem and enhance the development of positive attitudes toward physical activity.

Since body concept is an important part of self-esteem, students should be taught to define and accept realistic body concepts and to modify factors that can be affected through physical education activities. They should also be helped to respect themselves and others, regardless of appearance.[91]

Occasionally, teachers would do well to engage in skills for which they have little competence or expertise, thereby showing students how difficult it is for others to learn new and unfamiliar skills.

Harris emphasized the importance of students entering the "psychological door" through enjoyment in a specific physical activity that has meaning for them.[92] One of the main goals of physical education should be to get students to incorporate physical activities into their life-styles. Students must experience successful participation in physical activities in a warm, supportive, positive environment with teachers who care if they are to continue to participate outside of the school setting.

A number of different needs stimulate interest in physical activity. These needs may take the form of social affiliation, energy release, health and well-being, or self-fulfillment. As needs change from time to time, so do interests. When students are allowed to select their own activities, motivation to learn is increased considerably.

4. *Provide individual assistance and keep students active.* Teachers and parents have the task of helping adolescents direct their energies into socially acceptable activities that also enhance their personal worth. Adults do this by acting as positive role models, with clearly defined values. They establish limits and define procedures so students have the emotional security that comes from knowing what is expected. Gradually, students must learn to accept responsibility for their own actions, to set personal goals, and to learn self-discipline. Adults can facilitate this process.

The buddy system and peer tutoring are excellent ways to help special-needs students. A recent study by DePaepe found that the use of peer tutors significantly increased the academic learning time of students and created the best environment for enhancing motor performance for moderately mentally retarded students.[93]

The Physical Education Opportunity Program for Exceptional Learners (PEOPEL) teams fifteen student aids and fifteen exceptional learners on a one-to-one basis in physical education classes. The aids or peer-teachers are trained to understand the problems of the exceptional learners and to help their partners learn cognitive, psychomotor, and affective skills. Program results show that PEOPEL students improved significantly in physical fitness and in attitudes toward physical education, while similar students enrolled in traditional adapted physical education classes did not show significant improvements. Student aids improved in their understanding and appreciation of handicapped students.[94]

Skills should be presented in a developmental sequential manner and opportunities for engaged learning time should be increased by using all balls and equipment or using teaching stations. Some other validated programs designed to individualize learning are I CAN and Project Active.

> The I CAN program is a published, individualized, instructional management system for teaching physical education and associated classroom skills to all children, handicapped and nonhandicapped. It includes a set of sequential performance objectives, assessment instruments, instructional activities, games, class and individual records, and a Teacher's Implementation Guide. These diagnostic and prescriptive teaching resource materials are divided into four program skill areas: associated, primary, sport-leisure, and social.[95]

Eight activity notebooks and accompanying films are provided to teach fundamental skills, health, fitness, body management, and aquatics.

Traditional demonstration and practice learning strategies may not be appropriate for handicapped students. Teachers must learn to use a variety of teaching styles and activities to meet the diverse learning styles, needs and interests of students. Noncompetitive activities should be included in the curriculum.

Project Active was developed by the Township of Ocean School District, Oakhurst, New Jersey, under the direction of Thomas M. Vodola. Materials assist teachers in the assessment, prescription, and evaluation of the physical and motor needs of handicapped students.[96]

5. *Group students by ability to allow for mastery teaching.* Make certain skills are learned well before moving on to new skills. Provide remedial or challenge activities for students to practice the skills to be learned.

A challenge for every physical educator is to get each student on the avenue of success by planning situations in small, sequential steps so that all students can succeed as often as possible. Although this takes more time, it is rewarding because students progress more rapidly and there are fewer discipline problems. For a discouraged student, even a small success can be a boost, since often these students feel that they have never experienced success before. As skills are learned and small successes become big successes, self-esteem begins to increase.

Once students begin to experience success, they show a willingness to try new skills, they put forth greater effort, they obtain more success, and the circle continues as shown in figure 5.1. On the contrary, failure results in an unwillingness to try and little or no effort.

Activities should be provided on various skill levels. Group students by ability level within classes to help low-skilled students experience success while, at the same time, providing a challenge for the more highly skilled. Mastery learning, described in chapter 10, is an excellent way to meet the diverse needs of students, while giving all students an opportunity to achieve at a higher level. Individual contracts or units can also be used to individualize instruction. A number of learning activities that can be used to individualize instruction to meet the differing learning needs of students are presented in chapter 10.

Most activities can be adapted to meet the needs of students of varying abilities by decreasing time periods; modifying courts, fields, and equipment; and changing the rules.

6. *Alter and adapt.* Some activities are more readily adapted than others. The best activities are those in which success or failure is not dependent on the ability or performance of another person. Since many secondary schools now offer selective or elective programs, all students have the opportunity to select the activities that best meet their needs.[97]

Winnick suggested eight ways in which activities can be adapted so that handicapped students can participate effectively with their peers.[98] They are:

1. Modify activities to equalize competition by creating "handicaps" for students, as in golf and bowling; changing distance, height of basket, etc. (see the inclusion style in chapter 10); or reducing skill complexity (e.g., kicking a stationary rather than a moving ball).

What we need is . . .

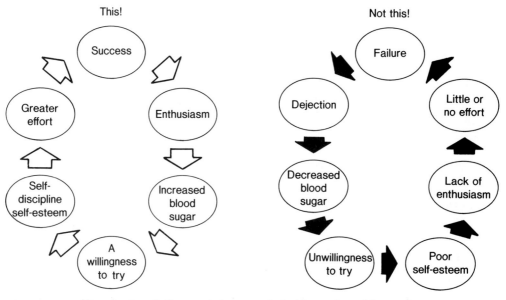

How about you? Can you help every student be a winner this year?

Figure 5.1 Failure and success cycles in students.
Source: Health, Physical Education and Recreation Newsletter, Utah State Office of Education.

2. Permit "courtesy" runners (or partner runners for the blind) for students who need them.
3. Include activities in which contact is maintained with a partner, small group, or object (such as square dancing, wrestling, tug-of-war, a rail for bowling). Contact helps the blind, deaf, or retarded student know what is expected.
4. Modify the activity to require regular students to assume the impairment of the handicapped, such as in relays when all students have only one leg or in a game in which all players are blindfolded.
5. Assign positions according to the abilities of the handicapped persons. (Field hockey goalies and softball pitchers do not have to move as quickly and are good choices for individuals with one leg. Catcher can be a good position for persons with one arm because they do not have to throw as quickly.)
6. Change elimination-type activities, such as dodge ball, to permit students to exchange positions with the thrower or count the number of times hit rather than be eliminated.
7. Limit the size of the playing area by reducing the court size or increasing the number of players on a team.
8. Use audible goals such as a horn or drum to allow blind students to compete in relays, basketball, archery, shuffleboard, or softball.

Other modifications might include:

1. Emphasize cooperative rather than competitive games.
2. Decrease the duration of the activity.
3. Increase or decrease the size of game objects (such as balls) or game implements (such as rackets or bats).
4. Increase or decrease the size of the target or hoop.
5. Players may only guard or block players of the same size.
6. Every player on the team must touch the ball before a goal is scored.
7. Players may choose the implement with which to hit and the object to be hit (softball-type games).
8. The pitcher (in softball) must be a member of the team at bat.

Encourage students to modify activities to ensure fair play. For the mentally retarded student, select games with simple rules and strategies. Rhythms and dance, swimming, and other individual activities are popular with these students.

The Education for All Handicapped Children Act

The Education for All Handicapped Children Act of 1975 (Public Law 94–142) came about through parental lobbying and court action. Two landmark court decisions (*Pennsylvania Association of Retarded Citizens v. Commonwealth of Pennsylvania* and *Mills v. Board of Education of District of Columbia*) resulted in a decree that all children of school age have a right to a free, quality education regardless of their handicap.[99]

Physical education is the only subject specifically mentioned in the law. Every handicapped student must have access to physical education as defined by the student's individualized education program (I.E.P.). According to the law, physical education includes the development of (1) physical and motor fitness; (2) fundamental motor skills and patterns; and (3) skills in aquatics, dance, individual and group games, and sports (including intramural and lifetime sports). In addition, P.L. 94–142 specifies that students receiving special education and related services must have access to extracurricular activities, including athletics, that are comparable to those received by their nonhandicapped classmates. Related services—such as recreation and school health services—or supportive services—such as athletics, physical therapy, or dance therapy—*must* be provided by the district or school or contracted from some other agency if such services are required to assist a handicapped student to benefit from special education.

The Individualized Education Program

Every student receiving special education and related services must have an I.E.P. This is a written statement that includes:

1. The student's present levels of educational performance
2. Annual goals and instructional objectives
3. Specific special education and related services to be provided to the student and the extent to which the student will be able to participate in regular educational programs
4. Projected dates for initiation of and anticipated duration of services
5. Objective criteria and evaluation procedures and schedules

Special care must be taken to meet the needs
of *all* students.

Other appropriate inclusions are activity sequences and progressions, appropriate class placement, teaching strategies, equipment and facility adaptations, motivational techniques, assessment techniques, and transportation.

The first step in the process of designing an I.E.P. is to identify handicapped students who also have special educational needs. A committee can then determine the student's eligibility for the program. Once the student has been accepted, a planning conference is convened, consisting of the student's teacher, a second school representative such as the principal, one or both parents, and the student (if appropriate). Since physical education is required by law, the physical educator should sit in on this meeting. This group develops the I.E.P. for that particular student. Because each student's needs and interests are different from those of other students (even with the same handicap), each I.E.P. will be different from all other I.E.Ps.

A review of each student's I.E.P. must be done at least annually, with a complete re-evaluation at least every three years. An agency, teacher, or other person cannot be held accountable if a student does not achieve the growth projected in the annual goals and objectives of an individualized education program.

Mainstreaming and the Least Restrictive Environment

Mainstreaming is the procedure whereby handicapped students are educated in the regular classroom along with their nonhandicapped peers, rather than in special education classes. The *least restrictive environment* refers to the education of handicapped students with their

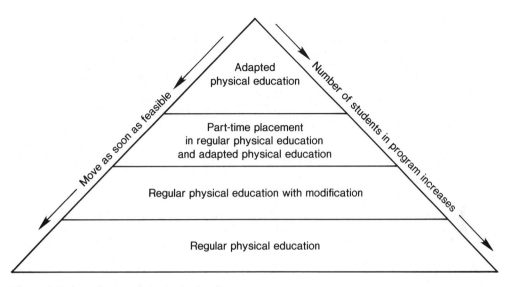

Adapted
physical education

Part-time placement
in regular physical education
and adapted physical education

Regular physical education with modification

Regular physical education

Move as soon as feasible

Number of students in program increases

Figure 5.2 A continuum of physical education
placement possibilities.

nonhandicapped peers when that environment is conducive to helping students reach their
full potentials. If a student cannot participate successfully in a regular class program, then
that student should be placed in a special class or school.

Most handicapped students can be successfully integrated into regular physical education if their individual needs are considered. Mainstreamed students generally have a more
favorable attitude toward physical education, adjust more adequately to the real world, and
do better both academically and socially than non-mainstreamed students.[100] Their nonhandicapped peers also learn to understand and appreciate them.

The inappropriate placement of severely handicapped students into a regular physical
education class, however, often results in a *more* restrictive environment because of the discrepancy between the teacher's expectations and the student's inability to perform as expected.[101] Adapted physical education classes were created to provide for needs that cannot
be met in the regular program.

To mainstream all handicapped students or to segregate all students into adapted physical education classes is to violate the principles on which the law was based. Placement in
a least restrictive environment must be made on an individual basis. Failure to do so could
result in a malpractice suit.[102] Physical educators must take the initiative to see that placement flexibility is maintained in individualized education programs so that each student participates in regular physical education activities where possible and in specially designed
programs as necessary.

Alternative Placement Possibilities

Since schools are now required to enroll students who possess a wide range of individual
abilities, a continuum of physical education services must be provided. This continuum ranges
from the most restrictive environment to the regular physical education class as shown in
figure 5.2.

Regular Physical Education Students who can safely and successfully participate in the regular physical education program should be encouraged to do so.

Regular Physical Education with Modification Some handicapped students can participate with their nonhandicapped peers if appropriate modifications are made, such as (1) a buddy or peer-tutoring system, which pairs a handicapped student with an able-bodied partner for specific activities, as in the PEOPEL program described earlier; (2) circuit or station organizational patterns; (3) contract-learning techniques; (4) team teaching, involving regular and adapted physical education teachers, resource teachers, or paraprofessional aids; or (5) preteaching certain activities to students with special needs. Students with special needs might work on such needs a specified amount of time each period, with the remaining time being devoted to regular activities with other members of the class.

Part-Time Placement Part-time placement is an arrangement in which students spend specified days each week in an adapted physical education class, where they concentrate on special needs as delineated in the I.E.P., and other days in regular classes. This type of placement may be especially useful in helping students gain the skills and confidence necessary to make the transition to a regular physical education program.

Adapted Physical Education Students with severe or multiple handicaps may need to be placed in an adapted physical education class in which they can receive corrective therapy or remedial help. Only in this setting can activities be adapted enough for students with severe handicaps to participate freely and successfully. Adapted physical education can occur as a separate class within the school, in a special school, in a home, or in a hospital.

Section 504 of the Rehabilitation Act

A second federal law that affects physical education programs and facilities is Section 504 of the Rehabilitation Act of 1973 (P.L. 93–112). This law provides that "no otherwise qualified handicapped individual . . . shall, solely by reason of his handicap, be excluded from participation in, be denied the benefits of, or be subjected to discrimination under any program or activity receiving federal financial assistance."[103]

This law requires schools to provide equal opportunities for the handicapped to participate in *all* programs offered by the school, including physical education, intramurals, clubs, and interscholastic athletics. Accommodations, adaptations, and adjustments expected so that individuals with handicapping conditions can participate in regular physical education programs and activities include:

1. Accessible buildings and other facilities
2. Appropriate transportation
3. Appropriate curricular adjustments, such as changing competency requirements, eligibility requirements, and rules that discriminate
4. Appropriate adaptations in activities, such as a bowling ramp or beeper balls

The major impact on the schools as a result of the two laws dealing with the handicapped is to modify existing curricula to include a wide spectrum of activities for the handicapped. In addition, architectural, administrative, and instructional barriers must be removed to allow handicapped students access to all programs offered by the schools.

Multicultural Education

Swisher and Swisher summarized multicultural education as it applies to physical education. The United States is a multicultural society. The number of Asian, Hispanic, black American, native American, and Asian American citizens is increasing. This means more minority students in the schools. Federal legislation and Supreme Court decisions require *equal educational opportunities* for all students regardless of gender, physical condition, socioeconomic level, racial or ethnic background, religion, or language. However, equal opportunity does not mean that all students should be treated equally. Sometimes equity requires *different treatments* to meet the *differing needs* of individual students. Multicultural education implies that teaching will capitalize on the strengths of student differences rather than on their weaknesses. This means that teachers need to learn to view cultural values from each group's perspective rather than from their own. This can be done by asking questions about family life, interpersonal interaction styles, health and hygiene, and similar items. Problems arise when the interaction style of the culture differs from the style of the school. For example, the culture of American Indians may tend to emphasize cooperation rather than competition; Mexican-American children tend to learn with a global rather than an analytical cognitive style; Asian children tend to hold the teacher in high esteem. All of these styles differ considerably from those of Caucasian children.[104]

Swisher and Swisher list things that teachers can do to adopt a multicultural approach to instruction.[105] They include:

1. Learning students' names and pronouncing them correctly
2. Accepting students' native languages, while patiently helping students develop proficiency in English
3. Using alternative teaching styles that allow for differences in the learning styles of students
4. Avoiding calling attention to individual students in front of their peers
5. Being aware of the different ways in which students of different cultures pay attention (e.g., eye contact or no eye contact)
6. Avoiding the choosing of teams during class time, thereby embarrassing students

Above all, teachers should accept student differences and communicate to students that these differences are not problems to be remediated. Swisher and Swisher conclude that multicultural education is an attitude that communicates to students "that diversity is desirable and to be different is okay."[106] Knutson published a sensitivity index to help teachers rate themselves on their ability to help all students. She also stressed the importance of student feedback to teachers about their teaching.[107]

Sex Equity and Title IX

Historically, physical education programs have been segregated by gender. The intent of Title IX was to provide equal educational opportunities for males and females. For physical education classes, the law provided that

1. Students may be grouped by ability using objective standards of individual performance developed and applied without regard to gender.
2. Students may be separated by sex within physical education classes during participation in contact sports—wrestling, boxing, rugby, ice hockey, football, or basketball.

3. Portions of classes dealing exclusively with human sexuality may be conducted separately for males and females.
4. When use of a single standard of measurement has an adverse effect on members of one gender, then appropriate standards may be used, such as in skill and fitness test norms.[108]

However, Geadelmann reported that the extent of implementation of Title IX has not reached the desired goal and "the content and conduct of coeducational classes. . . remain susceptible to sexist practices which perpetuate stereotypes and fail to realize the spirit of Title IX."[109] She noted that some schools have refused to offer certain activities to coeducational groups, others have eliminated controversial activities, and many offer activities on an elective basis with no previous exposure to both genders. These same problems were confirmed by Young in a 1986 report.[110]

Even when programs meet the requirements of the law, sex-role stereotypes are often reflected in differing teacher expectations for males and females. In a study by Geadelmann, 54 percent of the boys and 44 percent of the girls thought the teacher expected more of the boys.[111] According to Griffin, teacher expectation differences appear in programs in four ways: (1) class organization strategies, (2) teacher-student interaction patterns, (3) teacher language, and (4) teacher role modeling.[112]

For *class organization,* teachers used the command style of teaching almost exclusively and picked teams publicly without using ability grouping. Studies have consistently demonstrated that participation styles of boys and girls differ, even when the teachers' purposes favor nondiscrimination.[113] Boys tend to dominate team play, and girls tend to give scoring opportunities to boys. Girls and boys perceive boys as more highly skilled, even when objective tests show the girls to be more talented.[114] Boys have more contacts with the ball[115] and tend to see girls' events, such as gymnastics, as lower in status.[116] Boys tend to sit in front of girls in squads[117] and boys have higher active learning time.[118] Low-skilled boys and girls have less opportunities to practice skills.[119]

However, as Griffin pointed out, "A generalized description of student interaction and participation by sex . . . can ignore or minimize differences in participation among students within the same gender group." She concluded, "To rely on gender differences in describing participation styles . . . would have presented an inaccurate picture ignoring the variety of action and attitude among the boys and among the girls observed."[120]

Even when teachers adapt games to increase participation by girls, the changes may be discriminatory, according to Geadelmann. These changes favor the girls over the boys. She emphasizes that "without raised expectation levels regarding the physical performance of girls, it is unlikely that the girls will receive the necessary encouragement and assistance to reach new performance levels."[121]

Studies on *teacher-student interaction* patterns show that teachers interact differently with males and females. They interact more with boys in the areas of class management, discipline, physical contact, informal talk, feedback, and criticism.[122] However, teachers praise boys more for their performance and girls more for their effort.[123] Boys were chosen more often as class leaders, demonstrators, role models, and equipment managers.[124] Some teachers showed condescending behavior to girls.[125] Teachers rarely corrected sex stereotyping by students in language or behavior.[126]

Studies on *teacher language* showed that teachers occasionally made stereotyped comments about "girls'" pushups or throwing "like a boy," but they rarely made comments about girls being equal to boys. Although teachers generally used inclusive language to refer to students as a group (e.g., people, students), there was some use of stereotyped activity terms, such as "man-to-man." Occasionally girls were called "ladies," while boys were rarely called "gentlemen." Other teachers used boys' last names and girls' first names.[127]

Research demonstrates that *teacher role modeling* is stereotyped in that male teachers rarely teach activities such as dance and gymnastics, while female teachers teach a wide variety of activities. Few teachers team teach activities. A predominance of male athletes were pictured on bulletin boards and mentioned as role models by teachers.[128]

Sex equity depends on the teachers' awareness of sex stereotyping patterns, commitment to change, and specific action to change.[129] Effective teachers have learned that a wider range of motor abilities exists within each gender than between the sexes. Grouping students by ability can resolve the problems of students being intimidated or held back. Experimentation with rules can be done to find the best ones for both genders. Students can be challenged to experiment to find the best solution to the problem of appropriate rules.

Suggestions for increasing sex equity in physical education classes include activities to counteract the tendencies listed above.[130] For class organization, teachers can

1. Use a broader repertoire of instructional styles.
2. Change game rules to include all students, such as three-on-three basketball or seven-player soccer, or have every player touch the ball before scoring.
3. Use a variety of ways to divide students into teams.
4. Group students for instruction using simple objective tests.
5. Help students overcome sex stereotyping and learn to appreciate themselves and each other in physical education activities.
6. Base activities on individual needs rather than arbitrary male-female standards, since variations in abilities within gender are greater than between the sexes.[131]
7. Reduce the contact in contact sports, rather than gender-segregation for such activities, so all students can participate.[132]
8. Schedule equal numbers of boys and girls into physical education classes, thus permitting equal numbers of each gender on each team. This promotes equality and fairness in participation styles.[133]

For sex-equitable teacher-student interactions, teachers can

1. Become aware of whom they interact with and how, recognize their sex-stereotyped expectations of students, and monitor their behavior.
2. Choose boys and girls equally as class leaders, role models, skill demonstrators, and equipment managers.

Nonstereotyped teacher language can be improved by using the following:

1. Avoid "man" and "you guys" and consciously use inclusive language.
2. Use equivalent terms when referring to boys and girls.
3. Avoid reference to activities as boys' or girls'.

Sex-equitable role modeling should include the following:

1. Develop competencies in activities traditionally associated with the opposite gender.
2. Develop competence in and team teach activities traditionally associated with the opposite gender.
3. Include male and female models participating in a variety of nontraditional activities on instructional materials, such as bulletin boards.

Teachers should also elicit anonymous feedback from students about their feelings, preferences, and assessment of the results of instruction.[134]

Kneer suggested two methods for adjusting instruction for coed classes.[135] In differentiated instruction, students are introduced to new skills as a group but then provided different practice tasks and achievement levels. For example, some students might be working on right-handed lay-ups, others reverse lay-ups, and still others practicing lay-ups in a game situation. Students are grouped for play according to ability. In individualized instruction, students select different instructional programs to meet their various needs. Chapter 10 describes several strategies for individualizing instruction, as well as procedures for defining the tasks for differentiated instruction.

Griffin listed the factors necessary for successful coeducational programs as follows:

> In programs where coeducation is a success, where boys and girls are learning and enjoying physical activities together, students participate in a variety of competitive and noncompetitive activities, teachers spend as much time as they can helping students improve their skills, teachers step in to eliminate destructive student interactions and to change unfair game participation, and teachers frequently use ability grouping to even up competition and to match instruction to student needs. Teachers who have made coed physical education a success are enthusiastic about teaching, their students, and trying something new. They have a sense of their own power to change student behavior in their classes and know specific strategies to use in addressing problems they encounter.[136]

When planning coed programs, physical educators should teach many activities in which competition is not a critical factor. Lifetime activities, such as tennis, golf, badminton, fitness, and swimming, can be enjoyed on an equal basis by both boys and girls. Interest surveys will make teachers aware of the desires of students for instruction in specific activities.

Kneer expressed three ways in which the curriculum can be adapted to effectively implement coed activities.[137] They are:

1. The *traditional class pattern* in which two coed classes are taught the same activity at the same time by two teachers. Students can then be regrouped by gender for play involving contact sports. This arrangement also facilitates ability grouping and team teaching.
2. The *integrated pattern* consists of classes in which all students are integrated. When contact sports are played, students can be separated by gender within the class.
3. The *selective pattern* consists of placing all students into activities according to the interests of the students. Every few weeks, a new group of activities are offered for student selection. Activities can also be offered at beginning, intermediate, and advanced levels.

Some years ago, the members of the Educational Policies Commission summed up the purpose of education for all American youth, a purpose that still holds true today. They said:

> When we write confidently and inclusively about education for all American youth, we mean just that. We mean that all youth, with their human similarities and their equally human differences, shall have educational services and opportunities suited to their personal needs and sufficient for the successful operation of a free and democratic society. . . . Each of them is a human being, more precious than material goods or systems of philosophy. Not one of them should be permitted to be carelessly wasted. All of them must be given equal opportunities to live and learn.[138]

To implement all at once the suggestions offered for meeting the needs of all students would require a super teacher. While it is true that excellent teachers seriously attempt to improve their teaching, they do so by tackling a few ideas at a time rather than trying to implement everything at once. Wessel noted that "individualizing instruction does not necessarily require major changes in the class or school. Teachers can adjust existing instructional approaches to students' learning, personal and social, and physical and motor abilities within their own classrooms and within existing constraints," through the use of a variety of instructional cues, different groupings for different activities, and the modification of games and activities. Students can be given the responsibility of helping to assess, monitor, and record learning outcomes.[139]

Although the design of instruction by the teacher attempts to establish the conditions that will facilitate learning, the learner is responsible for taking advantage of them. Teachers cannot learn for their students.

An attempt should be made to place more and more of the responsibility for education on the learners. One seldom observes signs of friction or disorder in a classroom where the students are interested and actively engaged in meaningful school activity related to their needs and interests, especially if that schoolwork is a part of their own planning.

Studying Student Needs

Getting to know students implies taking the time necessary to find out what the similarities and differences are among students in a particular school. Some of this information will be available from school and student records. School records include data about the entire school population, such as total enrollment, age and gender distributions, race or ethnic backgrounds, dropout rates, and other essential information needed for developing educational programs. Student records include health and medical status, intelligence and achievement test results, grades, results of interest and attitude inventories, and other information.

Teachers should be aware of the Family Educational Rights and Privacy Act of 1974 (P.L. 93–380), which withholds federal funds from any school denying parents (or students age eighteen or over) access to student educational records or permitting third-party access to personally identifiable data in the records without prior consent. Persons permitted access to the records include teachers and school officials with legitimate educational interests and local, state, or national officials specified in the law. Parents have a right to challenge the content of the records.[140]

Observation of students in the school setting can be a valuable source of data. Parent-teacher conferences and back-to-school nights can be helpful in getting acquainted with family backgrounds.

Teachers could use the following questions to direct their observation of students in a selected class to better meet individual needs:

1. What would you guess to be the range in height in the class? In weight? Have you observed any students for whom size may be the source of potential problems? What problems do you foresee? Record ideas for dealing with these problems.
2. What is the age range of students in the class? Does age appear to be a problem factor for any student in this class? Explain.
3. Identify the student whom you consider to be the most aggressive in the class; the least aggressive. As you think about and observe these two, do you see a basic difference in the way they approach learning activities at school? Explain.
4. Which student, in your judgment, comes from the most affluent home? The least affluent? What implications do you see for instruction and learning?
5. What is the performance range of students in the class? The range in physical fitness? How would you adapt the instruction to meet the needs of each level?
6. Identify students who are handicapped physically, culturally, or otherwise. What would you do to help them achieve success?
7. List as many other ways as you can think of in which students differ. Which of these do you consider to be factors that might affect the way a student learns? Try ranking them in order of importance.

Observation of students in nonschool functions can also provide an insight into student activities, interpersonal relationships, and leadership abilities. The following questions might be used as a guide:

1. Who was the group leader? How could you tell?
2. Were the leaders in these activities also leaders in school activities? Why or why not?
3. How did the boys react to the girls and vice versa?
4. Who directed the activities officially? Unofficially?
5. How was attention shown? To whom was it shown?
6. How were the students' behaviors different from their behaviors in school?
7. What motivating factors influence students when they are not in school?
8. What group or individual values were in evidence?
9. How did the group values influence the individuals?
10. How were decisions made among the students?
11. What learning was taking place?
12. What was the nature of the activity (constructive, destructive, social, religious)? How did this help determine the type of behavior considered appropriate for the situation?
13. Why were these particular students together?
14. What methods of influence did you notice being practiced?
15. How will knowing this information about students change your behavior in the classroom?
16. How do students behave differently in adult company? With different teachers?

Questionnaires can provide insight into the actual interests, attitudes, and values of students. Some possible questions are given here. Other ideas are included in chapter 8.

Directions: Do not write your name on this paper. Answer the questions below in the best way you know how.

1. How do you feel about yourself? I am:
2. How do you rate yourself as a student?
3. Do you have a job? If so, what kind?
4. What do you do in your free time?
5. What are your favorite sports or activities?
6. Do you play a musical instrument? Take private lessons in dance, music, sports? If so, what kind?
7. Do you have a lot of friends? A few friends? Are they close friends? Casual friends? Both?

Teacher-student interaction before, during, and after classes provides one of the best opportunities for teachers and students to get to know each other on a more informal basis.

Questions and Suggested Activities

1. How can you meet the needs of all of the students in your classes? Must all instruction be individualized? What common learning needs do all students have?
2. Study or talk with youth in different environments, such as school, church, casual situations, and youth groups. Learn about their living styles, families, friends, interests, and attitudes. What general conclusions might you make?
3. Select one student and observe him or her very closely. Prepare an anecdotal record about the student over a period of several days or weeks.
4. Spend a day with someone who is concerned with young people in a nonschool situation, such as a truant officer, social worker, juvenile court judge, police officer, or camp counselor. How do students react to these authority figures? Why? Are there some who have good rapport with students? Why?
5. Tutor a student over a period of time. Does the student like you? How can you tell? Were you successful as a tutor? Why or why not?
6. Select a student who appears to have a low self-concept and talk with him or her about home life, social life, success in school, or other areas. How could you help this student develop more self-confidence?
7. Read the article "Cipher in the Snow" by Mizer (see Suggested Readings). How do we go about turning a boy or girl into a cipher? How can a teacher stop the slow eroding of students as persons of worth?
8. You are teaching a track and field lesson, and you have a girl who is asthmatic in your class. What will you do?
9. You are teaching volleyball, and you have a boy with one arm paralyzed in your class. What will you do?
10. What suggestions do you have for adapting games and activities to meet the needs of all students? You may want to read G. S. Don Morris, *How to Change the Games Children Play,* 2d ed., Minneapolis: Burgess Publishing Company, 1980.
11. Visit a school that has successfully integrated handicapped students into the physical education program. Study several individual education programs. How is the decision made for placement of students into the various physical education classes?

12. Put your dominant arm in a sling and use your other hand all day, borrow a wheelchair and get around as best as you can for an entire day, or blindfold yourself and let someone lead you around for an hour. How did the experience affect your self-concept? Did it change your feelings about handicapped persons?

13. It has been suggested that "Winning is not the most important thing. It is the only thing!" How does it feel to lose? Try the following activity:

    a. Have someone draw a diagram with squares or rectangles similar to the one shown here:

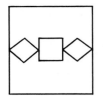

    b. Have the person *tell* you how to reproduce the diagram without showing it to you or answering any questions. Could you draw it? If you were successful, would you like to try again? If you failed, will you risk another try? Repeat the experience in competition with several others. Set a time limit. Then try working with a partner to complete the diagram. Which way did you like best? What did this experience tell you about winning and losing? About your self-concept?

    Source: Kneer, Marian E. "How Human Are You? Exercises in Awareness." *Journal of Health, Physical Education and Recreation* 45 (June 1974):32–34.

14. Put a check by the statements that best describe you in physical education activities:

    I'm always chosen first
    I cheat to win
    I do my best
    I usually lose
    I help my team win
    I usually sit on the bench
    I go to any extreme to win
    I'm always chosen last
    I'm a good winner
    I always win
    I play fair
    The coach thinks I'm great
    I'm a poor loser
    My team usually loses
    I'm not very good
    I'm a good loser
    I don't do as well as I'd like to
    I always drop the ball

I'm the best player
I always want to quit
I'm the best player on the team

How many positive sentences did you mark? How many negative ones? What kind of self-concept do you appear to have about sports activities?

14. Do the following activity: Your name is Michael. Take a piece of paper and write the letters IALAC (I am loved and capable) on it. This is your self-concept. Then, read the following story and tear off a piece of your self-concept each time it is attacked.

> A seventh-grade boy named Michael is still lying in bed three minutes after his alarm goes off. All of a sudden his mother calls to him, "Michael, you lazyhead, get your body out of bed and get down here before I send your father up there!" (rip!) Michael gets out of bed, goes to get dressed, and can't find a clean pair of socks. His mother tells him he'll have to wear yesterday's pair. (rip!) He goes to brush his teeth and his older sister, who's already locked herself in the bathroom, tells him to drop dead! (rip!) He goes to breakfast to find soggy cereal waiting for him. (rip!) As he leaves for school, he forgets his lunch and his mother calls to him, "Michael, you've forgotten your lunch; you'd forget your head if it weren't attached!" (rip!) As he gets to the corner he sees the school bus pull away and so he has to walk to school. (rip!) He is late to school and has to get a pass from the principal who gives him a lecture. (rip!) How would you feel if you were Michael? How does putting yourself in Michael's shoes help you to be a better teacher? Source: Canfield, Jack and Harold C. Wells. *100 Ways to Enhance Self-Concept in The Classroom*. Englewood Cliffs, N.J.: Prentice-Hall, 1976, p. 91.

Suggested Readings

Armstrong, Thomas. "How Real Are Learning Disabilities?" *Learning* 14 (September 1985):45–47.

Bayless, John, and Muriel Cutter. "Teacher Recognition of Child Abuse," *Journal of Physical Education, Recreation and Dance* 57 (January 1986):73–74.

Beezer, Bruce. "Reporting Child Abuse and Neglect: Your Responsibility and Your Protections." *Phi Delta Kappan* 66 (February 1985):434–36.

Forgan, Harry W. "Teachers Don't Want to Be Labeled." *Phi Delta Kappan* LV (September 1973): back cover.

Gerler, Edwin R., Jr. "Skills for Adolescence: A New Program for Young Teenagers." *Phi Delta Kappan* 67 (February 1986):436–39.

Gilbert, Evelyn H., and Richard R. DeBlassie. "Anorexia Nervosa: Adolescent Starvation by Choice." *Adolescence* 19 (Winter 1984):839–46.

Griffin, Pat. "Coed Physical Education: Problems and Promise." *Journal of Physical Education, Recreation and Dance* 55 (August 1984):36–37.

Griffin, Pat, and Judith Placek. *Fair Play in the Gym: Race and Sex Equity in Physical Education.* Amherst: University of Massachusetts, 1983, p. 53.

Griffin, Patricia S. "Teachers' Perceptions of and Responses to Sex Equity Problems in a Middle School Physical Education Program." *Research Quarterly for Exercise and Sport* 56 (June 1985):103–10.

Hafen, Brent Q., and Kathryn J. Frandsen. "Drug Behavior: The Factors Behind Drug Abuse," in *Addictive Behavior: Drug and Alcohol Abuse.* Englewood, Colorado: Morton Publishing Company, 1985, pp. 52–64.

Hafen, Brent Q., and Kathryn J. Frandsen. *Youth Suicide: Depression and Loneliness.* Provo, Utah: Behavioral Health Associates, P.O. Box 7527, University Station, 1986.

Harrison, Rebecca. "How You Can Help the Abused Child." *Learning* 14 (August 1985):74–78.

Hawley, Richard A. "School Children and Drugs: The Fancy that Has Not Passed." *Phi Delta Kappan* 68 (May 1987):K1–K8.

Hurwitz, Brian D. "Suspicion: Child Abuse." *Instructor* 94 (April 1985):76–78.

Jones, C. J., and Barbara Nelson. "Helping Students with Problems: What Physical Educators Can Do." *Journal of Physical Education, Recreation and Dance* 46 (February 1985):50–51.

Knutson, Marjorie C. "Sensitivity to Minority Groups." *Journal of Physical Education and Recreation* 48 (May 1977):24–25.

Mizer, Jean. "Cipher in the Snow." *NEA Journal* (November 1964):8–10.

Pangrazi, Robert. "Physical Education, Self-concept, and Achievement." *Journal of Physical Education, Recreation and Dance* 53 (November/December 1982):16–18.

Richardson, Peggy A., Kevin W. Albury, and Ruth E. Tandy. "Mirror, Mirror, On the Wall . . ." *Journal of Physical Education, Recreation and Dance* 56 (August 1985):62–65.

Roscoe, Bruce. "Sexual Abuse: The Educator's Role in Identification and Interaction with Abuse Victims." *Education* 105 (Fall 1984):82.

Swett, Walter E. "Helping Young People Survive in a Chemical World," reprinted from *Family & Community Health* (August 1984), in *Addictive Behavior: Drug and Alcohol Abuse.* Englewood, Colorado: Morton Publishing Company, pp. 359–69.

Wall, M. B. "Review of Childstress by M. S. Miller." *NEA Today* (October 1982):20.

Workman, Brooke. "Dear Professor: This Is What I Want You to Know." *Phi Delta Kappan* 67 (May 1986):668–71.

References

1. David Pratt, *Curriculum: Design and Development* (New York: Harcourt Brace Jovanovich, 1980), p. 270.

2. Brooke Workman, "Dear Professor: This Is What I Want You to Know," *Phi Delta Kappan* 67 (May 1986), pp. 668–71.

3. Carl E. Willgoose, *The Curriculum in Physical Education,* 4th ed. (Englewood Cliffs, New Jersey: Prentice-Hall, 1984), p. 255.

4. Janet A. Wessel and Luke Kelly, *Achievement-Based Curriculum Development in Physical Education* (Philadelphia: Lea & Febiger, 1986), p. 56.

5. Leslie J. Chamberlin and Ricardo Girona, "Our Children Are Changing," *Educational Leadership* 33 (January 1976), pp. 301–5.

6. Pat Griffin and Judith Placek, *Fair Play in the Gym: Race and Sex Equity in Physical Education* (Amherst: University of Massachusetts, 1983), p. 53.

7. Ibid., p. 54.

8. Chamberlin and Girona, "Our Children Are Changing."

9. Thomas Armstrong, "How Real Are Learning Disabilities?" *Learning* 14 (September 1985), pp. 45–47.

10. Carl Bereiter, "The Changing Face of Educational Disadvantagement," *Phi Delta Kappan* 66 (April 1985), pp. 538–41.

11. Carri P. Jenkins, "Brain Research Leads to New Teaching Methods," *BYU Today* 40 (February 1986), pp. 4–5.

12. Willgoose, *The Curriculum in Physical Education,* p. 9.

13. Charles A. Bucher and Constance R. Koenig, *Methods and Materials for Secondary School Physical Education* (St. Louis, Missouri: C. V. Mosby Company, 1983), p. 42.

14. Arthur W. Combs, "The Human Side of Learning," *The National Elementary Principal* (January 1973), pp. 38–42.

15. Richard E. Snow, Joseph Tiffin, and Warren F. Seibert, "Individual Differences and Instructional Effects," *Journal of Educational Psychology* 56 (1965), pp. 315–26.

16. James R. Johnson, "Development and Implementation of a Competency-based Teacher Education Module," paper presented at the annual meeting of the American Educational Research Association, Chicago, April 1974, cited in Pratt, *Curriculum: Design and Development,* p. 271.

17. Pratt, *Curriculum: Design and Development,* p. 273.

18. Bucher and Koenig, *Methods and Materials for Secondary School Physical Education,* p. 57.
19. Gregory R. Anrig, "Schools and Higher Education in a Period of Reform: Strengthening Standards and Performance," *National Forum: The Phi Kappa Phi Journal* LXVI (Spring 1986), p. 7.
20. M. Verzaro and C. B. Hennon, "Single-Parent Families: Myth and Reality," *Journal of Home Economics* (Fall 1980), pp. 31–33.
21. Sanford M. Dornbusch, J. Merrill Carlsmith, Steven J. Bushwall, Philip L. Ritter, Herbert Leiderman, Albert H. Hastorf, and Ruth T. Gross, "Single Parents, Extended Households, and the Control of Adolescents," *Child Development* 56 (April 1985), pp. 326–41.
22. U.S. Department of Labor, *Children of Working Mothers* (Washington, D.C.: U.S. Government Printing Office, 1981).
23. U. S. Department of Labor Statistics, 1984.
24. Jack McCurdy, "Schools Respond to Latchkey Children," *The School Administrator* 42 (March 1985), pp. 16–18.
25. Lloyd P. Campbell and Ann E. Flake, "Latchkey Children—What Is the Answer?" *Clearing House* 58 (May 1985), pp. 381–83.
26. Deborah Burnett Strother, "Latchkey Children: The Fastest-Growing Special Interest Group in the Schools," *Phi Delta Kappan* 66 (December 1984), pp. 290–93.
27. Alice Pecoraro, Judy Theriot, and Pamela Lafont, "What Home Economists Should Know About Latchkey Children," *Journal of Home Economics* 76 (Winter 1984), pp. 20–22.
28. McCurdy, "Schools Respond to Latchkey Children."
29. Pecoraro, Theriot, and Lafont, "What Home Economists Should Know About Latchkey Children."
30. Strother, "Latchkey Children."
31. Lloyd D. Johnston, et al., *Monitoring the Future,* NIDA (Washington, D.C.: Superintendent of Documents, U.S. Government Printing Office, 1986); and Lloyd D. Johnston, et al., *Use of Licit and Illicit Drugs by America's High School Students,* NIDA (Washington, D.C.: Superintendent of Documents, U.S. Government Printing Office, 1985), cited in Richard L. Towers, *How Schools Can Help Combat Student Drug and Alcohol Abuse* (Washington, D.C.: National Education Association, 1987), p. 18.
32. Towers, *Student Drug and Alcohol Abuse,* p. 18.
33. Ibid., pp. 29–30.
34. Ibid., pp. 18–26.
35. Robert L. DuPont, Jr., M.D., *Getting Tough on Gateway Drugs* (Washington, D.C.: American Psychiatric Press, 1984), cited in Towers, *Student Drug and Alcohol Abuse,* p. 28.
36. Towers, *Student Drug and Alcohol Abuse,* pp. 19, 26–27.
37. Diane Jane Tessler, *Drugs, Kids, and Schools: Practical Strategies for Educators and Other Concerned Adults* (Glenview, Illinois: Scott, Foresman and Company, 1980), pp. 39–40; and DuPont, *Getting Tough on Gateway Drugs,* pp. 34–39, cited in Towers, *Student Drug and Alcohol Abuse,* pp. 28–29.
38. Ardyth Norem-Heibesen and Diane P. Hedin, "Adolescent Problem Behavior: Causes, Connections & Contexts of Drug Abuse," reprinted from *Grassroots—Special Populations,* (2/84), in *Addictive Behavior: Drug and Alcohol Abuse* (Englewood, Colorado: Morton Publishing Company, 1985), pp. 39–48; and Brent Q. Hafen and Kathryn J. Frandsen, "Drug Behavior: The Factors Behind Drug Abuse," in *Addictive Behavior: Drug and Alcohol Abuse* (Englewood, Colorado: Morton Publishing Company, 1985), pp. 52–64.
39. Neil Postman, "Disappearing Childhood," *Childhood Education* 58 (November/December 1981), pp. 66–68; and David Elkind, "The Hurried Child," *Instructor* 91 (January 1982), pp. 40–43.
40. Norwood, "A Society That Promotes Drug Abuse: The Effects on Pre-Adolescence," *Childhood Education,* vol. 61, No. 4 (March/April 1985) pp. 267–71.
41. Norem-Heibesen and Hedin, "Adolescent Problem Behavior."
42. Hafen and Frandsen, "Drug Behavior," pp. 52–64.
43. Ibid.

44. Coryl Larue Jones and Robert J. Battjes, "The Context and Caveats of Prevention Research on Drug Abuse," in Coryl Larue Jones and Robert J. Battjes, eds., *Etiology of Drug Abuse: Implications for Prevention,* NIDA (Washington, D.C.: Superintendent of Documents, U.S. Government Printing Office, 1985), p. 3, cited in Towers, *Student Drug and Alcohol Abuse,* p. 40.
45. David Hawkins, et al., "Childhood Predictors and the Prevention of Adolescent Substance Abuse," in Jones and Battjes, *Etiology of Drug Abuse,* p. 85, cited in Towers, *Student Drug and Alcohol Abuse,* p. 40.
46. Norwood, "A Society That Promotes Drug Abuse."
47. Hafen and Frandsen, "Drug Behavior," pp. 52–64.
48. Norem-Heibesen and Hedin, "Adolescent Problem Behavior."
49. Zimbardo, quoted in Brent Q. Hafen and Kathryn J. Frandsen, "Preventing Drug Use and Abuse," in *Addictive Behavior: Drug and Alcohol Abuse* (Englewood, Colorado: Morton Publishing Company, 1985), pp. 373–76 [375].
50. Towers, *Student Drug and Alcohol Abuse,* p. 45.
51. Dr. Richard H. Blum, Stanford University, cited in Hafen and Frandsen, "Drug Behavior," p. 60.
52. Hafen and Frandsen, "Drug Behavior," p. 58.
53. Ibid., pp. 52–64.
54. Ibid.; and Towers, *Student Drug and Alcohol Abuse,* pp. 61–63.
55. Towers, *Student Drug and Alcohol Abuse,* pp. 64–65.
56. Ibid., p. 71.
57. Ibid., p. 186.
58. Ibid., p. 76.
59. Ibid., p. 76.
60. Ibid.; and Walter E. Swett, "Helping Young People Survive in a Chemical World," reprinted from *Family & Community Health* (August 1984), in *Addictive Behavior: Drug and Alcohol Abuse* (Englewood, Colorado: Morton Publishing Company, 1985), pp. 359–69.
61. Towers, *Student Drug and Alcohol Abuse.*
62. Ibid.
63. Brent Q. Hafen and Kathryn J. Frandsen, *Youth Suicide: Depression and Loneliness* (Provo, Utah: Behavioral Health Associates, P.O. Box 7527, University Station, 1986).
64. Ibid.
65. Ibid.
66. Eva Y. Deykin, Ruth Perlow, and John McNamarra, "Non-fatal Suicidal and Life-threatening Behavior among 13- to 17-Year Old Adolescents Seeking Emergency Medical Care," *American Journal of Public Health* 75 (January 1985), pp. 90–92.
67. Hafen and Frandsen, *Youth Suicide: Depression and Loneliness.*
68. Jerry Jacobs, *Adolescent Suicide* (New York: Irvington Publishers, 1980).
69. Mary M. Wellman, "The School Counselor's Role in the Communication of Suicidal Ideation by Adolescents," *The School Counselor* 32 (November 1984), pp. 104–9; and Hafen and Frandsen, *Youth Suicide: Depression and Loneliness.*
70. Jerome A. Motto, "Assessment of Suicide Risk," *Medical Aspects of Human Sexuality* 18 (October 1984), pp. 134, 153.
71. Hafen and Frandsen, *Youth Suicide: Depression and Loneliness.*
72. Murray A. Straus, Richard J. Gelles, and Suzanne K. Steinmetz, *Behind Closed Doors: Violence in the American Family* (New York: Doubleday, 1980), p. 73.
73. Gordon Solomon, "Child Abuse and Developmental Disabilities," *Developmental Medicine and Child Neurology* 21 (1979), pp. 101–8.
74. Bruce Beezer, "Reporting Child Abuse and Neglect: Your Responsibility and Your Protections," *Phi Delta Kappan* 66 (February 1985), pp. 434–36; and Brian D. Hurwitz, "Suspicion: Child Abuse," *Instructor* 94 (April 1985), pp. 76–78.
75. Beezer, "Reporting Child Abuse and Neglect."
76. Hurwitz, "Suspicion: Child Abuse."
77. Bruce Roscoe, "Sexual Abuse: The Educator's Role in Identification and Interaction with Abuse Victims," *Education* 105 (Fall 1984), p. 82.

78. Ibid.
79. Rebecca Harrison, "How You Can Help the Abused Child," *Learning* 14 (August 1985), pp. 74–78.
80. Hurwitz, "Suspicion: Child Abuse."
81. Roscoe, "Sexual Abuse."
82. Workman, "Dear Professor," pp. 668–71.
83. Edwin R. Gerler, Jr., "Skills for Adolescence: A New Program for Young Teenagers," *Phi Delta Kappan* 67 (February 1986), pp. 436–39.
84. Ronald C. Doll, *Curriculum Improvement: Decision Making and Process,* 4th ed. (Boston: Allyn & Bacon, Inc., 1978).
85. Dorothy Zakrajsek and Lois Carnes, *Learning Experiences: An Approach to Teaching Physical Education* (Dubuque, Iowa: Wm. C. Brown Company Publishers, 1981), p. 5.
86. Ann E. Jewett and Linda L. Bain, *The Curriculum Process in Physical Education* (Dubuque, Iowa: Wm. C. Brown Company Publishers, 1985), p. 109.
87. Darci Weakley Mizen and Nancy Linton, "Guess Who's Coming to Physical Education: Six Steps to More Effective Mainstreaming," *Journal of Physical Education, Recreation and Dance* 54 (October 1983), pp. 63–65.
88. James Stephens, *The Crock of Gold* (New York: Macmillan Publishing Company, 1942), p. 128.
89. Marion D. Hanks, "How to Listen," *The Improvement Era* 72 (March 1969), pp. 16–19.
90. John Gustafson, "Teaching for Self-Esteem," *The Physical Educator* 35 (May 1978), pp. 67–70.
91. Kathleen M. Haywood and Thomas J. Loughrey, "Growth and Development: Implications for Teaching," *Journal of Physical Education and Recreation* 52 (March 1981), pp. 57–58.
92. Dorothy Harris, *Involvement in Sport: A Somatopsychic Rationale for Physical Activity* (Philadelphia: Lea & Febiger, 1973).
93. James L. DePaepe, "The Influence of Three Least Restrictive Environments on the Content Motor-ALT and Performance of Moderately Mentally Retarded Students," *Journal of Teaching in Physical Education* 5 (October 1985), pp. 34–41.
94. Information about PEOPEL can be obtained from PEOPEL, 2526 West Osborn Road, Phoenix, Arizona 85017. It is sponsored by the U.S. Education Department National Diffusion Network and National Inservice Network, Washington, D.C., and the Phoenix Union High School District, Phoenix, Arizona.
95. Janet. A. Wessel, ed., *Planning Individualized Education Programs in Special Education with Examples from I CAN Physical Education* (Northbrook, Illinois: Hubbard, 1977). For additional information about the I CAN program, write to Hubbard Scientific Company, P. O. Box 105, Northbrook, Illinois 60062.
96. Anthony A. Annarino, Charles C. Cowell, and Helen W. Hazleton, *Curriculum Theory & Design in Physical Education,* 2d ed. (Prospect Heights, Illinois: Waveland Press, 1980), p. 333.
97. Julian Stein, "Sense and Nonsense About Mainstreaming," *Journal of Physical Education and Recreation* 47 (January 1976), p. 43.
98. Joseph P. Winnick, "Techniques for Integration," *Journal of Physical Education and Recreation* 49 (June 1978), p. 22.
99. *Federal Register,* vol. 42, August 23, 1977 (part II), p. 42480.
100. Janet Seaman, "Attitudes of Physically Handicapped Children Toward Physical Education," *Research Quarterly* 41 (October 1970), pp. 439–45.
101. Bruce A. McClenaghan, "Normalization in Physical Education: A Reflective Review," *The Physical Educator* 38 (March 1981), pp. 3–7.
102. Rita S. Dunn and Robert W. Cole, "Inviting Malpractice through Mainstreaming," *Educational Leadership* 36 (February 1979), pp. 302–6.
103. *Federal Register,* vol. 42, May 4, 1977, p. 22676.
104. Karen Swisher and Clark Swisher, "A Multicultural Physical Education Approach: An Attitude," *Journal of Physical Education, Recreation and Dance* 57 (September 1986), pp. 35–39.
105. Ibid.
106. Ibid.

107. Marjorie C. Knutson, "Sensitivity to Minority Groups," *Journal of Physical Education and Recreation* 48 (May 1977), pp. 24–25.
108. *Federal Register,* vol. 40, June 4, 1975, p. 24127.
109. Patricia L. Geadelmann, "Physical Education: Stronghold of Sex Role Stereotyping," *Quest* 32(2) (1980), pp. 192–200 (p. 193).
110. Judith C. Young, "Teacher Beliefs and Behaviors Concerning Coeducational Physical Education," *Abstracts of Research Papers 1986* (Reston, Virginia: AAHPERD, 1986).
111. Geadelmann, "Physical Education"; and Young, "Teacher Beliefs and Behaviors Concerning Coeducational Physical Education."
112. Patricia Scott Griffin, "One Small Step for Personkind: Observations and Suggestions for Sex Equity in Coeducational Physical Education Classes," *Journal of Teaching in Physical Education,* Introductory Issue (Spring 1981), pp. 12–17.
113. Beulah Marie Wang, "An Ethnography of a Physical Education Class: An Experiment in Integrated Living," Doctoral dissertation, University of North Carolina, Greensboro, 1977. *Dissertation Abstracts International,* 1978, 38 1980-A.
114. Helen Harris Solomons, "Sex Role Mediation of Achievement Behaviors and Interpersonal Interactions in Sex-Integrated Team Games," in Emmy A. Pepitone, ed., *Children in Cooperation and Competition* (Lexington, Massachusetts: D. C. Heath and Company, 1980), pp. 321–64.
115. Griffin, "One Small Step for Personkind."
116. Patricia S. Griffin, "Gymnastics Is a Girl's Thing: Student Participation and Interaction Patterns in a Middle School Gymnastics Unit," in Thomas J. Templin and Janice K. Olson, eds., *Teaching in Physical Education* (Champaign, Illinois: Human Kinetics Publishers, 1983), pp. 71–85.
117. Wang, "An Ethnography of a Physical Education Class."
118. Young, "Teacher Beliefs and Behaviors Concerning Coeducational Physical Education."
119. Griffin, "One Small Step for Personkind."
120. Patricia S. Griffin, "Girls' and Boys' Participation Styles in Middle School Physical Education Team Sport Classes: A Description and Practical Applications," *The Physical Educator* 42 (Late Winter 1985), pp. 3–8.
121. Geadelmann, "Physical Education."
122. Young, "Teacher Beliefs and Behaviors Concerning Coeducational Physical Education"; and Griffin, "One Small Step for Personkind."
123. Solomons, "Sex Role Mediated Achievement Behaviors and Interpersonal Dynamics of Fifth Grade Co-educational Physical Education Classes." Doctoral dissertation Bryn. Mawr College, 1976. Dissertation Abstracts International, 1977, 37, 5445A (University Microfilm No. DBJ77–06538).
124. Griffin, "One Small Step for Personkind."
125. Geadelmann, "Physical Education."
126. Ibid.
127. Griffin, "One Small Step for Personkind."
128. Ibid.
129. Ibid.
130. Ibid.
131. Vincent Melograno, *Designing Curriculum and Learning: A Physical Coeducation Approach* (Dubuque, Iowa: Kendall/Hunt Publishing Company, 1979), p. 216.
132. Ibid.
133. Judith Bischoff, "Equal Opportunity, Satisfaction and Success: An Exploratory Study on Coeducational Volleyball," *Journal of Teaching in Physical Education* 2 (Fall 1982), pp. 3–12 (p. 11).
134. Ibid.

135. Marian E. Kneer, "Sex Integrated Physical Education," *National Association of Secondary School Principals Bulletin* (April 1978), pp. 79–84.
136. Pat Griffin, "Coed Physical Education: Problems and Promise," *Journal of Physical Education, Recreation and Dance* 55 (August 1984), p. 37.
137. Kneer, "Sex Integrated Physical Education," p. 82.
138. Educational Policies Commission, *Education for ALL American Youth* (Washington, D.C.: National Education Association, 1952), p. 29.
139. Wessel, ed., *Planning Individualized Education Programs in Special Education with Examples from I CAN Physical Education,* pp. 57–58.
140. *United States Statutes at Large, 93rd Congress, 2nd Session, 1974* (Washington, D.C.: U.S. Government Printing Office, 1976), vol. 88, part 1, pp. 571–74.

6

Implications of Learning Theory for Teaching Physical Education

Study Stimulators

1. What is the best strategy for teaching motor skills?
2. How do the methods differ for teaching cognitive information, skills, and strategies?
3. How can attitudes toward physical education, self-esteem, self-efficacy, and moral education be influenced?
4. What is ALT-PE? Why is it important in instruction? How can ALT-PE be increased?

Strategies for each of the three domains of learning have been proposed to help students learn effectively. The strategies for psychomotor, cognitive, and affective learning will be followed by a section on learner involvement in instruction.

Psychomotor Learning

A well-rounded physical education program provides students with the opportunity to acquire skills in a variety of activities. This contributes to the students' enjoyment of physical activity and the development of positive attitudes toward the body.

Psychomotor Content

A critical factor in effective teaching is selecting an appropriate learning task for the developmental level of the learner. Units and lessons should ensure that the activities selected are ones for which students have the essential background knowledge or skills and that challenge students to improve existing levels of skill.

Instruction always needs to be adjusted to challenge students who have a high level of skill or to correct deficiencies so that poorly skilled students can benefit from instruction. Unit and lesson plans should include a progression of skills from simple to complex. Harter proposed the use of *optimum challenges* to match the difficulties of the tasks with the developmental capabilities of the learners.[1] Tasks that are too easy are boring and result in no additional learning. On the contrary, tasks that are too difficult produce learner anxiety, with a resulting deterioration of knowledge or skill.

According to Fitts, psychomotor skills can be classified into difficulty levels based on the degree of body involvement and the extent of external pacing of the activity. The simplest skills are done with the body at rest. Intermediate skills involve movement of the body or movement of an external object, but not both. The most complex skills involve movement of the individual and the external object simultaneously.[2] Merrill divided skills into four areas, as shown in table 6.1,[3] but there appears to be no difference in difficulty between levels II and III.[4] An example of a type I skill is a place kick in soccer. In a type II task, a stationary player kicks a moving ball, while a type III task consists of a moving player kicking a stationary ball. The most difficult task involves a moving player receiving and redirecting a moving ball.

Table 6.1 Merrill's task classification system

		Object	
		At Rest	**In Motion**
Learner's Body	**At Rest**	Type I task	Type II task
	In Motion	Type III task	Type IV task

Concepts from M. David Merrill. "Psychomotor Taxonomies, Classifications, and Instructional Theory." In Robert N. Singer (ed.) *The Psychomotor Domain: Movement Behaviors* (Philadelphia: Lea and Febiger, 1972), pp. 385–414.

Students should begin with skills at their present level and gradually move to higher levels of skill. This requires preassessing the current level of performance and starting instruction at the appropriate level for each learner. Practice can be manipulated to increase the difficulty of the task by[5]

1. Increasing the size of the "whole" to be handled by the learner.
2. Adding movement to a stationary skill.
3. Increasing the force requirements, such as the height or distance involved in producing or receiving force.
4. Receiving an object at different levels or from different directions, such as to the side of the receiver.
5. Decreasing the size of the target or goal.
6. Requiring a higher degree of accuracy in the placement of a hit or throw.
7. Involving more interaction with other people (e.g., offensive or defensive players).
8. Using larger or heavier equipment (e.g., bowling ball, racquet, bow).
9. Increasing the speed of the object to be received or redirected.
10. Involving sideways or backwards movement.
11. Receiving an object from one direction and redirecting it to another direction.
12. Increasing the speed of the body movement or the tempo.
13. Combining skills.
14. Using the skills in competitive or self-testing situations.

Graham and his colleagues have analyzed each skill into a number of levels that can be used to create task progressions.[6] An example of their progression for throwing is shown in figure 6.1.

Motor Learning Strategies

For learning selected skills, Fitts classified psychomotor skill learning into three overlapping phases: (1) cognitive—an attempt to understand the skill to be learned, (2) fixation or associative—an attempt to refine the movement by eliminating errors, and (3) autonomous—an automatic movement.[7] Gentile defined a practical model for teaching motor skills based

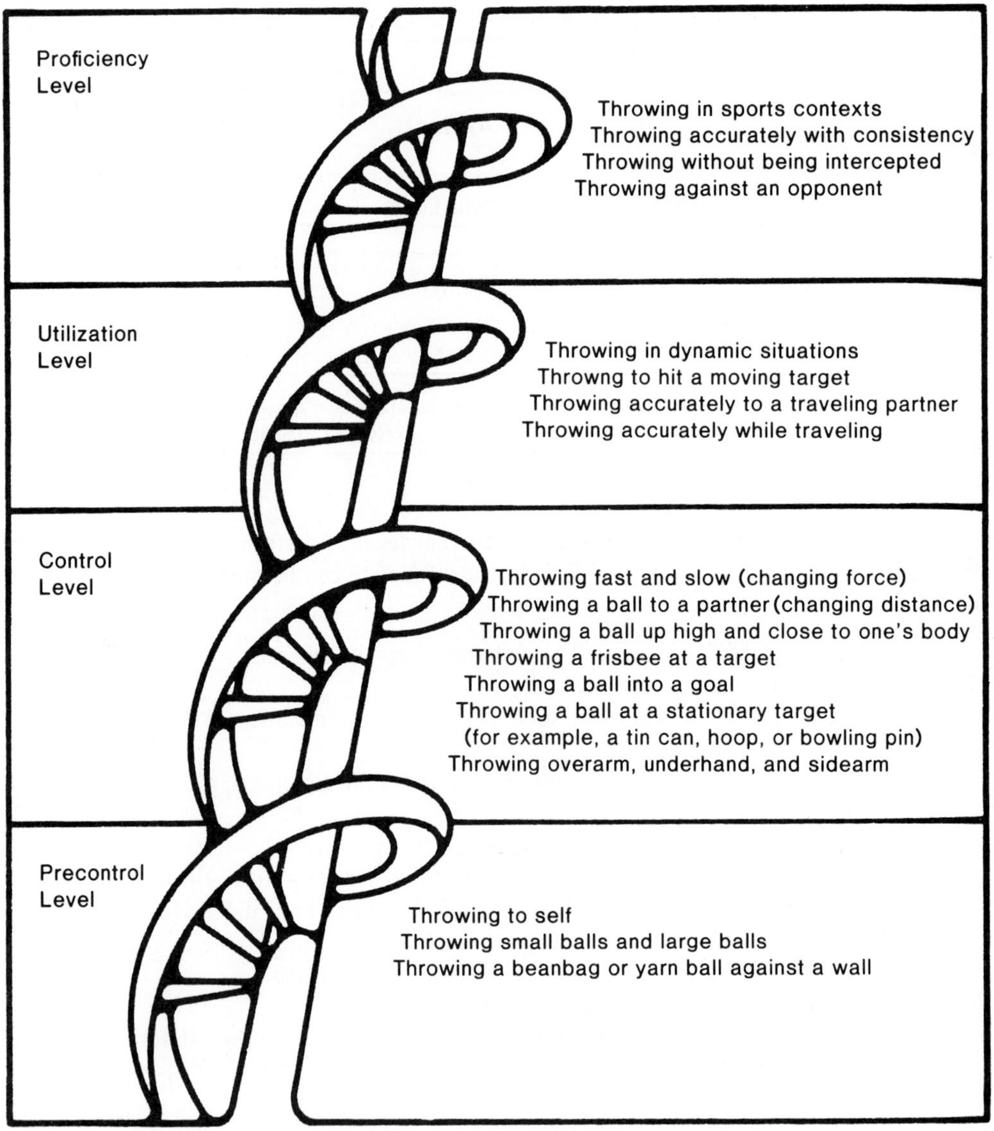
Proficiency
Level
Throwing in sports contexts
Throwing accurately with consistency
Throwing without being intercepted
Throwing against an opponent
Utilization
Level
Throwing in dynamic situations
Throwng to hit a moving target
Throwing accurately to a traveling partner
Throwing accurately while traveling
Control
Level
Throwing fast and slow (changing force)
Throwing a ball to a partner(changing distance)
Throwing a ball up high and close to one's body
Throwing a frisbee at a target
Throwing a ball into a goal
Throwing a ball at a stationary target
(for example, a tin can, hoop, or bowling pin)
Throwing overarm, underhand, and sidearm
Precontrol
Level
Throwing to self
Throwing small balls and large balls
Throwing a beanbag or yarn ball against a wall

Figure 6.1 An example of a progression for throwing in a spiral curriculum.
Source: George Graham, Shirley Ann Holt/Hale, Tim McEwen, and Melissa Parker. *Children Moving: A Reflective Approach to Teaching Physical Education* (Palo Alto, California; Mayfield Publishing Company, 1980), p. 374.

on these levels.[8] She divided skill learning into two stages: (1) getting the idea of the movement—the cognitive stage, and (2) fixation or diversification of the movement. Suggestions for teaching are included in the following description of the model.

Getting the Idea of the Movement

To help the learner get an idea of the movement to be performed, the teacher should follow the steps below:

The Goal Each unit or lesson should have one or more objectives, and students should be made aware of the objectives to be achieved. Students should understand the nature of the problem to be solved or the outcome to be produced and why it is important. Failure to ensure that the learner understands the goal results in goal confusion, in which the learner attempts to do something different from what was intended. A demonstration of a skill or a verbal statement about what is to be learned provides direction to the learning process. Students should demonstrate their understanding of the lesson objective by answering questions related to the objective.

Relationship of Parts to the Whole Skills to be taught should be the largest possible wholes that the learners can handle. Lay indicated the importance of the whole as follows:

> Students need to see the relationship of isolated skills to the game situation. Too often students practice skills without ever having an opportunity to perform those skills in a game. If actual participation in the activity is the ultimate goal, then students should have this experience early on in the learning of the skills.[9]

On student understanding of the relationship of the skills to be learned to the whole, Gentile mused:

> It has always been a source of wonderment . . . that within a few minutes to perhaps an hour, children can teach each other all there is to know about the conduct of a game. . . . The level of skill in the game performance after such a rapid initial exposure usually is not very high; but some things are evident. The participants seem to recognize the outcomes that have to be produced for success in the game and, therefore, understand what skills have to be learned and why. Further, there appears to be some immediate pleasure evident on the part of the participants, even if inversely related to degree of skill.
> In contrast to this play environment . . . physical education class instruction seems to be based on an inductive model: one skill, artificially removed from the normal game environment, is taught at a time, progressing from simple to complex. It may be a matter of weeks or months (or never) before the learner gets to play the game. Little wonder there are motivational difficulties.[10]

Establishment of the Conditions for Learning Verbal directions or cues tell the learner to recognize or recall previously learned facts, skills, or strategies for use in current learning. This involves reviewing concepts or skills that have previously been learned and may involve a brief practice at that level, perhaps as a warm-up.

Skills can be taught by creating environmental conditions in a microcosm of the total game or by playing the actual game and teaching skills as they arise. Telling students what will be encountered would seem to be a less-effective strategy. In any case, the learning environment must include all relevant stimuli needed for execution of the skill to be learned.

A correct model of the skill to be taught is
essential to successful performance by
students.

Gentile used the example of batting in which the regulatory stimuli are the bat, batter's box,
plate, and a pitched ball. Irrelevant stimuli, such as the fielders and spectators, might not
be included, but performance may be negatively influenced by these distractions when students are placed in the actual game situation. Exaggerations of the regulatory stimuli or
figure-ground relationships for instructional purposes, such as using yellow balls, may also
be disadvantageous later on if only white balls are allowed.

Irrelevant elements should be eliminated as much as possible until learners have mastered the beginning stages of a skill. Since students can handle only small amounts of information at a time, chunking information can promote retention. For example, in teaching
a folk dance, the grapevine step might initially be presented as four separate movements—
step to the side, step behind, step to the side, step in front. As soon as the students are familiar
with the sequence, it can be reduced to one piece of information—the grapevine. The same
thing may be done with the entire folk dance. As the sequences of the dance become automatic, the entire dance becomes "chunked" under one piece of information, the name of the
dance.

Selective Attention Reading, listening to a presentation, and observing a demonstration done
by the teacher, a student, or a loop film all involve the presentation of a new learning stimulus. In motor learning, the stimulus is usually a model of the skill so that students gain a
correct perception of the performance they are trying to achieve.

Factors that can interfere with the learner's attention on the model are visual, auditory, Visual difficulty can be poor eyesight, sighting into the sun or against a similarly colored background, or other activities occurring in the background. Yelling and talking by other students can interfere with the students' auditory perception. Internal factors include sleepiness, fatigue, boredom, or discouragement.

A good demonstration is worth a thousand words. Two or three short verbal cues help the student perceive the key points of the demonstration without being distracted by non-essential portions of the movement. Too much verbiage or too many cues can be distracting to the learner. Adding cues one at a time can facilitate absorption by the learner. By thinking of potential problem areas for the learner and counteracting those problem areas with positive cues, the most important points will be reinforced. An example of cues for the set in volleyball might be (1) look through the triangle, (2) keep your seat down, and (3) extend. For the badminton clear, the cues might be (1) scratch your back, (2) reach for the shuttle, and (3) make the racket whistle.

The kinesiological or biomechanical analysis of a skill by the instructor is used as a basis for developing cues that focus the students' attention on relevant parts of the skill and provide feedback during the guided practice following the demonstration. In no case should the kinesiological or biomechanical analysis be presented to the student while in the process of learning a new skill. This overloads the limited capacity of the learner with irrelevant details that have no meaning. The ability to select the best cues is learned by experience. However, beginning teachers have access to the experience of the experts in reference books.[11]

Students must be helped to identify and attend to regulatory stimuli such as ball direction, speed, height, spin, angle or distance from the goal, or the location of other players. For skills such as golf, the focus is on the position of the body and the implement and the kinesthetic awareness of the learner. Students need to know such items as where to position themselves in relation to other objects, where to look for relevant cues, how to discriminate the object from the background, and how to use the cues to predict changes in the environment. Although the learners may be told this information, a demonstration or guided discovery type of learning may be more appropriate. At the same time, the learner needs to learn to disregard irrelevant aspects such as the spectators, fatigue, and anxiety.

The Motor Plan or Schema Unless an exact movement is the outcome, as in gymnastics or diving, students should be allowed to organize the movement into a plan that best fits them and is compatible with the environment and the outcome. Undue emphasis on a specific form may cause goal confusion in which the learner fails to achieve the goal due to overemphasis on the movement. Decision making about the motor plan is based on the perceptions obtained; an analysis of the options available, such as passing, dribbling, or shooting; and the past experience of the player. The decision includes factors such as when to begin the response and where to hit the ball.

Response Execution Following the demonstration, the student should practice the desired concept or skill in the most appropriate environment. Once the concept of the skill has been acquired, the learning environment should include as many of the situations as possible in which the student will actually use the behavior (e.g., a moving rather than a stationary ball, as close to the real speed as possible). In activities involving a ball, speed and accuracy should be stressed rather than just speed or just accuracy. When the skill involves both accuracy and speed, a decision must be made as to whether to emphasize speed or accuracy. In most situations, the movement should be practiced at a moderate speed.[12]

Gymnastics Worksheet: This worksheet is a study aide to review the concepts and skills studied in P.E. It includes shapes, jumping and landing (flight), balance, and weight transfer. Answer the questions by circling the best answer, filling in the blank, or writing a sentence.

To balance well, one needs to know how the *base of support* and the *center of gravity* affect the body's balance. Look at the pictures below and circle the *most* stable position.

Why is it the most stable?

To remain balanced the center of gravity must be _____ the base of support.
If the body wants to roll, the center of gravity must fall _____ the base of support.

Figure 6.2 An example of a worksheet used with upper-grade children in gymnastics.
Source: Tom Ratliffe, "Using Worksheets in Physical Education." *Journal of Physical Education, Recreation and Dance* 53 (September 1982):48.

Practice drills used with interscholastic teams are generally not appropriate for physical education classes in which students are developing rather than refining skills. Research by Earls demonstrated a regression in skill development when students were challenged to move on to more complex patterns before their skills were sufficiently rehearsed.[13] Since most skills are learned best in an atmosphere of positive reinforcement and low muscle tension, a stressful learning situation should be avoided.

Students also need help with applying movement principles to a variety of situations. This can be achieved by pointing out activities in which the concepts apply and do not apply. Worksheets, such as the one in figure 6.2, can help students generalize concepts to various activity situations.

Just prior to execution of the skill, the teacher might direct the student to focus on specific feedback processes and how they can be used to improve the skill. Through analyzing the learning process, students will learn how to learn, as well as acquire the skills themselves.

Feedback Feedback is information about the learner's response. It may be provided by the learner or by the environment. The ability to provide meaningful feedback is one of the most important abilities a teacher possesses. Feedback might make use of the verbal cues used to

Table 6.2 Four possible outcomes for evaluating skill learning

Type of evaluation	Was the movement executed as planned?		
	Outcome	Yes	No
Was the goal accomplished?	Yes	Got the idea of the movement	Surprise!
	No	Something's wrong	Everything's wrong

A. M. Gentile. "A Working Model of Skill Acquisition with Application to Teaching," *Quest* 17 (January 1972), p. 9.

accompany the initial skill demonstration. Melville used checklists of the four or five most important aspects of performance to help students and teachers focus on skill essentials.[14] Visual feedback may also be structured by the teacher, such as a rope over a badminton net to encourage correct serving technique or a videotape replay.[15] Kinesthetic cues, such as moving a student's arms in the correct swimming pattern, can be useful with some students.

Another valuable feedback technique is a redemonstration of the skill following the initial skill attempts of the student. In all cases, the students' attention should be directed to the essential aspects of the skill or its consequences that will help them to correct initial attempts at skill achievement. Gradually, as the students' skills approximate the model, patterning is complete and the cues should be changed so that the skill performance will be more refined and fixation or diversification will occur.

Feedback is necessary to evaluate and modify the motor plan. Both intrinsic and extrinsic feedback must be considered in the decision-making process. Extrinsic feedback should not be given immediately following the performance to allow the learner to process feedback from the task itself. However, it should be given prior to the next response so that it can be incorporated into the next motor plan. Gentile proposed that the learner answer two questions about the response:[16] "Was the goal accomplished?" and "Was the movement executed as planned?" The possible answers are shown in table 6.2. If the answer to both questions is yes, then the learner should continue to use the same motor plan. If a "surprise" is obtained, the learner must make a decision. Either the original motor plan or the incorrect but successful movement may be tried. Perhaps both plans will be tried and compared. If the "something's wrong" response is obtained, the learner may need to reevaluate the regulatory conditions to determine if some stimuli have been ignored and establish a new plan. If the "everything's wrong" response occurs after several tries, the motivation of the learner may suffer. Possible strategies include revising the motor plan, reevaluating environmental conditions, or altering the goal.

Fixation/Diversity of the Movement

The second stage of skill learning is entered after the learner has been successful in acquiring the movement. The goal of this stage differs depending on the type of skill to be learned. Gentile divided skills into open and closed skills, although she indicated that a continuum of skills exists.[17]

A *closed skill* is done in a relatively stable environment. Examples of closed skills are archery, bowling, gymnastics, golf, the basketball free throw, the place kick in soccer, and hitting a ball off a batting tee. For closed skills, fixation of the motor skill is the goal. Learning consists of concentrating on the identical elements in the body and the environment and striving for consistency in the execution of the motor plan. Closed skills are not necessarily easier than open skills since they require extraordinary kinesthetic awareness. Students should begin to feel the correct movements through kinesthetic perception of their own body movements.

In an *open skill,* the environment is unpredictable, the players keep changing places, and objects move through space. Adjustments must be made in speed, timing, and space, such as in the height and speed of a softball pitch or the interaction of players on a basketball court. Other examples include tennis, racquetball, soccer, and the martial arts. Diversification of the skill is required to meet the multitude of environmental conditions. Decisions must be made in split seconds during the action. Therefore, practice must include a variety of situations, and the learner must be informed about the range of possibilities. At first, combinations of two or three variables may be practiced, but later practice must include all possible variables. If only three speeds, three directions, three ball heights, and three distances were considered, eighty-one different combinations must be rehearsed. Imagine how many might exist in an actual game.[18] Practice should not consistently occur with any particular combination or a fixation might occur. The student must learn to predict what conditions will be like from cues available in the environment and past responses and outcomes. An example is focusing on when the ball leaves the thrower's hands and how long it takes to arrive. When the ball gets there, it is too late to begin to catch it. The teacher may need to help the learner identify the important elements in the environment and the motor patterns that resulted in goal attainment for each of the different environmental conditions.

It is at this point that physical educators often make the mistake of introducing a new skill rather than refining the skill already presented. Students should be assisted in setting goals for accuracy, distance, speed, quality of movement, and reduction of errors. Practice situations can be modified to meet the needs of specific individuals as they work on their own goals. Another mistake is to jump from practice directly into competitive games before students have had the time to refine their skills. The complex nature of the game almost ensures a regression to less-desirable movement patterns.[19]

With both open and closed skills, practice should be as gamelike or competitionlike as possible, with a changing, unstable, unpredictable environment for open skills or a stable, predictable environment for closed skills.

Young discussed ways to improve practice drills to make them more gamelike. She suggested placing cones at random rather than in straight lines for dribbling practice, with several players moving at a time so that students learn to adapt to changing circumstances. Students could also play games called Three-on-Three or Bonus Ball rather than "lead-up games," which make secondary school students feel incapable of playing the real game. For Bonus Ball, points could be awarded for using the skill in game situations.[20]

The final result of skill learning is accurate, consistent, adaptable, and coordinated motor responses. Automatic skill execution enables the learner to devote more attention to the game plan and strategy. Instead of paying attention to each part of a skill, the elements are "chunked" into a skill or even a combination of skills. Performers learn where to look and what to look at, how to differentiate relevant and irrelevant information, and how to

Written examinations reinforce important
concepts of physical education.

predict outcomes from cues. In essence, the students learn to integrate movements and information into schemata that help them select appropriate movement responses to a wide variety of conditions, monitor outcomes, and guide their own learning.[21] These factors occur because the information-processing system improves its ability to process information. A schema is developed by practicing in a variety of situations and noting the outcomes that occur with different responses. By integrating information from the environment and the body, a rule or principle emerges to guide future behavior. Lichtman emphasized that transferability may be based on the student's "ability to generalize the appropriate motor schema to the set of conditions which are present."[22] She also suggested that helping students develop the ability to evaluate movement errors can speed up learning.[23]

Cognitive Learning

Traditionally, physical education teachers have relied on teaching skills and activities as the components of physical education. However, "being physically educated means having understandings about the body and physical activity that prepare each individual to want to live and be capable of living a physically active lifestyle."[24] Simplified concepts can be taught in elementary school with more in-depth analysis of the same concepts occurring in the secondary schools.

Teaching the cognitive aspects of physical education is not easy. It requires extensive planning to integrate concepts with psychomotor activity. However, knowledge learned through relevant experience is more lasting than that gained merely through reading or listening, and learning occurs faster when students understand the principles involved in skill performance.

Mohr emphasized the importance of integrating concepts with physical activity to enhance understanding and save time. She said:

> Our students do not have to stop motor activity in order to engage in cognitive activity. Students do not store their brains in their lockers along with their books and street clothes. . . . To develop physical education understanding we need to guide these cognitive activities, just as we guide the motor activities. In other words, we can accomplish the intellectual, aesthetic, and social objectives without moving into the classroom. However, in some parts of the country, during inclement weather, physical education classes must be held in classrooms or other confined spaces. The resourceful teacher will take advantage of these times to plan worthwhile cognitive activities related to the body of knowledge in physical education and to the motor activities involved in the unit of curricular content. Modern audio-visual aids and numerous innovative teaching techniques are available to motivate and challenge the students to exciting cognitive achievements.[25]

Mohr concluded with the following statement:

> In your undergraduate and graduate professional preparation programs you have learned many exciting and valuable concepts about principles of movement, how the body performs desired movements, the effects of activity on these wonderful bodies of ours, and the effects of numerous factors on performance. Why keep these learnings a secret? Why not let your students share these exciting understandings so that their lives will be enriched by them just as yours have been.[26]

What Can I Do While Participating?

Kinesiology

Spin results when force is applied off the center of the object.

The force can be applied by the hands, a racket, or the foot when kicking. The two factors which determine the behavior of the ball are where the force is applied relative to the center of gravity of the ball, and the amount of force applied.

Learning Activities:

1. Use any ball-type activity. Plan a drill or task which experiments with applying force off-center and with the amount of force. Plan applications of force above, below, and to the sides of the ball. Discuss how spin aids or inhibits performance of skill in the sport being studied and in other sports.
2. Select a variety of objects for experimenting with spin: volleyball, basketball, frisbee, golf ball, softball, and table tennis ball. Practice throwing or striking off center. Watch the spin and note the rebound.
3. Teach the application of force concept to produce spin in the sports where it is a performance factor: tennis, golf, basketball, volleyball, racquetball, softball and table tennis.

Figure 6.3 An example from *Basic Stuff Series I: Kinesiology.*
Source: *Basic Stuff Series I: Kinesiology* (Reston, Virginia: American Alliance for Health, Physical Education, Recreation and Dance, 1981), p. 25.

Cognitive Content

As in other areas of specialization, the knowledge explosion has dramatically increased knowledge of physical education. The *Basic Stuff Series* was written to help physical educators keep up with the knowledge from an expanding research base and to help teachers communicate that knowledge to students in physical education classes.[27] The series helps the teacher tell the student what, why, and how—knowledge about performance as well as skills and knowledge necessary to perform.[28] Series I includes six booklets on exercise physiology, kinesiology, motor development, motor learning, social and psychological aspects of movement, and movement in the humanities (art, history, and philosophy). Each booklet presents the body of knowledge in that area of physical education in concise, readable format, with numerous examples and applications.[29] An example from the booklet on kinesiology is shown in figure 6.3. Series II *Basic Stuff in Action* has three booklets designed to help teachers apply the concepts in Series I to specific age groups (K–3, 4–8, and 9–12).

Ley listed some concept areas that should be included in instruction. They include the following:

1. Statements of description that provide information about "what"—facts, knowledge, information
2. Statements of importance that answer "why"—simple reasons, values, justifications, worth

3. Statements of scientific analysis that answer "why it happens"—principles, relationships, laws
4. Statements of problem solving (what one can do about it)—application of facts, principles, and relationships[30]

Gagné noted the existence of three types of cognitive learning outcomes: (1) verbal information, (2) intellectual skills, and (3) cognitive strategies. *Verbal information* consists of stored knowledge or facts that can be used through *intellectual skills* that help the learner deal symbolically with the environment. The former are things the learner can *tell,* while the skills reflect things the students can *do.* Facts may be provided by the teacher at the time of learning, recalled by the learner from previous learning, or learned just prior to the task at hand. If both facts and intellectual skills have been mastered, the learner is said to have the appropriate readiness for learning.[31] *Cognitive strategies* are skills used by learners to manage their own "learning, remembering, and thinking." These strategies are used to help the learner decide what past knowledge and skills are to be used and how to implement them. During early learning experiences, the strategies are cued by the teacher. As the student's experience increases, the strategies may be expected to be self-activated by the learner.[32]

Verbal Information

Two principal divisions of verbal information are memorization or rote learning and meaningful verbal learning. The task of the teacher is to master teaching methods appropriate to each of these types of learning. Large amounts of information can be acquired through verbal learning in relatively short periods of time, thereby supplying the knowledge needed to solve problems.

Memorization or Rote Learning

The behaviorists emphasize the importance of associating the items to be learned with items already familiar to the learner. Repetition of the paired events is assumed to create a bond or association between them.

Learning a series of things in order is a common method of association. Almost everyone who has studied music has learned the sentence "Every good boy does fine" to learn the names of the lines on the staff. Learning the components of motor fitness is done easily in alphabetical order—agility, balance, coordination, endurance, flexibility, speed, and strength. Rhymes such as "i before e except after c or when followed by g" are also readily remembered. Another method is the use of a key word, phrase, or mental image to remind the learner of the idea to be learned. Examples of mental images are the cues used to remind students of specific aspects of performance, such as the back-scratch position in the tennis serve, the heart-shaped pull in the breaststroke, or the S-pull in the freestyle. Learner-generated memory devices are more effective than teacher-generated devices. However, when students are incapable of generating their own devices, instructor-generated devices can also be effective.[33]

A common practice method is the progressive-part method in which the student learns the first part; then parts 1 and 2; then 1, 2, 3; and so forth. For example, when learning the bones in the body, start with the foot, review the foot and learn the ankle, review the foot and ankle and add the leg, and so forth. Another practice method is to respond to the entire task on each trial by using some kind of prompts or cues as needed to get through the material. One way to do this is to gradually cross out parts of the material as it is practiced until the whole sequence of material has been learned. This method has been used in the programmed learning sequence in figure 10.8 on page 343. A third method is the use of questions spaced periodically throughout the practice phase to stimulate student attention to the material during practice. An example of this is to stop students during a game and have them identify the rule infraction.

Reinforcement or confirmation of correct responses is essential so that the learner knows that the material has been learned correctly. Feedback must be specific enough that the student knows whether the response is correct or incorrect and, if incorrect, how to change it to make it correct. Rote learning has only specific transferability. Identical elements must occur in the new situation to trigger retrieval.[34]

Although memory devices are adequate for learning facts, they are not necessarily effective in comprehension. A variety of learning strategies has emerged for helping learners generate relationships between previous knowledge and experience and information to be learned.[35] For example, students who summarized textbook information from the headings in the book doubled their comprehension over a control group.[36] Student generation of topic sentences from text also improved comprehension, but reduced the learning of facts.[37] Student underlining of words in texts produced greater comprehension when students selected and underlined the words.[38]

Meaningful Verbal Learning

According to Ausubel, a cognitivist, the key to comprehension lies in actively connecting new material to previously learned material to form a meaningful relationship.[39] The most general concepts are presented first, followed by progressively more specificity and detail. For example, in figure 6.4, the diagram shows the general components of physical education. Students should have an understanding of each of these areas before proceeding to each of the subdivisions around the outer borders of the diagram. The subdivisions may then be broken down into specific concepts, such as endurance training or the measurement of endurance.

Ausubel theorized that the way subject matter is organized and the way people organize ideas in their minds are identical. This organization forms a hierarchy with the most inclusive concepts at the top and the specific concepts at the bottom. When the structure is taught to students, they have a meaningful context to which newly learned information can be related. The information can then be used to analyze information and solve problems within the hierarchy. By organizing the information and attaching it to old information, more information-processing space is available. Learning is enhanced when the following steps are included: (1) the presentation of an advance organizer, (2) the presentation of the material to be learned, (3) the anchoring of the new ideas to the existing cognitive structure, and (4) the mastery of the new ideas.

An *advance organizer* is a verbal or visual expression presented before the learning task itself that clarifies the interrelationship of the knowledge to be learned with previously learned material. There are two kinds of advance organizers. The *expository organizer,* which is shown in figure 6.4, provides an overall view of physical education that includes the material to be presented and shows how it will relate to previously learned knowledge. The expository organizer is used when unfamiliar material is to be presented. A *comparative organizer* shows the relationship of the new concept to similar previously learned concepts by pointing out the similarities and differences between the two. A comparative organizer might help the student understand the football throw by comparing it with a softball throw.

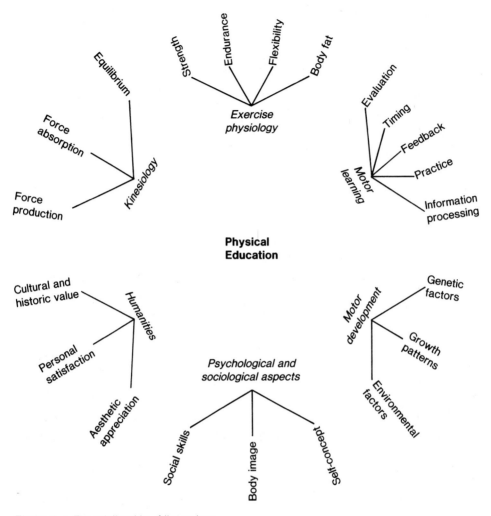

Figure 6.4 The relationship of the various components of physical education.

To facilitate anchoring the new learning material to that previously learned, the teacher must remind the learners of the previously learned skill, summarize the new material, and point out similarities and differences with the previously learned skill. The major difficulty lies in selecting the advance organizer. Advance organizers emphasize the context within which the content fits. For this reason, one of the best kinds of advance organizers is a diagrammatic portrayal of the relationships among the content variables.

The material to be learned may be presented in any of the traditional modes, including lectures, demonstrations, class discussions, films, readings, or experiments. Throughout the presentation, the students must be led to understand the logical relationships of the ideas to each other. An outline could facilitate the students' organization of the material and help to maintain the students' attention on the material. The most general information is presented first, followed by the details.

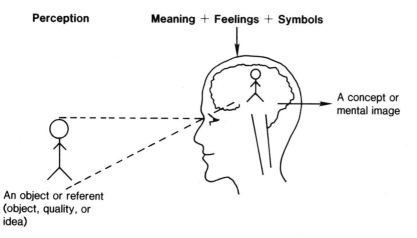

Perception   **Meaning + Feelings + Symbols**

A concept or
mental image

An object or referent
(object, quality, or
idea)

Figure 6.5 The origination of a concept.

Studies show that meaningful verbal material is learned more rapidly and retained more readily with less interference than rote learning. Meaningful verbal learning also has the potential for general transfer to many situations.

Intellectual Skills

Intellectual skills are rules that use verbal information to help the learner interact with the environment. Intellectual skills include concept learning, discrimination learning, rule learning, and problem solving. *Concept* learning involves organizing environmental input into categories for storage in the brain. *Discrimination* learning involves the ability to perceive features in an object or event that are the same or different. A *rule* is a meaningful relationship between two or more concepts. *Problem solving* involves the use of rules to help the learner interact with the environment.[40]

Concept and Discrimination Learning

A *concept* is an idea or picture in the brain that aids understanding. The origination of a concept is diagrammed in figure 6.5. Each concept consists of one's perceptions, the meanings given them, the feelings about them, and the words or symbols with which one discusses them. Most school learning is of concepts or the rules and principles that are made when concepts are linked together.

Concept learning involves the identification of objects, experiences, processes, or configurations (often of widely differing physical appearances) into a category of elements that share certain essential characteristics. A concept has

1. A name or label—a term given to a category or class of experiences, objects, processes, or configurations, such as "aerobic activities."
2. Examples—instances of the concept that contain all of the essential attributes of the concept, such as "jogging or walking."
3. Nonexamples—examples with none or only some of the essential characteristics, such as "sprinting or calisthenics."

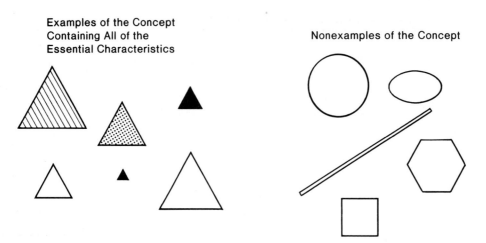

Examples of the Concept
Containing All of the
Essential Characteristics

Nonexamples of the Concept

Figure 6.6 Concept learning involves distinguishing relevant from irrelevant characteristics.

4. Essential or shared attributes—common features or characteristics of examples within a concept, such as "the constant use of oxygen without incurring an oxygen debt."
5. Irrelevant attributes—features that often accompany, but are not a required feature of, an element to be included in the concept, such as "where or when a person runs."
6. Definition—a statement specifying the essential attributes of the concept, such as "activities that develop oxygen transportation and utilization without incurring an oxygen debt are called aerobic activities."

Concept learning involves the ability to *discriminate* (1) essential characteristics from irrelevant characteristics and (2) essential characteristics of examples from essential characteristics of nonexamples, as shown in figure 6.6. Concepts can be taught by the following sequence:

1. Present a variety of labeled examples that incorporate all of the essential characteristics of the concept (simultaneously or in close time succession). "Jogging, stationary cycling, and walking are aerobic activities."
2. Compare examples and nonexamples (see definition above) to identify essential characteristics and develop a hunch or hypothesis. Within the examples and nonexamples, vary the irrelevant attributes. Start with examples that are least similar, with the fewest shared characteristics. "Is this an aerobic activity?" rowing—yes   sprinting—no   folk dance—yes
3. Verify the hypothesis formulated above by asking for several new examples of the concept. "List several aerobic activities."
4. Have students state a definition of the concept in their own words. Check to see that the definition includes all of the essential characteristics of an aerobic activity.
5. Reinforce correct answers.
6. Apply the concept to choose appropriate examples, such as "aerobic activities."
7. Test the concept. When the instructor wants to know if the students have acquired the concept, he or she must assess whether the students can generate examples with

the essential characteristics and distinguish examples from nonexamples (e.g., aerobic from anaerobic activities).

Concepts become more meaningful to students as they accumulate more experience with their objects or referents. Laboratory experiences and demonstrations are important in helping students gain the experiences needed.

Mohr provided some additional ideas for teaching concepts.[41] They are paraphrased here as follows:

1. Explain why one method of performance is better than another.
2. Omit some important feature of a skill, such as stepping in the direction of the throw, to help the students see what a detrimental effect this has on the force of the throw.
3. Incorporate the learning of fitness concepts, such as exercise heart rate, recovery rate, and respiration rate, into rest periods between vigorous exercise.
4. Conduct informal experiments by comparing conditions, such as heat, cold, or smog, as they affect exercise on different days.

Rule Learning

Concepts can be linked together in various ways to form rules or principles. Rules and principles can be taught best by applying them. Students who learn to say or write a rule usually forget it within a few weeks, while those who are able to apply rules or integrate them with prior learning retain them more easily. Rules and principles are best taught when the following procedure is followed.

1. Inform the learner of the performance to be expected at the conclusion of the lesson. It may later serve as a reinforcement to learning. "Traveling is a violation in basketball."
2. Recall the component concepts. "Traveling is . . . A violation is . . ."
3. Provide verbal cues that explain the relationships of the concepts. "Traveling is an unfair advantage with no body contact and is therefore a violation."
4. Ask each student to demonstrate one or more instances of the rule (e.g., show various examples of traveling such as taking more than a two-step stop or moving the pivot foot).
5. Request that each student state the rule verbally.
6. Apply the rule in more complex situations (e.g., play a game and identify traveling while officiating).

Students should be taught concepts and rules related to the activity at the same time as the psychomotor skill is learned. For example, rules involving the volleyball serve should be taught as soon as students are ready to practice the regulation serve. Principles relating to force production should be taught or recalled when hitting a tennis serve or throwing a ball. Several other ways to teach rules include:[42]

1. Give the rule and an example. Ask students to supply a second example.
2. Give one or more examples. Have students formulate the rule.
3. Give an example. State the rule. Ask students for a second example.
4. Give the rule and ask students for an example.
5. Give the rule and ask students to restate the rule.
6. Give an example. Ask students for a second example.

Problem Solving

Problem solving is the capacity to solve previously unencountered situations by combining old rules and principles into new higher-order ones. A problem is solved when the individual's previous knowledge or behavior is put together into a new relationship or added to new information to form an insight that resolves the new situation. The problem-solving approach can provide students with opportunities to develop game strategies, create new games, compose gymnastic routines, choreograph dances, and a host of other creative endeavors. The main concern about problem solving is whether problem-solving abilities can be transferred from the school to real-life situations.

The nature of the task determines the specific problem-solving behaviors, but certain general behaviors are essential. For a problem to be solved, the following must occur: (1) the student is presented with a problem that is worth solving; (2) the student recalls previously learned knowledge and behavior that relate to the problem; (3) the teacher provides assistance to channel students' thinking; and (4) the teacher reinforces both the problem-solving process and the solution.

Presentation of a Problem Recognition of a problem may occur as a result of teacher selection and presentation or student perception. Teachers often design problems to help students apply recently learned principles. Two important elements of the problem are (1) that the teacher and the student see some worth in its solution and (2) that the essential features of the solution can be inferred from the problem. The problem chosen must be one that can be handled within the limitations of time and the resources available.

The student should understand the problem and the performance expected. The essential features of the solution could be questions to be answered. A problem can be as simple as "How do I move my bowsight in archery?" or as complex as "Why are some people better performers in some activities, while others are better in other activities?"

Recall of Previous Learning Students must be taught the information or helped to identify and recall the knowledge and skills that relate to the problem. This may involve searching their long-term memory systems for the relevant schema.[43] The teacher could facilitate this process in the problem cited above by having the students shoot at thirty yards and asking them where they think they should place the bowsight based on their previous shooting at twenty yards.

Teacher Assistance Providing information about the method or the principles to be used leads to better problem solving by students. Students differ in their abilities to attack and solve problems. Bloom and Broder discovered a number of differences in problem-solving behaviors of successful and unsuccessful problem solvers.[44] Unsuccessful solvers

1. Experienced difficulty with reading comprehension and failed to understand the problem. Often they solved the problem only to discover that the problem they solved was not the one presented.
2. Were unaware that they possessed the knowledge necessary to solve the problem.
3. Approached problems as if the problems had pat solutions.
4. Lacked confidence in their ability to solve problems.

Teachers can facilitate problem solving by helping students understand the problem, break it down into manageable components, and select relevant knowledge and skills from their previously learned skills. They can reinforce the possibility of several solutions. The greater the repertoire of previously learned knowledge and skills and the easier it is to recall and apply them, the greater are the chances of solving the problem. Teacher assistance may take many forms—from listening to students' exploration of possible alternatives to providing students with cues to channeling their thinking.[45] For example, the teacher could ask, "What happened when you moved your bowsight up?" "Why not try moving it another direction to see what happens?" Group discussion and participation in problem solving appears to be superior to individual problem solving in assisting students to learn the problem-solving process and to use the principles learned to solve other problems.

One of the most important things a teacher can do is to establish an environment of acceptance and self-worth in which students feel free to explore alternative solutions to problems. Problem solving cannot occur when conformity is the norm. Teachers should ensure that students have the time necessary to solve problems without pressure.

Reinforcement Teachers who use problem solving must have confidence in their students' abilities to solve problems. Reinforcement of both the process of problem solving and the product or solution are important in encouraging students to continue to solve problems.

Cognitive Strategies

Cognitive strategies use networks of rules or schemata to achieve successful learning.[46] The use of cognitive strategies is especially effective in motor learning.[47] Teachers can help students recognize the correct strategies for given situations. A relative newcomer in the research arena is *metacognition,* which refers to conscious control over one's own cognitive actions or the theories used to study thinking. As expressed by Flavell:

> Metacognition refers to one's knowledge concerning one's own cognitive processes and products or anything related to them, e.g., the learning-relevant properties of information or data. For example, I am engaging in metacognition (metamemory, metalearning, metaattention, metalanguage, or whatever) if I notice that I am having more trouble learning A than B; if it strikes me that I should double-check C before accepting it as a fact; if it occurs to me that I had better scrutinize each and every alternative in any multiple-choice type task situation before deciding which is the best one; if I sense that I had better make a note of D because I may forget it.[48]

Metacognition involves knowing *when* you know something and when you do not, *what* you need to know and what you already know, and *how* to use learning strategies to acquire the information needed. Metacognition also helps you decide what information should be stored, how much information can be handled at a time in short-term memory, and how to link the new information with previously stored information. Metacognition increases as children mature.[49]

Closely related to metacognition is the concept of learning strategies, which are behaviors engaged in by the learner that are designed to influence the manner in which the learner selects, organizes, and integrates new with existing knowledge.[50] Examples of learning strategies are notetaking, underlining, and summarizing. Norman summarized the importance of helping students learn how to learn:

> It is strange that we expect students to learn yet seldom teach them anything about learning. We expect students to solve problems yet seldom teach them about problem solving. And, similarly, we sometimes require students to remember a considerable body of material yet seldom teach them the art of memory. It is time we made up for this

lack, time that we developed the applied disciplines of learning and problem solving and memory. We need to develop the general principles of how to learn, how to remember, how to solve problems, and then to develop applied courses, and then to establish the place of these methods in an academic community.[51]

Weinstein and Mayer concluded that "helping students to develop effective ways to handle the barrage of information coming from the environment, as well as their own thinking processes, is a major goal of our educational system that will only increase in importance in the future." They stated that the goals of education should include goals concerned with the products of learning, as well as with the processes of learning.[52]

A number of learning strategies exist, from the basic association strategies used for rote learning to complex strategies for organizing material such as outlining. Examples include:[53]

Rote learning:	using a key word or mental image
	reciting
	chunking or clustering items into groups
Meaningful verbal learning:	paraphrasing
	summarizing
	creating analogies between known and unknown information
	using advance organizers
	underlining
	listing chronologically
	notetaking
	questioning-answering
	outlining
	diagramming
	applying comprehension monitoring strategies using self-questioning

One recent learning strategy that relates well to Ausubel's concept of advance organizers is concept mapping, which represents the relationships among various concepts by linking lines as shown in figure 6.7.[54] In its simplest version, two concepts connected by a linking word are used to form a proposition. The propositions are then linked together in a hierarchical arrangement to form a schematic summary of the key ideas of what has been learned. Different learners may form the maps in different, though valid, ways because of their different perceptions and processing styles. Instructors and students can then talk about their concept maps and learn new meanings from each other. Concept maps can be used to explore what learners already know; map new learning routes; extract meaning from textbooks, articles, and laboratory or field studies; or plan a paper or talk. Studies on concept mapping show that it is a useful learning strategy.[55]

Students should be encouraged to make a conscious effort to apply learning to life's problems. Homework assignments might be used to encourage the transfer of school learning to problems in the home or community. Homework can play an important role in informing

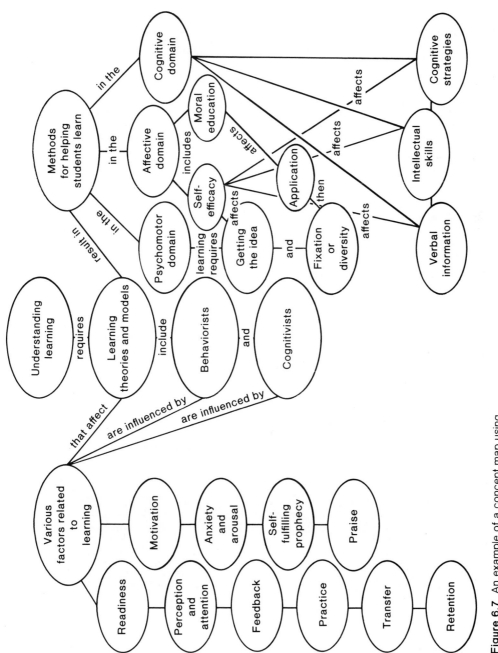

Figure 6.7 An example of a concept map using the concepts from chapters 4 and 6.

the family about physical education and can even involve them directly in physical education activities. It can be used to practice skills, learn or apply concepts, increase physical fitness, solve problems, and develop self-discipline. French listed a number of possibilities for homework in physical education.[56] They include:

1. Practicing skills using task sheets.
2. Attending sports events or watching them on television.
3. Coaching or officiating youth sports.
4. Tutoring another student in a skill.
5. Watching films or other media in a learning resource center.
6. Studying for tests and quizzes.
7. Interviewing well-known sports figures.
8. Reading books on sports and physical activities and writing book reports.
9. Reporting on current events.

Another possibility is working on individual physical fitness programs. Since one of the objectives of physical education is to encourage people to exercise on their own, teachers reward students who make a habit of self-directed fitness activity.[57]

Students can also be asked to solve problems, such as creating a gymnastics routine, a modern dance composition, strategies for a sports event, or a new game. Cameron tried a bonus incentive plan with extra-credit points earned for an optional out-of-class assignment each week. A maximum of three points could be earned based on the level of the problem selected. Problems consisted of self-testing and problem-solving activities, concept-related experiences, analysis of readings, and the interpretation and design of learning materials.[58]

Affective and Social Learning

Compared with cognitive and psychomotor learning, little affective learning has been deliberately introduced into the curriculum. One reason for this is that teaching cognitive facts and psychomotor skills is easy, but training is needed to incorporate affective learning into the educational process. The widespread attitude that the students' beliefs and values are private and should not be tampered with in the schools is a second reason. Third, society fluctuates in the affective objectives it wants or does not want taught in its schools. The constant change makes many teachers and administrators wary of teaching any values at all, so they resort to those areas of the curriculum with which they are more comfortable—knowledge and skills.

Affective strategies are used to focus attention, maintain concentration, establish and maintain motivation, manage anxiety,[59] develop self-esteem, and learn ethical and social behavior. The primary purpose of teaching students in the affective domain is to help them learn how to deal with their emotions and attitudes toward physical education and toward others.

Positive Attitudes toward Physical Education

One's tastes, preferences, attitudes, values, and ideals will ultimately affect how one chooses to behave. Because students are thinking, feeling beings, no intellectual or psychomotor learning can possibly occur without some sort of feelings being involved—feelings about

Table 6.3 Positive conditions and consequences

Content-Oriented Conditions

1. Providing challenging instruction that leads to success most of the time.
2. Helping students know what the course objectives are and where they are in relation to the goal.
3. Preassessing students and providing instructional tasks that will help students achieve course objectives.
4. Providing immediate, specific feedback in a positive way.
5. Helping students develop confidence in their performance by overlearning skills.
6. Keeping verbal instruction to a minimum.
7. Using only relevant test items for the specified objectives.
8. Allowing students to select some learning activities.
9. Basing grades on each student's achievement, not on how well the other students performed.

Student-Oriented Conditions

1. Expressing genuine interest in the students and in their individual successes.
2. Treating each student as a person.
3. Acknowledging students' responses as legitimate learning attempts even when incorrect.
4. Allowing students to learn without public awareness of errors.

Environment

1. Providing an environment in which students feel accepted, supported, and trusted.
2. Providing a wide range of activities in which students can choose to involve themselves with appropriate counseling.
3. Focusing on what students can do rather than on what they cannot do.

themselves, the subject matter, and the situation. In each student's feelings and values are powerful forces that control the individual. Sometimes these forces block learning; on other occasions they enhance it. When teachers are aware of the existence of students' feelings and their relationships to physical education, they can do a lot to ensure that appropriate learning situations are provided. When teachers ignore the affective domain and put pressure on students to learn apart from their feelings and interests, students often end up disliking physical activity.

Since one of the purposes of physical education is to promote the enjoyment of physical activity so that students will continue to engage in activity, an important objective of every teacher should be to develop as favorable an attitude toward physical education as possible. To accomplish this objective, teachers must ensure that when students are in the presence of any physical education instructional or extracurricular activity, they are, at the same time (1) in the presence of positive conditions and consequences and (2) in the presence of as few negative conditions and consequences as possible. This does not mean to imply that all physical education instruction should be fun, but rather that, given the appropriate conditions, students will work harder.

Although determining whether a given condition is positive or negative for a certain student is not always possible, Mager suggested a number of conditions or consequences that are generally considered to be positive or negative.[60] Examples are shown in tables 6.3 and 6.4.

Table 6.4 Negative conditions or consequences

Pain (Physical Discomfort)

1. Forcing students to overdo in a physical fitness program, resulting in nausea, sore muscles, etc.
2. Failing to provide adequate safety, with resulting injury.
3. Making students sit for long periods of time when dressed for activity.
4. Allowing the classroom to be too hot or too cold.
5. Forcing students to rush from one class to another or to dress more quickly than is reasonable.
6. Using subject matter as an instrument of punishment.

Anxiety (Mental or Emotional Discomfort or Anticipated Unpleasantness)

1. Being unpredictable about what is expected or how it will be graded.
2. Expressing that the student cannot possibly succeed.
3. Using vague, threatened punishment.

Frustration (Interference with Goal-Directed Activities)

1. Presenting information or skills faster or slower than the student can learn them or forcing all students to learn at the same pace.
2. Teaching one thing and testing another.
3. Failing to provide immediate and/or adequate feedback.
4. Stopping an activity just as the students are beginning to enjoy and be absorbed in it.
5. Overemphasizing competition during class time.

Humiliation and Embarrassment (Lowered Self-respect, Pride, or Painful Self-consciousness)

1. Making a public spectacle of a student, such as making the student do push-ups while the class watches or belittling the student's attempts to do well.
2. Allowing repeated failure.
3. Labeling students—"special ed.," "handicapped," etc.

Boredom

1. Repeating instructions that students have already had.
2. Failing to challenge students.
3. Failing to use variety in presenting course content.

A supportive classroom environment is one in which students are treated as individuals and in which they know that help is available. Brophy summed up the research by saying:

> Effective teachers maintain a strong academic focus within the context of a pleasant, friendly classroom. Highly effective teachers clearly stress . . . objectives, but they do not come across as slave drivers, and their classrooms do not resemble sweatshops. They maintain high standards and demand that students do their best, but they are not punitive or hypercritical. Instead, students perceive effective teachers as enthusiastic and thorough instructors whose classrooms are friendly and convivial.[61]

Self-esteem

Felker developed five keys for improving students' self-concepts based on helping students develop the language necessary to enhance and maintain self-concept.[62] They include (1) adults, praise yourselves, (2) help students to evaluate realistically, (3) teach students to set reasonable goals, (4) teach students to praise themselves, and (5) teach students to praise others.

Success in physical activities increases self-esteem.

Because students learn by imitating a model, teachers must learn to praise themselves in front of their students. They can begin by expressing how good they feel when they accomplished such and so. Later, they can expand to praise of their personal qualities. Environmental situations can also be praised. Teachers should try to use a variety of different phrases for praising.

Students need to learn to realistically evaluate actual achievement. Accurate evaluations can prove to be catalysts toward behavior change. One way of helping students evaluate realistically is to have them check off skills or grade and record test scores as they achieve them. (See chapter 8 for examples of check-off charts and other useful techniques.)

Research shows that students with poor self-concepts tend to set unrealistic goals (either too high or too low) and then perceive themselves as failures when they fail to achieve those goals or when they achieve a goal that anyone, even they, could reach. When students are taught to set realistic goals, their commitment to reaching them is increased. Goals should be set slightly higher than prior performances for the most effective learning to occur. Short-term goals are geared toward success and lend themselves to appropriate praise and reward for achievement. Students should then move step-by-step up the ladder toward long-term goals.

By teaching students to praise themselves, the teacher is released from the role of behavior-reinforcer and the students become the reinforcers for their own behavior. Teachers can help them do this by beginning with group praise such as "Didn't we do well. . . ?" and then moving to "Don't you think you did a great job on . . . ?" An "I'm okay day" in which students write or tell something nice about themselves can also help students begin to understand the concept of self-praise. Students could also be helped to evolve from self-encouraging statements such as "I am trying hard," or "I am improving," to self-praise such as "I did a good job," or "I am a good sport." As students praise themselves, they attach the label of "worthwhile" to themselves and their behavior, and their self-esteem rises.

Felker pointed out that self-praise and praise of others are positively correlated. Praising others tends to result in satisfying responses from others, but students need to be taught how to handle the few negative responses that might result. They also need to be taught how to receive praise—sometimes by praising in return, sometimes by a simple "thank you."

Self-efficacy
Self-efficacy is a person's belief in his or her ability to execute the behavior needed to produce a specified outcome or, in simpler terms, it is a situation-specific self-confidence. Efficacy expectations determine a student's selection of activities, expenditure of effort, and persistence at a task. Therefore, teachers should focus on developing competence which, in turn, develops self-confidence. Romance suggested three cues that teachers can use to detect students who lack confidence in physical education:

1. Performer uses extraneous or protective movements.
   a. Performer spends an inordinate amount of time warming up before trying a gymnastic trick.
   b. Performer goofs around—does not perform seriously—so as to mask unconfidence.
   c. Novice diver constantly reverts to a jump into the water at the moment of execution.

2. Performer uses inappropriate choice of tempo for moving.
   a. Performer rushes through a dance step, not staying with the music.
   b. Performer *walks* through the hurdling motion again and again.
3. Performer fixates on single element in environment.
   a. Performer continues to measure his or her jump rope and trade for new one.
   b. Performer is constantly tying shoe.
   c. Performer complains about condition of equipment (balls too slippery).[63]

Students who possess self-confidence generally persist in activities even when not directly supervised by the teacher. Activity competence depends upon a cognitive understanding of the nature of the task and a knowledge about one's own movement capabilities. Confident performers believe that they can handle the task and that it will be satisfying, while those who lack confidence anticipate unpleasant consequences. Students who think they can accomplish a task may be able to achieve tasks the teacher thinks are too difficult. However, students who think they cannot do something may avoid a task they could easily do. Dangers arise when students try activities beyond their capacities, resulting in injury or defeat.[64]

According to Feltz and Weiss, self-efficacy can be increased through (1) ensuring performance success, (2) communicating effectively, (3) modeling techniques, (4) encouraging positive talk, and (5) reducing anxiety-producing factors.[65]

Performance accomplishment is a result of activities that are challenging and yet at a level that permits students to experience success as early in the learning experience as possible. Success is one of the keys to effective motivation; therefore, teachers should ensure a logical progression of activities from simple to complex and choose activities for which students have the prerequisite skills. If tasks are too easy or done with the aid of outside help, the student attributes the success to outside forces, no self-efficacy results, and boredom may occur. If tasks are too difficult, anxiety and failure may occur. Only success attributed to effort on the part of the student results in self-efficacy.

Personally selected, specific, challenging, but realistic goals result in self-efficacy. Process-oriented goals, such as the ability to use specified strategies in a game situation or perform a certain skill in a gymnastics routine, things under the learner's control, should be emphasized rather than winning, over which the learner may have no control.

One means of effective communication involves using a compliment on what was correct, then instructions on how to improve, followed by encouragement to keep trying. This "sandwich" technique was developed to the pinnacle of success by Coach John Wooden, the Wizard of Westwood, and the "winningest" coach in basketball.[66] Teachers and coaches need to evaluate communication to determine if it is positive and equitable to all students.

Modeling is important for self-efficacy, especially when the models are similar in age, gender, and athletic ability, and demonstrate the ability to achieve success through effort. Models must exude confidence, however, to promote task persistence. Appropriate role modeling by teachers and coaches of what they teach wins student respect and encourages confidence in the teacher's ability to help them learn and in their own desire to achieve the modeled behavior.

Positive self-talk by students should be directed toward effort rather than winning. Students who perceive that effort results in success persist longer at learning in the face of difficulties.

Emphasis on effort over winning can help students reduce anxiety. Mental imagery can be used to envision successful performance in sport situations.

Moral Education

Oser noted that there is no integrated, highly developed strategy for values and moral learning. Different models and approaches tend to contradict each other. He attempted to analyze the different models and approaches and derive the common elements of all of them. His analysis followed four issues: (1) the desirability of moral education, (2) the concept of moral discourse, (3) the concept of a moral educational situation, and (4) the distinction between moral and values education.[67]

The Desirability of Moral Education

Parents and educators generally agree that children should receive moral education. Recent Gallup polls showed that approximately 70 percent of the American people expressed a desire that the schools teach values as part of the educational process.[68]

All societies have some values that permeate the society and, as an agent of society, the school is obligated to transmit them to the young. History demonstrates that many of these values have been those cherished by the American people, including loyalty, self-discipline, honesty, and hard work. The existing morality of a society is called the *moral consensus*. However, each individual must develop his or her personal system of values through applying rules and principles to moral situations and making decisions that result in a *moral sense*. Oser, expressing the views of Durkheim, stated that

> Society must protect moral and social values and not leave them to free rationalization. Values like the protection of life, the procedural forms of a democracy, and the dignity of a person cannot be reconsidered in such a way that everybody is free to choose or not to choose them. The core assumption is that nobody, as long as he is willing to be a member of a society, can reject fundamental societal and moral claims that are explicitly objects of the fundamental belief of such a society.[69]

At the same time, teachers and students as individuals are confronted day-by-day by different moral problems involving truth, integrity, and commitment.[70] Oser concluded that moral education has been greatly neglected in the schools.[71] He also said:

> The inescapable reality is that the school setting is always a moral enterprise; the inescapable fact is that social and political life is filled with moral content, and that history encompasses millions of moral decisions with which we as educators have to deal, not only as scientists but also as people. This burden stands against the claim that all education should be value free.[72]

Kahn and Weiss aptly summarized the conclusions of the proponents of affective education as follows: "Education cannot afford the luxury of having its most important affective outcomes occur as accidents or unintended effects of the curriculum and of school life in general."[73]

Physical education is an especially appropriate place to teach moral education. A position statement by the American Academy of Physical Education urged physical educators to encourage and support the following:

1. That the development of moral and ethical values be stated among the aims of the physical education program;
2. That the educational preparation of physical education teachers and athletic coaches emphasize moral and ethical values;
3. That the emphasis on the teaching of moral and ethical values by physical education teachers and athletic coaches be encouraged;
4. That the profession of physical education establish criteria for the selection of appropriate ethical and moral values, develop formal plans of instruction, and develop methods for the assessment of results.[74]

Klausmeier and Goodwin suggested that the following attitudes are worth fostering: a liking for the subject, teachers, classmates, and for school generally; starting work promptly; working with enthusiasm and vigor; following directions; taking care of property; observing safety rules; and being courteous to others. Few disagree with the idea of fostering self-respect in pupils, respect for others, open-mindedness, freedom from prejudice, and the promotion of individuality and self-actualization.[75]

Leona Holbrook, a prominent philosopher in physical education, espoused twelve action values for physical education. They are:

1. Enjoying life
2. Realizing self
3. Helping others
4. Practicing honor—sportsmanship
5. Using moderation—emotional control
6. Developing excellence
7. Establishing personal habits—physical fitness
8. Cultivating breadth—aesthetics
9. Applying conservation
10. Esteeming work
11. Increasing productivity
12. Living spiritually[76]

Other values that have been proposed include cooperation and teamwork, tolerance of and respect for others, loyalty, fairness, integrity, dependability, unselfishness, self-control, responsibility for the consequences of one's behavior, friendliness, and thoughtfulness.

The Concept of Moral Discourse

Moral discourse is the common denominator of moral learning. Members participate in a discussion about problems of justice, through which each person learns to develop a personal point of view and, at the same time, consider the point of view of others.[77] Any solution to a moral problem must be understood in terms of the following four principles governing moral discourse:

1. The principle of *justification*, which implies that it is necessary to justify any course of action which concerns us;

2. The principle of *fairness,* which guarantees a just balance in the distribution of efforts and sacrifices;
3. The principle of *consequences,* which implies that everybody should anticipate the consequences of actions and of omissions;
4. The principle of *universalization,* which implies consistency in judgment and the will to take the role of the concerned persons (Golden Rule).[78] (italics added)

The Concept of a Moral Educational Situation

A moral educational situation is a situation created for educational purposes that demands a moral decision and has real consequences. According to Oser, moral education involves

> Teaching the use of rules and principles, regarding justice and respect in discourse, that enable us to defer personal success in favor of another person, a community, or a society. . . . There is a difference between the situation itself and the moral discourse. The discourse is always a step back from the reality of the situation. It is an ideal form of solving a moral problem. The moral situation is always bounded by time and other pressures; a decision must be made, an action taken. In order to act, the discourse has to be terminated and the decision has to be planned and implemented.[79]

The moral education situation must look at the circumstances, needs, motives, and interests of the person involved and apply the four principles discussed above—justification, fairness, consequences, and universalization.

The Distinction between Moral and Values Education

Values education usually refers to helping people become aware of their own values. Exercises are designed to help students achieve this awareness, but they lack the ability to help students develop a moral consensus through discourse or moral interaction.

Moral education commonly refers to a Kantian concept of justice. According to Rest, morality includes behavior that internalizes and conforms with social norms, helps others, puts their interests ahead of one's own, arouses guilt or empathy, or includes reasoning about justice.[80] One must base the decision not on right or wrong, but on the universal principles that guide moral behavior.

Learning Strategies for Moral Education

Oser analyzed current learning strategies for moral education on the basis of seven elements of educational moral situations:

1. The discourse should be directed to the *moral* conflict and to the stimulation of a higher level of moral judgment.
2. The discourse should be directed toward moral *role taking* and moral *empathy.*
3. The discourse should be oriented to *moral choice and action.*
4. The discourse should be directed toward *shared norms* and to a moral community (positive climate).
5. The discourse should be directed toward the *analysis* of moral situations and of value systems.
6. The discourse should be oriented toward the student's own reasoning and attitude change and psychological disposition (coping and defending).
7. The discourse should be directed toward one's theoretical moral knowledge (i.e., moral psychology, moral philosophy).[81]

Hersh, Paolitto, and Reimer presented the situation of a nine-year-old boy with cerebral paralysis whom the other students teased. One day when Brian was absent the teacher explained that some people are born with diseases that prevent them from using their muscles in a normal way. She wondered what it would be like to be Brian. The children empathized and reacted. When Brian returned, they were much more receptive and helpful.[82] An analysis of this situation shows how the seven elements above were included and explains the components of each element.

Element 1 Brian's situation involved a conflict in which two moral options competed with each other. The children talked openly about the moral conflict and Brian's and their own points of view. By presenting different arguments and opinions, a state of disequilibrium is stimulated in the learner, which promotes the development of higher moral judgment.

Kohlberg's *cognitive-development approach* is probably the most well-known model.[83] He proposed six levels of moral judgment and encouraged teaching moral judgment by stimulating a moral crisis or disequilibrium to guide the person to the next higher stage of moral judgment. This procedure is called a *plus-one strategy*. Kohlberg's system has been shown to be more effective than values clarification, probably due to the lack of clarity of values clarification strategies.[84] Preston used the Kohlbergian process to teach moral education in once-a-week sessions in health and physical education, with positive results.[85]

Element 2 Some children empathized with Brian and expressed how he might feel. One problem regarding the second element of role taking and moral empathy is that children may not be able to put themselves in another person's shoes and completely integrate the point of view of the other person. Students should exhaustively seek to imagine and evaluate the claims of the other person. Personal and altruistic claims must be resolved into a state of equilibrium. Role playing helps students develop sensitivity to the needs and feelings of others.

Element 3 Discussion led to an evaluation of previous actions versus what was just, and children changed their behavior as a result of the discussion. Students need to consider a justification for the correct action, the means for carrying out the action, the responsibility they are willing to accept, the psychological and social obstacles they might confront, and the social consequences of the action.[86]

Element 4 The interaction allowed the freedom to react openly, along with listening to the point of view of others. To accomplish the goals of moral education, students must have a warm, accepting atmosphere in which conversation rules are maintained and aggression is minimized.

Element 5 The teacher related similar instances in literature, politics, or history. Students should be led to analyze their own values and then the values of their peers, families, schools, and places of employment. Through literature, history, and politics, students can examine the value systems of their own society and of foreign cultures.[87]

Element 6 The children reflected changes in attitudes and feelings. Very little research has been done about analyzing one's own moral growth. To achieve this, the learners must look at their transformation from a previous stage to a new level and evaluate their own moral thinking and the thinking of the group, their style of argumentation, reasons for change, and defense strategies.

Element 7 The theoretical moral positions of philosophers, psychologists, and sociologists should be discussed so that students can identify the relationship of their own moral positions with those reflected by these disciplines. The teacher helped students use the instance of Brian and the instances found in the literature to understand a theoretical position about moral behavior.

Moral and Ethical Issues in Physical Education

Physical education lends itself readily to instruction in ethical principles. Figley suggested using Kohlberg's cognitive-development approach to help students progress to higher levels of moral reasoning and behavior.[88] Sport provides its own moral dilemmas in which disequilibrium exists between the actual and desired behavior of students. The physical educator, acting in a warm, accepting environment, can guide or facilitate student discussions about these dilemmas based on a regard for the worth and dignity of human beings and a concern for justice. Figley suggested that teacher verbalization might include statements such as "(a) have you thought about. . . ?, (b) let's listen to Rusty's reason for. . . , (c) how would you feel if. . . ?, and (d) what would happen if. . . ?"[89] Whether interacting with an individual, small group, or class, the teacher would attempt to help students understand (1) why the action was taken, (2) alternative behaviors that might have been used, (3) how all of the persons involved would feel in each of the alternative solutions, and (4) the most just solution to the situation the students are ready to accept. Kohlberg's techniques work best in an environment in which students have learned to trust one another and have had some experience in democratic processes, such as in setting class rules, ruling on transgressions, and setting sanctions.

Giebink and McKenzie used three strategies (instruction and praise, modeling, and a point system) to encourage the development of sportsmanship in a softball class.[90] They then proceeded to study the transfer effects to a recreational basketball setting. After baseline coding of behavior, the instruction and praise phase was conducted for five days. Students were asked to define and give examples of sportsmanship and provide positive and negative examples. Every day before playing the game, the teacher stressed fair play, complimenting teammates and opponents, and accepting consequences. During the game, he provided feedback on sportsmanlike and unsportsmanlike behavior. After the games, the students discussed their sportsmanship. The five-day modeling phase involved instruction and praise plus role playing and teacher participation in game play with appropriate behavior. The last five-day phase involved rewards for displaying sportsmanship. Following all three phases, baseline coding was resumed.

The results demonstrated that sportsmanship can be taught in physical education classes, with unsportsmanlike behaviors decreasing dramatically. The point system seemed to have the most effect. However, since the phases followed each other, there was undoubtedly a cumulative effect of the three techniques. The sportsmanlike behavior persisted into the second baseline period, but not at the level of the previous weeks. The learned behavior did not transfer to the basketball setting. However, with instruction, praise, and rewards, the unsportsmanlike behavior diminished considerably and the sportsmanlike behavior increased in that setting also. Giebink and McKenzie concluded that sportsmanship training must occur over a long period of time and in a variety of settings.

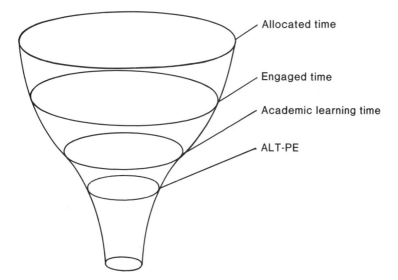

Figure 6.8 Measures of time.

Learner Involvement in Instruction

In describing the Beginning Teacher Evaluation Study (BTES) conducted in the mid-1970s, the research team concluded: "Teachers who find ways to put students into contact with the academic curriculum and to keep them in contact with that curriculum while maintaining a convivial classroom atmosphere are successful in promoting achievement. . . ."[91]

From these findings, the research team identified and studied three measures of time, each of which correlated more closely with academic achievement. *Allocated time* is the amount of time provided for instruction in a given subject area. Allocated time depends on the philosophy of the district, school, or department, as well as on the finances of the school.[92] *Engaged time* is the amount of time the student attends to instruction in a given subject. Engaged time primarily depends on the goals and managerial skills of the teacher.[93] *Academic learning time* (ALT) is the number of minutes the student is engaged with activities and instructional materials at an easy level for that student (generally a level of 80 percent success, which is essential for acquisition of the concepts and overlearning, both of which are essential for retention). Although the BTES showed a strong correlation between ALT and achievement, it varied for different subjects, objectives, grade levels, and teachers.[94]

Metzler modified the BTES instrument to measure ALT in physical education and measured the ALT-PE in a variety of physical education contexts.[95] His instrument measured student in-class behavior for the setting, content, learner movement, and difficulty level of the tasks being performed. He defined ALT-PE as "the amount of time students spend in class activity engaged in relevant overt motor responding at a high success rate." The variables of ALT-PE are task relevancy, motor engagement, and high success rate.[96]

Far less ALT was found in physical education than had previously been imagined and much of it was cognitive rather than psychomotor in nature. ALT-PE studies by Metzler and Godbout, Brunelle, and Tousignant found that about one-third of the allocated time was spent in activities at the appropriate level of difficulty.[97] Figure 6.9 graphically portrays their findings.

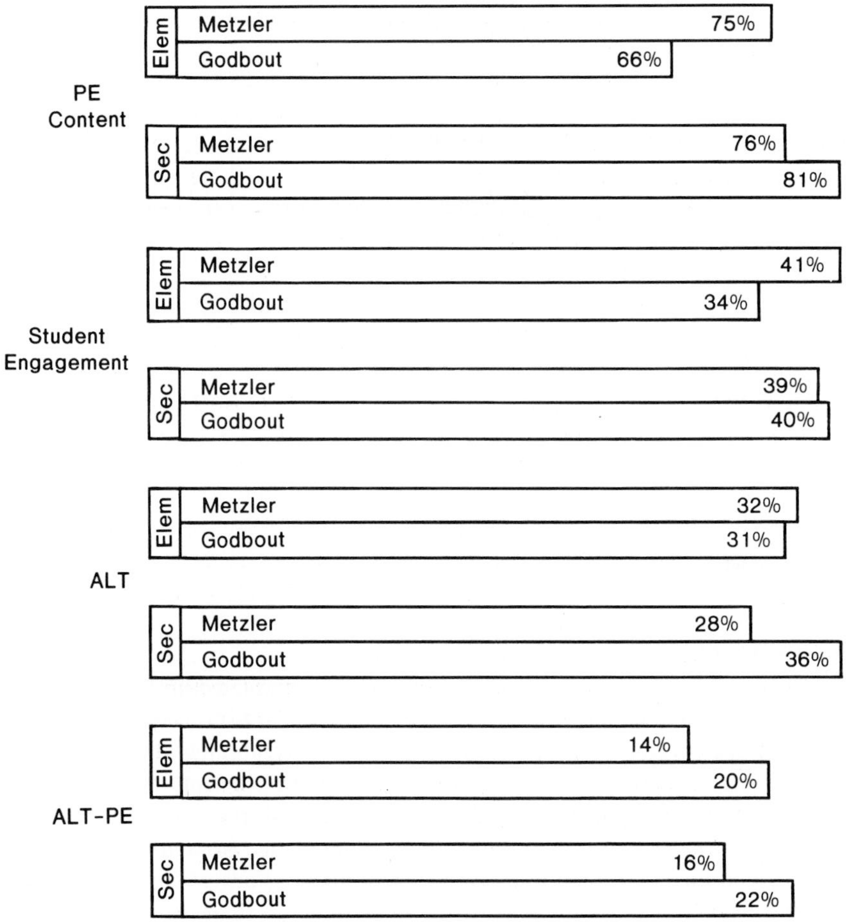

Figure 6.9 Comparison of "funneling effect" for students' time involvement in physical education classes.

Students have been found to spend a great deal of time waiting for turns, chasing balls, doing easy rather than challenging movement activities, and in management and transition between activities. Some studies have shown differences in ALT-PE between boys and girls and students of different skill levels, with boys and higher-skilled learners often having higher levels of ALT-PE. Differences in ALT-PE have also been noted for male and female teachers and for teachers using different instructional strategies.[98]

ALT-PE is an indirect strategy for evaluating teacher effectiveness. The effectiveness of ALT-PE research is contingent on the assumption that ALT in physical education correlates with student achievement as it does in academic subjects. A few studies have attempted to prove this relationship. Graham summarized five studies and found that practice time on the criterion task correlated with student learning.[99] Silverman found that the number and appropriateness of practice trials correlated significantly with student achievement.[100]

Recent studies involving cognitive learning have shown that student-reported attention and understanding and their use of specific cognitive strategies correlate with achievement better than time-on-task. In any case, student constructive use of time is more important than allocated time.[101]

Some relatively simple changes in teacher behavior have been shown to increase ALT-PE. Programs that teach teachers to reduce management and student nonengagement time and to increase feedback to students increase the engaged skill learning time. One study discovered that pupils of student teachers with early field experiences had significantly greater ALT than their counterparts with no prior experience.[102]

Because a highly active environment in physical education can exist without quality instruction, ALT-PE cannot be used exclusively to assess teacher effectiveness. Although ALT-PE is essential for learning, it is not sufficient by itself to cause learning.[103]

In addition to studying ALT, Dodds also analyzed the teacher behaviors that accompanied student engagement. They fell primarily into instruction (50 percent), praise (17 percent), and cues (15 percent). Some teacher behaviors regularly appeared with particular student behaviors. For example, instruction, criticism, and modeling mistakes correlated positively with students being in a content-PE knowledge mode. Praise correlated positively with student skill practice. Dodds suggested that future studies consider ways in which instructional time can be reduced and individual skill practice time increased, such as by praising students while they are waiting for turns.[104]

The results of this research indicate that instruction should be provided in a way that allows maximum participation by each student. With the reduction in funding for education, teachers must creatively manage large classes in limited spaces with inadequate equipment. The organization of time, space, equipment, rules, and group size all affect the amount of time each student has to participate in the activity and, therefore, to achieve success.

Involvement in challenging learning activities contributes to the opportunity for success and keeps students busily engaged in positive behavior with little or no time or incentive for irrational, unruly behavior. Talking rather than doing contributes to boredom, inattention, and deviant behavior. Bertel suggested an excellent way to obtain maximum participation and increase the fun of an activity. It involves starting an activity just as it might have been played by its inventors and then adding rules, skills, and strategies as the need arises. Once the students become involved, they will want to learn more. For example, basketball can be played with peach baskets or the old rules of three dribbles before passing or shooting.[105]

Time

Because time is at a premium in most physical education classes, time spent in noninstructional activities such as roll call, equipment distribution and collection, unnecessary showering, or dressing for activity should be minimized. Many physical educators could also reduce teacher talk by using more effective demonstrations with cues, thereby increasing student practice time.

Lay reminded teachers that "students learn by doing." However, observation of physical education classes might lead one to conclude that learning occurs through a magical verbal transmission from the teacher. She remarked:

> In some classes so much time is spent talking about a skill that there is virtually no
> time left to actually practice the activity. Beginning classes, particularly, suffer from a
> teacher who talks too much. For the most part, beginning classes could be conducted in

silence. Beginners need demonstrations and then opportunities to practice. It is useless to analyze skills for beginners until they have an opportunity to try the skill for themselves. An interesting study . . . indicated that students paid least attention when the teacher was talking and most attention when the students were actually performing.[106]

Well-planned lessons also eliminate time spent in transitions from one activity to another. Other suggestions for increasing the actual student learning time are included in each of the areas below.

Space

Facilities in physical education have not always kept up with the demand, resulting in large classes in facilities built for a few students. By making use of community and commercial facilities as well as hallways and multipurpose rooms, some additional space can be acquired. Often teachers can share a gym and a classroom and take turns teaching concepts or other activities that can be taught in a small room so that the other class can spread out in the gym to play activities requiring large areas. However, physical education teachers have often ignored the possibility of adjusting group sizes among themselves to fit the spaces available. For example, if two instructors have a class of eighty and only four tennis courts, they could divide the students into one group of sixty or more to learn soccer so that the other twenty or so can be instructed in tennis. Another possibility is to offer two units simultaneously. For example, a sport such as badminton and a fitness activity such as jump rope could be offered in one facility, or a team sport such as softball and an individual or dual activity such as tennis could be taught in adjacent teaching stations. Some students could jog while others work on skills. Students could then rotate between the activities.

Students could use inactive time to work on study sheets; learn rules or fitness concepts; take written, skills, or fitness tests; study films or videotapes of themselves or effective skill models; or work on personalized learning activities. Learning centers can be used to teach concepts. A learning center is a station at which students work individually or as teams to discover psychomotor or cognitive principles and skills related to sport.[107] Students could also officiate, mark ratings on incidence charts, or work on skill checklists. Students should rotate into games at planned intervals. An example of tennis stations incorporating this concept might include the following: At station one, a hitter-tosser-receiver drill is done. Tossers throw to the forehand or backhand side and hitters stroke the ball. Retrievers return the balls to the tossers. At station two, the ball-on-a-string drill is done. Students practice forehand and backhand strokes using a ball attached to a weight on the court with a string or shock cord. After each stroke the ball springs back to be hit again. Station three consists of balls attached by shock cords to the bottom of volleyball or other standards. Students serve and the ball comes back to the post. The fourth station consists of partner volley practice through a hula hoop attached to the net. Other students could be practicing on the courts.

Equipment

Maximum participation requires appropriate quantities of equipment. To experience success, each student must have an adequate opportunity to practice with sport-related equipment on a one-to-one basis. In drills and games, an attempt should be made to decrease the number of participants interacting with each piece of equipment and to increase the number of pieces of equipment. Teachers should provide for maximum use of equipment within the limits of safety and practicality. Using various kinds and sizes of balls can increase the chances of success and the amount of equipment available. A large number of inexpensive yarn balls, plastic balls, or foam training balls could replace a few of the more expensive balls. Jones summarized some of the problems of inadequate equipment as follows:

> . . . having students practice with balls, striking implements, bows, or other equipment that is too heavy or cumbersome may be particularly deleterious to proper acquisition of skill. For example, a bowling instructor may furnish a perfect demonstration model of the four-step approach and delivery and use excellent teaching cues, but all of this will go for naught on a student who is struggling just to hang on to a fourteen pound ball. Other examples observed far too often in physical education classes include: tennis racquets too heavy for youngsters to handle properly, archery bows too heavy to be drawn correctly, balls too big or heavy and baskets too high for correct execution of skills by the students involved. In volleyball, a student may be reluctant to practice the forearm or bump pass correctly because it hurts his arms.[108]

When appropriate quantities of equipment are unavailable, several options exist. The best is to obtain the needed equipment through the school budget. When this is impossible, students can be asked to bring equipment (such as softball gloves) from home. Parents are often willing to donate unused equipment cluttering their closets. Occasionally, hand-me-downs from college or professional teams can be obtained. Fund-raising or solicitations from local businesses are allowed in some districts, while booster clubs or parent-teacher organizations may supply the need in others. When all else fails, teachers and students should repair all usable equipment and adapt or make other equipment whenever possible. Many fitness activities work well with improvised equipment. Broomstick or wand activities can be used to develop agility, flexibility, and strength by jumping over the stick, or doing partner pull-ups or stick wrestling.

Activities that require little or no equipment include dance (aerobic, square, folk, social, modern), fitness (jogging, relays, races, calisthenics), and most team sports. Drills can be created in which players practice different roles at the same time, such as one student dribbling and one guarding; or one student shooting with several others rebounding.

Modified team sport games could include small-group activities such as "bull in the pen" or "volley keep-away" in which a player in the center of a circle attempts to intercept the basketball or volleyball, or "keep-it-up" in which five or six players count the number of consecutive volleys, or dribbling around live players (who may guard without moving their feet) rather than cones.

Dual sport drills can be made into games such as badminton "keep-away" in which two players near the net attempt to intercept overhead clears hit too low, or "racquet switch" in which foursomes hit overhead clears back and forth, with partners passing one racquet back and forth between them after each stroke. These drills use only two racquets for four players and stimulate correct use of skills. Wall or backboard volleys and fitness drills can also be used by those without room to play on courts.

Safety and legal liability should always be considered when using improvised equipment, especially in high-risk activities such as gymnastics or archery.

Students can be grouped in pairs with one tutoring the other and one piece of equipment per pair or in threesomes with a tosser, a hitter, and a retriever as in tennis or volleyball or with a performer and two spotters as in tumbling. Students can also be assigned as coaches, referees, scorekeepers, or statisticians for teams and rotated periodically.

Stations, at which students practice different activities, can be used to learn sport skills using different pieces of apparatus or equipment. For example, fitness stations could be alternated with one or two courts, a skills test station, a written quiz, videotape or loop film viewing, and wall or backboard hitting. Students rotate every three to five minutes.

Rules

By changing game rules, students can experience all of the facets of the game in a shorter period of time. For example, a seven-inning "one-swing" softball game can be played in one class period, whereas in a regulation game, some students will "sit" in left field for the entire period waiting for a turn at bat. When pitchers pitch to their own teams, batters learn to hit and offensive and defensive action increases significantly. Lowering the volleyball net allows players who have never been able to spike to enjoy that aspect of the game. Games can be played using only the overhead pass in order to practice it more, or only underhand serves to provide for better volleys. The game may be scored differently to achieve different purposes. For example, score the number of times students bump pass successfully. By eliminating the spike, the scoring could be changed so that instead of each team trying to be the first to gain fifteen points, the goal is to accumulate the highest number of hits back and forth across the net in a specified time period. This would get both teams cooperating and encouraging each other to perform well. This concept of rule adaptations can be applied to all activities. The number of players, the purpose of the game, the dimensions of the playing area, and the rules can all be changed to allow for greater numbers of students to participate and to concentrate on specific skills. In basketball, eliminate jump balls and free throws and play three-on-three. In tennis, play with four people on a side. Modified games such as pickle ball (similar to tennis on a badminton-sized court) and volley tennis (played with a volleyball or playground ball on a tennis court) can be excellent ways to develop both teamwork and sport skills. The book *How to Change the Games Children Play* outlines different ways to analyze and modify many contemporary activities taught in physical education.[109]

Group Size

By keeping teams small, students will have the opportunity to play the ball more often. The use of many smaller teams, on smaller fields if necessary, provides the opportunities students need to apply skills to game situations. Games such as five-pass keepaway (in which teams earn a point for every five consecutive passes by one team without an interception), three-on-three basketball, or seven-player soccer provide many opportunities for contact with the ball by each player. Relay teams should be kept to a few players to avoid waiting for a turn.

In this chapter, learning strategies advocated by educational researchers for each of the three domains of learning have been presented, followed by a discussion of how to maximize learner involvement in instruction.

Questions and Suggested Activities

1. What is an optimum learning task for students? How can a task be adjusted to increase or decrease its level of difficulty?
2. Explain Gentile's model for teaching motor skills.
3. What differences exist between rote learning and meaningful verbal learning? Which type is best for learning facts? For learning principles?
4. List some concepts that you might teach when explaining a sport or game.

5. List some examples of problem solving that might help students learn the principles of biomechanics in sport activities?
6. When might cognitive learning strategies be helpful in physical education?
7. Why is it important to teach the "why" along with the "how" of physical activity? How can this be accomplished?
8. Freud once said that "No one ever does anything unless he would rather." What does this statement suggest about affective learning?
9. How can you tell whether a student feels good about physical education? How can you increase the chances of a student feeling good about physical education?
10. Why is self-efficacy important in learning motor skills? How is it acquired?
11. How can moral and character education be increased? What values might best be taught in physical education?
12. What can be done to maximize student learning in the following situations:
    a. You are teaching a basketball unit to forty-five eighth graders. You have only one court and wish to let the students have the opportunity of playing a three-day tournament on a full court. What will you do with the students who are not active in the game?
    b. You are teaching a badminton unit to forty-five ninth graders. You have three courts. How will you provide for all players to practice fundamentals? How will you keep every student active and succeed in letting each student have the opportunity to play a regulation game?
    c. During inclement weather all physical education classes must be moved to the auxiliary gym because of water leakage. Repair to the main gym will not be completed for another four weeks. You have just started a volleyball unit with your ninth graders, and you barely have enough room for forty-five students participating on one full-size court. How will you make sure everyone gets an opportunity to play a regulation game? Consider time, space, equipment, rules, and group size.

Suggested Readings

American Alliance for Health, Physical Education, Recreation and Dance. *Basic Stuff Series.* Reston, Virginia: AAHPERD, 1981 and 1987.

Bean, David. "Outdoor Games Teaching: A Key to Effectiveness." *Journal of Physical Education, Recreation and Dance* 54 (November/December 1983):54–56.

Bertel, H. "Try What? Introduction of a New Activity in the Physical Education Class." *Journal of Health, Physical Education, and Recreation* 45 (May 1974):24.

Brown, Eugene W. "Visual Evaluation Techniques for Skill Analysis." *Journal of Physical Education, Recreation and Dance* 53 (January 1982):21–26, 29.

Corbin, Charles B., et al. *Concepts in Physical Education with Laboratories and Experiments,* 4th ed. Dubuque, Iowa: Wm. C. Brown Company Publishers, 1981.

Corbin, C. *Inexpensive Equipment for Games, Play and Physical Activity.* Dubuque, Iowa: Wm. C. Brown Company Publishers, 1972.

———. *Fitness for Life: Physical Education Concepts.* Glenview, Ill.: Scott, Foresman and Company, 1979.

Docherty, David, and Les Peake. "Creatrad: An Approach to Teaching Games." *Journal of Physical Education and Recreation* 47 (April 1976):20–22.

Edington, D. W., and Lee Cunningham. "More on Applied Physiology of Exercise." *Journal of Physical Education and Recreation* 45 (February 1974):18.

Feltz, Deborah L., and Maureen R. Weiss. "Developing Self-Efficacy through Sport." *Journal of Physical Education, Recreation and Dance* 53 (March 1982):24–26, 36.

Figley, Grace E. "Moral Education through Physical Education." *Quest* 36 (1984):89–101.

Gabbard, Carl. "Teaching Motor Skills to Children: Theory into Practice." *The Physical Educator* 41 (May 1984):69–71.

Gillam, G. McKenzie. "Back to the 'Basics' of Physical Education." *The Physical Educator* 42 (Fall 1985):129–33.

Kneer, Marian E. "How Human Are You? Exercises in Awareness." *Journal of Health, Physical Education, and Recreation* (June 1974):32–33.

Lamke, Gene G. "Leisure Sports for Family Participation." *Journal of Physical Education, Recreation and Dance* 55 (October 1984):61–62.

Lay, Nancy. "Practical Application of Selected Motor Learning Research." *Journal of Physical Education and Recreation* 50 (September 1979):78–79.

Lewandowski, Diane M. "Shoestrings and Shoeboxes." *Journal of Physical Education, Recreation and Dance* 55 (August 1984):34–35.

Lichtman, Brenda. "Motor Schema: Putting Theory into Action." *Journal of Physical Education, Recreation and Dance* 55 (March 1984):54–56.

Marlowe, Mike. "Motor Experiences through Games Analysis." *Journal of Physical Education and Recreation* 52 (January 1981):78–80.

McVaigh, Betty. "Lead with Rules, Don't Let Them Lead You." *The Physical Educator* 39 (May 1982):86.

Melville, Scott. "Teaching and Evaluating Cognitive Skills." *Journal of Physical Education, Recreation and Dance* 56 (February 1985):26–28.

Morris, G. S. Don. *How to Change the Games Children Play,* 2d ed. Minneapolis: Burgess Publishing Company, 1980.

Pangrazi, Robert. "Physical Education, Self-Concept, and Achievement." *Journal of Physical Education, Recreation and Dance* 53 (November/December 1982):16–18.

Peterson, Susan C. "Softball Without Strikes." *Journal of Physical Education, Recreation and Dance* 52 (September 1981):72.

Ratliffe, Tom. "Evaluation of Students' Skill using Generic Levels of Skill Proficiency." *The Physical Educator* 41 (May 1982):64–68.

Rich, Sarah M., and Deborah A. Wuest. "Self-Confidence and the Physically Handicapped Mainstreamed Child." *The Physical Educator* 40 (October 1983):163–65.

Rink, Judith E. "The Teacher Wants Us to Learn." *Journal of Physical Education and Recreation* 52 (February 1981):17–18.

Romance, Thomas J. "Observing for Confidence." *Journal of Physical Education, Recreation and Dance* 56 (August 1985):47–49.

Seidel, Beverly L., Fay R. Biles, Grace E. Figley, and Bonnie J. Neuman. *Sports Skills: A Conceptual Approach to Meaningful Movement,* 2d ed. Dubuque, Iowa: Wm. C. Brown Company Publishers, 1980.

Templin, Thomas J., and Maria T. Allison. "The Sportsmanship Dilemma." *The Physical Educator* 39 (December 1982):204–7.

Turner, Robert B., and William W. Purkey. "Teaching Physical Education: An Invitational Approach." *Journal of Physical Education, Recreation and Dance* 54 (September 1983):13–14, 64.

Young, Jane F. "When Practice Doesn't Make Perfect—Improving Game Performance in Secondary Level Physical Education Classes." *Journal of Physical Education, Recreation and Dance* 56 (October 1985):24–26.

References

1. Susan Harter, "Effectance Motivation Reconsidered: Toward a Developmental Model," *Human Development* 21 (1978), pp. 34–64.
2. Paul M. Fitts, "Factors in Complex Skill Training," in Robert Glaser, ed., *Training Research and Education* (Pittsburgh: University of Pittsburgh Press, 1962), pp. 177–97.

3. M. David Merrill, "Psychomotor Taxonomies, Classifications, and Instructional Theory," in Robert N. Singer, ed., *The Psychomotor Domain: Movement Behaviors* (Philadelphia: Lea and Febiger, 1972), pp. 385–414.

4. Shirl J. Hoffman, Charles H. Imwold, and John A. Koller, "Accuracy and Prediction in Throwing: A Taxonomic Analysis of Children's Performance," *Research Quarterly for Exercise and Sport* 54 (March 1983), pp. 33–40.

5. Judith E. Rink, *Teaching Physical Education for Learning* (St. Louis, Missouri: C. V. Mosby Company, 1985), pp. 101–10.

6. George Graham, Shirley Ann Holt/Hale, Tim McEwen, and Melissa Parker, *Children Moving: A Reflective Approach to Teaching Physical Education* (Palo Alto, California: Mayfield Publishing Company, 1980).

7. Fitts, "Factors in Complex Skill Training," pp. 177–97.

8. A. M. Gentile, "A Working Model of Skill Acquisition with Application to Teaching," *Quest* 17 (January 1972), pp. 3–23.

9. Nancy Lay, "Practical Application of Selected Motor Learning Research," *Journal of Physical Education and Recreation* 50 (September 1979), pp. 78–79.

10. Gentile, "A Working Model of Skill Acquisition," p. 15.

11. Rink, *Teaching Physical Education for Learning,* p. 218.

12. Anne Rothstein, Linda Catelli, Patt Dodds, and Joan Manahan, *Basic Stuff Series I: Motor Learning* (Reston, Virginia: AAHPERD, 1981), pp. 31–32.

13. Neal F. Earls, "Research on the Immediate Effects of Instructional Variables," in Thomas J. Templin and Janice K. Olson, eds., *Teaching in Physical Education* (Champaign, Illinois: Human Kinetics Publishers, 1983), pp. 254–64.

14. Scott Melville, "Process Feedback Made Simple," *The Physical Educator* 40 (May 1983), pp. 95–104.

15. Patricia DelRey, "Appropriate Feedback for Open and Closed Skill Acquisition," *Quest* 17 (1972), pp. 42–45; and Melville, "Process Feedback Made Simple."

16. Gentile, "A Working Model of Skill Acquisition," p. 15.

17. Ibid.

18. Rothstein, Catelli, Dodds, and Manahan, *Basic Stuff Series I: Motor Learning,* p. 52.

19. Earls, "Research on the Immediate Effects of Instructional Variables."

20. Jane F. Young, "When Practice Doesn't Make Perfect—Improving Game Performance in Secondary Level Physical Education Classes," *Journal of Physical Education, Recreation and Dance* 56 (October 1985), pp. 24–26; and Carl Gabbard, "Teaching Motor Skills to Children: Theory into Practice," *The Physical Educator* 41 (May 1984), pp. 69–71.

21. Young, "When Practice Doesn't Make Perfect," p. 93.

22. Brenda Lichtman, "Motor Schema: Putting Theory into Action," *Journal of Physical Education, Recreation and Dance* 55 (March 1984), pp. 54–56.

23. Lichtman, "Motor Schema: Putting Theory into Action."

24. Barbara D. Lockhart, "The Basic Stuff Series: Why and How," *Journal of Physical Education, Recreation and Dance* 53 (September 1982), pp. 18–19, (p. 18).

25. Dorothy R. Mohr, "Identifying the Body of Knowledge," *Journal of Health, Physical Education, and Recreation* 42 (January 1971), p. 23.

26. Ibid., p. 24.

27. American Alliance for Health, Physical Education, Recreation and Dance, *Basic Stuff Series* (Reston, Virginia: AAHPERD, 1981 and 1987).

28. Hal A. Lawson, "Change, Controversy, and Criticism in the Profession," *Journal of Physical Education, Recreation and Dance* 53 (September 1982), pp. 30–34.

29. Helen M. Heitmann, "Integrating Concepts into Curricular Models," *Journal of Physical Education, Recreation and Dance* 52 (February 1981), pp. 42–45.

30. Katherine Ley, "Teaching Understandings in Physical Education," *Journal of Health, Physical Education, and Recreation* 42 (January 1971), pp. 21–22.

31. Robert M. Gagné, *The Conditions of Learning and Theory of Instruction,* 4th ed. (New York: Holt, Rinehart and Winston, 1985), p. 47.

32. Ibid., p. 48.

33. Pauline Grippin and Sean Peters, *Learning Theory and Learning Outcomes: The Connection* (New York: University Press of America,® Inc., 1984), pp. 194–97.
34. Ibid., p. 208.
35. Merlin C. Wittrock, "Students' Thought Processes," in Merlin C. Wittrock, ed., *Handbook of Research on Teaching,* 3d ed. (New York: Macmillan Publishing Company, 1986), p. 308.
36. Marleen J. Doctorow, M. C. Wittrock, and Carolyn B. Marks, "Generative Processes in Reading Comprehension," *Journal of Educational Psychology* 70 (1978), pp. 109–18.
37. Scott G. Paris, Barbara K. Lindauer, and Gloria L. Cox, "The Development of Inferential Comprehension," *Child Development* 48 (December 1977), pp. 1728–33.
38. John P. Rickards and G. J. August, "Generative Underlining Strategies in Prose Recall," *Journal of Educational Psychology* 67 (December 1975), pp. 860–65.
39. David P. Ausubel, *The Psychology of Meaningful Verbal Learning: An Introduction to School Learning* (New York: Grune & Stratton, 1963), p. 16.
40. Grippin and Peters, *Learning Theory and Learning Outcomes,* p. 177.
41. Mohr, "Identifying the Body of Knowledge," p. 24.
42. Rink, *Teaching Physical Education for Learning,* pp. 123, 126–29.
43. Grippin and Peters, *Learning Theory and Learning Outcomes,* p. 141.
44. Benjamin S. Bloom and Lois J. Broder, *Problem-Solving Processes of College Students: An Exploratory Investigation,* Supplementary Educational Monographs, no. 73 (Chicago: University of Chicago Press, 1950), p. 25.
45. Bryce B. Hudgins, *Problem Solving in the Classroom* (New York: Macmillan Publishing Company, 1966), p. 43.
46. Grippin and Peters, *Learning Theory and Learning Outcomes,* p. 179.
47. Ibid., pp. 142–45.
48. John H. Flavell, "Metacognitive Aspects of Problem Solving," in L. B. Resnick, ed., *The Nature of Intelligence* (Hillsdale, New Jersey: Lawrence Erlbaum Associates, Publishers, 1976), p. 232.
49. Grippin and Peters, *Learning Theory and Learning Outcomes,* p. 137.
50. Claire E. Weinstein and Richard E. Mayer, "The Teaching of Learning Strategies," in Merlin C. Wittrock, ed., *Handbook of Research on Teaching,* 3d ed. (New York: Macmillan Publishing Company, 1986), pp. 315–27, (p. 315).
51. Donald A. Norman, "Cognitive Engineering and Education," in D. T. Tuma and F. Reif, eds., *Problem Solving and Education: Issues in Teaching and Research* (Hillsdale, New Jersey: Lawrence Erlbaum Associates, Publishers, 1980), pp. 97–107, (p. 97).
52. Weinstein and Mayer, "The Teaching of Learning Strategies," p. 315.
53. Ibid., p. 316.
54. Joseph D. Novak and D. Bob Gowin, *Learning How to Learn* (Cambridge: Cambridge University Press, 1984).
55. Joseph D. Novak, D. Bob Gowin, and Gerald T. Johansen, "The Use of Concept Mapping and Knowledge Vee Mapping with Junior High School Science Students," *Science Education* 67(5) (1983), pp. 625–45.
56. Ron French, "The Use of Homework as a Supportive Technique in Physical Education," *The Physical Educator* 36 (May 1979), p. 84.
57. Lowell A. Klappholz, ed., "Half the PE Grade Is Based on Outside Activity," *Physical Education Newsletter* (November 1980).
58. David A. Cameron, "Who Plays Basketball? Bonus Incentive Plans—A Learning Stimulus," *The Physical Educator* 42 (Late Winter 1986), pp. 151–55.
59. Weinstein and Mayer, "The Teaching of Learning Strategies," p. 324.
60. Robert F. Mager, *Developing Attitude Toward Learning* (Palo Alto, California: Fearon Publishers, 1965), pp. 50–57.
61. Jere Brophy, "Successful Teaching Strategies for the Inner-City Child," *Phi Delta Kappan* 63 (1982), pp. 527–30.
62. Donald W. Felker, *Building Positive Self Concepts* (Minneapolis: Burgess Publishing Company, 1974).
63. Thomas J. Romance, "Observing for Confidence," *Journal of Physical Education, Recreation and Dance* 56 (August 1985), pp. 47–49.

64. Elizabeth S. Bressan and Maureen R. Weiss, "A Theory of Instruction for Developing Competence, Self-Confidence and Persistence in Physical Education," *Journal of Teaching in Physical Education* 2 (Fall 1982), pp. 38–47.

65. Deborah L. Feltz and Maureen R. Weiss, "Developing Self-Efficacy through Sport," *Journal of Physical Education, Recreation and Dance* 53 (March 1982), pp. 24–26, 36.

66. Roland G. Tharp and Ronald Gallimore, "Basketball's John Wooden: What a Coach Can Teach a Teacher," *Psychology Today* 9 (January 1976), pp. 75–77.

67. Fritz K. Oser, "Moral Education and Values Education: The Discourse Perspective," in Merlin C. Wittrock, ed., *Handbook of Research on Teaching,* 3d ed. (New York: Macmillan Publishing Company, 1986), pp. 917–41.

68. George H. Gallup, "The 13th Annual Gallup Poll of the Public's Attitudes Toward the Public Schools," *Phi Delta Kappan* 63 (September 1981), p. 39.

69. Emile E. Durkheim, *Moral Education: A Study in the Theory and Application of the Sociology of Education,* (New York: Free Press of Glencoe, 1961), in Oser, "Moral Education and Values Education," p. 144.

70. Deana Pritchard Paolitto, "The Role of the Teacher in Moral Education," *Theory into Practice* 16 (April 1977), pp. 73–80.

71. Oser, "Moral Education and Values Education," p. 919.

72. Ibid., pp. 935–36.

73. S. B. Kahn and J. Weiss, "The Teaching of Affective Responses," in R. M. Travers, ed., *Second Handbook of Research on Teaching* (Chicago: Rand McNally & Company, 1973), p. 789.

74. American Academy of Physical Education, *The Academy Papers: Reunification,* Reston, Virginia (October 1981), pp. 107–8.

75. Klausmeier, H. J. and W. Goodwin, *Learning and Human Abilities,* 2d ed. (New York: Harper and Row, 1966), cited in Thomas A. Ringness, *The Affective Domain in Education* (Boston: Little, Brown & Company, 1975), p. 25.

76. Joy Griffin, "Developing Ideas for Teaching Values in the Physical Education Curriculum," Master's thesis, Brigham Young University, 1981.

77. Oser, "Moral Education and Values Education," p. 919.

78. Monika Keller and Siegfried Reuss, "The Process of Moral Decision-Making: Normative and Empirical Conditions of Participation in Moral Discourse," in Marvin W. Berkowitz and Fritz Oser, eds., *Moral Education: Theory and Application* (Hillsdale, New Jersey: Lawrence Erlbaum Associates, Publishers, 1985), pp. 109–23, (p. 110).

79. Oser, "Moral Education and Values Education," p. 920.

80. James R. Rest, "Morality," in John H. Flavell and Ellen M. Markman, eds., *Handbook of Child Psychology, Volume 3: Cognitive Development* (New York: John Wiley & Sons, 1983), pp. 556–629, (p. 556).

81. Oser, "Moral Education and Values Education," p. 921.

82. Richard H. Hersh, Diana Pritchard Paolitto, and Joseph Reimer, *Promoting Moral Growth: From Piaget to Kohlberg* (New York: Longman, Inc., 1979), p. 4.

83. Lawrence Kohlberg, "The Just Community Approach to Moral Education in Theory and Practice," in Marvin W. Berkowitz and Fritz Oser, eds., *Moral Education: Theory and Application* (Hillsdale, New Jersey: Lawrence Erlbaum Associates, Publishers, 1985), pp. 27–87.

84. James S. Leming, "Curricular Effectiveness in Moral/Values Education: A Review of Research," *Journal of Moral Education* 10 (May 1981), pp. 147–64; and Alan A. Lockwood, "The Effects of Value Clarification and Moral Development Curricula on School-age Subjects: A Critical Review of Recent Research," *Review of Educational Research* 48 (Summer 1978), pp. 325–64.

85. Diane Preston, "A Moral Education Program Conducted in the Physical Education and Health Education Curriculum," EdD dissertation, University of Georgia, 1979.

86. Oser, "Moral Education and Values Education," p. 929.

87. Ibid., p. 931.

88. Grace E. Figley, "Moral Education through Physical Education," *Quest* 36 (1984), pp. 89–101.

89. Ibid., p. 97.

90. M. Patricia Giebink and Thomas L. McKenzie, "Teaching Sportsmanship in Physical Education and Recreation: An Analysis of Interventions and Generalization Effects," *Journal of Teaching in Physical Education* 4 (April 1985), pp. 167–77.

91. David C. Berliner, "Tempus Educare," in Penelope L. Peterson and Herbert J. Walberg, eds., *Research on Teaching: Concepts, Findings, and Implications* (Berkeley, California: McCutchan Publishing Corporation, 1979), pp. 120–35.

92. Jere E. Brophy, "Teacher Behavior and Its Effect," *Journal of Educational Psychology* 71 (1979), pp. 733–50.

93. Ibid.

94. C. Fisher, N. Filby, R. Marliave, L. Cahen, M. Dishaw, J. Moore, and D. Berliner, *Teaching Behaviors, Academic Learning Time, and Student Achievement: Final Report of Phase III-B, Beginning Teacher Evaluation Study* (San Francisco: Far West Laboratory for Educational Research and Development, 1978).

95. Michael W. Metzler, "The Measurement of Academic Learning Time in Physical Education," Doctoral dissertation, Ohio State University, 1979 (University Microfilms No. 8009314).

96. Michael W. Metzler, "Adapting the Academic Learning Time Instructional Model to Physical Education Teaching," *Journal of Teaching in Physical Education* 1 (1982), pp. 44–55.

97. Metzler, "The Measurement of Academic Learning Time in Physical Education"; and Paul Godbout, Jean Brunelle, and Marielle Tousignant, "Academic Learning Time in Elementary and Secondary Physical Education Classes," *Research Quarterly for Exercise and Sport* 54 (1983), pp. 11–19.

98. Joyce M. Harrison, "A Review of the Research on Teacher Effectiveness and Its Implications for Current Practice," *Quest* (April 1987), pp. 36–55.

99. George Graham, "Review and Implications of Physical Education Experimental Teaching Unit Research," in Thomas J. Templin and Janice K. Olson, eds., *Teaching in Physical Education* (Champaign, Illinois: Human Kinetics Publishers, 1983), pp. 244–53.

100. Stephen Silverman, "Relationship of Engagement and Practice Trials to Student Achievement," *Journal of Teaching in Physical Education* 5 (1985), pp. 13–21.

101. Merlin C. Wittrock, "Students' Thought Processes," in Merlin C. Wittrock, ed., *Handbook of Research on Teaching,* 3d ed. (New York: Macmillan Publishing Company, 1986), pp. 297–314.

102. Joyce M. Harrison, "A Review of the Research on Teacher Effectiveness and Its Implications for Current Practice."

103. Rink, *Teaching Physical Education for Learning,* p. 268.

104. Pat Dodds, "Relationships Between Academic Learning Time and Teacher Behaviors in a Physical Education Majors Skills Class," in Thomas J. Templin and Janice K. Olson, eds., *Teaching in Physical Education* (Champaign, Illinois: Human Kinetics Publishers, 1983), pp. 173–84.

105. Budd Bertel, "Try What? Introduction of a New Activity in the Physical Education Class," *Journal of Health, Physical Education, and Recreation* 45 (May 1974), p. 24.

106. Lay, "Practical Application of Selected Motor Learning Research."

107. Joyce K. Espiritu and Thomas J. Loughrey, "The Learning Center Approach to Physical Education Instruction," *The Physical Educator* 42 (Late Winter 1985), pp. 121–28.

108. J. Richard Jones, "Modify—To Simplify the Learning of Sports Skills," *Utah Association of Health, Physical Education and Recreation Journal* (Fall 1977), pp. 4, 10.

109. G. S. Don Morris, *How to Change the Games Children Play,* 2d ed. (Minneapolis: Burgess Publishing Company, 1980).

Establishing the Environment for Learning

An appropriate environment for learning is essential to the achievement of the goals of physical education. In the broadest sense of the term, the environment is a product of many factors that may be determined by school boards, administrators, parents, and oftentimes circumstances that are beyond the control of the teacher. Once the general environment for learning has been established within the context of the school, however, the classroom emerges as the specific environment for learning. The classroom is the domain of the teacher, and the teacher alone must make many decisions that directly affect the learning of students. These decisions then become the essence of teaching and finally learning. Mosston described teacher behavior as "a chain of decision making."[1] Hunter defined teaching as a "constant stream of professional decisions made before, during and after interaction with the student; decisions which, when implemented, increase the probability of learning."[2] She found that, regardless of who or what is being taught, all teaching decisions fall into three categories: (1) what *content* to teach next, (2) what the *student* will do to learn and demonstrate that learning has occurred, and (3) what the *teacher* will do to facilitate the acquisition of that learning. Errors made when making any of these decisions can impede student learning.

Because "teachers operate in a. . .complicated and demanding world,"[3] the decision-making process may be difficult. Teachers must carefully plan for students to successfully reach the goals of physical education. Effective instruction and learning should be based on the needs of individual students as well as the demands of a changing environment and should stimulate the teacher to avoid doing the same things year after year.

Decision making that leads to student learning is most effective when it follows an organized system or model, such as the one shown in unit figure 3.1. Just as a traveler uses a map to reach a certain destination, teachers can use the model to plan the best route toward their destination. By following the model, teachers can be sure they do not leave out an essential part of the planning process.

A learning system consists of a collection of interacting and interdependent elements designed to maximize performance toward a goal. The task of the instructional designer is to organize the elements of instruction in the most effective way possible to achieve the goal, which is student learning.[4] Thus, all decisions are made as to whether they facilitate student learning. Teachers are in the best position to act as instructional designers because of their knowledge of the subject matter and their experience with students. However, to produce or improve a system, the teacher must understand each of the components and how they interact with one another to achieve the goal, as well as the context of the environment surrounding the system.[5]

The content of any instructional program cannot be implemented until: (1) the learning environment has been established, and (2) the learning experiences have been planned. Unit 3 addresses the component of establishing the learning environment.

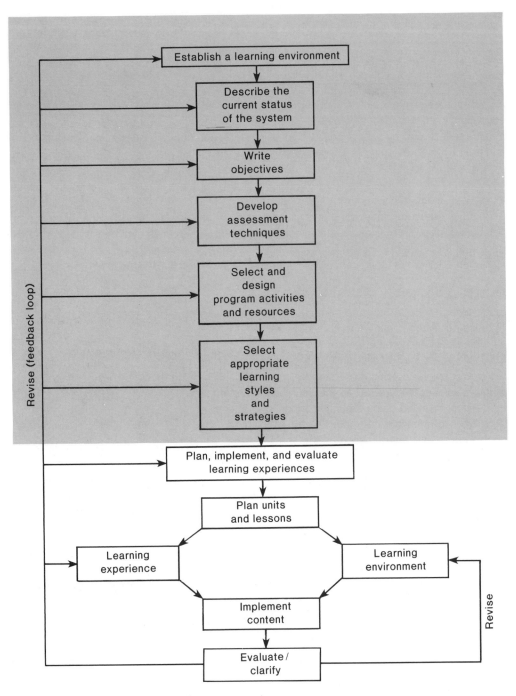

Unit Figure 3.1 A model for designing instructional programs.

Davis, Alexander, and Yelon defined the first step in designing the instructional process as "describing the current status of the learning system." Such a description would include "purposes, resources and constraints, the students entering the program, their skills, expectations and needs, and his (the teacher's) own capabilities."[6] Other factors include the time restraints of the school and the freedom to innovate. Many of these purposes and constraints were presented in units 1 and 2.

Once the current status of the system (i.e., the real world) has been defined, the instructional designer must next consider the ways in which students will use the knowledge, attitudes, and skills and then develop a set of clearly defined learning objectives to achieve these outcomes. The second step in designing the instructional program is the actual writing of performance objectives that set the stage for each successive step. Chapter 7 explains the process of writing objectives.

The third step is to develop assessment materials and techniques. Preassessment techniques tell the teacher where the students are at the beginning of instruction. Evaluation techniques tell whether the students have achieved the stated objectives. A variety of techniques that can be used for preassessment and evaluation are described in chapter 8. An explanation is also given as to how these techniques can be combined into a grading system.

The fourth step is to select or develop the resources that formulate meaningful learning activities to take students from where they are at the beginning of the instructional process to the achievement of the objectives of the unit or lesson. Unit 2 presented the theory and knowledge base necessary to make sound decisions. Chapter 9 presents various instructional resources, materials, and activities that could be included in the instructional program.

The fifth step is to incorporate the planning and designing done so far into the selection of specific instructional methods or strategies. A unit of instruction may incorporate several methods or strategies to ensure learning by individual students. Chapter 10 presents several such alternatives. The spectrum of teaching, mastery learning, individualized instruction, and other instructional techniques will be discussed.

The main charge of physical educators is to help young people improve their movement skills. All children are different as are schools and the school environment. For all children to succeed at improving their movement skills, the effective teacher must use a variety of teaching skills, strategies, and activities while interacting with the environment.[7] This unit provides teachers with many options for guiding students to become successful at performing movement skills.

References

1. Muska Mosston, *Teaching Physical Education,* 2d ed. (Columbus, Ohio: Charles E. Merrill, 1981).
2. Madeline Hunter, *Mastery Teaching* (El Segundo, California: TIP Publications, 1982), p. 3.
3. William G. Anderson, *Analysis of Teaching Physical Education* (St. Louis, Missouri: C. V. Mosby Company, 1980), p. 1.
4. Robert H. Davis, Lawrence T. Alexander, and Stephen L. Yelon, *Learning System Design: An Approach to the Improvement of Instruction* (New York: McGraw-Hill Book Company, 1974), p. 304.
5. Ibid, p. 305.
6. Ibid, p. 309.
7. George Graham, Shirley Ann Holt/Hale, and Melissa Parker, *Children Moving: A Teacher's Guide to Developing a Successful Physical Education Program,* 2d ed. (Palo Alto: Mayfield Publishing Company, 1987).

7

Writing Performance Objectives

Study Stimulators

1. Define and give an example of a goal, an objective, and a performance objective for each of the instructional domains. Why are both goals and objectives important?
2. What three elements must be included in a performance objective? How do these differ when evaluating affective objectives?
3. What is the difference between an explicit and an implicit performance objective? Which is more commonly used in education today?
4. What is the difference between open and closed objectives? When would it be appropriate to use each of these?
5. List at least ten acceptable verbs and ten unacceptable verbs that could be used when writing performance objectives.

Education has been defined as "a process that changes learners." This being the case, someone must decide what changes are "possible" and "desirable."[1] This charge most often falls to the teacher who may be contributing ideas to a curriculum guide or determining course direction for his or her class. Determining what is possible in education is not the prime consideration, because if teachers are convinced of the need and are provided with the necessary training and experience, they can effectively teach most of the important objectives. The more difficult problem is determining objectives that are desirable.[2] The process for doing this is the same, whether it be for a district curriculum guide, a school handbook, or an individual unit or lesson plan. General aims or purposes are shaped into goals, and goals are further refined into specific objectives that determine educational outcomes.

Defining Educational Outcomes

An *aim* or *purpose* is a broad statement of an ideal that is directed toward the total program. The following is an example of an educational aim:

> Physical education will contribute to the total education and development of each child as a complete program of physical activity is integrated into the school day.

An *instructional goal* is more specific than an aim. It is a broad, general outcome of instruction expressing the common learning expected of all students. However, it does not tell what the learner is to do at the end of instruction.[3] Goals are used as a basis for curriculum planning and for summarizing the purposes of the school or a specific program to the public. The following examples are instructional goals:

1. Students will be physically fit; have a desire to maintain physical fitness; and possess an understanding of how to assess, develop, and maintain physical fitness.
2. Students will develop skills sufficient to participate in several recreational activities of their own choosing, understand how to learn new skills, and have an appreciation for the value of participating in physical activity.

Objectives help teachers achieve specific
learning outcomes.

An *objective* is a relatively specific outcome of instruction that can be achieved within a short period of time. Objectives answer the question "what is worth teaching?"[4] Objectives are derived logically from goals and serve as "stepping stones to the achievement of a broader goal."[5] The following are examples of objectives:

1. The student will demonstrate cardiovascular fitness.
2. The student will execute sufficient skill proficiency and knowledge of the game of tennis to participate in a competitive match if he or she desires.

Objectives may be of two types: (1) instructional or (2) performance.[6] An *instructional* (process) objective tells what the teacher or coach will do during the lesson. The following is an example of an instructional objective:

The teacher will demonstrate the overhead smash.

A *performance* objective is a statement of an outcome that is attainable and is stated with enough specificity to identify what the learner is to do or produce, or what characteristics he or she should possess at the end of instruction.[7] The teacher and student can then determine whether a student has achieved the objective. Performance objectives are used more often than instructional objectives because they personalize the learning for the individual student. The following are examples of performance objectives:

1. The student will achieve the "good" or "excellent" category on the 1.5 mile run given several opportunities for doing so.
2. The student will execute correctly three out of five tennis serves into the service court (given a racquet, balls, and an official tennis court).

Table 7.1 Statements of educational outcomes and their uses

Statement	Use
Aim or purpose	Federal, state, district General policy statement
Instructional goal	District or school Curriculum guide
Objective	Department Program guide
Performance objective	Teacher Unit or daily lesson plan

These examples emphasize that students' actions should be directly observable. Performance objectives should demonstrate three characteristics:

1. A statement of behavior (what the learner will be able to do at the conclusion of instruction).
2. The conditions under which the learner will perform the task.
3. The criteria for successful performance.

The following example illustrates these characteristics:

The student will execute correctly three out of five tennis serves into the service court.

1. Behavior—*serve*
2. Conditions—*execute correctly into the service court*
3. Criteria—*three out of five times*

As shown in table 7.1, statements of educational outcomes usually progress from an aim or purpose produced at the federal, state, or district level down a hierarchy to the grassroots level at which the teacher is responsible for integrating performance objectives into the instructional process. However, because of their specific nature, performance objectives may be incorporated at any level of the hierarchy.

The Advantages of Performance Objectives

Performance objectives serve as a basis for the entire process of instructional design. Without objectives, preassessment would be unnecessary, learning activities would be like a map without a destination, and effective evaluation techniques could not be prepared. Expressing objectives in terms of performance provides the criteria for selecting and organizing the content and learning activities for the program of instruction.

Objectives also increase teacher accountability by focusing on specific behaviors that can be evaluated. Objectives convey to the parent, administrator, student, or teacher exactly what is to be accomplished. Parents and administrators are assisted in their understanding of school programs and their ability to gauge the progress of children.

Clearly stated objectives help students evaluate their own progress toward instructional goals and therefore serve as a motivating factor toward success. Pupils are more secure because they know what is expected and can spend more time on the important items and less time on unimportant items. They can readily focus on their strengths and weaknesses.

Students who know they need to shoot two hundred points in five ends on a forty-eight-inch target at a given distance in archery are much better able to evaluate their own progress in class than students who are told only to shoot a round each day. Students missing a class know exactly what skills and knowledge were missed and can take steps to make up the work.[8]

Teachers incorporating performance objectives are more secure because they know that what they are teaching has been carefully planned and that the evaluation is appropriate and specified. With clearly defined objectives, the teacher can preassess student behavior in relation to the objective, evaluate progress toward the objective, and determine the extent to which the objectives have been achieved by the learners. When a teacher has written performance objectives for a lesson or unit of instruction, clear purposes for both the teacher and students emerge. Nonessential items can then be removed from the lesson, thus providing more time to achieve what is considered to be the most important objectives. In addition, broad content is broken down into manageable, meaningful sequences and hierarchies; evaluation is simplified; and selection of instructional materials is clarified.[9]

Defining Performance Objectives

Writing performance objectives was defined very formally and with complexity through the seventies. It was at this time that *explicit* (behavioral) objectives were in the forefront. In the eighties, a much more simplified manner of writing *implicit* (experience) performance objectives was initiated. The following are examples:

1. *Explicit:* The student will correctly perform the overhead volley ten consecutive times against the wall above the eight-foot mark.
2. *Implicit:* The student will correctly perform the overhead serve, pass, and bump in a game situation.

Educators today are not in agreement as to the necessity of writing precise objectives.[10] Critics point out that objectives may be fallible, too many details hamper learning, and precision is emphasized at the expense of reaching new or untried applications.[11] Rink pointed out that measurable outcomes, especially in physical education, tend to restrict and narrow the learning experience. She suggested that the implicit objective is more common in education today, stating that

> Educational objectives should be specified to the degree that they provide direction for the design and evaluation of educational experiences without narrowing those experiences to what is most easily measured. Objectives still include the components of behavior, conditions, and criteria, but . . . the learning outcomes are more implicit than explicit.[12]

However, physical educators today are calling for more accountability in programs. Griffey stated, "We have failed to provide an experience that our students perceive as meaningful. The sense of mastering something important is denied most students in secondary physical education programs."[13] Precise objectives lead programs toward meaningful experiences and accountability. Annarino spoke of the need to stop incorporating the traditional or nonexplicit objective in favor of the more precise performance objective.[14] This text will take a formal approach to writing performance objectives that includes both explicit and implicit objectives.

Writing Performance Objectives

Performance objectives are generally divided into three types—cognitive (learning and application of knowledge), psychomotor (learning of physical or neuromuscular skills), and affective (concerned with interests, attitudes, appreciations, and values).

Performance objectives must describe the behavior of the learner. The key to writing objectives is the selection of the verb. As Bloom[15] pointed out, some verbs are directly observable and are better to use when formulating objectives. Others cannot be directly observed and are not suitable for use. The following are examples of observable and nonobservable verbs:

Observable (Appropriate)

Match (duplicate, equal, agree, fit)
Translate (decipher, interpret, explain, simplify)
Compute (calculate)
Name (identify, label, designate)
Diagram (draw, illustrate, picture, design, chart)
Classify (rank, rate, arrange, categorize)
Apply (pertain to, relate to, employ)
Construct (assemble, make, produce, build)
Identify (distinguish, recognize, associate, know)
Explain (define, decipher, illustrate)
Demonstrate (evidence, prove, be able to, perform)
Pass or (shoot, dribble, serve, catch, hit)
Improve (enhance, enrich, better)
List (catalog, index, enumerate, specify)

Non-Observable (Not appropriate)
Comprehend
Understand
Learn
Respect
Appreciate
Think
Grasp
Has an interest in
Has knowledge of

The taxonomies for each domain are reviewed in table 7.2, along with appropriate verbs for each level of behavior.

Since the general principles of writing objectives apply to both cognitive and psychomotor objectives, these two types will be considered simultaneously. Affective objectives will be considered later in the chapter.

Table 7.2 Appropriate verbs for performance objectives within each of the domain taxonomies

Cognitive Domain

Levels of Behavior	Verbs for Objectives
1. Knowledge	Define Match Spell Recite Who, what, where, when, why
2. Comprehension	Translate Paraphrase Tell in your own words Summarize Compare or contrast Predict
3. Application	Solve Apply
4. Analysis	Analyze Examine Break down Delineate Determine Identify
5. Synthesis	Compose Write Design Invent Hypothesize Plan Create Produce Organize
6. Evaluation	Judge Evaluate Defend

Table 7.2 (Continued)

Psychomotor Domain

Levels of Behavior	Verbs for Objectives
1. Generic movement	
Perceiving	Identify Recognize Discover Discriminate
Imitating	Replicate Duplicate Pantomime
Patterning	Perform (shoot) Demonstrate (pass) Execute (swim) Coordinate (jump)
2. Ordinative movement	
Adapting	Adjust Apply Employ Utilize
Refining	Control Synchronize Improve Synthesize Regulate Perform rhythmically (smoothly, efficiently)
3. Creative movement	
Varying	Alter Change Revise Diversify
Improvising	Interpret Extemporize Improvise Anticipate
Composing	Design Compose Symbolize

Table 7.2 (Continued)

Affective Domain

Levels of Behavior	*Verbs for Objectives*
1. Receiving	Notice Select Tolerate Be aware or conscious of Listen
2. Responding	Comply Follow Volunteer Enjoy Be satisfied Agree or disagree React Give opinion Sympathize with Appreciate Attend Read Accept responsibility
3. Valuing	Prefer consistently Support consistently Pursue activities Involve others Debate Argue Value Purchase Improve skills
4. Organization	Discuss codes, standards Formulate systems Weigh alternatives against standards Define criteria Base decisions on values
5. Characterization	Demonstrate consistent behavior or methods Integrate total behavior or values

Steps in Writing Performance Objectives (Cognitive and Psychomotor)

As stated earlier, writing performance objectives involves a statement of behavior, conditions of performance, and the criteria for successful performance. Some performance objectives are *closed* in that they demand a single correct response of all learners.[16] An objective that asks the student to name the thigh bone has only one answer—the femur. Some objectives are *open* and each learner could have a different response and yet meet the behavior specified in the objective. An example of an open objective might be to perform three new skills on a chosen piece of gymnastics equipment.

The teacher must practice writing performance objectives before it will feel comfortable. The following steps are designed to develop competence in properly stating performance objectives. Each step will add another piece to the soon-to-be-completed objective. Those desiring to write implicit objectives should follow only steps 1, 2, and 3.

Step 1. Define the area of instruction.
Step 2. Define what the student will be able to do (behavior) at the conclusion of instruction.
Step 3. Describe the conditions under which the student's performance will be evaluated.
Step 4. Specify the criteria for acceptable performance.
Step 5. Evaluate the objective.

Step 1—Define the Area of Instruction

Choose a lesson or unit of instruction that is relevant to the student population in real-world utility or preparation for future educational needs. Specify the target population by age, gender, and previous experience in the unit. Some examples are:

1. Archery—seventh-grade boys and girls, no previous experience.
2. Volleyball—ninth-grade boys and girls, two years experience.
3. Physical fitness—high school, coed, varied experience.

Step 2—Define What the Student Will Be Able to Do at the Conclusion of Instruction

In clear and concise terms, state what the student will be able to *do* at the conclusion of instruction. Include only those behaviors or products of behavior that can be observed through one or more of the five senses. Some examples of behaviors are:

1. Archery
   a. The student will define archery terms.
   b. The student will pass a test on the rules, etiquette, and basic skill techniques of archery.
   c. The student will shoot with correct form.
2. Volleyball
   a. The student will serve a volleyball.
   b. The student will set a volleyball.
   c. The student will write a paper on the history of volleyball.
3. Physical fitness
   a. The student will create an aerobic dance routine.
   b. The student will improve his or her 1.5 mile run score.
   c. The student will engage in a strength and flexibility program.

Step 3—Describe the Conditions Under Which the Student's Performance Will Be Evaluated (Implicit Objectives Will State In a Simple Way Both the Conditions and Criteria)

Include where, when, and with what equipment or materials and what set of rules. In informal units (e.g., those not programmed or written out for student use), some conditions may be implied and are not stated. Some examples of conditions follow:

1. Archery
    a. Given a list of definitions, the student will write the correct archery terms.
    b. The student will pass a test on the rules, etiquette, and skills of archery. (Implied conditions are that the student will have a copy of the test, a pencil, an answer sheet, and that the test will be closed-book.)
    c. The student will shoot using correct form as rated on the rating sheet by the instructor. (Implied conditions are the use of a bow, arrows, and target.)
2. Volleyball
    a. Using an overhand serve, the student will serve into the back half of the court. (A regulation ball and court are implied.)
    b. Using a legal volley, the student will volley a volleyball continuously against the wall so that it touches above the head. (A regulation ball is implied.)
    c. The student will write a one- to three-page paper on the history of volleyball. (Handwriting is implied, since typing has not been specified.)
3. Physical fitness
    a. Given class time daily, the student will join with two or three other students to create an aerobic dance routine to any music provided by the student or teacher.
    b. Given practice time for jogging, the student will improve his or her 1.5 mile run score. (A track or running area is implied.)
    c. The student will engage in a strength and flexibility program during class.

Step 4—Specify the Criteria for Acceptable Performance

State the criteria in such a way that a qualified person could use it to successfully choose students meeting the standard. Describe the performance or the result of performance in terms of the number of trials, number of successful completions, number of repetitions within a given time allotment, improvement on a given scale, percent or percentile achieved, raw score, or other observable standard. Describe a subjective performance in terms of the degree or quality of performance required. The following objectives are now complete performance objectives with behavior, conditions, and criteria:

1. Archery
    a. Given a list of definitions of twenty-five archery terms, the student will write in the correct term with fewer than four errors.
    b. The student will pass a multiple-choice test on the rules, etiquette, and skills of archery with a score of 80 percent or better.
    c. The student will shoot using effective form as rated by the instructor on a rating scale, with a minimum of two errors.

2. Volleyball
   a. Using the correct technique for an overhand serve, the student will serve eight out of ten serves into the back half of the court.
   b. Using the correct technique, the student will volley fifteen consecutive times against the wall so that it touches above a line marked seven feet from the floor.
   c. The student will write a one- to three-page paper on the history of volleyball that includes the origin, early rules and changes in the game, recent changes in the style of the game, and indications of current interest in volleyball.
3. Physical Fitness
   a. Given twenty minutes of class time, the student will create, with two or three other students, a two-minute aerobic dance routine to music that includes activities that raise the heart rate to the target heart rate (refer to formula given in class).
   b. The student will improve his or her 1.5 mile run score by at least one level or will maintain his or her endurance at the "good" or "excellent" level.
   c. Given twenty minutes three times per week, the student will demonstrate participation in a strength and flexibility program three times a week for six weeks by turning in a log of activities on the form provided by the instructor.

Step 5—Evaluate the Objective

Evaluate the objective by asking the following questions: (1) Is the expected behavior attainable as a result of learning in the unit of instruction? (2) Is the objective relevant or is it included merely because it is easy to state in terms of performance? (3) Are good objectives omitted because they are difficult to state in performance terms? (4) Can another competent person understand the objective well enough to use it to evaluate learners in the unit of instruction? (5) Are facilities and materials available for the attainment of the objective? (6) Is the objective motivating to the student? (7) Are both short-range and long-range objectives included for the unit of instruction?

If some students are functioning within all levels of a domain, care should be taken to ensure that objectives include all of these levels. An example of objectives for each level of the cognitive and psychomotor domains is shown in tables 7.3 and 7.4.

Self-check on Performance Objectives

Directions: Classify the following statements as (A) properly stated performance objectives or (B) improperly stated performance objectives. If the objective is classified as (B), identify the part of the objective that is incorrect or missing.

1. To teach the student to bat correctly.
2. The student will list five historically prominent persons in physical education.
3. The teacher will cover the rules of badminton.
4. The student should learn the reasons for using correct safety procedures in archery.
5. The Red Cross standards will be the model for student performance in swimming the five basic strokes.
6. The student will compute the percentage of body fat.
7. Given the specific data needed, the student will be able to solve six out of seven problems on body composition.

Table 7.3 A sample of objectives for each level of the cognitive domain

Knowledge

1. Match bowling terms and definitions on a written test at the 80 percent level.
2. Given a diagram of the human body, list the names of the bones and muscles shown.
3. List the six basic rules of archery.

Comprehension

1. Given ten game situations in a specified sport, select the correct referee's decision from a criteria sheet.
2. Describe in writing (define) the meaning of "intensity" in a physical fitness program.
3. Diagram a two-one-two zone defense in basketball.

Application

1. List the criteria you would use to purchase a quality tennis racquet for yourself based on the characteristics explained in class.
2. List the situations in which you would use a zone defense and those when you would use a man-to-man defense in basketball.
3. Write a physical fitness program for an individual who was rated "poor" after completing the AAHPERD tests. Include specific recommendations for intensity, duration, and frequency.

Analysis

1. Analyze ten exercises in *The Readers Digest* article handed out in class. List the muscles used for each exercise and determine if the exercise develops strength or flexibility.
2. Using the criteria sheet handed out in class, analyze the offensive player of your choice by watching a videotape of the NBA Championship game. List the strengths and weaknesses of this player during five consecutive plays executed by his team.

Synthesis

1. Create five new plays for flag football.
2. Choreograph a new dance lasting five minutes for three to six participants using music of your choice.
3. Create a gymnastics routine on the balance beam that includes at least five new stunts.

Evaluation

1. Using the criteria sheet, evaluate three fad diets from the following list to determine whether they meet minimum nutritional standards.
2. Judge a list of specific behaviors exhibited by the spectators at the league championship volleyball match to determine sportsmanlike behavior based on the following criteria (recognized values of society).

8. The course will provide the student with an understanding of physical fitness.
9. Given a pencil and paper, the student will pass a true-false quiz on the rules of bowling.
10. The student will appreciate the value of physical activity.
11. The student will shoot free throws from the foul line.
12. The student will understand basketball strategy.
13. The student will learn the overhead clear in badminton.
14. The student will demonstrate progress in weight training by keeping a progress log.
15. The student will demonstrate the serve in racquetball.

Table 7.4 A sample of objectives for each level of the psychomotor domain

Peceiving

1. Identify the tumbling skills performed by the teacher.
2. Discover how the lay-up shot is performed by asking questions after a demonstration of the skill.

Imitating

1. Duplicate the soccer dribble around three cones after watching a demonstration of the skill.
2. Imitate the performance of a synchronized swimming skill after watching a video of a simple routine.

Patterning

1. Perform a gallop.
2. Demonstrate a backward volleyball set into the basketball hoop.
3. Execute a headstand in good form (as determined by the criteria sheet) for ten seconds.

Adapting

1. Dribble a basketball in control from one side of the court to the other while being guarded.
2. Shoot five arrows at ten yards, twenty yards, and thirty yards on the archery field.
3. Bat a pitched ball to right, left, and center field.

Refining

1. Perform a bowling approach and release, until it is smooth, meeting the criteria listed on the checklist.
2. Improve a softball accuracy score at a target on the wall, until a score of fifty points in ten throws is achieved.
3. Perform a series of forward rolls in a straight line until three in good form can be executed from standing to standing.

Varying

1. Alter the forward roll until a straddle, pike, or other variation can be performed.
2. Modify the bowling stance to increase the speed of the ball three seconds from release until the pins are contacted.
3. Hit three pitched balls past the infield from the right batter's box and three from the left.

Improvising

1. Change offensive pattern #5a to involve the center more often and exploit the lack of height by the defense.
2. Add two new steps to the "That's Cool" aerobic routine.

Composing

1. Create a floor exercise routine using at least five stunts already learned.
2. Design five new flag football play patterns.

Answers to Self-Check
1. B, not stated in terms of observable performance.
2. A
3. B, not stated in terms of observable performance.
4. B, not stated in terms of observable performance.
5. B, not stated in terms of observable performance.
6. B, no stated conditions or criteria.
7. A

8. B, not stated in terms of observable performance.
9. B, no stated criteria.
10. B, not stated in terms of observable performance.
11. B, no stated criteria.
12. B, not stated in terms of observable performance.
13. B, not stated in terms of observable performance.
14. A
15. B, no stated conditions or criteria.

If you had difficulty with the self-check, review the preceding pages in this chapter before proceeding. Practice writing objectives until you feel that you have mastered the art of writing objectives. Have two of your classmates analyze your objectives in terms of the three criteria for writing objectives and the questions in step 5.

Steps in Writing Affective Objectives

Performance objectives in the affective domain differ from cognitive and psychomotor objectives in that attitudes, appreciations, and values cannot be measured directly but must be inferred by the behaviors of students toward or away from the desired behavior. These behaviors are called approach or avoidance behaviors. Lee and Merrill have delineated a method for writing affective objectives.[17] Their ideas have been incorporated into the following steps for writing affective objectives:

Step 1. Describe the attitude the student should acquire.
Step 2. List specific student approach or avoidance behaviors.
Step 3. Describe the conditions under which the approach or avoidance behaviors will occur.
Step 4. Specify the criteria under which the approach or avoidance behaviors will occur.
Step 5. Evaluate the objectives.

Step 1—Describe the Attitude the Student Should Acquire

Write a descriptive statement describing the attitude, including interests, desires, or appreciations.

1. Physical fitness: The student will have a desire to maintain physical fitness.
2. Dance: The student will enjoy participating in dance activities.
3. Sportsmanship: The student will demonstrate good sportsmanship.

Step 2—List Specific Student Approach or Avoidance Behaviors

Approach Behaviors   List the behaviors that students will most likely be expected to say or do that bring them into closer contact with the subject. These behaviors are called approach behaviors. Some examples of approach behaviors are:

1. Physical fitness:
   a. Reads fitness books, articles.
   b. Exercises daily.
   c. Tells everyone how exercise can improve their lives.
   d. Is always checking own heart rate during activity.
   e. Tries to get others to engage in fitness activities.
   f. Attends lectures about fitness.

2. Dance:
    a. Reads the fine-arts section of the newspaper.
    b. Subscribes to a dance magazine.
    c. Participates in dance instruction or activity other than during class.
    d. Knows the names and performance characteristics of professional dance performers.
    e. Watches dance events on television.
    f. Attends all local dance events.
3. Sportsmanship:
    a. Volunteers to officiate intramural basketball games.
    b. Reads an article or attends a lecture on sportsmanship.
    c. Calls own fouls during a competitive game.
    d. Controls own temper and behavior during any sports competition.
    e. Shakes the hand of all opposing players after the game or match.

In most school-related activities, approach behaviors are adequate for evaluating affective objectives and can be used exclusively if desired.

Avoidance Behaviors List the behaviors that students will most likely exhibit that will detract from or lead them away from the desired attitude. These behaviors are called avoidance behaviors. Some examples of avoidance behaviors include:

1. Physical fitness:
    a. Tries to convince physical education teacher that he or she is not supposed to run, but plays basketball later in the period.
    b. Does not dress for activity on days that fitness activities are conducted.
    c. Asks to substitute marching band for fitness unit.
    d. Refuses to turn in a record of eating kept for one week.
2. Dance:
    a. Says, "This is a dumb or sissy activity."
    b. Tells the teacher this is the only time the counselor is available and asks to be excused during dance class.
    c. Is often tardy to class or fails to attend class.
    d. Fails to study for quiz or turn in paper.
3. Sportsmanship:
    a. Gets involved in a fight during a game.
    b. Refuses to come out of a game to allow other team members to play.
    c. Blames others for unsportsmanlike behavior.
    d. Constantly argues with the referees.

Eliminate activities that cannot be observed either directly or indirectly. Direct observation includes student activities that are actually seen. Eliminate activities that are not commonly expected to occur among students or are inappropriate.

Step 3—Describe the Conditions under Which the Approach
or Avoidance Behaviors Will Occur
A testing situation for affective objectives must include a set of alternatives presented to the student that allow the student to make a free choice, unhindered by what the teacher may want the student to do. Stating the conditions or circumstances under which the behavior

will take place is the hardest part of writing an affective objective. Only when the conditions are known can the behavior be interpreted as a true approach or avoidance behavior. Students should be asked to choose between two behaviors, one of which is the behavior in question.

1. Physical fitness: Each student may run a mile and a half, swim three minutes, or play basketball.
2. Dance: Each student may choose to join the square dance group or play badminton.
3. Sportsmanship: Each student may shake hands with the opposing team or gather up the equipment.

Another possible set of alternatives would be to ask the student to choose between an approach or an avoidance activity, such as "Each student can choose to play basketball or fail the course." In this situation, no one would feel free to sit out. Free choice is an essential component of the testing situation. Teachers must do as little as possible to influence the alternative chosen by a student in the testing situation. Some other examples of teacher influence might include extra credit, praise, or special privileges. Although these might be appropriate in a learning situation, they are inappropriate in a testing situation, because they cause the student to approach the subject because of the teacher rather than because of a favorable attitude toward the subject.

When using questionnaires or other direct-observation techniques, care should be taken to make students feel free to express their true feelings, such as through anonymity or assessing feelings after the course grades have been submitted.

Step 4—Specify the Criteria under Which the Approach and Avoidance Behaviors Will Occur

The criterion statement indicates how well, how often, or how much of the approach or avoidance behavior must occur for the objective to be achieved. Two types of criterion statements can be used to indicate a complete objective:

A. This kind of criterion statement indicates the number of activities in which each student will participate.
   1. Physical fitness:
      Each student will engage in a fitness activity at least three times a week for one semester.
B. This kind of criterion statement indicates the number of students who will demonstrate the specified behavior.
   1. Dance:
      Eighty percent of the students will participate regularly (not more than three absences) in the dance class for a six-week unit.
   2. Sportsmanship:
      All of the students will shake the hands of the opposing team after a game whether they win or lose.

Using the number of activities as a criterion allows students with several interests or extenuating circumstances to demonstrate approach behaviors that might not occur in a single instance. For example, a student with a large number of sports-related behaviors had her tonsils out and could not participate in intramural basketball, although basketball was her favorite activity.

Table 7.5 A sample of objectives for each level of the affective domain

Receiving

1. Listens attentively to an analysis of the volleyball spike.
2. When asked (following a demonstration), identifies the position of the feet in a tennis serve.
3. Selects a position to play in soccer, given a choice of three positions. . . .

Responding

1. Voluntary assists in setting up apparatus equipment before a gymnastics class.
2. Responds to a request to work on a subject-related project, such as designing and organizing a football bulletin board.
3. Remains after a class in wrestling takedowns for additional instruction or practice. . . .

Valuing

1. Attends an optional class session to practice high jumping for the Spring meet.
2. Risks being late for the next class by continuing a discussion concerning a certain defensive strategy in basketball.
3. Volunteers to organize an intramural swimming meet during his or her free time. . . .

Organization

1. Volunteers to play for the opposing softball team so that there are an even number of players on each team.
2. Following instructional units in judo and karate, organizes and supervises a self-defense club for girls.
3. Proposes alternative safety and spotting techniques to be used when gymnastics equipment is available during a free-time activity period. . . .

Characterization by a Value or Value Complex

1. Requests additional information on ways to improve physical skills following each instructional unit.
2. Volunteers free time on Saturday mornings to coach an elementary-school basketball team.
3. Participates in all intramural events either as a player, team representative, council representative, official, scorekeeper, or equipment manager.

Source: Melograno, Vincent J. "Evaluating Affective Objectives in Physical Education," *The Physical Educator*, 31 (March 1974):8–12.

In either kind of criterion statement, the number indicates how much of the behavior will occur for the objective to be achieved. This number should be based on some realistic goal from what is already known about students, perhaps through a preassessment of student behaviors. Teachers should not expect miracles to occur by stating numbers that are impossible for students to achieve.

In addition, teachers should avoid using numbers so large that they cannot tabulate the responses for the number of students or activities involved. Teachers can get a general idea of achievement of the objectives by selecting only one class to evaluate each semester. Words such as *several, most,* or *often* should also be avoided since they are too vague to demonstrate goal achievement.

Because behavior in the affective domain is evaluated by inferred behavior, teachers may not need to tell students what the performance objective says. A knowledge of the general objectives in the affective domain is usually sufficient for students.

An example of objectives for each level of the affective domain is shown in table 7.5.

Step 5—Evaluate the Objectives

After writing several objectives, check them by referring to the following checklist, which incorporates each of the steps described by Lee and Merrill:[18]

1. Attitude:
    a. Is there a descriptive statement of interest, desire, or appreciation?
2. Behavior:
    a. Is a student approach or avoidance behavior specified?
    b. Can the behavior be directly or indirectly observed?
    c. Is the behavior a high-probability behavior?
3. Conditions:
    a. Is a situation described in which the approach or avoidance behavior may occur and can be observed?
    b. Are at least two alternatives presented to students?
    c. Is the situation a free-choice situation in which the teacher does not directly influence the student's choice?
    d. Are cues eliminated that might indicate the expected behavior?
    e. Do students feel free to express their true feeling if direct observation is used?
4. Criteria:
    a. Is a number of students or approach behaviors specified?
    b. Are indefinite words avoided?
    c. Is the criterion a realistic estimate of changes that can be expected in the students?
    d. Will the results indicate a trend or pattern of approach or avoidance?

Concerns about Performance Objectives

Now that guidelines for writing performance objectives have been explored, other concerns about the use of objectives can be examined.

Since writing performance objectives at the lowest levels of the taxonomies is easiest, many teachers have a tendency to leave out many worthy objectives that cannot be easily evaluated. Often these objectives are among the most important ones.[19] Knowing this, teachers can avoid a deficiency by using the taxonomies to check their objectives.

Some teachers complain that writing objectives before instruction prevents them from taking advantage of "the teaching moment." This is especially true in the affective domain in which teachers cannot plan the teaching of such behaviors as good sportsmanship at a scheduled time and place.[20] These unintended effects of education may be as important or more important than many of the specified objectives.[21] The specification of the objectives of instruction does not tell the teacher when it is to be taught. It can, however, make the teacher aware of the need to teach the behavior when the opportunity arises. A good teacher will continue to take advantage of "the teaching moment" to assist students in their learning rather than limit themselves to only those behaviors that will be evaluated.

Innovative efforts can be frustrated by an attempt to specify objectives too early in the program because the range of exploration is limited.[22] Teachers should specify minimal objectives and then add new objectives as they are discovered to be worthwhile.

In some fields, such as dance and the other arts, specifying measurable student behaviors is difficult. However, teachers do have criteria that they use for evaluation and it is only fair that students be told the criteria on which they will be evaluated.[23]

The use of performance objectives has been said to dehumanize learning. Actually, for many students, performance objectives serve to humanize learning by telling students what is expected.[24] The use of the open forms of objectives can also be used to individualize learning.

Questions and Suggested Activities

1. Write an aim or purpose for physical education. Develop it into a goal, the goal into an objective, and the objective into at least two performance objectives in each of the three domains.
2. Write three or more performance objectives for a lesson or a unit of instruction that are clearly stated and include the three essential components—behavior, conditions, and criteria. Include the cognitive, psychomotor, and affective domains.
3. Discuss the advantages and disadvantages of performance objectives from your point of view. How can some of the disadvantages be overcome?
4. Write a performance objective for each level of the taxonomy in each of the three domains for a specified unit of instruction.
5. The recent emphasis on accountability has emphasized the use of performance objectives and the specification of competencies for graduation. What problems might arise in physical education because of this emphasis?

Suggested Readings

Annarino, Anthony A. "Physical Education Objectives: Traditional vs. Developmental." *Journal of Physical Education and Recreation* 48 (October 1977):22–23.

Bloom, Benjamin S., George F. Madaus, and J. Thomas Hastings. *Evaluation to Improve Learning.* New York: McGraw-Hill Book Company, 1981.

Burns, Richard W. *New Approaches to Behavioral Objectives.* Dubuque, Iowa: Wm. C. Brown Company Publishers, 1971.

Davis, Robert. "Writing Behavioral Objectives." *Journal of Health, Physical Education and Dance* 44 (April 1973):47–49.

Gagné, Robert M. "Behavioral Objectives? Yes!" *Educational Leadership* 29 (February 1972):394–96.

Heitmann, Helen. "Curriculum Evaluation." *Journal of Physical Education and Recreation* 49 (March 1978):36–37.

Kneller, George F. "Behavioral Objectives? No!" *Educational Leadership* 29 (February 1972):397–400.

Mager, Robert F. *Developing Attitude Toward Learning.* Belmont, Calif.: Fearon Publishers, 1968.

———. *Measuring Instructional Intent: Or Got a Match?* Belmont, Calif.: Fearon Publishers, 1973.

———. *Preparing Instructional Objectives.* Belmont, Calif.: Pitman Learning, 1975.

Polidoro, J. Richard. "Performance Objectives: A Practical Approach Toward Accountability." *The Physical Educator* 33 (March 1976):20–23.

Quinn, Lee W. "Generic Competencies in Physical Education." *Journal of Physical Education and Recreation* 50 (April 1979):68–69.

Shockley, Joe M. "Needed: Behavioral Objectives in Physical Education." *Journal of Health, Physical Education, Recreation* 44 (April 1973):44–46.

Singer, Robert. "A Systems Approach to Teaching Physical Education." *Journal of Health, Physical Education and Recreation* 45 (September 1974):33–36, 86.

References

1. Benjamin S. Bloom, George F. Madaus, and J. Thomas Hastings, *Evaluation to Improve Learning* (New York: McGraw-Hill Book Company, 1981), p. 5.
2. Ibid., p. 8.
3. Richard W. Burns, *New Approaches to Behavioral Objectives* (Dubuque, Iowa: Wm. C. Brown Company Publishers, 1972), p. 3.
4. Bloom, Madaus, and Hastings, *Evaluation to Improve Learning,* p. 17.
5. Hal A. Lawson and Judith H. Placek, *Physical Education in the Secondary Schools: Curricular Alternatives* (Boston: Allyn & Bacon, Inc., 1981), p. 80.
6. Neil J. Dougherty and Diane Bonanno, *Contemporary Approaches to the Teaching of Physical Education,* 2d ed. (Scottsdale: Gorsuch Scarisbrick, Publishers, 1987), p. 144.
7. Robert F. Mager, *Preparing Instructional Objectives,* 2d ed. (Belmont, California: Pitman Learning, 1975), p. 2.
8. Joe M. Shockley, "Needed: Behavioral Objectives in Physical Education," *Journal of Health, Physical Education, Recreation* 44 (April 1973), pp. 44–46.
9. Martin Haberman, "Behavioral Objectives: Bandwagon or Breakthrough," *The Journal of Teacher Education* 19 (Spring 1968), pp. 91–94.
10. Shockley, "Needed: Behavioral Objectives in Physical Education," p. 45.
11. Ibid.
12. Judith E. Rink, *Teaching Physical Education for Learning* (St. Louis: Times Mirror/Mosby College Publishing, 1985), p. 142.
13. David C. Griffey, "Trouble for Sure a Crisis-Perhaps: Secondary School Physical Education Today," *Journal of Health, Physical Education, Recreation and Dance* 58 (February 1987), p. 21.
14. Anthony A. Annarino, "Physical Education Objectives: Traditional vs. Developmental," *Journal of Physical Education and Recreation* 48 (October 1977), pp. 22–23.
15. Bloom, Madaus, and Hastings, *Evaluation to Improve Learning,* p. 33.
16. Richard W. Burns, *New Approaches to Behavioral Objectives,* pp. 58–59.
17. Adapted from Blaine Nelson Lee and M. David Merrill, *Writing Complete Affective Objectives: A Short Course* (Belmont, California: Wadsworth Publishing Company, 1972).
18. Ibid., pp. 98–99.
19. Blaine R. Worthen and J. R. Sanders, *Educational Evaluation: Theory and Practice* (Worthington, Ohio: Charles A. Jones Publishing Company, 1973), p. 240.
20. Ibid., p. 241.
21. I. K. Davies, *Objectives in Curriculum Design* (New York: McGraw-Hill Book Company, 1976), p. 66.
22. Ibid.
23. Worthen and Sanders, *Educational Evaluation,* p. 236.
24. Ibid., p. 243.

Evaluating Student Performance

Study Stimulators

1. Why is evaluation an important part of instructional design?
2. What is the difference between norm-referenced and criterion-referenced evaluation as they relate to test construction, test evaluation, and learner performance? Which type of evaluation is preferable?
3. Define the following terms: reliability, validity, objectivity.
4. How might one go about developing evaluation materials for a written test, for a skills test, and for an affective assessment?
5. What is preassessment? Why is it important in the instructional setting?
6. What is a task analysis? Why is it important? How does one determine what tasks go where in the hierarchy?
7. What is the purpose of giving grades in physical education?
8. What is the process for determining grades in physical education?
9. What kind of grading system is best?

The primary purpose of evaluation should be to improve instruction. Teaching, learning, and evaluation are interdependent in the education process. Evaluation, therefore, plays an important part in instructional design. What is evaluated determines what will be taught and how it will be taught. Evaluation emphasizes the importance of the skills and knowledge being taught by expecting acceptable levels of comprehension and performance by students. It makes students accountable for their performance and teachers responsible for student achievement. Such accountability is vital to the credibility and effectiveness of the profession, but it is oftentimes lacking. "Effective student accountability procedures depend on the teacher"[1] and, for this reason, evaluation must be carefully planned. Teachers must have expectations for students and create ways for them to achieve success. Teachers must do more than expect students to be "busy, happy, and good," as Placek[2] pointed out they often do. Students should be expected to perform certain skills, know certain concepts, and behave in certain ways. This is what teaching is all about, and evaluation is the means of rating success at doing these things.

Evaluation fulfills the following purposes. It (1) confirms that students have completed the objectives of instruction, (2) provides information concerning student abilities and progress (often for the determination of grades), (3) aids in creating a more effective instructional process, (4) aids the teacher in providing individualized help for each student, and (5) aids in communicating objectives to the public.

At the beginning of instruction, evaluation provides the teacher with information concerning those students who have already achieved the objectives of the course by completing the criteria stated in the objective. Students who already possess the skills can be directed into advanced and challenging activities. Those students who lack adequate skills can be given help to improve their performance and eventually achieve the objectives of the course. When evaluation techniques are used effectively, students do not have to guess lesson objectives or their progress toward the objectives.

The primary purpose of evaluation is to improve instruction.

During instruction, evaluation should be a feedback tool for students, informing them of the course objectives and of their progress toward achieving the criteria. Grades should not be the means of informing students of these important factors. In effective instruction, students have been prepared for the test in advance and should not be surprised at what will be required. In such cases, a well-constructed test with a broad coverage of class content serves as a challenge for students to "put it all together" and as a summarizing experience that gives students a feeling of accomplishment by helping them realize how much they have learned.

Evaluation should also serve as a learning activity. It should arouse the student's interest, motivate class attendance to perform and study, and finally require the learner to use or apply information and skills in a real or simulated situation.

At the conclusion of instruction, evaluation helps teachers check the effectiveness of the teaching process and the teacher. It informs the teacher whether students have achieved the course objectives and the progress they made in doing so. When students are not performing well, as determined by evaluation materials, the teacher must examine the instructional design. Unit and lesson plans should first be critiqued to determine if the achievement of performance objectives was pursued in a meaningful way. Next, the teacher must critically decide if his or her own teaching techniques were effective.

Because evaluation is so important, it should be an ongoing process. One of the important roles of the present-day physical educator should be that of evaluator. Evaluation will be discussed first as an integral component of instructional design, second as it determines preassessment, and third as a grading procedure.

Evaluation in Instructional Design

Evaluation should be a vital component of instructional design. It transpires informally and formally throughout units of study during the entire school year. Two types of evaluation commonly used in education today are norm-referenced and criterion-referenced.

Norm-referenced evaluation refers to how well a student performs compared with others of the same age, gender, class, grade level, school, or geographic area. Standardized tests such as the AAHPERD Fitness Tests are norm-referenced and provide important information regarding the general school population as it relates to national norms.

Norm-referenced evaluation is based on the normal curve that assumes that achievement is in fact normally distributed around the average class performance. When the distribution of student performance deviates from the normal curve, which is often the case, something is assumed to be wrong with either the test (i.e., it was too hard or too easy) or the sample population tested. Therefore, the teacher is left to make a subjective evaluation of the "true" performance of the students.

Norm-referenced evaluation can be used to place students into ability groups for instruction or to establish the norms for criterion-based grading. Beginning teachers, who are not yet familiar with appropriate mastery levels for a given activity or content unit, may find norm-referenced evaluation easier to use.

Norm-referenced evaluation is often used for *summative evaluation,* which takes place at the end of a unit or course. It is comprehensive in nature and allows the teacher to evaluate student progress for an entire unit of work by determining the achievement of performance objectives. Summative evaluation is usually formal, involving such instruments as skills tests, written tests, records of performance, and final projects. On the other hand, *formative evaluation* is administered at the end of a learning task or segment within a unit of instruction and measures small chunks of learning. It is ongoing throughout a unit and is often informal. It usually assesses progress toward a final goal or performance objective.

Teachers must keep in mind that norm-referenced scores may not totally apply to a current situation. Comparing present students with norms derived from students evidencing differences in aptitude (low/high ability), environment (rural/urban, high/low economic status), and mix (all boys or all girls) may not be realistic. Also, students at one school may not fit the norm for students at another school. Students in a class one semester may not fit the norm for students in the class during a different semester. A class taught by one teacher will not fit the norm of the same class taught by a different teacher. One class taught by a teacher will not necessarily fit the norm of another class taught by the same teacher. Test scores from small classes or select populations (e.g., all athletes, all boys, or all girls) will usually not result in a normal distribution of scores. Teachers need to realize such differences and use norms as a reference point or when applicable in a current situation.

Criterion-referenced evaluation refers to how well a student performs in comparison with a predetermined and specified standard of performance. Ideally, given enough time for each student to learn the materials, students should pass most of the items on the test. Failure to pass often indicates that the student has not had adequate time for preparation and needs more time or instruction to achieve the objective.

Criterion-referenced evaluation can be used for evaluating cognitive, psychomotor, or affective objectives. Before this system can be used, the teacher must be able to set appropriate standards. This system of evaluation is used for both formative and summative evaluation. If it is used for summative evaluation, the criteria should not change as students become more proficient. The initial establishment of the criteria should be done with care. Establishing standards that are too high is better than too low. Students do not usually complain if the standards are lowered.

With increasing frequency, educators are using criterion-referenced evaluation materials to demonstrate the achievement of their students. Such measures demonstrate the extent to which a student has achieved competence in a given area of instruction (instead of what the student does not know). However, the complaint of grade inflation often prevents educators from adopting criterion-referenced systems. One type of criterion-referenced evaluation is called a mastery test. Mastery learning is explained in more detail in chapter 10.

Both norm- and criterion-referenced evaluation leave no doubt in the mind of students of what is expected of them. Some combination of criterion-referenced and norm-referenced assessment is recommended for assigning grades.[3]

Test Construction

Proper use of evaluation techniques requires an awareness of the strengths and limitations of the test. Although the focus of this book is not tests and measurements, several terms need to be reviewed before proceeding with a discussion of test construction because each is essential to a well-constructed, efficient test.

Validity is defined as the extent to which a test measures what it is intended to measure. *Content validity* is increased by creating a test "blueprint" so that the test items directly reflect course content. To determine the validity of any test, ask the question "Are the student behaviors asked for by the test the same as those called for in the course objectives?" A common error made by teachers is testing the easiest things to write questions on or adopting the easiest skills test to give rather than testing on the content and skills they desire the students to know. This destroys content validity.

When evaluating validity, the teacher should ask the questions "What might cause the student to get the wrong answer on the test when the student knows the answer if asked orally?" or "What might cause the student to perform poorly on a skills test when the student performs very well in a game situation?" Some reasons might be that the test is written on an inappropriate reading level, has vocabulary or instructions that are too difficult for the student to comprehend, or has a question type that confuses the student (such as the situation question that asks for the official's response). Tests given to foreign or bilingual students often create problems when given in written form, but they can be easily answered in oral form. Skills tests might require skills different from those in the game situation, such as in the tennis backboard test in which the ball returns at a rate much faster than in a regular tennis game. Test construction is demanding, and teachers should strive to construct valid tests.

A *reliable* test is one on which a student obtains similar scores on different trials of the same test. Reliability on norm-referenced tests is enhanced by increasing the number of test questions or trials or the number of students taking the test. For example, if only two questions or trials appear on the test and one day the student has a perfect score and another day misses one, the difference is 50 percent versus 100 percent. If one hundred questions or trials appear on the test, missing one would only make the difference of 99 percent versus 100 percent. In the same way, if ten students take the test, one student might change from ninth to tenth place, whereas with one hundred students, the difference in rank might be from ninety-ninth to one-hundredth place.

Criterion-referenced tests, such as mastery tests, are designed for a high percentage of students to achieve the criterion; therefore, the range of scores on the test is reduced and obtaining a high coefficient of reliability is very difficult. Reliability is not usually checked in such teacher-made tests.

An *objective* test is one in which a student obtains an identical score on the test regardless of who administers or scores the test. Because objective tests (e.g., true–false, multiple choice) are easier to score, they lend themselves to increased reliability over essay tests. The objectivity of essay-type tests can be increased by making up a scoring key before administering the test.

Although evaluation in education cannot always be as precise as some statisticians would like it to be, it can certainly be much more precise than many teachers have supposed it could be. The examples on the following pages are designed to at least make evaluation somewhat practical and objective for the teacher.

Steps in Developing Evaluation Materials
Step 1. Determine what to evaluate.
Step 2. Determine specific evaluation techniques.
Step 3. Construct written tests as needed.
Step 4. Construct skill evaluation techniques.
Step 5. Construct affective evaluation techniques.
Step 6. Evaluate the evaluation techniques.
Step 7. Try out the evaluation techniques.

Step 1—Determine What to Evaluate
If this has not already been done, refer to the chapter on writing performance objectives. Each performance objective should state the specific performance that is to be observed. Once the performance objective has been written, the question of what to evaluate has been solved.

Step 2—Determine Specific Evaluation Techniques
The teacher must decide how to know when the behavior specified in each objective has been achieved. If the objectives have been correctly written in terms of performance, the verb should describe what the student will be expected to do to demonstrate achievement of the objective. For example, if the objective is to throw a softball, swim a distance, shoot free throws, or improve time in running, some type of *skills test* to determine skill in throwing,

swimming, shooting, or running would be involved. However, if the objective is to define bowling terms, score an archery round, or recognize correct rules of etiquette, some type of *written test* would be necessary. Some objectives—such as writing a paper on the history of tennis or passing a multiple-choice test on the rules of badminton—are evaluated exactly as specified, by writing a paper or passing a test. Some examples of various general objectives and appropriate evaluation techniques follow:

badminton short serve	skills test
archery form	rating checklist
swimming skills—dive, tread water	checklist
knowledge of rules	written test
dance composition	subjective evaluation by teacher using specified criteria

Many objectives would be more accurately evaluated by using several techniques:

lifesaving	skills test, essay test, personal interview
feelings about fitness	anonymous questionnaire, observation of participation in fitness activities
tennis serve	skills test on accuracy, teacher evaluation of form

Each of these techniques will be discussed in detail in the following pages.

Step 3—Construct Written Tests as Needed

An example of a test construction "blueprint" is illustrated in figure 8.1. The following discussion will briefly explain the elements that are helpful in constructing a written test.

Element 1 Decide on the course or unit to be tested; in this case, racquetball has been selected.

Element 2 Summarize the course objectives, including skills, knowledge, and other goals. Decide which objectives can best be evaluated by written test items—objectives A and B have been included in this test.

Element 3 Outline the course content based on the list of objectives. Use a rules study sheet or text to make certain that all important rules have been included. Use class notes, text, or study sheet for other areas of instruction. Occasionally an objective will be discovered that is important but was not included in the evaluation. Go back and include it before continuing.

Element 4 Decide on the number (or percentage) of test questions to be included in each area of course content. Indicate this number beside each item listed in the course content. The number of items in each content area should usually reflect the emphasis placed on that area during class instruction or in study materials, or the most common problems experienced by students (such as illegal serves in racquetball).

RACQUETBALL

1. Objectives
   A. To use the following skills successfully in game play as rated on a rating scale by the teacher: power serve, lob serve, kill shot, passing shot, lob or ceiling shot, drop shot, backwall play.
   B. To demonstrate a knowledge of the rules, history, and strategy of racquetball by passing an objective test at the 70 percent level or above.
   C. To participate in tournament play.
2. Course Content
   A. Skills (15)
      a. Power serve--1
      b. Lob serve--1
      c. Kill shot--1
      d. Passing shot--1
      e. Lob or ceiling shot--1
      f. Drop shot--1
      g. Backwall play--1
      h. Grip--1
      i. Skill breakdown--6
      j. Ready position--1
   B. Rules (49)
      a. Game--2
      b. Match--1
      c. Court and equipment--6
      d. Serving--9
      e. Illegal services--13
      f. Return of serve--2
      g. Hinders--6
      h. Ball hitting players--4
      i. Rallying the ball--6
   C. History (1)
   D. Strategy (10)
      a. On the serve--3
      b. Home base--1
      c. Shots to use when--2
      d. Double's play--2
      e. General--2

TOTAL   75

Figure 8.1 A test construction "blueprint" for racquetball.

Rule	1	2	3	4	5	6	7	8	9	10	Etc.
1.1	✓										
1.2		✓									
1.3	✓	✓									
2.1			✓								
2.2				✓							
2.3					✓						
Etc.											

Figure 8.2 A comparison of test questions with course objectives to determine content validity.

Element 5 Write or collect test items on cards or slips of paper and check to see that each area of course content has been evaluated. An easy way to do this is to list the content or objectives in a column on the left and the number of the test question at the top and place a check in the appropriate box. This is shown in figure 8.2. Check questions for correct principles of construction by referring to common errors listed in a tests and measurements textbook. As test questions are constructed, put the rule number or content area in parentheses at the end of each question. For example:

1. In a match that goes three games, the winner of the second game serves first in the third game. (Rule 4.1)
2. In singles, it is considered desirable to return to the mid-court position after each play. (singles strategy)

This technique gives a double check with the "blueprint" to be sure the right number of questions have been included. It also gives a ready reference for checking to be sure the question accurately represents the rule.

Element 6 Arrange questions by groups according to item types and add appropriate test directions. Slips of paper can be taped on sheets of paper or cards can be arranged in order for typing.

Element 7 Select or construct an answer sheet and make an answer key from a copy of the test. Proofread the test while making the answer key and correct any errors on the test. Then, make sufficient copies for class use. Number each copy to make certain that none has been taken during the administration of the test. Provide a space on the answer sheet for students to record this number.

Element 8 Administer the test. Make certain that sufficient copies of the test and answer sheet are available as well as extra pencils. Be sure the answer key is in a safe place. A red pencil or pen is helpful to have for correcting the tests. To minimize the temptation to cheat, seat students in alternate seats or ask them to use the space of the entire room. Alternate forms of a test can also be used to discourage cheating. Review the testing procedures and the test directions orally to avoid needless questions. Include how to fill out answer sheets, how to get help if needed (e.g., raise hand or come to front desk), and what to do when finished. If possible, assign a student assistant to correct tests (if it is an objective test) as students complete them. Papers can also be collected when all students have completed the test and redistributed so no student gets his or her own paper. Then have students correct the exam. Whichever method is used, the test serves as a learning activity as well as a means of evaluation because students know the correct answer to the questions they missed. Make sure to collect all tests and answer sheets before dismissing the class.

Element 9 Evaluate the test by looking for and eliminating factors that might decrease its validity. Look for items such as unclear directions, complex vocabulary, poor sentence structure, poorly constructed questions, and materials that do not test course content as stated on the test "blueprint." Listen to students' questions as they attempt to take or correct the test and note problems with the directions or test items on a master copy for use when the test is revised. Record the amount of time needed to complete the test by indicating when the last student finished. Keep a tally of questions missed. Identify those questions no one missed or that were often missed. These questions may need to be eliminated or revised.

Variations of the written test include:

1. *True–false test.* Develop a true-false test in which the students change the questions so the answers are all true or all false. Tell the students which one of these conditions will exist.

2. *Take-home test.* Students are given questions to be answered outside of class. A deadline for submission is stated when the questions are handed out. Students may use whatever resources are available to answer questions, and they should be listed on the test answer sheet. Answers are expected to be comprehensive and grades reflect this criterion.

3. *Multiple-choice test.* By labeling options of a multiple-choice test with letters other than the usual a, b, c, or d, the correct answers can be grouped into words to spell out a phrase appropriate to a given holiday or activity.[4] For example, the answer to question one might be F; to question 2, I; to question 3, T, and so forth. Another variation is to label the responses themselves to form words as shown in this example:

What score would the server call out when she has scored three points and the opponent has scored two points?

X. 30–40
M. Ad In
A. 40–30
S. Deuce

4. *Nongraded exam.* Students are asked to answer questions that when completed serve as a study sheet. Answers are corrected but not graded. Such activities can be motivational. Examples include the crossword puzzle and the pyramid described in chapter 9.

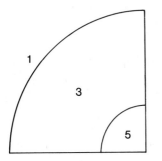

Figure 8.3 A target for the badminton short-serve skills test.

Step 4—Construct Skill (Psychomotor) Evaluation Techniques

Review the course objectives and select those involving the performance of psychomotor skills. Look to see if appropriate tests can be found in tests and measurements books or professional books and journals. AAHPERD has skills tests for many activities. These tests generally cite coefficients of reliability and validity. Always check to see if the norm group is appropriate for the students. It may be necessary to devise norms. This can be done once the test has been given to many students.

If no tests appear for the objectives being evaluated or if the tests cannot be used in the teaching environment, the teacher will be forced to create the tests. In this case, list the behaviors demonstrated by an outstanding player in the activity being tested. For example, in badminton, an "A" student should be able to

1. Hit a short serve as close to the corner of the service court as possible.
2. Hit an overhead clear and long serve that land as close to the back boundary line as possible.
3. Hit an effective smash.
4. Hit an underhand drop shot that lands as close to the net as possible.

Next, devise a means of testing for the behavior specified. Try to keep the test as close to the game situation as possible.[5] For example, for the short serve, mark the court or place a target (tape, paper, plastic, or cloth) in the corner of the service court. This target should give higher points to players serving closest to the corner to simulate an effective serve in a game (see figure 8.3).

Continue to formulate the tests in a similar manner, keeping the tests as simple as possible. Try out the tests with a few students to see how they work and revise them as needed. For example, a review of the short-serve test showed that students often hit the shuttle too high to achieve an effective short serve. A rope placed twenty inches above the net provided a solution to this problem. Also, after the review, the number of serves was reduced from twenty to ten to facilitate testing an entire class within one class period.

```
┌─────────────────────────────────────────────────────────────┐
│              BADMINTON SKILLS TEST CARD                       │
├─────────────────────────────────────────────────────────────┤
│                                                               │
│   Name _____ Period _____ Date _____         │
│                                                               │
│                                                               │
│   SHORT SERVE:                                                 │
│   Equipment: Rope--20" above net                              │
│                  Target--yellow, as shown                     │
│                                                               │
│   Directions: Serve 10 birds to the right court.             │
│                                                               │
│   Scoring:  Liners count higher number. (Serve must          │
│             go between ropes. Must repeat illegal            │
│             serves.) (Shuttle or racket above               │
│             waist.)                                          │
│    5 or 3   Scored depending on area on target.             │
│      0      For hitting net.                                 │
│      0      For passing over rope.                          │
│      1      For hitting in service area but not on          │
│             target.                                         │
│                                                              │
│   1. ____  2. ____  3. ____  4. ____  5. ____               │
│   6. ____  7. ____  8. ____  9. ____  10. ____              │
│   Have partners score as you serve.                         │
│                              Total _____                  │
│                                                              │
└─────────────────────────────────────────────────────────────┘
```

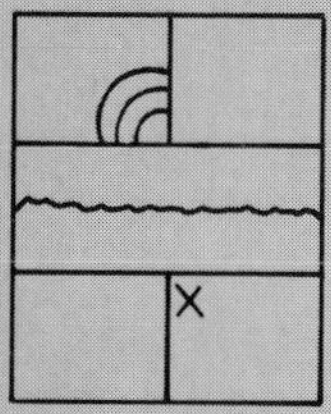

Figure 8.4 A skills test scorecard.

Before giving the tests to the class or classes involved in the activity, devise some method of scorekeeping that includes a management system. A sample scorecard for the badminton short serve is shown in figure 8.4. Administer the test and note any problems involved.

Be aware of the disadvantages of grading on a single administration of a skills test. A student might be ill, anxious about the test, or just not able to perform as well some days as others. This can be remedied to some extent by allowing the student to take the test several times and use the highest score achieved. In this way, it also serves as a learning activity.

When administering the skills tests, demonstrate each test, read and explain the directions on the card or test sheet, and answer any questions students might have. Carefully explain trials, scoring, and recording. Make certain areas are marked and equipment for all tests is set up in advance.

SWIMMING	Sculling	Ch. direction	Turn over	Jump--waist deep	Jump deep	Level off	Dive	Bobbing--25 times	Rhythmic breathing	Tread H₂O for 1 minute	Ch. position	Elementary rescues	Feet first surface dive	Pike or tuck surface dive	
Mark	✓	✓	✓	✓	✓	✓	✓	✓	✓	✓	✓	✓	✓	✓	A
Gregg	✓	✓	✓	✓	✓	✓	✓	✓	✓	✓	✓	✓	✓	✓	A
Tracy	✓	✓	✓	✓	✓	✓	✓	✓	✓	✓	✓	✓	✓	✓	A
Gary	✓	✓	✓	✓	✓	✓	✓	✓	✓	✓	✓	✓	✓	✓	A
Lance	✓	✓	✓	✓	✓	✓		✓	✓	✓	✓	✓			B

Figure 8.5 A checklist.

How does the teacher know what is realistic to expect from students in performance on psychomotor tests? The first time a unit is taught the teacher may have to use norm-referenced criteria. The results of the testing can then be used to determine criterion levels for future units.

Many physical education activities can be more appropriately evaluated through techniques other than written or skills tests. Some suggestions are presented here as a basis for planning.

1. *The checklist.* A simple way to use the checklist is to determine those skills that cannot be effectively graded on a quality or quantity basis but which need to be executed at a minimal level. A list of the skills to be performed and the students' names must appear on a card or paper. Then, simply check off the skills as they are achieved. The grade may consist of the number of skills completed. Examples of checklists are shown in figures 8.5 and 8.6.

2. *Scores.* Activities such as bowling and track lend themselves to direct forms of individual measurement because the score or time is the best indication of success in the activity. An example is shown in figure 8.7.

3. *Converted scores, percentiles.* In some activities, such as archery, raw scores cannot be averaged because of differences in the rounds shot. In these cases, norms of some kind may be used to convert the raw scores into a standard score that can be compared with scores on other rounds or averaged to get a composite score. Standard tests and measurements texts are a good source for learning how to calculate converted scores or

ARCHERY FORM CHECKLIST

Date _____

NAMES

Address	Feet not positioned properly	
	Weight unbalanced	
	Body twisted	
Nock	Arrow not perpendicular to string	
	Fingers grip nock	
	Archer's feet move to get arrow	
Draw	Fingers uneven on string	
	Finger or wrist curl	
	Grip on bow too tight	
	Forefinger above arrow rest	
	Forearm, wrist, hand not even with line of arrow	
	Bow canted	
	Bow elbow rotated downward	
	Head or body moves to meet anchor	
Anchor Aim	Incorrect eye closed	
	Unsteady bow arm	
	Not holding long enough to aim	
	Inconsistent anchor--no anchor	
Release	Body or head moves	
	Bow arm moves	
	String hand jerks	
Follow Through	Not holding form until arrow strikes target	
	SCORE	

Figure 8.6 A form checklist.

percentiles. Grades on each round can also be used as converted scores and can be averaged. An example of converted scores obtained by collecting scores from previous classes and the average calculated is shown in the Archery Progress Record in figure 8.8.

4. *The rating sheet.* The rating sheet is a form of checklist used to evaluate (rate) some ability. It can be constructed from a list of expected behaviors. The teacher places a check or number beside the appropriate item. Examples of rating sheets include the Evaluation of Individual Presentation Rating Sheet and the Tumbling Routines Rating Sheet shown in figures 8.9 and 8.10.

BOWLING	Game 1	Game 2	Game 3	Game 4	Game 5	Final average	Form	Scoring quiz	Written final	Grade
Glen	134	134	148	140	144	140 / A	B⁺	B	C	B
Jean	122	128	110	112	122	118 / B	B	D	B	B⁻
Jim	150	168		120	168	151 / A	A⁻	C	A	A⁻
Steve	121	83	114	112	104	106 / C⁺	B	C	D	C
Lois	141	150	149	166	124	146 / A	B⁺	C	B	B⁺

Figure 8.7 Grading with actual scores.

ROUND	ARCHERY PROGRESS RECORD GRADE										TOTAL POSSIBLE
	Boys A	A−	B+	B	B−	C+ C	C−	D+	D		
	Girls A	A	A−	B+	B	B−	C+ C	C−		D	
NAA 900*	600	510	480	460	430	400	340	280	230	150	900
Columbia	500	410	360	330	300	280	240	220	180	140	648
Jr. Columbia	500	450	410	380	350	330	310	270	240	210	648
Scholastic	330	260	230	210	190	170	150	130	110	100	432
Jr. Scholastic	380	340	320	310	300	280	260	240	210	180	432

*Others listed are noncompetitive rounds.

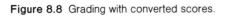

Figure 8.8 Grading with converted scores.

EVALUATION OF INDIVIDUAL PRESENTATION
RATING SHEET

Student presenting _____

Subject _____

CRITERIA	RATING				
	Excellent 5	Good 4	Satisfactory 3	Fair 2	Poor 1
I. *Preparation*					
A. Depth of material					
B. Breadth of material					
C. Accuracy of information					
D. Research information cited and reliability of sources					
II. *Procedure*					
A. Organization-- Logical Development of ideas					
B. Interesting, stimulating, provocative					
C. Visual aids, examples, and illustrations ..					
D. Level of class participation ..					
Column scores					

Highest possible score = 40

Highest possible average = 5.0

Total score

Average total / 8

Figure 8.9 A rating sheet for evaluating an individual presentation.

TUMBLING ROUTINES RATING SHEET

Rating to be given in each area: 4 = Very Good; 3 = Good; 2 = Fair; 1 = Poor

Group number	Entrance	Team work	Original- ity	Quality of skill	Stage poise	Exit	Evidence of prepara- tion	Comments
1								
2								
3								
4								
5								
6								
7								
8								
9								
10								

Period _____   Date _____   Signature of evaluator _____

Figure 8.10 A rating sheet for tumbling.

5. *The incidence chart.* The incidence chart is a list of skills performed in a given activity. The Badminton Incidence Chart shown in figure 8.11 is an example. The number of times each stroke is used is tallied during a specified time period. Incidence charts can assist the teacher in describing game performance to the student.

6. *Subjective evaluation of performance.* Subjective evaluation by the teacher is another method for evaluating performance. Keep in mind that evaluating a few students each day is easier than evaluating all of the students at the same time. Scores for several evaluations can then be averaged at the conclusion of the term. Discuss each individual rating immediately. This feedback to students helps to improve and motivate performance. It also opens the line of communication for those students who may not agree with the evaluation made by the teacher. Figure 8.12 shows a sample of scores from a badminton class. In the example shown, the students were graded in badminton as follows:

GRADE or POINTS

A or 4—Correct use of all strokes
B or 3—Correct use of clears, serves, and smash or drop
C or 2—Correct use of clears and serves
D or 1—Correct use of clear or serve

In swimming, each stroke can be divided easily into arms, legs, breathing, and coordination and one point assigned to each, the highest grade possible being A or 4. Never use a scale that is so detailed that it cannot be interpreted to students to show the difference between adjacent points on the scale. For sport skills, a description of each point on the scale would contribute to a more objective and reliable grade. An example might be as follows:

Points	Rating	Definition
5	Excellent	Technique and form mastered. Effective, polished, confident in execution of skills and strategies.
4	Above Average	Good technique and execution of skill but not highly effective or efficient. Some minor errors. Good use of strategy.
3	Average	Basic skill performed but not refined. Accuracy and effectiveness consistent enough to permit some use of strategy.
2	Fair	Executes skill with many errors that result in inconsistency, inaccuracy, and ineffectiveness. Lacks confidence and timing.
1	Poor	Basic mechanics in performance of skills lacking. Experiences very occasional success. Fails to apply strategy.

BADMINTON INCIDENCE CHART

Name	SERVE Short Out-of-court	SERVE Short Into net	Too high	SERVE Long Out-of-court	Too short	Too low	Into or below net	Out-of-bounds	Missed bird	Too low	CLEAR Too short	Out-of-court	Out-of-position
	Short			*Long*			SMASH				CLEAR		
Diane White			/	///	/				///		////// ////	//	
Gregg Charlton				//////					//////		//////// ////// ///	//////// ////// //	///

Figure 8.11 An incidence chart.
Source: Rudy Moe, Brigham Young University.

NAME	9/17	9/19	9/24	9/26	10/1	10/3	10/8	10/10	10/15	AVERAGE
Judy	2		2			2+		2-		2
Sally	3+			4			4-		4	4-
Vickie	2	3-			3		3	3		3
Bonnie	1		2-	2		2+				2
Kay				4				4		4

Figure 8.12 Subjective evaluation of performance.

MODERN DANCE COMPOSITION EVALUATION

Period ______________ Grade ______________

Names	*Floor patterns* (2)	*Coordination of movements* (3)	*Variations* (3)	*Performance* (2)
Janice				
Betty				
John				
Jerry				

Figure 8.13 Subjective evaluation in dance.

Subjective evaluations in dance can often be made more objective by defining the factors to be considered, as in the Modern Dance Composition Evaluation shown in figure 8.13. This also helps the student to discern what is to be included in the composition (ten points are possible).

7. *Tournament results.* Results of a comprehensive class singles tournament is generally a good indication of the playing ability of individual students. Otherwise, care must be taken to avoid grading one student on his or her team's or partner's ability or lack of ability. A detailed explanation of various kinds of tournaments is found in chapter 9.

8. *Accumulative record.* This evaluation technique (see figure 8.14) is one in which a cumulative record is kept of student performance. For example, the distance swum by each student is recorded daily in the Swim and Stay Fit program of the American Red Cross. In basketball, a student can shoot ten free throws each day and record the total number made on an accumulative record. This method of evaluation is most valuable as a motivational technique for many students. Caution should be used, however, when incorporating this technique for all students. Those who are doing poorly may be motivated to quit trying or give up. Such records can be very valuable to the teacher as the low-aptitude students quickly emerge and a general indication of such factors as skill,

Jogging Record

Name	¼	½	¾	1	1¼	1½	1¾	2	2¼	2½	2¾	3	3¼
Gail	■	■	■										
Lois	■	■		■									
Karen	■	■	■										
Penny	■												

Figure 8.14 An accumulative tournament.

endurance, and effort appear. Individualized programs can then be set up catering to the personal needs of students. Scores could be averaged at the end of a unit to be used for grading purposes.

Step 5—Construct Affective Evaluation Techniques

Because affective evaluation techniques are generally difficult to construct, they are often less precise than other evaluation techniques. However, these techniques can be used to determine student progress toward course objectives in the affective domain and to assist students through individual conferences and group instruction. In general, teachers are attempting to assess (1) whether student attitudes are positive or negative—toward physical education or the specific activity engaged in, or toward such principles as teamwork or sportsmanship, (2) whether students appear to be as willing to approach physical education or an activity as readily at the end of course instruction as when they began, and (3) what activities appeal to students.

For students to answer honestly on affective evaluation instruments, they must trust that results will not be used against them. To accomplish this, use questions that require checking or circling the responses instead of writing, tell students not to put their names on the papers, have students collect the papers and tabulate the responses, or ask for papers to be placed in a box in a nonthreatening place. At the beginning of the course, students can be told that their answers are needed to help organize the course to best meet their needs; at the conclusion of the course, they can be told that they are helping to improve instruction for classes to be taught at a future time.

Two types of techniques can be used—direct and indirect. *Direct techniques* use quantitative data such as statistics, questionnaires, checklists, rating scales, inventories, ranking, and paired comparison. *Indirect techniques* use qualitative data such as teacher observation, interviews, sentence completion, and student self-evaluation.

Statistics A comparison of student approach or avoidance behaviors during the first quarter of the course versus their approach or avoidance behaviors during the last quarter provide a general idea of student affect.[6] Items for analysis might include:

1. Avoidance behaviors
    a. Dropouts
    b. Tardiness
    c. Absences

2. Approach behaviors
   a. Nonrequired club, intramural, or extramural participation
   b. Unassigned library books on physical education topics checked out
   c. Number of students volunteering to help with physical education-related activities
   d. Number of students desiring to major in physical education in college
   e. Amount of money spent on sports equipment

Questionnaires The following possible items may be selected for student response to furnish evidence for making instructional changes. Others may be invented.

Student Goals and Interests
1. Indicate your interest in physical fitness *before* taking this class. highly interested/ interested/ neutral/ less interested/ highly uninterested
2. How long do you plan to continue your present exercise program? throughout life/ throughout school years/ until school is out this year/ this term only/ I don't plan to continue
3. Circle the subject you would be most interested in teaching. English/ physical education/ math/ science/ music/ other
4. I took this class for the following reasons:

I was curious	_____
It was required	_____
I needed the challenge	_____
I've always liked it	_____
I wanted to learn something new	_____
I needed some easy credit or an easy A	_____
Nothing else was available and I needed an elective	_____
I don't know	_____

5. If you were asked to give a short talk about your favorite school subject, which subject would you talk about?
6. If someone suggested that you take up physical education as your life's work, what would you reply?

Student's Perception of Teacher and/or Methods of Instruction
1. If I had it to do all over again, I (would/ would not) have taken this course.
2. To what extent will you use the things you have learned in this class? often/ sometimes/ seldom/ never
3. What are the two most important things you have learned in this class?
4. Which of the following helped you most in meeting your course goals? teacher/ practice drills/ playing games/ study sheet/ individual work on skills
5. The study sheet was helpful in preparing for the test. strongly agree/ agree/ neutral/ disagree/ strongly disagree

6. The homework assigned was a useful part of the course. yes/ no
7. The present system of grading is appropriate. strongly agree/ agree/ neutral/ disagree/ strongly disagree
8. What things would you have liked more help with in this unit?

Students' Perceptions of the Curriculum
1. I learned more this semester because I was able to take the activities I wanted.
   yes/ no
2. I like being able to select the teacher I want.
   yes/ no
3. There should be a limit on the number of times a student can take a given activity.
   yes/ no
4. With regard to activities, I wish we had a class in _____ .
5. In which of the following did you participate?

   intramurals _____

   extramurals _____

   varsity sports _____

   none of these _____

6. By which method do you prefer intramural teams be picked?

   homerooms _____

   physical education class _____

   personal selection _____

7. If physical education were not required, would you still have taken it this year?
   yes/ no

Checklists Checklists involve lists of activities or questions with brief responses that can be checked by students. Although they are relatively crude instruments, they can provide valuable data if they are carefully constructed. Checklists also run the risk of students "helping out" the result by marking what they think the teacher wants. An example of a checklist is shown in figure 8.15. To score the checklist, total the responses for each symbol and activity.

Rating Scales Rating scales provide a numerical value for each level of intensity on a scale. They can be used to provide information about the rater or the object of the rating. The danger in using rating scales is that they give the illusion of accuracy. There is also an implication that a high score on one factor can compensate for a low score on another. If a student scores low in skill, can this really be counterbalanced by high scores for attendance, attitude, and cooperativeness? Frequently, in practice, ratings tend to cluster on the high side with this system.

Labels used on the scales may not mean the same things to different people or to the same person on different occasions. Therefore, ratings or labels must be defined as to the frame of reference that students are expected to use. Otherwise, students will be influenced by what they think is the purpose of the scale, and since their guesses will be different from each other, ratings will diverge more than might be expected.

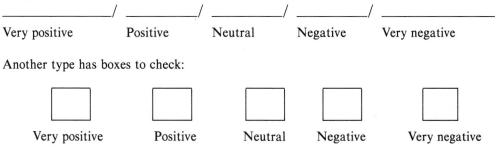

INSTRUCTIONS: Each activity is followed by a number of symbols. Circle all of the symbols for the words that describe you.

Sport	Spectator	Occasional participant	Frequent participant	Low skill	Average skill	High skill
Chess	(S)	(OP)	FP	(LS)	AS	HS
Archery	S	OP	FP	LS	AS	HS
Badminton	S	OP	FP	LS	AS	HS
Basketball	S	OP	FP	LS	AS	HS
Bicycling	S	OP	FP	LS	AS	HS
Others (list)						
_____	S	OP	FP	LS	AS	HS
_____	S	OP	FP	LS	AS	HS

Figure 8.15 An activity checklist.

Rating scales usually include from three to nine choices. The number should be based on the complexity of the information required. Fewer choices yield more reliable data. More choices provide more information. Generally, an odd number is used so the midpoint will be a neutral category. Several types of scales exist. One form of scale is the continuum, on which the rater places a mark as shown in this question:

Has positive attitudes toward self:

_____/ _____/ _____/ _____/ _____

Very positive   Positive   Neutral   Negative   Very negative

Another type has boxes to check:

☐   ☐   ☐   ☐   ☐

Very positive   Positive   Neutral   Negative   Very negative

Several scales for rating behavior have been developed. In the Blanchard Behavior Rating Scale, the rater rates the frequency of observation of such traits as leadership, self-control, cooperation, and other personal and social qualities.[7] Cowell has developed a Social Adjustment Index to measure similar qualities, and a Personal Distance Scale to measure social acceptance.[8] Another test of group status is Breck's Sociometric Test of Status.[9] Fox has developed a tool that can be used to screen out students with low self-concepts.[10] An example is shown in figure 8.16. Results of all of these scales will be influenced to some extent by the amount of trust that has been developed between teacher and students. Teachers should be aware of the possible lack of validity and reliability in using these measures. Therefore, caution must be exercised when using them.

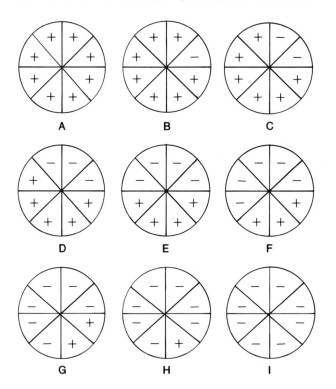

Date _____

Your Number _____

Class _____

How They See Me

Just as each part of the day is filled with positive, neutral, and negative things, each person is made up of things we like and things we do not like so much. Below are a number of circles showing persons with different amounts of positive (+) and negative (−) things about them. Which of these circles comes closest to the way you see yourself? Write the letter of the circle which most resembles you right here: _____ .

In the blank following each question, write the letter of the circle that you think each of the persons mentioned would pick for you.

1. Which circle do you think your closest friend would choose to describe you? _____
2. Which circle would the teacher in this class choose? _____

Figure 8.16 A self-concept scale.

Source: *Diagnosing Classroom Learning Environments*
by Fox, Luszki and Schmuck. © 1966, Science
Research Associates, Inc. Reprinted by permission of
the publisher.

Inventories Inventories are rating scales designed to yield two or more scores by grouping items in certain prespecified ways. Many personality tests take the form of inventories. The Thurstone[11] Likert[12] and Osgood[13] scales are some of the best known of the attitude inventories. Although each of these inventories has a carefully specified technique for formulation, teacher-constructed versions can provide useful information.

Several attitude inventories have been created to appraise student attitude toward physical fitness, exercise, and physical education. They are referred to in a number of tests and measurements textbooks. Attitude inventories generally contain three types of questions. The first type is based on the work of Thurstone and uses the following type of question:

	Agree	Disagree
1. Physical education is a waste of time. (2.00)	_____	_____
2. Physical education is helpful in one's life. (8.00)	_____	_____
3. Physical activity is important to my mental, physical, and emotional fitness. (9.00)	_____	_____
4. Physical fitness is no longer essential in today's world. (3.00)	_____	_____

The student's score is an average of the scale factors (in parentheses) for all of the questions marked "agree."

The second type of question is based on the Likert scales. An example of this type looks like this:

	Strongly agree	Agree	Uncertain	Disagree	Strongly disagree
1. I need a lot of exercise to stay in good physical condition.	( )	( )	( )	( )	( )
2. Following game rules helps me be a better citizen in the community.	( )	( )	( )	( )	( )
3. I prefer to engage in activities that require a minimum of physical activity.	( )	( )	( )	( )	( )

The third type of question is based on Osgood's semantic differential technique. An example of this type of question follows:

Physical education is:

Pleasant	: ___ : ___ : ___ : ___ : ___ : ___ : ___ :	Unpleasant
Good	: ___ : ___ : ___ : ___ : ___ : ___ : ___ :	Bad
Active	: ___ : ___ : ___ : ___ : ___ : ___ : ___ :	Passive

	Strong interest	OK	Neutral	Don't like
Archery	SI	OK	N	DL
Badminton	SI	OK	N	DL
Basketball	SI	OK	N	DL
Bicycling	SI	OK	N	DL
Bowling	SI	OK	N	DL
Others (list)				
_____	SI	OK	N	DL
_____	SI	OK	N	DL

Figure 8.17 An interest or valued activities inventory.

Another type of inventory is the interest or valued activities inventory. An example is shown in figure 8.17. To score the inventory, simply tally the responses for each activity.

Adjective checklists differ slightly from inventories. Students select those adjectives that apply to themselves or others from a list of those provided, as shown below:

Circle each of the words that tell how you feel about physical education:

interesting	dull	boring
fun	useful	very important
too hard	exciting	too easy
useless	tiring	

Ranking Ranking involves arranging items on a list in order of personal preference or some other specified quality. Items to be ranked should be limited to about ten items. Two examples of ranking are shown here:

Example 1: List all the subjects you are now taking and then rank them in order from most interesting to least interesting (1 is best).

Example 2: Rank order the following activities by placing a 1 by the activity you like to play best, 2 next, and so on down to number 10:

Archery	_____	Folk dance	_____
Badminton	_____	Golf	_____
Basketball	_____	Gymnastics	_____

Do you dislike the activity you rated last? Yes No
If yes, why?

To score, total the ranks from all students. The rank with the lowest score is indicative of the highest interest. One major disadvantage of ranking is that there is no way of knowing how much difference exists between items in adjacent ranks. Group scores, however, can provide valuable data.

Paired Comparison A relatively quick method for determining attitudes toward a subject or activity is the paired comparison technique.[14] To construct it, do the following:

1. List school subjects or physical education activities in the boxes as shown below:

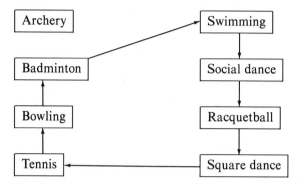

2. Keeping the top left box stationary, rotate all other boxes as shown in the arrows until each box has returned to its original location. List each rotation separately.
3. Ask the student to consider each pair that results by indicating which one he or she would prefer to learn, or play, or likes best.
4. To avoid a student's changing responses to ensure consistency, use numbered flashcards with each pair and have the student note A or B, or put the pairs on separate pieces of paper stapled together.
5. Sample question: Circle the subject you like best in each pair (if on paper) or write the activity beside the question number on your answer sheet.

Badminton—tennis	English—math
Archery—bowling	Math—science

6. To score, count the number of times each subject has been circled or written. When used with school subjects, the paired comparison can be used as a pretest/posttest to indicate how physical education stacks up with other school subjects. If the second score is at least as large as the first, attitude has not been seriously impaired. When used with physical education activities, it can tell teachers the rank order of activities preferred by students.

```
Sportsmanship Checklist for _____

                            Usually Sometimes Seldom  Never

Knows and obeys rules,
  even when not
  observed                  _____ _____  _____ _____
    Calls own violations, fouls, liners
    Plays "clean"
Respects officials          _____ _____  _____ _____
    Does not argue with officials or complain
    about misjudgments
    Compliments officials
Shows respect for
      opponents             _____ _____  _____ _____
    Applauds or congratulates good play by opponent
    Is courteous
    Shakes hands with opponents before the contest
    Congratulates opponents after the game
Maintains self-control      _____ _____  _____ _____
    Accepts victory without boasting
    Loses gracefully without complaint or alibi
    Does not make excuses
    Performs to the best of his or her ability regardless
      of the situation
    Does not use profanity
    Refrains from verbal or physical abuse of others
Shows respect for
      facilities and
      equipment             _____ _____  _____ _____
    Puts equipment away
    Respects property of others
    Takes appropriate care of equipment
```

Figure 8.18 A rating scale for sportsmanship.

Teacher Observation Teachers have almost unlimited opportunities to observe the students they teach. That teachers have so many opportunities for observing student behavior and attitudes does not necessarily mean their judgment will be objective and informed, however. If the assessment is to be thorough and truly useful, teachers should systematically plan both data collection and procedures for recording information. If teachers do not consciously identify the behaviors to be observed and take time to gather and record information, their impressions are more likely to be formed on the basis of extreme incidents and behavior patterns, rather than by a less-biased sample of the behaviors of interest.

Ideally, teachers should take the time to devise a system of recording individual student behavior. Rating scales, frequency counts, or anecdotal records can all be useful in achieving this. Examples of rating scales that could be used for evaluating sportsmanship or teamwork are shown in figures 8.18 and 8.19. Each of these rating scales could also be used for self-evaluation.

```
┌─────────────────────────────────────────────────────────────────┐
│                                                                   │
│        Teamwork Checklist for _____         │
│                                                                   │
│                       Usually  Sometimes  Seldom   Never          │
│     Shows respect for                                             │
│       teammates        _____ _____ _____ _____      │
│         Congratulates good play by teammate                       │
│         Puts team before self                                     │
│         Plays own position--does not hog ball                     │
│         Assists play by teammates                                 │
│         Talks or signals to teammates during play                 │
│         Does not argue with team members                          │
│         Demonstrates loyalty                                       │
│         Is courteous                                              │
│         Gets along with teammates                                 │
│         Works with teammates to improve skills                    │
│     Maintains self-control  _____ _____ _____ _____ │
│         Is punctual and in own place, does not keep others        │
│           waiting                                                 │
│         Does not use profanity                                    │
│         Puts in hard, honest practice                             │
│     Shows respect for                                             │
│       teacher or coach  _____ _____ _____ _____     │
│         Follows instructions without arguing                      │
│                                                                   │
└─────────────────────────────────────────────────────────────────┘
```

Figure 8.19 A rating scale for teamwork.

Interviews Interviews can be structured or unstructured. Much valuable information about student feelings toward physical education can be acquired through informal discussions with individuals or groups of students. Structured interviews involve asking students predetermined questions. The effectiveness of the interview technique hinges on the trust between teacher and students.

Sentence Completion Open-ended questions completed by students can provide information unobtainable in direct techniques because the teacher is completely unaware of the student's viewpoint. Questions might include such questions as "I wish this class . . ." or "I really like this class when . . . ."

Student Self-evaluation Student self-evaluation can be helpful in assisting students to focus on their personal effort and involvement in physical education and to learn to evaluate themselves realistically. Often students will have a different feeling about their effort and progress than the teacher does. Teacher-student conferences can be used to discuss these discrepancies and gain a better understanding of what goals each is trying to achieve. An attitude or effort inventory such as the one shown in figure 8.20 could be used for this purpose.

Step 6—Evaluate the Evaluation Techniques
Answer the following questions about each evaluation technique:

1. Does the evaluation agree with the performance objective stated for the activity (content validity)?
2. Are the directions and vocabulary simple enough for the students' maturity, and are the test items carefully selected or constructed (validity)?

INSTRUCTIONS: Answer the following questions by circling the best
response or filling in the blank.

1. I feel <u>really good</u>   good   ok   <u>bad</u>   about myself and what I
   have done.
2. I accomplished <u>all</u>   almost all   most   some   none of
   my contracted objectives.
3. I completed _____ elective objectives.
              (number)
4. My efforts on the objectives would be considered: <u>good</u>   fair
   <u>poor</u>.
5. My efforts in helping others would be considered: <u>good</u>   fair
   <u>poor</u>.
6. The grade that I contracted for was _____.
7. The grade I have earned is _____.
8. If you were to grade yourself on a ten-point scale for each of the
   following items, what score would you give yourself on:
   a. Your current skill level: _____
   b. Your skill improvement: _____
   c. Your physical fitness: _____
9. How can you improve in the following areas in this class?
   a. Achievement _____

   b. Effort _____

   c. Citizenship _____

Figure 8.20 An attitude or effort inventory.

3. Is the technique formulated so that another person with similar experience can use it
   for evaluation and get the same results (objectivity)?
4. Does the technique consistently result in the same score or grade for a student even
   when given on different occasions (reliability)?
5. Does the technique contribute to improved teaching-learning practices by enhancing
   teacher-pupil relations, encouraging students to devote attention to all areas of
   instruction, and serving as a fair and useful measure of achievement of outcomes
   emphasized in instruction?

Step 7—Try Out the Evaluation Techniques

After, or while using, the evaluation techniques with one or more classes, note how each one
was implemented or whether it was effective, and why. Then, make plans to remedy any
problems and increase the efficiency, validity, and reliability of the test. Repeat this process
each time the test is given. Remember, evaluation is a means to an end, not an end in and
of itself.

When the process of ongoing evaluation has been completed, some type of reporting
of results usually occurs. The assignment of a grade to each student is the most common
method of reporting evaluation results.

Preassessment

The process of evaluation begins with preassessment. Preassessment is any technique used at the beginning of instruction to determine where the learner is in relation to the instructional objective. Preassessment techniques can be used to determine

1. Whether the learner or learners can or cannot already perform the behavior of the instructional objective and, therefore, whether the objective is appropriate for the learner or group.
2. Whether the learner possesses the knowledge or skills necessary to succeed in learning the behavior of the instructional objective.

Why is preassessment important? It gives the teacher information needed to personalize instruction to the student or class. Preassessment aids the instructional process in the following ways:

1. Provides diagnosis or screening information to the teacher for grouping and individualizing instruction.
2. Clarifies objectives for the students while assisting them to increase their self-awareness of and reevaluate their own skills, knowledge, and attitudes.
3. Evaluates instructional objectives for accuracy and application to the specific situation.
4. Assists in the determination of student achievement and the effectiveness of teaching methods as the difference between pre- and posttests are calculated.

Students who have already achieved the objective, as evidenced by preassessment results, should be allowed to perfect the behavior by practicing for accuracy, by practicing an advanced form of the skill, or by going on to other activities. For example, if the objective states that the student will perform the lay-up shot in basketball successfully and with correct form, the teacher can quickly identify those students who can already perform successful lay-ups with correct form. These students can be sent to a separate court to work on consecutive lay-ups, left-handed or reverse lay-ups, or lay-ups in a game while the rest of the class learns to perform a basic lay-up successfully. In team-teaching situations, or when individualized instruction is available, these advanced students can move on to other objectives.

Those students who cannot perform the behavior specified in the objective, as determined by the preassessment technique, can be given help to develop the prerequisite skills. For example, students who do not have the hand-eye coordination necessary to hit a badminton shuttle are not ready to learn the overhead and underhand clears. Special help must be given these students so they learn to connect with the shuttle before instruction can take place on the strokes.

An instructor evaluating the application of performance objectives will want to employ preassessment techniques. For example, suppose that the class average (mean) on a pretest is fifty-five and the mean on a posttest is sixty. A class that showed very little improvement in performance from the beginning to the end of a unit might need to be challenged to achieve more difficult levels of knowledge or skill. On the other hand, the test could be too hard indicating performance standards were set too high. The teacher would need to carefully analyze the results of assessment in such a situation.

A teacher or administrator desiring to evaluate methods of teaching is aided by preassessment results. For example, Teacher A brags that students can shoot two hundred points at forty yards and, therefore, she is an excellent teacher. Without some other information, no judgment of her teaching ability can be made. Since two hundred points at forty yards is a good score for a beginning student, we can assume either that she taught the class well or that she began the class with students who were already highly skilled in archery. Teacher B, on the contrary, indicates that in his class no student scored two hundred points or better on the pretest at twenty yards, yet now all students can shoot two hundred points at forty yards. Because of the pretest scores, Teacher B can be pleased with the results of his teaching.

Preassessment can be done formally through written or performance tests or informally through observation, asking questions, or analyzing student records of previous work. Some preassessment techniques fall within the realm of instruction (i.e., some can occur following the demonstration of the skill). Whatever the method, the *preassessment should precede each new objective in the lesson or unit.*

Because of the safety factor in some cases, students should not be allowed to take a pretest until a certain level of fitness or skill has been achieved. For example, in tumbling, students should not be evaluated on higher-level skills such as the roundoff until they have demonstrated the ability to perform prerequisite skills such as the cartwheel. Students should not be asked to run continuously in a twelve-minute run/walk without engaging in a cardiovascular endurance program that gradually develops the ability to run that long without incurring adverse physical effects. The instructor should also stress that such a test is actually a run/WALK.

The information that follows is designed to help teachers develop practical preassessment techniques for instruction.

Steps in Developing Preassessment Techniques

Step 1. List what the students will have to be able to do or know to perform the objective.
Step 2. Write down how the teacher will know if some or all of the students have achieved the objective.

Step 1—List What the Students Will Have to Be Able to Do or Know to Perform the Objective

The key to a determination of prerequisite knowledge and skills is the question: "What will the students have to be able to do or know to perform the objective?" For example, if the objective of the course was "The students will be able to play tennis at a beginning level," then what will the students need to be able to do to play tennis? Teachers would probably agree that the students will be able to use (1) a forehand stroke, (2) a backhand stroke, and (3) a serve; that they would know how to (4) score, and (5) follow game rules; and (6) enjoy playing tennis.

The three taxonomies can assist teachers in placing the tasks into the hierarchy (see unit 2). The lowest, most easily learned tasks are placed at the bottom, with the higher-level tasks at the top of the hierarchy. This is called a *task analysis*. Such a task description explains step by step how a task is performed. An example of a task analysis for beginning tennis is shown in figure 8.21. The sequencing of this task analysis identifies skills and knowledge that must be mastered prior to engaging in a new activity. This task analysis shows that a player must know the grip, have eye-racquet coordination, and possess some degree

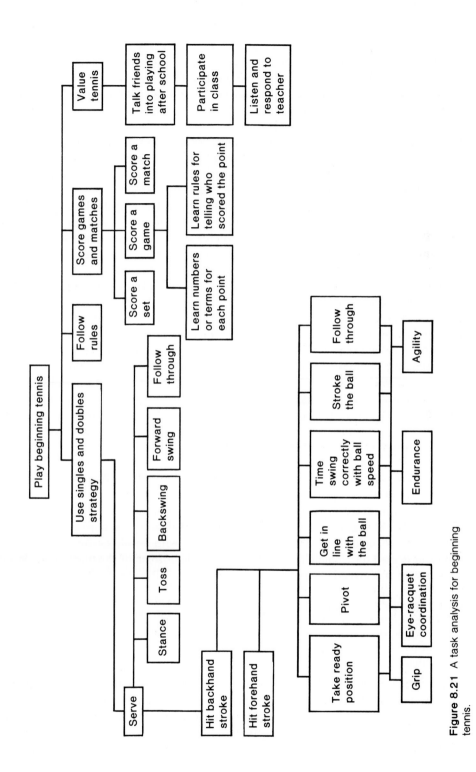

Figure 8.21 A task analysis for beginning tennis.

of endurance and agility to learn to play tennis. The teacher moves to the next level of the hierarchy to progress in teaching the beginning player the basic fundamentals of tennis. To perform both the backhand and forehand stroke, the player takes the ready position and performs each task in order at that hierarchy level. The same process is followed for the serve and finally for singles and doubles strategy that involve both psychomotor and cognitive tasks.

Each teacher might analyze an activity differently, and some disparity will be evidenced when placing tasks into a hierarchy. That is what makes teaching as much an art as a science. However, by writing out a task analysis, teachers are able to pretest students to determine at what point they are in the hierarchy.

Once a teacher determines what a student must know or do, he or she then has to determine performance standards before the preassessment process begins. For example, after deciding students should know how to serve, the teacher might use the preassessment criterion that students must be able to serve three out of five serves legally.

Most performance objectives require some adjunct type of knowledge or skill to benefit from instruction designed to reach the objective. For example, to perform the serve correctly, students must know the area of the court where balls are legally served (service court) and what constitutes a foot fault when serving. As the teacher preassesses serving ability, he or she can also determine student knowledge of a legally served ball.

Knowing where students are helps teachers choose activities that are challenging, yet still within the realm of success for them. It eliminates the need for starting over with beginning basketball each year. By deciding on prerequisite knowledge and skills, teachers can diagnose and provide remedial help to students who are deficient in these areas. Students who already have these skills can move on to practice skills in a way that will be challenging and motivating. A teacher who preassesses student abilities can plan and carry out a meaningful course of study for each individual class.

Step 2—Write Down How the Teacher Will Know If Some or All
of the Students Have Achieved the Objective
The preassessment technique used to determine how the students have achieved the objective will often be the same technique as that used for evaluating the objective. However, other less-formal techniques will be useful in conjunction with formal evaluation or when preassessment is used for a single lesson. An explanation of some of the more common forms of preassessment is given here and examples were included earlier in this chapter.

Pretest A formal test before instruction is a very accurate preassessment tool. A written test may be used to preassess knowledge or a skills test to check on skill achievement. These tests may be equivalent forms of a posttest or a simplified version if time is a factor. If a student passes an equivalent of the posttest, the student should not be asked to repeat the evaluation.

Teacher Observation Students are asked to perform a skill as they have previously learned it, and the teacher observes to see which students can already perform the skill according to the criterion established in the instructional objective. This can be informally done while students are engaged in a learning activity.

Question or Questionnaire A formal questionnaire or an informal question asked of the student by the teacher is often sufficient to tell the teacher which students at least think they have achieved the objective. For example, "How many of you can do a feet-first surface dive?" If no one thinks he or she can, then it is probably a waste of time to use a more formal preassessment technique.

Once student ability is known through preassessment and class instruction begins, evaluation is a much more comprehensive process.

Grading

Grading is often perceived as one of the most bothersome of all teaching duties. Perhaps this is because no consensus is held by members of the profession as to how or why it is to be done. Many grading practices seem to be educationally unsound. Dressel pointed out:

> A grade (is) . . . an inadequate report of an inaccurate judgment by a biased and variable judge of the extent to which a student has attained an undefined level of mastery of an unknown proportion of an indefinite amount of material.[15]

Given the uncertainty of grading, it is still a very important part of the educational process. Students, parents, employers, and institutions of higher learning all demand such accountability. Great care should be taken to ensure fairness and consistency in this process.

The Purpose of Grading

The primary purpose of a grade is to inform students, parents, and administrators concerning the present status and progress of students toward program objectives. Grades also tend to promote positive public relations with colleges, universities, professional schools, and employers, who depend on them for admission and hiring. Grades may also serve as a motivator for both teachers and students to improve the teaching-learning process. Finally, if used properly, grades help teachers evaluate the effectiveness of instruction. Under no circumstances should grades be given casually, based on the teacher's impression of the student, without evidence of student achievement.

Principles of Grading

Even though educators have never been able to agree on how to grade, certain procedures have emerged that, if followed, will make grading a more rewarding process for both teacher and student.

1. The grade should reflect individual student *achievement* as determined by declared course objectives.
2. Grades should be based on achievement of all of the objectives of physical education, such as psychomotor skills, physical fitness, knowledge, social skills, and attitudes and appreciations.
3. Grades should reflect educational aims and promote educational outcomes. The stress placed on marks in conventional practice tends to cause the student to believe that getting good marks is the aim of education and, therefore, the end of education.
4. The school or district grading system should be developed cooperatively by parents, students, teachers, and school personnel so the grades will be consistent with those given by other subjects in the school. A sample worksheet for developing the grading process is shown in figure 8.22.

CRITERIA FOR GRADING

Directions:
1. Choose the criteria you will use in grading by checking either the "Yes" or "No" column.
2. Give a brief explanation for your selection or rejection of each item.
3. Indicate the items from the class roll that you will use to determine the score or grade for each criterion.
4. Indicate the total number of points representing each criterion.
5. Indicate the percent of the total points for each criterion. (This must total 100%.)
6. Under "Comments" explain how you will determine the letter grade for each student.

Criteria	Yes	No	Explanation	Items on Class Roll to Be Used in Criteria	Points	Percent
Fitness						
Improvement						
Skill Tests						
Written Tests						
Other						
				Total		100%

Comments:

Figure 8.22 Criteria for grading.

Source: Moe, Rudy. Brigham Young University.

5. The department grading system should be established collectively by all physical education teachers and be applied consistently to every physical education class in the school.
6. Students should be informed in advance of the criteria and procedures used in assigning grades and receive adequate feedback on their progress toward objectives.
7. A variety of evaluation instruments, including both objective and subjective, should be used in the evaluation process.
8. Evaluation should be an ongoing process with students being adequately prepared. Grades should not depend on one test score or evaluation session.
9. Evaluation procedures should foster positive student attitudes toward physical education.
10. A grading system should be detailed enough to be diagnostic, yet compact enough to be practical in terms of time, understandability, ease of recording, and fair as a uniform measure of achievement.
11. Evaluation procedures should consider individual differences such as physical characteristics, maturity, background experiences, and ability.

The Process of Grading
The process for determining grades in physical education involves the following steps:

Step 1. Select a grading system.
Step 2. Select objectives and determine the emphasis to be placed on each objective.
Step 3. Select evaluation instruments for each objective.
Step 4. Measure the degree of achievement of each objective.
Step 5. Determine the grade based on the original percentage specified for each objective.
Step 6. Communicate the grade to the student.

Step 1—Select a Grading System
In the selection of a grading system or combination of systems, care should be taken to consider the advantages and limitations of each. No one method is superior in all situations; hence, some compromises or combinations of systems may need to be made. One arrangement would be to grade all students according to prearranged standards or criteria. A second arrangement would be to group students for instruction according to skill or fitness levels and grade each group according to different criteria. The following systems of grading are presented for consideration.

Norm-Referenced Evaluation ("Grading on the Curve") Norm-referenced evaluation is a measurement of individual performance as it compares with group or class performance according to a normal probability curve. Grades are distributed at different levels, usually A, B, C, D, or F. Such a system is ideal when students need to be ranked.

Several disadvantages of norm-referenced evaluation exist, however. First, it tends to assess the rate of learning of students rather than the ability to learn; therefore, the fastest learners get As. Second, grades are distributed over a curve whether this is appropriate or not. Third, grading on the curve is not consistent with evaluation based on performance objectives. It fails to tell whether the students have mastered the skills. Some skills cannot be graded on a curve, such as treading water in swimming. Consequently, most grading policies do not adhere to a strict norm-referenced evaluation system. Many grading policies are modifications of the norm-referenced system and a true curve is not strictly observed.

Criterion-Referenced Evaluation Criterion-referenced evaluation is a measurement of individual performance as it compares with a preestablished standard of performance, such as a score, number of tasks completed, or difficulty of tasks completed. Grades can be expressed in percentage scores, as pass/fail, or as letter grades of A, B, C, D, or F.

Criterion-referenced evaluation allows more students to earn a good grade. Grades are not influenced by the high skill levels of others or by the differing instructional abilities of teachers. Criterion-referenced evaluation facilitates the use of student-paced programs, competency-based programs of instruction, and contract grading.

Contract grading specifies the performance and criteria (quantity and quality) for which each student will receive a given grade. An example of contract grading is shown in figure 8.23. In individual contracts, each contract specifies the performance and criteria for that student and whether the student or teacher or someone else will determine when the criteria have been met.

Criterion-referenced grading reduces student anxiety and decreases subjectivity in grading. This is especially true of contract grading and mastery grading, which communicate

TENNIS CONTRACT

A GRADE

I, _____ , contract with AFJH physical education instructors for an A grade. In return for this grade I will complete the following requirements on or before May 26.

_____ 1. Twenty-five forehand ball bounces.
_____ 2. Twenty-five backhand ball bounces.
_____ 3. Twenty-five alternating ball bounces.
_____ 4. Twenty-five consecutive forehand strokes against the gym wall.
_____ 5. Twenty-five consecutive backhand strokes against the gym wall.
_____ 6. Rally with a classmate at least six forehand and backhand strokes.
_____ 7. Serve ten consecutive serves to each court.
_____ 8. Play a match with an *experienced* player.
_____ 9. Write a two-page report on the four most popular tennis tournaments and the history of the game.
_____ 10. Pass a quiz on scoring.

B GRADE

I, _____ , contract with AFJH physical education instructors for a B grade. In return for this grade I will complete the following requirements on or before May 26.

_____ 1. Fifteen forehand ball bounces.
_____ 2. Fifteen backhand ball bounces.
_____ 3. Fifteen alternating ball bounces.
_____ 4. Rally against the gym wall fifteen consecutive strokes using forehand and backhand strokes.
_____ 5. Serve seven consecutive serves to each court.
_____ 6. Play one game with a classmate.
_____ 7. Write a *short* report on the history of tennis and scoring.

C GRADE

I, _____ , contract with AFJH physical education instructors for a C grade. In return for this grade I will complete the following requirements on or before May 26.

_____ 1. Ten forehand ball bounces.
_____ 2. Ten consecutive backhand bounces.
_____ 3. Ten alternating ball bounces.
_____ 4. Serve five consecutive balls over the net to the correct court.
_____ 5. Read the tennis information in Mrs. Anderson's workbook and answer the corresponding questions in the test booklet.

Figure 8.23 A contract for grading.
Source: Dona Anderson, American Fork Jr. High,
American Fork, Utah.

```
     I, the undersigned, do forfeit all credit for this unit if I fail to
fulfill the terms of my contract and will accept a zero for this unit.




                                                    _____
                                                         (Name)

Procedures for Evaluation

  1. All tests must be taken on or before May 25. An appointment must
     be made with one of the instructors to take the test either during
     class or before or after school. The appointment must be made at
     least twenty-four hours before the desired testing time.
  2. All written reports and papers must be handed in to the instruc-
     tors on or before May 25.
```

Figure 8.23 *(continued)*

to the student exactly what is expected in performance, quantity, and quality. When students know what the objectives are, they are much more likely to achieve them.

The major disadvantages of criterion-referenced evaluation are twofold. Accurate standards cannot always be specified before the activity or unit has been taught. Grades may also become a reflection of test difficulty rather than of failure to achieve. For example, if no one got ninety or above on a test, that means the students did not learn or the test was too difficult. In mastery grading, drawing the line between what is passing and what is failing is often difficult. Standards may vary from one teacher to another.

Criterion-referenced methods of grading are sometimes accused of encouraging mediocrity. Critics maintain that grade inflation takes place when too many students receive high grades. Care must be taken to set standards high enough that the integrity of an A grade is not in question—no matter how many students earn that grade.

When *pass-fail* grading is used, students may lower their achievement to the level of the standard for passing, and motivation to excel is decreased. When pass-fail, criterion-referenced grading is used, it does not differentiate between students of different abilities, except at a minimum level. In some classes, an A-pass-fail system is used to distinguish those students who wish to do more than achieve the minimum specified level of performance.

Pass-no credit grading is a variation of the pass-fail system. It eliminates the need for students to cheat in order to pass because there is no stigma on failure. It encourages students to try new activities that they might be afraid to fail. However, students still have to repeat the experience if they wish to receive credit.

Improvement Grading on improvement is supposed to reflect individual progress, demonstrated by performance on a posttest compared with performance on a pretest. It is used to evaluate fitness objectives where high reliability exists and in individual sports where improvement is not based on the performance of others. It can also be used when student motivation is high enough to minimize students' purposely scoring low on the pretest. Its main advantage lies in the motivation of lower-skilled students, especially when they are included in classes with students who have high levels of ability.

Individual progress is determined by comparing performance on several occasions.

Grading on improvement favors the less-skilled students over the highly skilled students unless achievement plus improvement is included in the grade calculation. For example, a highly skilled student who scored fifteen baskets on a thirty-second timed test in basketball will probably not improve very much at the posttest. A score of seventeen on the posttest plus a score of two for improvement gives that student a total score of nineteen. A student who scored only six baskets on the pretest, but scores thirteen on the posttest receives a total score of nineteen, and both students have earned the same grade.

A disadvantage of this system is that many activity units do not permit adequate time for improvement to occur. Improvement scores then may be unreliable.

Student-Assigned Grades Because some teachers perceive grades as destroying student-teacher rapport, they favor student self-evaluation and grading. Students might be asked to write out their goals, criteria for evaluating goal achievement, ways in which the goals were achieved or not achieved, and the appropriate grade. Teachers may then add their own comments, negotiate with the student for a mutually acceptable grade, or average the student's and teacher's grades to arrive at a course grade. Student-assigned grades are most frequently used in individualized learning programs when time is available for individual student-teacher conferences, although they can be used in a group situation if students are provided with some type of form for self-evaluation.

For this type of evaluation to be used effectively, students must be taught goal-setting techniques and techniques for evaluating their own strengths and weaknesses. Often, teachers will discover that students are harder on themselves than the teacher would be. However, honest self-evaluation is tough because of the intense pressure on students to get high grades.

Step 2—Select Objectives and Determine the Emphasis
to Be Placed on Each Objective
List each of the objectives of physical education inherent in the unit or course of study and determine the percent of emphasis for each one. Consistent with the unique status of physical education, skill and physical fitness should be emphasized in the weighting (refer to figure 8.22).

Table 8.1 A sample grading plan

Objectives	Emphasis (%)	Instruments
Skill	35	Teacher observation checklists Rating scales Skills tests Student self-evaluation
Physical fitness	35	Objective physical fitness tests
Knowledge	15	Written tests Assignments Oral discussion Teacher observation of application in activities
Social skills	15	Teacher observation Student self-evaluation Anecdotal records

Step 3—Select Evaluation Instruments for Each Objective

A comprehensive review of evaluation techniques has been presented. Appropriate instruments should be selected to evaluate each objective. A sample plan for steps 1 and 2 is shown in table 8.1.

Step 4—Measure the Degree of Achievement of Each Objective

Student progress should be reported in terms of individual achievement of the objectives specified in each unit of activity. Care should be taken to record each test score or other data for each of the objectives. This information can be extremely valuable in interpreting student progress and grades to both students and parents.

Step 5—Determine the Grade Based on the Original Percentage Specified for Each Objective

Based on the example shown in table 8.1, if a student achieved a B+ on skill, C on fitness, A on knowledge, and A on social skills, the grade would be averaged as follows:

If
A+ = 12 points	35% B+ = .35 × 9 = 3.15
A = 11	35% C = .35 × 5 = 1.75
A− = 10	15% A = .15 × 11 = 1.65
B+ = 9	15% A = .15 × 11 = 1.65
B = 8	
B− = 7	8.20 = B
C+ = 6	
C = 5	
C− = 4	
D+ = 3	
D = 2	
D− = 1	

Students should also know and understand how the skill grade of 35 percent will be derived. If the fitness skill grade includes a run, some criteria for A, B, C should be stated. For example:

A = 8:29 min.

A − = 9:01 min.

B+ = 9:36 min.

B = 10:00 min.

Perhaps the fitness grade will be determined by the completion of an individual contract. Criteria for a grade will differ with each student. The grade might be pass-fail or specific standards of performance could be stated in the contract for A, B, or C work.

Another efficient method of figuring grades is done by assigning point values to the grade components. The final grade can then be tallied by adding all points together as shown below. Each component for the total grade has a point value. For example:

Component	Maximum Points
Skills tests	40
Pass	10
Bump	10
Serve	15
Spike	5
Physical fitness	40
Improvement	10
Cardiovascular	10
Strength	10
Other	10
Written work	20
Behavior	20
Improvement	10
Social	10

Total Grade

85 – 100 points = A

65 – 84 points = B

36 – 64 points = C

16 – 35 points = D

Below 16 = F

All criteria for the calculation of the grade should be determined and stated before beginning instruction in any activity or unit.

Step 6—Communicate the Grade to the Student

Many problems are eliminated by communicating grades to the students as soon as possible after the evaluation. Students are then able to see their own progress toward objectives instead of what the teacher "gave me." They can also average the grades themselves as a unit of instruction progresses. If the teacher can schedule a private moment with each student several days before the end of the grading period, the teacher can review the grades earned as well as the reasons for each grade and let the student know what grade will appear on the report card. By doing this, misunderstandings can be eliminated and, if necessary, changes can be made. All grades should be communicated to the student during the course of a grading period. Nothing should come as a surprise.

Grading in Coed and Mainstreamed Classes

With the introduction of Title IX and P.L. 94–142, the range of abilities within each class has widened considerably. This requires new insight into grading to provide equal opportunities for students to reach success. Stamm discussed three possible approaches to grading in coeducational and mainstreamed classes. These include (1) grading on improvement, (2) using separate performance standards, and (3) mastery learning.[16]

All of these approaches have been discussed previously. Teachers also need to remember that grading males and females using separate standards may result in perpetuating the stereotype that boys are capable of better performances than are girls. Perhaps a more equitable arrangement would be to group students by ability rather than by gender and then set the standards in terms of the abilities of each group. This plan might also prove more valuable in meeting the needs of the handicapped students in the class.

Record Keeping for Grading

A grading system is only as good as the records of student performance that are kept. Teachers must use a record-keeping system that facilitates calculation of the final grade and keeps track of all grade input. A comprehensive system also aids the teacher in explaining the grade to parents or administrators at a latter date. Examples of record-keeping systems are shown in figure 8.24 and figure 8.25.

Evaluation of student performance involves test and measurement theory. This chapter briefly mentions some applicable information. Excellent resource texts in the area of tests and measurement include *Practical Measurements for Evaluation in Physical Education* (4th edition) by Johnson and Nelson, and *Measurement for Evaluation in Physical Education* (2d edition) by Baumgartner and Jackson.

Questions and Suggested Activities

1. For a chosen objective in each domain, design a preassessment procedure. Explain how you will preassess quickly and meaningfully. Include recording sheets (if used). State how this information will be used further in the educational process.
2. Select a topic for a daily lesson. Include a psychomotor skill and related cognitive knowledge as well as an affective outcome. Write performance objectives and do a task analysis of each objective.
3. Select or develop evaluation materials in each of the three domains for the performance objectives specified in number 2 above.

Figure 8.24 Official class roll.

Source: Constructed by Rudy Moe and James Tyrrell, Brigham Young University.

NAMES	Fitness Test	VOLLEYBALL Serves	Spike	Set	Wall Volley	Written test	Total skill pts. V.b.	BADMINTON Long serve	Short serve	Clear	Drop	Smash	Written test	Total skill pts. Bad.	Total written pts.	Total skill pts.	COMMENTS	TOTAL POINTS	FINAL GRADE
Adams, J.	76	33	37	38	28	40	136	37	30	34	34	48	104	164	83	300	Average		
Alder, C.	68	38	40	41	33	41	152	36	42	38	37	37	198	178	78	350	Disrupts, highly skilled		
Bennett, A.	73	30	31	29	38	38	126	40	29	39	35	25	172	73	304		Average		
Boyle, D.	57	38	35	27	40	40	130	32	33	29	38	44	159	84	279		Tries hard		
Butler, N.	59	28	35	33	19	37	114	31	36	34	26	59	162	75	276		Dirty gym clothes often		
Cannon, R.	64	29	34	37	25	38	125	36	28	26	40	40	154	76	279		Refuses to follow directions		
Evans, W.	75	31	34	36	31	35	135	39	32	35	24	36	157	71	209		Above-average ability		
Garrick, S.	63	36	31	39	29	30	136	31	31	20	34	34	139	64	214		Low self-concept, lethargic		
Jensen, T.	78	40	38	33	20	37	141	36	37	37	36	36	175	73	336		Hardly ever notice student		
Jones, W.	68	37	33	30	39	39	139	36	36	28	24	34	159	73	223		Talks continually		
Madsen, G.	76	33	36	41	28	37	138	27	35	34	27	34	159	76	287		Average		
Nielsen, A.	70	20	27	28	20	38	105	38	36	18	44	44	170	76	253		Overweight—teased often		
Price, P.	89	43	41	38	36	57	158	46	28	39	43	41	206	82	304		Leader of class		
Pyne, K.	72	34	37	36	27	34	134	30	26	36	36	43	170	64	334		Disadvantaged background		
Reed, N.	80	40	37	30	30	41	143	37	20	39	31	30	171	78	334		Tries to impress me		
Rice, V.	93	46	41	39	34	46	160	43	41	46	39	39	212	85	322		Highly skilled		
Robins, E.	82	28	31	34	17	31	100	29	30	22	19	31	130	68	255		Parent often complains		
Robinson, H.	93	30	30	33	23	23	39	—	—	—	—	33	0	72	116		Always asks how he's doing		
Sandberg, B.	64	34	37	29	24	36	134	36	31	37	38	38	170	74	204		Likes to be in charge		
Saunders, P.	86	32	31	29	26	43	119	31	34	31	34	48	177	91	270		Very conscientious		
Schwartz, R.	77	28	28	29	27	33	112	27	28	17	30	40	136	84	240		Shy and hesitant		
Simons, J.	79	27	33	30	29	26	112	21	38	40	33	33	176	72	302		Average		
Snow, C.	80	30	31	34	17	46	112	27	22	20	18	19	42	116	89	204	Very uncoordinated		
Taylor, L.	85	27	33	30	20	40	122	24	28	36	18	20	41	166	81	288	Great improvement in skill		
VanBuren, T.	74	30	33	34	27	35	119	36	31	39	30	40	165	75	289		Average		
Wilcox, B.	71	35	28	27	29	39	119	32	36	37	30	27	39	162	78	291	Foul language, trys hard		

```
                    UNIT SUMMARY SHEET

    Name _____        Fourth-Term Grade
                                         Sheet
                                         Physical Education
    CLASS _____

    ROLL NUMBER _____
                        Possible     Points      Total Possi-
                                     Earned      ble: 100

    OBSTACLE COURSE TIME
    _____   35       _____

    TRACK AND FIELD SCORES
    50-yard Dash _____    10       _____
    Standing Broad Jump
    _____                 10       _____
    Running Broad Jump                            Your Total
    _____                 10       _____   _____
    Jogging _____         10       _____

                                                  Your Fourth-
                                                  Term
    TRACK AND FIELD QUIZ    10       _____   Grade _____

    WRITTEN TEST            15       _____   First _____

                                                  Second _____

                                                  Third _____

                          ___        _____   Fourth _____
               Total 100       Total _____    Final _____
```

Figure 8.25 A unit summary sheet.

4. Construct a short cognitive test of at least twenty-five questions on the topic of your choice. Administer it to three other people and evaluate its effectiveness with them.

5. One day during a department meeting, the department chairperson mentions that several parents and the school's principal think the grading system for physical education is too vague and subjective. The principal has asked that your group submit guidelines for a new grading policy. Construct the document that will be sent to the principal.

6. Role-play the following incident: The English teacher, Mrs. Frankel, gives her class a research assignment in which students choose their own topic and write a report. Dave, your outstanding receiver on the football team, fails to turn in a report and receives a failing grade. You need Dave to win the football game with Clearwater High on Friday and if he fails English, he will be unable to play.

7. Calculate the grades for the students in figure 8.25 by first determining a grading policy. (Use the policy in number 5 above, if available.) Justify in writing for Mrs. Robins the grade her son received by answering the attached letter.

Letter from a parent

Dear Mr. or Mrs. ————————— ,

I'm Mrs. Robins, the mother of Eddie Robins. I would like to know why my son received the grade you gave him for P.E. He has come home every day so excited about his badminton and volleyball class and has been quite conscientious about practicing both sports out in the backyard.

I would like to know what you based his final grade for the class on, and how you came to that decision.

Sincerely yours,

[Signature]

Mrs. Edward G. Robins

Suggested Readings

Arrighi, Margarite A. "Equal Opportunity through Instructional Design." *Journal of Physical Education, Recreation and Dance* 56 (September 1985):58–60, 64.

Barton, Grant E., and Andrew S. Gibbons. *Test Questions: A Self-Instructional Booklet,* 3d ed. Provo, Utah: Brigham Young University Press, 1973.

Baumgartner, Ted A., and Andrew S. Jackson. *Measurement for Evaluation in Physical Education,* 2d ed. Dubuque, Iowa: Wm. C. Brown Company Publishers, 1982.

Bayless, John. "Conflicts and Confusion Over Evaluation." *Journal of Physical Education and Recreation* 49 (September 1978):54–55.

Busch, William M. "Look! Instructors, Let's Improve Our Standards to Meaningful Objective Measurement." *The Physical Educator* 31 (October 1974):129–30.

Cotten, Doyice J., and Mary B. Cotten. "Grading: The Ultimate Weapon?" *Journal of Physical Education, Recreation and Dance* 56 (February 1985):52–53.

Davis, Myron W., and Vicki L. Hopkins. "Improving Evaluation of Physical Fitness and Sport Skill Performance: A Model Profile." *Journal of Physical Education and Recreation* 50 (May 1979):76–78.

Disch, James G., ed. "The Measurement of Basic Stuff." *Journal of Physical Education, Recreation and Dance* 54 (October 1983):17–29.

Dunham, Paul, Jr. "Evaluation for Excellence: A Systematic Approach." *Journal of Physical Education, Recreation and Dance* 57 (August 1986):34–36.

Gabbard, Carl. "Task Sheets—A Report Card That You Can Live With." *The Physical Educator* 37 (March 1980):42–43.

Geiger, William, and David Kizer. "Developing a Teaching Awareness." *The Physical Educator* 36 (March 1979):25–26.

Griffin, Patricia S. "Second Thoughts on Affective Evaluation." *Journal of Physical Education, Recreation and Dance* 53 (February 1982):25, 86.

Griffey, David D. "Trouble for Sure a Crisis—Perhaps: Secondary School Physical Education Today." *Journal of Physical Education, Recreation and Dance* 58 (February 1987):20–21.

Johnson, Barry L., and Jack K. Nelson. *Practical Measurements for Evaluation in Physical Education,* 4th ed. Minneapolis: Burgess Publishing Company, 1986.

Lambdin, Dolly. "Keeping Track." *Journal of Physical Education, Recreation and Dance* 55 (August 1984):40–43.

Locke, Lawrence F., and Patt Dodds. "How One Teacher Uses Student Records." *Journal of Physical Education, Recreation and Dance* 53 (September 1982):41–43.

Mager, Robert F. *Measuring Instructional Intent: Or Got a Match?* Belmont, California: Fearon Publishers, 1973.

Marsh, Jeanette Jewell. "Measuring Affective Objectives in Physical Education." *The Physical Educator* 41 (May 1984):77–81.

McDonald, E. Daron, and Marilyn E. Yeates. "Measuring Improvement in Physical Education." *Journal of Physical Education and Recreation* 50 (February 1979):79–80.

McGee, Rosemary. "Uses and Abuses of Affective Measurement." *Journal of Physical Education, Recreation and Dance* 53 (February 1982):21–22.

Melville, Scott. "Teaching and Evaluating Cognitive Skills in Elementary Physical Education." *Journal of Physical Education, Recreation and Dance* 56 (February 1985):26–28.

Mood, Dale. "Evaluation in the Affective Domain? No!" *Journal of Physical Education, Recreation and Dance* 53 (February 1982):18–20.

Noble, Larry, and Richard H. Cox. "Development of a Form to Survey Student Reactions on Instructional Effectiveness of Lifetime Sports Classes." *Research Quarterly for Exercise and Sport* 54 (September 1983):247–54.

O'Brien, Dianne Boswell. "Self-Grading to Develop Responsibility and Cooperation." In Ronald P. Carlson, ed. *IDEAS II for Secondary School Physical Education.* Reston, Virginia: American Alliance for Health, Physical Education, Recreation and Dance, 1984, 79–83.

Ratliffe, Tom. "Evaluation of Students' Skill Using Generic Levels of Skill Proficiency." *The Physical Educator* 41 (May 1984):65–68.

Reeve, Jean, and Craig Morrison. "Teaching for Learning: The Application of Systematic Evaluation." *Journal of Physical Education, Recreation and Dance* 57 (August 1986):37–39.

Rink, Judith E. "The Teacher Wants Us to Learn." *Journal of Physical Education and Recreation* (February 1981):17–18.

Safrit, Margaret J., and Carol L. Stamm. "Reliability Estimates for Criterion-Referenced Measures in the Psychomotor Domain." *Research Quarterly for Exercise and Sport* 51 (May 1980):359–68.

Shea, John B. "The Pass-Fail Option and Physical Education." *Journal of Health, Physical Education and Recreation* 42 (May 1971):19–20.

Shick, Jacqueline. "Written Tests in Activity Classes." *Journal of Physical Education and Recreation* 52 (April 1981):21–22, 83.

Siedentop, Daryl. "High School Physical Education: Still an Endangered Species." *Journal of Physical Education, Recreation and Dance* 58 (February 1987):24–25.

Stamm, Carol Lee. "Evaluation of Coeducational Physical Activity Classes." *Journal of Physical Education and Recreation* 50 (January 1979):68–69.

Stoner, Lela June. "Evaluation in the Affective Domain? Yes!" *Journal of Physical Education, Recreation and Dance* 53 (February 1982):16–17.

Taylor, John L., and Eleanor N. Chiogioji. "Implications of Educational Reform on High School PE Programs." *Journal of Physical Education, Recreation and Dance* 58 (February 1987):22–23.

Wiese, Cynthia E. "Is Affective Evaluation Possible?" *Journal of Physical Education, Recreation and Dance* 53 (February 1982):23–24.

References

1. Judith E. Rink, *Teaching Physical Education for Learning* (St. Louis: Times Mirror/Mosby College Publishing, 1985), p. 76.
2. Judith Placek, "Conceptions of Success in Teaching: Busy, Happy and Good?" in Thomas J. Templin and Janice K. Olson, eds., *Teaching in Physical Education* (Champaign, Illinois: Human Kinetics Publishers, 1983), pp. 46–56.
3. Kenneth H. Hoover, *The Professional Teacher's Handbook* (Boston: Allyn & Bacon, Inc., 1982), p. 502.
4. Larry J. Sullivan, "Campus Comedy," *Reader's Digest* 117 (November 1980), p. 203.
5. Mike Bobo, "Skill Testing—A Positive Step toward Interpreting Secondary School Physical Education," *Journal of Physical Education and Recreation* 49 (January 1978), p. 45.
6. Adapted from Blaine Nelson Lee and M. David Merrill, *Writing Complete Affective Objectives: A Short Course* (Belmont, California: Wadsworth Publishing Company, 1972).
7. B. E. Blanchard, "A Behavior Frequency Rating Scale for the Measurement of Character and Personality Traits in Physical Education Classroom Situations," *Research Quarterly* 7 (May 1936), pp. 56–66.
8. Charles C. Cowell, "Validating an Index of Social Adjustment for High School Use," *Research Quarterly* (March 1958), pp. 7–18.
9. June Breck, "A Sociometric Test of Status as Measured in Physical Education Classes," Master's thesis, University of California, 1947.
10. Robert Fox, Margaret Barron Luszki, and Richard Schmuck, *Diagnosing Classroom Learning Environments* (Chicago: Science Research Associates, 1966), p. 73.
11. L. L. Thurstone, "Attitudes Can Be Measured," *American Journal of Sociology* 33 (January 1928), pp. 529–54.
12. Rensis Likert, *A Technique for Measurement of Attitudes,* Archives of Psychology, no. 140, 1932.
13. Charles E. Osgood, George J. Suci, and Percy H. Tannenbaum, *The Measurement of Meaning* (Urbana, Illinois: University of Illinois Press, 1957).
14. Lee and Merrill, *Writing Complete Affective Objectives,* p. 75.
15. Paul Dressel, *Basic College Quarterly,* Michigan State University (Winter 1957), p. 6.
16. Carol Lee Stamm, "Evaluation of Coeducational Physical Activity Classes," *Journal of Physical Education and Recreation* 50 (January 1979), pp. 68–69.

Selecting Program Activities and Materials

Study Stimulators

1. What learning activities and materials should the teacher consider when planning the instructional program?
2. What media materials would you feel comfortable using in your program?
3. How might you incorporate the computer into your teaching?
4. How might you structure a content unit on fitness and wellness?
5. What motivation techniques would you use to encourage students to perform up to their potential in a content unit of movement skills?
6. What is a lead-up game?
7. How would you justify incorporating a "risk activity" into your program?
8. Design the playing schedule for eight teams in a round-robin tournament.
9. What adjunct activities would you incorporate into your school physical education program? Why?

Many avenues are open to the committed and innovative teacher in planning the instructional program to achieve the goals of physical education stated in chapter 2—to develop physical skills, physical fitness, knowledge and understanding, social skills, and attitudes and appreciations. This chapter will present numerous resources to aid the physical education teacher in planning a program that meets the needs of all students in a variety of circumstances. Whether it be a rainy day, shortened day, or a field day; with special education students, excited students anticipating a vacation break, or a team anxious to play a tournament game, business must proceed as usual. Teachers are always expected to make learning meaningful and motivating.

What is taught in a well-rounded physical education program should be determined by student needs and not by convenience or tradition. For example, softball should not be taught in the spring just because the baseball season is beginning or because it has always been taught at this time. Spring might be an ideal time to introduce adventure or initiative activities, with a club experience to enhance the offering. Fitness activities should be emphasized all year and not just during the first months of school to compensate for the long summer lay-off period.

This chapter will focus on the instructional aids and materials a teacher might select when planning both the regular content and the adjunct activities of a meaningful physical education program.

Selecting General Program Aids and Materials

The purpose of instructional aids and materials is to achieve instructional objectives more effectively and more economically. These instruments can increase student motivation and create heightened interest and enjoyment in learning by reducing the amount of teacher talk and increasing visual involvement. They can be used to introduce a lesson, present new material, clarify a subject or discussion, or summarize a lesson. Approximately 83 percent of

Table 9.1 A summary of the various types of instructional materials

Medium	Uses	Advantages	Disadvantages
Videotapes.	Evaluation of student performance. Self-evaluation of student or teacher. Magnification of small objects.	Instant replay. Can save for future use. Can prerecord. Inexpensive. Portable.	Need skilled production staff.
8-mm films and loops. Videodiscs.	Individual study. Homework. Students make own films. Stimulates verbal communication and creativity.	Highly portable—compact. Inexpensive, more accessible. Ease of operation. Versatility. Replay without rewinding.	Silent.
16-mm films.	Present meanings involving motion. Compel attention. Heighten reality. Speed up or slow down time. Enlarge or reduce size. Bring past or present into class. Build common denominator of experience. Influence and change attitudes. Promote understanding of abstract concepts.		Sound film is costly. Production time is long. Requires darkened room. Internally controlled pacing. Fixed sequence. Outdated soon after purchase.
Models. Mock-ups. Exhibits. Displays. Objects, specimens.	Examples of real-life situations. Comparisons.	Enlargement or reduction. High reality—3-D.	
Computers.	Programmed instruction. Record keeping.	High interest. Fast.	Relatively expensive unless terminals can be hooked up to a main computer. Software is currently limited.
Tape recorders. Audiotapes. Records.	Authority resource. Create a mood. Grading comments. Student interview. Exams.	High reality. Inexpensive software. Available equipment and tapes. Ease of production.	Low cost, accessible equipment.

Medium	Use	Advantages	Disadvantages
Slides or filmstrips.	History, geography. Concepts.	Magnification or reduction. Inexpensive software. Availability. Inexpensive hardware. High reality. Flexible sequence and pacing (slides). Can be combined with audio.	Requires darkened room. Fixed sequence (filmstrips).
Overhead transparencies.	Graphic presentations.	Inexpensive software. Availability. Project in light room. Flexible sequence. Base of operation at front of room. All advantages of chalkboard plus.	
Duplicated materials.	For important information: as a quiz; as a guide; as a reminder. To emphasize a point. For a complete explanation.	Can be prepared in advance. Can be retained for future reference and review.	
Opaque projections.	Still pictures.	High reality. Flexible sequence.	
Magnetic boards.	Sequence material. Tell stories with simple illustrations. Illustrate hard-to-understand concepts. Display materials. Strategy talks.	Inexpensive. Easy. Creative. Attention-getting.	
Chalkboards.	Clarify sequence of events. Focus attention. Stimulate discussion.	Flexibility and versatility. Availability. Size.	
Still pictures: Charts Posters Bulletin boards Flipcharts Graphs Maps Diagrams Cartoons	Attract attention. Arouse interest. Reinforce and add dimension. Provide concrete meaning to abstract ideas.	Very inexpensive. No equipment needed. Easy to use and store. Readily available.	Too small. Limited to two dimensions. No motion.

all learning occurs through sight, only 11 percent results from hearing, and less than 6 percent through the other senses. Retention of learning is increased fourfold over hearing only by the use of visual involvement and nearly sevenfold by combining the use of visual and auditory senses. Instructional aids and materials accomplish these tasks by involving the students in the learning process. An old Chinese proverb pointed this out very well. It said:

I hear, I forget.
I see, I remember.
I do, I understand.

When selecting instructional aids and materials, teachers should always attempt to choose those things that are as close to the real-life experiences as possible. Other considerations—such as student safety, money, and practicality—will restrict the teacher in making a selection. The selection of costly materials is a process that should be shared by teachers, students, parents, and administrators so that the needs of all are considered.

Sources of instructional materials include catalogs of instructional aids and printed materials such as tests, journals, newspapers, and learning packets from commercial outlets. Professional persons, parents, and friends are excellent sources, as are many students. A college or university media center or a district or school instructional materials center have access to many of these sources. The American Alliance for Health, Physical Education, Recreation and Dance also publishes catalogs of instructional materials. A summary of various types of instructional materials with their advantages and disadvantages is shown in table 9.1.

The use of a systematic evaluation guide will facilitate the selection of materials. The guide should consider the potential of the materials for relevant learning by asking the following questions about them:

1. Do they make a meaningful contribution to the topic under study?
2. Do they develop concepts that are difficult to convey through another medium?
3. Are they true to fact and life, accurate and authentic?
4. Are they up to date?
5. Are they worth the time, cost, and effort involved?
6. Do they develop critical thinking skills?
7. Are they appropriate for the age, intelligence, and experience level of the students?

A second consideration of the systematic evaluation guide is the technical quality of the materials. The picture and sound should be examined for quality. The mode of communication should be adequate for the intended purpose, and the message should be unbiased and free from objectionable propaganda or distractions.

The ease of presentation of media or other materials is the third consideration. Often, management problems associated with the use of instructional materials renders them useless when, in fact, it is the management system that is ineffective. When purchasing equipment, an evaluation of the ease of operation, ease of maintenance, quality, durability, and portability should be made before buying.

The following examples of instructional aids and materials should be helpful to the teacher seeking ways to enrich the program.

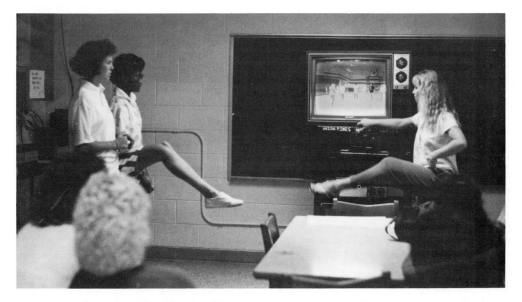

Instructional material can be used effectively to
enhance motivation of learners.

Media

Although instructional materials can be used effectively to enhance motivation and learning, research indicates that in many cases no increase in learning has taken place. Students are media-saturated. Teachers compete with the multimillion-dollar budgets of television and movies. Therefore, media has to be exceptional for students to respond positively toward it. Instructional media have proven to be of the most value when they have been closely correlated with the instructional objectives, so that they can supplement and increase the effectiveness of the teacher. In no way should media be used just to take up the time on a rainy day or when the teacher is unprepared. Teachers should remember that no medium can substitute for a concerned, well-prepared teacher.

A live demonstration is often more effective than a visual aid. However, a video, motion picture, or film loop can give the entire class the view obtained by the observer in the most advantageous position. Close-ups afford all members of a large class the opportunity to see the motion clearly. Another benefit of this type of media is that it can reproduce action that the observer rarely sees, such as an underwater view of a swimming stroke or a slow-motion view of a complex skill. Through the use of slow motion, sports skills can be analyzed in terms of body position, timing, and the relationship of skills to game play.

The instant-replay feature of the video recorder makes it a terrific teaching aid because the players can see themselves in action. Videotaping helps the learners see their own mistakes or successes. By helping students compare their own performance with the performance of a model, videotape feedback can be even more valuable.

When videotape machines are unavailable, Polaroid pictures can be used to provide feedback in activities such as archery and in posture classes. A Polaroid-type graphic-sequence camera can take a series of timed snapshots with a single shot, which can then be analyzed for feedback purposes.

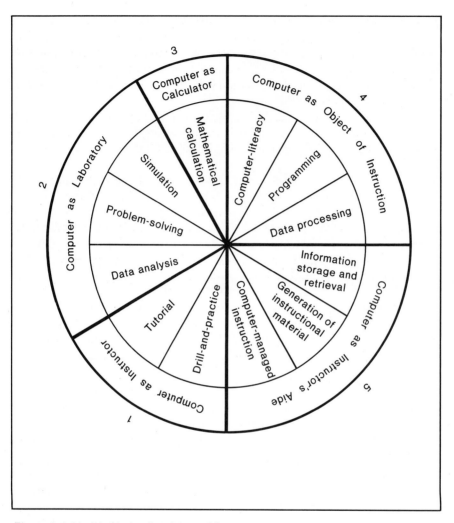

Figure 9.1 Model of instructional uses of the computer.
Source: Adapted from Judith B. Edwards, et al., *Computer Applications in Instruction,* Hanover, New Hampshire: Time Share (Houghton, Mifflin), 1978, p. 30.

Computers

In 1986 more than one million microcomputers existed in the schools.[1] Judith Edwards developed a model in 1978 for the instructional uses of the computer that has proven to be visionary.[2] Many projects and fads have come and gone, but Edward's model still encompasses the overall direction of computer use in education. The model, pictured in figure 9.1, indicates five instructional uses of the computer. These include (1) an instructor/teacher, (2) a laboratory, (3) a calculator, (4) an object of instruction, and (5) an instructor/teacher aid.

An explosion of computerization during the eighties saw the manufacture of hundreds of different computers and tens of thousands of software products for every conceivable application.[3] Available software is used by the teacher, coach, and researcher to enhance the quality and efficiency of their work. Available software in the areas of sport science, health, and dance have been indexed, and the titles may be retrieved from such sources as AAHPERD[4] and King and Aufsesser.[5]

In accordance with Edward's model, the computer is used in physical education as both an instructional aid and a data-management tool in the classroom and the laboratory. However, the use most often made of the computer in physical education today involves data management.

The microcomputer in the classroom was first used as an aid in cognitive instruction. Programmed learning or drill-and-practice programs produced a volume of software, most of which was extremely poor.[6] More and more computer software programs to facilitate learning are becoming available to physical educators, and the quality of the programs has improved.[7] A variety of programs is currently available for classroom application in fitness testing; grading and record keeping; test construction; on-line testing with questions for drill, practice, and formal testing; and simulation and modeling to graphically illustrate the principles of blood pressure or a sports skill such as the shot put.[8]

Cicciarella noted that physical educators have incorporated the computer as an instructional tool most effectively by interfacing it with other modern technology such as the videotape player, the videodisc, and the audiotape player to produce quite sophisticated programs. For example, a videodisc, computer, and electronic manikin in combination can teach cardiopulmonary resuscitation (CPR). He cautioned, however, that

> Although these programs can and have been developed for teaching sport strategy, rules, and skills such as refereeing, the physical setting or gymnasium, pool, or athletic fields does not adapt easily to the use of electronic equipment for instruction. It seems probable that the computer will not be heavily used for instruction in motor skills.[9]

In addition to a tutorial tool and its specialized use in the classroom setting, the computer is being used by professionals in specialized areas and in the laboratory to analyze human performance and behavior. Microcomputers assist specialists in motor learning, exercise physiology, sport psychology, and biomechanics.[10] Through the use of film motion analysis, significant and objective interpretation and comparison of selected sport skill techniques is possible.[11] Computer technology has also been applied to programs for dance notation.[12]

Countless graphics and word-processing software packages are available to the teacher to aid in creating classroom materials. They are constantly being improved and updated. Teachers need to become computer literate to take advantage of these programs.

The most practical and widespread use of the computer for physical educators is to assist with data generated from instructional activities. The mammoth organizational and record-keeping tasks of physical education programs warrant the use of the computer to aid in management tasks. Such software reduces countless hours of recording and analytical work on the part of the teacher, coach, and researcher. Excellent software is available to record and process grades and fitness data and provide immediate feedback and results. Fitness-testing and management programs usually carry a statistical-analysis package that also allows a curriculum reviewer to ascertain if the instructional programs are actually meeting intended learning outcomes.

```
                        GROUP'S TEST RESULTS
CLASS NAME: PERIOD 2
TEST NUMBER: 2
TEST DATE: OCTOBER 1986
RUN TYPE: 1 WHICH IS A 1 MILE RUN
SKINFOLD TYPE: 1. . . .TRICEP ONLY
```

NO.	NAME	AGE	SEX	HT	WT	RUN TIME	SKINFOLD TRI	SUB	SIT-UPS	REACH
1	Byron Anderson	13	F	−1	−1	12:24	−1	0	40	33
2	George Burke	13	F	−1	−1	11:54	−1	0	28	34
3	Paula Conlin	13	F	−1	−1	9:09	−1	0	35	35
4	Alecia Dayton	13	F	−1	−1	8:21	−1	0	41	41
5	Paige Evans	13	F	−1	−1	8:51	−1	0	31	29
6	George Fairchild	13	F	−1	−1	7:34	−1	0	48	43
7	Andres Garcia	13	F	−1	−1	8:42	−1	0	42	31
8	Jim Glass	13	F	−1	−1	10:43	−1	0	35	38
9	Bob King	14	F	−1	−1	9:37	−1	0	34	35
10	Kirsten Knight	13	F	−1	−1	12:45	−1	0	33	28
11	Glen Lott	13	F	−1	−1	10:45	−1	0	31	44
12	Tom Marks	13	F	−1	−1	7:34	−1	0	45	26
13	Jeff Matthews	14	F	−1	−1	11:26	−1	0	36	20
14	Erin McLaughlin	13	F	−1	−1	8:55	−1	0	42	38
15	Nina Monsen	13	F	−1	−1	8:22	−1	0	35	36
16	Kevin Moon	13	F	−1	−1	8:48	−1	0	43	21
17	Brad Norman	12	F	−1	−1	9:02	−1	0	33	33
18	Terri O'Connor	14	F	−1	−1	8:20	−1	0	45	40
19	Kathy Stevens	13	F	−1	−1	8:26	−1	0	36	35
20	Vicki Peterson	13	F	−1	−1	−1:	−1	0	37	28
21	Ferrill Rowley	12	F	−1	−1	8:48	−1	0	35	37
22	Carlos Sousa	13	F	−1	−1	8:56	−1	0	38	38
23	Claudia Taylor	13	F	−1	−1	8:54	−1	0	42	39
24	Tina Vickers	13	F	−1	−1	8:26	−1	0	39	40
25	Scott Walker	13	F	−1	−1	9:09	−1	0	37	38
26	Diane Zabriskie	14	F	−1	−1	8:29	−1	0	34	40

Figure 9.2 A class fitness score computer printout.

Software packages to aid the teacher in reporting and evaluating fitness scores can be obtained from several sources, including AAHPERD. Several software packages furnish class and individual results similar to the printouts shown in figures 9.2, 9.3, and 9.4. Engelhorn[13] has made available input programs for fitness testing allowing teachers to program their own packages.

The FITNESSGRAM, a physical fitness report card, is a computerized system of scoring and reporting the results of physical-fitness testing. Students and parents can visually see achievement results on specific tests and be instructed personally on techniques for maintenance and improvement of scores by viewing the FITNESSGRAM[14] (see figure 9.5).

```
                        PERIOD 2
                     AUGUST/1986
TEST 2
OCTOBER 1986
PAYSON JUNIOR

INSTRUCTOR: MISS AMES

JENNIFER JONES
_____

AGE: 14
SEX: F
HEIGHT: -1
WEIGHT: -1

                                                              1
                                    1 2 3 4 5 6 7 8 9 0
TEST ITEM   RESULT      %TILE  RATING    0 0 0 0 0 0 0 0 0 0 0
_____   _____      _____  _____    _____

                                         **************
RUN-1 MILE 8:29          68    ABOVE AVG  **************
                                          **************

SKINFOLD   NOT TESTED

                                          ++++++++++
SIT-UPS      34          45    AVERAGE    ++++++++++
                                          ++++++++++

                                          @@@@@@@@@@@@@@@@@@
REACH        40          85    EXCELLENT  @@@@@@@@@@@@@@@@@@
                                          @@@@@@@@@@@@@@@@@@
```

THE %TILE SCORE INDICATES YOUR RELATIONSHIP TO OTHER PEOPLE
OF THE SAME AGE AND SEX. FOR EXAMPLE, A SCORE OF 60 MEANS
THAT YOU SCORED EQUAL TO OR ABOVE 60% OF THE PEOPLE BUT ALSO
BELOW 40% OF THE PEOPLE.
IF YOU SCORED LESS THAN 50 %TILE, YOU ARE ENCOURAGED TO
BEGIN A PROGRAM OF DEVELOPMENT IN THOSE AREAS. SOME
GUIDELINES ARE PROVIDED IN THE HEALTH-RELATED PHYSICAL
FITNESS TEST MANUAL, PP. 37-58.

Figure 9.3 An individual fitness printout.

Teachers must keep in mind that entering the data into the computer can be very time consuming unless some type of scanner sheet or individualized card is used.[15] Secretaries or student aids can help with this task so that meaningful, personalized data is available to the teacher, student, and parent at the conclusion of the testing.

Coaches find the computer advantageous for statistical analysis of game play in basketball, baseball, football, and other sports.

> The reduction of time spent in paperwork and the accuracy of the data make microcomputer software a cost-efficient item and frees the coach, teacher, or administrator for quality time with the individuals involved.[16]

```
CHRISTENSEN/MELINDA

50 YARD DASH      SCORE: 7.2   SEC   85      %    :
600 YARD RUN      SCORE: 2:11        91-94   %    :
Long Jump         Score: 6'5''       95      %    :
Shuttle Run       Score: 9.9   Sec   95      %    :
Sit-Ups           Score: 55          96-99   %    :
Arm Hangs         Score: 21          85      %    :
''Ave Percentile'' =                 91.17
<Achieved 85 %ile in all Categories!>
```

Figure 9.4

FITNESSGRAM®

NAME **Martha Doherty**   GRADE **5**   SECTION **3**
SCHOOL **Westlawn Elementary School**   INSTRUCTOR **O'Neil**

SIT AND REACH		SIT - UP		SKINFOLD OR BODY MASS INDEX (BMI)			WALK / RUN		
CENTIMETERS	% RANK	NUMBER	% RANK	ⓘ SKINFOLD MM	BMI kg/m²	% RANK	MIN SEC OR YARDS	% RANK	ⓘ ·TYPE
25	35	36	75	14.0 ST		75	1830	85	9 mn

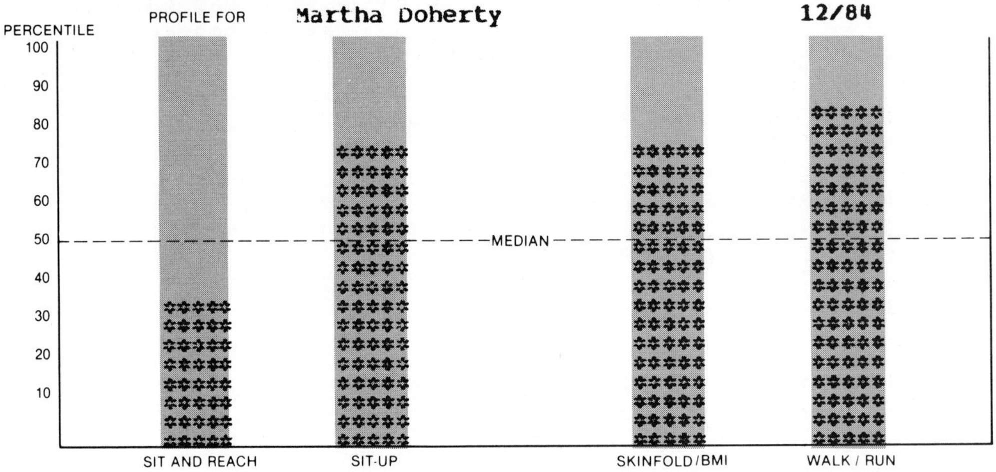

PROFILE FOR **Martha Doherty**   **12/84**

Figure 9.5 FITNESSGRAM.
Source: Campbell Soup Company, Campbell Place,
Camden, New Jersey 08103.

Computers are here to stay, and they can be a tremendous aid to the teacher. Certain guidelines should be followed, however, when using computers in the physical education setting:

1. Achieve an understanding of and facility in using the computer.
2. Become familiar with existing software and effectively evaluate that software before making any purchases.
3. Use computer-assisted instruction only if it is better than traditional methods and not in place of direct instruction.
4. Use the computer with other technological packages such as the videotape or videodisc.

Instructional Games

Instructional games add a new dimension to the learning process. These activities may not involve the psychomotor domain at all, thus giving variety to the usual methods of learning. They also add a viable option for involvement to those students who do not normally like to participate. They can be used individually or in groups and are especially effective when regular lesson plans cannot be used due to inclement weather, scheduling changes, or facility unavailability. Care should be taken to design games to meet specific course objectives and to keep the activities at the appropriate learning level of the students (e.g., vocabulary, spelling, content). Instructional games can lose their effectiveness if used too often.

The following games could be used as study sheets, as activities for extra credit, as activities to be done after completing regular assignments, and just for fun. Teachers should be on the lookout for instructional games in resource books, magazines, or at conventions and workshops. The creative teacher will not hesitate to make up original materials.

1. *The crossword puzzle* (see figure 9.6) The crossword puzzle can be created by printing the terms in the squares on a piece of graph paper and working out interlocking words. A ruler is used to transfer the squares to a ditto master by drawing around the squares on graph paper that has been placed over the ditto master. The numbers are added. (Do not forget to remove the tissue paper on the ditto master.) The puzzle must be proofread for accuracy before using it. Answers can be listed alphabetically for use by students who have difficulty spelling.
2. *Pyramid* (see figure 9.7) Another puzzle-type study aid or motivational device is the pyramid. The longest terms for recall are placed at the bottom of the pyramid, and it is built upward to the shortest terms. This works well for a test of knowledge of rules and terminology.
3. Other examples of instructional games are:
   a. Soccer Scrambled Words (see figure 9.8)
   b. Hidden Terms (see figure 9.9)
   c. Bingo Lingo (see figure 9.10)
   d. Sports Bowl (see figure 9.11)
   e. Baseball (see figure 9.12)

Name _____ Period _____ Date _____

Instructions: Fill in the puzzle using the list of possible answers given below.

Across
2. The amount of force required to pull the bow to full draw.
4. The practice of shooting with bows and arrows.
9. An arrow that strikes the scoring area and bounces off the target.
10. The third ring outside the gold, counting four or three points.
11. To sight for hitting the target with the left eye closed for right-handed archers.
12. To pull the bowstring back to the anchor point.
14. Plastic "feathers" on an arrow.
15. A device that provides force for shooting arrows.
16. Six arrows shot in a row.
17. The fiberglass, aluminum or wooden portion of the arrow.
18. A term for archery equipment.
21. The second ring outside the gold, counting six or five points.
22. Two feathers on the arrow shaftment that are not at right angles to the nock and are the same color are called _____ feathers.
23. To place the tip of the index finger of the string hand on the anchor point and hold it steady until the release.
27. The outer ring on the target face, counting two or one points.
28. A certain place on the face to which the index finger of the string hand is brought consistently (every time) on each draw (two words).
30. The round object, marked with circles, at which the arrows are shot.
31. The side of the bow away from the string.
34. The upper and lower parts of the bow, divided by the handle.
35. Colored stripes used for identification that are placed near the feathers on an arrow.
37. The plastic portion of the arrow into which the bowstring is fitted.
39. A leather protection worn on the forearm to keep the string from hurting the arm (two words).
40. The arm, the hand of which holds the bow during shooting.
41. A device for holding arrows.
42. A leather piece worn on the shooting hand to protect the fingers (two words).
43. The center of the target, counting ten or nine points.
44. The side of the bow toward the string.

Down
1. The edge of the target face beyond the white ring, counting 0 points, sometimes marked "P" on the scorecard.
3. The center part of a bow that the archer grips with her hand.
5. The first ring outside the gold, counting eight or seven points.
6. To shoot the arrow from a position of full draw by straightening the fingers of the string hand.
7. Vanes are substitutes for this material.
8. The feather on an arrow that is set at right angles to the nock; usually of a different color from the hen feathers (two words).
13. To stand ready to shoot.
19. The middle section of an arrow.
20. Archery "games."
21. The string of the bow.
24. The part of the bow on which the arrow rests while shooting.
25. The line upon which the archer stands while shooting at a target.
26. The metal point of an arrow, on the forward end.
29. To brace the bow.
32. The object that is shot.

Figure 9.6 An archery crossword puzzle.

33. A method of recording hits and the total score on a score card.
36. The thread wrapped around the bowstring to keep the arrow or the fingers from wearing out the string where the arrow is nocked.
38. An archery ground.
40. To string a bow.

Possible Answers

Address	Belly	Crest	Hen	Red	Shooting line
Aim	Black	Draw	Hold	Rest	String
Anchor	Blue	End	Limbs	Rounds	Target
Anchor point	Bow	Face	Nock	Release	Tackle
Arm guard	Bowarm	Feathers	Rebound	Quiver	Tip
Archery	Bowstring	Finger tab	Petticoat	Serving	Vanes
Arrow	Brace	Gold	Pile	Scoring	White
Back	Cock feather	Handle	Range	Shaft	Weight

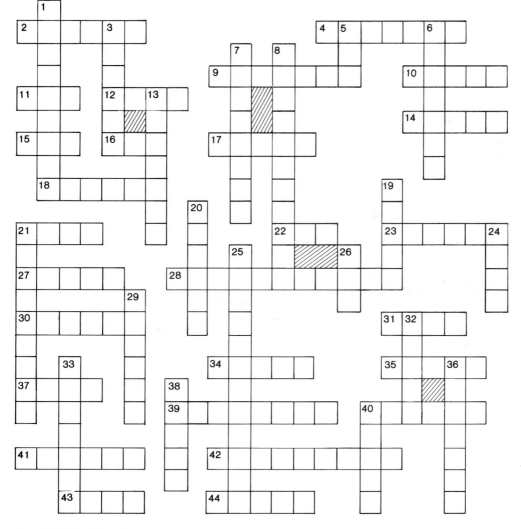

Figure 9.6 *(continued)*

Pyramid Volleyball Quiz

Name _____

Period _____

Date _____

Instructions: Fill in the pyramid with the appropriate word or words to complete each sentence.

1.

2.

3.

4.

5.

6.

7.

8.

9.

10.

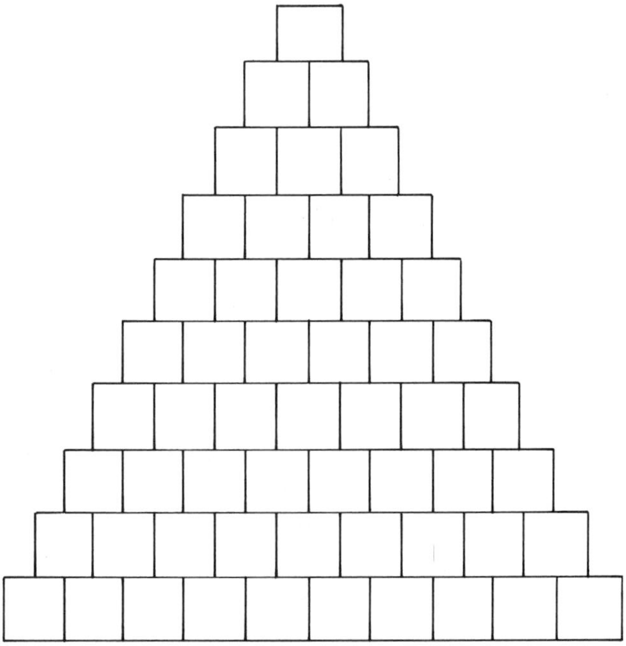

1. The winner of an official game must have at least a _____ point lead. (number)
2. The player in the _____ _____ position is the server. (initials)
3. An official team has _____ _____ _____ players.
4. A ball that lands on a court line is _____ _____ _____ _____ .
5. Except on a _____ _____ _____ _____ _____ the ball may be played out of the net.
6. To _____ _____ _____ _____ _____ _____ , is the moving of all players into position to begin serving.
7. _____ _____ _____ _____ _____ _____ _____ is called when the serving team loses turn of service.
8. The plan of attack used by a team to score points is called _____ _____ _____ _____ _____ _____ _____ _____ .
9. When the _____ _____ _____ _____ _____ _____ _____ _____ _____ team loses the rally, a point is scored.
10. In playing the ball, a player may step on but not over the _____ _____ _____ _____ _____ _____ _____ _____ _____ .

Figure 9.7 A pyramid test.

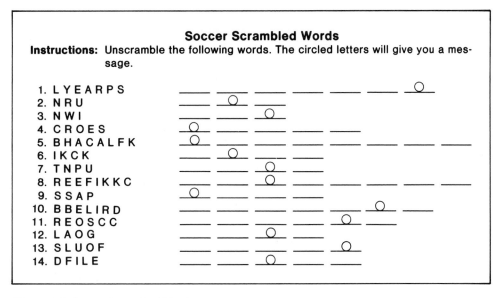

Figure 9.8 Soccer Scrambled Words.

Study Guides

Study guides, such as study sheets, workbooks, or journals, are useful in promoting cognitive learning. Students involved in completing a study sheet, a workbook assignment, or a journal entry have moved to the "I do, I understand" level of learning. These aids allow another chance for information to be remembered. They are a good review help for a test or before competing in tournament competition. An example is the Archery Study Sheet shown in figure 9.13.

Study guides can be used for individual study or review or as an adjunct to class instruction. They can focus student attention on important instructional points. Care should be taken to simplify instructions and to use variety in their construction to prevent boredom. Procedures include the following:

1. Use appropriate vocabulary and reading level for students.
2. Eliminate nonessential items.
3. If possible, write so that the student is actively involved in learning by filling in the blanks or working through the material to be learned, or so that the material is programmed with immediate feedback.
4. Answers to study guides can be provided through class instruction, individual units, "A Rule a Day" bulletin boards, or individual study of text materials or loop films.

Hidden Terms—Track and Field

Instructions: Circle the terms that have to do with track and field. Words may read horizontally, vertically, or diagonally and forwards or backwards.

```
B R A K O S T S H O T A R T A L B U F A
T A R T A N B A U V A B A T O N A L I L
S T R O M M I N R A V E N D S Y L V N C
T J A V E L I N D U L I L I T A L S I R
E L S T R O M B L I A E X S R W S U S O
E X R I S T A H E F I I S C O N T N H S
P I T A N D R O S F H U L U N U A D A S
L E V A B E L D D A M O F S P R I N T C
E R I K M A D N U M C I T A O S D T R O
C I A M A M A D I K B A T L L I Y U I U
H U A N A K I L O L R O R O E L A T P N
A H S O C I T R O T K O N F V A R T L T
S T I A X L V Y E F H G N F A D D A E R
E L R E L A Y R G H J K L I U N S W J Y
B T A P E X S T V U O L N C L R T E U H
G N I R U S A E M Y N L O I T U T I M E
M E T E R U S P O U N D S A P S T G P J
D A M A R K E R N U O D F L A Y D H M D
S K C O L B G N I T R A T S R L C T D U
```

Bar	Pit
Baton	Polevault
Clock	Pounds
Cross Country	Relay
Discus	Runway
Distance	Shot
Finish	Sprint
Hammer	Starter
High Jump	Starting Blocks
Hurdle	Steeplechase
Javelin	Tape
Kilo	Tartan
Long Jump	Time
Marker	Track and Field
Measuring	Triple Jump
Meter	Weight
Officials	Yards

Figure 9.9 Hidden Terms.

Bingo Lingo—Diving

Instructions: The teacher draws a card one at a time and reads the definition. The first student to circle five terms in a row—either vertically, diagonally, or horizontally—wins.

Approach	Back Dive	Backward Take-off	Cutaway Dive	Degree of Difficulty
Entry	Forward Dive	Header	Hurdle	Free
Inward Dive	Jackknife	Layout	Lift	Opening
Pike	Press	Rotate	Somersault Dive	Spin
Swan	Straight	Takeoff	Tuck	Twist Dive

Figure 9.10 Bingo Lingo.
Source: Romine, Jack and Joyce M. Harrison. Brigham Young University.

Sports Bowl

Instructions: Follow the procedure below to play "Sports Bowl."
1. Divide class into two teams of equal size.
2. Read a question.
3. The first person to raise his or her hand gets to answer the question. If the question is answered correctly, a bonus question is directed to the answering team; if it is answered incorrectly, the other team may attempt the answer (and the bonus).
4. There is a thirty-second time limit on questions.
5. The scoring is as follows:
   Correct answer—10 points
   Correct bonus answer—5 points
   Incorrect bonus—no penalty

Questions can be created from sports, history, current events, game rules, etc. Typical questions and bonus questions might be:

Q. Who holds the record for lifetime home runs?

B. What is the record?

Q. How many points can be scored on a penalty bully in field hockey?

B. When is a penalty bully awarded?

Figure 9.11 Sports Bowl.

Baseball

Instructions: Follow the procedure below to play "Baseball."

1. Mark a diamond on the floor of a classroom or locker room area or use a magnetic board.
2. Write a list of questions about a sport.
3. Divide the class into two teams—designating one as the batting team and the other as the fielding team.
4. Ask the first batter a question. If correctly answered, the batter moves to first base. If incorrectly answered, the fielding team is allowed to answer. If the fielding team answers correctly, the batter is out. If not, the batter sits down and the next batter is up.
5. Continue until three outs are made or all batters have been up, then exchange teams.
6. Points are scored as runs are "batted" in.

Figure 9.12 Baseball.

Skill Checklists

Skill checklists are used to motivate students to practice tasks and keep a record of their learning activities. Checklists shift some of the decisions for learning to the student, thereby involving students in on-task behavior and eliminating standing around or goofing off. Some students require extra help to succeed in working on their own, but they will grow by doing so, and students will learn to accept the consequences of their learning decisions. The checklists include lists of skills or tasks to be checked off, with instructions for performance, such as quantity, quality, and use of equipment. Task checklists are of three types:

1. A checklist of skills in which the grade is determined by categories. Students are given a new sheet for each grade they are attempting to earn. An example of this type of checklist is the tennis checklist shown in figure 9.14.
2. A checklist that is not divided into categories but merely specifies the grade from the number of items passed. For example, checking off ten items is a C, fifteen items is a B, etc. The Swimming Class Record Sheet in chapter 8 is an example of this style (see figure 8.5 on page 230).
3. A checklist in which certain tasks are graded pass or fail, such as the Badminton Skill Checklist in figure 9.15.

Although extra preparation time is necessary for creating the checklists, they can be an extremely valuable teaching strategy both for preclass activities and during class time. There are two ways of using the checklist method:

1. A dittoed checklist can be issued to each student and items can be checked off by partners, team captains, student assistants, or the teacher.
2. A check-off card, which lists each student in the class and the skills to be performed, can be maintained by the teacher.

Checklists may form part of the grade for a unit or may be used as a record of performance.

An inclusion skill checklist is a list of skills in which multiple levels of performance are available from which students choose. It is used to ensure participation and success by all students. It accommodates individual differences by including the highly skilled or fit as

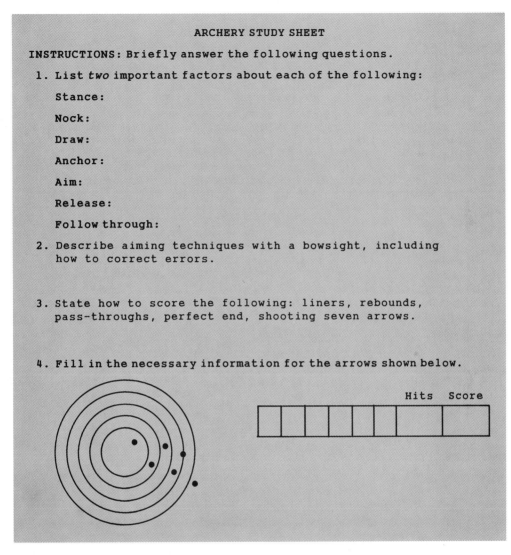

ARCHERY STUDY SHEET

INSTRUCTIONS: Briefly answer the following questions.

1. List *two* important factors about each of the following:

   Stance:

   Nock:

   Draw:

   Anchor:

   Aim:

   Release:

   Follow through:

2. Describe aiming techniques with a bowsight, including how to correct errors.

3. State how to score the following: liners, rebounds, pass-throughs, perfect end, shooting seven arrows.

4. Fill in the necessary information for the arrows shown below.

Hits   Score

Figure 9.13 Archery study sheet.

well as the less skilled or fit and handicapped students. It increases students' awareness of their own abilities and the ability to set realistic goals. Because students select their own levels of participation, learner anxiety is reduced. Although the preparation of an inclusion skill checklist may be time consuming and equipment may need to be adjusted, both teachers and students will benefit from the use of the inclusion skill checklist. Some examples include:

1. Archery—Shoot two hundred points in five consecutive ends at
   a. twenty yards
   b. twenty-five yards
   c. thirty yards
   d. thirty-five yards

```
            SKILL REQUIREMENTS FOR TENNIS

Rally Rascals--  C  Grade              Name _____

        Exercises
_____  1.  Fifty down bounces using forehand grip.
_____  2.  Fifty up bounces using forehand grip.
_____  3.  Twenty-five reverse bounces using forehand grip.

     Wall or Backboard Practice
_____  4.  Return at least ten consecutive forehands. One bounce only
           from baseline.
_____  5.  Return at least five consecutive backhands. One bounce only
           from baseline.

     Tossed Balls
_____  6.  Return five moving forehands in a row from no man's land to
           no man's land without an error. Repeat three times.
_____  7.  Repeat above for backhand.
_____  8.  Return eight out of ten moving forehands from baseline to
           baseline.
_____  9.  Return five out of eight moving backhands from baseline to
           baseline.
_____ 10.  Return five out of eight moving forehand volleys to no man's
           land.
_____ 11.  Return five out of eight moving backhand volleys to no man's
           land.

     Self-Tossed Balls
_____ 12.  Put ten consecutive forehands into play from the baseline to
           the baseline.
_____ 13.  Put five out of ten backhands into play from the baseline to
           the baseline.
_____ 14.  Serve five out of ten fast serves into either court.

     Rally Practice
_____ 15.  Short court rally for at least ten times.
_____ 16.  With an experienced player, play a pro set.
```

Figure 9.14 A skill checklist—tennis.
Source: Ann Valentine, Brigham Young University.

2. Badminton—Do ten consecutive underhand drop shots with a partner under a rope placed
   a. twenty inches above the net
   b. sixteen inches above the net
   c. twelve inches above the net
3. Volleyball—Volley the ball consecutively against the wall above a line eight feet high
   a. five times
   b. ten times
   c. fifteen times

BADMINTON SKILL CHECKLIST

Name _____

_____ Twenty consecutive underhand drop shots in a rally with a partner.

_____ Eight out of ten short serves between short service line and white line.

_____ Score twenty-five short serves on court with rope twelve-inches above net and target in right court.

_____ Eight out of ten long serves on court with target in right court.

_____ Score twenty long serves on court with target in right court.

_____ Eight out of ten smashes with partner setting up (shots that can be returned with some effort by the partner cannot be counted).

_____ Eight out of ten clears (overhead) with partner setting up (must land between the two back boundary lines).

_____ Eight out of ten clears (underhand) with partner setting up (must land between the two back boundary lines).

_____ Read the handout on scoring and score one game.

Complete the following play patterns with a partner (you should be player A and player B in each case).

_____ Player A--Serve
        B--Clear to deep backhand
        A--Drive down sideline
        B--Clear to deep forehand
        A--Clear to deep backhand
        B--Drive cross court

_____ Player A--Serve
        B--Clear to deep backhand
        A--Drop to the forehand
        B--Clear to the deep forehand
        A--Clear to the deep backhand
        Repeat

Figure 9.15 Badminton skill checklist.

4. Swimming—Tread water
   a. fifteen seconds
   b. one minute
   c. two minutes

Procedures
1. Determine the tasks.
2. For each task, determine one or more factors that change the level of difficulty of the skill.

3. Make a checklist of the tasks, quantity to be done, multiple performance levels, and criteria for successful performance.
4. Have students circle or put an x through the starting level and the level completed.

Personal Resource File

A personal resource file is a file in which instructional materials are located and where they can be easily obtained for use and replaced for future reference and use. Every teacher should devise a system of filing that is practical in the situation in which he or she is working. Materials should include items such as pictures, items for lesson and unit planning, skill analyses, evaluation materials, handouts, study sheets, instructional media lists, books, and pamphlets. Each item should be labeled as to its location so it can be returned when not in use. Files should include community resources and lists of people who might be willing to assist in developing or conducting learning activities, or for special reports or projects.

One of the simplest methods of filing is to have a file folder for each sport or topic taught. This might be expanded later as in the following examples of file titles:

Archery—Unit Plans
Archery—Equipment
Archery—Skill Evaluation
Archery—Knowledge Evaluation

The filing system must follow a plan that agrees with the teachers' personal style and with which materials can most easily be located.

Selecting Program Aids and Materials for Specific Content Areas

The general instructional aids and materials just presented are designed to help teachers plan meaningful physical education programs. Teachers should be up to date and aware of the many options available when incorporating them into the instructional experience. Specific ideas for the content areas of fitness and wellness, movement skills, and adventure activities are included in this section. In a concentrated effort to meet the goals of physical education, the following components should be included in the teacher's planning: (1) motivation, (2) instruction and practice, and (3) evaluation.

Fitness and Wellness

"Fitness is the capacity to achieve the optimal quality of life." It includes intellectual, social, spiritual, and physical components.[17] Physical fitness is a reflection of the ability "to work with vigor and pleasure without undue fatigue, with energy left for enjoying hobbies and recreational activities, and for meeting unforeseen emergencies."[18] Physical fitness is built on a foundation of five major factors—cardiovascular endurance, strength, flexibility, proper body weight, and relaxation.[19] Students need to know the importance of optimal physical fitness in their lives, whether or not they are fit, and how to become fit. Such instruction should be treated as an explicit objective rather than as an activity.[20] Teach *why* physical fitness is important and provide guidelines for choosing activities. Then, let students choose their own fitness activities, invent or name their own exercises, bring their own music, and develop aerobic dance or other exercise routines. Use varied and exciting ways to develop fitness.

Motivation

Developing and maintaining good physical fitness is a demanding and challenging task. Students need to be supported and rewarded in their efforts to have physically fit bodies. Students first must realize a *need* for such a condition. The administration of a pretest is one means of helping students understand the need for optimal physical fitness in their lives. Pretests may include a written questionnaire or a fitness test battery.

A written questionnaire that is not graded, but used to stimulate interest and point out needed areas of instruction, is an effective way to introduce a unit of instruction. Questions might include the following:

1. The emphasis in the United States today on healthy life-styles has resulted in a more physically fit nation, especially the youth.   T   F
2. Exercising three days per week will maintain an adequate level of physical fitness.
   T   F
3. Children and youth under the age of eighteen need not worry about coronary heart disease.   T   F
4. A person burns more calories jogging one mile than walking the same distance.
   T   F
5. One must exercise at least sixty minutes per session to develop and maintain adequate physical fitness.   T   F
6. Performing exercises involving the hips and waist will reduce the fat in those areas.
   T   F
7. Children who engage in a vigorous exercise program score higher on academic tests.
   T   F
8. Exercise increases the appetite.   T   F
9. One should not exercise outside when temperatures reach zero degrees because the lungs may be damaged.   T   F
10. Golf is good aerobic exercise for those walking the course.   T   F

Other motivational techniques include:

1. *Special award programs*—to recognize participation and achievement. Teachers may award certificates or other awards to students who achieve their own predetermined goal in jogging, bicycling, or swimming or who achieve predetermined standards.[21]
2. *Fitness club*[22]—Fitness can be further promoted in a club devoted exclusively to engaging in and learning about physical fitness.
3. *Posters, charts, and banners* displaying test results and improvement—A chart, such as the one shown in figure 9.16, is unique and very motivational. Each class has a chart with a square block area for each student. Stickers or dots may be earned by students participating in acceptable fitness activities for thirty minutes outside of class. (Flexibility participation must be thirty minutes in the same week). Students may earn stickers in any way they choose and arrange them on the chart. Other stickers may be earned in ways decided on by the class and/or teacher (e.g., complete a three-day self-study of dietary habits and appropriate changes).
4. *Unusual events*
   a. Have a team jogging meet. Divide the class into teams of two or three people. Set a timer for a given time period, such as fifteen or thirty minutes. Team members alternate laps, one runner at a time, and report to a scorer at the conclusion of

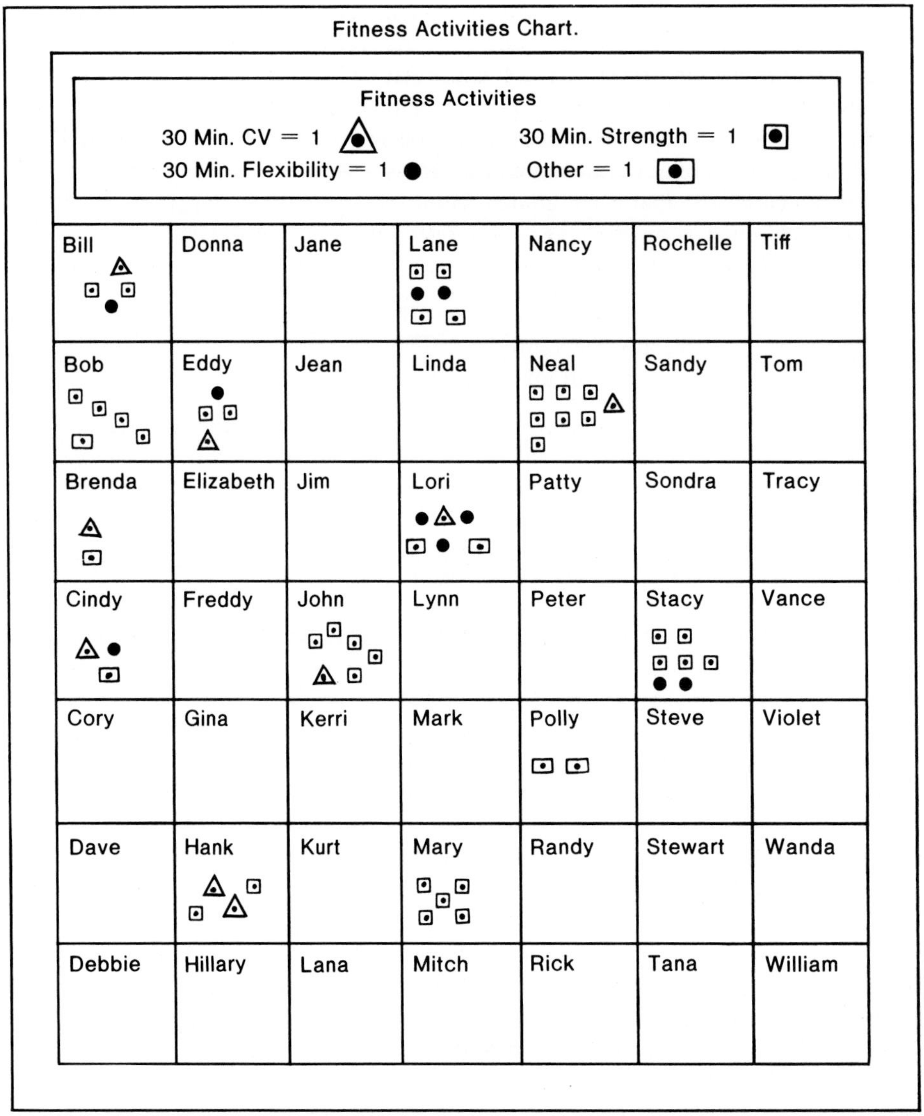

Fitness Activities Chart.

Fitness Activities

30 Min. CV = 1 ▲ (triangle with dot)   30 Min. Strength = 1 ▣ (square with dot)
30 Min. Flexibility = 1 ●   Other = 1 ▣ (square with dot)

Bill	Donna	Jane	Lane	Nancy	Rochelle	Tiff
▲ ▣ ▣ ●			▣ ▣ ● ● ▣ ▣			
Bob	**Eddy**	**Jean**	**Linda**	**Neal**	**Sandy**	**Tom**
▣ ▣ ▣ ▣ ▣	● ▣ ▣ ▲			▣ ▣ ▣ ▲ ▣ ▣ ▣ ▣		
Brenda	**Elizabeth**	**Jim**	**Lori**	**Patty**	**Sondra**	**Tracy**
▲ ▣			● ▲ ● ▣ ● ▣			
Cindy	**Freddy**	**John**	**Lynn**	**Peter**	**Stacy**	**Vance**
▲ ● ▣		▣ ▣ ▣ ▲ ▣			▣ ▣ ▣ ▣ ▣ ● ●	
Cory	**Gina**	**Kerri**	**Mark**	**Polly**	**Steve**	**Violet**
				▣ ▣		
Dave	**Hank**	**Kurt**	**Mary**	**Randy**	**Stewart**	**Wanda**
	▲ ▣ ▣ ▲		▣ ▣ ▣ ▣ ▣			
Debbie	**Hillary**	**Lana**	**Mitch**	**Rick**	**Tana**	**William**

Figure 9.16 Fitness Activities Chart.

each lap. Joggers are allowed to walk, skip, run, or move as they wish, but the team with the most laps completed within the time period wins the meet.

b. Have competition among classes to see who can run the farthest in one month's time. Students record their laps each day. Awards may be given to individuals with the highest distance in each class and to all students who completed the goal.[23]

c. Have a treasure hunt in which students run from point to point as directed by a series of clues. Students can pick up a marker at each point to show that they covered the entire course.[24]

d. Sundberg suggested participation races in which students run to a given point and back, picking up a marker at the midpoint. Students are encouraged to pace themselves so they do not have to stop and walk.[25] Only those who finish are eligible for awards. Awards could be given for the fastest times and the team with the most finishers (divide the number of finishers by the number of starters). This type of race should be used at the end of a fitness unit after students have learned to pace themselves and have the endurance to last the entire distance.

e. Corbin suggested prediction races in which students attempt to run as close as possible to their predicted times. Individuals or teams can be used. The individual or team coming closest to its predicted time wins.[26]

f. Stein described a "Run for Fun" in which students run a specified distance and then record their overall finish place and category on a card. Awards are given to those finishing first in each category. Although he suggested age and gender for the categories, many other categories could be selected—such as eye color, color of tennis shoes, or birth month.[27]

5. *Fitness programs* involving the school and community
   a. Fair: including displays, lectures, testing
   b. Contest: involving runners, walkers, cyclers, swimmers, wheelchair participants (e.g., Jump Rope for Heart)[28]

The real test of student motivation is the continued pursuit of health-related exercise. Lambert suggested a self-management model that uses goal setting and attainment of goals, evaluation, and the setting of new goals to ensure continued participation by students.[29]

Teachers need to be examples of fitness. *Keep yourself physically fit!* Exercise with the students, not just in front of them. Point out how other prominent people, such as movie stars and astronauts, stay physically fit.[30] Be enthusiastic about physical education.

Instruction and Practice

"Students must understand why as well as how to exercise."[31] Fitness programs should be carefully planned and structured to include opportunities to learn basic concepts and principles as well as to progress in the performance of fitness components. Table 9.2 illustrates a plan for implementing fitness instruction, assessment, and development.

Of the three components that operate to meet the goals of physical education, practice or experience is critical when designing physical fitness activities. Students must be motivated to perform so that the evaluation phase is meaningful.

Fitness activities may be planned for part or all of a period. Such activities might include exercise routines, circuit training, obstacle courses, aerobic dance, jogging, cycling, swimming, and weight training. Exercise routines to music add a new dimension to the workout. Students often are more willing to be active for longer periods of time with music in the background.

Teachers should not forget to include some fun. "Without fun the program and the kids get the blahs."[32] A fun, but challenging, obstacle course can be set up to meet the demands of developing fitness. Such courses can be designed for inside the gymnasium or at an outside station (see figure 9.17).

Table 9.2 A teaching schedule for a fitness unit

Design for Lifetime Fitness
Scope and Sequence Chart

Episode: 1 Introduction to Physical Fitness	Episode 2: Improving Physical Fitness	Episode 3: Flexibility: Meaning and Values	Episode 4: Flexibility: Assessment and Safety
Episode 5: Developing Flexibility	Episode 6: Muscular Strength: Meaning and Values	Episode 7: Muscular Strength: Assessment and Weight Training	Episode 8: Muscular Strength: Development
Episode 9: Muscular Endurance: Meaning and Values	Episode 10: Muscular Endurance: Assessment and Activities	Episode 11: Developing Muscular Endurance	Episode 12: Cardiorespiratory Endurance: Meaning and Values
Episode 13: Cardiorespiratory Endurance: Safety and Aerobic Activities	Episode 14: Cardiorespiratory Fitness: Assessment	Episode 15: Cardiorespiratory Fitness: Development	Episode 16: Body Composition: Meaning, Values, and Assessment
Episode 17: Body Composition: Control	Episodes 18, 19, and 20: Personal Program Development and Activities		

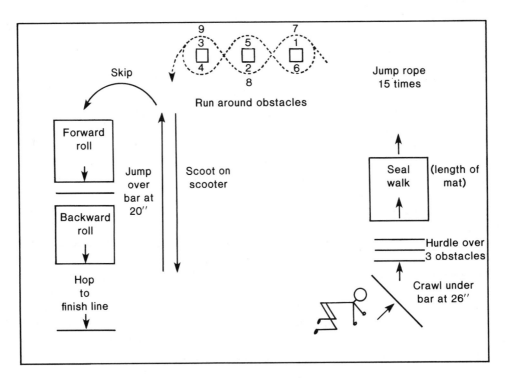

Figure 9.17 An example of an obstacle course.

Name _____ Date Begun _____										
Event	1-min Score	Training Dose	Workout Score							
			1	2	3	4	5	6	7	8
Jump rope-- forward	40	20								
Jump rope-- backward	35	18								
Push-ups	18	9								
Curl-ups	21	12								
Burpees	22	11								
Trunk twister	30	15								
Running in place (count each foot)	53	27								
Shuttle run (count laps)	13	7								

Completion Date of First Circuit _____
Completion Date of Second Circuit _____

Figure 9.18 Ten-minute circuit training record sheet.

Circuits are another fitness activity that can be challenging and motivating. Tasks are performed either for time or by work load. An example of a circuit set up by work load and time is shown in figure 9.18. The work load or "training dose" for each task is the score obtained after performing the task for one minute and dividing the score in half. For example, if the student performs ten curl-ups, the training dose is five. After the training dose is determined for each task, students perform the circuit for a specific amount of time. The time of the circuit is equal to one minute for each task (eight tasks requires an eight-minute circuit). The student attempts to perform the circuit three times at the training dose for each task. At the end of eight minutes, the student records how many times each task was performed. When the student is able to complete the circuit three times in the allotted time (which may take several weeks), the training dose is recalculated by once again obtaining a one-minute score for each task. If weight-training equipment is available, the circuit could employ that equipment.

Evaluation

Testing and evaluation are vital to the success of a physical fitness program. Tests should be a learning experience so students understand what results mean. The test program should emphasize aerobic fitness, but should also test other aspects of fitness such as abdominal and upper-body strength and flexibility.[33] Tests can also be a good motivational tool for the student who feels good about the results. Care must be taken with those students who are not fit so results do not cause them to react negatively.

Teachers wanting to preassess student fitness levels and stimulate awareness and motivation should administer all or part of a standardized test battery such as the AAHPERD Fitness Test. The updated and revised test battery includes an awards program that should be motivating to students. The AAHPERD test and awards program[34] includes the following:

1. AAHPERD Basic Test (girls and boys ages six to seventeen)
   a. one-mile run/walk
   b. modified sit-ups
   c. pull-ups
   d. sit and reach
   e. skinfolds—with Body Mass Index (BMI) alternate
      (AAHPERD offers videos to assist teachers in administering skinfold tests.)[35]
2. Recognition Categories
   a. Participation Award—Earned by students who participate in designated physical activities outside the classroom and within the framework of the assessment and educational program; designed to award participation and effort.
   b. Personal Goals Award—Earned by students who meet their contractual agreement established by the teacher and student after pre-testing; designed to reward effort and achievement of individual goals.
   c. Health-Fitness Award—Earned by students who successfully achieve criterion standards for all five test items; designed to reward effort and achievement in reaching a healthful fitness standard.

Participants are entitled to certificates, patches, and computer printouts of results as part of this program. Other organizations such as the President's Council on Physical Fitness and Sports (PCPFS), the Institute for Aerobics Research (IAR), and the Amateur Athletic Union (AAU) publish similar fitness and award programs. The President's Council on Physical Fitness and Sports offers a Presidential Sports Award based on participation or standard of achievement in 43 different sports (Presidential Sports Award, AAU House, P.O. Box 68207, Indianapolis, Indiana 46268).

Accurate records of participation, both in class and outside, are helpful. Figure 9.19 is an example of a physical fitness record-keeping form.

The success of any fitness program lies with the teacher. "Excellent leadership can overcome poor equipment and facilities but the opposite is seldom true."[36] Nothing can substitute for the example and enthusiasm of a good teacher.

| Philadelphia Physical Fitness Test Score Report |

School _____ Class _____ Instructor _____

Student Gender _____ (make a separate list for boys and girls)

S = score (number, time, distance)   % = percentile rank

Students	1st Test										2nd Test									
	S&R		Jump		Sit-Up		Chin/Hang		Run		S&R		Jump		Sit-Up		Chin/Hang		Run	
	S	%	S	%	S	%	S	%	S	%	S	%	S	%	S	%	S	%	S	%

Figure 9.19 Philadelphia Physical Fitness Test
Score Report.

Movement Skills

The major emphasis of any physical education program is the development of movement skills. Whether the thrust is sport skills or rhythms and dance, the teacher spends the majority of program time concentrating on improving skill execution. The skill emphasis in programs over the past two decades has been that of "lifetime sports." These sports are primarily individual or dual activities that have carryover value for the participant after the school years. Approximately 75 percent of the nation's secondary schools emphasize lifetime sports such as bowling, badminton, tennis, frisbee, and racquetball in their physical education programs.[37] The concept of team sports has expanded to include more than the traditional favorites, such as team handball,[38] New Games,[39] and modified games such as speed-a-way[40] or volley tennis.[41] Aerobic dance gained popularity in the eighties and is noticeable in physical education programs throughout the United States. These exercises set to music emphasize cardiorespiratory fitness, strength, and flexibility.

Although the activities that are popular change as time passes, the basic thrust in physical education programs still remains that of teaching movement skills. The effective teacher needs useful program aids and materials to enhance curricular offerings.

Motivation

Carron[42] cited many factors affecting motivation. One factor that has application to the learning of movement skills is that of reward. The following examples are ideas for reward incentives to motivate students that are inexpensive and easy to administer.

1. *Recognition clubs* such as the Bull's-Eye Club for archery students or the 100-Mile Club for swimmers or joggers.
2. *Skill charts* used in multi-event activities such as gymnastics or track and field. Students decide from a list what skills they wish to practice and progress at their own rate. Skills are checked off on the charts as they are completed.
3. *Spotlight board* recognizes individuals or teams for performance, sportsmanship, leadership, or honors.
4. *Awards* such as certificates, trophies, or t-shirts are given to outstanding performers.[43]

A second motivational factor mentioned by Carron was the introduction of novelty or change in routine. One means of incorporating this factor is through the introduction of nontraditional games such as Team Ball, a game developed by a middle school faculty to teach students skills and strategies for use in other situations. The game is played on a basketball court with a goal placed directly in the middle of each baseline. A restraining line is placed parallel to the free-throw lane seven feet from the baseline to mark an area in which no players are allowed. The goalie plays in front of this line within the free-throw lane and is the only player allowed in the lane. The objective is to throw the ball (preferably a volleyball) into the opponents' goal. Such a score counts one point. A player may advance the ball only by passing and may not be in possession of the ball for more than three seconds. Offensive and defensive players are designated, and after a goal is scored these players trade positions. The game is started by a jump ball at center court. After a goal the other team brings the ball in from the end line. Playing time is divided into four equal periods.[44]

Nothing motivates students more than success. Teachers should select instructional strategies that ensure success for all students. Instructional strategies will be discussed in chapter 10.

Instruction and Practice

Movement skills should be taught in an orderly teaching progression with activities chosen according to student ability. The teacher may decide to use any or all of the following activities to teach physical skills:

1. Demonstration: Students are shown the movements they are expected to reproduce. Demonstrations are used to create interest or to show how something is to be done, such as a sports skill or safety procedure. They help students avoid misconceptions. Procedures include the following:
   a. Plan a meaningful demonstration for the audience involved.
   b. Practice the demonstration or acquire a good demonstrator. Demonstrations can involve live models, films, loop films, videotapes, or other media. When demonstrating sports skills, remember to use the mirror-image technique—that is, say "right hand" to the students and use the left hand—or face away from the students so they will see the image as they will be doing it.
   c. Assemble and set up equipment and the seating arrangement so all can see and hear.
   d. Briefly explain the purpose of the demonstration.
   e. Demonstrate using key points to enhance perception.
2. Drills: Drills are contrived situations used to learn or review skills. They provide a large number of practice trials in a short amount of time. Skills tests can be used as drills when students are allowed to repeat the tests over and over to achieve higher levels of skill. Examples of drills are a partner volley in volleyball, a three-person weave in basketball, or a toss-and-hit drill in tennis. Procedures include:
   a. Demonstrate and/or explain the learning activity.
   b. Organize small groups for maximum participation.
   c. Make drills as gamelike as possible to ensure transfer to game situations.
   d. Provide continuous feedback to ensure correct learning of skills.
   e. Adjust or change drills to provide for individual differences in student learning.
3. Lead-up games: Students usually need a transition from drill practice to the competitive game situation so they feel comfortable in an official game. Lead-up games bridge this gap by allowing students to practice skills in gamelike settings, in which interest can be maintained while learning to refine and apply skills. Lead-up games are modified team games that involve one or more of the fundamental skills, rules, or procedures used in a major team game.[45] Procedures are as follows:
   a. Present games from simple to more complex.
   b. Use games to complement drills, not replace them.
   c. Organize the game to provide maximum participation.
   d. Provide evenly matched competition.
   e. Match the game to the ability of the students.
   f. Make maximum use of time and space.
   g. Rotate players so all get an opportunity to play all positions.[46]
4. Game or team play: Games are played using official rules.
5. Competition: Competitive game situations are provided with an expected winner and loser.

Endless possibilities exist when teaching movement skills as the components of the game or activity are changed or varied. For example the number of players, type of equipment, rules, organizational patterns, movements, limitations, and purposes can be altered to change the outcome of the activity.[47]

Teachers should not be fearful of straying from the traditional curricular offerings. Valuable learning experiences can result for students engaged in the following nontraditional activity units:

1. *Work:* Students are taught certain tasks that facilitate the performance of work in lifting, carrying, pushing, pulling, striking, and the like. The topics of stability, force, leverage, momentum, and friction are taught through such activities as "tray relay races." In this activity, students weave in and out of markers carrying various objects (an empty bottle, a bottle one-third full of water, and a bottle three-fourths full of water) on a tray to determine the differences they feel.[48]
2. *Stress management:* The topics of stress diseases, promoters, and results are discussed. Students are taught relaxation responses, techniques of exercise, recreation, and diet to cope with stress.[49]
3. *Self defense:* Students are taught the skills and strategies to protect themselves when physically attacked.[50]
4. *Aquatic exercise:* Fitness conditioning using in-water movement is the goal of such a program.[51]
5. *Movement awareness:* Activities such as yoga, karate, aikido, or t'ai chi chuan are taught.[52]
6. *Cycling:* Students are taught about equipment, safety, riding courses, and such skills as balancing.[53]

Activities not usually performed in the gymnasium can be adapted to the school site. For example, tennis and bowling can be simulated in the gym so students get a very authentic experience.[54] Where adequate room exists, a miniature golf course can be set up so students get the experience of keeping score and learning the rules and etiquette of the course. Whiffle balls are used to ensure safety. Cross-country skiing can be taught during the winter months using both the outside playing fields and the gymnasium.[55]

Evaluation

The aim of the evaluator should be to give skills tests that simulate the game situation as closely as possible. A volleyball skills test in which the participant executes the bump, set, and spike sequentially is an example of this principle. Upon receiving the ball, students alternate a bump and a set to themselves, working the ball into spiking position, until six series have been completed. The ball is spiked over the net to complete the test.[56]

In addition to the evaluation procedures discussed in chapter 8, teachers might also consider a feedback checklist when evaluating student performance of movement skills. For example, specific proficiencies are checked off when they are executed. Students are expected to have all proficiencies checked off. Figure 9.20 illustrates such a checklist.

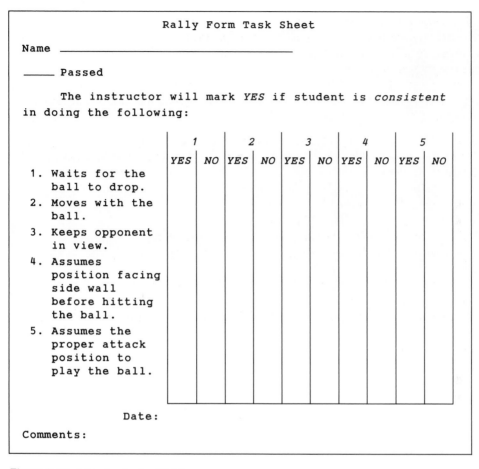

Figure 9.20 A feedback checklist for evaluating student performance of movement skills.

Adventure Activities

Adventure activities are relative newcomers to the physical education program. They include activities that invoke the emotions of excitement, challenge, apprehension, and fear. They are included in the curriculum to meet the need for adventure and to build self-confidence, self-reliance, and independence.[57] Such outcomes are possible because students learn to think clearly and make wise decisions, to have the courage to act, and to control the emotion of fear.[58]

Motivation

The adventure activity itself is often motivation enough for student participation. However, some students will be overwhelmed by the risk or challenge of the activity and must be carefully directed until they gain the necessary confidence, trust, and skill to participate. All students must be diligently supervised so that trust is developed by the apprehensive student and caution is evoked in the fearless student. Motivation is enhanced by offering students a

Challenge activities develop cooperation,
problem solving ability, and fitness.

choice in the activities in which they participate. The teacher might further ensure motivation and participation by following a systematic progression. First challenge activities would
be introduced, followed by initiative activities, and finally several choices of risk activities.

Instruction and Practice

Instruction and practice in adventure activities should be geared to the level of the students.
Students must have the necessary skills and abilities to participate safely in any venture.
Some students are ready to immediately engage in risk activities, but students should have
the option of deciding if they want this type of experience.

Challenge Activities Students participating in challenge activities develop the ability to cooperate in a group, learn to solve problems, and improve individual fitness.[59] Games are one
means of offering adventure and challenge to students. The nature of some games equalizes
competition and makes everybody a winner. The New Games Foundation pioneered this concept. From this beginning has emerged cooperative sports and games and the multicultural
physical education approach. Examples of challenge activities include the following:

1. *Knots*—Approximately twelve players stand in a circle, shoulder to shoulder, and
   place hands in the center of the circle. Everyone grabs a couple of hands of people
   who are *not* next to them. They cannot grab both hands from the same person. The
   objective of the game is to untie the knot without releasing hands. The game is
   complete when all players are standing in one circle facing each other holding
   hands.[60]

2. *All on One Side*—A team of four or five players on one side of a volleyball court (with no one on the other side) attempts to move back and forth to the other side of the net as many times as possible without the ball touching the floor. Using a balloon for a ball, each player volleys the balloon to another player on the same side of the net and then scoots under the net to the other side. The last player to touch the balloon taps it over the net and scoots under. The receiving players try to keep the balloon in play on the new side of the net as they repeat the process. As the team gets better, two balloons may be put into play at one time.[61]

Teachers might want to vary the components of an activity to cause one to perceive risk and feel a sense of fear while participating in a safe environment. For example, the group is divided into pairs. One person in each pair puts on a blindfold and stands behind a starting line. The partner stands ten feet behind. Other partners are at least six feet apart. On the starting signal, the blindfolded persons are guided by the verbal directions of the partner around an obstacle course or to perform certain activities such as walking backwards.[62]

Initiative Activities Group initiative activities are designed to provide adventure while incorporating problem-solving experiences involving a cooperative effort. Participants should get to know and understand each other better while developing a trust for group members and a sense of group belonging. Groups should comprise no more than twenty participants. Success is measured by group accomplishment rather than individual achievement. Simulation of the activity setting is stressed and little sophisticated equipment is required. The following are examples of initiative activities:

1. *Prisoners of War*—Participants are brought into a dimly lighted handball court. A five-foot high badminton net is stretched across the court to represent a fence. A six-foot pipe or fifteen-foot rope is on the floor on the prisoner's side of the net. A mat is under the net for safety. Participants are told that guards are coming to execute them in twenty minutes. The task is to get all prisoners over the fence and up a fifteen- to eighteen-foot high wall into the observation gallery before the guards arrive. Anyone touching the net is electrocuted. The mat may be moved to the wall for safety, but it may not be used to aid in the escape.[63]
2. *River Crossing*—Participants are brought to a stream of water or a gap between two platforms, representing a fourteen-foot wide river. Materials available are three, two-by-eight inch planks with lengths of six, nine, and eleven feet. Participants are told the enemy is pursuing twenty minutes behind. The task is to successfully get everyone across the river using only the three planks. The water (or ground) may not be touched. The group is successful when all participants and the three planks are on the opposite bank.[64]
3. *The Chain Gang*—Participants form a circle around a stationary tetherball or volleyball standard (or a ten-foot pole set in a tire filled with cement). Short ropes or strips of cloth are used to tie each team member's hands together (right hand to left hand). Mats may be placed around the base of the pole. The group is being held for ransom by international terrorists who have left momentarily, giving them time to escape. The object is to become free of the pole in the center while the pole remains upright and fixed to the ground with all hands tied together[65] (see figure 9.21).

Figure 9.21 The chain gang.
Source: Allan C. Boyer, Brigham Young University
Master's Thesis, 104 E. State Highway, Copperton,
Utah 84006.

4. *Mission Impossible*—An entire physical education class divided into teams is challenged to get across the gym in the shortest possible time without touching the floor. A high stage area or bleachers folded into the wall with the top seat accessible might be used as the start or finish point. Other aids to the class might be climbing ropes suspended from the ceiling (hanging straight down or suspended eight to ten feet above the floor from one point to another), a plastic waste can, an old tire, tumbling mats, a gym scooter, two-by-eight plank, small tarpaulin, small blocks of wood. The students are told they can use anything in the gymnasium with the exception of their shoes and uniforms to aid them with the task. Each team is timed.[66]

Risk Activities "Risk sports are characterized by physical and psychological challenges encountered by participants as they confront elements of the environment."[67] These activities usually take place in a natural setting and contain an element of perceived risk or physical danger.[68] Although some aspects of teaching these activities can be done during a regularly scheduled class period, they are often conducted after school, on weekends, and during vacations.

Activities range from low risk (fishing, cycling, orienteering) to medium risk (backpacking, cross-country skiing, horseback riding) to high risk (rock climbing, white water canoeing, winter camping).[69] Other activities of varying degrees of risk include: bicycle touring, scuba diving, cross-country cycling, caving, rafting, field archery, group initiative activities, high-ropes courses, indoor or outdoor climbing walls, and camping.

Risk activities cause participants to confront
elements of the environment.

Such activities are performed in a noncompetitive atmosphere sparked by intrinsic motivation. The activities are active, not passive, and this component alone has the potential to increase physical skills and physical fitness. The development of social skills such as leadership, trust, cooperation, esprit de corps, and enhanced interpersonal relationships are inherent in risk activities. Personal development, including knowledge of personal limits, pride in achievement, increased problem-solving ability, and enjoyment are listed as benefits. Other values include an appreciation of nature, an experiential knowledge of survival and emergency-care skills, and the application of nutrition and personal-health information. The teacher must weigh the benefits against the risk factors and decide if a safe environment can be created. Rademacher and Cruse stress that risk management is perhaps the most important key to the success of all such programs.[70] Personal safety of the participants must be ensured.

Protection of participants in risk activities, as well as the program, hinges on two guidelines:[71]

1. Reduce or eliminate programs with a high potential for accidents. Activities with a high potential for risk include hang gliding, ice climbing, parachuting, sky jumping, mountaineering, and spelunking.[72]
2. Maintain well-planned, carefully carried out, safe activities.
   a. Publish policies and procedures of operation.
   b. Continually analyze trip goals versus the limitations or abilities of participants and leaders.
   c. Screen participants.

d. Provide in-service training for staff, maintaining experienced, well-trained personnel. Be committed to readiness and rescue training. Provide a carefully defined progression of activities.

e. Inspect equipment and facilities regularly.

f. Keep track of accidents and near misses and publish records of safety. Analyze the major causes based on unsafe conditions, unsafe acts, or judgment errors.

g. Provide a program leader who provides direction and expertise (consistent, directive, nonpermissive).

h. Repeat operations in known areas.[73]

Evaluation

Objectives inherent in adventure activities are often from the affective domain and should be evaluated by appropriate methods (see chapter 8). Cognitive concepts may be tested through written exams or other appropriate means. Certain psychomotor skills are often formally evaluated using skills tests, checklists, or other testing procedures, especially when risk activities are the focus. Evaluation of adventure activities is often informal, however, and the successful completion of the activity is the method of evaluation used by the teacher.

Selecting Program Aids for Adjunct Activities— Intramurals and Tournament Play

The icing on the cake for meaningful physical education programs is often the adjunct activities that allow students complementary experiences to those activities offered in class. Ideas for such projects are presented in the following section. Intramurals, which includes tournament play, is recognized as an integral part of a balanced physical education program because it contributes to achieving the five goals of physical education mentioned earlier. The Calgary Curriculum Action project defined intramurals to include four dimensions of activity: (1) leagues and tournaments, (2) clubs, (3) special days, and (4) self-directed activities.[74] All of these dimensions can be motivational to students while promoting physical education programs.

Leagues and Tournaments

The teacher should not limit tournaments to intramural play. Explanations of tournament possibilities are described here giving the teacher information necessary to include them as activities in the regular physical education class.

Round-Robin

The round-robin tournament is played by having each player compete against every other player. The victor is the player who wins the most games and loses the fewest. This structure is very time consuming, but provides maximum participation for participants. After players or teams have been ranked by previous competition, a smaller ability-grouped round-robin competition is effective for participants of like ability. A round-robin schedule for six teams is shown here:

```
 1–6      1–5      1–4      1–3      1–2
↓2–5↑    ↓6–4↑    ↓5–3↑    ↓4–2↑    ↓3–6↑
 3–4      2–3      6–2      5–6      4–5
```

Team	1	2	3	4	5	6	Wins	Loses	Rank
1				15-8	6-15		1	1	
2									
3									
4	8-15							1	
5	15-6						1		
6									

Figure 9.22 A round-robin tournament chart.

This schedule was easily formulated by keeping team 1 stationary and moving every other team one place counter clockwise on the schedule. This procedure is repeated for each round until the teams rotate back to their original positions. To compute the number of games, use the following formula:

$N(N-1)$ divided by 2

$$\frac{6(6-1)}{2} \quad = \quad \frac{6 \times 5}{2} \quad = \quad \frac{30}{2} \quad = \quad 15$$

Another representation of a round-robin tournament graphically illustrates the standings of each player or team. This structure allows players or teams to select the order in which they play opponents and permits longer or shorter games to be played (see figure 9.22).

Elimination

When elimination tournaments are used, all competitors except the winner are eliminated after one or two losses depending on the type of tournament selected. Tournaments are set up with a standard number of open slots, with the total number of teams being divisible by two (e.g., 2, 4, 8, 16, 32). If the exact number of teams needed for the brackets is not available, some teams must be given a *bye* (an exemption from playing a game in a round). To determine who gets the byes, teams are *seeded* (ranked according to how they are expected to finish based on their record from previous play). Byes should be placed as far apart as possible on the tournament chart so seeded players are not playing each other in the first round.

Single Elimination A single-elimination tournament is a short tournament with half of the teams being eliminated in the first round. The winner is determined quickly, but it may not be the best team. An example of a single-elimination tournament with six entries is shown in figure 9.23. Figure 9.24 shows an example with thirteen entries.

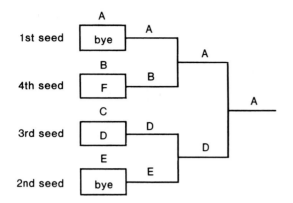

Figure 9.23 A single-elimination tournament for six entries.

Consolation A consolation tournament allows teams to compete for third place after losing in the first round. When a team loses one game after the first round, it is eliminated. Winners move to the right on the bracket tournament chart and losers move to the left. An example of a consolation tournament with four teams is shown in figure 9.25. Figure 9.26 shows an example of a tournament with sixteen teams.

Double Elimination A double-elimination tournament requires that each team must lose two games before being eliminated. It is nearly as effective in producing a true winner as a round-robin tournament and is less time consuming. Examples of double-elimination tournaments for four and fourteen teams are shown in figures 9.27 and 9.28. Note that for fourteen teams, sixteen slots are required.

To determine the number of games to be played, compute $2N - (1$ or $2)$. For example, $2 \times 24 = 28 - 1$ or $2 = 27$ or 26 games.

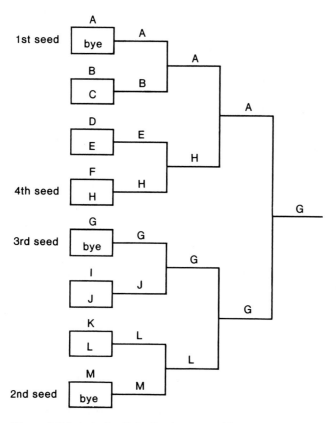

Figure 9.24 A single-elimination tournament for thirteen entries.

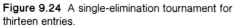
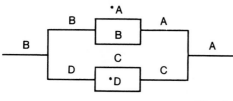

*Seeded players or teams

Figure 9.25 A consolation tournament for four entries.

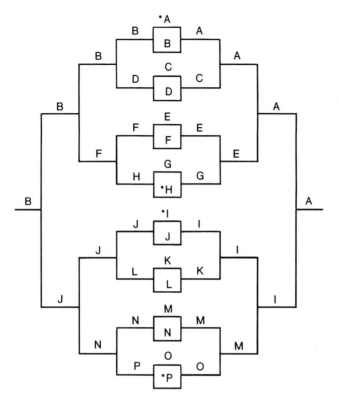

*Seeded players or teams

Figure 9.26 A consolation tournament for sixteen entries.

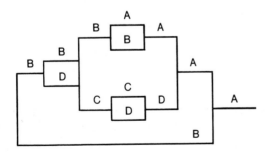

Figure 9.27 A double-elimination tournament for four entries.

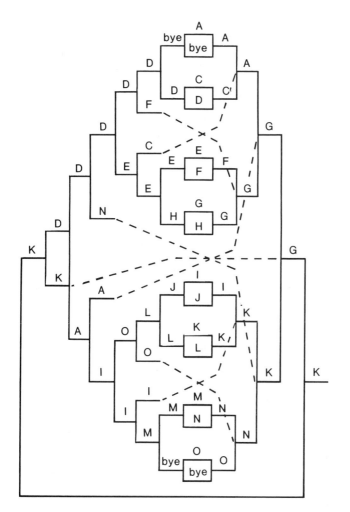

Figure 9.28 A double-elimination tournament for up to sixteen entries.

Challenge

Challenge tournaments are played by having each student challenge as many other players as possible within the class or group. A win allows students to change places with the loser. The best teams move to the top of the tournament chart. Players can be placed in an initial order by a draw, seeding, or in the order they signed up. It is sometimes fun to put the best players at the bottom of the chart so they have to win to advance to the top.

Ladder A ladder tournament places teams directly above one another on a chart. Challenges should be limited to one or two places above. Usually the team judged to be the best will be placed at the top of the ladder (see figure 9.29).

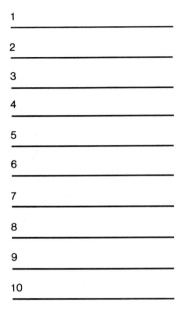

Figure 9.29 A ladder tournament.

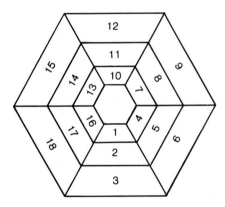

Figure 9.30 A spider-web tournament.

Spider Web A spider-web tournament, as shown in figure 9.30, is a unique variation of a ladder. Participants in each section of the web engage in their own challenge. Challenges are made one level above. Winners advance toward the middle of the web. On an ending date, winners are placed in an elimination tournament. Participants at each level could also be placed in their own elimination tournament.

Pyramid A pyramid tournament is designed to accommodate large numbers of participants. A team may challenge any team on the same line with it on the tournament chart as well as those to the immediate left or right on the line above (see figure 9.31).

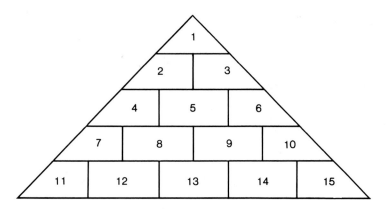

Figure 9.31 A pyramid tournament.

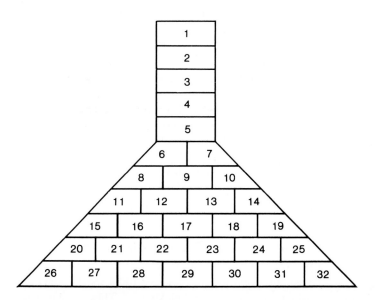

Figure 9.32 A funnel tournament.

Funnel A funnel tournament combines the best features of both the ladder and the pyramid by accommodating large numbers of participants while also ranking them. The lower half of the funnel is governed by the rules for a pyramid and the upper half by the rules of a ladder. An example is shown in figure 9.32.

Clock A clock tournament is an animated version of a challenge tournament. Participants challenge no more than two numbers ahead. The tournament ends when any player advances full circle. More or less numbers may be used (see figure 9.33).

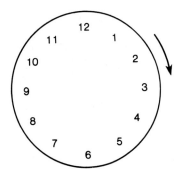

Figure 9.33 A clock tournament.

Clubs

Intramural clubs are another way to extend the class program and meet the special needs and desires of students. Almost any activity might be conducted outside of class. For example, badminton, backpacking, dance, or jogging might be directed after the school day under supervised conditions.

Special Days (or Weeks)

A special theme may serve as the basis for conducting activities such as a "Sports Day" or "Olympics" as a special event. Such events might be executed in the regular class or as a schoolwide project. When such events are conducted as a school activity, they become an excellent public relations tool.

A fun type of field day for students is a "Super Kids' Day" in which students compete as partners, rotating about from one event to another.[75] Each student has a "Super Kids' Day" certificate (see figure 9.34) on which the event and place—first or second—is recorded at each station.

Tenoschok listed a number of schoolwide contests that might be conducted during National Physical Education and Sport Week or at another appropriate time. He included a physical education essay contest; a poster coloring contest; a sports-in-action drawing contest; a physical education slogan contest; an invent-a-game contest; and a sports safari contest, which asks students to identify athletes by their animal nicknames. These activities can stimulate an overall school awareness of the objectives of physical education while encouraging students to achieve in other areas in the curriculum.[76] All-school activity days or weeks can be designed to include all curriculum areas of the school. They can be both fun and profitable to students and faculty alike.

Self-directed Activities

Students who are self-motivated will welcome the opportunity to check out equipment during free-play hours. Such activities may also serve as incentives to swim one hundred miles or jog five hundred miles. The time to do this is determined by the students. When the final number of miles is reached, recognition such as a certificate or an award such as a t-shirt is made. These activities can be very stimulating to students.

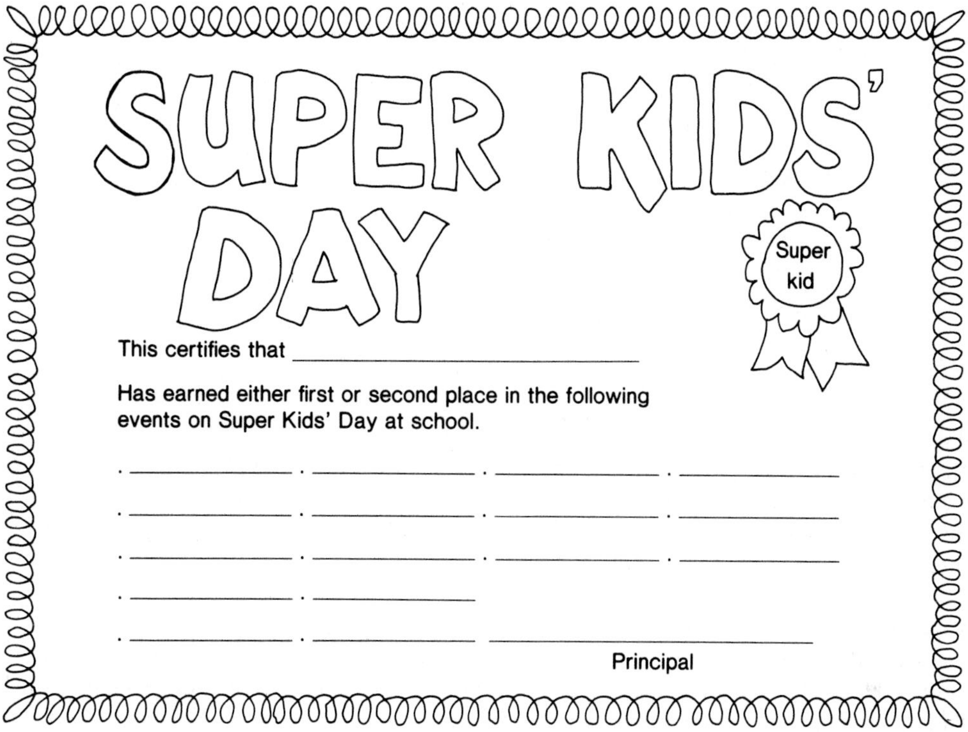

SUPER KIDS' DAY

Super kid

This certifies that ______________________

Has earned either first or second place in the following events on Super Kids' Day at school.

· ________ · ________ · ________ · ________

· ________ · ________ · ________ · ________

· ________ · ________ · ________ · ________

· ________ · ________

· ________ · ________ ______________________

Principal

Figure 9.34 A "Super Kids' Day" certificate.
Source: Pat Sawley, Woods Cross High School, Woods Cross, Utah.

Questions and Suggested Activities

1. Write down the instructional activities and materials explained in this chapter that you would like to incorporate in your teaching. Add to this list other activities and materials you have collected. Be sure explanations for these are complete. List the media you are qualified to operate. File all of these with your resource materials. If you have no such system, initiate a resource filing system at this time.
2. Begin a bulletin board file of sketches, ideas, newspaper and magazine clippings, cartoons, pictures, objects, color book ideas, and so forth. Make a bulletin board and evaluate it in terms of its effect on the viewers.
3. Using the partial list of computer software programs applicable to physical education compiled by King and Aufsesser (Suggested Readings), write down the possible programs you would like to use. Compile a list of the software vendors most available to you.
4. The athletic alumni support group has offered to buy the department a computer and printer with appropriate software if such a purchase can be justified. Prepare a request for the computer including what it will be used for, who is qualified to use it, and how it will benefit the students.

5. Outline a physical fitness activity that will involve students in improving their fitness proficiency. You might want to make this an instructional unit, a community project, a special project, or some other idea. Include record sheets and awards.

6. Mrs. Jones has just contacted the principal of your school to arrange a conference with everyone concerned with the wilderness program you direct. Her son broke his leg while backpacking with the school-sponsored group. Prepare materials to take to the conference explaining the program, its goals, activities, safety precautions and liability insurance, and emergency procedures.

7. Outline the intramural program you would set up in your school. List all activities, estimated student participation, and personnel needed to support the program.

Suggested Readings

Bonnano, Diane (ed). "Intramural and Recreational Sports: Perspectives Beyond the Competition." *Journal of Physical Education, Recreation and Dance* 58 (February 1987):49–61.

Carlson, Ronald P. (ed.) *Ideas II: A Sharing of Teaching Practices by Secondary School Physical Education Practitioners*. Reston, Virginia: American Alliance for Health, Physical Education, Recreation and Dance, 1984.

Cicciarella, Charles F. "Getting Into the Computer Game: Guidelines and Pitfalls." *Journal of Physical Education, Recreation and Dance* 55 (April 1984):46–47.

Darst, P., and G. Armstrong. *Outdoor Adventure Activities for School and Recreation Programs*. Minneapolis: Burgess Publishing Company, 1980.

Donnelly, Joseph E. *Using Microcomputers in Physical Education and the Sport Sciences*. Champaign, Illinois: Human Kinetics Publishers, 1987.

Fluegelman, Andrew. *The New Games Book*. Garden City, New York: Headlands Press, 1974.

Hawkins, Jerald D. "An Analysis of Selected Skinfold Measuring Instruments." *Journal of Physical Education, Recreation and Dance* 54 (January 1983):25–27.

Howley, Edward T., and B. Don Franks. *Health/Fitness Instructor's Handbook*. Champaign, Illinois: Human Kinetics Publishers, 1986.

Jenkins, David, and Joseph Staub. "Student Fitness: The Physical Educator's Role." *Journal of Physical Education, Recreation and Dance* 56 (February 1985):31–32.

Kelly, Luke. "Computer Assisted Instruction: Applications for Physical Education." *Journal of Physical Education, Recreation and Dance* 58 (April 1987):74–79.

King, Harry A., and Kathryn Summa Aufsesser. "Microcomputer Software to Assist the School Physical Education Teacher." *The Physical Educator* 43 (Spring 1986):90–97.

Kuntzleman, Charles T. *Fitness Discovery Activities*. Spring Arbor, Michigan: Arbor Press, 1978.

Lacy, Ed, and Barbara Marshall. "Fitnessgram: An Answer to Physical Fitness Improvement for School Children." *Journal of Physical Education, Recreation and Dance* 55 (January 1984):18–19.

Levitt, Stuart L. "Fitness on Your Own Time." *Journal of Physical Education and Recreation* 51 (November–December 1980):79–80.

Lohman, T. G., and B. H. Massey (eds.) "A Fit America in the Coming Decade: 1985–1995." *Journal of Physical Education, Recreation and Dance* 55 (November–December 1984):24–60.

Londeree, Ben R. (ed.) "Microcomputers in Physical Education." *Journal of Physical Education, Recreation and Dance* 54 (November–December 1983):17–50.

Michelin, Donald L., and William Albrecht. "Super-Star Physical Fitness Program." *Journal of Physical Education and Recreation* 50 (September 1979):74.

National Intramural Sports Council. *Intramurals and Club Sports: A Handbook*. Reston, Virginia: AAHPERD, 1986.

Orlick, Terry. *The Cooperative Sports and Games Book*. New York: Pantheon Books, 1978.

"Outdoor Adventure Activity Programs." (series of articles) *Journal of Physical Education, Recreation and Dance* 57 (May–June 1986):56–69.

Pangrazi, Robert P., and Douglas N. Hastad. *Fitness in the Elementary Schools: A Teacher's Manual*. Reston, Virginia: AAHPERD, 1986.

Research Consortium, AAHPERD. *Directory of Computer Software with Application to Sport Science, Health, and Dance.* Reston, Virginia: AAHPERD.

Rohnke, Karl. *Cowstails and Cobras.* Project Adventure, P.O. Box 157, Hamilton, Massachusetts 01936.

Rupnow, Allan. "Upper Body Strength: Helping Kids Win the Battle." *Journal of Physical Education, Recreation and Dance* 56 (October 1985):60–63.

Sanders, Harry J. "Motivation Through Special Events." In Patricia E. Barry, ed. *Ideas for Secondary School Physical Education.* (Reston, Virginia: AAHPERD), 1976, 70–71.

Spindt, Gary. "Fitness is Basic." *Journal of Physical Education, Recreation and Dance* 56 (September 1985):68–69.

Stein, Eric L. (ed.) "Starting Intramural Programs in Elementary/Secondary Schools." *Journal of Physical Education, Recreation and Dance* 54 (February 1983):19–31.

Stein, Julian U. "Physical Education Selective Activities: Computerizing Choices." *Journal of Physical Education, Recreation and Dance* 58 (January 1987):64–66.

Steinhardt, Mary A., and Patricia M. Stueck. "Personal Fitness: A Curriculum Model." *Journal of Physical Education, Recreation and Dance* 57 (September 1986):23–29, 32.

Stewart, Michael J. "Eloquent Bulletin Boards." *Journal of Physical Education and Recreation* 51 (November–December 1980):80–81.

Torbert, Marianne, and Lynne B. Schnieder. "Positive Multicultural Interaction: Using Low Organized Games." *Journal of Physical Education, Recreation and Dance* 57 (September 1986):40–44.

Torbert, Marianne. *Follow Me.* Englewood Cliffs, New Jersey: Prentice-Hall, 1980.

Wendt, Janice C., and James R. Morrow, Jr. "Microcomputer Software: Practical Applications for Coaches and Teachers." *Journal of Physical Education, Recreation and Dance* 57 (February 1986):54–57.

Zakrajsek, Dorothy. "Premeditated Murder: Let's 'Bump-Off' Killer Ball." *Journal of Physical Education, Recreation and Dance* 57 (September 1986):49–51.

References

1. Harry A. King and Kathryn Summa Aufsesser, "Microcomputer Software to Assist the School Physical Education Teacher," *The Physical Educator* 43 (Spring 1986), p. 94.
2. Judith B. Edwards, et al., *Computer Applications in Instruction* (Hanover, New Hampshire: Time Share [Houghton Mifflin Company], 1978).
3. Research Consortium, AAHPERD, *Directory of Computer Software with Application to Sport Science, Health, and Dance* (Reston, Virginia: AAHPERD), p. 3.
4. Ibid.
5. King and Aufsesser, "Microcomputer Software to Assist the School Physical Education Teacher."
6. Charles F. Cicciarella, "The Computer in Physical Education: Its Promise and Threat," *Journal of Physical Education, Recreation and Dance* 54 (November–December 1983), p. 18.
7. King and Aufsesser, "Microcomputer Software to Assist the School Physical Education Teacher," p. 94.
8. Joseph E. Donnelly, (ed.), *Using Microcomputers in Physical Education and the Sport Sciences* (Champaign, Illinois: Human Kinetics Publishers, 1987).
9. Cicciarella, "The Computer in Physical Education," p. 18.
10. Donnelly, *Using Microcomputers in Physical Education and the Sport Sciences."*
11. David A. Barlow and Patricia A. Bayalis, "Computer Facilitated Learning," *Journal of Physical Education, Recreation and Dance* 54 (November–December 1983), p. 29.
12. David Sealy, "Computer Programs for Dance Notation," *Journal of Physical Education, Recreation and Dance* 54 (November–December 1983), pp. 36–37.
13. Richard Engelhorn, Chapter 6, "Classroom Applications for Microcomputers," in Joseph E. Donnelly, ed. *Using Microcomputers in Physical Education and the Sport Sciences* (Champaign, Illinois: Human Kinetics Publishers, 1987), pp. 81–90.

14. Ed Lacy and Barbara Marshall, "Fitnessgram: An Answer to Physical Fitness Improvement for School Children," *Journal of Physical Education, Recreation and Dance* 55 (January 1984), pp. 18–19.
15. Victor P. Dauer and Robert P. Pangrazi, *Dynamic Physical Education for Elementary School Children* (Minneapolis: Burgess Publishing Company, 1986), p. 202.
16. Janice C. Wendt and James R. Morrow Jr., "Microcomputer Software: Practical Applications for Coaches and Teachers," *Journal of Physical Education, Recreation and Dance* 57 (February 1986), p. 54.
17. Edward T. Howley and B. Don Franks, *Health/Fitness Instructor's Handbook* (Champaign, Illinois: Human Kinetics Publishers, 1986), p. 4.
18. Philip E. Allsen, Joyce M. Harrison, and Barbara Vance, *Fitness for Life: An Individualized Approach,* 3d ed. (Dubuque, Iowa: Wm. C. Brown Company Publishers, 1984), p. 5.
19. Ibid.
20. James E. Misner, "Are We Fit to Educate About Fitness?" *Journal of Physical Education, Recreation and Dance* 55 (November–December 1984), p. 27.
21. John J. McCarthy, "Boy's Graded Physical Fitness Teams," in Patricia E. Barry, ed. *Ideas for Secondary School Physical Education.* Reston, Virginia: American Alliance for Health, Physical Education, Recreation and Dance, 1976), pp. 68–69.
22. Tom Romance, "The Century Club: Beyond the Fitness Test," *Journal of Physical Education and Dance* 57 (April 1986), pp. 14–15; and Corlee B. Munson, "A Club-Oriented Incentive Program," *Journal of Physical Education, Recreation and Dance* 53 (September 1982), pp. 40, 42, 55.
23. Ron Marquardt, "Voluntary Jog-a-Thon," *Journal of Physical Education and Recreation* 49 (November–December 1978), p. 68.
24. Joyce A. Gallery, "Orienteering with a Map and Clues," *Journal of Physical Education, Recreation and Dance* 54 (May 1983), pp. 73–74.
25. Howard E. Sundberg, "A Running Program that Works," *Alliance Update* (July–August 1981), p. 7.
26. David E. Corbin, "Prediction Races and Relays," *Journal of Physical Education and Recreation* 50 (June 1979), pp. 58–59.
27. Eric L. Stein, "Run for Fun—A Program for All Ages," *Journal of Physical Education and Recreation* 49 (November–December 1978), p. 70.
28. American Heart Association and American Alliance for Health, Physical Education, Recreation and Dance, 1900 Association Drive, Reston, Virginia 22091.
29. Leslie Lambert, "A Self-Management Model for Health Related Fitness Instruction," *Journal of Physical Education, Recreation and Dance* 56 (September 1985), pp. 47–50.
30. Daniel H. Ziatz, "How Do You Motivate Students to Learn?" *Journal of Physical Education and Recreation* 48 (March 1977), p. 26.
31. David Jenkins and Joseph Staub, "Student Fitness: The Physical Educator's Role," *Journal of Physical Education, Recreation and Dance* 56 (February 1985), pp. 31–32.
32. Ibid.
33. Ibid.
34. AAHPERD, *Fitness Test Manual* (Reston, Virginia, 1987 and new 1988 tests).
35. ARAPCS, *Physical Fitness Council Newsletter* III (Fall 1986), p. 2.
36. Misner, "Are We Fit to Educate About Fitness?" p. 27.
37. Robert P. Pangrazi and Paul W. Darst, *Dynamic Physical Education Curriculum and Instruction for Secondary School Students* (Minneapolis: Burgess Publishing Company, 1985), p. 15.
38. Mike Homsy, "Team Handball: A Budget Sport for Any Program," *Journal of Physical Education, Recreation and Dance* 55 (May–June 1984), p. 90.
39. Andrew Fluegelman, *The New Games Book* (Garden City, New York: Headlands Press, 1974).
40. Marjorie S. Larsen, *Speed-A-Way: A New Game for Boys and Girls* (Minneapolis: Burgess Publishing Company, 1960).

41. Andy Kostick and Dave Gehler, "Volley Tennis," in Ronald P. Carlson, ed. *Ideas II: A Sharing of Teaching Practices by Secondary School Physical Education Practitioners* (Reston, Virginia: American Alliance for Health, Physical Education, Recreation and Dance, 1984), pp. 99–100.

42. Albert V. Carron, *Motivation Implications for Coaching and Teaching* (Sports Dynamics, 11 Ravenglass Crescent, London, Ontario, N6G 3X7, 1984).

43. Sue Whiddon, "Reward Incentives," in Ronald P. Carlson, ed. *Ideas II: A Sharing of Teaching Practices by Secondary School Physical Education Practitioners* (Reston, Virginia: American Alliance for Health, Physical Education, Recreation and Dance, 1984), pp. 52–53.

44. Patricia M. McCann, "Breaking Away from Tradition: A New Game for Middle School Students," *Journal of Physical Education, Recreation and Dance* 58 (March 1987), pp. 76–79.

45. O. William Blake and Anne M. Volp, *Lead-up Games to Team Sports* (Englewood Cliffs, New Jersey: Prentice-Hall, 1964), p. 1.

46. Ibid., p. 3.

47. G. S. Don Morris, *How to Change the Games Children Play,* 2d ed. (Minneapolis: Burgess Publishing Company, 1980).

48. "Work: An Instructional Unit in Physical Education," CEC Publishers, 6 Lexington Avenue, Merchantville, New Jersey 08109, 1987.

49. Gretchen Koehler, "Teaching Stress Management," in Ronald P. Carlson, ed. *Ideas II: A Sharing of Teaching Practices by Secondary School Physical Education Practitioners* (Reston, Virginia: American Alliance for Health, Physical Education, Recreation and Dance, 1984), pp. 108–109.

50. Ibid., pp. 117–20.

51. Betty Evenbeck, "Aquatic Exercise: Taking Shape," *Journal of Physical Education, Recreation and Dance* 57 (October 1986), pp. 22–25.

52. Paul Linden, "Aikido: A Movement Awareness Approach to Physical Education," *Journal of Physical Education, Recreation and Dance* 55 (September 1984), pp. 64–65.

53. Mountain Bicyclists' Association, Inc., *Comprehensive Bicyclist Education Program: Course Guide,* 1290 Williams Street, Denver, Colorado 80218, 1981.

54. Melinda Krumm, "Tennis, Despite Weather and Site Restrictions," in Ronald P. Carlson, ed. *Ideas II: A Sharing of Teaching Practices by Secondary School Physical Education Practitioners* (Reston, Virginia: American Alliance for Health, Physical Education, Recreation and Dance, 1984), pp. 38–39; and Linda S. Fairman and David Nitchman, "A Bowling Program in the Gymnasium," in Ronald P. Carlson, ed. *Ideas II: A Sharing of Teaching Practices by Secondary School Physical Education Practitioners* (Reston, Virginia: American Alliance for Health, Physical Education, Recreation and Dance, 1984), pp. 66–68.

55. Jonathan E. Nelson, "Teaching Cross-Country Skiing," *Journal of Physical Education, Recreation and Dance* 55 (March 1984), pp. 58–64.

56. Joyce F. Barker, "A Simplified Volleyball Skills Test for Beginning Level Instruction," *Journal of Physical Education, Recreation and Dance* 56 (May–June 1985), pp. 20–22.

57. Jay H. Naylor, "Honey & Milk Toast," *Journal of Physical Education and Recreation* 46 (September 1975), p. 20.

58. CEC Publishers, "Adventure Without Ropes," 6 Lexington Avenue, Merchantville, New Jersey 08109.

59. Linda Kelly Smith, "Using Challenge Activities to Develop Group Cooperation in Physical Education," *Physical Education Newsletter* (P.O. Box 8, 20 Cedarwood Lane, Old Saybrook, Connecticut 06475, August 1980).

60. Andrew Fluegelman, ed., *The New Game Book* (New York: Doubleday and Company, 1976), p. 69.

61. Terry Orlick, *The Cooperative Sports and Games Book* (New York: Pantheon Books, 1978), p. 54.

62. "Adventure Without Ropes," CEC Publishers, 6 Lexington Avenue, Merchantville, New Jersey 08109.

63. Naylor, "Honey & Milk Toast."

64. Ibid.

65. Allan C. Boyer, "Initiative Activities," Master's thesis, Brigham Young University, 104 E. State Highway, Copperton, Utah 84006.

66. Floyd Lorenz, "Mission Impossible," *Journal of Health, Physical Education and Recreation* (September 1974), p. 98.

67. James W. Tangen-Foster and Calvin W. Lathen, "Risk Sports in Basic Instruction Programs: A Status Assessment," *Research Quarterly for Exercise and Sport* 54 (September 1983), p. 305.

68. Dennis R. Latess, "Physical Education and Outdoor Adventure: Do They Belong Together?" *Journal of Physical Education, Recreation and Dance* 57 (May–June 1986), pp. 66–67.

69. Ibid.

70. Craig E. Rademacher and L. Dale Cruse, "Planning Success for Small College Outdoor Programs," *UAHPERD Journal* 18 (Autumn 1986), pp. 12–14.

71. Jay H. Naylor, "Recreation Without Litigation." Provo, Utah: Brigham Young University, 1986. Handout.

72. Tangen-Foster and Lathen, "Risk Sports in Basic Instruction Programs," p. 306.

73. Daryl Siedentop, Charles Mand, and Andrew Taggart, *Physical Education: Teaching and Curriculum Strategies for Grades 5–12* (Palo Alto: Mayfield Publishing Company, 1986), p. 223.

74. Phil Carlton and Rob Stinson, "Achieving Educational Goals through Intramurals," in *Intramurals and Club Sports: A Handbook* (Reston, Virginia: AAHPERD, 1986), pp. 4–6.

75. Pat Sawley, Woods Cross High School, Woods Cross, Utah.

76. Michael Tenoschok, "Physical Education Appreciation," *Journal of Physical Education and Recreation* 50 (November–December 1979), p. 18.

Selecting Instructional Styles and Strategies

Study Stimulators

1. What is direct and indirect instruction? When would each be used?
2. What factors influence the selection of a teaching style?
3. What is the Spectrum of Teaching? Describe a situation in which you would use each of the styles.
4. How would you incorporate individualized instruction into your teaching?
5. What is mastery learning and what are its components?
6. How do problem-solving strategies fit into the physical education learning environments?
7. Which instructional strategies would you feel comfortable using in a class?

"Great instructors nourish individual differences."[1] They are aware that each student has unique aptitudes and needs that must be addressed. Teaching is said to be both an "art" and a "science." It is an art in the sense that each teacher decides what will work best in guiding students to learn while adding a personal touch to the process. It is a science in that when certain principles of learning are operating a distinct outcome is usually the result.

Excellent teachers become experienced at making wise decisions. They select objectives at the correct level of difficulty for students; they select and use teaching activities that are directly relevant to the daily objective(s); they monitor student learning continuously; and they apply known principles of learning.[2] No teaching strategy or behavior has been shown to enhance learning for all students. The best physical educators develop a repertoire of styles and strategies to aid them in the teaching process. Many such options are presented in this chapter to give teachers alternatives to maximize the efficiency with which all the students achieve the desired objectives of the program.

Teaching Styles

Styles can be arranged on a continuum and range from those designated as *direct instruction,* or teacher-centered, to those designated as *indirect instruction,* or student-centered. Styles that result in direct instruction are implemented when the acquisition of basic skills is the instructional goal.[3] Styles reflecting indirect instruction are selected to enhance creativity and independence or change the attitudes of students.[4] The direct style of teaching is the one used most often by teachers. This may be explained by research findings substantiating that direct instruction (lecture/demonstration, drill, practice, feedback) has been consistently found to be more effective than indirect instruction for students learning basic academic skills in the elementary schools.[5]

Direct instruction implies a structured teaching-learning environment that contains the following:

1. A focus on appropriate academic goals and content.
2. Teacher-controlled coverage of extensive content through structured learning activities and appropriate pacing.
3. Sufficient time-on-task for student success.

4. Monitoring of pupil performance.
5. A task-oriented, but relaxed environment.
6. Immediate, academically oriented feedback.

Selecting a Teaching Style

The selection of a teaching style depends on a thoughtful evaluation of the learning situation, including such factors as (1) the students, (2) the subject matter to be taught, (3) the teacher, (4) the learning environment, and (5) time.

Students

The first consideration in choosing a learning activity is the total educational needs of students—physical, intellectual, emotional, and social. Younger children will need a much more structured learning environment with the teacher directing most of the activities. Sooner or later the teacher should encourage students to take the initiative for their own learning. Since it is the individual student who does the learning, consideration must be given to the different ways in which students learn best. Different personalities, aptitudes, experiences, and interests combine to make each learner unique in the way he or she responds to a given style of teaching. Tyler emphasized that a teacher must have some understanding of the interests and background of students to set up the desired learning environment.[6] Rink pointed out that low-ability students, as well as those who are unmotivated, unsociable, and nonconforming, seem to perform better in more unstructured environments. High-ability, motivated, sociable, conforming students perform better in more structured environments.[7]

Joyce and Weil provided a formula for tailoring learning environments to individual student learning styles. They translated student characteristics into two dimensions: "a need for and tolerance of structure, and a need for and tolerance of task complexity." They defined structure as "the degree of prescription in the environment," and task complexity as the complexity or intricacy of the task, with more complex tasks demanding higher levels of skill.[8] Teachers must consider the variety of needs of individual students when programming both the environment of the learning situation and the learning task.

Hunt suggested striving for an "optimal mismatch" between the present capacity of the learner and the strategy chosen, so as to "pull" the learner toward greater capacity without overstressing the capabilities of the learner.[9]

Hawley suggested that by being exposed to a variety of teaching styles, the learner will find one suited to his or her own learning style and will be more motivated toward achievement of the goals of the class. He also suggested that many students are only familiar with the more traditional styles of teaching and will need to be taught that learning can occur in a variety of ways.[10]

Subject Matter

A second consideration in planning instruction involves the specific ideas or skills to be taught. Obviously, some methods work best for some activities while others prove better with other activities. For example, teaching an idea or skill at the lower levels of the cognitive or psychomotor taxonomy (refer to unit 2) might utilize a more structured approach whereas the upper levels of the taxonomies might incorporate student experiences using the creativity and problem-solving techniques of learning. Affective behaviors suffer with some teaching styles and blossom with others. A knowledge of concepts and skills in activities can be a valuable aid to the physical education instructor in the selection of teaching strategies.

Teacher

The teacher is the third consideration in the selection of learning activities. Some methods work better for some teachers than for others. Each teacher should select a comfortable teaching style for his or her own personality and talents. The best teachers, however, experiment with many styles until they are comfortable with a wide range of styles from which they can choose as the learning situation changes. They must also learn to be sensitive to feedback from the students and the learning environment and use that feedback to modify their teaching behavior.

Learning Environment

The fourth consideration is the learning environment. A school or class that focuses on basic skills or academic skills would predominantly use a direct instructional style. Brophy concluded that students who receive most of their instruction from the teacher do better than those expected to learn on their own or from each other.[11] Each teaching style establishes a unique social environment with a specific group of learners. The social system becomes a part of the learning experience along with the subject matter to be taught. Students learn competitiveness, cooperation, democratic processes, and other social skills as environments change within the school. The teaching style influences the way students react to each other, to the teacher, and to others outside of the class environment.

Time

Time is the fifth consideration. Early in the school year or in a new unit of activity, the teacher may choose to use a more structured teaching style. Later on, as the teacher gets to know the students' capabilities and learning styles, the teacher may choose a more informal approach.

Another variable of time is the allocation of practice minutes built into the teaching style. Graham substantiated that students who learned more had teachers who provided them with more time to practice the criterion skill. Students who learned less spent more time waiting, listening, managing, and organizing than higher achievers.[12]

The Spectrum of Teaching Styles

A useful approach for classifying teaching styles and learning activities according to direct or indirect is Mosston's *Spectrum of Teaching Styles*.[13] The concept of the spectrum of styles proposes a number of alternative styles of teaching that provide teachers with a knowledge of the roles of teacher and learner and the objectives that can be achieved with each style. This permits teachers to move back and forth along the spectrum as needed to meet the changing needs of students, environments, and subject matter.

Mosston described teaching behavior as a "chain of decision making." As can be seen in figure 10.1, the anatomy of a style categorizes decisions as being made before (pre-impact), during (impact), or following (post-impact) the interaction between teacher and learner. The teaching style is identified by specifying who, teacher or learner, makes which decisions. Each style has been identified by name and letter and is called a *landmark* style. Ten styles have been identified, so far, ranging from Style A (command), which is a complete teacher decision-making style, to Style J (self-teaching), which is a complete learner decision-making style. An infinite variety of other styles exists that exhibit characteristics of two adjoining styles and fall under the canopies of these landmark styles.

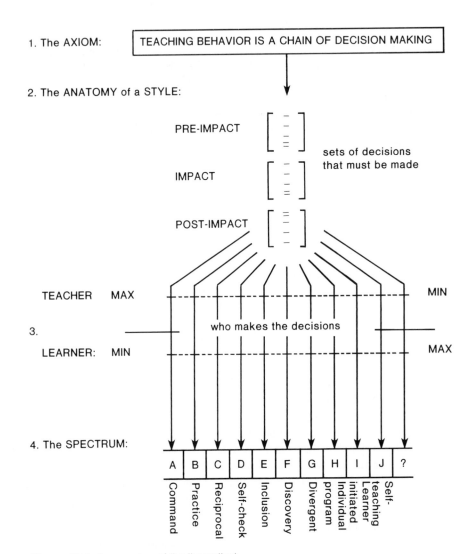

1. The AXIOM:

TEACHING BEHAVIOR IS A CHAIN OF DECISION MAKING

2. The ANATOMY of a STYLE:

PRE-IMPACT

IMPACT

POST-IMPACT

sets of decisions
that must be made

TEACHER   MAX   MIN

3.   who makes the decisions

LEARNER: MIN   MAX

4. The SPECTRUM:

| A | B | C | D | E | F | G | H | I | J | ? |

Command
Practice
Reciprocal
Self-check
Inclusion
Discovery
Divergent
Individual program
Learner initiated
Self-teaching Learner

Figure 10.1 An overview of the theoretical
structure of the spectrum of teaching styles.
Muska Mosston and Sara Ashworth, *The Science and
Art of Teaching:* From *Command to Discovery* (a book
soon to be published).

Style		Pre-impact	Impact	Post-impact	Maximum Teacher Decision Making	Minimum Learner Decision Making
Command style	A	T	T	T		
Practice style	B	T	L	T		
Reciprocal style	C	T	D	O		
Self-check style	D	T	L	L		
Inclusion style	E	T	L	L		
Guided-discovery style	F	T	T–L	T–L		
Divergent style	G	T	L–T	L–T		
Learner-designed program	H	T	L–T	L–T		
Learner-initiated style	I	L	L–T	L–T		
Self-teaching style	J	L	L	L		
					Minimum Teacher Decision Making	Maximum Learner Decision Making

Figure 10.2 Pre-impact, impact, and post-impact decisions in each of the learning styles on the Sepctrum of Teaching.
Concepts from Muska Mosston and Sara Ashworth, *Teaching Physical Education,* 3d ed. (Columbus, Ohio: Charles E. Merrill Publishing Company, 1986).

Each style of teaching creates different conditions for learning founded on the decision-making process. Figure 10.2 illustrates who makes decisions at what stage of impact. Based on who makes these decisions, the styles then appear to form organized clusters along the spectrum. For example, styles A through E represent, in general, direct instruction. Styles F and G call upon the learner to exhibit different recall levels of cognitive behavior and represent indirect instruction.[14]

Research validating specific application of the spectrum is sparse and sometimes conflicts with other studies. Goldberger and his associates found in studies of fifth-grade children using the direct styles of B, C, and E that all of the styles facilitated learning. In one study, style B produced the most effective results.[15] Another study revealed that average-aptitude children responded best to the conditions provided by style B, whereas exceptional children, the combination of children with above- and below-average aptitude, profited more from the conditions provided by style E.[16]

Griffey studied students in a volleyball unit using Mosston's command and task styles of instruction. In this situation, students with high initial ability were found to achieve higher posttest scores on the forearm pass with task instruction (some student decision making), while low-ability students did better with command instruction (teacher decision making).[17] Cronbach and Snow obtained similar results.[18]

Salter and Graham found that when elementary school children were taught a novel golf task using the command, guided discovery, and no instruction methodologies, no significant differences existed between the groups on skill improvement or self-efficacy. Cognitive understanding improved significantly for the groups taught by the command and guided discovery approaches, however.[19]

Pettigrew and Heikkinen reported that on twelve measures of achievement for students taught using a variety of spectrum styles as compared with those taught by one style, nine measures showed significantly higher achievement by students. The authors recommended that to effectively accommodate the learning needs of students a teacher should use a variety of instructional styles.[20]

The teacher incorporating the spectrum should move freely along the spectrum of styles, as students are ready to make more and more decisions, selecting one or more applicable styles for use during a particular lesson or unit of activity. An attempt should be made to involve the students as much as possible in the selection of methods that affect them and in the application of methods on the higher cognitive levels. The use of a variety of methods provides students with different learning styles the opportunity to find their niche in the learning experience. It also prevents boredom and the "inverted U" phenomenon from overuse of a single style. (The inverted U phenomenon refers to a teacher behavior or strategy that has a positive effect on learning but, if continued past a certain point, turns negative.)[21]

The following presents a brief description of the landmark styles of the Spectrum of Teaching. A teacher using each style should be able to incorporate the appropriate decisions of the anatomy.

The Command Style (A)

In the command style, the teacher makes all of the decisions on what, where, when, and how to teach, and on how to evaluate learning and provide feedback. The teacher should tell the class that "the purpose of this style is to learn to do the task accurately and within a short period of time."

Pre-impact decisions:

1. Identify subject matter (e.g., swimming, soccer).
2. State the overall lesson objectives.
3. Design the episode (learning experience).

Impact decisions:

1. Explain roles of teacher and learner.
2. Deliver subject matter.
3. Explain logistical procedures.

Post-impact decisions:

1. Offer feedback to learner about performance and role in following the teacher decisions.

The command style capitalizes on the expertise of the teacher through such teaching-learning strategies as lecture and other verbal presentation modes, demonstration, and drill. Homogeneous grouping can be used advantageously during drills to individualize learning. Instructional games can also be used to drill students on such items as terminology and rules. Students are expected to respond as they have been "commanded" to do. This style reaches the objective of precision, synchronization, and uniformity. It is especially applicable when safety, efficient use of class time, and teacher control are essential.

The Practice Style (B)

In the practice style, the teacher determines what is to be taught and how the activity will be evaluated. The students are then given a number of tasks to practice and each learner decides which task to begin with, where to do it, when to begin and end the practice of a particular task, how fast or slow to work, and what to do between tasks. Styles A and B and the canopy bridging these styles are the ones most often used by physical educators. In style B, students are encouraged to clarify the nature of the tasks by asking questions as needed. The teacher moves around the class, offering feedback to each individual. The teacher should state, "the purpose of this style is to offer you time to work individually and privately and to provide me with time to offer you individual and private feedback."

Pre-impact decisions:

1. The same as style A.

Impact decisions:

1. Student—practice tasks.
2. Teacher—offer feedback individually or in a group.

Post-impact decisions:

1. Teacher—offer feedback to all learners.

By using a variety of tasks, including fitness activities and testing activities, the teacher and students can make use of all of the available space. Skill checklists, study guides, workbooks, journals, and progress charts are some of the teaching-learning strategies that can be employed within this style.

Social interaction among students is increased with this style.

The Reciprocal Style (C)

In the reciprocal style, students provide the feedback for each other. One student performs while the other observes and provides feedback. Then, the students exchange roles. The teacher decides what tasks are to be accomplished, designs the criteria sheet that will guide the observer in giving feedback, gives the assignments to the students, and helps the observers improve their ability as observers and their ability to communicate with their partners. The teacher states, "the purposes of this style are to work with a partner and to offer feedback to your partner."

Pre-impact decisions:

1. The same as style A.
2. Design and prepare criteria sheet for observer.

Impact decisions:

1. Teacher—set up logistics; set scene for new roles.
2. Student—understand and perform role of doer and observer.
3. Student—perform the task.

Post-impact decisions:

1. Student—(observer) receive criteria; observe doer's performance; compare and contrast performance with criteria; conclude correctness of performance; communicate results to doer; initiate communication with teacher, if necessary.
2. Teacher—answer questions of observer (do not usurp role of observer).

Socialization between students is an inherent part of the reciprocal style.

The Self-check Style (D)

In the self-check style, the feedback is provided by the individual learner instead of by the teacher or another student. The selection of tasks is important so that students can evaluate their own performance. Events that provide external feedback—such as making baskets, kicking a football over the goalposts, or hitting a target with an object—facilitate student self-evaluation. The role of the teacher is to help the students become better self-evaluators. The teacher should state, "the purpose of this style is to learn to do a task and check your own work."

Pre-impact decisions:

1. The same as style A.
2. Prepare subject matter.
3. Prepare criteria sheet for self-check.

Impact decisions:

1. Teacher—set up logistics, set scene for new role, answer questions.
2. Student—understand role as a doer.
3. Student—perform the tasks.

Post-impact decisions:

1. Student—assess one's performance against criteria.
2. Teacher—offer feedback to learner about his or her role in self-check.

The self-check style can increase student self-esteem for students who are comfortable working independently. One disadvantage of this style is that student interaction with the peer group and with the teacher are at a minimum. A computer can be used to monitor student progress in the self-check style.

A number of different teaching-learning strategies can be employed within the self-check style, including the use of testing activities as learning activities, programmed learning, individualized learning packets, and contract learning.

The Inclusion Style (E)

The major difference between the inclusion style and the styles previously discussed is that in this style the learner selects the level of performance for each task and alters it according to each self-assessment of the performance. The teacher selects the task and defines the various levels of the task according to the degrees of difficulty. The learner performs the skill at the level of difficulty at which it is possible to achieve success. Some factors that contribute to differences in difficulty include distance, height of basket or net, size of ball or implement, weight of ball or implement, size of the target or hoop, angle of shot or kick, quantity of tasks to be done, and body positions. The task to be done remains the same in this style (e.g., all push-ups or all striking skills). The degree of difficulty varies, however. The teacher should state, "the purpose of this style is for everyone to be successful."

Pre-impact decisions:

1. The same as style A.
2. Present the concept.
3. Prepare the individual program for the tasks.

Impact decisions:

1. Describe the role of the learner.
2. Present the subject matter.
3. Explain logistics.

Post-impact decisions:

1. Teacher—observe class, offer feedback to individual learners.
2. Student—assess performance using criteria sheet.

The purpose of the inclusion style is to permit all students to be successful at the task to be performed, thereby increasing each student's self-esteem and enjoyment of physical activity. For this reason, the inclusion style is especially important when teaching classes that are coed and also have handicapped students mainstreamed within them. The inclusion style can be combined with other styles.

The Guided-Discovery Style (F)

The main purpose of the guided-discovery style is to lead the learner in a particular process of discovery. The role of the teacher is to determine the concepts and principles to be taught and the best sequence for guiding the students to the specific response. As the students are involved in these strategies, the teacher varies the size and interrelationship of the steps and the speed of the learning sequence so that students are constantly moving toward the desired objective. The teacher should state, "the purpose of this style is to evoke the correct answer or response."

Pre-impact decisions:

1. The same as style A.
2. Determine a sequence of questions or clues building on each other to lead student to the end result.

Impact decisions:

1. Teacher—present questions or clues to elicit the desired response (never tell the answer).
2. Student—respond to sequential questions or clues.

Post-impact decisions:

1. Teacher—provide feedback.
2. Student—discover correct response.

The guided-discovery style requires a warm, accepting environment in which students are allowed time to think through their questions or responses and helped to experience success in the discovery process. This style also requires a certain amount of risk on the part of the teacher. The teacher must be able to trace backward from the desired objective to get the first question and the sequence from which to proceed. Whenever a student response deviates from the desired response, the teacher must be able to ask a question that brings the students back into the desired sequence.

The advantage of the guided-discovery style is its ability to help students understand the basic concepts of physical activity.

The Divergent Style (G)

In the divergent style, the student is encouraged to come up with multiple solutions to a given problem. The teacher selects the subject and designs the problem. The student discovers alternative solutions to the problem and evaluates his or her ability to solve the problem. In some situations in which the quality of the movement is part of the solution, verification must be done by the teacher. The teacher should state, "the purpose of this style is to engage in producing multiple responses to a single question. There is not one correct answer. It is all right to produce different responses."

Individual problems can be offered to students, or problems can be clustered in groups. Students can also be allowed to select from a list of problems those relevant to their own interests.

Pre-impact decisions:

1. Identify the general subject matter (e.g., tumbling, golf, modern dance).
2. Identify the specific topic (e.g., headstand, putt).
3. Identify the specific problem or series of problems that will elicit solutions (e.g., variations, downhill lie, in groups).

Impact decisions:

1. Student—discover alternate answers to the problem.
2. Student—decide which multiple and divergent solutions are applicable to the problem.

Post-impact decisions:

1. Teacher—observe solution.
2. Student—evaluate the solution by asking, "Is my solution answering the question?"
3. Teacher—offer feedback about the learners' role in producing divergent ideas.

The divergent style requires an environment in which the teacher feels secure enough to accept a wide variety of alternative solutions to problems. The teacher should respond to the *process* of discovery, not to the *value* of the particular response. Students must have time and a supportive environment in which to work out solutions. The major advantage of the divergent style is its ability to help the student develop creativity. Social development depends on whether the student is working in a group or individually.

Styles H, I, and J

The purpose of these styles is to increase the creativity of the student by allowing the learner to choose the problem and design the learning activities. Because of this, these styles can be used only with individual students who are ready to take the initiative for their own behavior.

The teacher's role is to facilitate the student's formulation of the problem, the learning activities, and the final presentation and evaluation. During learning, the student checks in periodically to keep the teacher up to date on the learning process.

Strategies

As teachers utilize teaching styles in the classroom, they also incorporate various teaching strategies or instructional delivery systems to enhance the process. The word strategy originally described the placement of an army in an advantageous position in relation to the enemy. As adopted by business and industry, strategy involves the advantageous relationship of an organization to its environment. An instructional strategy is a particular arrangement of the teacher, learner, and environment to produce desired learning outcomes. Hurwitz defined an instructional strategy as "a plan for a pattern of actions aimed at one or more students achieving and demonstrating mastery of a specific goal or objective."[22] His plan of action defines eight instructional steps arranged in a sequence forming a macrostructure that incorporates any instructional strategy. Predicted and measurable outcomes are the result of strategies that plug into the model (see figure 10.3).

Since learners vary in their response to various strategies and since distinct strategies produce diverse outcomes, a number of strategies are presented to facilitate selecting the appropriate one for the subject, the learner, the teacher, and the instructional environment.

Selecting a Teaching Strategy

Consideration must be given to selecting appropriate strategies for students who lack self-motivation or discipline and for situations in which large classes are taught in limited facilities. There is no one best strategy for any one teaching style on the spectrum. Rather, those strategies should be selected that best meet the needs of the instructional situation and each strategy should be adapted to the parameters of that particular style. Teachers selecting strategies to amplify the learning process should have as a prime consideration high engaged time for students (refer to chapter 6).

The best teaching strategy is one that "pulls"
the learner toward greater capacity without
overstressing the capabilities of the learner.

> *Introduction:* An action that motivates students or acquaints them with the objective or content to be covered.
>
> *Structuring:* An action that organizes, schedules, or specifies procedures to be used to interact with content. This can be accomplished through teacher talk or demonstration, or through instructional media.
>
> *Model Communication:* A demonstration of expected performance accomplished through teacher or student demonstration or through demonstration by another person or by instructional media.
>
> *Information Communication:* The presentation of content to students with which they are expected to interact. Such items as rules, strategies, examples, theories, or definitions may be presented by the teacher, student, another person, or instructional media.
>
> *Problem Communication:* The presentation of a challenge, by the teacher or instructional media, to students that requires cognitive interaction at higher levels on the cognitive taxonomy such as comprehension, application, analysis, synthesis, or evaluation.
>
> *Content Interaction:* Active student interaction with the content of instruction. Types of content interaction include practice, drill, problem-solving, guided discovery, experimentation, recitation, discussion, worksheets, role playing, simulations, games, reports, projects, and similar experiences. Students can work individually, in partners, or in small, medium, or large groups. Interactions can be non-interactive; cooperative, competitive, or both. Feedback can be provided by oneself, other students, media, or the teacher. Decisions can be made by the teacher or student concerning such factors as task selection, location of practice, group size and composition, equipment used, starting and stopping time, pace, performance goals, and repetitions.
>
> *Application/Assessment:* An action in which students can demonstrate mastery of the objective. Possible assessment techniques include written, oral, or skills tests; game play, or a report, performance, demonstration, or simulation. Assessors may include the teacher, oneself, other students, or other persons.
>
> *Closure:* An action used to summarize, review, synthesize, or relate the instruction to future content, or evaluate the steps involved in the instructional episode.

Figure 10.3 Hurwitz's model for the structure of instructional strategies.
(Concepts from Dick Hurwitz, "A Model for the Structure of Instructional Strategies," *Journal of Teaching in Physical Education* 4 (April 1985), pp. 190–201).

Many strategies fit nicely into the physical education instructional process. Included for further discussion will be: (1) lecture, (2) individualized instruction, (3) peer tutoring and team learning, (4) simulation, (5) problem-solving strategies, and (6) affective learning strategies.

Lecture

A lecture is a verbal presentation to an audience of a defined segment of information by one or more persons. Lectures include special reports, outside speakers, and panel discussions. A teacher might use a lecture to present rules, a panel discussion to elaborate on health concepts, or a police officer to speak on the dangers of drugs. Lectures can introduce, summarize, explain, or create interest in a topic. They can be used to impart information to a large group of students in a short period of time. When classes are large and the student-student and student-teacher interactions are limited, the opportunities for misunderstanding the information can occur. Teachers using the lecture method in the classroom need to prepare in such a way that the experience is meaningful and is not limited to memory learning.

Procedures
1. Know the material.
2. Define the segment of material to be presented.
3. Organize the material to fit the time available.
4. Proceed from simple or familiar to complex or abstract.
5. Present the information in a motivational way.
   a. Use visual aids to support the topic.
   b. Relate the lecture to real life.
   c. Use humor.
   d. Repeat important points.
   e. Pace the material at the middle-level student.
6. Speak clearly and succinctly.
7. Be sensitive to feedback from listeners and modify the delivery accordingly.

Procedures for Special Reports or Outside Speakers
1. Make assignments well in advance.
2. Define the assignment clearly. Explain the topic and information wanted (and the ages and background of the class for outside speakers).
3. Help students make reports interesting by suggestions of topic, tips for presentation, and so forth.
4. Thank the speaker.

Procedures for Panel
1. Select and define the problem.
2. Choose and prepare panel participants in advance. All class members can be assigned to prepare and the panel is then chosen extemporaneously, or panel members can be assigned in advance.
3. Select a moderator who can stimulate questions and guide the discussion.

Individualized Instruction
Individualized instruction programs enable each learner to progress at his or her own pace. Such programs assume that students are capable of learning independently with minimum direction from teachers. "A major goal of individualization is to promote self-directed learners who are capable of engaging effectively in the process of decision making."[23] Teachers are then free to act as consultants to students who need or desire their assistance. Educators conceiving individualized methodologies must consider what the student already knows, what the student wants to know, and what the student needs to know.[24]

A teacher attempting to formulate an individualized approach to teaching physical education should be familiar with mastery learning, contract learning, quests, individualized learning packets, and programmed learning.

Mastery Learning Mastery learning, as conceptualized by Benjamin Bloom,[25] is a theory of school learning based on the premise that almost all students can learn at a high level what the schools have to teach if given sufficient time and instructional help. Bloom asserted that children in schools are being taught as "good and poor" learners rather than "fast and slow" learners, and when students are provided with favorable learning conditions most of them have similar learning ability. Students taught using mastery learning techniques are expected to succeed. Torshen suggested this is the case because in mastery learning individual differences are taken into account.[26]

Mastery learning is not a new concept. Its roots go back to the Jesuit schools before the seventeenth century. Bloom and other twentieth century theorists have structured the concepts into a well-known educational paradigm. The mastery model includes the following components:

1. *Performance objectives,* including criterion levels for student achievement that are set high enough to be demanding and challenging for all students. These objectives are made known to the students prior to instruction.
2. *Instructional activities,* including demonstration, explanation, and learning tasks that emphasize skill acquisition and application to the point of overlearning.
3. *Diagnostic assessment,* using formative tests that students repeat until mastery is achieved. Either the formative tests or a summative test administered at the end of a unit may be used for grading purposes.
4. *Feedback,* including test results so students know how they are progressing.
5. *Prescription,* including "correctives" for students who did not attain mastery and "enrichment activities" for those who did.

Correctives are those activities engaged in by students who did not attain mastery, which enable most of them to do so on future formative tests. Such activities include practicing the tests, practicing the test skills in other ways, and personalized instruction from the teacher or a peer.

"Enrichment activities" are those activities provided for the student who has passed the mastery tests and is waiting to move on to the next task. Such activities include probing deeper and more completely into the instructional task at hand, peer tutoring between students, and independent learning.

Mastery learning is a group-based model. Students engage in learning activities involving correctives and enrichment activities until 80 to 95 percent of the class has attained mastery before moving on to a new task. More time to learn is needed in the initial phases of instruction because some students take longer to learn than others. Block pointed out that this time is reduced by the end of the course.[27] Students use time more efficiently as they become familiar with mastery learning procedures, and they also learn more advanced skills faster once basic skills are mastered. Short units of one or two weeks are not sufficient for mastery learning principles to take effect.

Over the years research on mastery learning has produced an impressive legacy of positive results. A number of literature reviews have consistently reported the beneficial effects of mastery approaches on a variety of learning outcomes.[28] However, most of the research has been done in the cognitive and affective domains, and research documenting the effects of mastery learning on the acquisition of psychomotor skill is lacking.

Both Annarino[29] and Heitmann and Kneer[30] have emphasized mastery learning principles in physical education. However, very few studies have been done to substantiate their theories. Ashy and Lee conducted a study with kindergartners and first graders.[31] Summative scores on throwing showed no significant differences between the mastery and non-mastery groups, although the mastery group did better.

Chambless, Anderson, and Poole concluded that mastery learning produced a high rate of psychomotor learning in stunts and tumbling for the mentally retarded child.[32]

Blakemore conducted three studies using mastery learning to teach physical education skills.[33] The conclusions based on the results of all three studies were: (1) mastery learning produces significant gains in student achievement, (2) low-aptitude students do better when taught with mastery learning methods, and (3) mastery learning equalizes the difference between the performance of males and females, although males consistently score higher. She also found that the results of mastery learning did not take effect until at least the fourth week of a unit. Teachers must allot sufficient instructional time for mastery techniques to be productive.

Procedures

1. Complete a unit plan that is at least six weeks long.
2. Divide the unit of instruction into small teaching segments or subunits including tasks to be learned (e.g., Volleyball: volley and bump, serve, spike and block). Decide on a hierarchial order to teach these tasks.
3. Preassess students on each task to determine entry levels and mastery criteria.
4. Devise specific objectives stating performance standards (scores) for each task based on preassessment results and previous testing (if possible).
5. Design formative tests to assess student competence for each task.
6. Teach the first subunit and allow students to practice.
7. Test all students to determine who mastered (passed) the formative tests included in the first subunit.
8. Provide feedback to each student based on the results of the formative tests.
9. Prescribe correctives or enrichment activities for each student. Provide individualized corrective activities to improve the skill of those who have not mastered a task. Direct students who have mastered or passed a task to expand their performance of the specific skill in game situations, in more advanced drills, and in peer-tutoring circumstances.
10. Monitor students carefully as they engage in correctives or enrichment activities. Repeat the formative tests regularly for those who have not passed.
11. Teach a new subunit when 80 percent of the students have mastered the tasks of the present subunit.
12. Repeat this process of direct instruction, practice, diagnostic testing, mastery, and enrichment activities or correctives until the unit is complete.
13. If Bloom's formal model is followed, administer a summative test.

Task sheets similar to the example shown in figure 10.4 could be used to monitor the progress of each student toward mastery of the subunit tasks. The task sheet includes mastery scores and spaces to record results for several evaluations. It also includes corrective procedures (tasks 1–4), enrichment activities (tasks 5–7), and skill execution tips. This sheet

```
┌─────────────────────────────────────────────────────────────────────┐
│                        Mastery Learning                               │
│              Racquetball Forehand/Backhand Task Sheet                  │
│                                                                       │
│   Name _____ Treatment _____     │
│                                                                       │
│                       Mastery Test Results                            │
│                                                                       │
│               30 Second Wall Volley Behind Short Line                 │
│                                                                       │
│   Passed:                                                             │
│   _____ A. Long Wall Volley: MASTERY IS 15 points for FOREHAND   │
│                 (Record score and date)                               │
│                 1. _____ 2. _____ 3. _____ 4. _____ 5. _____ │
│              Date:                                                    │
│   _____ B. Long Wall Volley: MASTERY is 13 points for BACKHAND   │
│                 (List score and date)                                 │
│                 1. _____ 2. _____ 3. _____ 4. _____ 5. _____ │
│                                                                       │
│              Date:                                                    │
│   IF YOU HAVE PASSED A AND B, GO TO TASK 5 BELOW:                     │
│   Check Off Tasks as They Are Passed                                  │
│                                                                       │
│   Passed:                                                             │
│    1. Drop 20 balls; hit 15 correctly (as stated below). You or a     │
│       partner may drop the balls. Catch the ball after each hit. The  │
│       ball should hit the wall at the same height and straight ahead  │
│       of where it is contacted. It should rebound to within an arm's  │
│       length of where you are standing. An assistant should evaluate  │
│       consistency/control, slicing, hooking, and height of ball.      │
│   _____ 15 correctly hit balls with forehand standing mid-court. │
│   _____ 15 correctly hit balls with backhand standing mid-court. │
│   _____ 15 correctly hit balls with forehand standing 6 feet from│
│              the back wall.                                           │
│   _____ 15 correctly hit balls with backhand standing 6 feet from│
│              the back wall.                                           │
│    2. Stand at the side court and move to hit 20 balls that come to   │
│       center court. Hit 15 correctly (as stated below). Your partner  │
│       should hit or throw the ball to the front wall so it bounces    │
│       to center court. Catch the ball each time it is hit.            │
│   _____ 15 correctly hit balls standing mid-court with the       │
│              forehand.                                                │
│   _____ 15 correctly hit balls standing mid-court with the       │
│              backhand.                                                │
└─────────────────────────────────────────────────────────────────────┘
```

Figure 10.4 Example of a mastery learning
task sheet.

3. Drop the ball from behind the short line and continuously hit it off the front wall as stated below.

_____ 10 continuously hit balls with forehand.
_____ 10 continuously hit balls with backhand.
_____ 25 continuously hit balls with forehand in 2 minutes.
_____ 25 continuously hit balls with backhand in 2 minutes.

4. Practice the Long Wall Volley Test using either the forehand _____ or backhand for 1 minute. Retake the test when you are ready.

5. With a partner, rally the ball continuously off the front wall using either forehand or backhand 25 times. Alternate hits _____ with your partner.

6. With two or three other people, rally the ball continuously, establishing a sequence of hitting that is followed each time _____ (e.g., John, Sally, Bill; John, Sally, Bill.

7. With a partner, play a modified game. The server stands between the red lines and puts the ball into play by bouncing it and then hitting so it rebounds off the front wall. The ball must then bounce on the floor beyond the red lines. The receiver may stand anywhere beyond the red lines to receive the ball. The server scores a point if the receiver makes an error. The receiver becomes the server if the server makes an error. The receiver does not score points. Play continues to 15 points.

Forehand Form
1. Face side wall, with racquet arm away from front wall. The feet are a shoulder's width apart with the left foot slightly closer to the side wall (right-handed player).
2. Bend knees comfortably.
3. Hold racquet arm back and perpendicular to body with the racquet head pointing to ceiling about shoulder level.
4. Contact ball between waist and knee as you step forward (skilled players will contact the ball at the knee).
5. Snap wrists and follow through to opposite shoulder so body now faces the front wall.

Backhand Form
1. Face side wall, with racquet arm close to front wall. The feet are a shoulder's width apart with the right foot slightly closer to the side wall (right-handed player).
2. Band knees comfortably.
3. Bring racquet across mid-section of body with elbow bent to form a 90° angle with the upper arm (L) a few inches from the body.
4. Point the racquet head to the ceiling near the shoulder.
5. Contact the ball between the knee and waist as described above for the forehand.
6. Snap wrists and follow through to head height away from the body.

Figure 10.4 *(continued)*

allows the student to work independently, engaging the teacher only when specific help is needed. The teacher is then free to interact in the class with those students requiring assistance.

Teachers often find teaching for mastery is very time consuming at its inception, but discover the rewards in the end worth the effort. The rewards of mastery learning include: (1) individual student success, (2) willingness by students to practice, (3) progress easily identified, and (4) high levels of achievement.

Teachers incorporating mastery learning or other individualized learning techniques often desire to group students homogeneously by dividing students into smaller groups of similar ability levels. The following examples point out the practical application of such a strategy as well as its pros and cons.

Example (Lay-ups)
1. Demonstrate lay-ups to the class.
2. Have all students go to baskets to practice the lay-up progression.
3. As soon as a student can do successful lay-ups, have the student put on a pinnie, but continue to practice.
4. As soon as enough students are wearing pinnies, start a half-court game with these players and move players left at those baskets to other baskets.
5. Continue with 3, 4, and 5 until all players are successful.

Example (Archery)
1. Have all students shoot at twenty yards and score the best five consecutive ends.
2. Have students who score two hundred points at a given distance move back five yards.
3. Students will soon be shooting at various distances designated by the teacher. The students at the closest distance need the most help.

Uses
1. To preassess students needing help with skill development.
2. To enrich the learning of advanced students.
3. To enhance safety.

Advantages
1. It permits the teacher to work with students who need the most help.
2. It permits advanced students to move on to new objectives.
3. It increases student effort.
4. It rewards student effort.

Limitations
1. It necessitates advance planning.
2. It is difficult to supervise many groups doing different things at the same time.

Procedures
1. Write objectives for each skill.
2. Preassess students on one skill.
3. Group together the students who pass the preassessment to apply the skill in an advanced situation (e.g., game play), to work on accuracy, or to work on advanced skills in an individual program.

4. Work with all of the other students until another group can pass the evaluation. Send them to do the same thing as the first group.
5. Continue working with less-skilled students and regrouping until 85 to 100 percent of the students can pass the evaluation.
6. Teach the next skill.

Contract Learning Contract learning is the use of an individual learning packet in which a student contracts (or agrees) with the teacher to complete specified objectives to receive a specified grade. Contracts individualize learning by allowing students to select different tasks or learning activities and to take responsibility for their own learning and self-assessment. They permit students to work at their own pace on clearly defined tasks. Types of contracts include: (1) teacher-controlled contracts in which the tasks and reinforcers are determined by the teacher, (2) transitional contracting in which decision making is shared by the student and the teacher, and (3) student-controlled contracts in which the tasks and reinforcers are determined by the student. An example of a contract is the Gymnastics Grade Contract shown in figure 10.5.

Some limitations of contracts might include the necessity of using additional media and outside facilities, the time-consuming preparation involved, and the fact that some students are not ready to work on their own without constant teacher direction.

Procedures
1. Specify the performance and/or process objectives for a given unit of study. Identify the level (e.g., A, B, C).
2. Specify possible learning activities and learning materials.
3. Devise the contract. The teacher may do this or teacher and student might work together.
4. Develop evaluation methods and materials, including progress checks that tell students when performance objectives have been accomplished. (They also serve as reinforcers.)
5. Divide the instructional unit into blocks that provide ample time for activities to be taught, practiced, and evaluated.
6. Meet together as teacher and student or teacher and class to discuss the conditions of the contract and specify proposed dates for the completion of various phases of the contract.
7. Begin the instruction or activity phase with the teacher serving as a resource person when needed.
8. Evaluate the achievement of the stated objectives in terms of the stated criteria. The teacher and student may need to recontract along the way. Performance that does not meet acceptable standards should either be redone or receive a lower grade.
9. Award a grade based on the specified criteria.

Quests
A quest is an individualized learning activity in which the student writes the objectives and learning activities (subject to teacher approval). In other ways it is similar to contract learning. Quests allow students to set and pursue their own goals at their own pace and to take responsibility for their own learning. They encourage individual initiative and creativity and decrease unhealthy competition between students, since each student has different goals.

```
┌─────────────────────────────────────────────────────────────────┐
│                     Gymnastics Grade Contract                     │
│                                                                   │
│         Please read the following contract carefully and ask any  │
│   questions you may have. Remember: teachers do not give students │
│   grades; students earn the grades they receive.                  │
│                        * * * * * * * * * *                        │
│   Name _____ Period _____       │
│   I contract for an A B C (circle one) based on the criteria below:│
│   Starting date _____ Ending date _____     │
│   Student signature _____ Teacher signature _____  │
│   Requirements for an A:                                          │
│    1. Attend class regularly, be dressed, and participate each day.│
│    2. Actively participate in all activities taught by your       │
│       instructor.                                                 │
│    3. Earn a minimum score of fourteen out of twenty on the written│
│       examination.                                                │
│    4. Learn and perform for the instructor fourteen stunts from any│
│       or all of the events at the advanced level.                 │
│    5. Select and complete fourteen Learning Experience points from │
│       the class list.                                             │
│                                                                   │
│   Requirements for a B:                                          │
│    1. Attend class regularly, be dressed, and participate each day.│
│    2. Actively participate in all activities taught by your       │
│       instructor.                                                 │
│    3. Earn a minimum score of twelve out of twenty on the written │
│       examination.                                                │
│    4. Learn and perform for the instructor twelve stunts from any or│
│       all of the events at the intermediate level.                │
│    5. Select and complete twelve Learning Experience points from the│
│       class list.                                                 │
│                                                                   │
│   Requirements for a C:                                          │
│    1. Attend class regularly, be dressed, and participate each day.│
│    2. Actively participate in all activities taught by your       │
│       instructor.                                                 │
│    3. Earn a minimum score of ten out of twenty on the written    │
│       examination.                                                │
│    4. Learn and perform for the instructor ten stunts from any or  │
│       all of the events at the beginning level.                   │
│    5. Select and complete ten Learning Experience points from the │
│       class list.                                                 │
└─────────────────────────────────────────────────────────────────┘
```

Figure 10.5 A gymnastics contract.
Source: Linda Fleming and Joyce M. Harrison,
Brigham Young University.

```
                        A Quest Contract
    1. My objectives


    2. My learning activities

    3. My plans for evaluation
           _____ videotape recording
           _____ expert or professional
           _____ other:


    4. I plan to present evidence of my achievement of each objective by

       _____
              (Date)

    5. My contract is for an _____ grade.


                                  _____    _____
                                  Signature of student       Date
                                  _____    _____
                                  Signature of instructors   Date
```

Figure 10.6 A quest contract.

However, since students are doing different types of projects, stating or measuring the quality of each quest can be difficult. Some teachers have difficulty letting students do their own thing. An example of a quest contract is shown in figure 10.6.

Procedures
1. Select a topic to be pursued.
2. Write performance objectives (with the teacher's help) describing what is to be done.
3. Decide on evaluation criteria.
4. Select the learning tasks and the materials or resources to be used.
5. Create a schedule of progress checks and completion dates.
6. Submit completed contract and evaluate progress in terms of the criteria agreed on.

Individualized Learning Packets Individualized learning packets are packets of materials prepared in such a way that they can be used with little or no direct teacher supervision. They are used to individualize instruction and increase student responsibility for learning. Some advantages of this technique are self-pacing, adaptability to various interests or levels of development of different learners, and the ability to study a specific area of interest in greater depth than allowed in the normal classroom. Students also learn to provide their own feedback. Challenges imposed by this technique are finding time to write, evaluate, and update programs and managing classes in which students are working individually. Some students may perceive individualized units as busy work. An example of an individualized unit is Elementary Rescues (see figure 10.7).

Elementary Rescues

Objective

The student will demonstrate self-rescue skills to a partner, as follows (in seven feet of water):
a. Treading water—five minutes
b. Floating on back—minimum of movement of hands—remain in five-foot circle—one minute
c. Survival floating—ten minutes fully clothed
d. Disrobing and shirt and trouser inflation—without touching the side
e. Staying afloat with inflated clothing—five minutes
f. Jumping in and swimming in clothing, fully dressed—one length
g. Releasing a cramp
h. Removing self from weeds

Preassessment

1. Skills you already should know:
   a. Back float
   b. Treading water—two minutes
   c. Survival floating—two minutes
   d. Jellyfish float

   Note: Clothes must be brought from home for skills requiring them.

2. Completion by having partner initial passed requirements on Skills Check-off Card.

Skill Statements (Example from total unit)

1. You will tread water for five minutes using any one of the following kicks and a sculling motion with the arms. (Floating is not permitted.)
   a. Whip or frog kick
   b. Scissors kick
   c. Bicycle kick
2. You will survival float for ten minutes fully clothed.
   a. Assume a prone float or jellyfish float position in the water.
   b. Breathe by lifting the head while pushing gently down with the hands.
   c. *Sink* into the prone or jellyfish position and let the water buoy you to the surface. Exhale.
   d. Repeat b and c alternately with less than five breaths per minute.

Learning Activities

1. Read pages 120–27 in *Swimming and Water Safety*.
2. Read pages 20–29 in *Life Saving and Water Safety*.
3. Study and try to do the skill statements as they are outlined for you.
4. Have a partner check you off on each skill as you pass it.
5. If you have difficulty inflating clothing, ask for a demonstration by your instructor.

Evaluation

Have a partner initial passed skills on Unit IV Skills Check-Off Card.

Figure 10.7 An individualized unit.

Procedures

1. Choose a project that will be a meaningful learning experience.
2. Write units that include the following:
    a. Performance objectives—cognitive, psychomotor, and affective.
    b. Preassessment procedures.
    c. Ideas to be learned or skill statements.
    d. Learning activities designed to provide for individual differences in
        1) Rate of learning.
        2) Amount of practice needed to perfect skills.
        3) Mode of instruction preferred.
        4) Optional enrichment activities.
    e. Evaluation of achievement of the objectives.
    f. Instructions on how to use the unit—how, where, when, with whom, what, why, and how to get help.
3. Provide a wide variety of learning activities that require the student to read, view, discuss, listen to, analyze, do, identify, describe, construct, use media, survey, demonstrate, visit, participate in, or videotape.
4. Models of skills in individualized units can be provided in advance by the teacher or by photos, loop films, videotapes, drawings, or highly skilled students.
5. Evaluate in terms of the goals.

Programmed Learning Programmed learning is a method of organizing instruction into small steps that can be readily learned by a student. It is a process of learning rather than a product. Programmed learning consists of the following characteristics: (1) the subject matter is carefully organized into a logical sequence with each step building on the one preceding it, (2) the subject matter is divided into small steps, (3) the student is presented with and actively responds to one question or skill movement at a time, (4) the student receives immediate knowledge of results, (5) each student can progress at his or her own rate within the parameters defined by the unit, and (6) programs are written or created to ensure a minimum of error.

Programmed learning encourages student responsibility for learning. Immediate knowledge of results yields higher motivation and learner confidence. Programming frees the teacher to provide individual help and to help the students apply the learning gained. Programs insist that each point be thoroughly understood before proceeding on. Therefore, programmed learning works well for slower students and results in efficiency in learning per unit of time. Some well-constructed programs compensate for weaknesses on the part of instructors.

Despite its advantages, programmed learning cannot be used to teach attitudes, opinions, or values. Students can easily lose interest or cheat, especially with linear programs.

There are several methods of programming that are fairly simple to use. One type is *recall,* and it can be programmed by the teacher who will take the time. An example of this first method is to place the words of a song on the chalkboard. Sing the song several times. Erase one or more words. Continue to sing the song, erasing several words at the conclusion of each trial, until all of the words are erased and the song is learned. Method I is excellent for teaching facts such as terminology. An example of its use in physical education is Archery Terms (see figure 10.8).

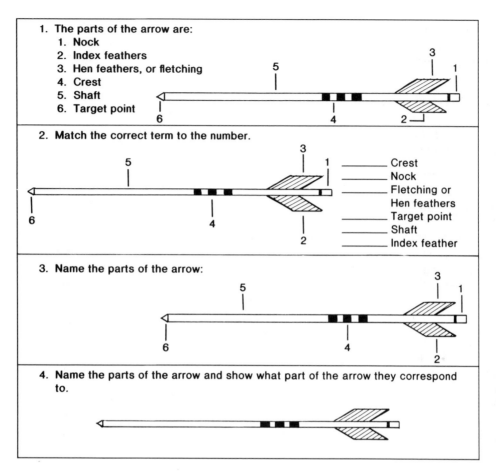

1. **The parts of the arrow are:**
   1. Nock
   2. Index feathers
   3. Hen feathers, or fletching
   4. Crest
   5. Shaft
   6. Target point

2. **Match the correct term to the number.**

   _____ Crest
   _____ Nock
   _____ Fletching or Hen feathers
   _____ Target point
   _____ Shaft
   _____ Index feather

3. **Name the parts of the arrow:**

4. **Name the parts of the arrow and show what part of the arrow they correspond to.**

Figure 10.8 Archery terms programmed unit.

Procedures for Method I (Recall)

1. Identify the objective and state it.
2. Compose a test question based on the objective. This will be the last frame or segment.
3. Answer the test question. This will be the first frame.
4. Write several practice frames in between, each time providing less information and requiring the student to supply the necessary information.
5. Place the frames one behind the other on separate pages. Read through all of the top frames, then begin again with page one. Continue until all frames have been read.
6. Add a title sheet, instructions, and answers to frames.
7. Try out on a few students. Revise.

The second programming method, Identification, is used to teach concepts. An example of the second method is Bowling-Split Recognition (see figure 10.9).

Split Recognition: A Programmed Unit

Objective

You will be able to pass a ten-item quiz on split recognition with 90 percent accuracy.

Preassessment

Read item 1. Then, take the quiz in 2. If you have all items correct, go to 6 for practice, if desired; then proceed to 7. If you missed any items, continue with frame 3.

Instructions

Cover the answers on the left with your hand or a card, uncovering them in turn as you proceed through the frames.

Evaluation

See Objective.

	1. A split is a leave of two or more pins when the headpin (#1) is down and one or more spaces remain between or in front of standing pins. Examples: 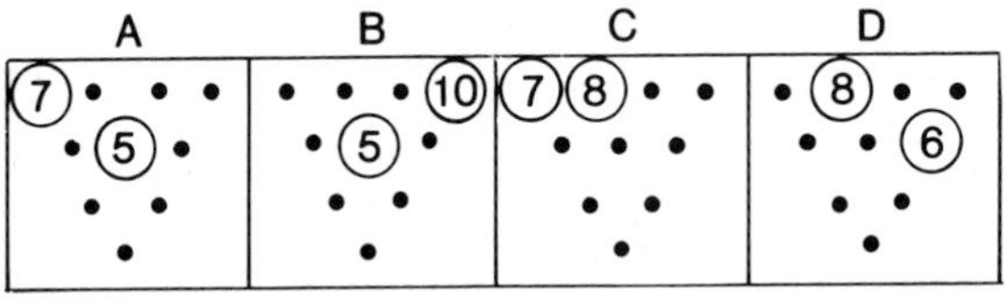
	2. Identify the splits below. (Cover the frame above.) 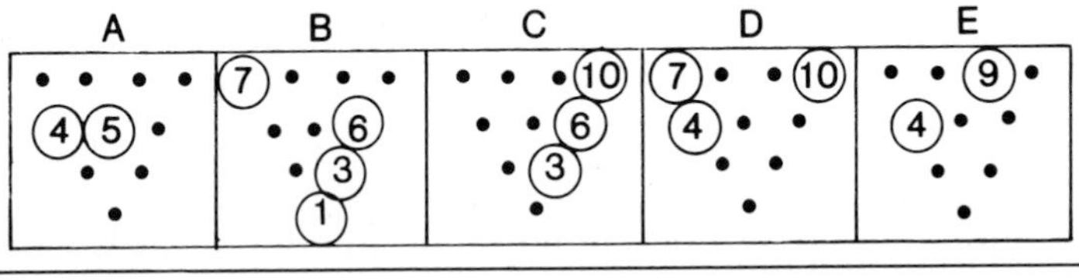
A, D, E If you have all 3 correct you may go to #6	3. Remember, to be a split, the headpin must be down. Which of the following are *not* splits? 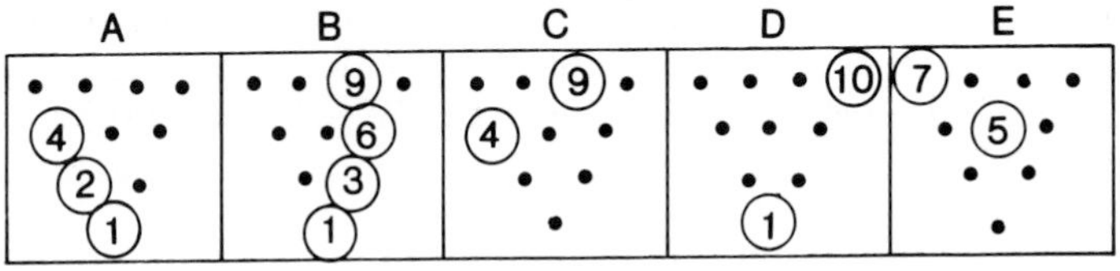

Figure 10.9 A programmed unit.

A, B, D are *not* splits

4. A split may have at least one pin down between standing pins, *as you look from the front.* Which of the following are *not* splits?

A   B   C   D   E

B, C, E are *not* splits

5. Instead of having spaces between pins, a split may have no intermediate pins left standing in front of the pins. Example:

Which of the following are *not* splits?

A   B   C   D   E

B, C, D, E are *not* splits

6. (Cover the frame above.) Identify the splits below by circling the letters for leaves that are splits.

A   B   C   D   E

F   G   H   I   J

A-No
B-Yes
C-Yes
D-No
E-Yes
F-No
G-No
H-Yes
I-Yes
J-Yes

7. If your answers were correct, you are ready to take the quiz on recognition of splits. Ask your instructor for the quiz. If your answers were incorrect, go back to 3 and review the frames again. Then, if needed, ask your instructor for assistance.

Figure 10.9 *(continued)*

Procedures for Method II (Identification)
1. Define the concept (e.g., A split is . . .).
2. List as many examples of the concepts as possible (all kinds of splits).
3. List as many nonexamples of the concept as possible (all pin set-ups that are not splits). Be sure to include all necessary nonexamples.
4. Create a test question that indicates understanding of the concept. (For example, "Identify all of the splits below.") This is the last frame.
5. Define the characteristics of the concept for the students. (For example, the head pin is down and one or more spaces exist between or in front of standing pins.)
6. Identify characteristics that may be confusing (for example, the space must be viewable from the front, not the side) or problem examples (such as the 9–10 split).
7. Using one characteristic at a time, build one upon another to arrive at the test question.
8. After presenting the material in each frame, ask the learner to identify examples and nonexamples of the concept, being careful not to include examples and nonexamples that do not meet the characteristics already presented.
9. Add instructions, answers to frames, and a concluding frame. Try out and revise.

The third method of programming is used to teach rules and principles. Programs can be written in a linear style, in which everyone reads the same frames at different speeds, or in a branched style, in which multiple-choice questions are used that have alternatives leading to different frames. Branched programs can speed up the learning process by skipping material or slow it down by providing remedial detours. Two examples of the third method of programming are Archery Scoring (see figures 10.10 and 10.11), one of which is linear and one of which is branched.

Methods of programming psychomotor skills are limited in quantity and quality because programming the practice of psychomotor skills is more difficult.

Programmed learning, along with learning packets and other individualized materials, is often administered through a learning center. The learning-center approach may be used to aid learning in the traditional movement activities and in the cognitive areas relating to the discipline of physical education.[34]

Teachers should be alert to sources for programmed learning information. Professional conventions and programs can provide opportunities to purchase these materials.

Peer Tutoring and Team Learning

Peer tutoring and team learning are strategies that work well in combination with other strategies. Peer tutoring is when one partner helps another learn a skill, such as when partners provide feedback to each other on swimming skills. Team learning is when a team works together to help its members achieve a certain goal and progresses only as fast as all members have achieved each skill or passed each quiz. Both peer tutoring and team learning can be used to save the teacher's time to handle special cases and to provide enrichment materials. However, some planning for or with tutors or groups is necessary. Although both types of learning may be more time consuming than the more teacher-directed strategies, they significantly increase student social interaction and develop group participation and leadership skills. Peer tutoring promotes learning by students who seem to learn better from their peers

Archery Scoring—Linear
(Frames 6-9)

	6. Arrows are always scored in order from the *highest to the lowest*. 10, 9, 8, 7, 6, 5, 4, 3, 2, 1 Place the following arrows in the correct order by numerical value: inner white, inner black, outer red, inner blue, outer red, outer gold. _____ _____ _____ _____ _____ _____
9, 7, 7, 6, 4, 2	7. Mary shot the following arrows: outer gold, outer red, outer white, outer black, outer blue, outer red, outer red. Her scores are recorded as follows: __7__ __7__ __7__ __5__ __3__ __1__ The rule to follow when shooting seven arrows instead of six is: _____ Subtract the lowest scoring arrow. _____ Subtract the highest scoring arrow. _____ Subtract the last arrow shot.
Subtract the highest scoring arrow.	8. 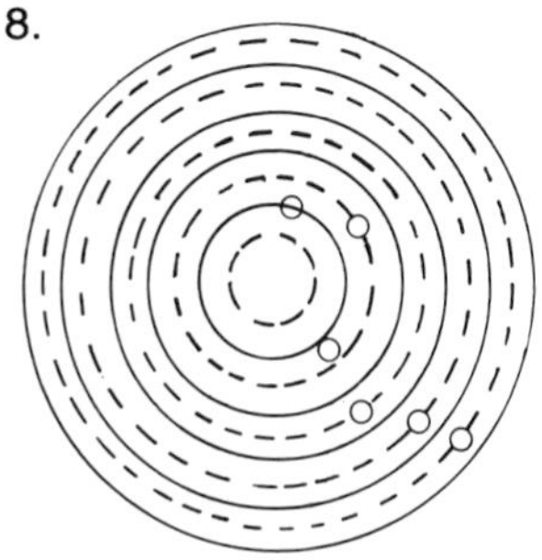 9, 9, 8, 6, 4, 2 Which rule best describes how to score an arrow on a line? _____ An arrow on a line scores the higher value. _____ An arrow on a line scores the lower value.
An arrow on a line scores the higher value.	9. Score the following arrows. 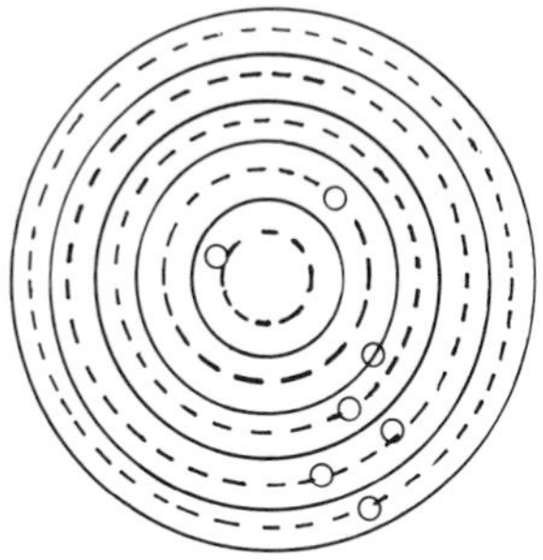

Figure 10.10 Archery scoring—a linear program.

Archery Scoring—Branched

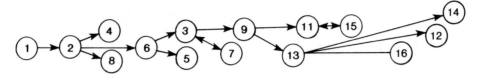

1. **Layout of a target archery face:**

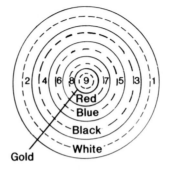

Give the color and value for each of the arrows shown.

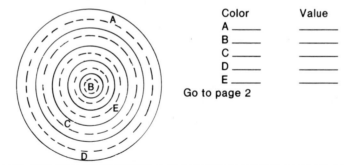

	Color	Value
A	_____	_____
B	_____	_____
C	_____	_____
D	_____	_____
E	_____	_____

Go to page 2

3. If an archer shot a perfect end of six arrows, the resulting score would be

_____ .

   a. 60. Turn to item 7.
   b. 54. Turn to item 5.
   c. Any other score. Turn to item 9.

4. That's right!
   Mary shot the following arrows: gold, red, white, black, blue, red, red. Her scores are recorded as follows:

   7, 7, 6, 5, 3, 2

   The rule to follow when shooting seven arrows instead of six is:
   a. Subtract the lowest scoring arrow. Turn to item 8.
   b. Subtract the highest scoring arrow. Turn to item 10.
   c. Subtract the last arrow shot. Turn to item 8.

Figure 10.11 Archery scoring—a branched program.

5. That would be correct if you were shooting on a target face divided into five scoring rings. This target face, however, had ten scoring rings. Recalculate your answer from the information given you on page 1. Return to page 2 and choose again.

6. Oops! Go back and look at the numerical order shown in the examples. Then, choose again.

7. That's right, 6 × 10 = 60.
Some examples of scores recorded by Barbara Bowslinger follow:
7, 7, 2, 1, 1, 0
10, 9, 6, 5, 3, 2
10, 4, 3, 2, 1, 1
The rule to follow when recording scores is:
   a. Record scores in order from highest to lowest. Turn to page 4.
   b. Record scores in order from lowest to highest. Turn to page 6.
   c. Record scores in the order shot. Turn to page 6.

8. You should have converted each color to a score, then looked to see which arrow was eliminated when the scores were recorded. Go back to item 4 and try again. Then, select another answer.

9. Perhaps you don't know how to figure the score for a perfect end. Six arrows multiplied by ten points (All arrows were in the bull's eye or inner gold ring) equals _____ .
Turn to item 6.

Figure 10.11 *(continued)*

than from the teacher. These types of learning increase student involvement in the learning process and motivate slower learners to improve their performance while reinforcing the learning that has already occurred by the faster learners. Always asking faster learners to tutor slower learners can be discouraging to the faster learners.

Procedures
1. Select appropriate instructional objectives.
2. Preassess to find learning problems.
3. Select activities in terms of objectives and learning problems. Tasks should be relevant to group members.
4. Create task sheets that include
   a. A description of the tasks, including diagrams or sketches.
   b. Specific points to look for in the performance.
   c. Samples of possible feedback.
5. Check to be sure students understand the purpose of the tasks and the criteria for correct performance.
6. Provide for facilitation of the observation by incorporating a system of
   a. Comparison of the performance with the criterion for correct performance.
   b. Communication of the results to the performer during and after the completion of each task.
7. Select partners or groups. Have students select a partner they have not worked with before.

Partner tutoring works well in combination with other strategies.

Simulation

An excellent teaching aid is a simulation of an event. Once again the *doing* aspect of learning is built into the learning experience. Students not competing on an athletic or intramural team may never have the experience of playing with official rules, referees, and scorers. Simulation activities are selective simplifications or representations of real-life situations in game or laboratory-type settings. They can be used to promote the learning of skills, knowledge, attitudes, strategies, and social skills. Possible experiences include a simulated track or gymnastics meet in which students might never have the opportunity to participate. Figure 10.12 illustrates a simulation of a diving meet that also involves students in the administration of the event.

Activities not usually performed in the gymnasium can be adapted to the school site. For example, tennis and bowling could be simulated in the gym so students get a very authentic experience.[35] Cross-country skiing can be taught during the winter months using both the outside playing fields and the gymnasium.[36] By contacting local carpet stores for pieces of carpet and using discarded or broken pieces of sports equipment, one teacher designed a nine-hole golf course in the locker room areas of the physical education building. A floor plan of the course was first designed and then transferred to the carpet. The carpet was then cut to fit the appropriate area. Scorecards, similar to those on a regulation golf course, were duplicated, and golf course courtesy was used. The course design is limited only by the imagination of the individual.[37] The same type of ingenuity might create a course outside on a grassy playing area using whiffle balls for safety.

Disadvantages of simulation are the increased time needed for preparation and learning and the expense involved in providing actual equipment in some instances. Some complain that simulation activities result in an oversimplification of life situations.

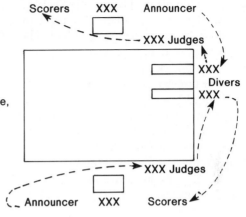

Simulation—Diving Meet

There are three students at each station. The rotation from station to station is illustrated here. Students change stations after three divers have each performed two dives. The teacher roves back and forth between the two scoring tables to offer needed assistance. Eighteen people can participate at one time, and more can be added.

Equipment Needed
1. Extra diving forms
2. Ten sharp pencils with erasers
3. Two diving calculators
4. Six judges scoring cards
5. Two tables and twelve chairs
6. Extra towels
7. Instructions taped to the announcer's and scorer's tables. (In case they have trouble remembering their duties.)

There are six teams (assigned by the instructor to assure the teams are evenly divided as far as diving ability). Each team (consisting of three members) should select a captain and a name. Each team captain has the responsibility to write each team member's two (2) dives on the diving sheet with their names in the left margin.

Figure 10.12 A simulated diving meet.
Source: Jack Romine and Joyce M. Harrison, Brigham Young University.

Procedures
1. Counsel students on how to accomplish the objectives of the assignment.
2. Tell what the results have to do with real life.
3. Supervise student activities.
4. Progress from simple to complex.
5. Emphasize the meaning of the simulation activity through preassessment and follow-up.
6. Assign heterogeneous teams.
7. Allow teams to select their own positions in the group.
8. Place faculty in legitimate roles, not as advisors to teams.
9. Define rules.
10. Play game.
11. Evaluate the results and provide feedback.
12. Discuss principles involved.
13. Allow students to create their own games.

Problem-Solving Strategies

Problem-solving strategies can be used to develop the ability to solve problems and verify solutions to problems. They can also be used to encourage the application of concepts already learned. If done in a group, they can encourage student interaction and teamwork. They encourage the use of cognitive processes other than memory and increase retention. However, this strategy is more time consuming than teacher-dominated instruction and can take time away from practicing psychomotor skills.

The problem-solving techniques that will be discussed further include: (1) questioning, (2) inquiry learning, and (3) brainstorming and buzz sessions. Other examples of problem-solving strategies are choreographing dance or gymnastics routines, developing new games with given parameters, or thinking up and sharing new plays for games. Most of the affective learning activities also fall into the category of problem solving. Problem solving has been discussed previously in chapter 6.

When problem-solving strategies are used, teachers need to keep in mind that involving some students meaningfully (e.g., slow learners, culturally disadvantaged, and students who lack the knowledge necessary to solve the problem) in problem-solving situations can be difficult.

Procedures

1. Define the problem in a few words.
2. State conditions necessary for the problem to be considered solved.
3. List possible solutions.
4. Find the best solution based on the desired outcomes.
5. Evaluate success in solving the problem.

Questioning Strategies Teachers use questions to arouse interest and hold attention; to help learners perceive the referent of a concept or discover a specific relationship or principle; to stimulate thought, develop understanding, apply information, develop appreciations and attitudes; or to emphasize a point or clarify a misconception. Questioning can also be used to evaluate student understanding and learning. Its use during a lecture increases individual student participation and understanding. Questioning requires considerable skill on the part of the teacher to accomplish the objective without embarrassing students or limiting the responses to only a few students. The following are some examples of questions at the various levels of the cognitive taxonomy:

1. Knowledge or fact questions: who, what, where, when. Involves recognition or recall of facts, events, places, or person's names.
2. Comprehension: Compare the belief in (subject) of . . . and. . . . Explain in your own words. Involves understanding of what was expressed.
3. Application: If you were . . . , what might you do? How does this apply in our lives? Involves using knowledge in new ways.
4. Analysis: Give evidence. . . . Explain. . . . What caused. . . ? What effect was caused by. . . ? Tell why. . . . Involves breaking information into parts.
5. Synthesis: Write a journal of your reactions to your fitness program. Describe how physical education makes a difference in your life. Involves combining parts to make a whole.
6. Evaluation: Should people. . . . Judge whether behavior was right or wrong. Defend the. . . . Involves making judgments based on standards.

Procedures
1. Prepare questions that
    a. Relate to the purpose of the lesson.
    b. Are clear, definite, easily understood.
    c. Engage the attention of the whole class.
    d. Relate to the students' world and interests.
    e. Cause students to stretch their minds.
    f. Take into account individual differences in such areas as intelligence, background, and experiences.
    g. Avoid manipulation of student responses.
    h. Build upon knowledge students now have.
    i. Can be answered in the time available.
    j. Are phrased in such a way as to obtain a discussion answer.
2. Inform students prior to instruction that they will be expected to answer questions. It may be well to introduce the discussion session with a story, diagram, chart, filmstrip, film, record, tape, object, case study, or a well-planned question written on the chalkboard to stimulate thinking.
3. Ask questions by
    a. Directing the question to the entire class, pausing, and then calling on volunteers.
    b. Directing the question to the class, pausing, and then calling on a specific student.
    c. Directing a question from one student to another student or the entire class.
4. Encourage student involvement by
    a. Pausing after each question to encourage thoughtful and meaningful responses (at least three seconds). Say, "Think carefully before you answer," wait, then call on someone.
    b. Using nonvolunteers. Inform students that they will be encouraged to contribute and they might be called whether or not their hands are raised. If a student hesitates, say, "Think about it for a minute, and we'll come back to you."
    c. Redirecting questions. Ask one question, then ask "Jane, can you add anything else?" or just nod at another student. Encourage students to direct questions to other students.
    d. Rephrasing. Listen to the student's answer and then attempt to restate what was heard. For example, "Barry, do you mean. . . ?" Avoid inserting personal reactions into the answer.
    e. Probing. Accept the student's initial response and then ask the student to extend, justify, or clarify it by asking, "Can you tell me more, Nathan?" Probing helps the student think more carefully and express a more complete answer.
5. When answers are off the subject, only partially complete or correct, or wrong, treat responses with courtesy and tact.
    a. Say something such as, "That's not quite right. Let's think it through together."
    b. Avoid rejecting good ideas that were not the hoped-for answer. Instead, rephrase the question.
    c. Avoid negative responses that might lower the student's self-esteem or discourage future responses. Always attempt to make the student feel good about responding.
    d. Avoid praising answers excessively. Other students may assume their answers were no good.

6. Keep the discussion organized by relating questions to the previous answers or to questions students raise about the topic under discussion.
7. Summarize often to show students the progress they are making toward a solution, to focus the class on the solution, and to emphasize truths students are learning. Give credit to students who make important contributions. Use students to summarize when appropriate, and list the main points on the chalkboard.
8. Show how the solution can be applied to real life. Challenge the students to apply it.
9. Evaluate any questions against the following criteria:
   a. Did the sequence of questions display a logical development of ideas leading students directly to the heart of the problem and to its solution?
   b. Was each question related in some useful way to the problem statement?
   c. Was the question accurately stated, specific, and to the point?
   d. Was the question within the ability of the student to whom it was addressed?
   e. Was the question relevant to students?
   f. Did the question stimulate students to think and investigate?[38]

Inquiry Learning Inquiry learning is a process through which students learn how to seek out answers scientifically by asking thought-provoking questions. The most commonly used example is "Twenty Questions." Although inquiry learning is more time consuming than conventional learning, it tends to help students learn how to learn by putting the responsibility for learning directly on the students, thereby providing more meaningful learning.

Procedures
1. Provide and introduce the focus of the lesson—a puzzling or unfamiliar object, event, or situation.
2. Define the rules of questioning.
   a. All questions must be answered by yes or no.
   b. Ask only one question at a time.
   c. One student may ask a series of questions until a train of thought has been completed.
   d. Students may confer or call for a summary at any time.
3. Answer questions to help students gather data and verify information, reminding students of the rules when necessary.
4. Help students organize the information they have obtained, identify relationships among the variables, and create hypotheses to explain the situation. For example, if x is true, then would y be so?
5. Summarize the questioning procedure and identify how it can be improved.

Brainstorming and Buzz Sessions Brainstorming is the generation of solutions to a defined problem by stating any idea relevant to the parameters of the subject matter that comes to mind. For example, a small group of students might generate ideas for a new game or dance. In a buzz session, a large group is divided into small groups of people who generate ways to solve a case study or problem. Group members can be rotated to increase the diversity of ideas. Both techniques can be used to solve a specific problem or to define creative approaches to problem solving. They can result in individual creativity, maximum group participation, and unique, creative solutions to problems.

Procedures

1. State the problem clearly.
2. Establish a time limit of five to ten minutes.
3. List ideas about the subject on a chalkboard or paper as they come to mind with no attempt to evaluate them. Try to get as many as possible.
4. At the end of the time specified, the teacher should restate the problem and help students evaluate the ideas.

Affective Learning Strategies

Although affective learning surrounds the teaching-learning process at all times, some specific strategies can be used to enhance the teaching of affective behaviors. Although activities can take time away from physical activity, many of them are important to the acquisition of affective skills.

Affective behaviors can be learned during actual situations that arise during classroom interaction or during planned activities. The preferred method in physical education is through actual experience in situations as they arise. However, some affective activities can be used on rainy days, during assembly schedules, and on other days when time does not permit dressing for activity.

Developing attitudes toward activities necessitates knowing something about the activity; therefore, the instructional sequence should begin with learning skills and knowledge relevant to that activity. By pairing a new skill or bit of knowledge with a preferred or rewarding activity, students may acquire a liking for the new skill or knowledge. Gagné generalized that "success in some learning accomplishment is likely to lead to a positive attitude toward that activity."[39]

A number of techniques for learning affective behavior have been included within the teaching strategies in unit 2. Their use will be more effective in a democratic classroom environment.

Reaction and Opinion Papers Reaction and opinion papers are papers submitted by students expressing their feelings, opinions, or reactions to something. They can be used to increase student awareness of their own feelings and to increase teacher awareness of student feelings. Since there is no one right answer, every student can be included. However, some students may not feel free to express their true feelings when names are included on papers. Writing can sometimes be done as homework to decrease time spent in lieu of physical activity. Some examples of reaction and opinion papers include:

1. I Urge Telegrams: Send a "telegram," urging someone to do something, change something, or stop doing something. For example: To Mother, "I urge you to stop smoking. Your loving daughter."[40]
2. "I Learned" Statements: Write a brief statement of what you learned by doing a specific activity—such as going on a field trip or participating in a challenging activity, such as rapelling.[41]
3. Write reactions to a statement or quote such as "It's not whether you win or lose, but how you play the game," or "Winning is not the most important thing; it is the only thing," or "When the going gets tough, the tough get going," or "They didn't really lose the game; they only lost the score."

Procedures

1. Establish a nonthreatening, supportive environment in which students feel free to express their feelings.
2. Have students write their feelings about some specific topic.
3. Avoid grading reaction papers.

Goal Setting Students learn to set realistic goals through practice. Since students have different abilities and backgrounds, they should be helped to set goals that are challenging and yet can result in successful achievement. Students will often set goals lower than their true expectations so they will not be penalized by failure to meet their goals. Some ideas for goal setting include:

1. The Goalpost[42]
   a. Decorate the bulletin board in the form of a goalpost.
   b. Have students record goals on footballs (3 x 5 cards) and post them below the crossbar.
   c. Each day students achieve their goals, they can move the football above the goalpost.
   d. Allow students time to share their successes with the class.
2. The Envelope
   a. Have students record long-term goals.
   b. Place them in a sealed envelope for each class.
   c. Open the envelope at the end of the unit and redistribute them so students can see their progress.
   d. Allow students to share their successes.

Procedure

1. Help students get ideas for goals using some of the following techniques (or make up some).
   a. Questions.
      1) What skill would you like to be able to do better when we complete this unit?
      2) What talent do you wish you had?
   b. Suppose a doctor just told you that you have only one year to live. What would you do differently? How would you change your life? What is stopping you from doing these things now? Let's set a goal to achieve some of them.[43]
2. Help students clarify goals. Goals should be
   a. Clearly defined.
   b. Desirable, worthwhile, challenging.
   c. Achievable.
   d. Measurable in terms of time and quantity.
   e. Controllable. (Goals involving someone else should have their permission.)
   f. Achievement should result in a better self.[44]

Discussion Group consideration of a question or real-life problem situation can help students clarify values and concepts by discussing their implications and their similarities and differences with known referents. Through individual participation, students have opportunities to organize and communicate their thoughts and to learn respect for the viewpoints of others. Care must be taken, however, to encourage everyone to participate, rather than allowing a few talkative students to monopolize the conversation or reverting to a question-answer session. The following ideas can help to initiate a discussion:

1. Continuum
   a. Draw a continuum on the chalkboard.
   b. Label 0 in the center, degrees toward the ends, and name the ends:

Cooperative									Competitive
Clark	40	30	20	10	0	10	20	30	40	Connie

   c. Have students place themselves on the continuum. (Do not let them position themselves in the center.)
   d. Discuss where the most popular, happiest, or capable student would be and why.
2. Priority or ranking[45]
   a. Rank order a list of three to five situations from best to worst.
   b. Think of an idea that is better than and one that is worse than the situations given.
   c. Discuss the rankings.
   d. Example: Rank the actions you might take when you see another student cheating off your paper on a test.
      1) Do nothing.
      2) Hide your paper.
      3) Tell the teacher.
3. Value voting[46]
   a. Read questions and have the class vote for or against each one.
   b. Sample questions:
      1) Would you try rapelling?
      2) Would you turn in a friend who cheated on a test?
4. Case studies or moral dilemmas—Situations that need a decision and a plan of action (see example in chapter 6).
5. Devil's advocate—Teacher takes a nonpopular view of an issue and encourages reactions from students.
6. Incomplete sentences—Have students complete sentences such as the following and discuss them: Competition is. . . . Winning is. . . .

Procedures
1. Make sure students have the learning on which the discussion will be based.
2. Define the topic.
3. Work from an idea such as a visual aid, demonstration, quote, provocative question, or film.
4. Keep to the topic.
5. Involve everyone who wants to participate; avoid required participation.
6. Summarize periodically.
7. Draw conclusions.

Role Playing Role playing is an exploration of interpersonal relations problems by re-creating or acting out real-life situations and then discussing them. Problems can include social events, personal concerns, values, problem behaviors, or social skills. Some examples are:

1. A coach kicks a player off the team for not conforming to the rules regarding length of hair. The student threatens the coach's safety.
2. A football player fails a test in English and is ineligible for the championship game this weekend. You are the player's best friend and the English teacher is your aunt.

Sensitivity modules, such as staying in a wheelchair for a day to experience being handicapped or swimming without the use of the legs, can increase student empathy for others. Through playing the roles of other people, students can explore and begin to understand the feelings, attitudes, and values of others in social situations, as well as the consequences of their behavior on others. As they become more aware of the values of society, they also develop an awareness of alternative ways to solve problems. Some students are comfortable with role playing, since they can act out their own feelings without fear of reprisal. Others, however, have difficulty portraying feelings, and care should be taken to avoid embarrassing these students.

Procedures

1. Define the problem situation, which might include social problems, personal concerns, values, problem behaviors, or social skills. Choose easy problems first.
2. Prepare role sheets that describe the feelings or values of the character to be played (optional).
3. Introduce students to a problem through a real-life situation far enough away from the students to remove threat or stress yet close enough to draw out the relationship between the behavior in the problem and parallel behavior within the class or school. Ask students to think about what they would do under the same circumstances.
4. Select participants from volunteers. Avoid assigning roles based on peer pressure or the natural role of the student. Assign minor roles to the shy individuals. Use role sheets if desired.
5. Clarify the setting—i.e., place, time, situation, roles.
6. Assign observers specific things to look for, such as feelings of certain players or alternative endings.
7. Role-play, several times if needed, to bring out possible alternative behaviors and their consequences.
8. Discuss behaviors and feelings. Relate the role-playing situation to students' actual behavior in a nonthreatening way.
9. Discuss the role-playing situation, successes and failures, and how it could be improved.

Summarizing and Reviewing Lessons

A carefully prepared summary at the end of a lesson ties together the loose ends and highlights the important points. It also gives the students an opportunity to ask questions and provides the teacher with an opportunity to correct any inaccuracies acquired by the students. Some ideas for summarizing a lesson include:

1. Summarize the main idea of the lesson with a short statement and tell what the students should realize as an outcome.
2. Assign one or two students to listen carefully and tell the class afterwards what the lesson was about.
3. Have students write or tell in their own words what they think the main idea is.
4. Use a worksheet to help students summarize the main idea of the lesson.
5. Have several students in turn tell one thing learned from the lesson.
6. Divide the class into small groups. Each group in turn acts out a part of the lesson while the other groups try to guess what is being depicted (charades).
7. Present a real-life situation that could be resolved by using lesson ideas.
8. Give an oral or written quiz.
9. Use instructional games to test the information taught.

Some ways to review a lesson include:

1. Have students keep records of their progress with lesson objectives.
2. Have students write briefly on a previous lesson topic.
3. Have students perform any specific skill previously taught.

The way is clear for each and every physical education instructor to be creative and design new styles and strategies for teaching in the future. The committed teacher is limited by only one criterion—is it successful in teaching students?

Questions and Suggested Activities

1. Prepare a lesson plan for each of the first seven styles of teaching.
2. Teach a lesson using at least three of the ten styles of teaching. Record your lesson on videotape for further analysis, if this is possible.
3. Identify different teaching styles and strategies you have experienced. Which ones enabled you to learn best? Ask other students which ones enabled them to learn best.
4. Design a mastery learning task sheet for any skill you wish.
5. The principal of your school has given a student permission to get credit for your physical education class by fulfilling a contract until his competitive season for diving is over. How would you set this up?
6. The parent-teacher association in your school is making available money for individualized instruction materials. Prepare a request for funds including program objectives, justification, procedures, and sources of materials.
7. Plan two learning situations in which you would incorporate problem-solving strategies.
8. Discuss those affective teaching strategies you might use in an effort to change some negative attitudes about your physical education class to positive ones.

Suggested Readings

American Alliance for Health, Physical Education and Recreation. *Ideas for Secondary School Physical Education: Innovative Programs from Project Idea.* Washington, D.C.: AAHPER, 1976.

Arrighi, Margarite A. "Equal Opportunity through Instructional Design." *Journal of Physical Education, Recreation and Dance* 56 (September 1985):58–60, 64.

Beale, Judith C. "Task Sheets for Badminton and Racquetball." *The Physical Educator* 39 (May 1982):87–90.

Beland, Robert M. "Simulation Techniques that Work." *Journal of Physical Education, Recreation and Dance* 54 (November–December 1983):58–60, 68.

Carlson, Ronald P., ed., *IDEAS II for Secondary School Physical Education: A Sharing of Teaching Practices by Secondary School Physical Education Practitioners.* Reston, Virginia: American Alliance for Health, Physical Education, Recreation and Dance, 1984.

Darst, Paul W., and Randy L. Model. "Racquetball Contracting: A Way to Structure Your Learning Environment." *Journal of Physical Education, Recreation and Dance* 54 (September 1983):65–67.

Ellson, Douglas. "Improving Productivity in Teaching." *Phi Delta Kappan* 68 (October 1986):111–24.

Francke, Eleanor. "Excellence in Instruction." *Journal of Physical Education, Recreation and Dance* 54 (September 1983):55–57.

Goldberger, Michael. "Effective Learning through a Spectrum of Teaching Styles." *Journal of Physical Education, Recreation and Dance* 55 (October 1984):17–21.

Hurwitz, Dick. "A Model for the Structure of Instructional Strategies." *Journal of Teaching in Physical Education* 4 (April 1985):190–201.

Metzler, Michael W. "On Styles." *Quest* 35 (1983):145–54.

Mosston, Muska, and Sara Ashworth. *Teaching Physical Education,* 3d ed. Columbus, Ohio: Charles E. Merrill, 1986.

Netcher, Jack R. "A Learning System: What Is It, Why Is It, How Does It Work?" *Journal of Physical Education and Recreation* 47 (June 1976):29–30.

Youngberg, Linda, and Dee Dee Jones. "Performance Contracts Help Teach Tumbling." *Journal of Physical Education and Recreation* 51 (November–December 1980):63.

Zakrajsek, Dorothy, and Lois A. Carnes. *Individualizing Physical Education: Criterion Materials,* 2d ed. Champaign, Illinois: Human Kinetics Publishers, 1986.

References

1. Dugan Laird and Forrest Belcher, "How Master Trainers Get That Way," *Training and Development Journal* (May 1984), p. 73.
2. Eleanor Francke, "Excellence in Instruction," *Journal of Physical Education, Recreation and Dance* 54 (September 1983), pp. 55–56.
3. N. L. Gage, "The Yield of Research on Teaching," *Phi Delta Kappan* (November 1978), pp. 229–35.
4. Penelope L. Peterson, "Direct Instruction Reconsidered," in Penelope L. Peterson and Herbert J. Walberg, eds. *Research on Teaching: Concepts, Findings, and Implications* (Berkeley: McCutchan Publishing Corporation, 1979), pp. 57–69.
5. Michael Goldberger, "Effective Learning through a Spectrum of Teaching Styles," *Journal of Physical Education, Recreation and Dance* 55 (October 1984), p. 17.
6. Ralph W. Tyler, *Basic Principles of Curriculum and Instruction* (Chicago: University of Chicago Press, 1949), p. 64.
7. Judith E. Rink, *Teaching Physical Education for Learning* (St. Louis: Times Mirror/Mosby College Publishing, 1985), p. 269.
8. Bruce Joyce and Marsha Weil, *Models of Teaching,* 2d ed. (Englewood Cliffs, New Jersey: Prentice-Hall, 1980), p. 478.
9. David E. Hunt, *Matching Models in Education: The Coordination of Teaching Methods with Student Characteristics* (Toronto, Ontario: The Ontario Institute for Studies in Education, 1971), pp. 9–10.

10. Robert C. Hawley, *Human Values in the Classroom: Teaching for Personal and Social Growth* (Amherst, Massachusetts: Education Research Associates, 1973).
11. Jere Brophy, "Successful Teaching Strategies for the Inner-City Child," *Phi Delta Kappan* 63 (April 1982), pp. 527–30.
12. George Graham, "Review and Implications of Physical Education Experimental Teaching Unit Research," in Thomas J. Templin and Janice K. Olson, eds. *Teaching in Physical Education* (Champaign, Illinois: Human Kinetics Publishers, 1983), pp. 244–53.
13. Muska Mosston and Sara Ashworth, *Teaching Physical Education,* 3d ed. (Columbus, Ohio: Charles E. Merrill, 1986).
14. Michael Goldberger, "Direct Styles of Teaching and Psychomotor Performance," in Thomas J. Templin and Janice K. Olson, eds. *Teaching in Physical Education* (Champaign, Illinois: Human Kinetics Publishers, 1983), pp. 211–23.
15. Ibid, p. 221.
16. Michael Goldberger and Philip Gerney, "The Effects of Direct Teaching Styles on Motor Skill Acquisition of Fifth Grade Children," *Research Quarterly for Exercise and Sport* 57 (September 1985), pp. 215–19.
17. David Griffey, "Hunting the Elusive ATI: How Pupil Aptitudes Mediate Instruction in the Gymnasium," in Thomas J. Templin and Janice K. Olson, eds. *Teaching in Physical Education* (Champaign, Illinois: Human Kinetics Publishers, 1983), pp. 265–76.
18. L. J. Cronbach and R. E. Snow, *Aptitudes and Instructional Methods: A Handbook for Research on Interactions* (New York: John Wiley & Sons, 1977).
19. Wallace B. Salter and George Graham, "The Effects of Three Disparate Instructional Approaches on Skill Attempts and Student Learning in an Experimental Teaching Unit," *Journal of Teaching in Physical Education* 4 (April 1985), pp. 212–18.
20. Frank E. Pettigrew and Michael Heikkinen, "Increased Psychomotor Skill through Eclectic Teaching," *The Physical Educator* 42 (Fall 1985), pp. 140–46.
21. Goldberger, "Effective Learning through a Spectrum of Teaching Styles," p. 17.
22. Dick Hurwitz, "A Model for the Structure of Instructional Strategies," *Journal of Teaching in Physical Education* 4 (April 1985), pp. 190–201.
23. Dorothy Zakrajsek and Lois A. Carnes, *Individualizing Physical Education: Criterion Materials,* 2d ed. (Champaign, Illinois: Human Kinetics Publishers, 1986), p. 33.
24. Ibid.
25. Benjamin S. Bloom, *Human Characteristics and School Learning* (New York: McGraw-Hill Book Company, 1976).
26. K. P. Torshen, *The Mastery Approach to Competency Based Education* (New York: Academic Press, 1977).
27. James H. Block, "Mastery Learning in the Classroom: An Over-view on Recent Research," in James Block, ed. *Schools, Society and Mastery Learning* (New York: Holt, Rinehart and Winston, 1974).
28. James H. Block and R. B. Burns, "Mastery Learning," in L. S. Shulman, ed. *Review of Research in Education* (Itasca, Illinois: F. E. Peacock Publishers, 1977); Bloom, *Human Characteristics and School Learning* K. Cotton and W. G. Savard, "Mastery Learning, Topic Summary Report," ERIC Document Reproduction Service, no. ED 218 279 (June 1982); D. W. Ryan and M. Schmidt, *Mastery Learning: Theory, Research and Implementation* (Available from Ontario Department of Education, Toronto, 1979); and Torshen, *The Mastery Approach to Competency Based Education.*
29. Anthony A. Annarino, "Accountability—An Instructional Model for Secondary Physical Education," *Journal of Physical Education and Recreation* 52 (March 1981), pp. 55–56.
30. Helen J. Heitmann and Marian E. Kneer, *Physical Education Instructional Techniques: An Individualized Humanistic Approach* (Englewood Cliffs, New Jersey: Prentice-Hall, 1976).
31. Madge Ashy and Amelia M. Lee, "Effects of a Mastery Learning Strategy on Throwing Accuracy and Technique," Paper presented at the AAHPERD National Convention, Anaheim, March–April, 1984.

32. J. P. Chambless, E. R. Anderson, and J. H. Poole, *Mastery Learning of Stunts and Tumbling Activities for Mentally Retarded* (Oxford: Mississippi University, North Mississippi Retardation Center, 1980).

33. Connie L. Blakemore, "The Effects and Implications of Teaching Psychomotor Skills Using Mastery Learning Techniques," Paper presented at the International Conference on Research in Teacher Education and Teaching in Physical Education, University of British Columbia, May 30–June 1, 1986.

34. Joyce K. Espiritu and Thomas J. Loughrey, "The Learning Center Approach to Physical Education Instruction," *The Physical Educator* 48 (Fall 1985), pp. 121–27.

35. Melinda Krumm, "Tennis, Despite Weather and Site Restrictions," in Ronald P. Carlson, ed. *Ideas II: A Sharing of Teaching Practices by Secondary School Physical Education Practitioners* (Reston, Virginia: American Alliance for Health, Physical Education, Recreation and Dance 1984), pp. 38–39; and Linda S. Fairman and David Nitchman, "A Bowling Program in the Gymnasium," in Ronald P. Carlson, ed. *Ideas II: A Sharing of Teaching Practices by Secondary School Physical Education Practitioners* (Reston, Virginia: American Alliance for Health, Physical Education, Recreation and Dance, 1984), pp. 66–68.

36. Jonathan E. Nelson, "Teaching Cross-Country Skiing," *Journal of Physical Education, Recreation and Dance* 55 (March 1984), pp. 58–64.

37. Kathryn Wright and Joy Walker, "Rainy Day Golf," *Journal of Health, Physical Education and Recreation* 40 (November–December 1969), p. 83.

38. Charles R. Hobbs, *The Power of Teaching with New Techniques* (Salt Lake City, Utah: Deseret Book Company, 1972), p. 117.

39. Robert M. Gagné and Leslie J. Briggs, *Principles of Instructional Design* (New York: Holt, Rinehart and Winston, 1974), p. 64.

40. Merrill Harmin and Sidney B. Simon, "How to Help Students Learn to Think . . . About Themselves," *The High School Journal* (March 1972), pp. 256–64.

41. Ibid.

42. Jack Canfield and Harold C. Wells, *100 Ways to Enhance Self-concept in the Classroom* (Englewood Cliffs, New Jersey: Prentice-Hall, 1976), p. 187.

43. Ibid., p. 72.

44. Ibid., pp. 188–89.

45. Hawley, *Human Values in the Classroom*, p. 16.

46. Ibid., pp. 60–61.

Planning, Implementing, and Evaluating the Instructional Program

There once was a teacher
Whose principal feature
Was hidden in quite an odd way.
    Students by millions
    Or possibly zillions
    Surrounded him all of the day.

When finally seen
By his scholarly dean
And asked how he managed the deed,
    He lifted three fingers
    And said, ''All you swingers
    Need only to follow my lead.

''To rise from a zero
To Big Campus Hero,
To answer these questions you'll strive:
    Where am I going,
    How shall I get there, and
    How will I know I've arrived?''[1]

This poem emphasizes the importance of planning the instructional program. This text attempts to help teachers make meaningful decisions in the quest for productive student learning. As pointed out by Hunter[2] these decisions are aimed at the content, student, and teacher. Content decisions are discussed in units 3 and 5. Student decisions are discussed in units 2 and 3. The discussion of teacher decisions begun in unit 3 will be completed in this unit. Hunter stated, ''When those professional decisions are made on the basis of sound psychological theory and if those decisions also reflect the teacher's sensitivity to the student and to the situation, learning will be increased.''[3]

A critical factor in any decision made by the teacher is that teacher's attitude. A teacher with a deep sense of commitment to the profession and the goals of physical education will carry that commitment into the decision-making process. The result will be an atmosphere of learning established by an enthusiastic teacher. Students will pick up this enthusiasm and reflect it in the activities they perform both at school and away. A teacher who does not have a real excitement and zeal for the art of teaching physical education will have difficulty motivating students to perform physical activities no matter what decisions are made.

The model for designing instructional programs introduced in unit 3, and shown again in unit figure 4.1, illustrates that the content of any instructional program is determined by the learning environment and the planned learning experiences.

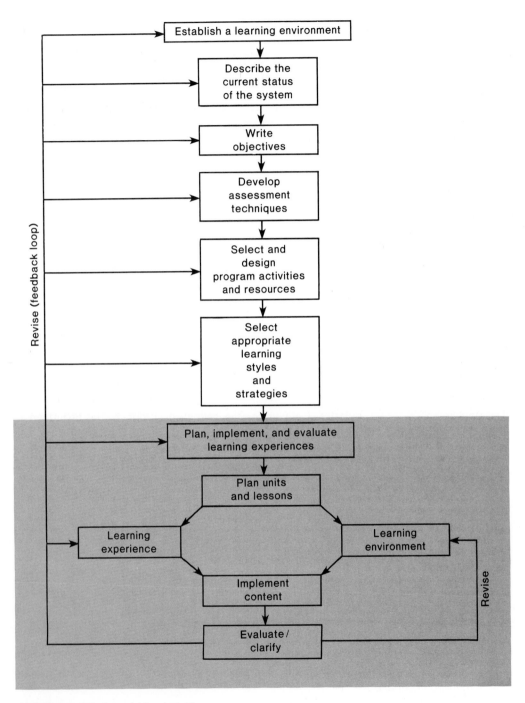

Unit Figure 4.1 A model for designing
instructional programs.

Once teachers have established the learning environment, they are ready to plan the instructional process for a specific group of students. This is accomplished through unit and lesson planning. Chapter 11 guides the teacher through this planning phase. Unit and lesson planning combines two elements of effective instruction—the educational environment and the subject matter—to best meet the needs of the learners.

Teachers must remember that effective planning also involves modification of the existing plan. Teachers may return to the same stage many times before the planning phase has been completed. Teachers must continually move back and forth among the stages of the model to include items that were inadvertently omitted or change items that are later considered to be inappropriate. A continual check is necessary to make sure the elements of the system fit together properly.[4] Teachers must also be open to change during the implementation stage. Anderson pointed out that if teachers are to continue to develop competence in teaching, they must develop skill in the analysis of teaching.[5]

Planning also involves decisions concerning classroom management. Chapter 12 discusses the organization and management of the instructional environment for effective learning. The areas of legal liability, departmental policies and procedures, class management techniques, and record keeping will be presented. Effective classroom management is the ability to organize the components of the classroom so that effective instruction occurs. Teachers must make sound decisions about the management of the classroom environment based not only on experience but also on research. Research shows that effective teachers manage classes in ways that increase academic learning time. They minimize time spent on nonacademic tasks, transitions between activities, and dealing with disruptions.

Kounin[6] identified several principles of effective management that correlated significantly with high task involvement and low deviancy of students. These were (1) with-it-ness and overlapping, (2) smoothness and momentum, (3) group alertness and accountability, and (4) challenge and variety. With-it-ness was defined as teachers' communicating to students by their actions that they know what is going on in the classroom. Overlapping refers to the ability of a teacher to attend to two activities simultaneously without neglecting one or the other. Smoothness and momentum involve the ability to move students quickly and smoothly from one activity to another at a good pace, without losing the focus on learning. Group alertness is created by using techniques that keep students actively participating in the content of the lesson. Accountability is created when students feel that they are held accountable for their time in class. The effectiveness of group alertness and accountability has *not* been well supported in the literature.[7]

Soar and Soar[8] reviewed four studies on classroom management and concluded that effective teachers select and direct learning tasks while, at the same time, allowing limited student freedom to move about, gather into subgroups, and socialize. They concluded that the most effective mixture of structure and freedom depends on the complexity of the learning tasks (i.e., the more complex the tasks, the more freedom needed).

Gage[9] emphasized the importance of teachers having a system of rules to minimize direction giving and class organization, while providing maximum drill and feedback. Teachers should select a variety of challenging learning activities, monitor student work closely, and ensure that students have an equal opportunity to respond.

Sanford and Evertson[10] studied the management skills of junior high school teachers and concluded that effective managers spent the first day discussing class rules and procedures and assigned some work the first day in which students could experience initial success. They devoted some time each day to presenting, reviewing, and discussing rules and acted consistently to stop off-task behavior. Good teachers understood students' backgrounds, abilities, interests, and attention spans; provided appropriate assignments for student success; and used logical, step-by-step instructions at an appropriate vocabulary level. They established accountability by monitoring work and providing appropriate feedback.

Teachers who operate a structured teaching-learning environment are more effective. In addition, Brophy indicated that the most effective teachers select material at the appropriate level of difficulty for their students and move the students through the material at a rapid pace while maintaining a very high success rate.[11] Oxendine noted that physical education teachers probably spend too much time reviewing skills that have already been learned.[12] On the other hand, Earls cautioned against leaping from simple drills to complex games.[13]

The key to effective classroom management appears to be the ability to minimize off-task and deviant behaviors through presenting appropriate learning activities, moving at a good pace, monitoring student responses, and providing instruction and practice in classroom procedures and routines.

Chapter 13 deals with one of the major problems of public school teachers—class control or discipline. The chapter reviews various discipline techniques and tells how to select an appropriate approach for a given situation.

Teachers who follow the model for designing instructional programs (see unit figure 4.1) soon realize that "teaching is, after all, as much science as it is magic."[14] Skill in making wise decisions based on the model increases with experience and is validated by one's creativity or "spark of magic."

Teachers should discuss the ideas shared in this unit with others and expand or modify ideas to fit their own situations. Research shows that students benefit academically when their teachers share ideas, cooperate in activities, and assist one another's intellectual growth.[15] Research also points out that teachers welcome professional suggestions about improving their work, but they rarely receive them.[16]

One of the purposes of an instructional model is to provide a structure for reviewing and analyzing instruction so that it can be improved. Once the program has been implemented, an evaluation should be conducted to determine weaknesses in each of the preceding levels of the model. Chapter 14 delineates a number of ways in which teachers can evaluate their effectiveness in providing instruction. Teacher evaluation will be the main focus of this chapter. (Chapter 18 details the methods of program evaluation.) Feedback loops indicate revisions that might need to be made in the various steps of the model following the evaluation process.

References

1. Robert F. Mager, *Developing Attitude Toward Learning* (Belmont, California: Fearon Publishers, 1969), p. vii.
2. Madeline Hunter, *Mastery Teaching* (El Segundo, California: TIP Publications, 1982), p. 3.
3. Ibid.
4. Robert H. Davis, Lawrence T. Alexander, and Stephen L. Yelon, *Learning System Design: An Approach to the Improvement of Instruction* (New York: McGraw-Hill Book Company, 1974), p. 313.
5. William G. Anderson, *Analysis of Teaching Physical Education* (St. Louis: C. V. Mosby Company, 1980), p. 2.

6. Jacob S. Kounin, *Discipline and Group Management in Classrooms* (Huntington, New York: Robert E. Krieger Publishing Company, 1977).
7. Jere E. Brophy, "Teacher Behavior and Its Effect," *Journal of Educational Psychology* 71 (1979), pp. 77–82.
8. Robert S. Soar and Ruth M. Soar, "Emotional Climate and Management," in Penelope L. Peterson and Herbert J. Walbert, eds. *Research on Teaching: Concepts, Findings, and Implications* (Berkeley, California: McCutchan Publishing Corporation, 1979), pp. 97–119.
9. N. L. Gage, "The Yield of Research on Teaching," *Phi Delta Kappan* (November 1978), pp. 229–35.
10. Julie P. Sanford and Carolyn M. Evertson, "Classroom Management in a Low SES Junior High: Three Case Studies," *Journal of Teacher Education* 32 (January–February 1981), pp. 34–38.
11. Jere Brophy, "Successful Teaching Strategies for the Inner-City Child," *Phi Delta Kappan* 63 (April 1982), pp. 527–30.
12. Joseph B. Oxendine, *Psychology of Motor Learning,* 2d ed. (Englewood Cliffs, New Jersey: Prentice-Hall, 1984), p. 179.
13. Neal F. Earls, "Research on the Immediate Effects of Instructional Variables," in Thomas J. Templin and Janice K. Olson, eds. *Teaching in Physical Education* (Champaign, Illinois: Human Kinetics Publishers, 1983), p. 261.
14. Leonard O. Pellicer, "Effective Teaching: Science or Magic?" *Clearing House* 58 (October 1984), p. 56.
15. U.S. Department of Education, *What Works: Research About Teaching and Learning* (Washington, D.C.: U.S. Department of Education, 1986), p. 51.
16. Ibid., p. 52.

11

Putting It All Together—Unit and Lesson Planning

Study Stimulators

1. Why is it important for teachers to write unit plans and daily lesson plans? How detailed should they be?
2. What components are included in a unit plan?
3. What components are included in a daily lesson plan that are not found in a unit plan? How should a daily lesson plan be written?
4. Define episode.

"Teaching is an act, and teachers are actors."[1] If one accepts this premise, then it follows that teachers need a script. The script teachers use in their daily performance is an instructional plan, and the better the script, the better the performance. As Siedentop stated, "Planning is crucial to effective teaching."[2] Although effective planning does not guarantee a flawless show, the chances for success are much greater when the teacher has adequately prepared to teach a lesson.

Once the yearly curriculum has been designed, as described in unit 5, the teacher must then follow up with two kinds of instructional plans—unit plans and daily lesson plans. Although both of these phases of planning serve a different function, they are mutually interdependent. Basically, these plans include the answers to three questions expressed by Mager as follows: (1) where am I going?, (2) how will I get there?, and (3) how will I know I've arrived?[3]

Where am I going? The plan should specify the performance objectives of the lesson or unit in the cognitive, psychomotor, and affective domains.

How will I get there? The plan should delineate the learning experiences that will be used to help students meet the objectives specified.

How will I know I've arrived? Evaluation techniques must be included that will help the teacher determine whether the students have achieved the objectives.

How to Write a Unit Plan

The teaching unit directs the teacher in providing purposeful chunks of learning for students. It "centers the work of the class around meaningful patterns and focuses the work of different days on a central theme until some degree of unified learning is attained."[4] The amount of time spent on the unit and on various aspects of the unit should be based on curricular objectives, as well as on the previous experience and expertise of the students. Teachers should take advantage of the possibilities of transfer from previous units and teach units concurrently that provide transfer. Sufficient time should be provided in some units so that students can learn the necessary skills to achieve high levels of performance and retention. Other units may be taught to introduce students to various skills and not be designed for all students to attain high levels of performance. The teacher must decide the teaching emphasis of each unit so that low levels of student proficiency in many skills is not the result at the end of the school year.

The teacher who fails to plan, plans to fail.

Before a unit plan can be devised and Mager's questions can be answered, certain preliminary considerations need to be identified. The following considerations must be listed on the unit plan form shown in figure 11.1.

1. An identification of subject matter and teaching time.
2. An identification of student characteristics. Special considerations such as physical limitations, foreign-speaking students, and low-ability students may need to be identified through surveys, school guidance materials, or informal assessment.
3. An identification of skills and concepts to be taught.
4. An identification of instructional materials and preparations.
5. An identification of preassessment techniques, if any. Interests and needs may need to be determined through surveys or informal assessment (review chapter 8).

Where Am I Going?
Before any learning experiences are planned, performance objectives should be formulated. Write down what the student is expected to *do* at the completion of the unit. Objectives should be included for the psychomotor, cognitive, and affective domains. Objectives might include the following outcomes:

1. Skills: These are psychomotor skills that the student will be able to do:
   a. Shoot three types of shots
   b. Bat and bunt successfully
   c. Bowl a score of 120
   d. Play safely
   e. Officiate a game (both psychomotor and cognitive)
   f. Achieve or maintain "good or excellent" on the 1.5-mile run

Unit Plan

Preliminary Considerations

Unit: Beginning Volleyball   Number of Days: 20

Class: Size 40   Grade 7th   (Boys ____   Girls ____   Coed __X__)   Skill Level: Beg

Special Considerations: None

Skills/Principles to be taught: Forearm pass, overhand volley, underhand serve, spike, volleyball rules, strategy.

Facilities needed: Gym, walls

Equipment needed: 40 volleyballs, tape for wall markers, volleyball nets

Media or other materials needed: Projector, film

Preassessment: The students will be asked about their previous experience in volleyball. After each skill is demonstrated, the teacher will have the students practice and make an assessment of the skill level of the class and how fast to move to the next skill.

Objectives

Psychomotor performance objectives   *Evaluation*

The student will:

1. Hit 6 consecutive legal hits alternating the overhead pass and the forearm pass.   Skills test
2. Serve 5 legal overhead serves anywhere in the court area.   Skills test
3. Execute the skills (set, bump, serve, hit) correctly and play with proper court positions during a game.   Checklist

Cognitive performance objectives   *Contract Evaluation*

1. Pass a written test with 50 percent or better on the playing skills and strategy that are discussed.   Written test

Affective performance objectives   *Evaluation*

1. Have a desire to become a more skilled volleyball player.   Record of games played in intramurals and freetime games.

Day-by-Day Decisions

Day (When)	Content (What)	Learning Activities (How)	Evaluation
1	Forearm pass	Explanation, drills, film	Pretest
2	Forearm pass	Drills	Partner observation
3	Overhand pass	Explanation, drills, film	Pretest
4	Overhand pass	Drills	Partner observation
5	Underhand serve	Explanation, drills, film	Pretest
1	Underhand serve	Drills, game	Partner observation
2	Spike	Explanation, drills	Pretest
3	Written test	Written test	Test results
4	4–2 offense	Explanation, drills	Successful performance in a game
5	Defense	Explanation, drills	Successful performance in a game

Figure 11.1 An example of a unit plan.

1	Offense, defense	Drills, games	Successful performance in a game
2	Play game	10 min. games/rotate	Teacher observation
3	Play game	Rotate teams	Teacher observation
4	Summative skills test	Skills test	Test results
5	Summative skills test/game	Skills test	Test results

1	Tournament and skill execution in game	Completed games/checklist
2	Tournament and skill execution in game	Completed games/checklist
3	Tournament and skill execution in game	Completed games/checklist
4	Tournament and skill execution in game	Completed games/checklist
5	Tournament and skill execution in game	Completed games/checklist

Motivational techniques

Tournament the last week of the unit. Winner receives written certificate. All other teams receive participation certificate. Players will be selected as tournament Most Valuable Player and Most Inspirational Player by students in the class.

Grading policies

Physical fitness	40 pts	40 pts
Physical skill	20 pts/test	60 pts
Knowledge	50 pts	50 pts
		150 pts

Grading breakdown

$$150 - 128 = A\ 85\%$$
$$127 - 105 = B\ 70\%$$
$$104 - 75 = C\ 50\%$$
$$74 - 53 = D\ 35\%$$
$$\text{Below } 53 = F$$

Skills test

1. Students will stand in a 3' × 3' area and alternately hit legal overhead and forearm passes as many times consecutively as they can. No time limit.
2. Students will serve 10 times legally into the court.

Figure 11.1 *(continued)*

Grading breakdown for skills tests

Skills tests 1 & 2

			Grade from Game Checklist		
Score of	10 =	20 pts	A	=	20 pts
	9 =	18 pts	A−	=	18 pts
	8 =	16 pts	B+	=	16 pts
	7 =	14 pts	B	=	14 pts
	6 =	12 pts	B−	=	12 pts
	5 =	10 pts	C+	=	10 pts
	4 =	8 pts	C	=	8 pts
	3 =	6 pts	C−	=	6 pts
	2 =	4 pts	D+	=	4 pts
	1 =	2 pts	D	=	2 pts

Physical fitness contract

Completed	= 40 pts
Almost complete	= 30 pts
Some completed	= 20 pts

25 pts = Tournament MVP (Most Valuable Player)
25 pts = Most Inspirational Player (team player, tries hard, encouragement, leadership)

Figure 11.1 *(continued)*

2. Knowledge: These are cognitive skills or ideas that the student will be able to use in some way:
   a. Select the proper golf club for each distance
   b. Demonstrate a knowledge of the rules
   c. Use correct strategy in game play
   d. Describe a fitness program for a given situation
   e. Keep a log of his or her strength training program
3. Attitudes, appreciations, and social skills: These are affective skills that will be realized:
   a. Demonstrate sportsmanship in game play
   b. Act as a squad or other leader when requested
   c. Express a joyful feeling about participating in physical education activities

Preassessment techniques, if appropriate, should be included and specified for each of the objectives—cognitive, psychomotor, and affective. Such screening devices might include questioning, skills tests, written tests, interest inventories, or goal-setting activities.

Once the objectives have been stated, unit grading policies can be formulated. Grading and reporting procedures should include what to grade, the emphasis on each area, and the process (specific percentage or points) to be used. Review chapter 8 to determine how to grade students in the unit of instruction.

How Will I Get There?

Certain preliminary considerations must be determined before a unit plan can be formulated and desired learning outcomes achieved. Such considerations include an appropriate facility, adequate equipment, length of the unit, and qualified faculty. Class size may have an effect on these factors. Weather may determine the facility and the dress requirements.

When preliminary considerations for the unit have been completed, the teacher is ready to make day-by-day decisions. Remember that unit plans are skeleton plans. Such plans simply list a meaningful progression of learning experiences that will be taught in a unit, stating when, what, and how. Organizational strategies and specifics for skill analysis are included later in the daily lesson plans.

The teacher might want to include specific activities in the plan to introduce the unit. These might consist of a videotape replay or film, a demonstration by several advanced players, results of recent college or professional competition, highlights of well-known performers, or playing the game the way it was in years past.

A daily progression of content (what and when) must be planned that is appropriate and logical. Such a progression provides for the following:

1. Progression from simple to complex
2. Maximum student participation
3. Successful learning
4. Safety
5. Motivation
6. Pacing of instruction commensurate with individual skill levels

Learning activities (how), which translate content into meaningful learning experiences for students, can now be added to the unit plan beside the appropriate daily content. Learning activities should be selected in terms of

1. Student needs and learning characteristics
2. Subject matter to be taught
3. Teacher characteristics
4. Learning environment—facilities, equipment, weather
5. Principles of learning
6. Teaching styles
7. Variety of learning activities

Examples of learning activities include the following:

1. Psychomotor
   a. Demonstration with cues
   b. Skills check-off chart
   c. Drills
   d. Games
   e. Practice with feedback
2. Cognitive
   a. Brief explanation
   b. Visual aid
   c. Question-answer session
   d. Study sheet
   e. Programmed unit
   f. Quiz

3. Affective
    a. Role play
    b. Brainstorming
    c. Case study
    d. Questionnaire

A variety of teaching and learning activities should be included to keep students involved and meet individual needs. (Review unit 2 and chapters 9 and 10 for additional learning activities that are appropriate.) Teachers should have a contingency plan to use for inclement weather (a rainy-day plan) or an emergency situation. This plan should be formulated as part of the unit plan.

Units are often terminated with formal culminating activities such as tournaments, field trips, interclass games, or faculty-student activities. When students know from the onset of the unit what these activities will be, motivation is often enhanced.

How Will I Know I've Arrived?

After planning the teaching and learning activities, the teacher is ready to write down the techniques to be used, specifying when the performance objectives have been achieved. Provision should also be made for evaluating the unit and the teacher (see chapter 14). The following examples of evaluation techniques may be used and might be based on norm-referenced or criterion-referenced standards:

1. Skills tests: on skills such as baserunning, batting, throwing, and fielding
2. Teacher observation: of form, use of strategy, officiating, playing ability
3. Checklist or rating sheet: in such activities as swimming or gymnastics
4. Game scores: in individual sports, such as bowling, archery, badminton
5. Times: in activities such as track or fitness testing
6. Written test: on rules and strategy
7. Incidence chart: for recording the number of correct spikes, free shots made, or hits landing out of bounds
8. Tournament results
9. Accumulative record: of miles run or swum in a "stay fit" program
10. Attitude or effort inventory, questionnaire, or interview

Motivational techniques that will enhance the day-by-day learning experience should be identified at this stage of unit planning. Such techniques might be intrinsic or extrinsic. The following examples list the end result of both types of techniques:

Intrinsic:

1. Success
2. Challenge
3. Self-confidence
4. Self-fulfillment

Extrinsic:

1. Competition
2. Ribbons for winners
3. Unique drills
4. Unusual warm-ups
5. Challenging learning strategy

(See chapters 9 and 10 for specific ideas.)

Once the unit plan has been completed, the teacher should finalize preparations for the learning experiences. Teaching stations such as the gym, field, classroom, or community facility need to be reserved and scheduled. Films should be ordered and guest speakers secured. Handouts and examinations may be prepared. With all of this preparation completed, the teacher should feel secure about the unit of instruction that will be presented to students.

The Resource Unit

Resource units are master plans to which teachers refer when developing units for their specific classes. They are usually formulated by state departments of education or district committees and are often found in curriculum guides. They contain much more material and information than would be used in a single unit of instruction. The resources they include give teachers many ideas from which to make choices for their own unit plans. Resource units generally contain the following:

1. Title page and introduction
2. Table of contents
3. Specific performance objectives
4. Details to consider before teaching
5. Preassessment techniques
6. Introductory activities
7. Subject matter content
8. Teaching and learning activities
9. Culminating activities
10. Evaluation techniques and grading
11. Resources
12. Index (if needed)

How to Write a Daily Lesson Plan

A daily lesson plan is written for each specific day of a unit plan. It is an expanded version of a unit plan, providing a detailed analysis of a particular activity described in the unit plan.[5] Each daily lesson plan fits into a scheme derived from the unit plan and is based on unit objectives, but it provides "for the realities of day-to-day teaching."[6] As shown in figure 11.2, teacher considerations and performance objectives, along with their evaluation techniques, are listed. A detailed analysis of the teaching experience is the main thrust of the daily lesson plan. This analysis should provide a maximum of student activity through efficient use of facilities, equipment, and time to provide guided practice so the learner can achieve and retain what is being taught.

Lesson Plan

Activity Softball-batting   Name _____

Preassessment In plan (Pepper-Self Scoring)   Date _____

Objectives	*Evaluation of Objectives*	Equipment needed: All softballs, gloves, eight tees, eight bases, eight to sixteen bats
1. Students will use correct batting form to hit 3 out of 5 balls	1. Results	Play space needed: Field--two diamonds
2. Students will develop cooperative group atmosphere	2. Teacher observation	Special markings: Bases
		Media to be used: None

Sources of Information: Dynamic PE Curriculum and Instruction for Secondary School Students, Pangrazi and Darst
Handout--"Rules for One-Swing Softball"

Time	Teaching and Learning Experiences	Teacher and Student Class Organization	Skill Analysis-- Description of Skills and Activities	Teaching Cues
5 minutes	I. *Warm-ups*	Before class-- throwing and catching X----------X X----------X X----------X X----------X		Safety, Motiva- tion, and Indi- vidual Differences, etc. Adequate space between groups All throwing north and south

Figure 11.2 An example of a lesson plan.

Time	Activity	Cues
No time	**II. Roll call** Student assistant marks each student as they enter the field.	
2 to 3 minutes	**III. Batting with cues** Demonstration	**Batting** A. Grip
	sitting—squad order X X X X X X X X X X X X T X X X X X X X X X X X X	1. Right hand above and close to left, 2 to 3 inches from end of bat. 1. Firm but not tense grip. Facing away from sun or other distractions.
		2. Trademark up—even with "v's." 2. Check trademark.
		B. Stance
		1. Body and knees easy, feet apart comfortably, left shoulder to pitcher. 1. Assume a natural position.
		2. Right foot opposite the back corner of the plate. 2. Elbows away from body.
		C. Contact
		1. Elbows away from body, wrist cocked. 1. Keep eye on ball.
		2. Bat is back as far as left arm can reach easily across chest. 2. Swing level.
		3. Step simultaneously with left foot. 3. Follow through. 4. Step and swing.

10 minutes	IV. *Pepper (drill)*	8 Groups: rotate after every 5 hits.
		
		A. With tee.
		
		X[B]
		[C]X Tee------X [P]
		
		B. Without tee as students show proficiency.
		
		       X
		X[B]------X
		       X
		
		C. Work-up game on nearby field as they reach objective. Those still practicing drill combine groups.
			See above.
			
			Meet the ball. Guide it to a teammate.
				Spaced far enough to avoid collisions. But in same direction.
				Gloves for retrievers.
				Keep eye on ball.
				
				Success.
				Individual help. Play game when successful.

15 minutes	V. *Play "One-Swing Softball"*	Teams 1 and 2 play on Diamond 1. Teams 3 and 4 play on Diamond 2.	Rules on handout (attached). Use "Teamwork."	No bat throwing. Do not block baseline. Call for fly balls. No sliding. Choose best pitcher to pitch for you. Competition, fun, different.

Culminating Activities (Lesson Conclusion):
Review teaching cues
Report scores
Gather equipment

Figure 11.2 *(continued)*

A daily lesson plan must be easy to follow and understand because it is often referred to by teachers during a class. After the completion of a lesson, it should be revised immediately, if found to be unsatisfactory in any area, and filed for future reference.

Where Am I Going?

The daily lesson plan contains a more detailed version of unit performance objectives that once again answer Mager's question of "where am I going?" The teacher should state what the students will be able *to do* after instruction. Incorporating one or two objectives that can be accomplished in a class period is better than including many objectives that can only be introduced. Although all domains will be represented in unit objectives, daily lesson plans may focus on only one.

The following examples of behavioral objectives might be included in a daily lesson plan:

1. Hit correctly three out of five balls
2. Use correct rules during tournament play
3. Perform one lay-up with correct form as specified
4. Refrain from arguing with the official

Preassessment techniques can be included in a daily lesson plan so that the teacher will know if students have already achieved the objective or are ready to begin learning what has been planned. The following examples of preassessment techniques may be used by the teacher:

1. Pretest—A written or skills test is given before instruction
2. Observation—Students are observed performing the desired behavior
3. Questioning—Students are asked about their experience or if they can perform a skill

Preassessment techniques may take an entire class period with the results being analyzed and used as the basis of a later daily lesson plan. They may also be incorporated as part of a single daily plan. In this case, the teacher needs to include several choices of activities in the plan to be selected based on the results of the preassessment. For example, if the teacher finds out from a pretest that swimming students will not put their faces in the water, instructional strategies must begin with activities in which students learn to function with water covering their faces. On the other hand, if students are already comfortable in doing this, instruction could begin with breathing drills for the front crawl. Both options would be included in the lesson plan with the appropriate one being selected after the results of the pretest.

How Will I Get There?

The meat of the daily lesson methodically progresses through the learning experiences of one class period in the order they will be taught. This part of the plan may be outlined but should be detailed enough that a substitute teacher could teach the lesson. Each teaching-learning experience in the plan should be handled as an *episode*. Anyone reading the plan should be able to read directly across the plan to include all components of each episode. The following components should be included and are graphically pointed out in figure 11.2:

1. Time allotment: Write down the *approximate* amount of time to be spent on each teaching or learning activity. Remember to plan time for a maximum amount of activity. Students learn by doing not by being told. For example:
    a. 8:05–8:07—Roll call
       8:07–8:15—Warm-ups
           or
    b. Two minutes—Roll call
       Eight minutes—Warm-ups
       Three minutes—Demonstration
2. Teaching and learning activities: Briefly state a description of what will be taught in each episode. For example:
    a. Warm-ups
    b. Skill or activity being taught (e.g., forehand stroke, 2–1–2 zone defense)
    c. Drill
    d. Game
    e. Mimetic drill (pantomime)
    f. Practice with feedback
    g. Skills test
    h. Written test
    i. Check-off chart
3. Class organization: Diagram or explain each separate pattern of organization that will be used during the period. Use Xs for students, T for teacher. For example:

a.
```
        x  x
     x        x
     x    T    x
```

b.
```
     x   x   x   x
     x   x   x   x
     x   x   x   x
     x   x   x   x

         T
```

c.
```
┌─────────┬─────────┬─────────┐
│ x  x  x │ x  x  x │ x  x  x │
│ x  x  x │ x  x  x │ x  x  x │
│  ~~~~   │  ~~~~   │  ~~~~   │
│ x  x  x │ x  x  x │ x  x  x │
│ x  x  x │ x  x  x │ x  x  x │
└─────────┴─────────┴─────────┘
```

Tell how the class will be moved from each formation shown into the one following (transitions). For example:

a.
```
x   x   x   x      Squad 1 go to
                      court 1,
  x   x   x   x    Squad 2 go to
                      court 2,
  x   x   x   x       etc.
  x   x   x   x
  1   2   3   4
```

b.
```
xxxxxxxxxxxxxxxxx   one's stay
1234 1234 1234 1234   two's take five steps



                    three's take ten steps



                    four's take fifteen steps
```

4. Skill analysis: Describe a complete analysis of the skill or activity to be taught. Remember to describe these in enough detail so that a substitute teacher will feel confident teaching. The components can be written down in outline form to conserve space. For example:
   a. Forehand drive
      1) Starting position
         Face net
         Racquet in front of body
         Racquet head up
      2) Backswing
         Racquet back
         Pivot
         Shoulder to net
      3) Contact
         Eyes on ball
         Transfer weight to forward foot
         Contact ball even with body
         Swing, do not hit
         Keep ball on racquet as long as possible
      4) Follow-through
         Face net
         Weight forward
         Racquet reaches in direction of ball

5. Teaching cues: Write a brief cue (one to four words) for each skill or activity that expresses what the performer should do. Limit the cues to three or four per skill. For example:
   a. Overhead pass—volleyball
      1) Look through the triangle
      2) Get under the ball
      3) Extend
   b. Badminton—overhead clear
      1) Scratch your back
      2) Reach for the birdie
      3) Make it whistle
   c. Swimming—breast stroke
      1) Pull
      2) Kick
      3) Glide

   Cues may be visual, verbal, or kinesthetic. For example:
   a. Moving a student's arms in front crawl motion
   b. Placing a hand on the student's string hand to prevent jerking to the side in archery
   c. Visual diagram of how to change lanes when league bowling
   d. Visual cues for footwork drill in badminton

6. Safety, motivation, and individual differences
   a. Safety: Write in appropriate safety provisions. For example:
      1) Safe spacing
      2) Rules enforced
      3) Surfaces free from obstacles, such as around walls that might be run into or balls, pinnies, vests, or other objects on the floor that might be stepped on
      4) Glasses guards
      5) No jewelry, long nails
      6) Shoelaces tied, shoes on
      7) Equipment in good repair and used properly
   b. Motivation techniques: Write down appropriate motivation techniques. For example:
      1) Fun! (How will this be promoted?)
      2) Competition
      3) Grades—sometimes
      4) Written or skills tests—sometimes
      5) Success! (How will this be ensured?)
      6) Extrinsic rewards—treats, ribbons
      7) Desire for activity
      8) Playing the game (not drills, but the real thing)

The teacher may want to think of himself or herself as one of the students and write those items that would make the teacher want to participate in the learning activities if not required to do so.

c. Individual differences: Write in how individual differences will be dealt with. For example:
    1) Handedness—Help left-handers with converting bowling leaves because the switch is not exactly opposite to that of right-handers.
    2) Handicaps—In a swimming unit, the blind student will be placed next to the outside wall (to get bearings by feel) when swimming across the pool.
    3) Skill level—Students who can already do the underhand serve will move to court 3 and practice overhead serves.
    4) Social abilities—Try to promote group acceptance of Robbie.
    5) Mental abilities—Assign partners so that Mary can help Dwayne with drills.
7. Culminating activities: The class should be concluded in a meaningful way. Assignments for equipment collection and class dismissal might also be given at this time. Examples of culminating activities include:
  a. Review basic teaching cues, game rules, strategies
  b. Ask questions about activities performed
  c. Collect scores
  d. Highlight good play or performance
  e. Make assignments for participation outside class

How Will I Know I've Arrived?

Evaluation of performance objectives determines if the teacher has accomplished what he or she set out to do. Techniques for accomplishing this must be incorporated in the plan at the time objectives are written or at the conclusion of fashioning the learning experience. The teacher should write how he or she will know when the behavior specified in the objective has been achieved. If more than one objective has been included, more than one evaluation technique will need to be included. For example:

1. Skills test—The student will hit eight out of ten serves into the back of the court as scored by a partner.
2. Teacher observation—The teacher will evaluate each student on lay-up form using a criteria checklist.
3. Game scores—The game scores will indicate a knowledge of how to pick up leaves in bowling.
4. Written test—A written test will indicate knowledge gained by the student.
5. Check-off chart—A check-off chart will be used to record negative comments to officials.

Once the class period has been planned, several final steps are included in the preparation of a daily lesson plan. First, write in the equipment needed for that day. Be sure to plan for maximum activity for each student. For example, list:

1. Balls
2. Bats
3. Cones
4. Score sheets

Next, write in the facilities or playing area that will be needed. Make a note of any special markings or preparations that need to be done to facilitate instruction. For example:

1. Three volleyball courts, tape line fifteen feet from net on north side
2. Two basketball courts, no markings
3. Four badminton courts, tape lines at six-inch intervals from short service line back

Finally, write in any media to be used. For example:

1. 8-mm loop film projector, screen, film
2. Magnetic chalkboard, chalk, magnets

The equipment, facilities, and media should have been secured or scheduled after the unit plan was completed. When the daily lesson plan is formulated, the teacher is reminded to double-check the availability of these things and to secure specific items for class.

The daily lesson plan is now complete. One final item should be added to aid the teacher. Write down *sources of information,* listing where the material for this lesson was acquired. For example:

1. Book—Allsen and Harrison, pp. 36–37
2. Handout—"Defensive Strategy: Marking" (in-service training, Sept. 1986)
3. Colleague or teacher—Ms. Jones
4. Resource file—pictures from magazine

If no sources were used or needed, write "previous experience."

With the daily lesson plan completed, the teacher should feel secure and ready to face a class of eager students.

Questions and Suggested Activities
1. Write a unit plan for a selected activity. Include a contingency plan (rainy-day plan).
2. Prepare three daily lesson plans to be used in a formal unit plan (see #1) in which skills are reviewed and taught.
3. You have been charged with neglect because of an accident suffered by one of your students in class. You have been advised to bring relevant unit and lesson plans to the hearing. How might these documents be used in a review of the charges?

Suggested Reading
Ritson, Robert J. "A Lesson Plan Is Like a Menu." *The Physical Educator* 35 (December 1978):208.

References
1. Hal A. Lawson, "Paradigms for Research on Teaching and Teachers," in Thomas J. Templin and Janice K. Olson, eds. *Teaching in Physical Education* (Champaign, Illinois: Human Kinetics Publishers, 1983), p. 345.
2. Daryl Siedentop, Charles Mand, and Andrew Taggart, *Physical Education: Teaching and Curriculum Strategies for Grades 5–12* (Palo Alto, California: Mayfield Publishing Company, 1986), p. 322.
3. Robert F. Mager, *Developing Attitude Toward Learning* (Palo Alto, California: Fearon Publishers, 1968).
4. Kenneth H. Hoover, *The Professional Teacher's Handbook,* 3d ed. (Boston: Allyn & Bacon, Inc., 1982), p. 23.
5. Ibid., p. 26.
6. Siedentop, Mand, and Taggart, *Physical Education,* p. 347.

12

Organization and Management of Instruction

Study Stimulators

1. What is "tort liability"? How can teachers defend themselves in a tort liability case?
2. How can teachers keep from getting sued in the first place?
3. What school and departmental policies and procedures are essential to a smooth operation of the department of physical education? How can these policies be communicated to students and parents?
4. What is classroom management? Why is it essential to good instruction in physical education? What governs the choice of a management technique?
5. What methods can be used to enhance classroom management?
6. Why is record keeping important? What types of records should teachers keep?

Effective physical educators stand out because of their ability to organize and manage the dozens of components that make up an effective learning environment. Effective policies and procedures must be in place on the first day of school so teachers can establish an appropriate learning environment. Teachers determining classroom policies and procedures should know the legal implications affecting their implementation. For this purpose, legal liability in physical education will introduce the chapter. Suggestions for classroom management procedures, along with record-keeping tips to facilitate this process will also be examined in this chapter.

Legal Liability in Physical Education

Physical educators must be ever diligent in maintaining a safe environment for students. Over half of the accidents occurring in the schools occur during supervised physical education activities.[1] A recent survey of lawsuits involving sport or recreation showed that 46 percent of the accidents occurred in an instructional setting, 40 percent occurred in recreational programs, and 14 percent involved team sports. The most commonly named activities in these suits were gymnastics (24 percent), softball/baseball (12 percent), playground activities (12 percent), basketball (7 percent), track and field (6 percent), and exercise and fitness programs (6 percent).[2] Accidents in physical education are usually less severe than those in intramural and athletic activities.[3] However, even one accident involving a loved one is one too many. Through a knowledge of the law, accompanied by intelligent action, many of these accidents and lawsuits could be prevented. As a result of society's reliance on the courts to resolve controversies and the intrusion of the federal government into areas previously considered to be the province of local governments or boards of education, the topic of legal liability has dynamically affected physical education programs.[4]

Liability refers to a legal responsibility that can be enforced by a court of law in a civil action, which is an action involving a relationship between citizens or between citizens and an institution such as a school or district. A basic understanding of the laws governing liability in physical education is essential to the preservation of physical education programs in the schools.

From 1961 to 1970, the number of lawsuits in physical education doubled from those of the previous ten years.[5] Again in the decade of the seventies, the number of reported cases more than doubled.[6] The eighties reflects a continuation of these same escalating trends. The *Sports and the Courts: Physical Education and Sports Law Quarterly* emerged as a publication to inform professionals of actual cases and settlements in the courts. Its pages document an average of twenty cases each issue. The Summer Law and Sports Conference came into being in the early 1980s to prepare physical educators to deal with the issues of legal liability.[7] Settlements now reach millions of dollars, and a single case can wipe out the entire year's budget of a school district.[8] In the light of these facts, some states have now passed legislation limiting awards to the maximum amount of insurance coverage. With this turn of events have come escalating insurance costs with which the schools must also deal. "Many schools report that the price of insurance is increasing to a point that it is becoming prohibitive."[9]

What Happens in a Legal Liability Case?

The parents of a senior high school student filed a one million dollar suit against her physical education teacher and the board of education for injuries the young woman suffered in a physical education class-related accident (in which the student disobeyed the teacher's orders and was jumping on a trampoline between classes). In the suit, the parents complained that she was required to take the class in order to graduate and that reasonable safety precautions were not taken to prevent injury.

In the above incident, the injured girl and her parents were the *plaintiffs*—the person or group initiating the action against another party. The teacher and school board were the *defendants*—the person or group against whom the action is brought. The complaint summarized the reasons why the plaintiff felt she was entitled to compensation for her injury. As the legal process continued, the defendant filed an answer stating why she felt she was not at fault. After a period of time, the case came before the court.

The entire case was based on the assumption that a wrong had been committed resulting in an injury. In this case, the parents charged the teacher with the commission of a tort.

Tort

A *tort* is a civil or legal wrong, an action that results in injury to another person or to that person's reputation or property. A tort can be caused by an act of *omission,* or the failure to perform a legal duty, such as failure to close the outside doors during a fire drill when instructed at an earlier time to do so. A tort can also be caused by intentional interference, or *commission,* such as the following:

1. *Negligence* is the failure to act as a reasonably prudent person would act under the same circumstances.
2. *Assault* is a threat to inflict harm on someone.
3. *Battery* is the unlawful use of physical force against another person.
4. *Defamation* involves a malicious intent to injure a person's reputation through
   a. *Slander*—the spoken word.
   b. *Libel*—the written word.

Negligence

Most liability cases involving the schools are based on negligence. Negligence may be caused by any of the following:

1. *Nonfeasance* involves failure to do what is required, such as failure to instruct the students properly in the use of the trampoline or failure to administer first aid to an injured student.
2. *Misfeasance* involves doing something incorrectly, such as moving an injured student when it is improper to do so, thereby injuring the young person further.
3. *Malfeasance* involves doing something illegal, such as using corporal punishment in a state where it is against the law.

Negligence involves a comparison of the situation with an acceptable or established standard of conduct for persons in similar situations. To determine negligence, the courts generally ask four questions.[10] The questions are:

1. Duty—Did one person owe a duty to another?
2. Breach—Did that person fail to exercise that duty?
3. Harm—Was a person actually injured?
4. Cause—Was the failure to exercise due care the direct or proximate cause of the injury?

A *duty* is a legal responsibility to act in a certain way toward others to protect them from physical or mental harm. It includes the expectation that a teacher will provide appropriate instruction, supervision, and a safe environment in which students can learn. A *breach* is failure to exercise a standard of care equal to the risks involved. However, the breaching of a duty does not constitute negligence. Cause and harm must also be shown. A causal relationship must exist between the breach of duty and the injury of another person. *Foreseeability* is involved when a teacher could have anticipated or foreseen a potential danger and fails to eliminate the danger. If a person is injured as a result, the teacher is liable. In the case cited above, the teacher could have seen that leaving a trampoline available for student use would result in students jumping on it even when advised not to do so.

Finally, an actual injury or loss must occur as a result of the breach. *Harm* can exist in many forms. Physical injury is most often the result, such as a broken bone, but sometimes the end result of a condition initiated by negligence is the harm. For example, permanent paralysis, death, or emotional distress may not be evidenced until a later time. These conditions are still grounds for court action.

To establish negligence, it must be demonstrated that the teacher's actions were the direct or *proximate cause* of the injury. In the case just cited, the fact that the trampoline was left out by the teacher could be considered to be the proximate cause of students jumping on it and, therefore, of the accident.

Defenses against Negligence

When defending a case involving possible negligence, lawyers generally rely on one or more of the following defenses.

Governmental Immunity Governmental immunity is based on the English common law premise that "the King can do no wrong" and is therefore immune from suit. In a few states, the government still enjoys this privilege. Therefore, even though the school district was negligent, no damages or money could be awarded. However, beginning in 1959, when an Illinois state court abolished governmental immunity in a school transportation case,[11] approximately 80 percent of the states have lost their immunity through legislative or court action.[12] Although boards of education were not previously liable for tort, individual administrators, teachers, or other employees of the district have never been immune from tort liability.

Contributory Negligence Contributory negligence occurs when the injured person directly contributes to the injury. In the case discussed earlier, the student contributed directly to her injury by jumping on the trampoline even though she knew she was violating the safety rules that were established by the teacher and repeatedly reemphasized. Participants must act for their own protection as a reasonably prudent person of that age level would act.

Comparative Negligence Comparative negligence happens when both the injured person and the defendant are jointly responsible for the accident. The court generally determines the percentage of responsibility held by each person and distributes the money accordingly. For example, in the case involving the trampoline, the student, the teacher, and a medical doctor could be held responsible for 50 percent, 25 percent, and 25 percent of the injuries, respectively. Although comparative legislation is fairly new, approximately one-half of the states have enacted legislation providing for it.

Assumption of Risk Assumption of risk occurs when a person understands and accepts that participation in an activity involves a certain amount of risk of injury that a teacher or supervisor cannot prevent. Despite the risk, the person voluntarily agrees to participate. This applies particularly to activities that are potentially dangerous such as football, gymnastics, rappeling, and rock climbing. However, a person never assumes the risk of negligent behavior of another person in any activity.

Act of God An act of God is an unforeseeable or unavoidable accident due to the forces of nature. If a student were suddenly struck by lightning while playing softball, the accident would be considered an act of God. However, a teacher allowing students to remain in an outdoor swimming pool during an electrical storm is, undoubtedly, negligent.

Legal Precedents Legal precedents are court decisions made previously in similar cases. They are used by both the plaintiff and the defendant to defend their particular points of view. Cases often depend on previous legal decisions for their solutions.

Preventing Negligence

Because of the large settlements occurring in court cases, more and more lawsuits involving physical education are being settled out of court. However, when they do come to court, the courts are showing less tolerance for mistakes by teachers and demanding greater responsibility than ever before.

Negligence generally arises from one of five sources. They are: (1) the failure to supervise students properly; (2) the failure to instruct students properly; (3) unsafe facilities, grounds, or equipment; (4) the failure to take proper first aid measures in an emergency; and (5) failure involving transportation. By increasing their awareness of these five areas, teachers can considerably decrease the chances of becoming a defendant in a lawsuit and the damages awarded if such a case does occur.

Supervision

More than 50 percent of all lawsuits involving physical education and sports are a result of improper supervision.[13] Henderson stated, *"By far the most crucial responsibility of physical education teachers is that of supervision."*[14] Berryhill and Jarman listed two basic questions frequently asked by the attorney for the plaintiff in a suit involving supervision:

1. If the supervisor had been present, would the accident have occurred?
2. Did the supervisor perform his or her assigned duties or abide by the rules and regulations?[15]

If the above principles have been put into practice, teachers should not have a major reason for concern. Appenzeller summarized the area of supervision as follows:

> Enough cases have been decided that help give a clear pattern for teachers to follow. Most courts do not expect superhuman effort by teachers in this area. No one can reasonably expect teachers to be everywhere at the same time. The court does expect teachers to remain in the general area of play, however, and will not tolerate teachers who leave the vicinity to gossip with fellow teachers. The teacher should also use common sense and stay in the locality in which the greatest risks are present.[16]

The quantity and quality of supervision needed depends on the circumstances and should consider (1) the age and maturity of the students, (2) the amount of risk inherent in the activity, (3) the skill level of the students, and (4) the previous preparation of the students.

Age and Maturity Younger, less mature students need more supervision; older, more mature students generally need less. However, teachers should consider the tendency of older students to engage in horseplay.[17]

Amount of Risk in the Activity Activities that involve greater risk—such as gymnastics, wrestling, swimming, archery, and initiative activities—need closer supervision and fewer students per teacher than activities with less risk.

Skill Level Students who are just beginning to learn a new skill need more direct supervision than advanced students.

Preparation of Students Students should be gradually prepared by the teacher to assume responsibility for their own behavior. Students should earn the opportunity to participate in the more student-directed styles of learning.

Administrators have the responsibility to (1) assign qualified teachers for each activity taught in the curriculum, (2) communicate to teachers what is expected of them, and (3) supervise the teachers to determine whether the expectations have been met. They also have the responsibility to regulate class sizes to meet the needs of the students.

Teachers have a responsibility to remain with their classes at all times. When an emergency occurs, a student should be sent to the physical education or administrative office for help. The teacher should not leave the room to assist an injured student unless a second, qualified teacher is in the room. Classes should never be dismissed early or late without supervision. Teachers are liable for unsupervised students in gymnasiums, dressing rooms, halls, or on the school grounds.

Instruction

Several principles apply when designing the instructional situation. They relate to (1) the selection of the activity, (2) safety precautions, (3) planning, (4) direct instruction, and (5) grouping.

Selection of the Activity Potential activities must be evaluated in terms of their educational value and their appropriateness for students. Educational value is determined by the ability of the activity to help students meet the objectives of physical education. Appropriateness for students is determined by the age, maturity, skills, and fitness levels of students. Students should be carefully screened for such high-risk activities as combatives and gymnastics and for fitness activities in which students might be compelled to push themselves beyond their normal limits.[18]

Health problems should be evaluated to prevent students from participating in activities that are beyond their abilities. Students should not be allowed to participate in activities following a serious illness or injury without medical approval. Particular care must be taken in the evaluation of activities when handicapped students are mainstreamed with regular students.

Safety Precautions Students should be warned of the possible dangers inherent in the activities in which they participate and be cautioned not to try things that they have not yet been taught. This is especially true in gymnastics, in which the plaintiff has usually been favored in court cases.[19]

Safety rules and regulations should be carefully formulated and taught to students. They should be few in number and well-enforced. To ensure that students have learned the safety rules, they should be distributed to students, reviewed with students, and posted as reminders. Then, students should be tested to determine their knowledge of the rules before being allowed to participate in the activity. Failure to follow the rules should result in exclusion from that activity.

Safety equipment—such as fencing masks and body protectors, catcher's masks and chest protectors, helmets, and other game-related safety equipment—should be required of all participants. Eyeglass protectors should be strongly encouraged when not required by policy or law. Teachers should also check to make sure that all equipment is used properly and safely. Ground rules can be used to help students learn safety rules, such as requiring softball players to lay the bat in a marked area on the way to first base or be called out.

Students should be taught that they have a responsibility to be careful, to respect possible dangers, and to prevent accidents from occurring by using appropriate means of prevention. Instructors should provide a handout and review it with the class explaining the responsibility of participants to report bad equipment, to rest when fatigued, and to ask for help when experiencing difficulty in performing a new skill. Students should be reminded that the instructor cannot be present at all times to help individuals and, therefore, they must accept some responsibility for their own safety.

Planning Teachers should follow accepted procedures for instruction contained in a state, district, or school course of study or in a recognized text. Deviations from such procedures should be based on sound reasons, such as research demonstrating that the previous procedure was unsound or that a new procedure is better. Unit and lesson plans can be extremely valuable in providing evidence that sound planning for teaching has occurred. Such plans should be readily accessible to the teacher and available to substitute teachers coming into the class.

Direct Instruction Instruction in proper techniques and progressions should precede participation in any activity. Students should progress gradually from less-strenuous and simple tasks to more demanding, complex, and higher-risk activities. Instruction should include proper techniques for the performance of the activity, the proper use of equipment, the inherent dangers in the activity or the equipment, and information on how to avoid those dangers.[20]

Drowatzky provided several guidelines regarding instruction, which are:

1. The care exercised by the teacher must increase as the risks involved in the activity increase. . . . If the activity is compulsory because of a curricular requirement, the need to complete it for a grade, or the teacher insists that the student perform it, the amount of care required on the part of the instructor increases dramatically. When the dangerous and compulsory features are both present in a given situation, the instructor must be most diligent and careful.
2. Skill level of the students is an important consideration; beginners should have closer supervision and be placed in situations that can be controlled to prevent any injuries that may be caused by their inexperience.
3. Instruction must include proper techniques of performance, safety precautions, and pertinent characteristics of the equipment. The instructor must follow progressive, professional procedures and instruction should not be delegated to advanced students. . . . If students are used as spotters, they must be taught how to spot before they are given any responsibility.[21]

Grouping To prevent unnecessary injuries in contact sports or combative activities, students should be grouped for competition by similar characteristics such as height, size, skill, or gender.

Unsafe Facilities, Grounds, and Equipment

Essential components of accident prevention are safe facilities, grounds, and equipment. Administrators should set policies and make plans for periodic inspection of facilities, grounds, and equipment to determine possible hazards and defects. The line of responsibility should be clearly delegated to a specific person.[22] Records listing the inspector, date, condition of the equipment, and recommendations for repair should be retained. Complete inventories of equipment should be maintained, including dates of purchase and repair.

Physical educators should inspect facilities, grounds, and equipment frequently and take note of any potential hazards. These should be reported promptly to the principal and followed by a written letter to the principal (and superintendent, if necessary), stating the date and the nature of the problem. A copy should be retained by the teacher. Administrators are responsible to see that the facilities and grounds are maintained and that defects are corrected.

While waiting for the defect to be corrected, the teacher should use temporary measures to protect students from injury. This can be accomplished by posting signs warning of the danger, warning students to stay away from the area, closing off or locking the area, or stationing a supervisor nearby to keep students away. No facility should be used while unsafe conditions exist. Appenzeller sums up one of the major problems with equipment as follows: "Too often teachers try to get by just one more day with obsolete and outdated equipment that should have been discarded years ago. These teachers are either indifferent to the needs of their pupils or are totally unaware of the serious consequences that may lay ahead."[23]

An *attractive nuisance* is a dangerous situation that attracts the attention of children or youth. Swimming pools, gymnastics apparatus, jumping pits, and excavation areas are all attractive nuisances. To prevent injuries, teachers and administrators have a responsibility to keep such areas and equipment locked up when not in use.

First Aid Versus Medical Treatment

The law both requires and limits the medical treatment of students to first aid—the immediate and temporary care needed to preserve the student's life or prevent further injury until medical care is available. This legal duty is imposed because the teacher stands *in loco parentis,* or "in the place of the parent," and also because physical education teachers are expected to be qualified to administer this aid.

Two common errors occur in giving first aid—doing too much or doing too little. An example of doing too much is moving an injured student before medical help has arrived. Cases of spinal injury and paralysis have resulted from this particular error. On the other hand, failure to obtain medical help for students suffering from heat exhaustion, a broken bone, or other injury can also be harmful. Students who have been seriously ill or injured should be required to obtain a doctor's release before resuming normal physical activity.

To help prevent accidents, proper medical examinations are often required of students at various school levels. Physical educators should take note of students who have medical problems or handicaps and may need close supervision or adapted instruction to meet their needs.

If an accident does occur, administer first aid while sending a student to summon medical help and inform the principal. An emergency plan should be formulated and reviewed frequently so that it can be followed quickly without further mishap. An accurate report of each accident should be kept, including a detailed report of the activity and the circumstances of the accident, the nature of the injury, the first aid treatment given, medical attention obtained, the names of persons rendering service, and the names of witnesses. A sample accident report form is shown in figure 12.1.

Appenzeller summarized the expectations of the court regarding first aid as follows:

> As a coach, the court expects you to handle emergencies when they arise. The court
> will set a much higher standard of first aid for the coach than the average classroom
> teacher. The court will demand emergency treatment but nothing more. Do not go
> beyond the emergency stage; avoid attempting to treat your players; [italics in original]
> *let the professional do this!*[24]

Medical treatment includes the dispensing of any medication. Teachers and coaches need to be extremely cautious in this regard, even to the extent of giving students aspirin.

Accident Report

INJURED PERSON

NAME (last, first, middle)

ADDRESS

TELEPHONE NUMBER

AGE

SEX □ Female □ Male

CLASSIFICATION □ Student □ Faculty □ Visitor

DATE AND HOUR OF ACCIDENT

SEVERITY □ Nondisabling (loss of less than a full day of normal activity) □ Disabling (loss of one or more full days of normal activity)

JURISDICTION □ On school property □ Off campus in school-conducted activity

ACCIDENT

DEPARTMENT SUPERVISING ACTIVITY

ACTIVITY AT TIME OF ACCIDENT (e.g., driving auto, diving from low board, lifting crate, etc.).

DETAILS OF ACCIDENT (Describe fully the events, conditions, factors that contributed to the injury)

ACTION TO PREVENT SIMILAR ACCIDENTS (Indicate if taken)

TYPE OF FACILITY
- □ Athletic or physical education
- □ Instruction
- □ Exterior walk or sidewalk
- □ Other, specify _____
- □ Street or highway
- □ Service or maintenance
- □ Undeveloped area

LOCATION
- □ Gymnasium
- □ Sports arena or play field
- □ Swimming pool
- □ Bath, shower, or locker room
- □ Interior stair or ramp
- □ Interior hall or corridor
- □ Classroom, lecture hall
- □ Auditorium or library
- □ Laboratory
- □ Shop (mechanical)
- □ Home economics
- □ Storeroom
- □ Food preparation/ service
- □ Cafeteria or dining room
- □ Public transportation
- □ Private transportation
- □ Bldg. exterior or grounds
- □ Water area
- □ Farm, field, or woods
- □ Other, specify _____

NATURE OF INJURY

INJURY

- ☐ Amputation
- ☐ Bruise
- ☐ Burn, scald
- ☐ Concussion
- ☐ Open wounds
- ☐ Dermatitis, infection
- ☐ Other, specify _____
- ☐ Exposure, frostbite
- ☐ Fracture
- ☐ Foreign body
- ☐ Heat exhaustion, sunstroke
- ☐ Inhalation (dust, fumes, gases, etc.)
- ☐ Internal injury
- ☐ Poisoning, internal
- ☐ Shock, electrical
- ☐ Shock, fainting
- ☐ Sprain, strains, dislocation
- ☐ Suffocation, drowning, strangulation
- ☐ Rupture, hernia

PART OF BODY INJURED

- ☐ Generalized
- ☐ Skull or scalp
- ☐ Eye
- ☐ Nose
- ☐ Mouth
- ☐ Jaw
- ☐ Other head
- ☐ Other, specify _____
- ☐ Neck
- ☐ Spine
- ☐ Chest
- ☐ Abdomen
- ☐ Back
- ☐ Pelvis
- ☐ Other trunk
- ☐ Shoulder
- ☐ Upper arm
- ☐ Elbow
- ☐ Forearm
- ☐ Wrist
- ☐ Hand
- ☐ Finger
- ☐ Hip
- ☐ Thigh
- ☐ Knee
- ☐ Lower leg
- ☐ Ankle
- ☐ Foot
- ☐ Toe

WITNESSES

WITNESSES AND THEIR ADDRESSES

TREATMENT

EMERGENCY CARE & PATIENT STATUS

- ☐ First aid only, not at hospital or by doctor
- ☐ Treatment by school nurse
- ☐ Treatment at hospital
- ☐ Confinement at hospital or at residence

This report prepared by (signature) _____
Title or status _____
Address _____
Date _____

DISTRIBUTION: White,   Yellow, Originating Department

Figure 12.1 An accident report form.

Transportation and Field Trips

When transportation is necessary to and from off-campus facilities or during a field trip, school officials should approve all travel arrangements. The preferred arrangement is to use school buses or commercial vehicles. However, in an emergency situation when these are unavailable, several precautions should be taken.

When teachers or adults drive their own cars, administrators should ensure that they have adequate liability insurance in case of student injury. They should also be aware that many automobile insurance policies do not protect the car owner who is paid for transporting passengers, even if the pay is only reimbursement for gas and oil. An insurance rider on the policy must be purchased to provide this protection.[25] School or district transportation should be used by teachers except in emergency situations.

Extreme caution should be used when allowing students to drive to or from school functions. Only when drastic circumstances arise should this be allowed. Administrators must then examine the student drivers' reputations and records for safe and careful driving and the cars for freedom from defects that might make them unsafe when student drivers are used. Such drivers should also be cautioned to obey all traffic laws and not to overload their cars or to allow students to drive who have not been approved by the administration. The students' insurance policies should be checked for adequate coverage.[26]

School boards would be wise to protect their students by establishing rules and regulations for student transportation and by securing liability insurance for their employees who transport students. It is also good public relations to let parents know exactly what is and is not covered.

Consent forms are often sent home to parents before students are allowed to go on field trips permitting a child to participate. Bucher and Koenig indicated that "waivers and consent slips are not synonymous." A parent cannot waive the rights of a child who is under twenty-one years of age; the parent is merely waiving his or her right to sue for damages. The child can still sue the individual, however.[27] Although these waivers do not stand up in court,[28] they serve a valuable purpose of informing parents and receiving their permission for the trip. They may also reduce the possibility of a lawsuit.

Protection

The guidelines for protection against legal liability presented in this chapter should be studied and applied by teachers in their own environments. Because of the abrogation of governmental immunity, more students are now able to recover damages for injuries caused by the negligence of school employees. Although this is a positive outcome for the injured person, it also means that teachers may be involved in more nuisance suits with resulting stress, professional embarrassment, and financial loss. School districts will also be involved in paying higher rates for insurance and sports equipment.[29] The result is a higher cost to the taxpayers for the support of their schools.

That physical education teachers are held legally responsible for their actions should not cause prospective or practicing educators to "throw in the towel." Rather, it should make them take their responsibilities as educators seriously and use common sense in their interactions with others. Teachers should make a point of becoming acquainted with the tort liability laws as they apply in their particular states.

In addition, the wise physical education teacher will also obtain liability insurance to protect against catastrophic personal loss. Personal liability insurance is available from the American Alliance for Health, Physical Education, Recreation and Dance or the National Education Association. In some states, *save-harmless* legislation requires or permits districts to provide teachers with protection against the financial losses resulting from a job-related liability suit.

Departmental and class operations should be governed by legal and safe procedures. Student welfare should be of prime concern.

Departmental Policies and Procedures

Departmental policies and procedures should be developed to regulate those elements that must be consistent for all students taking physical education. These policies and procedures govern such components as: (1) uniforms, (2) excuses from activity, (3) locker-room policies, (4) locks and lockers, (5) towels, and (6) showers.

A departmental handout or handbook can be developed to include each of these components, thereby reducing misunderstandings between home and school concerning the policies. A creative example of a departmental handout is the work contract shown in figure 12.2. Signatures on these forms can also be used to verify that parental requests for excuses from physical activity have indeed come from the parent. Items that might be included in such a handout are:

1. The department's philosophy.
2. Physical education objectives.
3. Registration procedures and course offerings.
4. Policies concerning uniforms, dressing, showers, locker room, and laundering uniforms.
5. Policies for medical excuses, safety, accidents, and first aid.
6. Grading standards and policies.
7. Policies for making up absences.
8. Physical fitness appraisals.
9. Policies concerning student leaders.
10. Extra-class activities.

Uniforms

The use of a required uniform for physical eduction is a controversial issue. Many states now have laws restricting the use of a specific uniform. Many schools have stopped requiring students to dress in a standard outfit to participate in class activities while others still require a specific outfit to be worn. Whatever the policy, students should be required to change into clothing that allows active, comfortable, and safe participation.

Students with special needs should always be considered when establishing a dress policy. For example, students who are overweight, handicapped, unable to afford a uniform, or restricted due to religious reasons, should not be made to feel uncomfortable or conspicuous in class because of the uniform. Several options should be provided for uniforms to teenagers who are at a time in their lives where they are experiencing their own independence. In a recent poll of twenty-three public school teachers in a graduate class at Brigham

---

Work Contract

Wanted—Students
Ninety days of work available

Type of Work
Preparation for lifetime physical fitness, team sports skill development, and individual sport skill development

Wage
One-half unit of physical education credit

Payroll Issued
After forty-five days and after ninety days

Qualifications
Must be willing to work, be properly dressed, be cooperative, possess the ability to get along with fellow workers, and be punctual

Hours
One hour per day at the scheduled time

Special Requirements
A uniform will be needed each day consisting of:
Shorts—White, yellow, or black—no cut-offs
Shirts—T-shirt, either white or yellow—no tank tops or bare midriffs
Gym Shoes—in good condition
Socks—preferably white
Long hair must be tied back from the face to prevent injuries
Long pants and sweatshirt for cold weather outside

Sick Leave and Vacation Time
The State of Utah requires a minimum of seventy-five class hours before credit can be issued (this would allow a maximum of fifteen days absent time). No credit will be given if exceeded.

Make-up Time
All make-up work will be due *one week* after the day you return from an illness or excused absence. No make-up will be allowed if you cut (sluff) class without being properly excused.

Figure 12.2 A work contract.

Types of Overtime Accepted

Equal to one hour's work for the hour missed in terms of—(1) a poster, (2) written report, (3) teach a new game, (4) organize and direct a ten-minute exercise routine for class, or (5) anything else with *prior* approval of the instructor.

(Running miles, swimming, hiking, bowling are things you do for fun, *not* for make-up after you've been ill. You need recuperation time.)

Extended absence for illness is covered by a doctor's excuse, which is honored, and no make-up is required. Your grade will be based on work completed up to that time.

Failure to complete this employment will result in termination of contract.

If interested in applying for this work, please sign after carefully reading the terms of the contract. Parent or guardian should be aware of your commitment. Have them sign one copy and return it to your new employer.

____________________ Parent / Guardian

____________________ Employee

Figure 12.2 *(continued)*

Young University, 4 percent taught in schools that required a specific uniform and 96 percent taught in schools where "anything goes." These same teachers said that if they could control the dressing policy, 66 percent of them would require a standard uniform and 33 percent said they would have a policy of "anything goes with some restrictions."

Whatever uniform is provided should be marked with the student's name in permanent ink or label to facilitate recovery in case of loss. The uniform (whatever it is) should be kept at school and used only during the physical education class. This discourages students from participating in street clothes. Uniforms should be laundered regularly to promote good hygiene.

When a specific uniform is included because of departmental policy, teachers should explain to students and parents what type of uniform is requested, why it is necessary, and possible purchase locations. An example of the uniform should be available in class for students to see. A handout could be prepared to explain the uniform, marking, and laundry policies to parents.

Teachers should also dress in appropriate activity clothes as an example for students to follow. Clothing should be such that the teacher can immediately be located within the activity area.

Excuses from Activity

A sound policy should be established regarding excuses from activity, and the policy needs to be communicated to students and parents at the beginning of the school year. Excuses from activity generally consist of two types: (1) medical excuses and (2) nonmedical excuses.

```
┌─────────────────────────────────────────────────────────────────────┐
│                                                                       │
│              Temporary physical education excuse form                 │
│                                                                       │
│        To physical education instructor:                              │
│                                                                       │
│        Please excuse _____ Section _____     │
│                                                                       │
│        from:                                                          │
│        ☐  participation ____                                          │
│                                                                       │
│        ☐  showers ____                                                │
│                                                                       │
│        ☐  dressing for class ____                                     │
│                                                                       │
│        From _____        To _____    │
│                                                                       │
│        Reason _____   │
│                                                                       │
│        Recommended by:                                                │
│                                                                       │
│        Physician's note _____ Parent's note _____             │
│                                                                       │
│        School nurse _____                                        │
│                                                                       │
│                        _____              │
│                                            School nurse               │
│                                                                       │
└─────────────────────────────────────────────────────────────────────┘
```

Figure 12.3 A temporary physical education excuse form.
Source: Walker, June. *Modern Methods in Secondary School Physical Education,* 3d ed,; Boston: Allyn and Bacon, Inc. 1973.

Medical Excuses

All medical excuses should be cleared through the school nurse if possible, using a form such as the one shown in figure 12.3. In this way, a record of the frequency of illness can be kept for each student. Notes from the parent or physician should be kept for future reference either by the nurse or the teacher. After three or four days of excuses in a row, the student should be asked to obtain a note from his or her physician or a parent contact should be made to verify the nature of the illness.

When a student brings a note from a parent or doctor asking that he or she be excused from activity, some alternate way of meeting the physical education objectives must be considered. Often students can be scorekeepers, equipment managers, or a teacher aid. When a long-term disability exists, students are often placed in a class for students requiring modified activity or excused from the class until unhampered participation is possible. In either case, a physician should monitor all activity.

Nonmedical Excuses

When students consistently fail to dress for activity, teachers need to look for the cause behind the behavior. Hardy identified three underlying causes for failure to dress for activity. They are (1) physical, (2) moral or religious, and (3) defiance of authority.[30]

Physical excuses include stomachaches, headaches, and menstrual cramps. They may also include personal embarrassment, such as obesity, or peer ridicule. These latter excuses can often be remedied by allowing these students to dress before or after the other students or in a private area, or by allowing them to wear a different uniform, such as longer pants or a long-sleeved shirt.

A second reason students fail to dress can be moral or religious. In *Mitchell v. McCall,*[31] the court ruled in favor of a school policy requiring a girl to attend physical education classes dressed in a uniform of her choice and to participate in activities that she considered appropriate. Undoubtedly, the fact that the school allowed her freedom to choose her uniform and activities helped it to win the case.

A third reason for failure to dress is defiance of authority. Although very little can be done with some students, others will respond positively to activities that they have had a part in choosing and to a teacher who they know cares.

Hardy also suggested some remedies to the problem, including: (1) making classes so exciting that students will look forward to participating in them, (2) setting an example of appropriate dress, (3) exhibiting a genuine desire to understand and help students resolve self-consciousness about their bodies or their performance skills, and (4) refusing to punish students who fail to dress for activity.[32]

Teachers need to explain to students why dressing for activity is important. If students have forgotten their own uniforms or desire not to dress on a particular day, a system of "loaner" uniforms often solves the problem. Suits left by students at the end of the year or uniforms donated by a parents' group can be loaned to students. With this system they know that not dressing, without a medical excuse, is not an option. Loaned uniforms can be washed and returned by the students or washed in the home economics room.

Students with minor excuses can be encouraged to dress and do what they can. Students who are not dressed should not be allowed to participate in activities or to sit on the sidelines, often being an "attractive nuisance." Students who are ill, idle, or disturbing should leave the class and be sent to an appropriate place such as the nurse's or counselor's office. Students who remain should be actively engaged in the class in some way. Completing a written report or answers to questions or a series of questions on articles related to sport or physical fitness might be an activity done during class time to encourage learning and avoid noninvolvement.

Dressing for activity should not be used as the chief tool of evaluation. If students fail to dress, they will usually fail to do well on written, fitness, and skills tests and in other evaluative measures. There is really no need to use dressing as a part of the evaluation system. Pease increased the percentage of students dressing for activity by rewarding students with weight training and aerobics when the percentages of students dressed reached specified goals.[33]

Locker-Room Policies

Locker-room policies should be clearly defined to students at the beginning of each term. Policies should include (1) traffic patterns to ensure safety; (2) use of lockers (usually long lockers to secure clothing and books during class and small lockers to secure gym clothing at other times); (3) lost and found for locks, uniforms, clothing, and other items; (4) procedures for showering; and (5) guideline policies for locker clean-out, laundering of uniforms, responsibility to keep lockers locked, and valuables. In some situations, teachers will wish to have students assist in making these policies.

The locker room should be checked regularly for clothing and towels left out and locks left open. One teacher can be assigned to supervise the locker room each period or a para-professional aid can be used for this responsibility. Student leaders should not be given the responsibility of supervising students in the locker room. Some teachers prefer to lock the locker room during class to prevent thefts.

Locks and Lockers

Since considerable time is spent each year managing dressing facilities, sound policies need to be made to reduce management time so that instructional time can be maximized.

Lockers

Two types of lockers are generally used for securing students' clothing and possessions. The first is the wire basket. The basket is the least expensive and has the advantage of good air circulation for drying clothes. However, it has the disadvantage of being too small to include all of the students' possessions such as coats, boots, and books. Also, small items can be removed between the wires.

Metal lockers are often supplied in banks of six small lockers to one large locker to solve the storage problem as shown in figure 12.4. Gym uniforms can be stored in the small lockers and street clothing can be placed in the long lockers during class time. By locating them together in this manner, traffic in the locker room is minimized.

Locks

Locks can be built into metal lockers or combination locks can be used. Although built-in locks reduce the problem of distribution, collection, and loss of locks, they can often be opened with a knife. Because they are built-in, they cannot be transferred to the large locker to secure valuables during class time. They are also difficult to repair.

Locks are available with changeable combinations that can be changed from year to year to prevent theft. *Combination locks are preferred over key locks because students tend to lose keys while participating in activity.*

Locks can be provided by the school or the student. When locks are provided by the school, a lock deposit is often required to ensure that the locks are returned in good condition. Locks provided by the school provide easy access by the teacher in case of emergency because a master key is usually provided. When students purchase locks, teacher access is more difficult unless locks are purchased that have a master keyhole built in for emergency use.

1	2	3	4	5	6
1A Kristi Anderson 12–6–22	**2A** Sheila Ballard 1–10–39	**3A** Sue Boucher 7–22–14	**4A** Lida Crowder 30–15–9	**5A** Shauna Foster 5–7–25	**6A** Gloria Jensen 22–38–7
1B Nancy Alexander 7–38–12	**2B** Sandy Andres 21–18–12	**3B** Dana Bergstrom 31–18–9	**4B** Chris Bindrup 11–36–3	**5B** Audree Dixon 8–26–17	**6B** Georgina Edwards 38–17–6
1C Karin Cardon 8–13–29	**2C** Barbara Durrant 16–24–6	**3C** Kristin Goodwin 28–2–37	**4C** Sharane Hepworth 3–18–9	**5C** Terrie Jarvis 32–11–6	**6C** Cindy Jemmett 17–3–26
1D Renee Baker 7–17–24	**2D** Debbie Bemis 6–4–29	**3D** Janis Brock 3–12–16	**4D** Kay Brown 3–22–6	**5D** Laura Cameron 35–9–27	**6D** Paula Campbell 20–4–33
1E Carole Brisbin 20–13–7	**2E** Cheri Clark 18–20–36	**3E** Janiece Dee 7–19–34	**4E** Donna Dupaix 14–33–12	**5E** Kelly Fredericks 2–8–16	**6E** Jennifer Kee 8–29–16
1F Elsie Bishop 8–23–9	**2F** Rosa De la Cruz 13–36–27	**3F** Debra Evans 29–18–26	**4F** Shelley Huber 18–23–9	**5F** Maria Vasquez 14–38–2	**6F** Alana Walker 3–36–15

Figure 12.4 A master locker list and example of physical education lockers.

```
┌─────────────────────────────────────────────────────────────────────┐
│                          Locker Card                                  │
│                                                                       │
│  Name _____ Locker # _____    │
│  (Print)  (Last)     (First)       (Middle)                           │
│                                                                       │
│  Teacher _____     Lock # _____      │
│                                                                       │
│  Period _____        Combination _____          │
│                                                                       │
│  Address _____                     │
│            (Street)                        (Apt. #)                   │
│                                                                       │
│          _____                     │
│            (City)          (State)      (Zip)                        │
│                                                                       │
│  I understand and agree that I will not share the locker assigned     │
│  to me with anyone else.                                              │
│                                                                       │
│  Signed _____                       │
│                                                                       │
│  For Locker # _____ Date _____                    │
└─────────────────────────────────────────────────────────────────────┘
```

Figure 12.5 A locker card.

An accurate record of lock ownership, identification number, combination, and student locker number is vital for any physical education department. Locks will get lost and students will forget combinations. A reliable file (discussed in the next section) must be kept to provide necessary information to return lost locks, restate combinations, and locate lockers. Marking students' names on individual locks is usually difficult and temporary. Keeping track of the lock by the lock number engraved on the lock is often easier.

Assigning Locks and Lockers

Lockers should be assigned to students in horizontal rows by class period. This spreads students throughout the locker room each period and prevents overcrowding with its resulting safety hazards. It also facilitates dressing quickly. If the lowest rows are assigned to the lower grades and the higher rows to the higher grades, differences in height can be easily accommodated.

A master list of lockers such as that shown in figure 12.4 can be kept, showing each bank of lockers, with students' names and combinations written in pencil. Using pencil makes erasing easy when students move out.

Locker cards can be used to record the student's name, lock number, combination, and assigned locker. A sample locker card is shown in figure 12.5. A second card, which is shown in figure 12.6, can be used to record the combination of each lock when locks are collected for redistribution at the end of each semester or year. If students use the same lock from year to year, a place for the name should be on the card. It is usually desirable to have two files. In one file, cards are filed by lock number. In the other file, cards are filed alphabetically by students' last name. The information found in either file provides access to information that is usually needed quickly.

```
┌────────────────────────────────────────────────────────────────────┐
│                    LOCKER COMBINATION CARD                           │
│   DATE ISSUED:                                                        │
│                                                                      │
│    . . . . . . . . . . . . . . . . . . . . . . .                     │
│                          LOCKER NO.   . . . . . . . . . . . . . . . . . . . . . . . . . . . . . . .   │
│                          LOCK NO.   . . . . . . . . . . . . . . . . . . . . . . . . . . . . . . .     │
│                                        R.   . . . . . . . . . . . . . . . . . . . . . . . .           │
│                      Combination:  L.   . . . . . . . . . . . . . . . . . . . . . . . .               │
│                                        R.   . . . . . . . . . . . . . . . . . . . . . . . .           │
│   Name: _____                     │
└────────────────────────────────────────────────────────────────────┘
```

Figure 12.6 A locker combination card.

A master lock book can be acquired from the manufacturer. This lists the lock serial numbers and their combinations. This book, in tandem with the lock card and student identification card, allows teachers a three-way system to locate locks and lockers by student name, locker number or location, or lock serial number. Lost locks can be locked on to a towel bar placed in or near the teacher's office or on the wire screen of an issue room cage. Some teachers charge students a small fee of five to twenty-five cents for retrieving their locks or telling them their combinations. The money collected can go into a fund for purchasing loaner suits, equipment of student choice, or adding to funds for field trips. Students should have a voice in how such monies are used.

Towels

Three decisions need to be made with regard to towels. They are (1) the method of acquisition of towels, (2) the laundering of towels, and (3) the distribution and collection of towels.

Acquisition of Towels

Towels can be purchased by the school or district, leased from a towel service, or students can be asked to bring one or two towels each year for the school supply.

Laundering of Towels

Towels purchased by the school are often laundered at a school or district facility. This requires purchasing laundry equipment and hiring someone to launder towels. Leased or purchased towels may be laundered by the towel service. This requires a bid by local laundries for pick-up, laundry, and delivery. Students are often charged a towel fee for this service. Fees for indigent students are often paid by welfare or other community services or absorbed by the school.

In some cases, students are required to bring a towel each week and launder it at home. This generally results in mildew and odor problems as towels are left in lockers throughout the week. It also results in students missing showers because of failure to bring a towel. Some districts, however, prohibit charging towel fees to students and, therefore, the cost must be absorbed into the regular budget or a system such as this one must be used.

Distribution and Collection of Towels

Towels can be distributed to students by their roll call numbers and checked in after showers as in this example:

Distributed   1   2̸   3   4̸   5   Collected   1   2̷   3   4̷   5

                        6   7̸   8   9   1̸0̸   6   7̷   8   9   1̸0̸

Towels were distributed to numbers 2, 4, 7, and 10, but number 7's towel has not yet been returned. This system helps to keep stray towels off the locker room floor and can also be used to check on which students took showers. Other more informal procedures are often used. For example, a towel is issued to each student at the beginning of the school year. Each time the student showers a dirty towel is exchanged for a clean one.

Showers

Required showers have often resulted in negative attitudes toward physical education. This is because some teachers require showers unnecessarily and do not consider the students' feelings when developing policies for showers.

Students should be taught the health-related concepts about exercise and showering and helped to understand when a shower should be taken and when one is not necessary. Showers should never be required when students have been relatively inactive during the period, such as in archery or golf.

When showering is necessary, make certain students have enough time to do it right. The amount of time will depend on the number of students in the locker room and the number of showers available, but ten to fifteen minutes is usually adequate. More time is needed after swimming for drying hair. Private showers should be provided for students desiring privacy.

Safety should be emphasized and students should dry off in a specified area to prevent students from slipping on water near the lockers. Glass bottles should never be allowed in the locker room.

Showers should not be used as a factor for determining grades.

Effective Classroom Management

Good classroom management is essential to quality instruction in physical education. In fact, it is even more vital than in the academic classroom. This is partly due to the variety of activities provided, often in different facilities and with different equipment, and partly due to the larger numbers of students in physical education classes. The need for safety is an essential consideration in most of these activities. Another factor is the restricted amount of time often allotted to physical education and the additional limits imposed by dressing and showering. Because of this, class time must be carefully planned to provide the maximum instructional benefit.

Classroom management in physical education involves (1) preparing the environment, (2) distributing and collecting equipment, (3) planning preclass activities, (4) calling roll, (5) leading warm-up and fitness activities, (6) getting students' attention and giving directions, (7) teaching and utilizing class formations, (8) organizing groups or teams, (9) supervising class activities, (10) adapting to interruptions, (11) using student leaders, and (12) increasing motivation through classroom management. Techniques for managing each of these activities will be discussed in this section of the chapter.

Teachers should teach students self-management skills and provide practice in using them just as other skills are practiced. On the first day of class, procedures for assembly, dismissal, roll call, excuses, tardies, collecting and distributing equipment, organizing teams and getting into formations should be taught. Also, students need to know why each of these procedures is used. During instruction, whenever a difficulty occurs with one of the management skills such as students getting into the proper formation, teachers should take time to stop and review the skill or procedure before proceeding. If resistance to any policy remains, student feelings should be examined to determine if modification or discontinuance would solve the problem. This attention to the problem will save instructional time in the long run and will reduce the incidence of serious discipline problems.

There is no one best way to manage a class. Each teacher needs to develop a wide variety of management techniques from which to choose as the situation changes. The choice of a management technique depends to a large extent on the experience and personality of the teacher and the maturity and self-management capabilities of the students.

As the style of teaching changes from the more teacher-directed styles to the more student-directed styles, the management style will also proceed from the use of formal to more informal techniques. Other factors that influence the selection of a management technique include the subject matter to be taught, the facilities and equipment available, the size of the class, and the school or department policies under which the teacher works.

A good teacher will select the best technique for a given situation, carry it out effectively, and modify it as the need arises. When choosing any technique, a balance must be achieved between concern for the student and efficiency of instruction.

The true test of a successful management technique is whether the objectives of the lesson or unit in question have been realized. Whenever the objectives are not being accomplished, the teacher should select a new plan of action.

Preparing the Environment

Prior to teaching each day, facilities and equipment should be inspected for safety, proper lighting, adequate towels, and comfortable room temperature. Nets can be set up, baskets raised or lowered, apparatus arranged, and special markings put in place by paraprofessional or student aids before class begins or by students who come in before school or prior to class time. Instructional time should not be used to accomplish these tasks unless it is absolutely necessary.

A wise teacher will always check the equipment prior to starting a new unit or activity and make sure each day that enough equipment is available and that balls are pumped up, arrows are repaired, pinnies are washed, and other essentials are attended to.

Adequate teaching stations should be available for all instructors. If a specialized area is needed to show a film, administer a test, or present a guest speaker, arrangements should be made well in advance of the activity. A plan of operations for inclement weather should already be part of departmental procedures. Teachers can then make last-minute adjustments and present an uninterrupted teaching program. All teachers in a department should share in these decisions so they feel they have a fair share of department facilities.

Storage facilities for loose equipment should include movable bins or racks. Plastic trash cans attached to a piece of plywood with wheels on it could be used for this purpose. Ball racks or bags that can be moved to and from the classroom for ease of distribution should be part of the department inventory. To avoid loss, equipment must often be moved to and from the classroom each hour. Student assistants or squad leaders can be assigned to assist with the movement of equipment.

Distributing and Collecting Equipment

A number of techniques can be used for distributing and collecting equipment. When choosing an equipment distribution and collection technique, always consider the relationship of the technique to the safety of the students and to effective learning.

The Teacher

The teacher or an aid distributes and collects equipment as students enter and leave the gymnasium or playing area. Students can sign the roll as they pick up equipment. The system should not "tie up" a teacher who could be helping students with other needs.

Squad Leaders

Squad leaders acquire the equipment needed for their individual squads and return it at the end of the practice period.

Numbers

Students are assigned equipment numbers that correspond to their roll-call numbers. Student #1 picks up bow #1, arrows #1, and armguard #1. If equipment is numbered in such a way that it would not correspond to a roll-call number, the number of the assigned equipment is recorded by the roll-call number. The person distributing equipment checks the roll-call number of the person receiving equipment each day. Equipment can be picked up in the locker room, as students enter the gymnasium, or as they complete warm-up and fitness activities. One advantage to this technique is that students feel more responsible for returning the equipment in good condition each day. A second advantage is that students can become accustomed to a particular racquet, bow, or glove.

Grab Bag

Students can be asked to get a piece of equipment and return to their space. This often results in students converging on a given box of equipment and grabbing out the best they can find. Chaos and a loss of instructional time usually result and the less-aggressive students may feel cheated by getting the worst equipment. This can be avoided by sending one squad or student at a time (changing squads each day) and by ensuring that all equipment is in good condition. When sending a few students at a time, have students pick up or return equipment as they enter the gym or as they complete an activity in which students finish at different times, such as after jogging or completing self-check activities.

Handing in Assignments

Assignments can be collected very efficiently by placing a basket or box for each class in a convenient location. Students can place their assignments in the box as they enter or leave the gymnasium. Handouts for students who have been absent can be placed in a different colored or labeled box.

Planning Preclass Activities

A good deal of time is often wasted by students between the time they enter the gymnasium and the time for roll call or instruction. If this is the case, students who come in last are rewarded by not having to sit around doing nothing. When students are allowed to begin activity the minute they enter the area, they also begin to dress faster and come to class earlier. Motivational devices such as a preclass activity chart, listing skills that students can practice, might be posted. The accumulative tournament described in chapter 9 is an effective preclass activity as are many other self-testing activities.

Teachers should always be close by to supervise student safety and equipment loss or damage. Teachers in larger departments can take turns supervising the locker room and the gymnasium, or a teacher aid can be used to supervise one of the two areas. At a given time or signal, students can report to roll call or a posted or preannounced area for instruction or practice.

Calling Roll

A fast, effective roll-call system gets things started on the right track. Generally, roll-call can be taken in only one or two minutes at the most. A number of different roll-call techniques can be used, depending on the class size, maturity of the students, and the learning situation. The major criteria for selection of a roll-call technique are time and accuracy. Since most schools receive some funding based on the average daily attendance (ADA) of students, schools insist on accuracy in attendance taking.

Time spent in roll call reduces the learning time for students, so efficient use of time is essential. When too much time is taken for roll call, students become bored and discipline problems can arise.

Five general techniques are commonly used. They include (1) numbers or spots, (2) squads, (3) student check-in, (4) silent roll, and (5) oral roll call.

Numbers or Spots

Each student is assigned a number or a spot. Students sit or stand in a specific spot, either in a line or in squad order. When numbers are painted on the floor, on a bench or bleacher, or on the wall, a blank number indicates a student who is absent. When no numbers are available, students can be asked to call out the numbers in sequence. Although this method is rather impersonal, it is very fast. Having students call their numbers and last names, as in "1-Allen," "2-Bacon," "3-Barr," can help teachers learn names.

Squads

Each student is assigned to a squad and a leader is chosen for each squad. Each day, the squad leader records the attendance of the squad members on a squad card. This could be done while students are participating in warm-ups or another squad activity.

Student Check-in

In this technique, students check in as they enter the gymnasium by signing their name and time of entry, by checking in with the teacher, by handing in an assignment, or by removing their name tags from a board or box and placing them in a specified location or wearing them. When using name tags, those remaining indicate absent students.

A variety of warm-up techniques should be
included to increase motivation.

A fast, effective roll call gets things started on the right track.

Silent Roll
In this technique, the teacher or a teacher's aid takes roll silently while students are participating in activity. This permits students to remain active.

Oral Roll Call
In this technique, the teacher calls out the students' names and listens for a response. This technique is only effective when used with very small classes or when employed to get acquainted with students during the first few days of instruction before rolls have been finalized. Another use is as an accuracy check by calling out only the names of those students who have been marked absent by one of the other methods.

Leading Warm-up and Fitness Activities
A variety of warm-up techniques and fitness activities should be employed to increase student motivation. Some ideas include:

1. Students exercise to popular music, using choreographed routines or "follow the leader." Music can be taped, with cues on the tapes, to free the teacher to provide individual assistance.
2. Squad leaders direct warm-up activities for their squads. Squad leaders change regularly so many students are afforded this opportunity.
3. Students warm up on their own.
4. Students rotate through a number of fitness stations.
5. Selected student leaders direct warm-up activities for the entire class.

6. Students alternate jogging and weight training at specified time intervals (e.g., every two minutes).
7. Students run three days a week and weight train two days.
8. Students run daily with a timed run once a week.
9. Students participate in an obstacle course.
10. Students participate in relays or games to emphasize certain fitness activities.

Innumerable other techniques can be invented by the creative teacher for warm-up and fitness activities (see also chapter 9).

The following tips for leading exercises will aid the student leader or the teacher who is directing the class:

1. Give a preparatory command, such as "ready-now."
2. Give a command to begin such as, "go," "begin."
3. During the exercise, repeat the sequence or cadence aloud, so the group is together (e.g., forward, side, forward, down; or 1, 2, 3).
4. Provide a model. If the leader is facing the class, try to mirror the actions (e.g., move the left arm when the class is moving the right).
5. Provide encouragement.
6. Have a sense of humor—smile, display enthusiasm, relax.
7. Give a command to stop. With exercises done to a cadence, a preparation to stop is also helpful (e.g., "and, stop").

Getting Students' Attention and Giving Directions

There are times when teachers must get students' attention, assemble students, give directions, dismiss students, and handle emergencies. Either verbal signals such as "roll call" or "ready, go!" or nonverbal signals such as a whistle or raised arm can be used to gain attention or give directions. One teacher got effective results by calling out "HEY." The students responded with "HO." Students seemed especially responsive to this system. Be sure students understand what system will be used during class. If a whistle is used for such situations, use it sparingly at other times so students do not tune out the sound.

Verbal Signals

A teacher who speaks softly, yet loudly enough to be heard, encourages students to listen carefully when he or she talks and also leaves room for a future increase in volume for gaining attention. In contrast, when a teacher consistently shouts at students with a loud voice, they tend to increase their noise level to a level that prohibits the use of verbal signals. A general rule for the teacher is to gather the students around and talk so that the student farthest away can hear clearly.

In addition to volume, effective teachers vary the speed, inflection, and vocabulary to either calm students or incite them to action. Such terms or phrases as "hustle," "quickly," and "Let's go!" are built-in motivators when used with appropriate inflection and enthusiasm. When teachers want students to do something, they should not ask "Susie, do you want to pick up the balls?" Rather, they should say "Susie, please put the balls away in the basket."

The voice can be saved by using a number of nonverbal attention-getters. A lesson taught completely by gestures and written instructions can be highly effective on occasion in getting students to pay attention.

Teachers of physical education need to develop a "gym voice" if they expect to talk all day to large classes in open spaces. They need to get used to speaking with a push from the diaphragm to project the voice, as singers are taught to do. Additional tips for teachers include: speak directly at students who are gathered closely around; avoid raising the voice or yelling; if possible, try to speak with a wall behind the listeners to trap the voice; and try to keep the voice at a low octave. Women especially need to avoid raising the pitch as they try to increase the volume. The result is a piercing sound that is hard to hear and very distracting.

Nonverbal Attention Signals

A whistle, horn, hand clap, drum beat, or raised hand can be used effectively to gain attention once students have become accustomed to its use. Flicking the lights off and on quickly is effective when teaching activities such as racquetball where students are dispersed in a wide indoor area.

When using a whistle, a sharp blast done by placing the tongue over the end and quickly removing it as the air is blown, is easily discernable and motivating. On the other hand, a long, drawn-out rumble denotes a lack of authority.

Students should be taught what behavior is expected when the attention signal is given. For example, students can be taught to sit or kneel where they are and wait for instructions or to gather to an appointed place for direction. Once the students learn the signal and the expected response, time can be saved by praising those who respond quickly or by rewarding them with extra time for activity. Feedback can also be provided on the amount of time spent, such as "You were ready five seconds faster than yesterday."

Giving Directions

When giving directions, the teacher should gather the students close enough so all of them can see and hear and face them away from the sun and other distractions. Students not able to stand quietly should be asked to sit.

Directions should be given in a clear, concise manner telling students the location to move to, the signal for moving, and what to do when they get there. For example, the teacher might be as specific as "On the signal, 'Ready, go!' move quickly to the black line and line up facing the net." If students are given options in class procedures, the teacher might say, "On my signal, find a partner, get one ball between you, and locate a space on the floor where you can safely practice the volley."

Occasionally, directions can be written on the chalkboard, posted on a bulletin board, or written on a skill checklist or individual contract. Such methods may allow more student time-on-task.

When complex directions are given, the teacher might ask students if they have any questions or ask questions to see if the students understand the directions. Avoid repeating the directions to students. They will learn not to listen the first time.

La Mancusa listed some pitfalls in giving directions.[34] They are (1) using words that students do not understand, (2) saying the same thing over and over, instead of using a few brief statements, in hopes the students will "catch on," (3) using extraneous words such as "well" and "okay," and (4) failing to wait until everyone is listening before talking. She stated: (italics in original)

> It is the wise teacher who will *not speak* until *everyone* is listening. If it means that the teacher will be forced to stop what he is saying and wait, then by all means WAIT. If it means that the teacher will have to stop a second time, or a third time, then stop and WAIT. Silent teacher disapproval and exasperated peer disapproval is too strong a factor to override. Soon enough the offenders will understand that when *their* teacher talks, *everyone listens* because *their* teacher *means it* when he says, "I will not repeat this a second time."
>
> There is nothing more to it than that. If a teacher allows himself to overlook rudeness, he will receive rudeness in return. Children will respond either to the *highest* or to the *lowest* of teacher-expectations.[35]

The key to avoiding these pitfalls is proper planning before speaking and careful evaluation of one's own ability to give directions. One of the best methods for evaluating the effectiveness of giving directions is to record a class session on a tape recorder. When it is played back, the teacher should ask "Would I like to be a student in my own classroom?"

Finish of an Activity

An activity or class period should always finish on a positive note. Teachers should include a culminating activity that capitalizes on enthusiasm and interest or reviews points taught in the lesson. This is a time when students are given an opportunity to ask questions, and it also provides the teacher with an opportunity to correct skill or reiterate important information. Some ideas for summarizing a lesson include:

1. Summarize the main idea(s) of the lesson with a short statement and tell what the students will be expected to realize as an outcome.
2. Ask the students questions in which responses summarize the lesson.
3. Assign one or two students to listen carefully and tell the class afterwards what the lesson was about.
4. Use a worksheet to help students summarize the main idea of the lesson.
5. Have several students in turn tell one thing learned from the lesson.
6. Present a real-life situation that could be resolved by using lesson ideas.

A teacher desiring to use activities that require more time might incorporate the following:

1. Give an oral or written quiz.
2. Use instructional games to test the information taught.
3. Have students write or tell in their own words what they think the main idea is.
4. Divide the class into small groups. Each group in turn acts out a part of the lesson while the other groups try to guess what is being depicted (charades).

Noteworthy performance and effort, and team or individual winners could be recognized at this time. The stage is now set for an orderly dismissal. The teacher might request that students get ready to leave in a certain fashion. For example, "The team sitting quietly in squad order will be the first to leave."

Teaching and Utilizing Class Formations

Innumerable class formations can be created to assist students and teachers in the instructional setting. The choice of a formation is determined by the needs of the instructional situation. A number of types of formations follow.

Circles and Semicircles

Circles can be formed by asking students to form a circle on a painted line on the playing surface, such as a free-throw circle, and then taking three giant steps backward. With younger students, students can follow the teacher into a circle as the teacher purposely catches up with the last person in line. In folk dancing, students can be asked to join hands to form a circle. (Avoid holding hands in other activities. It usually leads to giggling and tugging.)

Circles can be used for practice drills or lead-up games and for relays. The teacher should be careful to stay on the edge of the circle when giving directions, so that students are never behind.

The semicircle can be formed by asking students to gather around the teacher. It is often used for giving directions to small classes or for demonstrating to a group of students.

Lines and Columns

Lines are formed by asking students to line up facing the net or wall on a particular line on the floor, or between several cones or chalk marks. Lines are often used for roll-call formations and for some lead-up games, such as line soccer.

Columns are formed by selecting four to eight students as leaders and having other students line up behind one of the leaders in designated areas of the floor. Cones or other pieces of equipment can be used instead of leaders. Columns are used to create relay teams or squads.

Extended Formation

The extended formation is formed from a line. For example, students number off in fours. The ones stay where they are. The twos move forward five steps, threes move ten steps, and fours move fifteen steps. The extended formation is often used for warm-up and fitness activities, for demonstrations that students cannot see when grouped close together, and for mimetic drills (pantomime). An example of this is shown in chapter 11.

A variation of the extended formation is "waves," in which all the ones move (e.g., swim across the pool), then the twos, etc. This technique permits the teacher to observe and give feedback to a small group of students at one time.

Partners or Small Groups

Partners and groups can be assigned, or students can be asked to simply find a partner or get in groups of three or four. The teacher should ask students to raise their hands if they need a partner or to sit down with their partner as soon as one is found. When an extra person exists, be specific on how that person is to be included. If the teacher needs to be a partner, he or she should select a well-skilled student so the individual will not feel slighted on practice time as the teacher helps the rest of the class. Partners and small groups are often used for warm-up and fitness activities and for practice drills or peer tutoring.

Variations

The formations above can be combined into any number of formations for use in various drills. Some examples include:

1. Double lines for use in passing or volleying drills

2. "Teacher"-class formation for passing and volleying drills. Rotate "teacher" each time through. Use two balls for agility.

3. Shuttle for relays or practice drills.

X X X ⟵⟶ X X X

In the command style of teaching (see chapter 10), formal formations are used. As instruction moves toward the less teacher-dominated styles, teachers are more apt to ask students to move out, find a partner, or find a space on the floor.

Whatever formations are used, students should be taught how to assume them quickly on a brief, consistent signal. The teacher should always specify exactly where students are to be, such as on the red line; what formation they are to assume; and the direction they are to face. Painted lines and circles can be used when they are available. If there are none, chalk marks, traffic cones, or masking tape can be substituted.

Transitions between formations should be kept to a minimum. Transitions such as from a line to a circle to a line can be avoided by thinking through how students will get from one formation to another. *Xs* and *Os* might be used to plot out formations and to help visualize the movement of the class from formation to formation. An example of an effective class transition is shown in figure 12.7.

Organizing Groups or Teams

There are as many ways to choose teams as there are teachers to choose them. However, many teachers resort to only one or two techniques. A little variety here could be more motivating. Some common techniques and ideas follow.

Roll call X X X X X X X X X X X X X X X X X X X X X X X X
          1 2 3 4 5 6 7 8 9 10 11 12 13 14 15 16 17 18 19 20 21 22 23 24

Warm-ups X ' ' ' X ' ' ' X ' ' ' X ' ' ' X ' ' ' X ' ' '

           X ' ' X ' ' X ' ' X ' ' X ' ' X ' '

             X ' X ' X ' X ' X ' X '

                X X X X X X

Teams X-------X   X-------X   X-------X   X-------X   X-------X   X-------X
       X----X   X----X   X----X   X----X   X----X   X----X
       X--X   X--X   X--X   X--X   X--X   X--X
       X   X   X   X   X   X
       1   2   3   4   5   6

Move to drill

Figure 12.7 A class transition map.

Counting Off

Students line up, count off by fives, and are asked to remember their number. Then, all the ones become one team, the twos another team, and so on. This method takes too much time to be recommended. Also, students tend to change their numbers or position themselves to be on the same team as their friends.

Choosing Teams

Team captains might be elected by class members or chosen by the teacher. This responsibility should be rotated among as many students as possible. Self-esteem and leadership traits can be encouraged and developed in students by the wise and caring teacher.

Teachers should *never* allow team captains to choose teams with each captain in turn picking a member of the class until all are chosen. This results in some students always being chosen last. This ruins self-esteem. It also wastes valuable class time. One method is for captains to choose the teams in private using the class roll as a guide. Still another method is to have captains select team members for each other or draw a team at random from teams already chosen. Teachers can then alphabetize the list for posting.

Students within a class can select teams quickly if the following system is incorporated in an orderly manner. After the captains have been chosen, students are instructed to line up behind the captain of their choice. On the command "GO" they must *walk* to form this line. No more than seven (or any number) persons can be in a line. When the designated number is reached students must go to another line. With this method, best friends, highly skilled players, and goof-offs tend to end up on the same team. Teachers should intersperse this method with other methods of choosing teams.

Assigned Teams

Teams can be assigned by the teacher and posted or read to the class. Squads can be used as assigned teams.

At Random

Students are told to "get in groups of four" or to stand behind a number of markers. A second method is to say, "You five go to court one, you five to court two," and so forth, while indicating certain students as they happen to be grouped around the teacher.

Variations

Give each student a card with a color, shape, and number on it, such as:

Triangle	Circle	Square
Orange	Red	Blue
2	3	1

By varying the number of colors, shapes, and numbers, groups of different sizes can be formed. For example, if only three groups are desired, limit shapes to triangle, circle, and square. If five groups are desired, use orange, red, blue, yellow, and green. If ten groups are necessary, use the numbers one to ten. Groups can then be formed by calling out shapes, colors, or numbers, and students move to join others who have the same shape, color, or number in a designated spot.

Other variations might include birthday, height, eye or hair color, right-handed, or left-handed, depending on the size of teams wanted or the purpose for grouping students. Teachers are only limited by their own creativity to think of other variations for special occasions.

Whatever technique is used for selecting teams, the method should be changed often for variety and to encourage positive social interaction among students. Leadership responsibilities for teams should be traded regularly so most students are afforded this responsibility. Teachers should also divide the various abilities of students as evenly as possible among the teams. When teams are used for game play, colored vests or pinnies can be used to distinguish one team from another.

Supervising Class Activities

The teacher must employ both vision and movement in supervising class activities. A wide range of vision should be used as the class is scanned and that "sixth sense" or "eye in the back of the head" is called on. Never get so involved in the subject matter that students are forgotten.

The teacher should keep moving along the edges of the class when not involved in direct instruction. This permits all of the students to be in constant view and avoids favoring students in one part of the playing area. The center of the class is not a good place for the teacher to stand. Doing so means some students are out of view. If instructions must be given, some students may have trouble hearing. When a discipline problem exists, the teacher can more easily move from the perimeter toward the offenders and stand beside them, and if necessary, quietly speak to them.

Teachers should provide students as much freedom as possible, considering the nature of the task and the maturity of the students. As the teaching style moves toward the student-directed styles of the spectrum (see chapter 10), more and more freedom should occur, with increased student responsibility for learning. Students should be allowed to work together as long as they work cooperatively. Teachers need to keep an eye on students causing a disturbance, often separating them or locating attention-getters away from students who reinforce them.

Teachers are responsible for all students in the class. *Never leave students unsupervised.* Classes not working together as an entire group present problems in this regard. Teachers must work out team teaching/supervising schedules or get adequate help when supervising individualized class programs.

Teachers need to be sure all students are accounted for when class is in session. Some students might attempt to sneak off after roll call. If the class is a meaningful and motivational experience, this should not occur; but students sometimes have behavior problems for which a teacher is not responsible. Once teachers know of such students, adequate precautions must be taken during class or additional help from the counseling office might need to be secured to account for the student.

Adapting to Interruptions

A number of interruptions that reduce instructional time occur during school hours. They include such things as emergencies and injuries, assemblies, school dances, field trips, testing, and fire drills. Some of these activities reduce the length of the instructional period, often making it impractical to dress for activity. Others take students away from physical education classes, thereby leaving the teacher with only a few students in class. Another deviation is caused by inclement weather.

Dealing with Emergency Interruptions

Planning for emergencies is essential so that when they occur the teacher can act in the most efficient manner. For example, plans should be formulated for action when the fire alarm sounds and students are in the shower or for serious injuries occurring in class. An accident plan might include sending one student for first aid supplies, another to the office for the principal or school nurse, and a third to call the paramedics. First aid supplies, phone numbers, and so forth must be prepared in advance so they are readily available when the emergency strikes. Teachers should be prepared to give first aid if needed, wait for the paramedics, and then make sure the parents are called. Students should not be allowed to stand around to witness the drama of an accident or emergency situation.

When the emergency is over, an accident report should be completed as soon as possible while the incident is fresh. A sample accident report is shown in figure 12.1 on page 394. Accident reports should be kept for many years in case of lawsuits. They should be reviewed each year to analyze problem areas that could be resolved.

Dealing with Shortened Periods or Inclement Weather

Three types of activities can be used when the planned lesson must be changed. One type is an adaptation of the activity currently being taught to an indoor facility; a lesson on terms, rules, strategy, or other cognitive concepts related to the activity; or an evaluation activity such as a skill or written test.

If the use of an activity-related lesson is not feasible, a fitness-oriented lesson could be taught. This might include teaching fitness concepts, teaching a fitness activity such as an aerobic dance or circuit training, giving physical fitness tests, or evaluating posture.

A third activity is the use of a values-oriented activity from the affective domain. Chapter 10 includes a number of activities the teacher might use.

Dealing with a Small Class

Teaching a small class is an excellent time to provide practice time for skill development, since students are given an opportunity for individual help from the teacher. An alternative plan is to play a recreational or lead-up game using the skills that have been taught in the class.

Using Student Leaders

The physical education program should provide numerous opportunities for students to develop leadership skills. Within individual classes, students can serve as squad leaders, team captains, officials, equipment monitors, and in many other capacities. Student leaders should be rotated often to allow every student a chance to develop leadership skills.

In addition to these in-class leaders, student assistants can be assigned to assist the teacher with various nonteaching activities. Student assistants have proven to be an inexpensive method for improving teacher effectiveness and morale in large classes. In addition to helping teachers, student assistants can improve themselves in the following ways:

1. Develop and improve physical activity skills.
2. Develop social skills, such as leadership, followership, responsibility, and cooperation.
3. Develop improved skills in written and oral communication.
4. Learn more about the teaching profession and about physical education as a profession.
5. Grasp the significance of serving others and working with others to accomplish stated objectives.
6. Develop a better understanding of students who are less able.
7. Learn how to plan and lead activities.

Student assistants should be selected because of their interest, scholarship, physical ability, character, ability to get along well with others, and willingness to do what is required.

The experience afforded students is often enhanced if they can be assigned to a specific class section other than their own and if they have uniforms distinct from the other students—perhaps a different shirt—to set them apart.

Because student assistants are students and, therefore, lack professional training and experience, they must be prepared for their new role. Much of this preparation can precede the actual experience, while some of it must continue throughout the term in which the duties are performed. A leader's club or class can be used to instruct student assistants in their duties. Students should thoroughly understand the policies and procedures of the department and the duties that they will be expected to perform.

The major duty of the student assistants is to assist the instructor in any way possible, consistent with their own capabilities and potential. Some possible duties include:

1. Preparing the play area.
2. Distributing, collecting, and caring for equipment.
3. Taking roll.
4. Making out squad cards.
5. Checking uniforms.
6. Recording tardy and absence slips.
7. Checking showers.
8. Leading exercises and drills.
9. Demonstrating skills.
10. Officiating.
11. Assisting with media hardware.
12. Turning showers on and off.
13. Assisting with test administration and scoring.
14. Providing individual assistance to students.
15. Assisting with other duties, according to interests and abilities.

During their period of service, student assistants should be brought together periodically to discuss experiences, solve problems, and determine new and better ways to approach their assignments.

Some problems have been associated with the use of student leaders. These problems include students not being adequately prepared for their assignments, students doing teachers' "dirty work," students placed in situations where they "know too much," students assisting during their own physical education period losing out on practice needed to improve their own skills, and students losing friends by attempting to cope with grading or discipline problems. Each of these problems can be prevented by adequate preparation and by recalling that the duties of the student assistant are to assist with the class work and not to be responsible for grading or disciplining students.

Periodic evaluation of student assistants and the program should be made and a follow-up made of the results. An evaluation form that could be used for this purpose is shown in figure 12.8.

Increasing Motivation through Classroom Management

The discussion here is limited to those aspects of classroom management that relate directly to motivation (see chapter 13 for other suggestions). Some teacher behaviors that can be used to enhance classroom management include:

1. Be efficient, while keeping the emphasis on the activity rather than on the organization.
2. Keep distractions to a minimum.
3. Begin lessons promptly.
4. Be alert for boredom or inactivity.
5. Be consistent about requirements.

In addition to these behaviors, norm setting and classroom management games can be effective in many situations.

Norm setting involves students and teacher in setting rules for the health, safety, and mutual welfare of all concerned. When students participate in setting rules, they are generally more responsible for implementing them. (For a complete explanation of norm setting, refer to chapter 13.)

Management games are generally based on Grandma's Law, which states, "First clean up your plate, and then you may have your dessert." Translated into physical education terminology, it states, "By accomplishing certain classroom management tasks quickly, you will have more time for play." Teachers need to clearly specify a few rules that tell what is expected to earn the reward. The reward may be based on the behavior of the entire class or of each squad. For example, all squads quiet, sitting in place, and ready for roll call within five seconds from the teacher's signal, earn a point. A stopwatch can be used to record the amount of time used. A variety of reinforcers to reward appropriate behaviors often set a positive atmosphere in a class. Ideas for behavior modification are discussed in chapter 13.

Record Keeping

The main purposes of record keeping are to provide information to administrators, parents, and guidance counselors; and to help teachers evaluate students, themselves, and the curriculum. Only pertinent, up-to-date records should be kept.

Types of records include: (1) attendance records; (2) records of achievement, including grades; (3) health and medical records; and (4) equipment and locker records.

EVALUATION OF THE TEACHING ASSISTANT

Name: _____
       (Last)   (First)

Instructions: Rate the student on each of the items listed below. If there is no basis for determining a rating on an item, write "no basis."

	Strong	Average	Weak
I. *Personal Qualities*			
Adaptability, flexibility	_____	_____	_____
Initiative, originality	_____	_____	_____
Responsibility	_____	_____	_____
Well-mannnered, well-groomed	_____	_____	_____
Punctual, dependable	_____	_____	_____
II. *Teacher--Teaching Assistant*			
Friendly	_____	_____	_____
Asks for and accepts suggestions	_____	_____	_____
Acts upon suggestions	_____	_____	_____
Cooperates well	_____	_____	_____
III. *Teaching Assistant--Students*			
Likes students	_____	_____	_____
Understands students	_____	_____	_____
Students respond well to her or him	_____	_____	_____
Fair and impartial	_____	_____	_____
IV. *Teaching Skills*			
Knowledge of subject	_____	_____	_____
Demonstrates well	_____	_____	_____
Officiates well	_____	_____	_____
Communicates knowledge to students	_____	_____	_____
Keeps accurate records	_____	_____	_____
V. *Class Management*			
Effective organization of groups	_____	_____	_____
Good control	_____	_____	_____
VI. *Professional Growth*			
Interest in the profession	_____	_____	_____
Growing knowledge of the profession	_____	_____	_____

The teaching assistant was:

Valuable--a great deal of help   _____

Some help   _____

A burden--little or no help   _____

Comments: _____

Signature: _____

Figure 12.8 A student assistant evaluation form.

Attendance Records

Teachers are required to keep an accurate record of the daily attendance of all students assigned to them. The record should be kept up to date each day. Because pencil tends to blur, the records should generally be kept in ink.

Attendance Register

Figure 12.9 shows a sample page from an attendance register. The top section identifies the class as Mrs. Jackson's second period physical education class at Younowhere Junior High School during the fall semester. No text is required. In the left-hand column, the students are listed in alphabetical order. Next to their names are their sex, grade, entry code, and exit code. The entry codes are as follows:

E1—Enrolled from within the state
E2—Entered from another state this school year

The exit codes are as follows:

T1—Transferred to another class
T2—Transferred to another school
D1—Dropped out of school

Attendance markings may differ from state to state or district to district. Two common sets of markings follow. The first set has been used in this sample:

Absence	—	/
Excused absence	(—)	⊘ or x
Tardy	⊹	⋏
Excused tardy	(⊹)	⋋ or Ⓐ
Excused for another school event	Ex	Ex

Days enrolled includes the total number of days each student was enrolled in the class. Absences and tardies are also summarized for the term.

Squad Cards

Squad cards are often used to take roll, and the attendance record can be transferred to the attendance register after class. A sample squad card is shown in figure 12.10.

Records of Achievement

Records of student achievement are usually kept on class record cards and on individual permanent record cards. A discussion of each of these types of records follows.

Class Record Cards

A class record card is a record of the achievements of all students in a particular class. It provides information to the teacher and to the student on each student's progress in the class. A sample class record card is shown in figure 12.11.

Period	Instructor(s)	Course Title	Text(s)
2	Mrs. L. Jackson	Physical Education	None
Fall (Term)	Younowhere Jr. High (School)		9/8 (Date Class Began) to 1/12 (Date Class Ended); 80 (Total Days Held)

Ref.	Pupil	Sex	Grade	Entry Code	Exit Code	Sept. Wk. 1 8 T	9 W	10 T	11 F	Wk. 2 14 M	15 T	16 W	17 T	18 F	Wk. 3 21 M	22 T	23 W	24 T	25 F	Oct. Wk. 4 28 M	29 T	30 W	1 T	2 F	Wk. 5 5 M	6 T	7 W	8 T	9 F	TERM SUMMARY Days Enrolled	Days Absent	Times Tardy	YEAR-END SUMMARY Days Enrolled	Days Absent	Final Mark	Credit
1	Alexander, Claudia	F	8	E1			—																		⊖					44	2	0				
2	Bishop, April	F	8	E1																										44	0	0				
3	Carter, Susan	F	8	E1										⊖												⊖				44	2	0				
4	Dixon, Lonnie	M	8	E1	T1		⊖																				[T1]			21	1	0				
5	Dove, Jim	M	8	E1																·										44	0	1				
6	Eden, Sherron	F	8	E1																										44	0	0				
7	Giles, David	M	8	E1							⊖			⊖									(—	—	—	—	—	—)		44	8	0				
8	Herton, Giles	M	8	E1																										44	0	0				
9	Johnson, Kyle	M	8	E1										Ex																44	0	0				
10	Killian, Teresa	F	8	E1																										44	0	0				
11	Lance, Cathy	F	8	E1																										44	0	0				
12	Limb, Susan	M	8	E1	D			(—	—)					⊖		(—	—	—	—)		(—	—	—	—	—	—	—	—)		44	16	0				
13	Peery, Phyllis	F	8	E1																										44	0	0				
14	Rasmus, Jody	F	8	E1	T2									Ex												T2				19	0	0				
15	Skinner, David	M	8	E1												·														44	0	1				
16	Sousa, Pepe	M	8	E2																[E2]						⊖				28	1	0				
17	Stevens, Jim	M	8	E1						⊖·																				44	0	1				
18	Walden, Heather	F	8	E1										Ex																44	0	0				
19	Wardell, Mark	M	8	E1													⊖													44	1	0				
20	Wilson, Rosalie	F	8	E1																										44	0	0				
21	York, Ryan	M	8	E1					(—	—	—	—)		—	—				—			—	—							44	9	0				

Figure 12.9 An attendance register.
Source: Marilyn Harding, Springville Junior High School, Springville, Utah.

Figure 12.10 A squad card.

BADMINTON PERIOD 4	Serves	Clears	Drops	Smashes	Strategy + Positioning	FORM	Skills Test Clears	Skills Test Smashes	Skills Test Drops	Skills Test Serves	SKILL TEST	TOURNAMENT	QUIZ-RULES	FINAL TEST	SKILL	KNOWLEDGE	GRADE
Babbett, Mark R.	3	2	2	3	3	A	35	35	36	25	A-	A	B	A	A	A	A
Bagat, Devendra	2	3	1	1	2	C	13	26	20	25	C	B	C+	A	C+	B+	B-
Bushman, Virnell	3	3	3	3	3	A	36	30	17	14	C	A	B	A	B+	A-	B+
Crow, Craig J.	3	3	2	2	3	A	27	39	41	23	A-	B	A	A	B+	A	A-
Davis, Karen A.	3	2	3	3	2	A	34	38	10	43	B	B	B	B	B+	B	B+
Erickson, Craig A.	2	3	2	3	2	B	34	44	40	21	A	C	B	A-	B+	B+	B+
Gold, Lu Anne	3	3	2	2	2	B	31	40	29	38	A	B	C	B	B+	B-	B
Hansen, Marilyn A.	3	2	3	2	1	B	22	38	36	32	B	B	A	A-	B	A-	B
Hendrickson, Jan	3	3	1	1	1	C	4	30	25	36	C	C	C	B	C	B-	C+
Jackson, Linda A.	1	3	1	2	2	C	36	33	34	15	B	B	B-	A	B-	B+	B
Kramer, Terry May	3	3	2	3	2	A	20	43	24	31	C	A	B	B	B+	B	B+
Liscom, Leslie J.	3	2	2	2	1	C	24	31	15	34	B	C	C-	B	C+	C+	C+
Melner, Eric C.	3	3	2	3	2	A	27	33	29	29	B	B	A-	B	B+	B+	B+
Nielson, Lucy A.	2	3	3	1	2	B	32	29	32	14	B	A	C	C	B+	C	B-

Figure 12.11 A class record card.

Individual Permanent Record Cards

A permanent record card for each student provides a valuable source of information about student progress in the physical education program. It provides a record of the parents' names and phone number for emergencies, the students fitness test results, all of the activity or content units completed by the student, and awards and honors in the extra-class programs. Individual record cards should be filed alphabetically in the department office. Samples of two types of individual permanent record cards are shown in figure 12.12.

The computer provides an alternative method of keeping information about student progress. A printout can be used to obtain information about individual or class achievement in any area of physical education.

Health and Medical Records

In the first part of this chapter, medical excuses for temporary or long-term illness or injury were discussed and forms were presented for each of these situations. Each of these forms should be kept on file in the physical education department office.

Another type of record that should be kept on hand is a record of health status for each student. The school nurse can be helpful in collating this information from permanent school records. Such conditions as asthma, allergies, diabetes, heart conditions, muscular or orthopedic disorders, and many other conditions can affect student participation in the physical education program.

Equipment and Locker Records

Locker records were discussed earlier in the chapter under school policies and procedures. A record should be kept in the department by the department head, or some other faculty member, of all departmental transactions. Equipment purchases and maintenance are especially important. Equipment records include a yearly equipment inventory, copies of purchase orders, and check-out forms for athletic equipment. For further information regarding these subjects, refer to a textbook on administration.

Questions and Suggested Activities

1. You read the following court settlement case in the newspaper: "A student, excused from physical education for medical reasons, came out of the bleachers during class to wrestle another student. He was injured, sued his instructor for alleged lack of supervision, and was awarded $5 million by the New York Supreme Court."[36] What precautions would you take as a teacher to ensure against such a settlement at your school? What precautions should the district take?
2. Define the following terms: legal liability, tort, plaintiff, defendant, attractive nuisance, and *in loco parentis*. Determine your understanding of negligence. Explain negligence by omission, by commission. List the sources of negligence. What six possibilities exist for a defense of negligence?
3. Read cases from a book on school law in your state about uniforms and list what can or cannot be required.
4. Talk to a principal and the physical education department head in a secondary school regarding the policies and procedures of operation. Read the faculty handbook and student handouts from the school and become familiar with school and department policies and procedures. Do you agree with them? What policies would you change and why?

AN INDIVIDUAL RECORD CARD

Name _Carol Duncan_   Date of Birth _21 June 1972_

Address _234 S. Glassell_

Parents' Names _Lloyd & Karen Duncan_   Phone _358-9308_

PHYSICAL FITNESS TESTING

Grade	1.5 mile run R.S.	%	% Fat R.S.	%	Flexibility R.S.	%	Strength R.S.	%
9 Pre	17:19	45	18	75	29	30	35	50
9 Post	16:34	55	18	75	30	35	35	50
10 Pre	16:14	60	17	85	30	20	35	40
10 Post	15:50	65	18	80	32	30	37	50
11 Pre	15:26	70	18	85	32	35	37	65
11 Post								
12 Pre								
12 Post								

AN INDIVIDUAL RECORD CARD

Activity	Fitness & Skills	Knowledge	Citizenship	Grade	Year Taken
Archery					
Badminton	B+	A	A	A-	1986-7
Basketball	B	A	A	B+	1985-6
Flag Football					
Folk Dance	A-	A	A	A-	1986-7
Golf	B-	A-	A	B+	1986-7
Gymnastics	A-	A	A	A-	1986-7
Modern Dance	A-	A	A	A-	1987-8
Soccer	B	A	A	B+	1985-6
Social Dance	A	A	A	A	1987-8
Softball					
Swimming	A	A	A	A	1985-6
Tennis					
Volleyball	B	A	A	B+	1985-6

Intramural participation--Activities and awards:

Extramural participation--Activities and awards:

Figure 12.12 An individual record card (front and back).

5. After completing one of the following evaluation procedures, choose one or more components of teaching you need to work on and repeat the evaluation until you have improved your performance to a satisfactory level:
   a. While teaching a practicum class, have a student or another practicum student evaluate your classroom management techniques by using a stopwatch to record the amount of time students in your class are *actively* engaged in learning (see chapter 14).
   b. Tape record or videotape yourself while teaching a class or working with a group of children or youth. Analyze your management skills, using the suggestions in chapter 14.
6. Visit several public schools and talk to the physical education teachers to obtain ideas for (1) adapting activities for large groups, (2) learning students' names, and (3) adapting for interruptions. Take a tour of the equipment room. Study how equipment is stored and note the care techniques that are used. Obtain sample record-keeping forms used in the program.
7. You are a junior high school physical education teacher. In the middle of the semester, you get a new student who is the only minority member in the class. It is a rule in your class that each boy must take a shower, but the new boy refuses to do so. You are receiving much static from other students over this situation. When talking to the new student, you sense that he seems very concerned about showering with the other boys. You want to be fair to all. What will you do?

Suggested Readings

Appenzeller, Herb. *Physical Education and the Law.* Charlottesville, Virginia: The Michie Company, 1978.

Appenzeller, Herb. *The Right to Participate.* Charlottesville, Virginia: The Michie Company, 1983.

Appenzeller, Herb, and Thomas Appenzeller. *Sports and the Courts.* Charlottesville, Virginia: The Michie Company, 1980.

Arnold, Don E. "Legal Aspects of Off-Campus Physical Education Programs." *Journal of Physical Education and Recreation* 50 (April 1979):21–23.

Bayless, Mary Ann, and Samuel H. Adams. "A Liability Checklist." *Journal of Physical Education, Recreation and Dance* 56 (February 1985):49.

Blucker, Judy A., and Sarah W. J. Pell. "Legal and Ethical Issues: Essential for Professional Preparation Curricula." *Journal of Physical Education, Recreation and Dance* 57 (January 1986):19–22.

Brandon, Jim. "Discipline, Choosing Teams, Square Dance, and Rope-Skipping." In Ronald P. Carlson, ed., *IDEAS II for Secondary School Physical Education: A Sharing of Teaching Practices by Secondary School Physical Education Practitioners.* Reston, Virginia: American Alliance for Health, Physical Education, Recreation and Dance, 1984, 72–73.

Carpenter, Linda Jean, and R. Vivian Acosta. "Negligence: What Is It? How Can It Be Avoided?" *Journal of Physical Education, Recreation and Dance* 53 (February 1982):51–52, 89.

Clumpner, Roy A. "Maximizing Participation and Enjoyment in the PE Classrooms." *Journal of Physical Education and Recreation* 50 (January 1979):60–62.

Dougherty, Neil J. "Liability." *Journal of Physical Education, Recreation and Dance* 54 (June 1983):52–54.

Garcia, Robert Andrew. "Affecting Positive Behavior in Nondress Students." In Ronald P. Carlson, ed., *IDEAS II for Secondary School Physical Education: A Sharing of Teaching Practices by Secondary School Physical Education Practitioners.* Reston, Virginia: American Alliance for Health, Physical Education, Recreation and Dance, 1984, 77–78.

Garcia, Robert Andrew. "Time Use of Nondressers in Physical Education Class." *Journal of Physical Education, Recreation and Dance* 55 (October 1984):74–76.

Hellison, Don. *Beyond Balls & Bats.* Washington, D.C.: American Alliance for Health, Physical Education and Recreation, 1978.

Henderson, Donald H. "Physical Education Teachers: How Do I Sue Thee? Oh, Let Me Count the Ways!" *Journal of Physical Education, Recreation and Dance* 56 (February 1985):44–48.

Kaiser, Ronald A. "Program Liability Waivers: Do They Protect the Agency and Staff?" *Journal of Physical Education, Recreation and Dance* 55 (August 1984):54–56.

Lewandowski, Diane M. "Shoestrings and Shoeboxes." *Journal of Physical Education and Recreation* 55 (August 1984):34–35.

Nygaard, Gary, and Thomas H. Boone. *Law for Physical Educators and Coaches.* Salt Lake City: Brighton Publishing Company, 1981.

Placek, Judith H. "Involving the Nonparticipant: Motivation and Make-ups." *Journal of Physical Education, Recreation and Dance* 55 (August 1984):27–29.

References

1. Charles A. Bucher and Constance R. Koenig, *Methods and Materials for Secondary School Physical Education* (St. Louis: C. V. Mosby Company, 1983), p. 153.
2. Neil J. Dougherty and Diane Bonanno, *Contemporary Approaches to the Teaching of Physical Education,* 2d ed. (Scottsdale: Gorsuch Scarisbrick, Publishers, 1987), p. 207.
3. Charles Peter Yost, ed., *Sports Safety: Accident Prevention and Injury Control in Physical Education, Athletics, and Recreation* (Washington, D.C.: AAHPER), p. 9.
4. Don E. Arnold, "Positive Outcomes of Recent Legislative and Case Law Developments Which Have Implications for HPER Programs," *The Physical Educator* 37 (March 1980), pp. 24–25.
5. Larry Berryhill and Boyd Jarman, *A History of Law Suits in Physical Education, Intramurals and Interscholastic Athletics in the Western United States: Their Implications and Consequences* (Provo, Utah: Brigham Young University Publications, 1979), p. 2.
6. Arnold, "Positive Outcomes," p. 25.
7. Herb Appenzeller and C. Thomas Ross, eds., *Sports and the Courts: Physical Education and Sports Law Quarterly* 4 (Fall 1983), p. 1.
8. Herb Appenzeller, *From the Gym to the Jury* (Charlottesville, Virginia: The Michie Company, 1970), pp. 83–84.
9. Herb Appenzeller and Thomas Appenzeller, *Sports and the Courts* (Charlottesville, Virginia: The Michie Company, 1980), p. 4.
10. H. C. Hudgins, Jr., and Richard S. Vacca, *Law and Education: Contemporary Issues and Court Decisions* (Charlottesville, Virginia: The Michie Company, 1979), p. 72.
11. *Molitor v. Kaneland,* 163 NE 2d 89 (Ill. 1959).
12. Arnold, "Positive Outcomes," p. 25.
13. Berryhill and Jarman, *A History of Law Suits,* p. 2.
14. Donald H. Henderson, "Physical Education Teachers: How Do I Sue Thee? Oh, Let Me Count the Ways!" *Journal of Physical Education, Recreation and Dance* 56 (February 1985), p. 44.
15. Berryhill and Jarman, *A History of Law Suits,* p. 3.
16. Appenzeller, *From the Gym to the Jury,* pp. 68–69.
17. John N. Drowatzky, "Liability: You Could Be Sued!" *Journal of Physical Education and Recreation* 49 (May 1978): 17–18.
18. Appenzeller, *From the Gym to the Jury,* pp. 8–9.
19. Ibid., p. 171.
20. Hudgins and Vacca, *Law and Education,* p. 84.
21. J. N. Drowatzky, "On the Firing Line: Negligence in Physical Education," *Journal of Law and Education* 6 (1977), pp. 481–90.
22. Appenzeller, *From the Gym to the Jury,* p. 174.
23. Ibid., p. 115.
24. Ibid., p. 146.
25. Ibid., p. 139.
26. Ibid., p. 137.

27. Bucher and Koenig, *Methods and Materials for Secondary School Physical Education,* p. 164.
28. Ronald A. Kaiser, "Program Liability Waivers," *Journal of Physical Education, Recreation and Dance* 55 (August 1984), p. 55.
29. Arnold, "Positive Outcomes," p. 25.
30. Rex Hardy, "Dressing Out in Physical Education: Probing the Problem," *The Physical Educator* 36 (December 1979), pp. 191–92.
31. *Mitchell v. McCall,* 273 Ala 604, 143 S (2d) 629 (1962).
32. Hardy, "Dressing Out in Physical Education."
33. Paul C. Pease, "Effects of Interdependent Group Contingencies in a Secondary Physical Education Setting," *Journal of Teaching in Physical Education* 2 (Fall 1982), pp. 29–37.
34. Katherine C. La Mancusa, *We Do Not Throw Rocks at the Teacher!* (Scranton, Pennsylvania: International Textbook Company, 1966), p. 116.
35. Ibid., pp. 116–17.
36. Herb Appenzeller and C. Thomas Ross, eds., *Sports and the Courts: Physical Education and Sports Law Quarterly* 4 (Winter, 1983), p. 15.

13

Establishing Effective Class Control— Motivation and Discipline

Study Stimulators

1. Why are motivation and discipline studied together?
2. What is motivation?
3. What variables influence motivation?
4. How can effective classroom management increase motivation?
5. What are reinforcers and how might they be used to motivate students?
6. What is discipline?
7. Why is a study of discipline so important?
8. What disciplinary techniques are generally considered to be acceptable? Which ones would you use and when?
9. What disciplinary techniques are generally considered to be unacceptable?

According to Doyle, teaching basically involves a combination of instruction and order.[1] Assuming the teacher has the expertise to model and convey subject matter, he or she must then plan the instruction in such a way that order is maintained and learning occurs. Inherent in this process are both motivation and discipline. Both are discussed in this chapter because one often dictates the outcome of the other.

Teachers set the stage for both motivation and discipline. The meaningful organization of instruction is vital to the maintenance of order in the classroom. Of equal importance is the attitude, including motivation, of each individual learner. The teacher is not solely responsible for this attitude, but does exercise some control in this regard.

Hellison pointed out that "physical education teachers and coaches have expressed increasing concern over discipline and motivation problems in their gyms and on their playing fields."[2] He maintained that if physical education and sport leaders want to prevent or reduce discipline and motivation problems, they must adjust to the changing world and incorporate the following needs:

1. Improve control in our classes and on our teams.
2. Help students make responsible choices.
3. Help students lead more stable lives.
4. Counter the ineffectiveness of schools.
5. Accomplish these needs without minimizing participation in physical activity.[3]

Teachers working with students who lack motivation and discipline and those who want to increase these traits in students would do well to study Hellison's model. He outlined some nontraditional goals of physical education including teaching students self-control, to take responsibility for their own learning, to make wise choices, to develop a meaningful and personally satisfying life-style, and to cooperate and support and help one another. His model for teaching involves developmental levels of progression for students involving attitudes and behavior, and interaction strategies for both teachers and students.

Glasser maintained that "the major problem of the schools is a problem of failure."[4] He further suggested that educators need to examine why children fail and provide schools in which children can succeed. Youth who feel the concern and acceptance of a teacher can gain in self-confidence which, in turn, enhances self-motivation. These factors constitute the foundation for success. A student experiencing success is much more likely to anticipate each learning activity and participate in an orderly way. Once the cycle of success within each student is in operation, class control is more effective.

Teachers must be committed to helping students succeed through a genuine concern for each of them. This concern for learners involves the following:

1. *Caring:* helping students feel they are liked.
2. *Understanding:* creating an atmosphere of empathy and tolerance.
3. *Identification:* considering students as separate, worthy individuals.
4. *Recognition:* appreciating students' unique contributions.[5]

This chapter will present suggestions to promote student motivation, as well as discipline tactics to aid students in their quest for success.

Motivation

According to Joe Cybulski, a ten-year-old at Ballwin Elementary School in Ballwin, Missouri, motivation is "to convince someone he always wanted to learn something he never even knew he wanted to learn."[6] Madeline Hunter maintained that "no one can make a child or anyone else learn." What is done is to arrange circumstances in the environment so a child will be encouraged to do something that will result in learning. She defined motivation as "a state of need or desire that activates the person to do something that will satisfy that need or desire." Teachers cannot motivate students. They can only manipulate environmental variables that may result in an increase or decrease of motivation.[7] Motivation, then, is influenced both by personal factors within the student and by external environmental factors manipulated by the teacher.[8] Variables known to be related to the amount of motivation include the following:

1. The degree of concern or tension that exists within the learner. When tension increases to an undue degree because of excessive anxiety, anger, hostility, or compulsion, motivation decreases.
2. The feeling tone (pleasant or unpleasant). Pleasant feeling tones increase motivation to a high degree. Unpleasant feeling tones will also increase motivation, but to a lesser degree. The absence of or neutral feeling tones will not influence motivation.
3. Interest. People are motivated to do things that interest them.
4. Success. People are usually more successful in activities that interest them. Success in turn tends to stimulate interest. The degree of success becomes an important variable in motivation.

5. Knowledge of results (How am I doing). The more specific the feedback, the more one becomes motivated to improve performance.
6. Intrinsic-extrinsic motivation (refer to chapter 4). Most examples of these are not completely one or the other and both may be effective.[9]

Students are not unmotivated. As McKeachie indicated, "They are learning all the time—new dance steps, the status hierarchy on campus, football strategy, etc."[10] Teachers need to realize this and capitalize on "what turns students on." Students are much more motivated to learn material that is meaningful. This is a significant factor in retention, also. Students are more apt to remember material that is meaningful.[11] Teachers need to put themselves in the shoes of their students to determine what is meaningful to them.

Motivation results in an urge or desire to achieve a specific goal. In chapter 7, the importance of teachers defining objectives and setting goals was discussed. Locke and his colleagues found that, in 99 out of 110 research studies, specific, hard goals produced better performance than easy, do-your-best, or no goals.[12]

Students who are motivated engage in approach behaviors toward the activity or subject involved. Unmotivated students engage in avoidance behaviors and do not perform the desired responses; therefore, they learn slowly or not at all. The process of learning is more rapid when students are motivated. It works somewhat like a mathematical equation, in which skill $=$ performance $\times$ motivation. Learning increases geometrically as motivation increases.

Increasing Motivation through Classroom Management

Motivation can be increased by effective classroom management. Some teacher behaviors that can be used to enhance classroom management were included in chapter 12.

Increasing Motivation through the Use of Reinforcers

Teachers have at their disposal a variety of reinforcers that can be used to reward behavior and motivate future actions. The same techniques often overlap with discipline practices and should also be thought of in these terms. The way in which the teacher uses a reinforcer frequently determines its success, because teachers themselves are one of the major sources of motivation in a class. Enthusiasm, facial expression, animation, and vocal intensity are some of the qualities a teacher can exhibit that are important. Since some events or things are rewarding to some students and other events or things are rewarding to others, several suggested ideas for reinforcers follow.

Praise

The effects of praise or criticism vary with the experience, personality, and previous successes and failures of the students. Some students find praise embarrassing; others encourage and even elicit praise from teachers. Teachers should be careful to use praise only when it is sincere. Ignoring a student is less motivating to many students than either praise or criticism.

Tokens or Points

Tokens or points are collected to be exchanged at a later time for a specific reward. The object is not only to reward behavior, but also to change it. Tousignant and Siedentop found that students who were rewarded for effort or performance reduced the quantity of off-task behaviors.[13] Certificates, ribbons, stickers, special events, and other rewards might be used to reward and motivate students. Siedentop specified a series of guidelines to implement this system:

1. Define the target in observable units.
2. Explain the target behaviors clearly to the participants.
3. Monitor the target behaviors consistently.
4. State the contingency (reward) clearly.
5. Use a simple reward system.
6. Think small. Make the system manageable.
7. Be consistent.[14]

The following examples illustrate the use of tokens or points:

1. Points are awarded during tournament play for game results. The following point system might be used:

   1 point = a loss
   2 points = a tie
   3 points = a win

   At the end of round-robin competition, points are totaled to award first, second, third, or other place honors. Points might also be given for acts of courtesy and sportsmanship.
2. Colored tickets are awarded for events in track and field throughout the unit (see figure 13.1).

   Blue   = 1st place (running events)
   Red   = 2nd place (running events)
   White   = 3rd place (running events)
   Orange   = Jogged a lap

   Blue, red, white, yellow, and green ribbons are also awarded for designated heights or distances in field events. Students are able to earn ribbons even though they might not place first, second, or third.

   At the conclusion of a unit, the point values of each ticket are calculated and students record their total score.
3. Extra-credit points or tokens are awarded for participation outside of school hours for activities from archery to water skiing. One hour outside of school might be equal to ten hours in school. Have students keep a log of dates and hours spent in each activity. The Institute for Aerobics Research (12330 Preston Road, Dallas, Texas 75230) has a point system for 21 sports.
4. Points are awarded to units within a team for outstanding plays or goals achieved. For example, on the basketball team the guards, forwards, and centers would compete as three separate units. An average unit free-throw percentage would be kept, and the unit with the lowest average would buy pizza for the other two units.
5. Grades are based on a point system for completing learning tasks and policy requirements. When such a system is used, students know exactly what is required of them to earn a grade.

Name _____ Period _____ Total score _____

INDIVIDUAL TRACK RECORD

Staple tickets below:
Blues on top, reds
next, etc.

	Blue	Red	White	Yellow	Green	Orange	Ticket totals for each event
High jump	4	2	3	2	1	1	13
Standing long jump							0
Running long jump		2	1	2	1		6
All dashes (50-75-100)	2	2	1	1			6
All relays (440 and Shuttle)	2	1		1			4
Total number of tickets for each color	8	7	5	6	2	1	29

To calculate your total score:
    Count 10 points for *each* ticket.   <u>290</u>
    Count 3 more points for each *blue* ticket.   <u>24</u>
    Count 2 more points for each *red* ticket.   <u>14</u>
    Count 1 more point for each *white* ticket.   <u>5</u>

Total score   333

Figure 13.1 Individual track record.

Source: Kathryn Alldredge and Mary Taylor.

Contingent Activities

Contingent activities come about as a reward for a goal fulfilled. Such activities should always be incorporated in a positive manner. Physical activity should never be negative, such as using running or push-ups as punishment for the losers of a game or for inappropriate behavior. Some possible activities include:

1. Reward class effort by letting students play novelty games or make up their own games.
2. Allow students who complete assigned tasks early to set up a game or match of their choice, practice on their own, or use specialized equipment (e.g., a ball machine).

Increasing Motivation through Social Approval

Activities that bring social approval to students not only increase motivation, but also individual self-esteem. Activities that can be used to show social approval of students include:

1. Post a "player of the week" type award on the bulletin board for any specified behavior such as leadership, sportsmanship, effort, or skill performance.
2. Conduct a "move-up" tournament. The tournament is played by having winners move up one court, lane, or target, and having losers move down except on the first court where winners stay, and on the last court where losers stay.
3. Award fun prizes for unusual accomplishments, such as the golden arrow for the most bull's eyes (an old arrow sprayed gold) or the belle of the ball for most matches played (a tennis ball dressed in a gown) or the sneaker award (an old sneaker) to the most improved runner on the physical fitness test.
4. Select new team captains often so all students eventually get a chance to act in this capacity. Some students, who normally would be chosen last, might be selected to do this very early in the year.

Many of the motivational techniques discussed promote effective discipline in the class. The two areas complement each other and should be thought of together.

Discipline

Of the major problems facing the public schools, discipline has been ranked number one by the annual Gallup poll for sixteen of the past seventeen years. The 1987 poll showed 30 percent of the respondents mentioned drugs as the most important problem facing the schools. Discipline problems ranked second and were mentioned by 22 percent of the respondents as the most important problem.[15] Many teachers leave the teaching profession because of their inability to discipline.

Schools and teachers must further be concerned about discipline because research shows that schools contribute to their students' academic achievement by establishing, communicating, and enforcing fair and consistent discipline policies.[16] Educators, then, have a responsibility to organize and carry out effective discipline procedures. This responsibility includes providing a productive learning atmosphere and also teaching acceptable behavior practices. If a student is to behave in a disciplined manner, such behavior must be taught and ultimately learned. The schools are not solely responsible to teach and monitor discipline because discipline provides for social order and individual productivity,[17] but the results of such efforts are always in the public eye.

Students are critical of teachers who do not maintain adequate control of classroom behavior. They indicate that few teachers can teach well without establishing good class discipline. They are aware that often beginning teachers have less control than experienced teachers.

The most important concern of discipline is the establishment of a good learning environment—one in which students can grow in both knowledge and self-control. Each student has a basic right to an educational experience free from the unnecessary distractions caused by a few unruly students. Good order, based on a cooperative effort of all of those involved, contributes both to the teacher's goal of optimum learning and to the student's growth as a responsible member of society.

What is discipline? Is it a set of rules, controlled behavior, a systematic method to obtain obedience, punishment, or moral and ethical behavior? Discipline is difficult to define because its meaning has evolved over the years to include many aspects of behavior. Some authors have equated the word discipline with specific behavior. Discipline is often thought of as a cut-and-dried situation of good versus bad. However, because each individual reacts differently to his or her environment, many variations in behavior must be accepted as normal.

Historically, classroom discipline could have been defined primarily as an unquestioning, immediate, and strict obedience imposed by a teacher to create a teaching-learning environment through the maintenance of good order. This order was probably maintained by fear. Although the intelligent application of psychological principles to the maintenance of order has increased the chances of success with this type of discipline, it is best used only for restraint of the immature learner.

Children go through various stages as they mature and come to understand control. Preschool children are trained to follow established rules and procedures. Children learn to relate to nonpersonal objects, becoming familiar with natural laws and governing themselves so as to use those laws for their own purposes. As children enter school, they are helped to develop a certain amount of conformity to group patterns, which we might call social control. They learn to relate to the culture and its institutions—the sociological, political, and economic laws of force. They develop the capacity for some reciprocal adjustment with their environment. Finally, children learn to interact with others through a process of self-control. They interact on a psychological level and need no extrinsic reward or punishment.

Thus, discipline becomes a process of assisting youngsters to adjust to their environment and develop acceptable inner controls. For purposes of discussion, discipline will be defined as *orderly social behavior in an atmosphere that allows meaningful learning to transpire.* The process involves a slow progression from the direct, authoritative control of behavior needed by some learners to the level of desirable self-control experienced by only a few. In education today, the emphasis is often on the student's natural ability to interpret the situation and react accordingly, reaping the natural consequences of any undesired act, rather than on a strict code of behavior for all students.

Discipline involves both the students and the teachers. Teachers must know when to be authoritative, when to be permissive, and when to straddle the middle ground. Classes can change dramatically from one hour to the next or one week to another. Pep rallies, assemblies, lunchtime activities, weather, or the activities of the previous classes can cause normally quiet students to stampede into the room. Success or failure with homework or previous assignments can affect the attitude of students before the lesson has even begun.

As students and teacher embark on a day's activities, many results can occur. The ideal situation is one in which both teacher and students are successfully engaged in teaching and learning activities, neither interfering with the activities of the other. However, since teachers and students often have different personalities and values, conflict might occur, resulting in behavior unacceptable to either the teacher or the student.[18] If the problem is on the part of the student, the teacher must listen to the student's problem and attempt to understand and resolve it if possible. If the problem is a hindrance to the teacher's activities, the teacher must communicate to the student how he or she feels in an attempt to resolve the conflict. For example, the teacher might say, "I'm trying to help everyone learn the. . . , but I can't when I'm constantly interrupted." Sometimes the student will understand and alter the behavior. Oftentimes the school or teacher has a specific policy for handling the behavior. If not, the teacher will be forced to (1) take a stand and authoritatively decide what to do to solve the problem, (2) allow the student to continue the behavior at the expense of the teacher and often of the other students, or (3) attempt to work out a solution that is acceptable to both parties.

The wise teacher realizes that discipline problems are most often preventable. The students and the environment can be programmed to avoid many problems.

Preventive Discipline

The responsibility for discipline lies with the teacher. Preventive discipline involves more than just the establishment of sound methods of control. The following variables must also be considered: (1) the personality, self-confidence, and attitudes of the teacher; (2) the development of proper interpersonal relations; (3) a psychological insight into the background and characteristics of students and the causes of behavioral problems; (4) the use of routine (rules, conduct code) for recurring situations; (5) proper planning and preparation, both long range and short range; (6) a wholesome, attractive, and well-managed environment; (7) the establishment of a relevant, challenging curriculum; and (8) proper instructional techniques (e.g., keep the class moving). Each of these items is discussed in another section of this book.

The key to classroom control comes from understanding the worth of each individual student and communicating this to each student. No matter how effective a teacher has been at preventive discipline, students still need the guidance and security provided by well-defined rules of expected behavior and the knowledge that adults care enough about them to enforce those rules. A study of appropriate behavior in a low socioeconomic level junior high school revealed that the teacher with discipline problems failed to enforce rules and monitor behavior of students.[19] The results substantiated Durkheim's premise that "children themselves are the first to appreciate good discipline."[20] Teachers need to remember that it takes *courage* to discipline, but that students want this and they will still respect and like the teacher who is a disciplinarian.[21]

Until teachers and students know each other, discipline usually begins in a serious, no-nonsense vein with adult rule and pupil obedience. The teacher then attempts to work toward student self-control by planning with the individuals in the class. Teacher-directed group planning, in which the scope and area of planning are predetermined, is the next step toward self-direction. Self-management through group planning is achieved only after all of the other skills and understandings needed have been achieved.

However, even after self-direction in known areas has been achieved, some students will fail to be self-directing when a new situation presents itself. For this reason, patterns of control must be applied according to the appropriateness of the situation. At times, the teacher needs to provide the students with a choice between self-direction and teacher direction and let them decide which will be more valuable to them in the specific learning environment.

Teachers with good discipline in their classes exhibit some similarities in their authority style, but no specific formula will produce good discipline for all teachers. Effective discipline tends to emanate from teachers who are

1. Positive role models. They
   a. Are assertive rather than aggressive.
   b. Act rather than react.
   c. Are consistent rather than inconsistent.
   d. Clearly communicate expectations rather than being vague.
   e. Convey interest and enthusiasm rather than disinterest and boredom.
   f. Set realistic goals rather than unrealistic goals.
2. Efficient planners.
3. Effective communicators.
4. Thorough assessors of behavior for
   a. Their own teaching behavior, which they modify when needed.
   b. Students and their learning styles.
5. Consistent in their expectations of children.[22]

Teachers must decide what discipline practices work for them. Many acceptable practices can be incorporated into the teaching routine. On the other hand, some unacceptable practices should be avoided by teachers. These will be presented in the following pages.

Acceptable Practices

Each student is an individual, so teachers may need to vary actual practices or consequences according to individual needs. Students who have been disciplined should not be made to feel uneasy. Teachers need to interact with these students in an accepting way. Teachers striving to incorporate acceptable practices should also remember the following guidelines: (1) solve your own problems whenever possible, (2) be available and visible, (3) admit mistakes, (4) take advantage of the teaching moment, and (5) look for causes of misconduct. Several acceptable discipline practices will be discussed in the next few pages.

Waiting Aggressively

Waiting aggressively is a teacher tactic that lets students know they need to pay attention. Such waiting needs to be obvious. Waiting signals can include a frown, a shake of the head, a clearing of the throat, a disapproving look at an offender, a mild reproof, or movement toward the trouble spot. Often these techniques will resolve problems before they become difficult.

Individual Conference

The individual conference with a student outside of class time is one of the most effective techniques that can be utilized. A serious and frank talk would appear to be the logical first

An individual conference is one of the most
effective disciplinary techniques.

step in the understanding of behavior problems. Conferences help the teacher understand
the causes of misbehavior and problems the student faces. They can also be useful in interpreting school or class regulations to the student.

Cooperation between Home and School

Genuine cooperation between home and school through conferences, home visits, and social
contacts can achieve remarkable results, provided both parties are willing to understand the
student's behavior and are sincere about wanting to help the student. Home-school cooperation can produce fruitful information and lead to correction of misbehavior. A positive,
cooperative effort is usually most successful. Keep a record of behavior problems. Written
records can help to identify patterns of behavior and provide objective data for parents.

Loss of Privileges and Time-Out

The loss of privileges, particularly those of a social nature, is generally a well-accepted method
of discipline. When this method is applied, it should follow as a natural, logical form of
correction with no sort of retributory attitude on the part of the teacher. Ways must be made
available so that, after the student has had time to examine the misbehavior, the student
can be restored to full privileges. Often students will plead to be allowed to work after being
excluded.

Time-out consists of cutting off all reinforcement for a period of time.[23] Usually, the student is required to sit out away from other students until the decision is made to engage in appropriate behavior. Some teachers use time-out to help students resolve interpersonal-relationship problems such as fighting. Students are asked to leave the group until they have settled their differences so that other students can continue to learn. The lack of an audience can be very effective in quieting emotions. This process has been used effectively with students who are asked to sit on a bench together and agree on what the problem is about which they are complaining. This process helps children learn to resolve their own differences.

Isolation

Isolation removes the offender from the class and facilitates instruction to the other students. However, it also bars the student from necessary instruction. Occasionally it creates a scene in which the offender may be humiliated or, on the contrary, become a hero to classmates. This method is justified only in severe cases. Isolation from the activity while watching the enjoyment of the other students can be effective.

Administrative Assistance

Administrative assistance should only be secured after the teacher has been unsuccessful while trying to correct a disturbing situation or after repeated incidents of misbehavior. A principal once told a teacher, "After you've done everything you can and the student doesn't improve, don't let it bother you out of proportion. Let it give the principal an ulcer." The administration has the duty to do everything possible to help the teacher deal with discipline problems for the sake of the student, the teacher, and the school as a whole. However, the teacher should seldom refer a student to the administration until all the resources at hand have been exhausted. Procedures for using administrative assistance include the following:

1. Know the student. A trip to the office may be just what the individual wants at that moment in order to get out of a difficult assignment.
2. When it becomes necessary to send a student to the office of the administrator, send along a note (with another student) that states the difficulty and the depth of treatment expected.
3. See the administrator as soon as possible to discuss the situation.
4. Do not send more than one student to the office at a time.
5. If the student is sent back to class, calmly readmit the student and ignore any face-saving behavior the student displays.

Behavior Modification and Contingency Contracting

Behavior modification is an inclusive term for a number of techniques designed to reinforce the desired behavior of individuals or groups and to eliminate undesired behavior. It is based on the premise that people will repeat behaviors that are reinforced or rewarded and will not repeat behaviors that are consistently ignored. Behavior modification is especially helpful to teachers who have lost control of classroom behavior since desirable behavior is rewarded and encouraged.[24] Critics maintain that teachers are bribing students and that once the reward for desired behavior is removed, the undesirable behavior will return. They also point out that the system demands more time and effort by teachers than it is worth. Carron cited research that refutes these claims, as well as studies supporting the positive outcomes of behavior-modification techniques.[25]

Some techniques used to modify behavior include conditioning, shaping, reinforcement, extinction, and punishment. *Conditioning* is getting students to respond in a specific way to a specific stimulus. An example is roll call, to which students respond by standing on their numbers. *Shaping* involves rewarding behavior that is closer and closer to the desired goal. It is used to teach sports skills by rewarding first a gross motor skill and then increasingly refined movements until accuracy and efficiency are obtained. *Reinforcement* uses a thing or event following a behavior to increase the likelihood that a person will repeat the behavior for which it is given. *Extinction* occurs when a response or behavior is no longer reinforced. *Punishment* applies negative consequences to a behavior to decrease its frequency.

Most people have practiced behavior modification on themselves. For example, one might say, "As soon as I finish reading this chapter, I'm going to eat a cookie." That is an example of contingency contracting. *Contingency contracting* is reinforcement that is contingent on the performance of the desired behavior. An example of the technique is Grandma's Law discussed in the last chapter. A more sophisticated explanation was developed by Premack and is called the Premack principle. It suggests that any behavior that occurs frequently can be used to reinforce a behavior that occurs less frequently. For example, "obtaining high performance scores" (a highly desired result) becomes a reinforcer for practicing one's skills (a less desired result).

Since preferred activities can serve as reinforcers, all instructors have to do is observe students to determine what activities they like to do best. Teachers can even ask students what activities are worth working for. Contingency contracting places the responsibility on students for decisions regarding their behavior. It can be used along with extinction to reduce undesirable behavior, develop new behavior, or strengthen and maintain existing behavior. Joyce and Weil described contingency contracting as "the heart of effective classroom management."[26]

The major advantage of contingency contracting is a feeling of accomplishment on the part of students and teachers.[27] Teachers who worry about using behavior-modification techniques in the classroom should remember that reinforcement is a part of life. Adults are rewarded with paychecks, recognition by society, praise from friends or bosses, and many other types of reinforcement. Modifications in behavior are constantly being made by those who interact with others in the environment. It is the same with school. Teachers must take students where they are and assist them in trying out new kinds of behavior until they learn the satisfaction that comes from success in the activity itself. As La Mancusa stated, "The teacher does neither himself nor his students a favor by perpetuating the climate of failure."[28] Giving students attention for good behavior is far more desirable than giving them attention for misbehavior. Reprimands tend only to increase the behaviors they are intended to eliminate. Consistently ignored behaviors tend to increase in frequency initially and then weaken and disappear.

According to Homme,[29] contingency contracts should be

1. Clear—The directions should be stated in explicit terms that are easily understood by the student, such as:
   If you do . . . , then you will get. . . .
   If you do . . . , then I will do. . . .
   If you do . . . , then you may do. . . .
   (Note: *You* is a student or a group.)
2. Fair—The two sides of the contract must be of relatively equal importance.
3. Honest—The reward should be given immediately *after* the performance but *only* for the performance specified in the contract.
4. Positive—The contract *should not* say, "If you do . . . , then I will *not* do. . . .
5. Systematic—The instructor should be consistent in reinforcing only the desired behavior.

When establishing a contract, the following procedures should be employed:

1. Clearly specify a few rules that tell exactly what is expected. Limit rules to five or less.[30] Establish the target behavior in terms of performance and criteria for achievement. Establish what the reward will be for correct performance. Stress academic achievement rather than obedience.[31] Academic achievement is usually incompatible with disruptive behavior. Maintain a fair contract.
2. Initiate a contract with students. The contract may be a short statement by the teacher that states the consequences to be gained by certain behaviors.
3. Ignore disruptive, nondestructive behavior.
4. Reward the student immediately after completion of the desired behavior. Initial rewards should be given for behavior that approximates the goal (e.g., small, simple tasks). Later, behaviors should be increasingly close to the final objective.
5. Use a variety of reinforcers to reward appropriate behaviors. Work toward the use of higher-order reinforcers and an intermittent reinforcement schedule (random or unpredictable reinforcement) to increase resistance to extinction. This reduces teacher approval to only a few times a day. The needs of each individual will determine what things or events will serve as reinforcers. Therefore, teachers need to plan in advance to see what is reinforcing and what is not for their particular students. To be worthwhile, rewards must be highly desirable and not obtainable outside the conditions of the contract.[32]
6. Be consistent in following the plan.
7. Progress from teacher-directed contracts to mutually directed contracts to student-initiated contracts.

Becker identified three ways in which reinforcers lose their effectiveness.[33] One is *competing reinforcers.* These are reinforcers available from a source other than the teacher, such as those from the peer group. Second is *satiation,* in which the reinforcer has been used so often that it loses its effectiveness. Third is the *lack of transfer* of reinforcers to new situations. When learning a new task, the learner may fail to understand that the rules for achieving reinforcement are the same. Several solutions to these problems include withholding reinforcement for a short time to make it worthwhile again, changing the reinforcer, or strengthening the reinforcer. Reinforcement is not effective with all students. Different personalities of teacher and student, different student learning styles, and different environmental conditions can affect the success or failure of contingency contracting.

Examples of Reinforcers Some suggestions for reinforcers are listed below, from highest to lowest. Higher-order reinforcers are found more frequently in the normal environment.

1. Competence (skill acquisition).
2. Being correct (feedback).
3. Social approval (praise).
4. Contingent activity (for example, "Do . . . and then you can have five minutes of free time").
5. Tokens or check marks (exchanged for other reinforcers).
6. Tangibles (ribbons, trophies).
7. Edibles (food, candies).[34]

Punishment Punishment is negative contingency contracting—"if you do x, you will get y," y being undesirable. Punishment usually implies mental or physical pain or discomfort. *Restitution* of things taken and *reparation* for things damaged or destroyed willfully are generally conceded to be fair forms of punishment. To be effective, this form of punishment must educate the student to realize that when something is destroyed it affects the welfare of the entire group. This technique also teaches the student to make amends. The teacher's responsibility lies in explaining the reasons for the punishment and in following through to see that restoration is made. If the student is financially unable to pay expenses for reparation, the school should find a way in which the student can work off the debt. Where parents are too free with money, the school should solicit their cooperation to make the punishment effective by permitting the student to work out the debt to society.

Punishment has some undesirable side effects. Teachers should weigh the impact of these side effects before incorporating punishment into a system of discipline. Although a behavior may be temporarily suppressed when punishment or the threat of punishment follows behavior, it will often reappear later. One possible reason for this is that punishment tells the student what not to do, but gives no direction as to the appropriate behavior. Therefore, the student will probably experiment with a whole range of inappropriate behaviors while searching for the appropriate behavior. Reward, on the contrary, immediately tells the student what the appropriate behavior is. In addition, undesirable side effects, such as a negative self-concept or a dislike of school, the subject, or the teacher, can develop. These negative feelings may predispose the student to retaliate or withdraw. Further, punishment reduces the behavior only in the presence of the punishing agent. Students may learn how to avoid getting caught by more sophisticated cheating or lying. Finally, punishment teaches students to be aggressive through imitation of the aggressive behavior of adults.

Punishment should only be used in a planned, careful way to deal with problems that cannot be resolved with the alternative measures discussed or when students know ahead of time that certain results come from their actions. Some school districts have a discipline code that categorizes student misbehavior and identifies administrative or teacher actions that may be taken. Becker suggested two circumstances in which punishment may be needed: (1) when direct reinforcement procedures are likely to fail because the negative behavior is so frequent that there is no positive behavior to reinforce and (2) when someone might get hurt.[35]

Punishment, when it is used, should result primarily as a natural consequence of the choices made by students. Students should be counseled as to the consequences of alternatives when they make their choices. Negative reinforcement should never be used to punish one student in front of a group of students. The following procedures are suggested when using punishment.

1. Allow an undesirable act to continue (or insist that it continue) until the student is clearly bored with it. For example, a teacher could insist that a student throwing spit wads continue to make spit wads until the student has clearly learned how unattractive the behavior is and can make a decision to follow a desired behavior.
2. Always accompany punishment by a suggestion of something positive to do (i.e., the desired behavior).
3. End the punishment with the student's decision to perform the desired behavior.
4. Reward the positive behavior or the student will revert to the bad behavior in order to get recognition, even if it takes the form of punishment.

Reality Therapy

Reality therapy was developed by Glasser to help students assume the accountability for their own behavior.[36] Persons who can fulfill their needs through responsible behavior will have no need to act irresponsibly. These needs, according to Glasser, are the need to know that one is of worth to oneself and to others and the need to love and be loved. A person who is unable to fulfill these needs through responsible behavior is forced to fulfill them in irresponsible ways. Glasser's technique is dependent on three factors: (1) acceptance as a person but rejection of irresponsible behavior; (2) a meaningful relationship between teacher and student; and (3) education of the student into better ways of behaving by fulfilling the student's needs in responsible ways.

Reality therapy requires the teacher to become involved with and care about students. The teacher must work in the present and toward the future, ignoring the student's excuses. The teacher helps the student (1) identify the inappropriate behavior, (2) identify the consequences of the behavior, (3) make a value judgment about the behavior, (4) make a plan, and (5) follow the plan. The procedure is for the teacher to ask the following questions:

1. What is your goal? What do you want to happen?
2. What are you doing? *or* What did you do?
3. Is that what you should be doing? *or* How will that help you?
4. What is your plan? *or* What will you do that will help you?
5. What will be the consequences?
6. What can I do to help you?

If the student fails to apply the plan, the student should be allowed to suffer the consequences of the irresponsible behavior, but within a framework of love and understanding. The student should then be helped to reconsider the commitment that has been made. An example of reality therapy follows.

This reality-therapy session takes place in a tenth-grade gymnastics class. The students have been assigned to develop an individual routine on a chosen piece of apparatus. The routine is to be completed by the end of the hour. A substantial portion of the student's grade will be based on the routine. Louise sits over in the corner. She has not even attempted to create a routine. Instead, she is staring into space. The teacher approaches Louise and confronts her with the situation.

Teacher: Louise, what are you doing?
Louise: I'm just sitting here. [a]
Teacher: What are you supposed to be doing?
Louise: I don't know.
Teacher: What is the rest of the class doing?
Louise: I guess they're working on the routine.
Teacher: What are you supposed to be doing?
Louise: I guess I'm supposed to be working on the routine. [b]
Teacher: How far will sitting around get you?
Louise: Probably nowhere.
Teacher: What will happen if you don't do the routine?
Louise: I'll probably flunk the class. [c]
Teacher: Do you want to fail?
Louise: I don't know.
Teacher: What will happen if you do fail?
Louise: I'll probably have to take the class over.
Teacher: Is that what you want?
Louise: No.
Teacher: What can you do to keep from failing?
Louise: I guess I better work on the routine. [d]
Teacher: What can I do to help you?
Louise: Tell me what skills to do.
Teacher: That's not acceptable. What else can I do? [e]
Louise: Explain what things I'm supposed to have in my routine. [f]
Teacher: Okay. Will that help you?
Louise: I think so.
Teacher: Will you be ready to perform tomorrow?
Louise: I guess so.
Teacher: Okay.

Notes: a. Student identifies behavior.
        b. Student makes a value judgment.
        c. Student identifies the consequences of behavior.
        d. Student makes a plan.
        e. Teacher guides development of the plan.
        f. Teacher helps the student with the plan.

Norm Setting

When reality therapy is used with a group of students, it is known as *norm setting*. Norm setting is based on the principle that students are more responsible for implementing behavior expectations or goals that they have participated in selecting. Teachers and students work together to formalize and publicize essential rules and regulations. Rules should be clear, brief, reasonable, easily applied to all, and enforceable by teacher observation. For norm setting to work, the teacher must recognize the worth and intelligence of students.

Norm setting can be used with groups of all ages and in many different settings. The procedures include the following.

1. Help students share their goals or expectations regarding either learning or behavior. Focus on what students *need* to learn or do, not what they *want* to do.
2. State goals that students need to achieve.
3. Refine goals into one set of mutually acceptable goals by eliminating undesirable goals (those that cannot be achieved within the course) and adding any desirable goals that were omitted.
4. State goals in such a way that students and teacher will know what each goal is and when it has been achieved.
5. State what you, as the teacher, are willing to do to help students achieve the class goals (such as availability, being prepared, willingness to admit mistakes, caring for students or listening to students). Do not promise to do anything you will not do. Teachers who really care are willing to risk asking students to share additional expectations they may have for the teacher.
6. Help students describe what they need to do and are willing to do to ensure attainment of class goals.
7. Identify consequences for nonattainment of goals.
8. Commit yourself and your students to the class goals. Agreements may be written down and signed on a contract.
9. Use various motivational techniques to reward behavior that is consistent with the norms or standards previously agreed upon.
10. Use reality-therapy techniques to help the misbehaving student judge behavior in terms of the commitments made by the class.
11. Review goals and commitments from time to time and make changes when necessary.

Handling Explosive Situations

An explosive situation is a situation requiring immediate action to prevent personal injury or property damage. An explosive situation should be prevented from occurring whenever possible by using the following suggestions.

1. Do not let misbehavior go too far before attempting to handle the problem.
2. Do not lose your cool. Explosive situations become volcanic when the teacher and student are not in control of themselves.
3. Be decisive, act quickly, and disarm the situation. The teacher might use a time-out period or, if possible, remove the student or students from the classroom situation.

4. Do not use too harsh a punishment as that action can result in later aggressive behaviors being manifest.
5. Avoid confrontations with students. Do not accept a challenge as a personal matter.

When an explosive situation occurs, however, the following procedures may be helpful.

1. Decide whether help is needed or if the situation can be handled alone.
2. If help is needed, get it! Send a student for another teacher, principal, or counselor.
3. Move toward the problem.
4. Insist calmly but firmly that the behavior be stopped immediately.
5. Suggest an alternative behavior—an "out" by which the student can save face.
6. Act to stop the problem if it can be done safely. Do not touch the student if this can be avoided.
7. Remove the student from the area, if appropriate.
8. Calm the class by restructuring the incident or using it as a topic for discussion. Introduce humor.

Unacceptable Practices

Some disciplinary practices used by teachers are generally considered to be unacceptable. They are often initiated because the teacher is feeling the stress and tension of the situation. The use of such tactics normally generates resentment on the part of the student or causes the student to withdraw. Teachers need to decide ahead of time that the following practices will not be employed no matter what the intensity of a circumstance might be. These practices include (1) coercion; (2) ridicule; (3) forced apologies; (4) detention without a specified purpose; (5) imposition of schoolwork or homework for punitive purposes; (6) punishment instigated on the spot, including grades; (7) group punishment for misbehavior by one or a few; and (8) corporal punishment. Other methods that generally result in a lack of control on the part of the teacher include appealing to the student's sympathy; using vague, unfulfilled threats; and excluding the student from the room without supervision. To avoid unpleasant situations caused by a disciplinary action, the teacher needs to have in mind appropriate techniques that will be triggered automatically by the situation.

Selecting the Appropriate Disciplinary Technique

Teachers need to be prepared to act instinctively when a disciplinary incident arises in class. Outcomes are often unpredictable. Predetermined rules and regulations might provide the solution to the problem, but the teacher still must react with a cool head and conclude the incident. Whatever the problem might be that arises, proper action depends on (1) the teacher, (2) the students, and (3) the incident.

The Teacher

An understanding of a variety of suitable techniques and success in carrying out different methods allows the teacher to shift positions as conditions change. Teachers should experiment to see what works best for them, because what works for one teacher may not work for another. Administrative policy may limit the choices from which a teacher is allowed to select. Often, the teacher must deal with the incident, as well as direct students not involved in the action.

The Students

It is easy to assume that all students are alike, but no method of control is effective with all students. One must consider the age, gender, personality, and social values held by the student or group. Teachers should be alert to the individual needs of students. Occasionally, deafness, poor vision, or other handicapping conditions create supposed discipline problems.

The Incident

An attempt to determine the cause of the behavior and what actually happened should be made without relying too heavily on statements made by students. Often the cause of the incident results from the environment within the classroom itself. Poor, haphazard, and unproductive instruction or a curriculum that is too easy, too hard, or not relevant to the needs of students may cause many discipline problems.

With these items in mind, the teacher will first need to stop the ineffective behavior and then help to overcome individual problems, thus preventing a recurrence of the problem. The action must be clear, definite, and one in which the teacher truly believes. By continually being alert to the early signs of trouble and dealing with them firmly, calmly, and with consistency before they become serious, major discipline problems can be avoided.

The teacher who is inexperienced or new to a school must still deal with discipline problems in a confident, controlled manner. The following hints for new teachers are aimed at avoiding beginning pitfalls:

1. Learn school policies and procedures thoroughly.
2. Be an example the students can emulate.
3. Be a teacher—not a pal—to students.
4. Plan and organize.
5. Be flexible but consistent in carrying out plans.
6. Respect and appreciate students as individuals.
7. Let students know from the start what the payoff will be for working hard in class.[37]

Questions and Suggested Activities

1. What is the relationship between discipline and motivation?
2. You have just been hired as the long-term substitute in a high school physical education program. You discover that most of your students are apathetic. A high percentage of students are not dressed for activity each day, and those who are dressed cause many discipline problems. What would you do to remedy the situation?
3. Role-play the following discipline techniques with a partner: waiting aggressively, conference, time-out, behavior modification, and reality therapy.
4. Create a plan defining the discipline techniques you would use in the following situations: general policy for a regular class, a special education class, problems arising during intramural competition, and when an explosive situation occurs.
5. Devise a behavior-modification system to improve the disruptive atmosphere that has suddenly emerged in your class.
6. Several teachers in your district have been sued for what was termed "abusive and inhumane treatment of students." What tactics would you employ to counteract such charges?

Suggested Readings

Barr, Norman J. "The Responsible World of Reality Therapy." *Psychology Today* (February 1974):64–67.

Bauer, Gary L. "Restoring Order to the Public Schools." *Phi Delta Kappan* 66 (March 1985): 488–91.

Brandon, Jim. "Discipline, Choosing Teams, Square Dance, and Rope-Skipping." In Ronald P. Carlson, ed., *IDEAS II for Secondary School Physical Education: A Sharing of Teaching Practices by Secondary School Physical Education Practitioners*. Reston, Virginia: American Alliance for Health, Physical Education, Recreation and Dance, 1984, 72–73.

Carron, Albert V. *Motivation: Implications for Coaching & Teaching*. Kingswood, South Australia: Sports Dynamics, 1984.

Evans, Jane. "Implications of Behavior Modification Techniques for the Physical Education Teacher." *The Physical Educator* 31 (March 1974):28–32.

French, Ron, Barry Lavay, and Hester Henderson. "Take a Lap." *The Physical Educator* 42 (Early Winter 1985):180–85.

Gallahue, David L. "Punishment and Control, Part I. Negative Results." *The Physical Educator* 35 (May 1978):58–59.

Gallahue, David L. "Punishment and Control, Part II. Alternatives to Punishment." *The Physical Educator* 35 (October 1978):114.

Gallahue, David L. "Toward Positive Discipline in the Gymnasium." *The Physical Educator* 42 (Late Winter 1985):14–17.

Glasser, William. *Reality Therapy: A New Approach to Psychiatry*. New York: Harper & Row, Publishers, 1965.

Glasser, William. *Schools Without Failure*. New York: Harper & Row, Publishers, 1969.

Hellison, Donald R. *Goals and Strategies for Teaching Physical Education*. Champaign, Illinois: Human Kinetics Publishers, 1985.

Hunter, Madeline. *Motivation Theory for Teachers*. El Segundo, California: Tip Publications, 1971.

Jansma, Paul, Ron French, and Michael A. Horvat. "Behavioral Engineering in Physical Education." *Journal of Physical Education, Recreation and Dance* 55 (August 1984):80–81.

Johnson, Les. "Looking for a Fence." *Scout Magazine* (December 1964):14–15, 27.

Kennedy, Edward F. "Discipline in the Physical Education Setting." *The Physical Educator* 39 (May 1982):91–94.

Lavay, Barry. "Behavior Management in Physical Education, Recreation, and Sport: A Bibliography." *The Physical Educator* 43 (Spring 1986):103–12.

Martin, Robert J. "Avoiding Help That Hinders." *Today's Education* 70 (September–October 1981):58–61.

McDaniel, Thomas R. "A Primer on Classroom Discipline: Principles Old and New." *Phi Delta Kappan* 68 (September 1986):63–67.

Olson, Janice K. "Keeping Cool: Be a Teacher Who Disciplines LEAST." *Journal of Physical Education, Recreation and Dance* 55 (August 1984):38–39.

Schwager, Susan M., and Mark C. Mante. "Three Simple Rules: The Key to Cooperation." *Journal of Physical Education, Recreation and Dance* 57 (August 1986):85–87.

Vogler, E. William, and Ron W. French. "The Effects of a Group Contingency Strategy on Behaviorally Disordered Students in Physical Education." *Research Quarterly for Exercise and Sport* 54 (September 1983):273–77.

References

1. W. Doyle, "Classroom Organization and Management," in Merlin C. Wittrock, ed. *Handbook of Research on Teaching,* 3d ed. (New York: Macmillan Publishing Company, 1986), pp. 392–431.
2. Donald R. Hellison, *Goals and Strategies for Teaching Physical Education* (Champaign, Illinois: Human Kinetics Publishers, 1985), p. 1.
3. Ibid, pp. 2–3.

4. William Glasser, *Schools Without Failure* (New York: Harper & Row, Publishers, 1969), pp. 6–7.
5. Kenneth H. Hoover, *The Professional Teacher's Handbook: A Guide for Improving Instruction in Today's Middle and Secondary Schools,* 3d ed. (Boston: Allyn & Bacon, Inc., 1982), p. 64.
6. Harold Dunn, "Listen to Kids!" *Today's Education* 70 (November–December 1981), p. 37.
7. Madeline Hunter, *Motivation Theory for Teachers* (El Segundo, California: Tip Publications, 1971).
8. Albert V. Carron, *Motivation Implications for Coaching & Teaching* (Kingswood, South Australia: Sports Dynamics, 1984), p. 7.
9. Hunter, *Motivation Theory for Teachers.*
10. Wilsbert J. McKeachie, *Teaching Tips—A Guidebook for the Beginning College Teacher,* 7th ed. (Lexington: D. C. Heath and Company, 1978), p. 222.
11. Madeline Hunter, *Retention Theory for Teachers* (El Segundo, California: Tip Publications, 1974), p. 5.
12. E. A. Locke, K. N. Shaw, L. M. Saari, and G. P. Latham, "Goal Setting and Task Performance: 1969–1980," *Psychological Bulletin* 90 (1981), pp. 125–52.
13. M. Tousignant and D. Siedentop, "A Qualitative Analysis of Task Structures in Required Secondary Physical Education Classes," *Journal of Teaching in Physical Education* 3 (1983), pp. 47–57.
14. Daryl Siedentop, "The Management of Practice Behavior," in W. F. Straub, ed. *Sport Psychology: An Analysis of Athlete Behavior* (Ithaca: Movement Publications, 1978).
15. Alec M. Gallup and David L. Clark, "The 19th Annual Gallup Poll of the Public's Attitudes Toward the Public Schools," *Phi Delta Kappan* 68 (September 1987), p. 44.
16. U.S. Department of Education, *What Works: Research About Teaching and Learning* (Washington, D.C.: U.S. Department of Education, 1986), p. 47.
17. Charles H. Madsen, Jr. and Clifford K. Madsen. *Teaching/Discipline: Behavioral Principles Toward a Positive Approach* (Boston: Allyn and Bacon, Inc.), p. 9.
18. Thomas Gordon with Noel Burch, *T.E.T., Teacher Effectiveness Training* (New York: Peter H. Wyden, Publisher, 1974).
19. Julie P. Sanford and Carolyn M. Evertson, "Classroom Management in a Low SES Junior High: Three Case Studies," *Journal of Teacher Education* 32 (January–February 1981), pp. 34–38.
20. Emile Durkheim, *Moral Education: A Study in the Theory and Application of the Sociology of Education* (New York: Free Press, 1961), p. 152.
21. Madsen and Madsen, *Teaching/Discipline,* p. 10.
22. David L. Gallahue, "Toward Positive Discipline in the Gymnasium," *The Physical Educator* 42 (Late Winter 1985), pp. 14–17.
23. Wesley C. Becker, Siegfried Engelmann, and Don R. Thomas, *Teaching: A Course in Applied Psychology* (Palo Alto, California: Science Research Associates, 1971), p. 157.
24. Darwin Dorr, "Behavior Modification in the Schools," in W. Doyle Gentry, ed. *Applied Behavior Modification* (St. Louis: C. V. Mosby Company, 1975), p. 38.
25. Carron, *Motivation Implications for Coaching & Teaching,* pp. 10–14.
26. Bruce Joyce and Marsha Weil, *Models of Teaching,* 2d ed. (Englewood Cliffs, New Jersey: Prentice-Hall, 1980), p. 332.
27. Homme, et al., *How to Use Contingency Contracting,* p. 21.
28. Katherine C. La Mancusa, *We Do Not Throw Rocks at the Teacher!* (Scranton, Pennsylvania: International Textbook Company, 1966), p. 146.
29. Homme, et al., *How to Use Contingency Contracting,* pp. 18–21.
30. Becker, et al., *Teaching,* p. 171.

31. John P. Glavin, *Behavioral Strategies for Classroom Management* (Columbus, Ohio: Charles E. Merrill, 1974), p. 52.
32. Homme, et al., *How to Use Contingency Contracting,* p. 9.
33. Becker, et al., *Teaching,* p. 97.
34. Murray Tillman, Donald Bersoff, and John Dolly, *Learning to Teach: A Decision-Making System* (Lexington, Massachusetts: D.C. Heath and Company, 1976), p. 361.
35. Becker, et al., *Teaching,* p. 158.
36. William Glasser, *Reality Therapy: A New Approach to Psychiatry* (New York: Harper & Row, Publishers, 1965).
37. Becker, et al., *Teaching,* p. 177.

14

Clarifying the Physical Education Program—
Evaluation and Public Relations

Study Stimulators

1. Who has the responsibility for worthwhile outcomes of physical education programs?
2. Why is teacher evaluation important?
3. List the steps in teacher evaluation.
4. What are the advantages and limitations of evaluation that is based on student achievement or improvement, informal analysis, informal analysis by students, descriptive analysis, and interaction analysis?
5. Why is public relations important?
6. What methods can be used to enhance public relations?

The eighties will be documented in history books as the years of educational reform. The barrage of reports in the early part of the decade challenging the competency of our national education system sparked marked improvement by the schools. The "Education Report Card" released by the U.S. Department of Education showed four years of improvement by the schools with a leveling off in 1985–86. Student test scores were up, as were teachers' salaries; the number of pupils per teacher was down; and expenditures per pupil were up.[1] Even with the positive gains by the schools, the cry to do better was still heard. Secretary of Education William J. Bennett emphasized, "We have to do better. Our children deserve better."[2] Legislators reinforced these words. Lawsuits claiming inadequate education forced state legislatures to pass laws requiring schools to be accountable for educating students. The majority of the states now require students to pass minimum competency tests to graduate from high school.[3]

Accountability, according to the law, tends to be limited to accountability of teachers and administrators for learning by students. However, accountability is more than that. Schools have a responsibility to educate students. Parents and taxpayers have a responsibility for providing the resources necessary for adequate learning experiences. Students must be accountable for their own behavior.

Enochs set forth several principles for education in his Modesto, California, district. The principles included:

> The development of responsible adults is a task requiring community involvement. It cannot be left solely to the public schools. . . . Parents must consistently support the proposition that students have responsibilities as well as rights, and the schools have an obligation to insist upon both. . . . The full responsibility for learning cannot be transferred from the student to the teacher.[4]

Today the worth of physical education programs is being challenged as never before. On the other hand, the public has never been more active physically than at the present time. People are spending millions of dollars to look and feel better. More than one hundred million people in the United States are actively engaged in fitness activities, an estimated thirteen

Teacher evaluation can be enhanced by
videotaping specific teaching experiences.

hundred books on fitness are currently in print, and fifty thousand firms spend an estimated two billion dollars a year on fitness and recreation programs for their employees.[5] The obstacle of survival that the profession of physical education faces, then, is not one of justification but rather clarification. The goals of physical education must be clarified and confirmed on three fronts: (1) the student, (2) the teacher, and (3) the public. The clarification process should start with the students. First, students need to understand the worth of physical education activities to the extent that they become committed to improving their own performance. Class instruction must be more than "free play" and organized games. Students must be evaluated and results of achievement made available to parents, administrators, the general public, and the students themselves. Second, teachers must improve their effectiveness. Third, the public must be convinced of the worth of physical education programs in order to pledge support for them.

Physical education programs are costly. Physical educators must face the possibility of their programs being eliminated if outcomes cannot be demonstrated. The fight against such a probability is indeed clarification involving both evaluation and public relations. Evaluation is necessary so that results can be demonstrated and public relations must follow to make the results known. Student evaluation was discussed in chapter 8. Teacher evaluation and public relations will be presented in this chapter.

Teacher Evaluation

Teachers must be able to state performance objectives, assess student achievement of objectives, and use strategies that help students achieve objectives. They must also learn to evaluate and remediate weaknesses in their own teaching and in their programs. Administrators must be able to evaluate teachers' performance and help teachers improve their effectiveness.

Table 14.1 Goals, behaviors, and suggested evaluation techniques

Goals	Teacher Behavior	Suggested Evaluation Techniques
Teacher warmth	Calls student by name.	Event recording
	Provides more positive than negative feedback.	Event recording
	Interacts with students.	Student evaluation of instructor Interaction analysis
Teacher expectancy	Facilitates achievement of instructional objectives.	Student performance
	Facilitates improvement in student learning.	Student improvement
	Select tasks in terms of student abilities.	Student evaluation of teacher Informal analysis
Task-oriented climate	Helps students spend a large amount of time in productive behavior.	Time analysis Spot-checking Time sampling
	Provides feedback on behavior.	Event recording
	Decreases time spent on class management.	Time analysis Time sampling
Effective instruction	Provides appropriate model and explanation.	Informal analysis Event recording
	Provides appropriate feedback for skills.	Event recording
	Provides opportunity for student practice.	Time analysis Time sampling Number of practice trials/person

Effective teachers have the ability to adapt their teaching behaviors to meet the needs of their students. Studies demonstrate that teacher evaluation increases their awareness of these different instructional behaviors and helps them to improve both student achievement and teacher morale. This is true because teachers often perceive their teaching behavior quite differently from that which actually occurs. Teacher evaluation enables the teacher to retain effective teaching behaviors and eliminate ineffective behaviors, thereby making actual behavior more congruent with desired behavior. Teacher evaluation involves the following steps.

Step 1. Determine what to evaluate.
Step 2. Choose or construct specific evaluation techniques.
Step 3. Use the appropriate techniques to record information.
Step 4. Evaluate or interpret the data.
Step 5. Make changes and reevaluate.

Step 1—Determine What to Evaluate

The first step in any evaluation plan is to specify goals. This can be done by examining what one believes to be the most important goals of teaching and the behaviors one should assume to achieve those goals.[6] Some examples of goals and related behaviors, which are based on the characteristics of effective teachers discussed in chapter 3, are shown in table 14.1.

Step 2—Choose or Construct Specific Evaluation Techniques

Because teaching is so complex, a variety of formal and informal observation and recording techniques must be used to describe the total teaching process. The techniques discussed in this chapter include: (1) student achievement or improvement, (2) informal analysis, (3) informal analysis by students, (4) descriptive analysis, and (5) interaction analysis. These techniques generally assess either the performance of the students or the performance of the teacher.

Student Achievement or Improvement

The principal duty of teachers is to help students learn. Therefore, the key to evaluating teaching is to determine the extent to which learning has taken place. The use of performance objectives facilitates this process by providing an observable student behavior for each skill or content area to be learned. If students are learning and have positive feelings toward activity, then the teacher is effective, no matter how unorthodox the instruction appears to be. However, if students are not learning or do not have positive attitudes toward activity, then an analysis of the teacher's performance can help to pinpoint possible problem areas for remediation.

Common techniques for evaluating student achievement include knowledge tests, skills tests, and various affective measurements. Each of these techniques was discussed in chapter 8.

Another method for evaluating student learning is to record student performance each day and compare it with the objectives of the daily lesson plan. This can be as simple as having students check off skills as they accomplish them, such as in gymnastics or swimming; count the number of successful attempts, such as basketball free throws or tennis serves; or turn in a score, such as in archery or bowling (see chapter 8 for examples). If the lesson has been well planned, most of the students should be able to achieve the lesson objectives.

An accountability log can be kept each day, which shows student achievement not only toward the objective for that day but also the achievement of previous unit objectives. An accountability log can be a tremendous eye-opener into how much review and practice students need to achieve course objectives. The log might include a list of objectives and the number of students who have completed each one.

A second method is to preassess students, teach, and then evaluate the improvement. Again, a knowledge or skills test or an affective measurement can be used. Examples include:

1. Sprint—Check for improvement in time.
2. Knowledge—Check the number of students improving scores on a quiz or the class average on a quiz.
3. Attitude—Check the number of students changing from a negative to a positive attitude toward an activity. (Review chapter 8 for specific suggestions on evaluating affective behavior.)
4. Basketball strategy—Count the increases in successful passes per team.

Evaluating teachers based on student performance does have some limitations. One of the major limitations is the difficulty of accurately evaluating student performance. Weather, time of day, illness, fatigue, and innumerable other factors can influence student performance scores. Subjective evaluation techniques and teacher-constructed tests may be unreliable. Measurements may not be sensitive enough to determine improvement during short units of instruction. A second limitation is that a cause-and-effect relationship is difficult to establish between a specific teaching behavior and learning. Students may have learned from a parent, a friend, or private lessons. If skills were not preassessed, students may have begun with the skill level being evaluated. Students may learn because of or in spite of a teacher. When they do learn, proving which teaching behaviors may have caused the improvement is difficult.

These limitations, however, should not keep teachers from making some educated guesses about their own teaching based on student achievement. Checking for achievement or improvement each day will provide a better idea of which teaching behaviors helped to create the changes in student behavior.

Informal Analysis

The most common method of teacher evaluation is informal analysis by oneself, a supervisor or administrator, another teacher, or by students. By videotaping the class, the observation can be recorded for self-evaluation and follow-up and decisions can be made as to changes needed to improve future teaching performance. Such evaluations are based on the subjective opinions of the observer. More than one observer should evaluate the teacher when an informal analysis is used. Some informal analysis techniques that can be used include a written or verbal description of a lesson, a checklist, or a rating scale.

A written or verbal description of a lesson is generally influenced, either consciously or unconsciously, by the biases of the observer; therefore, several observers should be used and the behavior evaluated should be explicitly defined. The description may focus on only one portion of the teaching-learning situation, such as on discipline or on teacher-student interaction. Sometimes a recording form is used to direct the observer's attention to various aspects of the teaching situation. An example of a recording form is shown in figure 14.1.

Informal analysis serves a useful purpose because it focuses on aspects of performance that are important to the teacher in making day-to-day decisions. Although it is limited by its subjectivity and narrow focus (i.e., people see what they want to see), it is convenient for a quick look at teaching each day. Informal analysis is most useful when comments are highly specific, such as "The light drained from Paul's face when you started the next relay before he was finished," or when a record is kept over a period of time. Written records, tape recordings, or videotape recordings can provide a valuable journal of progress when kept for periodic review.

Because of its lack of validity and reliability, informal analysis alone should *not* be used to evaluate a teacher for retention or tenure. It should be combined with the other methods of evaluation discussed in this chapter to form a profile of the teacher's instructional abilities.

A checklist can be used to direct the observer's attention to specific parts of the lesson. The observer simply "checks" each item that was included in the teacher's behavior during the lesson. An example of a checklist is shown in figure 14.2.

The checklist provides the appearance of scientific accuracy; however, vague, undefined statements or characteristics result in a very low level of reliability for most checklists. A checklist such as the one in figure 14.2 provides no information concerning the frequency with which a given behavior occurs.

```
                    EVALUATION OF TEACHING

    Name _____     Activity _____

    School _____     Date _____

    Time _____


    Instruction:
          Objective clear
          Demonstration
          Practice
          Correction
    Selection of Activity:
          Success potential
          Challenging-motivational
          Progression
    Maximum Participation:
          Time
          Transitions
          Organization-space-equip-
          ment
          Opportunity for all
    Safety:
          Progressions
          Safety rules
          Equipment
    Teacher Relating to Class:
          Aware of class
          Aware of individuals
          Rapport
          Personal appearance
          Voice
```

Figure 14.1 A recording form for informal analysis.

Rating scales can be valuable as a tool for self-evaluation and goal-setting by teachers. They can also be completed by both teachers and supervisors and the results compared to encourage discussion of different points of view concerning the teacher's performance. Goals should then be set to evaluate and correct specific areas needing attention.

An advantage of rating scales is that they take a minimum of time to complete and can provide information sufficient to get a teacher started on a personal improvement plan. However, as an evaluative device, the rating scale is generally less valid and reliable than many of the other techniques that will be presented in this chapter.

When constructing a rating scale, remember that fewer choices increases reliability. However, enough points must be included to make the scale useful for its intended purpose. By having two observers complete the scale independently and then talking over discrepancies, items can be changed so that differences in understanding of the characteristics in question can be corrected. Then the differences are more likely to be related to teacher performance than to understanding the scale.

TEACHER EVALUATION FORM

Name _____ Date _____ Evaluator _____

Personal Qualifications

_____ Displays knowledge of the subject
_____ Projects enthusiasm and interest
_____ Maintains confidence and respect of the students
_____ Is easily heard and understood
_____ Displays self-confidence

Organization

_____ Lesson flows smoothly into activity, from activity to activity, (1) equipment available and ready (2) teacher doesn't talk too much
_____ Students know where to go and what to do
_____ Students understand the objective of the activity or lesson
_____ Available equipment and space is used effectively
_____ Time allotment is appropriate

Instruction

_____ Adequate safety precautions are taken
_____ Individual and group help is given
_____ The activity is challenging, enjoyable, and has success potential
_____ Students are motivated, interested, and involved (not standing too long)
_____ Teacher uses appropriate disciplinary techniques so students are controlled

Comments (Includes strengths, suggestions for improvement, clarification of above)

Lesson Plan

_____ Instructional objectives stated in behavioral terms
_____ Performance cues sufficient for skill execution
_____ Estimate of instructional time is appropriate
_____ Practice situations specified in detail (with diagrams)
_____ Sufficient equipment provided to maximize participation

Figure 14.2 A checklist of teacher functions.

Any of the types of rating scales presented in chapter 8 can be used to assess teaching performance. The choice depends on how one feels about a specific tool.

Many schools, districts, and universities provide rating scales of various standards of performance that can be used for self-evaluation or by peers or supervisors. The rating scale in figure 14.3 is one part of such an evaluation tool. The results can be compared to determine areas that might need improvement.

Rating scales can be developed to evaluate specific items such as execution of teaching styles, demonstrations, or questioning skills. Rosenberg and Knutson developed rating scales to investigate interpersonal relations.[7]

TEACHER EVALUATION RECORD

Name _____ Date _____ Evaluator _____

Instructions: Rate yourself (or have someone else rate you) on each of the major items by placing an "X" on the lines provided.

	Always	Usually	Sometimes	Seldom or Never	Doesn't Apply	Comments
Works Well with Associates						
Is friendly and cordial	____	____	____	____	____	
Possesses tact and courtesy	____	____	____	____	____	
Gains the respect of associates	____	____	____	____	____	
Promotes cooperative action among individuals and groups	____	____	____	____	____	
Listens attentively when associating with others	____	____	____	____	____	
Has a genuine desire to help others without concern for personal benefit or credit for achievement	____	____	____	____	____	
Is sensitive to own effect on others	____	____	____	____	____	
Accepts and utilizes suggestions from others	____	____	____	____	____	
Keeps informed on policies and procedures and follows them	____	____	____	____	____	
Asks questions to clarify assignments and responsibilities	____	____	____	____	____	
Carries own share of school responsibilities willingly and cheerfully	____	____	____	____	____	
Keeps commitments reliably	____	____	____	____	____	
Serves on committees and participates in other group projects	____	____	____	____	____	
Is prompt and accurate with reports	____	____	____	____	____	
Goes through regular "channels" on matters affecting the welfare of associates or of the institution	____	____	____	____	____	
Is loyal to associates, school, and district	____	____	____	____		

Figure 14.3 A portion of a teacher evaluation record.

Informal Analysis by Students

Because informal analysis relies on each person's individual perceptions, it can be used to help teachers see things as others see them. Thus, informal analysis can be especially helpful in determining how students feel about what they have learned and their perceptions about the learning situation. To be most effective, informal analysis by students should be written, not oral, and should be kept anonymous to allow for free and honest responses. Caution should be used in asking young students to analyze teacher behavior. Questionnaires should not be used with students who do not have the ability to understand the intent of the questions and to provide valid answers. Some examples of questions that might be asked on a student questionnaire include the following:

1. What are the two most important things you have learned in this class?
2. What factors helped you learn them? (Be specific. Who did what to help you?)
3. How could this class be improved to make it better?
4. List the strengths of your teacher.
5. Tell how your teacher could help you learn better.

To score the analyses, simply tally the number of times a similar response was given to each question. Then, look seriously at the ones listed most often. Also, take note of perceptions that may not have occurred previously.

Checklists can also be used to obtain an overall estimate of student feelings toward specific aspects of teacher performance. Items might include some of the following:

1. Place a check beside *each* characteristic that describes your teacher:

_____ Interesting   _____ Organized   _____ Strict

_____ Smart   _____ Pushover   _____ Disorganized

_____ Uninformed   _____ Dull

2. Place a check beside the answer that best describes your feelings toward the teacher:
   a. The teacher helps me learn or improve my skills.

      Yes   No   I don't know.
   b. The teacher has good discipline.

      Yes   No   I don't know.

Each of the different categories of rating scales discussed in chapter 8 can be used for student evaluation of teachers. Questions using the semantic differential scale to score student attitudes toward the teacher might appear as follows:

Friendly	1	2	3	4	5	6	7	Unfriendly

Boring	1	2	3	4	5	6	7	Interesting

Items are scored from 1 to 7, with 7 being the most positive. An average of the scores for the entire class on each item would undoubtedly provide the most information.

The Likert scale can be used to determine student attitudes toward the teacher or to compare how the students feel versus how the teacher feels about each characteristic. For example, in the following questions, x marks how the student feels, and o marks how the teacher feels on each item.

	Mostly true	Usually true	Neutral	Usually false	Mostly false
1. The teacher is concerned about student learning.	o			x	
2. The teacher likes teaching.		x	o		

When a serious discrepancy exists between the teacher's and the student's feelings, as in item 1, the teacher becomes aware of the need to communicate feelings differently.

Students' perceptions about the instructional system can also be acquired via a rating scale. An example of this type of rating scale is shown in figure 14.4. This scale could be used as a report card for students to grade the teacher at the end of a unit of instruction or grading period. The scale could be written at a lower level of reading ability for use by younger students.

Descriptive Analysis

One way to avoid the subjectivity inherent in informal analysis is to use descriptive analysis. Descriptive analysis is used to collect data that describe various components of the teaching performance. The data are then analyzed to determine the extent to which the intended teaching behavior actually occurred during teaching.

The primary purpose of descriptive analysis is to collect objective data that accurately describe events occurring in the classroom. The data must be recorded in such a way that they can be used to analyze one or more components of the teaching-learning process.

Literally hundreds of analytic systems have been developed to encode student and teacher behaviors. Some are relatively easy to learn and use; others are so complex that only trained researchers can use them. In this chapter, the simpler kinds of descriptive analysis that can be used for self-improvement will be presented. These systems require only an observer, a paper and pencil, and a stopwatch. A tape recorder or video recorder can be valuable if teachers wish to analyze their own teaching behavior rather than having an outside observer evaluate them.

Descriptive analysis is generally limited to a description of what the teacher and students were doing. It tells very little about the quality of the performance. Other limitations are the limited sample size (sometimes only one student), the limited time sample, and the limited set of categories used for describing behavior. For this reason, descriptive analysis should be accompanied by other forms of evaluation.[8]

Descriptive analysis uses the techniques of time analysis, time sampling, spot-checking, and event recording. A discussion of each technique follows.

STUDENT OPINIONNAIRE—
BASIC INSTRUCTION PHYSICAL EDUCATION PROGRAM
KNOWLEDGE—CLARITY—ENTHUSIASM

1. The instructor effectively explained or demonstrated the skills of the activity.
   INEFFECTIVE A_____ B _____ C _____ D _____ E VERY EFFECTIVE

2. The instructor was perceptive in diagnosing and skillful in correcting individual errors in performance.
   OBLIVIOUS/NOT HELPFUL A_____ B _____ C _____ D _____ E PERCEPTIVE/HELPFUL

3. The instructor clearly explained the rules, scoring and strategies involved in the activity. (May not apply to dance, gymnastics, skating, etc.)
   VAGUELY A_____ B _____ C _____ D _____ E CLEARLY

4. The instructor was enthusiastic and interested in teaching the subject matter.
   APATHETIC A_____ B _____ C _____ D _____ E ENTHUSIASTIC

5. The instructor demonstrated a comprehensive knowledge of the activity.
   UNINFORMED A_____ B _____ C _____ D _____ E VERY KNOWLEDGEABLE

6. The instructor encouraged and motivated you to attain a higher skill level.
   UNCONCERNED A_____ B _____ C _____ D _____ E VERY PERSUASIVE

7. The instructor seemed capable of teaching the more highly skilled performers.
   INCAPABLE A_____ B _____ C _____ D _____ E VERY CAPABLE

ORGANIZATION AND PREPARATION

8. The instructor provided, verbally or via a course outline, the course objectives, expectations, assignments, examination information, and grading procedures.
   UNDEFINED A_____ B _____ C _____ D _____ E CLEARLY DEFINED

9. The instructor's lessons reflected planned learning sessions and efficient utilization of class time.
   DISORGANIZED A_____ B _____ C _____ D _____ E WELL PLANNED

10. Within the limitations of the facilities, the instructor provided maximal active participation time for all students.
    INACTIVE A_____ B _____ C _____ D _____ E VERY ACTIVE

11. The textbook and other instructional materials were of value in the course.
    NO BENEFIT A_____ B _____ C _____ D _____ E VERY VALUABLE

12. A safe learning environment was provided for the class.
    HARMFUL A_____ B _____ C _____ D _____ E VERY SAFE

INSTRUCTOR-STUDENT INTERACTION & RAPPORT

13. The instructor provided evaluative feedback concerning your skill development.
    UNINFORMATIVE A_____ B _____ C _____ D _____ E INFORMATIVE

14. The instructor was impartial and fair in dealing with students.
    UNFAIR A_____ B _____ C _____ D _____ E VERY FAIR

15. The instructor was interested in you and your skill development.
    DISINTERESTED A_____ B _____ C _____ D _____ E VERY INTERESTED

16. The instructor was understanding of and helpful to students who experienced difficulty acquiring the activity skills.
    NO HELP A_____ B _____ C _____ D _____ E VERY HELPFUL

GENERAL EVALUATION

17. Fun and enjoyment were experienced throughout the course.
    BORING A_____ B _____ C _____ D _____ E VERY ENJOYABLE

18. Based on your experience in this course, would you enroll in another physical education course and/or recommend activity courses to others?
    ABSOLUTELY NOT A_____ B _____ C _____ D _____ E DEFINITELY

19. Considering all aspects of the course, how would you rate this course?
    POOR A_____ B _____ C _____ D _____ E EXCELLENT

20. Considering all of the instructional aspects of this course, how would you rate the instructor?
    POOR A_____ B _____ C _____ D _____ E EXCELLENT

Figure 14.4 A student rating scale.
Source: Zakrajsek, Dorothy B. and Ronald R. Bos.
"Student Evaluations of Teaching Performance,"
Journal of Physical Education and Recreation, 49 (May 1978): 64–65.

Class __Badminton__ Date __March 16__

Total class time __35 minutes__

Instruction	Management	Participation with feedback	Participation without feedback
4:30	3:06	6:18	2:06
1:10	1:24	3:50	6:00
1:10	2:50	9:08	8:06
2:00	1:50		
8:50	:46		
	9:56		
25.14%	25.43%	26.00%	22.89%

Suggestions for improvement

1. I should try to reduce the time spent organizing students during each management episode to less than 1 minute.
2. I should provide more feedback during student practice.

Figure 14.5 A time-analysis form.

Time Analysis Time analysis is useful for determining the amount of time spent on the various functions that teachers perform.[9] Such functions include instructing students (e.g., demonstrating, explaining, or questioning); class management (e.g., roll call, organizing students, distributing equipment, discipline); active student practice with feedback from the instructor; and student practice with no feedback from the instructor. A stopwatch is used to record the amount of time spent in each category. The stopwatch is restarted each time the teacher changes functions. An example of time analysis is shown in figure 14.5.

At the conclusion of the lesson, the time in each category is totaled and divided by the total class time to obtain the percentage of time spent in each category. Then, the results are analyzed to see if the time has been spent in the best way. Individual functions, such as roll call or demonstrations, can also be analyzed by time analysis to determine where the time is going and changes can be made to eliminate the nonproductive use of time.

Another variation of time analysis is to record the amount of time spent in actual practice by an individual student. The teacher may discover that, while the class is engaged in what appears to be a large amount of practice time, individual students spend a large amount of time waiting for a turn or "standing out in right field."

Time analysis can also be done for several brief periods of time spaced throughout a lesson. For example, three five-minute samples can provide a valid indication of the percentage of time spent in each type of behavior.[10] To obtain a percentage, merely divide by fifteen minutes instead of the total class time.

Time Sampling In time sampling, the observation session is divided into a number of equal intervals and a specified behavior is observed and recorded at the conclusion of each interval. For example, in a thirty-five-minute period, there are thirty-five one-minute intervals or seventy thirty-second intervals. The number of intervals selected will depend on the behavior to be sampled. Because time sampling occurs only at the end of each interval, it saves considerable time. Some time samples can even be done while teaching, such as checking on a student every five minutes to determine student involvement in activity.

The easiest kind of time sampling involves only two categories—such as active or passive, productive or nonproductive. A student is selected and at the end of each interval, a check or tally indicates the behavior the student demonstrates. Several students can be observed by observing the first student during intervals 1, 4, 7, . . . ; the second student during intervals 2, 5, 8 . . . ; and the third student during intervals 3, 6, 9. . . . The intervals can be recorded on a tape recorder or a watch or stopwatch can be used to determine the end of each interval.

To code a number of behaviors, an average student is selected and what the student is doing at the end of each interval is coded. To make it easier, coding can be done for three minutes, followed by resting three minutes, and repeating the coding and resting throughout the period.

Figure 14.6 shows a time-sampling form designed by Anderson to determine how students are spending their time during a class session. It uses a five-second interval for coding. The categories include the following:

1. Performs motor activity—Plays game or sport, practices skill, does exercises or calisthenics, explores movement.
2. Receives information—Listens, watches demonstration, uses media, reads written material.
3. Gives information or assists—Talks to teacher or student, demonstrates, spots.
4. Waits—Waits for turn, waits for game or drill to begin.
5. Relocates—Moves from one place or activity area to another.
6. Other—Ties shoes, gets equipment, gets a drink.

At the end of each three-minute period, notes can be recorded to help the teacher recall information explaining the recorded behaviors. At the end of the period, each column is totaled and a percentage calculated. The behavior is then analyzed and goals set for improving teaching.

Teacher behaviors can also be coded using time sampling and the categories used for time analysis. An example of a time-sampling form for teacher behavior appears in figure 14.7.

Sample Coding Form and Record

TIME SAMPLING OF A SINGLE STUDENT'S BEHAVIOR

RECORD A CHECK (✓) FOR EACH
5 SECONDS OF STUDENT ACTIVITY.

STUDENT'S NAME: Alice Smith
CLASS: Elementary Gymnastics

SEGMENT (3-MIN)	PERFORMS MOTOR ACTIVITY	RECEIVES INFOR- MATION	Gives INFOR- MATION OR ASSISTS	WAITS	RELOCATES	OTHER	NOTATIONS
I 9:00– 9:03	✓✓✓ ③	✓✓✓✓✓ ✓✓✓✓ ✓✓✓✓ ✓✓✓✓✓ ⑳		✓✓✓✓✓ ✓✓✓✓ ⑩	✓✓ ②	✓ ①	Waited for teacher to begin Rec. info on class organization
II 9:06– 9:09	✓✓✓✓✓ ✓✓✓ ⑧	✓✓✓✓ ✓✓✓✓ ✓✓✓✓ ✓✓✓✓✓ ✓✓ ㉓		✓✓ ②	✓✓✓ ③	✓ ①	End instruction / began tumbling and head stand
III 9:12– 9:15	✓✓✓✓ ✓✓✓✓✓ ✓✓✓✓✓ ✓✓ ⑰	✓✓✓✓✓ ⑤	✓✓✓✓✓ ③	✓✓ ③	✓ ①	✓✓✓✓✓ ✓ ⑥	Cont'd. tumbling "Other" = replaced mats
IV 9:18– 9:21	✓✓✓✓✓ ✓✓✓✓✓ ✓✓✓✓✓ ✓✓✓✓✓ ✓✓ ㉒	✓✓✓ ③	✓✓✓ ③	✓✓✓✓✓ ⑤		✓✓✓ ③	Performed on ropes
V 9:24– 9:27	✓✓✓ ③	✓✓✓✓✓ ✓✓✓✓✓ ✓✓✓✓ ✓✓✓✓✓ ㉓		✓✓✓ ③	✓✓✓ ③	✓✓ ②	Recd. instruction on bars
VI 9:30– 9:33	✓✓✓ ③	✓✓✓✓✓ ✓✓✓✓✓ ⑩		✓✓✓✓✓ ✓✓✓✓✓ ✓✓✓✓✓ ✓✓✓✓✓ ✓ ㉑		✓✓ ②	Waits turn on bars and performs
TOTALS	f = 56 %= 56/216 = 26%	f = 85 %= 85/216 = 39%	f = 8 %= 8/216 = 3%	f = 43 %= 43/216 = 19%	f = 9 %= 9/216 = 4%	f = 15 %= 15/216 = 7%	

SUMMARY COMMENTS AND EVALUATION (made by teacher of class)
Too much time spent waiting for teacher and getting organized.
Good activity levels on mats and ropes — too much waiting around on bars.
Overall, a greater proportion of time should be spent in performing activities.

Figure 14.6 A time-sampling form for student behavior.

Source: From Anderson, William G. *Analysis of Teaching Physical Education,* St. Louis, 1980. The C. V. Mosby Co.

TIME SAMPLING OF TEACHER BEHAVIOR

Class _____ Date _____

Total Class Time _____

Instructions: Record a check (✔) for each five seconds of teacher activity.

Segment (3 min.)	Instruction			Management Activities	Student Participation	
	Class	Group	Individual		With Feedback	Without Feedback
I						
II						
III						
IV						
V						
Totals						

Summary Comments and Evaluations:

Figure 14.7 A time-sampling form for teacher behavior.

Spot-Checking Spot-checking is time sampling applied to a group.* It is useful when a teacher wants to know what most of the students in a group or class are doing. Spot-checking involves counting the number of students engaged in a particular behavior at the conclusion of a specified interval of time, such as every two or three minutes. Behaviors to be checked should be limited to two or three so that the spot-check takes only about ten seconds to do. The observer should scan from left to right each time and record the number of students who are engaged in the less-frequently occurring behavior. For example, in an actively involved class, the inactive students are counted and subtracted from the total number of students to get the number in the actively involved category. A sample spot-checking record is shown in figure 14.8.

Anderson suggested the use of the following categories for spot-checking: "active/inactive, on-task/off-task, safe/unsafe, attentive/unattentive, cooperative/disruptive, and interacting with others/isolated."[11] Siedentop indicated that 90 to 100 percent of the students should be engaged in appropriate and productive behavior for teaching to be effective.[12]

At the conclusion of the class, the percentage of students in each category is calculated by dividing each column total by the sum of the two or three columns. The data are then analyzed and changes planned for improving teaching behavior.

Event Recording Event recording is merely tallying the frequency with which a given behavior occurs during a specified time period. It is done by identifying one person to observe (the teacher, an average student) and one or more behaviors to tally. The observer then proceeds to put down a mark each time the specified behavior occurs. For simple behaviors, a golf counter can be used to record frequency. Five three-minute intervals, spaced throughout the period, are usually adequate for event recording.

Event recording can be used to collect meaningful data on a wide variety of teacher or student behaviors. It produces a numerical value that can be converted into rate per minute. The rate per minute on different occasions can then be compared to determine whether improvement in the behavior has occurred. Event recording can be used to record items involving instruction, class management, student practice, use of first names, and feedback.

Instruction The extent to which the intended concepts are conveyed to the students can be determined by listing each concept and recording a check beside the concept each time it is mentioned by the teacher. An example of content evaluation is shown in figure 14.9.

Class Management Event recording can be used to tally the number of times the students have to be told how to assume a formation for roll call, drill, or game play. For each transition from one activity to another, only one teacher behavior should be emitted. In the example shown in figure 14.10, the teacher spent three minutes and six seconds organizing drills and told the students how to get organized seven times. This teacher needs to clarify instructions so that they are communicated to students on the first try.

*Called Pla-chek by Siedentop.

SPOT-CHECKING RECORD FORM

Class _Track and Field_   Date _May 10_

Time / Categories	Off-task	On-task active	On-task waiting	Comments
8:50	1	2	7	tieing shoes
8:56	0	3	7	
9:02	0	3	7	
9:08	3	2	5	talking
9:14	4	3	3	playing around
8:52	0	1	9	
8:58	0	1	9	
9:04	2	1	7	talking
9:10	5	1	4	talking
9:16	4	1	5	wandered off
8:54	0	4	6	
8:00	0	4	6	
9:06	0	4	6	
9:12	1	3	6	getting a drink
9:18	2	4	4	talking
Column Totals	22	37	91	
Total of All Columns	150			
Percent of Total	14.7%	24.7%	60.7%	

Row labels (left margin): High Jump (rows 8:50–9:14), Long Jump (rows 8:52–9:16), Hurdles (rows 8:54–9:18)

Summary Comments and Evaluation:

on-task, active = performing or helping
on-task, waiting = watching performance
off-task, = talking, wandering around,
        daydreaming

Students are spending a lot of time waiting
and seem bored, especially at end of period.

Figure 14.8 A sample spot-checking record.

Sample Coding Form and Record

CONTENT OF TEACHER'S INSTRUCTIONS

A check (✓) is recorded each time the teacher refers to a listed item of content

TENNIS LESSON ON BACKHAND DRIVE	BASIC MOVEMENT LESSON ON THROWING

1. Entire stroke (general) ✓✓
2. Grip (general) ✓
  – ⅛th turn ✓
  – 45% angle
  – other (list) too loose ✓
3. Back swing (general)
  – Short ✓
  – Help with left hand ✓
  – Body pivot ✓✓✓✓✓✓✓✓
  – Elbow position ✓
  – Other (list)
4. Forward swing (general) ✓
  – Arc of racket ✓
  – Point of contact ✓✓✓✓✓✓✓✓✓✓✓
  – Angle of contact
  – Other (list) eye on ball ✓✓✓✓✓
5. Follow through (general) ✓
  – Racket head rises
  – Topspin
  – Other (list) smoothness ✓
6. Common errors
  – Excessive body action
  – Chopping
  – Other (list) backswing too long ✓✓
        elbow push ✓
7. Other (list)
 	
  getting into position ✓✓✓✓✓✓✓
  anticipating flight of ball ✓✓✓✓
              ✓✓✓✓
	1. Performance elements
	  – Eyes on target ✓
	  – Feet apart ✓✓
	  – Rotate trunk
	  – Weight to back foot
	  – Elbow bent
	  – Transfer weight to front foot
	  – Point of release ✓✓
	  – Follow through ✓✓
	2. Major concepts
	  – Point of release affects direction ✓✓✓✓
	  – Transfer of weight gives power
	3. Common errors
	  – Facing front ✓✓✓✓✓✓✓✓✓✓✓
	  – No rotation ✓✓✓
	  – Pushing
	4. Other (list)
	  forgot to snap wrist ✓✓
	  "stride" toward target ✓
	  angle of projection ✓

SUMMARY COMMENTS AND EVALUATION I neglected the "follow through". I forgot to include "eye on ball" in initial plan, but covered it with individual students. "Positioning" and "anticipation" came up frequently, include in future presentations. Emphasized "point of contact" and forgot about "angle of contact."	**SUMMARY COMMENTS AND EVALUATION** Tried to cover too much with these third graders so purposely left out some things. Forgot to cover weight transfer = greater power. Too many students had to be corrected for facing front, emphasize sideward stance next time. Performance elements were covered at beginning, but not during later practice.

Figure 14.9 A sample content evaluation record.

Source: From Anderson, William G. *Analysis of Teaching Physical Education,* St. Louis, 1980, The C. V. Mosby Co.

RECORD OF TEACHER MANAGEMENT BEHAVIORS

Length of Each Episode	Number of Teacher Management Behaviors	Types of Management Behaviors
3:06	ℋℋ //	Organizing drills
1:24	///	Changing drills
2:50	////	Starting games
1:50	///	Rotating teams
:46	//	Ending class

Total Management Time = 9:56

Average Time Per Episode = abt 2 min

Average Number of Teacher Behaviors Per Episode = 3.8

Summary Comments and Evaluation:

I need to clarify my expectations so that I don't need to repeat instructions more than once.

Figure 14.10 A sample record of management behaviors.

STUDENT PRACTICE RECORD

Class __Soccer_____ Date __Oct. 15_____

Skills	Student #1 Period _1_	Student #2 Period _1_	Student #3 Period _1_	Student #4 Period ___
Number of times each student touches the ball	TH TH TH III	II	TH IIII	

Summary Comments and Evaluation:

Apparently student #2 rarely touches the ball. Perhaps I need to use smaller teams or rotate players so each student has an equal opportunity for skill development.

Figure 14.11 A sample record of student practice.

Student Practice The number of practice trials a student attempts or the number of times a student touches the ball or uses a piece of equipment can be easily tallied as shown in figure 14.11. This can be done during practice drills, in lead-up games, or during actual game play. A list of skills or tasks to be accomplished with a check by each one attempted provides an overall view of the distribution of practice over the entire range of tasks inherent in the activity. Figures 14.11 and 14.12 show how this can be done. A study of the record aids the teacher in determining the adequacy and distribution of practice trials.

STUDENT PRACTICE RECORD

Class *Badminton*   Date *March 17*

Skills	Student #1 Period _1_	Student #2 Period _2_	Student #3 Period _2_	Student #4 Period ___
Short serve	①①①11①1	⓪⓪⓪11⓪⓪	⓪⓪⓪⓪⓪⓪⓪ ⓪⓪⓪	
Overhead clear	1①11①1①⓪	⓪①①①⓪	⓪⓪⓪⓪⓪⓪1 ⓪1⓪⓪	
Underhand clear	111①111⓪	⓪⓪⓪11① 1⓪⓪1⓪1	⓪①11⓪①①⓪	
Smash				
Drop				

Summary Comments and Evaluation:

I circled the successful attempts in a five-minute game. Student #1 needs to review basic skills. No student attempted drops or smashes. Perhaps I need to reteach the drop and smash.

Figure 14.12 A record of student trials on key skills.

Feedback Feedback has been defined as one of the key elements in the acquisition of psychomotor skills. Feedback also occurs regarding appropriate and inappropriate student behavior. Event recording can be used to record the extent to which both kinds of feedback occur. Both skill feedback and behavior feedback can be analyzed in the following ways by using the form in figure 14.13.

1. Rate of feedback per minute.
2. Ratio of positive to negative feedback.

Skill Feedback ___
Behavior Feedback ✓

Five-minute Event Recording	Tone Pos./Neg.		Kind General/Specific/Value	To Whom Individual/Group		Skill-Feedback Type Verbal	Visual and Verbal	Kinesthetic and Verbal	Behavior-Feedback Type Reinforces Appropriate Behavior	Punishes Off-Task Behaviors
I	II	++++ I		++++	II				I	++++
II	I	++++ ++++		II						II
III		III		++++ III II	I				II	++++ III
IV	II	++++		II	I				I	II
V	III	II		++++ ++++	I					++++ ++++
Totals	8	26		29	5				4	27

Summary:

Feedback per minute =
Ratio of positive to negative feedback = 8/26
Percent of specific feedback =
Percent of feedback that explains why = 14.7%
Percent of group-directed feedback =
Percent of nonverbal feedback =
Ratio of reinforcement to punishment = 4/27

Comments and Evaluation:

Feedback is generally negative in tone and directed toward individuals. I need to look for what students do well and rein-force them, especially in group situations.

Figure 14.13 Event recording of behavior or skill feedback.

3. Percent of specific feedback.
4. Percent of value feedback.
5. Percent of group-directed feedback.
6. Percent of nonverbal feedback.
7. Ratio of reinforcement of appropriate behavior to punishment of off-task behavior.

Each column of the form can be used separately or several columns can be recorded at once. Categories can be defined as follows:

1. Positive—A tone that conveys acceptance of a student's performance or behavior.
2. Negative—A tone that conveys rejection of a student's performance or behavior.
3. General—Feedback with no specific information given about the skill or behavior.
4. Specific—Feedback with specific information given about how to perform the behavior or skill.
5. Value—Feedback that tells why a specific behavior or skill should be done in a certain way.
6. Individual—Feedback to one student.
7. Group—Feedback to more than one student.
8. Verbal—Feedback that is only verbal.
9. Visual and verbal—Feedback that demonstrates how the skill or behavior should be performed.
10. Kinesthetic and verbal—Feedback that uses touch or manipulation of body parts to correct the movement (such as spotting in gymnastics).
11. Reinforces appropriate behavior—Feedback that rewards appropriate behavior.
12. Punishes off-task behavior—Feedback that is nonreinforcing or punishing for inappropriate behavior.

Creating a Personalized Descriptive System Often evaluation instruments are not appropriate for specific situations. Those who know the situation best should not hesitate to create or adapt an appropriate tool for evaluation. Once an instrument has been formulated, it should be tried out and checked for reliability. Modifications should be made until it brings the desired results. Anyone preparing a descriptive system should incorporate the following components: (1) a single behavior focus, (2) a definition of categories, (3) an observation and coding system, and (4) reliability.

The Behavior Focus A single teaching component should be selected for analysis. Trying to analyze too much can defeat the system. The component should be defined to identify what is and what is not included in the behavior focus. An example for one teacher was to reduce the use of distracting words or phrases.

Definition of Categories Categories within the behavioral focus must be defined so that any observable behavior can be assigned to only one category. Examples of behaviors falling into each category should be provided. For example, *okay* or *all right* fit into the category of distracting words or phrases.

An Observation and Coding System A decision must be made as to the technique to be used, such as time analysis, time sampling, spot-checking, or event recording. A form should then be developed for recording the data.

Reliability Reliability results when two observers obtain similar results after independently rating the same lesson or when one observer obtains the same results on two separate occasions from a videotaped recording. When this occurs, it reveals that the definitions of the behavior categories are sufficiently clear to ensure that behaviors are recorded accurately by the observer and reflect the actual behavior that occurred during the lesson.

Interaction Analysis

Interaction analysis provides objective feedback about the type and quality of teacher-student interaction. Most of the interaction analysis systems have been based on verbal interaction and nearly all of them are based on teacher dominance of instruction. The best-known tool for interaction analysis is the Flanders system.[13] This system does not differentiate those behaviors used most by physical education teachers. A number of adaptations of the Flanders system have been produced. However, they made the system cumbersome to use for teacher improvement.

Anderson identified a simpler method for recording the interaction of teachers and students.[14] It is based on Morgenegg's findings that interaction in physical education classes focused on the three behaviors of teacher solicitations of movement, student movement responses, and teacher reactions to the movement responses.[15] A sample coding form is shown in figure 14.14. Each entry shows who solicited the response (the teacher or the student), who reacted and how (motor activity, verbal activity, or other behavior), and the reaction caused by the behavior. For example, the teacher asks students to get ready to shoot and the students respond; or the teacher asks a student to shoot an arrow, the student responds by shooting, and the teacher replies, "Good!"

Coding should include four or more five-minute coding periods. At the conclusion of the lesson, the amount and direction of the interactions are evaluated. The following questions should be answered to direct the teacher toward an analysis of the results: Are all solicitations initiated by the teacher or are students encouraged to seek out solutions to their problems? Is there a balance between teacher-directed instruction and student-directed instruction? Does the teacher react enough? Or too much?

Step 3—Use the Appropriate Techniques to Record Information

Table 14.1 listed possible evaluation techniques for the teaching goals and behaviors specified in step 1. The best evaluation technique is the one that provides precise feedback related to the specific teaching goal. Since only a few events can be recorded during each lesson, a plan should be formulated to use the most effective techniques for the objectives of the specific lesson. A sample evaluation plan for a lesson is shown in figure 14.15. The plan should be kept simple. Two or three evaluation techniques at a time are probably as many as can be checked accurately.

Step 4—Evaluate or Interpret the Data

So far, research has been unable to find one best way to teach. Therefore, teachers need to experiment to determine the best combination of teaching skills to create the desired results for their particular students and situation.

Sample Coding Form and Record

TEACHER - STUDENT INTERACTION

CLASS: Jr. H.S. Archery   TEACHER: Dick Martin

SOLICIT	RESPOND	REACT
T	S_O	
T	S_O	
T	S_O	T
S	T_V	
T	S_M	
T	S_M	T
T	S_M	T
T	S_M	T_M
	S_M	T_M
		T
T	S_O	
T	S_M	
T	S_M	
T	S_M	
T	S_V	T
T	S_M	T_M
S	T_V	
T	S_M	
T	S_M	T
T	S_M	T_M
		T_M
		T_M
T	S_O	
T	S_O	
T	S_V	
T	S_M	T
T	S_M	T
T	S_M	
T	S_M	
T	S_M	T_M
		T_n
S	T_O	
T	S_M	
T	S_M	
T	S_M	
T	S_O	
T	S_O	

CODES: (T) Teacher, (S) Student
(M) Motor activity
(V) Verbal activity or response
(O) Other behavior

TOTALS:

SOLICITATIONS: 32					
By teacher: 29			By students: 3		
of verb.	mot.	oth.	of verb.	mot.	oth.
2	19	8	2	1	0

RESPONSES: 32					
By teacher: 3			By students: 29		
to verb.	mot.	oth.	to verb.	mot.	oth.
2	0	1	2	19	8

REACTIONS: 16					
By teacher: 16			By students: 0		
to verb.	mot.	oth.	to verb.	mot.	oth.
0	15	1	0	0	0

MOST COMMON PATTERNS:
$T \rightarrow S_M = 13$
$T \rightarrow S_M \rightarrow T = 6$
$T \rightarrow S_O = 8$
$T_M = 8$

SUMMARY COMMENTS AND EVALUATION (by observed teacher)
I do virtually all the soliciting and reacting; the students
do almost all the responding.
I focus on eliciting student motor responses - which is OK - but
I virtually never elicit verbal responses from students - which
is not OK.
I seem to be reasonably conscientious about reacting to
what students do.
Overall, I'm concerned that I seem to start (solicit)
and end (react) all the interactions.

Figure 14.14 A sample coding form for
teacher-student interaction.

Source: From Anderson, William G. *Analysis of
Teaching Physical Education,* St. Louis, 1980, The
C. V. Mosby Co.

AN EVALUATION PLAN

Lesson Plan	Evaluation Plan	Data
Objectives		
1. Students will hit three out of five balls pitched to them during drill.	Students record number of successful hits during a specified time period.	
2. Students will hit 100 percent of the times at bat in one-swing game.	Tally number of students at bat and number of successful hits.	
Teaching and Learning Activities		
1. Demonstrate and explain batting.	Event recording of content of teacher's instruction.	
2. Pepper drill for maximum participation with teacher feedback.	Event recording of student trials during drill and skill feedback of teacher.	
3. One-swing softball game for application to game situation.	Event recording of student trials and successes during game.	
Specific Teacher Goals		
1. Reduce management time.	Time analysis of management time.	
Summary Comments and Evaluation		

Figure 14.15 A sample evaluation plan.

The major purpose of the evaluation is to determine how close the actual teaching behavior matches up with the intended behavior. This can be done by referring to the plan established in step 3. Some questions to ask are:

1. What teaching behaviors are satisfactory?
2. What changes in teaching behaviors might improve student learning?
3. Which changes are practical?
4. Which one or two changes in teacher behavior would result in the most important changes in student performance?
5. What will have to be done to implement these changes?
6. What target goal for the change would be indicative of a successful change effort? (e.g., call ten students by name each period)

Anderson delineated some problems with attempting to interpret the match between actual and intended behaviors:

> There will be a natural tendency to be pleased when reality matches your plans and to be disheartened when there is a mismatch. . . . That's as it should be, most of the time—but not always. There are times when unfolding events in class signify the need for a change of plan in midstream. A teacher who is tuned in to such signals is likely to digress from his or her original plan. In such cases the record will show a mismatch. Is that bad? There are times when unfolding events in class signify the need for a change of plan but the teacher is *not* tuned in to such signals, and so he or she plows ahead as originally planned. (Some teachers who *are* tuned in plow ahead anyway.) Such behavior will produce a record that shows a close match with the original plan. Is that good?
> Sometimes, in the midst of a lesson you come up with a brilliant idea that you hadn't thought of before. You try it out and it works. So you continue to pursue it and in the process abandon your original intentions. The lesson turns out to be a smashing success. The record shows an enormous mismatch. So? . . .
> Interpreting matches and mismatches can be tricky business. Be careful.[16]

Evaluating teacher effectiveness is complex and tricky. One research study concluded that the instrumentation to measure effectiveness was not sensitive to differences in the way individual skills were handled by individual teachers. The instruments used to evaluate instruction indicated that instructional characteristics did not change from skill to skill, but student learning did.[17]

Step 5—Make Changes and Reevaluate
An attempt should be made to incorporate the selected changes into the teaching repertoire. Only one or two changes should be made at a time. The same or a similar lesson should be taught, concentrating on the intended changes, and the lesson reevaluated to determine whether the changes produced the desired results. If not, a new procedure should be selected and tried.

An Example of Teacher Evaluation

Step 1—Determine What to Evaluate
For a softball unit, the teacher selected the following evaluation goals: (1) to increase student skill achievement and (2) to reduce class management time.

Step 2—Choose or Construct Specific Evaluation Techniques

The specific evaluation techniques selected were (1) student achievement, (2) time analysis and event recording of management time as shown in figures 14.5 and 14.10, (3) event recording of student practice using the technique demonstrated in figure 14.12, and (4) event recording of skill feedback as shown in figure 14.13.

Step 3—Use the Appropriate Techniques to Record Information

Student assistants were used to record student achievement and practice by tallying successful trials. Several lessons were videotaped for evaluation of management time and skill feedback. A sample evaluation plan for one of the lessons is shown in figure 14.15.

Step 4—Evaluate or Interpret the Data

The results of the data showed that students were spending too much time practicing without the help of teacher feedback and the feedback when given was primarily verbal. For class management, the analysis showed that the teacher had to tell students several times before they proceeded to do what they had been told.

Step 5—Make Changes and Reevaluate

The teacher decided to use a golf counter to keep a tally of the number of feedback attempts during one period each day to increase the frequency of feedback. Later, an event recording of skill feedback also showed an increase in the number of nonverbal feedback attempts.

The second result of the evaluation occurred in class management. The teacher told the students what they were to do, asked several questions to determine whether they understood, and then refrained from repeating instructions. Students were timed to determine how long it took to get into the next formation, drill, or game, and feedback provided on the length of time it took. The result was a rapid decrease in management time.

Evaluation techniques can be very useful tools to upgrade teacher effectiveness. A good teacher is the impetus behind good programs. Good programs should be the stimulus for productive public relations. The results of good public relations often come full circle and provide support for the program, resulting in an enhanced learning environment.

Public Relations

Since motivation is contagious, it is worth taking some time to promote a cycle of motivation among the various school publics. Figure 14.16 shows the interrelationships among these groups. Some ideas for motivating students, families, teachers, and the community are presented here.

Students

Students are the most important public. They are the only ones teachers see from day to day. When students experience a sound instructional program, they will "sell" it to their parents through their enthusiasm. Students grow up into community and school leaders and will have an influence on physical education in the future. Students who have a positive experience in physical education will be more supportive of it in the future.

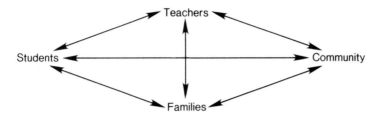

Figure 14.16 The interrelationships among the various publics of the school.

A number of ways to enhance student learning have already been discussed. Some other events that can promote public relations within the school include demonstrations of physical activities in school assemblies, interdisciplinary units with teachers of other subject areas, field days such as the "Super Kids' Day" presented in chapter 9, and contests for the entire school. Implementing interdisciplinary units with teachers of mathematics, foreign languages, home economics, health, and physiology can be effective in promoting student and faculty interest in physical education activities.

Administrators, Faculty, and Staff

Far too often, physical education teachers divorce themselves from the total school environment. Effective teachers make the effort to emerge from the gymnasium to share experiences with the rest of the faculty. They take time each year to discuss the physical education program with the principal, including an overview of the program, goals for the year, changes that have been implemented, achievements, and new trends or ideas.[18] They volunteer to serve on faculty committees, from which they gain new ideas and through which they have a positive effect on the rest of the school. Physical educators need to be aware of opportunities to integrate physical education concepts with other subject areas in the curriculum. Administrators, faculty, and staff can be invited to participate in faculty fitness programs, clinics to learn new skills, tournaments, and free-play activities.[19] One's personal appearance, manner of speech, and enthusiasm can affect the entire school.

Parent and Family Participation and Interest

A number of methods can be used to help parents understand what is happening in physical education classes. A "back-to-school night" is held in many schools. Teachers should take this opportunity to point out the objectives of physical education and provide an outline of activities in which students will be involved. Samples of the students' work and mini-demonstrations by students could also be provided along with a schedule of future events. Parents should also be invited to visit classes during a back-to-school day or week.

Parent-teacher conferences are helpful in discussing mutual problems and goals for individual students and for the program as a whole.

Demonstrations are valuable in showing what students are learning and are generally well attended when all of the students participate in some way. These can be as simple as two teams playing speed-a-way or team handball during halftime at a football or basketball game or as complex as a demonstration night for parents in which every student in the school

Public relations efforts should concentrate on
interrelationships among groups.

participates. The important thing to remember is to let everyone participate regardless of skill level or physical disability. Each class can be asked to demonstrate some aspect of the program. This provides parents with a realistic view of physical education in contrast to that of athletics.

Posters in downtown stores, notices to parents, and announcements in the local paper can be used to invite the public. A public-address system should be used. The principal should welcome parents and introduce the physical education faculty, who can take turns introducing the various numbers. A simple mimeographed program such as the one in figures 14.17 and 14.18 can be handed out at the door.

Parent or family participation in student homework can stimulate families to become more involved in outside activities, such as bike riding or jogging, and to be more supportive of student involvement in completing extra-class assignments or activities. Inviting families to participate in contests in which students earn points by participating in family recreational and fitness activities has also been very effective in some areas.

McLaughlin reported a "Chip-N-Block" bowling tournament in which a parent and student form a team and compete against other teams.[20] Parent-student participation nights can include everything from movement education to sports to fitness activities. Aerobic activities have become increasingly popular in recent years. Other possibilities include mother-daughter, father-son, father-daughter, and mother-son activities. Parents can also be involved as paraprofessional aids in the physical education program.

Figure 14.17 "Spring into Fitness" program.
Source: Artwork by Marjorie Ann McClure.

A brief newsletter to parents or an article in the district newsletter several times a year can be valuable in describing school and community programs and promoting parent and family involvement in these programs. The newsletter might contain a description of the physical education program, objectives, evaluation and grading; physical fitness goals and achievements; extra-class programs; programs for handicapped students; and special events for parents. A portion of the newsletter could provide tips for better performance in a particular activity such as tennis, bowling, or physical fitness (see figure 14.19).

Newsletters should represent the best effort of the department in terms of spelling, grammar, layout, and use of pictures. Poorly written materials cast a poor image on the profession of physical education, as well as on the teachers involved. Consult with the English faculty for help if needed. In some locales the newsletter should be printed in both English and Spanish.

In addition to newsletters, letters can be sent to parents describing the specific fitness test results of their children and what they mean, or progress in learning other skills. Schuman mentioned sending home red, green, or yellow cards each week for extremely unmotivated

```
              EASTMONT MIDDLE SCHOOL
                    PRESENTS
                 Spring into Fitness

   1.  Tumbling    ............................ 1st Period--7th Grade
   2.  Pyramids    ............................ 5th Period--8th Grade
   3.  Lummi Sticks  .......................... 2d Period--7th Grade
   4.  Gymnastics Exhibition  ........................ Special Team
   5.  Square Dancing  ....................... 6th Period--6th Grade
   6.  Tinikling  ............................. 2d Period--7th Grade
   7.  Jump Rope Routine  .................... 3d Period--7th Grade
   8.  Parachutes  .......................... 7th Period--6th Grade
   9.  Dance Aerobics  ...................... 4th Period--8th Grade

                    Acknowledgments

   Principal  ................................... Mr. Glayde Hill
   Vice-principal  ................................ Mr. Tom Hicks
   Cover Design  ............................. Mrs. Marge McClure
   Girl's Physical Education Department  .......... Miss Robyn Graham
                                                   Mrs. Karen Quinn
                                                   Mrs. Bell Breen
```

Figure 14.18 "Spring into Fitness" program.
Source: Karen Quinn, Bell Breen, Robyn Johnson,
Eastmont Middle School, Sandy, Utah.

students. Green meant "great work," yellow meant "caution," and red said "stop and change your work habits." On the cards she listed all tasks completed during that week. Parents were asked to sign the cards and return them each Monday. Cards were stopped when students no longer needed them.[21] When students know that they will be "paid" each week, they seem to work harder.

Letters or phone calls to parents can also be used to point out student's accomplishments. The following story is about a boy who had not had much success in school. The teacher sent home a letter to the boy's parents commending something he had done. Later, the teacher asked, "Did you give the letter to your mother?" "Yes," the boy responded. "What did she say?" "Nothin'," he replied. "Nothing? Why, it was a lovely letter—and your mother said, nothing?" The child nodded, "She didn't say nothing! She just bawled."[22] Generally, such parents make such a fuss over these students that they would not dare do anything to get in trouble with such a teacher or principal.

Herman suggested another practical way of gaining the support of parents—have a junk day, in which parents can contribute items such as old tennis racquets, golf clubs, or shuffleboard sets. Parents get rid of these space-wasters, and the school gains some usable equipment. After gaining the approval of the principal, a note can be sent home on which parents can list what is being donated and sign it so they know what their children are contributing.[23] One school asked for old brooms for broom hockey and was surprised to discover that many parents went out and purchased new brooms just so they could help out.

PHYSICAL
EDUCATION
NEWSLETTER

Dear Parents:

May I take this opportunity to tell you about our
new physical education program at Podunk High
School. During this past summer the members of
our Physical Education Department, with the
help of several students, completely updated
our curriculum. We are very excited about the
new course of study that will be implemented
this Fall. Let me tell you about it!

The program is lifetime sports-oriented. That is, we have decided to teach a wide variety of sports that may be played
throughout life. For example, tennis, golf, bowling, badminton,
archery, skiing and other sports with high carryover value are
now included in the curriculum. In addition, at grades 10 and 11,
students may select those sports which they enjoy the most. Instruction will be given at beginning, intermediate and advanced
levels so that students may become highly skilled in the sports
they have selected. It is our opinion that unless boys and girls
acquire a fairly high skill level they will not participate during the adult years.

At the 10th and 11th grade levels, the curriculum is completely
elective in nature. It is also coeducational in non-contact
sports. We see no reason why boys and girls can not learn sports
skills together. We are hopeful that this change will produce
better socialization and lead to increased understanding among
young people.

We are still very much concerned about physical fitness but our
approach to it has changed. In brief, the new program requirements call for a "gentle" approach to exercise. That is, we hope
that students will become physically fit through participation
in enjoyable activities. We still plan to give fitness tests
twice a year but we are not trying to condition your son or daughter the way we prepare our athletes for interscholastic sports
competition.

In the very near future we plan to hold "open house" so that you
may come to school and see our program in operation. At that time
you may ask questions, participate yourself if you like, and
meet the members of our physical education faculty. We look forward to meeting you at this function.

Sincerely yours,

William F. Straub
Director of Physical Education

Figure 14.19 A physical education newsletter.
Source: William F. Straub, THE LIFETIME SPORTS-
ORIENTED PHYSICAL EDUCATION PROGRAM,
© 1976, p. 138. Reprinted by permission of Prentice-
Hall, Inc., Englewood Cliffs, N.J.

The Community

Two factors are involved in community-school relations. They include (1) getting the school involved in the community and (2) getting the community involved in the school.

Getting the School Involved in the Community

Teachers can take the lead in community involvement by participating in institutional, civic, and neighborhood activities or projects. Educators often participate in local business-education exchanges by touring various commercial institutions.

Students can also be encouraged to participate in community-oriented projects and in work-experience programs. Youth sports provide an excellent opportunity for service in the community.

To carry out a lifetime sports curriculum, many schools must rely on resources within the community. The first step is to survey the community to see what is available and whether it is appropriate for an instructional situation. The cost of the facility and the cost of transportation must then be determined. Once permission from the school and district administration is obtained, a specific legal agreement should be drawn up to clarify the dates and times the facility is to be used, the cost, the roles of the school and the institution with regard to the instructional situation, and legal liability. The legal implications of transportation to and from the facility must also be considered. The use of community facilities is one more way in which schools and communities can develop a better understanding of one another.

Getting the Community Involved in the School

Passive involvement of the community in the schools generally occurs through the mass media, speeches, and exhibits.

PEPI—the Physical Education Public Information program developed by the American Alliance for Health, Physical Education, Recreation and Dance—has performed a great service by producing materials and sharing techniques for use in the public-relations effort.[24] Another organization that has played a prominent role in public relations is the President's Council on Physical Fitness and Sport. Both groups have produced films and television spots that have been well received.

Publishing articles in school and local newspapers about intramural activities, fitness projects, and class activities can stimulate community interest in physical education just as it has in athletics. All news articles should be approved by the administration to prevent embarrassment to the school from improper timing or undue controversy. Whenever possible, action photos should accompany the articles. Another way to inform the community about the physical education program is by speaking to parent-teacher organizations and civic groups. Talks can be accompanied by slides, videotapes, or actual performances by students. Exhibits in local stores, the public library, or other community buildings can be used to draw attention to special events.

Other active methods of involving the community include community-school programs, community involvement in curriculum planning, and the use of community sponsors and paraprofessional aids.

The use of school facilities for adult education and family-oriented recreation programs is increasing in many areas. Programs range from supervised recreation to instructional programs in physical fitness and skill development. They may be sponsored by the city recreation department or the school district. Adults who become involved in these programs are more supportive of school programs.

Another possible service to the community is a fitness fair in which booths are set up to show what the students have learned in the various areas of physical fitness. Fitness-evaluation activities can be conducted at such events. It is often fun for children to test their parents. Legislative fitness days have been sponsored in Washington as well as in individual states. Participants are tested and the actual scores as well as prescriptions for maintenance and improvement are presented.

Citizens can provide valuable input to school advisory committees, curriculum committees, and as resource persons. Many districts are realizing the importance of these committees in discussing school problems and making recommendations, serving as "sounding boards" for new ideas or programs, and reviewing films and books for adoption into the school curriculum. Whenever these committees are used, sound policies should be established as to the purposes of the committee and the role to be played by each member.

Just as many community groups contribute to athletics through booster clubs, a number of service clubs, commercial institutions, and government agencies, along with many lay citizens, contribute to school programs either financially or by donating their time and resources. Demonstrations, health and fitness fairs, safety clinics, and many other programs have been sponsored by these groups. Clay described an "adopt-a-school" program in which various businesses have each adopted a specific school and helped them with facility and equipment needs.[25] Government and other public-service agencies have donated innumerable hours teaching first aid, safety, and health skills to students.

Invitations of prominent athletes, sportscasters, sports journalists, and commercial recreation leaders to speak in physical education classes, parent-teacher organization meetings, and other school groups can extend the relationship. A file can be kept on citizens who possess skills needed by the department. Foster grandparent programs provide a double service by helping senior citizens to serve in useful endeavors and through the many services they can provide to the schools. Parents and other lay citizens can also serve as paraprofessional aids.

No one technique works for every situation. By understanding a variety of techniques, teachers can find the best one for each situation. Gray suggested a number of rules that might be helpful:

1. Borrow, steal, or gain inspiration any way you can, but mainly by sharing ideas freely with teachers within your own school.
2. Never stick with a losing game plan any more than a basketball coach would.
3. "Carrot-and-stick" your classes to the limit. Reward whatever assists student progress; discourage whatever does not.
4. Don't be trapped by rules for motivation; keep them flexible.
5. Change your approach often, even when things are going well.[26]

Questions and Suggested Activities
1. Use two different evaluation techniques to evaluate yourself as a teacher. Report on what you did and what you learned about your teaching. Tell what you will do to become a more effective teacher.

2. This is the first year that you have been the department chairperson of physical education in your school. You have observed that teachers have become lax in their duties and decide that it might be because of a lack of evaluation. What methods of evaluation might you consider implementing to improve the situation?
3. Develop an evaluation plan for a lesson using appropriate evaluation techniques.
4. Role-play the following situation: The school board wants to implement an accountability plan in which teachers are evaluated strictly on student performance.
5. What publics are important in a public-relations program? Which group is the most important?
6. Obtain some PEPI materials from your local AAHPERD leaders. How could you use them to promote physical education?
7. Make a bulletin board and evaluate it in terms of its effect on the viewers. Consider such items as the following: technical presentation, effectiveness in getting the idea across, and integration with the unit of instruction. How could it be improved?
8. Begin a bulletin board file of sketches, ideas, newspaper and magazine clippings, cartoons, pictures, objects, and color book ideas.

Suggested Readings

Alexander, Kenneth. "Beyond the Prediction of Student Achievement: Direct and Repeated Measurement of Behavior Change." *Journal of Teaching in Physical Education* Monograph 1 (Summer 1983):42–47.

Allard, Ray, and Frank Rife. "A Teacher-Directed Model of Peer Supervision in Physical Education." *The Physical Educator* 37 (May 1980):89–94.

Ellis, Deca B. "Using the Community to Enhance Your Physical Education Program." *Journal of Physical Education, Recreation and Dance* 53 (March 1982):77.

Griffey, David. "ALT in Context: On the Nonlinear and Interactional Characteristics of Engaged Time." *Journal of Teaching in Physical Education* Monograph 1 (Summer 1983):34–37.

Hall, W. Dianne. "Improving Instruction through Positive Performance Evaluation." *The Physical Educator* 37 (March 1980):7–10.

Lerch, Harold A., and Mabel M. Byrd. "Out-of-School Learning: A Physical Education Program." *Journal of Physical Education, Recreation and Dance* 57 (August 1986):40–42.

Marsh, David B., John L. Smith, David Jenkins, and Edward Livingstone. "Program Promotion." *Journal of Physical Education, Recreation and Dance* 52 (June 1981):24–26.

Nelson, Jonathan E. "Communication—The Key to Public Relations." *Journal of Physical Education, Recreation and Dance* 57 (April 1986):64–67.

Noble, Larry, and Richard A. Cox. "Development of a Form to Survey Student Reactions on Instructional Effectiveness of Lifetime Sports Classes." *Research Quarterly for Exercise and Sport* 54 (September 1983):247–54.

Quarterman, Jerome. "An Observational System for Observing the Verbal and Nonverbal Behaviors Emitted by Physical Educators and Coaches." *The Physical Educator* 37 (March 1980):15–20.

Rolloff, Bruce D. "Public Relations: Objectives for Physical Education." *Journal of Physical Education, Recreation and Dance* 56 (March 1985):69–71.

Smith, Nancy W. "Community Involvement through a Curriculum Study Project." *Journal of Physical Education, Recreation and Dance* 52 (June 1981):16–17.

Stewart, Michael J. "Eloquent Bulletin Boards." *Journal of Physical Education and Recreation* 51 (November–December 1980):80–81.

Tenoschok, Michael, and Steve Sanders. "Planning an Effective Public Relations Program." *Journal of Physical Education, Recreation and Dance* 55 (January 1984):48–49.

References

1. U.S. Department of Education, "Education Report Card." Washington, D.C., 1987.
2. *The Daily Universe,* February 11, 1987.
3. Robert Benjamin, *Making Schools Work: A Reporter's Journey through Some of America's Most Remarkable Classrooms* (New York: The Continuum Publishing Corporation, 1981), p. 119.
4. Ibid., p. 177.
5. Charles A. Bucher and Constance R. Koenig, *Methods and Materials for Secondary School Physical Education,* 6th ed. (St. Louis: C. V. Mosby Company, 1983), p. 184.
6. Daryl Siedentop, *Developing Teaching Skills in Physical Education* (Boston: Houghton Mifflin Company, 1976), pp. 271–75.
7. Max Rosenberg, "Test Your HRQ (Human Relations Quotient)," *Teacher* 90 (March 1973); or Marjorie C. Knutson, "Sensitivity to Minority Groups," *Journal of Physical Education and Recreation* 48 (May 1977), pp. 24–25.
8. William G. Anderson, *Analysis of Teaching Physical Education* (St. Louis: C. V. Mosby Company, 1980), p. 33.
9. Siedentop, *Developing Teaching Skills,* p. 30.
10. Anderson, *Analysis of Teaching Physical Education,* pp. 23–24.
11. Ibid., p. 32.
12. Siedentop, *Developing Teaching Skills,* pp. 99, 265.
13. Edmund J. Amidon, Ned A. Flanders, and Irene G. Casper, *The Role of the Teacher in the Classroom* (St. Paul, MN: Paul S. Amidon and Associates, Inc., 1985).
14. Anderson, *Analysis of Teaching Physical Education,* p. 76.
15. B. L. Morgenegg, "Pedagogical Moves," in *What's Going on in Gym? Descriptive Studies of Physical Education Classes,* a special monograph of *Motor Skills: Theory into Practice,* 1978.
16. Anderson, *Analysis of Teaching Physical Education,* pp. 109–10.
17. Judith E. Rink, Peter H. Werner, Richard C. Hohn, Dianne S. Ward, and Helen M. Timmermans, "Differential Effects of Three Teachers Over a Unit of Instruction," *Research Quarterly for Exercise and Sport* 57 (June 1986), pp. 132–38.
18. Doris A. Mathieson, "Interpreting Secondary School Physical Education—Take the Initiative," *Journal of Physical Education and Recreation* (January 1978), pp. 51–52.
19. Dianne S. Ward and Bruce A. McClenaghan, "Special Programs for Special People: Ideas for Extending the Physical Education Program," *The Physical Educator* 37 (May 1980), p. 66.
20. Robert D. McLaughlin, "Chip-N-Block for Parental Involvement," *Journal of Physical Education, Recreation and Dance* 52 (June 1981), pp. 22–23.
21. Marilyn E. Schuman, "Enrich the Curriculum and Your Own Style," *Today's Education* 70 (November–December 1981), p. 36.
22. Katherine C. La Mancusa, *We Do Not Throw Rocks at the Teacher!* (Scranton, Pennsylvania: International Textbook Company, 1966), p. 80.
23. William L. Herman, "Have a Junk Day," *Journal of Physical Education and Recreation* 46 (October 1975), p. 35.
24. For more information on PEPI, contact the AAHPERD, 1900 Association Drive, Reston, Virginia 22091.
25. Walter B. Clay, "First Class and Getting Better," *Journal of Physical Education, Recreation and Dance* 52 (June 1981), pp. 19–21.
26. John M. Gray, "Enjoy Yourself and Be Flexible," *Today's Education* 70 (November–December 1981), pp. 34–35.

Designing the Curriculum

In the past, the study of curriculum theory and design has been delayed until graduate school. However, since even beginning teachers are involved in curriculum development, this text integrates the process of curriculum design with that of designing instructional strategies.

What Is a Curriculum?

Bain describes the physical education curriculum as follows:

> The physical education curriculum is an overall plan for the total physical education program, which is intended to guide teachers in conducting educational activities for a specific group of students. The curriculum specifies the program content in terms of objectives and activities.[1]

What Is the Relationship between the Curriculum and Instruction?

The curriculum should be a reflection of the society within which it operates. It should take into account the philosophy of that society, as well as knowledge handed down by that society that has an influence on students and how they learn.

The teacher becomes the intermediary whereby the curriculum (the blueprint) is translated into the instructional methods and strategies (the delivery system) that influence student learning. The personality and abilities of the teacher will, of necessity, influence his or her ability to translate curricular content into student learning.

The students' interests and abilities will, in turn, influence their input into the instructional system. Unit figure 5.1 demonstrates graphically how this interaction occurs.

What Is Curriculum Design?

Curriculum design is the creation of a plan of action that eliminates guesswork and translates educational knowledge and philosophy into teaching methodology by establishing principles for guiding the faculty in all phases of the program. Curriculum design is an applied science, based on theory, that develops operating principles to guide decision making in practical situations.[2]

Why Is Curriculum Design Important?

Of the problems confronting the public schools, the Gallup poll has listed poor curriculum as third for four of the six years, 1981 to 1986, and fourth for two of those years[3] (see figure 1.1 on page 12). Parents and students can become dissatisfied with curricular offerings when programs lack an orderly plan for achieving the objectives of education. One reason for this is that the basic needs of students and, therefore, the purposes of education change as the culture undergoes modifications.

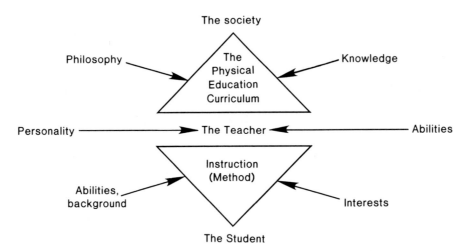

Unit Figure 5.1 The relationship of curriculum and instruction.

Until the twentieth century, social patterns and values changed almost imperceptibly from generation to generation. With the acceleration of social change in the twentieth century, schools are preparing youth for adulthood in a society not yet envisioned by its members. As Hawley stated:

> It's not a question of whether or not to change, but whether or not we can control the way we are changing. We are living in an *Alice in Wonderland* world where you have to run just to stay where you are. To get anywhere you have to run even faster than that. The pieces on the chess board keep changing and the rules are never the same.[4]

As educators, then, we must accept fundamental differences in the role of the curriculum we previously considered to be appropriate. In a society that is characterized by change, it is imperative that the curriculum change to meet the needs of the learner in a constantly changing environment.

Other factors that force curriculum change are cuts in financial resources, outdated and inadequate facilities and equipment, changes in student populations, reduction in and lack of turnover of faculty with the resulting need to retrain those available, changes in student needs and interests, and other environmental and technological changes.

Progress is not possible without change. However, all change does not result in progress or improvement. Some changes may be worse than no change at all. Therefore, change efforts must be carefully considered and evaluated before implementing them on a full-scale basis. At the same time, schools that continue to lag behind in curriculum development may be forced to implement changes not of their own choosing. The National Governors' Association's "1991" report on education, *Time for Results,* suggested a state intervention procedure for school systems that fail to meet acceptable standards of performance.[5]

Curriculum change should be based on a well-informed evaluation of past, present, and future, with consideration of the best thinking of professionals who have researched and tested each proposal. That which has proven effective should be retained. That which has proven ineffective should be discarded. New ideas should be tried on a small scale (perhaps with only one or two classes) before being adopted.

Planning and preparation are the keys to a successful and meaningful program. Traditionally, educators have made two mistakes in curriculum design. They have either just let things happen in the "curriculum," or have looked around for a good curriculum and adopted it, whether or not it fit their particular needs. Lawton described the problems of curriculum design as follows:

> If we wish to be completely frank we would probably say that the typical curriculum is a mess—an uneasy compromise between traditions (of doubtful pedigree) and various pressures for change; a mixture of high-sounding aims and classroom practice which could not possibly attain the aims and sometimes flatly contradicts them. . . .
> One of the problems of curriculum, as with many other aspects of education, is the enormous gap between theory and practice. . . . The difference between what teachers suggest should happen and what can be observed in the classroom, the gap between educational theory as taught in colleges and universities and the "commonsense" practical approach of teachers in schools.[6]

The task of the curriculum designer, then, is to carefully merge cultural elements, both old and new, into a curriculum that fits the existing students, school, and community. Since the American society is in a state of perpetual change, a continuous, systematic process of evaluating and designing the curriculum is essential so that program objectives can be realized.

Models of Curriculum Design

The classical model of curriculum design was presented by Tyler in 1949.[7] He asked four questions to be answered by curriculum planners: (1) What educational purposes should the school seek to attain? (2) What educational experiences can be provided that are likely to help attain these purposes? (3) How can these educational experiences be effectively organized? and (4) How can we determine whether these purposes are being attained? The steps he proposed for curriculum design included stating objectives, selecting learning experiences, organizing the experiences, and evaluating results.

Tyler's model has been criticized in that it does not describe the way most educational curriculum committees actually proceed. Walker observed curriculum designers and described their actions.[8] Their first step was to establish a platform of beliefs and values to guide the planning process. The second step was to "deliberate" by identifying facts, generating alternative solutions, determining consequences, weighing alternatives, and choosing the best solution. The result was a curriculum "design" or product.

Steps in Curriculum Design

The steps of the curriculum process presented here are based primarily on Tyler's classical design for curriculum development.

1. Establish a curriculum committee.
2. Study the basic principles of curriculum planning and determine the philosophy, aims, and objectives of the school and of physical education.
3. Determine the scope and sequence of the program.
4. Schedule.
5. Implement the program.
6. Evaluate and revise.

To make the learning meaningful, students should form a curriculum committee, choose a school with which to work, and study these chapters as a basis for designing a curriculum.

In chapter 15, basic principles of curriculum design are discussed, including the persons responsible for the curriculum, the information needed to make sound curriculum decisions, and the most common curriculum patterns for physical education. Much of the information was discussed in more detail in units 1 and 2, with implications for the curriculum presented here. A number of resources for the curriculum committee are also included.

Chapter 16 identifies the process for determining the scope of the curriculum and the sequence of instructional activities. A well-balanced program that meets the objectives established for the program is essential. Examples of the scope and sequence for various school levels are also included.

A number of scheduling considerations are presented for review in chapter 17. The chapter then outlines the procedures for scheduling.

The processes for evaluating a curriculum are presented in chapter 18, along with a variety of techniques that can be used for that purpose. A program evaluation of the existing curriculum could be done by making a visit to the school selected for the curriculum project.

The curriculum committee could also present its curriculum to the "board of education" in a simulated board meeting in which other students assume the roles of board members, superintendent, principals, other faculty members, and local citizens.

As indicated in units 3 and 5, the next step after evaluation is to follow the feedback loops back to the beginning of the cycle and reexamine the objectives and instructional programs to determine how to improve them through the new information gained.

Suggested Readings

Lawson, Hal A. "A Model for the Development of Innovative Physical Education Programs." *The Physical Educator* 39 (May 1982):59–66.

Tyler, Ralph W. *Basic Principles of Curriculum and Instruction.* Chicago: University of Chicago Press, 1949.

Walker, Decker F. "A Naturalistic Model for Curriculum Development." *School Review* 80 (1971):51–65.

References

1. Linda Bain, "Status of Curriculum Theory in Physical Education," *Journal of Physical Education and Recreation* 49 (March 1978), pp. 25–26.
2. David Pratt, *Curriculum: Design and Development* (New York: Harcourt Brace Jovanovich, 1980), p. 9.
3. Alec M. Gallup, "The 18th Annual Gallup Poll of the Public's Attitudes toward the Public Schools," *Phi Delta Kappan* 68 (September 1986), pp. 43–59.
4. Robert C. Hawley, *Human Values in the Classroom: Teaching for Personal and Social Growth* (Amherst, Massachusetts: Education Research Associates, 1973), p. 70.
5. National Governors' Association, Center for Policy Research, *Time for Results* (Washington, D.C.: National Governors' Association, Center for Policy Research and Analysis, 1986).
6. Denis Lawton, *Social Change, Educational Theory, and Curriculum Planning* (London: University of London Press LTD, 1973), p. 7.
7. Ralph W. Tyler, *Basic Principles of Curriculum and Instruction* (Chicago: University of Chicago Press, 1949).
8. Decker F. Walker, "A Naturalistic Model for Curriculum Development," *School Review* 80 (1971), pp. 51–65.

15

Basic Principles of Curriculum Design

Study Stimulators

1. What is the role of administrators in curriculum design? Of teachers? Of students? Of other resource persons? Why are all of these important on a curriculum committee?
2. What information should be considered before designing a curriculum?
3. Describe the influence of government legislation on curricular decisions.
4. Name the common curriculum patterns of physical education and give an example of each. How are the patterns used to build physical education programs?
5. What resources will be of most value in designing a curriculum for a particular school?

To be effective, a curriculum must be built on a solid philosophical foundation that answers the question of what educational purposes the school should seek to achieve. Bain described the value of studying curriculum theory as follows:

> Curriculum theory describes potential criteria for selection and structuring of content and predicts the impact of such criteria upon the instructional process.[1]

How are goals selected? Persons responsible for the curriculum meet to consider the information and knowledge available to them and, guided by a sound educational philosophy, seek to make value judgments about what is best for the learners who will attend that school.

Persons Responsible for Curriculum Design

Persons responsible for curriculum decisions include administrators, teachers, students, parents, and community leaders. Most of the major innovations in the public schools are introduced by teachers and administrators. Accrediting agencies and local education associations also play a direct role. In their role as teacher-trainer institutions, colleges and universities assume an indirect form of educational leadership. Private philanthropic foundations provide teachers with released time from school to develop and promote innovative instructional programs. Commercial enterprises such as textbook publishers and instructional materials producers have a powerful effect on the curriculum in that changes are quickly adopted with each new product. However, once adopted, they can be a deterrent for change because of the costs involved in product revision. State boards of education or departments of education sometimes provide leadership for promoting educational change. However, many departments are too small to promote or enforce all of the changes needed.

The Role of Administrators in Curriculum Design

The instructional program, or curriculum, is the most important responsibility of all school administrators, including superintendents, principals, and department heads. All other tasks are subservient to the instructional program. The National Association of Secondary School Principals listed some challenges that administrators should consider in attempting to upgrade the curriculum in physical education. They stressed the importance of creating instructional programs that contribute to the intellectual, physical, and emotional growth and well-being of all young people; the selection and assignment of competent teachers in ways that fully use their individual expertise; and the adoption of innovative instructional practices.[2]

Administrators at different levels provide the leadership required for curriculum initiation, planning, implementation, evaluation, and revision. Direct leadership occurs when department chairpersons, principals, or district supervisors help teachers assess program needs, define goals and objectives, and evaluate the quality of the curriculum. Once a decision has been made to develop or revise a curriculum, the department head or district supervisor selects a curriculum committee and presents it with goals and guidelines for action. This process is more formal at the district level or in a large department; in a smaller department, all teachers might compose such a committee. Administrators should continue to work closely with the committee by providing input based on experience and knowledge and by reviewing proposals for new programs. Released time should be arranged for committee meetings and provision should be made for adequate resources, including equipment and supplies, secretarial help, and the assistance of experts and consultants if needed.

The department head should preside at faculty meetings when the changes are presented and present proposals to the principal, who interprets the program to the public or invites the department head to do so. Administrators at each level are responsible for facilitating the implementation of approved programs and directing the development of curriculum materials.

Indirectly, all administrators, and especially principals, have the responsibility to provide a climate in which personal and group growth can occur. This requires the establishment of effective communication, time and resources for personal and group study, and freedom to experiment with new ideas. Communications between teachers and administrators are increased when administrators work with teachers and not over them. Teachers who have the time and resources available for studying and experimenting with new ideas and practices generally are more innovative than teachers who perceive little support for innovation. The provision of a teachers' study area with books and journals, opportunities to attend conferences or visit innovative schools, regular discussions about innovations during faculty meetings, and clerical help motivate teachers to continue their personal study of new ideas. Freedom evolves from the confidence of administrators in the ability of teachers to resolve their own problems.

The Role of Teachers in Curriculum Design

Although supervising the instructional program is an administrative responsibility, teachers are vital to the curriculum development process. Since teachers have daily contact with students, they are the first to notice a need for change. Many curriculum changes occur, almost unnoticed, as teachers work together to revise course content and schedule or reschedule classes as needs, weather, and conflicts require adaptations.

A current trend is the adoption of school *curriculum leaders,* master teachers with additional training in curriculum development and leadership skills. Since teachers have an intimate knowledge of learners, classrooms, and the school environment, they are in a position to make and implement practical curriculum changes. Participation in curriculum development also provides them with a clearer picture of exactly what is to be done to implement

A curriculum committee should include
administrators, teachers, parents, and students,
as well as a curriculum consultant.

program changes. Unless teachers are given the responsibility and authority to make curriculum decisions, they will be relegated to the role of technicians in the schools. Moreover, the valuable insights of teachers that may well be critical to the success of the schools would be lost.

Physical educators have more flexibility within the school system for curriculum development than other teachers because of the nature of the program and facilities. Because they share facilities, rather than being assigned to specific classrooms, physical educators often become responsible for their own curriculum and need to use sound curriculum development principles and practices to prevent the curriculum from "just happening." Students can be grouped and regrouped by ability levels or interests more easily than in intact classrooms, and class sizes can be altered to fit the activity to be taught and the facilities available.

Teachers have a responsibility to study and keep abreast of changes in physical education and how it can be taught most effectively. They should take the opportunity to attend conventions and in-service meetings, visit other schools, read professional journals, and discuss ideas with other teachers in their school and in other schools. Whenever possible, teachers should serve on school or district committees to develop instructional materials, write curriculum guides, and evaluate and revise curricular offerings. Released time should be provided for these types of professional development.

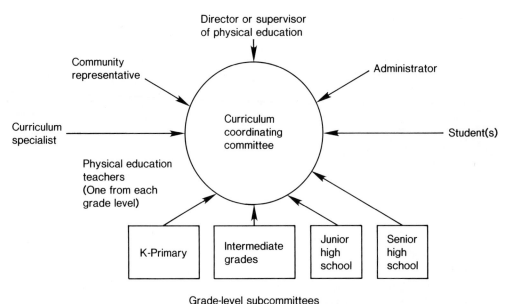

Figure 15.1 A possible organization for a
district curriculum development program.

The Curriculum Committee

The number and kinds of curriculum committees depend on the grade level or extent of the curriculum project. For a large school curriculum development project, committees might include a coordinating committee, with subcommittees for each grade level as shown in figure 15.1. Representatives from each of the various schools make up the *coordinating committee*. In smaller school systems, each member of the physical education staff might take part on this committee. The coordinating committee acts as a clearing house of ideas and suggestions. The functions of the coordinating committee are as follows:

1. Establishes the overall philosophy of physical education for the school district or school.
2. Explores satisfactions and dissatisfactions with the present program.
3. Schedules meetings, establishes sequence of work, and coordinates activities of all committees.
4. Selects members for subcommittee assignments.
5. Serves as a clearing house for proposals from subcommittees.
6. Provides for evaluation of the curriculum.

Subcommittees can be organized to give input at specific grade levels or for input into intramural, extramural, and athletic program needs. Such committees should be temporary and might consist of the following personnel:

1. Elementary—A principal, nonphysical education teacher(s), parent, elementary physical education specialists.
2. Secondary—Physical education teachers, coaches, principal, community representative, parents, students.

The functions of the subcommittees might be to

1. Establish specific grade-level objectives.
2. Establish the scope and sequence of programs for each grade level.
3. Make teaching suggestions, including specific lesson and/or unit plans.

Although program development can be a product of individual teachers, administrators, or supervisors, experience shows that a curriculum cooperatively planned by all of those involved in its implementation will yield the best results. The committee should include the following individuals:

1. Administrators, who can provide insights into time schedules, budgets, facilities, resources, and other administrative details.
2. Teachers, both men and women, who represent the grass-roots level, work daily with students, and know what will or will not work.
3. Students, who can provide information regarding their own interests, obstacles to desired learning, relevance of learning experiences, and recommended extra-class programs.
4. Parents and community leaders, who can provide varied, fresh ideas based on their experiences with school and life and their aspirations for children. Many of these people can be influential in promoting curriculum change if they have been consulted during the planning stages.
5. Recent graduates, who can be especially helpful in evaluating the relevance of the curriculum to real life.
6. Curriculum specialists, who can provide expertise in curriculum design and ideas that have worked well in other schools.
7. Clerical help, who can record, type, copy, collate, and distribute information.

Persons chosen to serve on curriculum committees should be representative of and have the respect and support of their peers and of the administration. Committees should be small enough so that a consensus can be achieved and the work can get done. Membership on committees should rotate periodically to avoid fatigue and to promote a fresh attack on the problems at hand. The secret of group action is that when several people of various backgrounds join together in a group effort, synergy occurs; that is, the result is greater than the sum of its members. Since curriculum development is a time-consuming process, released time or pay for extra work should be considered for committee members.

Information Needed to Make Curriculum Decisions

To make curriculum decisions, the committee must attempt to learn all it can about the environment, the school, the learners, and the subject matter and how it is learned; and then attempt to integrate this information and its implications with the philosophy of education espoused by the district and school involved. Governmental activity also has an influence on curriculum decisions.

Information about the Environment

A large number of social forces that affect the lives of students and, therefore, the school curriculum were discussed in chapters 1 and 5. Increases in the incidence of one-parent families and mothers in the work force has resulted in large numbers of latchkey children. Drug use, alcoholism, and suicide are increasing among American youth. Increased leisure time brings with it an increase in individual, family, and community recreation. Other cultural forces that affect the schools include the nuclear freeze movement, racial and sexual inequalities, television violence, and teenage pregnancy.

As social forces change, the demands placed on the school also change. Decisions about societal implications must consider the purposes of the curriculum with regard to the culture. In chapter 1 these purposes were delineated as follows:

1. To preserve and maintain the desirable aspects of the society or culture by transmitting them to the young.
2. To teach the skills and competencies needed to function effectively as an adult member of society, both socially and vocationally.
3. To help the individual function within society to the fullest extent possible, both currently and in the future, through intelligent self-direction, group deliberation, and action.
4. To teach the individual to constructively evaluate societal issues and to influence the social order by contributing to ordered, purposeful change.

Jewett and Bain described five value orientations for curriculum development that fit with the purposes described above.[3] They are disciplinary mastery, social reconstruction, learning process, self-actualization, and ecological validity.

Disciplinary mastery emphasizes the transmission "of the cultural heritage from one generation to the next." The current Back-to-the-Basics movement is a reflection of this emphasis, as is the emphasis on mastery of basic movement and sport skills in physical education.

Social reconstruction stresses instruction for "creating a better society" and emphasizes interpersonal and problem-solving skills. The "new games" emphasis on cooperation, rather than competition, agrees with this value orientation. Social reconstructionists include nontraditional activities such as outdoor and adventure education in the curriculum in an attempt to broaden the recreational interests of the community.

For the *learning process,* Toffler's emphasis on learning how to learn acknowledges that the knowledge explosion makes it impossible to learn everything that is important.[4] By learning how to learn, graduates will be equipped to deal with rapid changes in knowledge and technology. Content includes the basic knowledge of physical education and problem-solving skills.

Self-actualization, as stressed by Maslow, was reviewed in chapter 4.[5] Curriculum developers who advocate this value orientation attempt to provide experiences through which students can direct their quest for personal excellence and satisfaction.

In the fifth orientation, *ecological validity,* self-actualization is sought as a means toward a holistic interaction between the individual and the environment. This orientation is directed toward a global interdependent society and emphasizes self-confidence, creativity, outdoor education, and leadership skills.

Despite the increasing mobility of society, each community still shares certain values, attitudes, and beliefs that influence curriculum development. Local resources and interests also influence the selection of learning activities. The current emphasis on physical fitness and lifetime sports reflects a general commitment to preparing students for effective adult life-styles. The recent concern for fitness and life-style change has invaded the schools in many areas as Fitness for Life or similar courses mandated by state boards of education. Other purposes may depend more on local values. For example, local commitments to promote equality of opportunity for students of both sexes and all races and for handicapped students may not be strong enough to overcome the value toward excellence of athletics, especially if finances are limited. Thus, curriculum developers must consider local attitudes and values as well as national ones.

Needs and priorities can be assessed through brainstorming, observation, interviews, questionnaires, surveys, inventories, public hearings, available statistics, prior needs assessment research, and objective tests. Asking people to indicate priorities in terms of critical, important, or desirable can be helpful, as can classification as long-range or immediate needs.

A survey of the community can provide information concerning the following:

1. The historical background of the community.
2. The philosophy of community members and their willingness to support education and physical education programs.
3. The economic and tax base factors of the community—such as major employers; average family income; incidence of unemployment; and educational, recreational, health, and other services.
4. The social, cultural, and political factors—such as population and prospective changes in population, age distribution, ethnic and racial makeup of the population, social and cultural attitudes, religious orientation, educational background, crime, political pressures, and form of government.
5. Geographical and locational factors, including regional factors (climate, altitude, and the availability of lakes, mountains, and seashores) that affect the activity interests of students and the time that can be spent out-of-doors, and environmental factors (urban, suburban, or rural) that affect personal and family income and, therefore, the activities students can engage in outside of school.
6. The resources of the community, including centers of higher education, private and parochial schools, public libraries, parks and playgrounds, swimming pools, cultural programs, government agencies, citizens' groups, and commercial ski resorts, bowling lanes, and equestrian clubs.

Data obtained from studies of social and cultural forces in the community should be carefully analyzed for implications related to the curriculum. Students will need to be taught to fit in with some conditions, to resolve or eliminate problems in the current environment, and to prepare themselves to make future decisions about problems that have not yet arisen.

From community to community, and even within the same community, conditions may range from poverty to riches. Learning more about the community increases one's understanding not only of its organization, but also of the climate of life that takes place there. Sensitivity will increase to the feelings of the people and to the fear, insecurity, poverty, hunger, and disease that exist, as well as to the individuals and groups who are trying to bring about constructive changes. Once social forces have been analyzed, implications for curricular needs can be made. Hass provided a list of curriculum criteria to consider when dealing with social forces.

1. What social or cultural factors contribute to the individual differences of the learners?
2. How can the curriculum and/or teaching provide for these differences?
3. What values are we teaching?
4. What values do we wish to teach?
5. What can the curriculum do to assist learners in their goals of social self-understanding and self-realization?
6. How can the curriculum and teaching be planned and organized so that learners are assisted in confronting personal and social problems?
7. How can learners be helped to develop the problem-solving skills needed to cope with problems?[6]

Information about the School

External conditions directly affect the resources in the schools, which then have an impact on the physical education curriculum. These resources include finances, staff, facilities and equipment, school and department policies, and the total school curriculum.

Finances affect nearly every aspect of the school. Most of school monies go to the construction and maintenance of buildings and administrator and teacher salaries. Whatever is left is used for equipment and supplies. Therefore, when finances are low, teachers and students may be left without essential instructional materials.

The number and characteristics of the administrative and instructional staff have a tremendous impact on teaching. The age, gender, socioeconomic background, and philosophies of administrators and teachers affect the morale and cohesiveness of the staff and its ability to work together to achieve a common goal. The interests and expertise of the physical education faculty directly affect what is taught.

The type and location of facilities also affect the physical education curriculum. The number and size of gymnasiums, multipurpose rooms, swimming pools, dance studios, wrestling rooms, and outdoor fields, courts, and tracks should be noted. If school facilities are not available, local community resources such as bowling centers, skating rinks, ski slopes, and gymnastics studios should be considered. State and national parks and forests often provide resources for adventure and outdoor education activities.

Two problems exist with facilities—trying to establish a curriculum without the proper facilities and failing to include activities that could be provided with a little creativity. Facilities and equipment can be obtained if the desire is great enough. Governmental, community, business, and philanthropic agencies and foundations are often willing to aid the schools in obtaining resources.

The organizational structure of the school, relationships between teachers and administrators, power structure, and school policies stifle or encourage creativity in curriculum planning. Values, attitudes, and policies of the administration toward learning, student behavior, and faculty freedom affect student and teacher morale.

The school curriculum pattern, schedule, and time distribution dictate the limits within which the physical education program must operate. Local courses of study may define the boundaries of the curriculum in any given subject area.

Information about the Learners

The characteristics and needs of students at different ages were reviewed in chapter 5. Educational goals and curricular objectives arise from the needs of students. These needs are generally of two types. The first kind arises from needs within the organism itself, such as those suggested by Maslow's hierarchy of needs discussed in chapter 4.[7] To solve problems relating to physical and psychological safety, Kehres suggested providing a safe progression of curricular activities to help students develop self-confidence and skill in basic movement skills, and security to try activities requiring higher levels of skill.[8] Students should never be forced to try activities that they feel are dangerous. Standards for measuring performance should consider differences in skill level. Kehres listed four guidelines for teachers to use in planning group interaction experiences for students to increase social approval. They include:

1. Games and activities should allow for both competition and cooperative interaction among students.
2. Games and activities should at times be structured so that low-skilled individuals are not at a disadvantage.
3. Opportunities should be provided for experiencing both individual success and success as a member of a group.
4. Students encountering social rejection by peers should be given special assistance in developing acceptable social behavior and physical skills so that their status in the group may be improved.[9]

The need for self-esteem dictates the value of adapting activities to meet the needs of students with a wide range of abilities so that each student experiences success and enjoyment. Students should also be counseled to select those activities best suited to their individual needs and interests. According to Maslow, the role of the school is to create an environment in which students can strive to satisfy their basic needs so that they will be free to move on to self-actualization. For the development of self-actualization in physical education, Kehres emphasized the following principles:

1. The relationship of vigorous movement to health and well-being in adulthood should be taught to students.
2. Each student should be placed in a position of leadership and responsibility, during which time his decisions influence the behavior of others.
3. Participants in both physical education and athletic programs should be allowed to make decisions; the teacher or coach should not be the sole authority.[10]

Once the needs of the individual have been considered, the second type of needs is determined by comparing the current status of the learner with the status desired by society. The gap between these two levels defines an educational need. For example, if people are expected by a particular society to be able to swim and the students have not yet learned how, then there is a need that might be attended to by the curriculum. Some educational needs are common to most children or adolescents of a particular age level, no matter where they might live, while other needs are specific to the environment in which the students live.

For example, one can easily generalize that all seventh graders need instruction in team sports and all twelfth graders need to develop skills in individual and dual sports for use in their leisure time. It is not that simple, however, since students vary considerably within a single grade level in both age and intellectual, physical, social, and emotional development. Youth in Hawaii may need to be adept at swimming and surfing, while children in Colorado may need to be good snow skiers.

Students who differ dramatically from group norms, including potential dropouts, bilingual students, the mentally and physically handicapped, and the gifted, also need to be considered. The courts have ruled that schools must begin to meet the needs of all learners, whatever their differences might be. Programs need to be flexible enough to adapt to the individual differences of learners. Physical educators must consider the needs of the athletic, as well as the quiet, sensitive student who needs activity just to have a healthy body. George Leonard, in his book *The Ultimate Athlete,* expressed the idea that *every* human being has a right to move efficiently and joyfully.[11] Students' interests and purposes for enrolling in physical education must be considered. Curriculum designers need to plan for a variety of learning modes to accommodate the individual learning styles of students.

Data concerning both the whole student population and the individual students are essential. Curriculum designers must consider the nature of the student body—the number of students, their ages, gender, grade levels, socioeconomic levels, racial composition and ethnic background, personal and family characteristics, interests, achievements, talents, and goals. Data from physical fitness, knowledge, skill, and attitude tests can be helpful in describing students' past achievements. Health assessments can also provide essential information about students. Questionnaires to determine student interests can help determine readiness for learning specific activities. Other methods for studying learners include observations, interviews, and school and community records concerning attendance, delinquency, health, social status, discipline, extracurricular activity, and participation in recreation programs. Hass listed the following questions to ask about how well programs have been planned to meet the needs of students:

1. Does the planned curriculum provide for the developmental differences of the learners being taught?
2. Does the planned curriculum include provisions so that learning may start for each learner where he or she is?[12]

The data about students should be compared with norms considered to be desirable by the curriculum committee and any deviations noted as possible needs for school attention. The committee should distinguish between needs and wants. Social needs are not always the things students want. Decisions must be made by the committee about those needs appropriately met by the school and those best met through other social agencies. For instance, the school can teach appropriate health behaviors, but if facilities for maintaining proper health are unavailable, other agencies may need to resolve that situation.

The Subject Matter and How It Is Learned
When dealing with the subject matter of physical education, curriculum designers must consider all of the domains of learning, including the cognitive, psychomotor, and affective, and the various levels of learning within each domain. Each of these domains was discussed in some detail in unit 2. Each student selects from the subject matter those areas of perceived

importance and organizes them in a way that is most meaningful to him or her. Students should be helped to discover how physical education relates to them and how they can use the information gained to solve problems that have personal meaning for them.

Some questions to consider when planning the subject matter and instructional methodology include the following:

1. What does a physically educated student know? Do?
2. What subject matter is of most worth: physical skills? fitness? concepts? movement?
3. Does the curriculum allow students to develop at all levels in each of the domains of learning?
4. Does the curriculum help the learner identify and organize the key concepts and principles of physical education?
5. Does the curriculum prepare the student to use the content of physical education to solve personal problems, now and in the future?
6. Does the curriculum provide alternative approaches to learning to accommodate individual learning styles?

Physical educators generally agree on five instructional goals for physical education. They include the development of (1) physical skills for participation in a wide variety of activities, (2) physical fitness, (3) a knowledge and understanding of fitness, principles of movement, and the importance of exercise, (4) social skills, and (5) attitudes and appreciations that encourage participation in and enjoyment of physical activity.

The curriculum designer has an obligation to study the trends, innovations, and research that have implications for physical education and to use the ideas learned without being dominated by them. Care should be taken to take the best of the old and the new and to avoid change for change sake, without proving the worth of the new idea. Toffler made a strong case for this when he said:

> The adaptive individual appears to be able to project himself forward just the "right" distance in time, to examine and evaluate alternative courses of action open to him before the need for final decision, and to make tentative decisions beforehand.[13]

One societal trend that influences the school curriculum is the emphasis on preventive medicine and total health and fitness. Physical education programs are also emphasizing fitness and the concepts involved in taking care of one's body through changes in life-style. One state has changed the name of physical education to "Healthy Life-styles" in its K–12 curriculum. The FITNESSGRAM discussed in chapter 9 is an outcome of the emphasis on fitness.

Another trend is the Back-to-the-Basics movement with its emphasis on academic, rather than physical, achievement. In physical education, this is reflected in the emphasis on sport studies or cognitive learning, with themes developed around disciplinary concepts. Several examples are included in the next section of this chapter. Even the name of physical education has been changed in many institutions of higher learning to kinesiological studies or exercise and sport science. Many states have adopted criteria for promotion or graduation to ensure educational accountability. The emphasis on these tests, as well as on college-entrance exams such as the ACT and SAT, make "teaching to the tests" a high priority.

Some recent innovations in the secondary school curriculum include outdoor pursuits such as cross-country and alpine skiing, hiking, backpacking, camping, and orienteering; new or cooperative games; and adventure or risk activities such as climbing walls and rappelling. Leisure-time activities such as scuba diving, canoeing, sailing, and bicycling are popular. One school even has its own circus. Many of these activities involve concerns about teacher expertise, safety, transportation, and legal liability, which must be dealt with before these programs are implemented. However, with appropriate planning, the foregoing activities can be safely introduced in the curriculum. Professional journals and associations and state departments of education can provide a lead on programs or facilities that teachers can visit or write to for help in implementing new programs.

Research in the psychology of learning and motor learning, in exercise physiology, and in other areas of education have implications for curriculum development. It is up to the curriculum designer to determine the effects of research on the curriculum. Chapters 4 and 6 reviewed the research in the cognitive, psychomotor, and affective domains with their implications for learning. The research on academic learning time and mastery learning were presented in chapters 6 and 10. A knowledge of the psychology of learning helps educators select those objectives that are attainable at certain age levels and the conditions and amount of time necessary for learning to occur. Research indicates that applied learning and learning that is integrated with other learning tend to be retained longer than isolated or compartmentalized learning.

Governmental Activity

Federal and state legislation; judicial decisions such as those on legal liability, integration, and busing; and government regulations and supervision, including the power to allot or withdraw funds, play a major role in the educational process. Three federal laws that have had a tremendous effect on school programs include P.L. 94–142, Section 504 of the Rehabilitation Act, and Title IX. These laws, with implications for teaching, were discussed in chapter 5. Policy constraints often dictate what can be done, leaving little latitude for innovation. Legislation can be one of the quickest forms of change. For example, by reducing the state per-pupil expenditure, schools can be forced to cut programs. On the other hand, when legislation is enacted without public support, the schools or the public may resist government attempts to enforce compliance. Such was the case in some schools with P.L. 94–142 and Title IX.

AAHPERD has prepared a guide, *Shaping the Body Politic,* to help physical educators change public opinion and influence political decisions that affect physical education.[14]

Philosophy of Education and Physical Education

The philosophical orientation of those persons responsible for curriculum decisions is undoubtedly the greatest variable influencing the selection of school goals and objectives. The progressive philosopher studies the learner and selects curricular purposes and content for the needs and interests of the student. The essentialist derives goals and subject matter from the body of knowledge that has been handed down over thousands of years. Sociologists view the school as a means to help people deal with contemporary problems. In reality, all of the sources presented in this chapter should be considered before making decisions about the purposes of the school.

Educational philosophies must also determine whether to educate persons to adjust to the culture or to improve the culture and whether to provide a general education for all students or vocational training for those who wish to leave early or immediately after high school to go to work. The board of education is generally responsible for establishing the overall philosophy and goals of the schools within their jurisdiction.

Geiger and Kizer recommend that teachers gain an awareness of their own philosophies to form a philosophical base on which to build a meaningful program. To accomplish this, they suggest that teachers grapple with the following issues:

> What is the purpose of education?; what is physical education and how does it relate to education in general?; what is the role of a teacher?; should the learning situation be teacher centered or student centered?; is the purpose of physical education to teach sport skills or is there another purpose?; what is the humanistic physical education?; is conceptual teaching possible in physical education?[15]

The district goals should be broken down into subgoals and performance objectives that are consistent with the general educational goals. Physical education goals and objectives should be formulated in the same manner. Unless the goals are explicit, they will have no value in the curriculum.

Not all of the objectives suggested for the school by the preceding analyses can possibly be implemented in the time available; therefore, curriculum designers must select the most important ones and ensure that they are achieved. Pratt identified seven criteria that curriculum objectives should meet. Objectives should identify learning outcomes, be consistent with the curriculum aim, and be precise, feasible, functional, significant, and appropriate.[16] The proposed objectives must be evaluated in terms of the values (stated or implied) in the philosophies of the district, school, and department. Objectives that do not match the philosophy should be deleted. Those that match well should be retained.

Even though objectives are stated at this point in the curriculum process, they will undoubtedly be revised over and over again as decisions are made about scope and sequence, selection of learning activities, and evaluation. They should be refined into a usable state before implementing the curriculum, even though some of them may be revised after evaluating the new program.

Once the objectives have been selected, they should be stated in terms of the behaviors to be exhibited by the students and in a way in which educators, parents, students, and other interested persons can understand what behaviors are intended.

Hass listed some guidelines for evaluating goals and objectives as follows:

1. Have the goals of the curriculum or teaching plan been clearly stated, and are they used by the teachers and students in choosing content, materials, and activities for learning?
2. Have the teachers and students engaged in student-teacher planning in defining the goals and in determining how they will be implemented?
3. Do some of the planned goals relate to the society or the community in which the curriculum will be implemented or the teaching will be done?
4. Do some of the planned goals relate to the needs, purposes, interests, and abilities of the individual learner?

5. Are the planned goals used as criteria in selecting and developing learning activities and materials of instruction?
6. Are the planned goals used as criteria in evaluating learning achievement and in the further planning of learning subgoals and activities?[17]

Curriculum Patterns

For learners to achieve the objectives selected for the curriculum, learning experiences must be selected and organized in such a way as to provide reinforcement of concepts, values, and skills. Some common school organizing structures include the separate subjects curriculum, the broad fields curriculum, and the core curriculum. Elementary school curricula generally follow the broad fields pattern, including such areas as language arts, social studies, and natural science. Middle schools often combine some areas into core or general education courses, such as language arts to study the social and natural sciences; and study physical education, art, music, and other subjects in separate periods of the day. Several high schools have adopted core courses in which physical education is combined with the physical and biological sciences and English. Students spend up to one-half of the school day and some weekend trips hiking, backpacking, and bicycling to natural environments where they study science and then write about their findings.[18] The most common secondary school organizational pattern is the separate subjects curriculum in which a different subject is encountered by the learner during each period of the school day. No attempt is made to relate principles learned in courses such as chemistry, biology, and health to each other. The broad fields curriculum tends to be more learner-centered and promotes greater integration of concepts learned, while the specific subject pattern tends to be primarily subject-centered.

No one curriculum pattern is adequate to serve the varied populations of all schools. Curriculum designers must select elements from several patterns and combine them to form a curriculum pattern that suits the needs of the particular school or system within which they are working. This requires a knowledge of the elements of each of the curriculum patterns and the creativity to adapt them to the needs of the situation. Curriculum developers should study curriculum patterns as a basis for intelligent action.

In physical education, curriculum patterns have evolved from either a subject-centered or a student-centered approach. Subject-centered curriculum patterns include the traditional activity-based and the more recent movement-based and concepts-based curriculum patterns. Student-centered patterns include the developmental needs and the student-centered patterns.

Activity-Based Curriculum Patterns

In the most common pattern, the curriculum is organized around activity units, including dance, fitness, and sports. Meaningful participation in activities is the goal. It is not a means toward other goals, such as physical fitness or social development. Since not all possible activities can be included, a percentage of the total time is usually established for each activity category. Local considerations and the school situation influence specific selections within each category. Progression is from basic skills in the elementary grades to specialization in a few selected activities at the high-school level.

The foremost advocate of play for its own sake is Siedentop. He defined physical education as "any process that increases human abilities to play competitive and expressive motor activities."[19] Play is seen as an important part of human existence. Students need instruction to develop the fundamental motor patterns needed for participation in all activity and counseling to help them match their interests and abilities to suitable activities. Although few curricula publicly advocate a play philosophy, most demonstrate adherence to the characteristics of the play pattern, with the exception that some appear to emphasize recreation rather than learning.

Sports education is an activity-based approach that stresses learning to be good sportspeople through participation in competition in ways similar to athletic participation. Students participate in formal schedules of competition with pre-"season" instruction, team practice sessions, a culminating event, and publicized records and standings. Teachers assume the role of coaches. Sports education may occur in single classes, with competition between classes scheduled during the same class period or other class periods, or during time formerly planned for intramural activities. Sports education teaches skills, rules, strategies, appreciation for play in our society, and proper ethical principles involved in *good* sport.[20]

Another activity-oriented curriculum approach is *wilderness sports and adventure education.* Wilderness sports include activities conducted in wilderness settings such as backpacking, canoeing, and scuba diving. Adventure education uses contrived obstacles or environments as problems or challenges for students to solve. While physical skill is the primary objective of wilderness activities, group or individual problem solving under stress is the major purpose of adventure education. Although instruction can be taught in physical education classes, weekend or overnight outings are essential for skill application in wilderness or adventure settings.[21] Some activities for this approach were presented in chapter 9.

The advantage of activity-based patterns is ease of administration. Disadvantages include boredom, caused by repetition, and the failure to develop skills beyond the basic level of instruction when programs are inadequately planned and implemented. Students often fail to develop the concepts necessary for a total understanding of the purpose of physical education throughout life. This type of program is difficult to justify to administrators and taxpayers.

Movement-Based Curriculum Pattern

The movement-based curriculum is based on the work of Laban and is used primarily in elementary school programs.[22] The curriculum is organized around themes involving the body and its interrelationship with space, time, effort, and flow. Both movement skills and movement concepts are included in the instructional process. Emphasis is on the exploration of a large variety of movement skills in the areas of dance, gymnastics, and sports. Students use problem solving or discovery learning to create new ways of using their bodies to achieve specified goals with various pieces of equipment or with each other.

Graham and his associates have developed a framework that is relatively easy to use in developing a movement-based curriculum.[23] It is shown in figure 15.2.

Concepts-Based Curriculum Patterns

Curriculum patterns that deal with the concepts and skills of human movement at the secondary school level include various concepts approaches based on the body of knowledge about human movement. These approaches are organized around key ideas or principles,

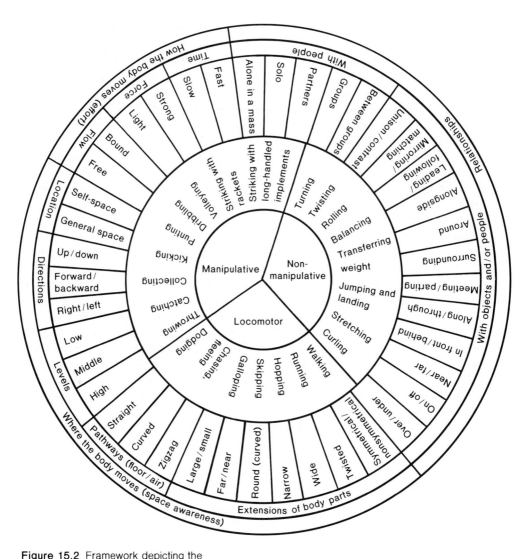

Figure 15.2 Framework depicting the interaction of movement concepts and skill themes.

Graham, George, Shirley Ann Holt/Hale, Tim McEwen, and Melissa Parker. *Children Moving: A Reflective Approach to Teaching Physical Education,* Palo Alto, California: Mayfield Publishing Company, 1980.

which must be broad enough to permit instruction in a wide variety of activities and meaningful enough to justify the time and effort expended. The goal is to help the students understand the what, why, and how of physical education through problem solving in laboratory and activity settings. Any or all appropriate sport and movement skills can be used to teach concepts. Progression is from simple to more complex knowledge.

Concepts approaches are based on two assumptions: (1) that transfer of concepts to new skills and situations occurs and (2) that students learn concepts better by emphasizing the concept (e.g., force production) rather than by teaching the concept within each activity unit.

Concepts-based curricula are more easily justified in an academic sense and help physical education achieve a more respected place in the school curriculum. They adapt readily to individual differences in students and to different locales. Students who do not excel in physical education activities like the concepts approach. Another advantage may be the carryover of basic concepts about health and fitness into real life.

The main disadvantage of concepts approaches is that students never experience a complete unit of instruction in a given activity and may never learn the skills needed to participate in each activity. Another disadvantage is that these approaches are based on the assumption that concepts will transfer to new skills and situations, while research shows that transfer usually occurs only when the application is made clear in the new situation.

In the *subdiscipline* approach to physical education, units are based on the six areas covered by the *Basic Stuff* series—exercise physiology, kinesiology, motor development, motor learning, social and psychological aspects of movement, and movement in the humanities (art, history, and philosophy).[24] Although there has been some controversy over the *Basic Stuff* series, teachers would do well to implement the teaching of concepts along with whatever curriculum pattern is chosen.

Lawson and Placek gave several examples of concept-oriented instructional units that follow a subdiscipline approach.[25] The following example deals with biomechanics.

Week 1: Center of gravity and base of support
Week 2: Balance
Week 3: Spin and angle of rebound
Week 4: Newton's laws of motion
Week 5: Force production
Week 6: Summary of the use of biomechanics in sport

Several variations of the concepts-based curriculum include: (1) integrating concepts with the traditional activity-based curriculum; (2) teaching a separate unit on concepts, along with the traditional activity units; and (3) teaching concepts on special occasions such as rainy days and shortened periods. An example of activities in which concepts are integrated with sport skills is shown in table 15.1.

With the recent emphasis on physical fitness, wellness, and healthy life-styles in the media, physical educators have created a *fitness-based curriculum approach*. Most programs emphasize fitness concepts, as well as skills in activities for developing healthy life-styles. *Fitness for Life* by Allsen, Harrison, and Vance[26] and similar programs have been

Table 15.1 Commonalities of fundamental movement skills and related mechanical principles

Moving the Body through Space + (Initiating Movement, Locomotion, Absorbing Momentum)		Moving an Object through Space = (Altering the Pathway, Sending, and Receiving)		Moving the Body and an Object through Space		
Activities	**Locomotor Skills**	**Activities**	**Manipulative Movements**	**Activities**	**Manipulative Movements**	**Locomotor Skills**
Badminton	Starting (staying ready to move)	Softball		Basketball	Dribbling (hands)	Starting
Basketball	Running	Field Hockey				Running
Field Hockey	Sliding	Badminton				Stopping
Gymnastics	Jumping	Tennis	Striking	Soccer	Dribbling (feet)	Changing directions
Soccer	Stopping	Golf				Sliding
Softball	Changing directions (flexible pathways)	Volleyball				
Tennis	Landing	Soccer	Kicking	Sending	Field Hockey	Dribbling (stick)
Track and Field	Propulsion					
Volleyball		Softball	Throwing	Basketball	Juggle (air dribble)	
Swimming		Basketball				
		Field Events				
		Archery	Projecting			
		Softball	Catching			
		Basketball				
		Soccer	Blocking and trapping	Receiving		

| **Control of Body** | + | **Control of Object** | = | **Control of Body and Object** | | |

From Seidel, Beverly L., Fay R. Biles, Grace E. Figley, and Bonnie J. Neuman. *Sports Skills: A Conceptual Approach to Meaningful Movement*, 2d. ed. © 1975, 1980 Wm. C. Brown Publishers, Dubuque, Iowa. All Rights Reserved. Reprinted by permission.

popular with college and adult populations for many years. Corbin and Lindsey's *Fitness for Life*[27] was developed to teach the concepts of fitness to secondary school students. These programs are generally supplemented with units of instruction in activity skills, designed to encourage participation in physical activity throughout life. Steinhardt and Stueck proposed a personal fitness model composed of physical fitness components and health-related objectives.[28] They stressed the importance of teachers understanding the characteristics of students as they influence behavior toward or away from fitness. These characteristics include perceived benefits and barriers, individual values, intentions, personal efficacy, and self-regulatory skills.

The Developmental Needs Curriculum Pattern

The *student needs curriculum* is based on the developmental stages and growth patterns of children and youth including cognitive, psychomotor, and affective development. The various taxonomies already presented and the characteristics of children and youth should be studied as a basis for developmental curriculum planning. Basic skills are taught in elementary school programs, team sports are emphasized in middle and junior high school programs, and lifetime activities in senior high school and college curricula, along with appropriate cognitive and affective objectives for the students' developmental levels. The curriculum is often divided into activity or theme units chosen by the faculty to meet student needs. This curriculum pattern is primarily based on the assumption that students go through the same stages of development at the same rate, although some programs attempt to provide a variety of learning experiences to provide for individual variation in these developmental levels. The developmental needs curriculum is widely accepted and often combined with the activity-based curriculum under the assumption that development will occur automatically through participation in motor activities.

Student-Centered Curriculum Patterns

Student-centered curriculum patterns are based on the student's own purposes for enrolling in physical education activities such as for social interaction, adventure, emotional release, physical fitness, self-discipline, or personal expression. They are based on the assumption that students are capable of assessing their own purposes and making appropriate choices. Counseling should be used to help students make choices appropriate to their values and interests. A wide variety of activities with beginning, intermediate, and advanced levels of instruction should be available to meet student needs.

The advantages of student-centered programs are that students have better attendance, are more cooperative, learn more when they are allowed to concentrate on activities in which they have real interest, and develop competence in activities in which they will participate outside of school hours.

One disadvantage lies in teachers being forced to teach activities that are of interest to students, but for which they were never prepared. A second disadvantage is that teachers may not get to know students if they continually shift from one teacher to another. Some students can get lost in such a system.

One student-centered pattern, *humanistic physical education,* stresses the uniqueness of each individual student. It uses physical activity to assist students in their search for personal meaning and self-actualization. Mastery of the subject matter is played down and an emphasis placed on providing a program based on the needs of the students. Self-understanding and interpersonal relations are stressed.

Hellison developed a humanistic or *social development* curriculum model for physical education. He identified five levels of awareness of students: (0) irresponsibility, (1) self-control, (2) involvement, (3) self-responsibility, and (4) caring. In *Goals and Strategies for Teaching Physical Education,* he proposed a number of strategies for helping youth progress through the five stages.[29] One of these techniques is shown in table 15.2.

Humanistic physical education requires a caring, authentic teacher who can establish a close teacher-student relationship and who facilitates learning for the students. In their text *Physical Education Instructional Techniques: An Individualized Humanistic Approach,* Heitmann and Kneer presented a humanistic approach to public school instruction in physical education.[30] They based their approach on the fact that children differ in how they learn, their growth and learning rates, their interests and goals, and their physical and psychological makeup. They emphasized the importance of teaching students the skills needed to direct their own behavior and encouraging them to accept responsibility for their own learning. They suggested that teachers facilitate instruction by providing a variety of teaching styles and resources from which the students could select those appropriate for themselves.

Another student-centered curriculum pattern is the *personal meaning approach,* in which the focus is on the satisfaction gained from participation in the movement experience or from the use of movement activities to achieve personal goals. Jewett and Mullan defined a purpose-process curriculum framework (PPCF) for the personal meaning approach.[31] The framework consists of seven groups of purposes for moving—physiological efficiency, psychic equilibrium, spacial orientation, object manipulation, communication, group interaction, and cultural involvement. It assumes that students have the same purposes. However, the emphasis may change from school to school depending on the students. The curriculum content can be arranged within activity or concept units, with an emphasis on one or more selected purposes within each unit. Students also study the processes for learning psychomotor skills (as defined in the taxonomy in unit 2). Very few practical examples of the PPCF exist. One is a program developed for a Canadian school district. The tenth-grade plan is shown in table 15.3. Students must take one unit each in fitness, personal development, and dance, along

---

Table 15.2 Big ideas sheet

A. Goal

Caring

B. Definition of the Goal:

We are not hermits. We look to others to fill many of our emotional, social and physical needs. Likewise, we can fill these needs for others.

C. Reasons for Valuing the Goal:

Realization of the fact that you need other people will help you build ties with others. Other people will value you if you help them in meeting their goals, just as you feel a tie towards anyone that assists or helps to make you feel good.

Table 15.2 (Continued)

D. Self-Inventory (Circle one)

CODE:	5	(Very often)
	4	(Frequently)
	3	(Occasionally)
	2	(Seldom)
	1	(Never)

I understand caring if:	I don't understand caring if:
I'm quiet when the teacher is talking.	I talk and interfere with others' rights and responsibility to teach.
5　　4　　3	2　　1
I helped someone recently.	I can't remember the last time I helped someone.
5　　4　　3	2　　1
I let people help me learn new or difficult things in PE and other classes.	I don't let people help me because I'll look weak or inferior to that person.
5　　4　　3	2　　1
I compliment people on things that they do well.	I never compliment anyone because they'll think they have the one-up on me.
5　　4　　3	2　　1
I thank people who have helped me.	I don't thank anyone because I'm too tough and cool.
5　　4　　3	2　　1
I'm humble about the talents I have.	I flaunt my talents and wipe them on others.
5　　4　　3	2　　1
I shared something with someone recently.	I never share anything because I might not get it back or they might not repay me.
5　　4　　3	2　　1
I stuck up for or found something good about someone everyone else was putting down.	I like getting into a group and tearing someone apart that everyone agrees is a jerk.
5　　4　　3	2　　1
I can accept compliments graciously.	I can't accept compliments because I think they're trying to get something from me.
5　　4　　3	2　　1

Hellison, Donald R. *Goals and Strategies for Teaching Physical Education* (Champaign, Illinois: Human Kinetics Publishers, Inc., 1985).

Table 15.3 Core program outline—grade 10

Subject Area	Concepts	Possible Activities
Fitness: 1 unit	Circulo-respiratory efficiency (A-1) Self-knowledge (B-5)	Cross country running, cross country skiing, jogging
Personal development: 1 unit	Neuro-muscular efficiency (A-3) (balance, agility, co-ordination) Challenge (B-7)	Tumbling, floor routines Apparatus—trampolining
Games: 5 units 2 goal types	Object manipulation (D)/projection (D-12) reception (D-13) a) one using the body to manipulate the object b) one using an implement to manipulate the object Group interaction (F) teamwork (F-17), competition (F-18)	Body: a) Basketball, soccer, team handball, flag football, rugby b) Ice hockey, floor hockey, lacrosse, broomball, field hockey
2 net types	Object manipulation (D)/projection (D-12) reception (D-13) a) one net game using the hands to manipulate the object b) one net game using an implement to manipulate the object Spacial relationships (C-10)	a) Volleyball b) Badminton, tennis
1 of: target or combative types	Target Object projection (D-12), catharsis (B-6) Combative Maneuvering weight (D-11), neuro-muscular efficiency (A-3) (agility)	Curling, golf, archery, bowling Wrestling, self defense, judo
Dance: 1 unit	Participation (G-20), joy of movement (B-4), clarification (E-15)	Folk dancing, social dancing, square dancing, modern dancing

Jewett, Ann E., and Marie R. Mullan. *Curriculum Design: Purposes and Processes in Physical Education Teaching-Learning.* Washington, D.C.: American Association of Health, Physical Education and Recreation, 1977.

with two goal-type games, two net games, and one target game or combative activity. Adventure activities might also fit in well with a personal meaning oriented curriculum. The major problem with the PPCF is that it is difficult to use for persons not familiar with the framework.

Building a Program from Curriculum Patterns

The process of curriculum development involves choosing one or more curriculum patterns that will meet the goals and objectives of the school or district for which the curriculum is being designed. For example, a movement approach may be chosen for the elementary schools, with activity-based programs dominating the secondary programs. Fitness-oriented concepts units could be taught in the junior and senior high schools, with other concepts integrated with the appropriate activity units. The important thing to remember is that programs and patterns should be compatible with the philosophies of the school and community. Avoid taking the "easy way out" when, with a little effort, a more appropriate pattern could result in greater benefits to students.

Annarino and his colleagues listed the following practical considerations when designing or selecting curriculum patterns and programs:

1. The needs and interests of students
2. The number and type of students
3. The preentry skills of the students
4. The terminal objectives to be achieved
5. The type, expertise, and number of instructional personnel
6. The grouping of students
7. The availability of equipment and supplies
8. The number of teaching stations
9. Time allotments
10. School and state requirements
11. Type of instructional strategy to be employed
12. Availability and types of instructional aids
13. Seasonality[32]

Siedentop and his colleagues suggested the following considerations:

How adequate are the school facilities? How adequate are the community opportunities? How easy is it for students to get from school to the community sites? Do students have to catch buses right after school? Is the school district willing to provide supplementary compensation for faculty leadership in intramurals, clubs, and drop-in recreation? What is the state law regarding physical education? What support is there for going beyond the requirements of the state law with an elective program? *How motivated are the physical education teachers to build a program that really counts?* The answers to these questions will provide the background information for making decisions about how much a program can accomplish.[33] [italics in original]

Whatever program is selected, do it well. It may be worthwhile to implement program components in small steps and work with one portion until success is achieved before starting another part.

Resources for the Curriculum Committee

Persons responsible for curriculum design should become aware of the many resources available, such as people, organizations, professional journals, curriculum guides, commercial publications, facilities, and media.

People

Curriculum and instruction specialists at colleges and universities are often more than willing to be of service as consultants. If none are available, write to authors of curriculum articles in professional journals. Researchers, housed in universities and commercial institutions, conduct basic research that is often rejected by teachers because of a failure by researchers to make their findings adaptable to the school setting. Teachers, who could do applied research that is directly applicable to the schools, often lack the time, training, or money to do so. A solution might be a joint arrangement in which researchers and teachers work together to identify and investigate problems and alternatives for resolving them.

Organizations

Two national organizations that can provide tremendous resources are the American Alliance for Health, Physical Education, Recreation and Dance (AAHPERD), and the President's Council on Physical Fitness and Sports. The AAHPERD has four excellent position papers outlining guidelines for physical education. They are:

Essentials of a Quality Elementary School Physical Education Program
Guidelines for Middle School Physical Education
Guidelines for Secondary School Physical Education
Guide to Excellence for Physical Education in Colleges and Universities

AAHPERD also publishes *The Research Quarterly for Exercise and Sport*, the *Journal of Physical Education, Recreation and Dance, Completed Research in Health, Physical Education, and Recreation*, and a number of other pertinent publications. The President's Council provides speakers, public-relations help, bulletins, and films on various areas of interest to physical educators.

A large number of national agencies also have materials or journals of value to physical education. Check *your* university or local library for addresses and publications. A few of them include:

Amateur Athletic Union
American Academy of Physical Education
American Association of School Administrators (NEA)
American Camping Association
American Cancer Society
American College of Sports Medicine
American Heart Association
American Medical Association
American Public Health Association
American Red Cross
American School Health Association

Association for Supervision and Curriculum Development (NEA)
Athletic Institute
Lifetime Sports Foundation
National Association of Secondary School Principals
National Education Association
National Federation of State High School Athletic Associations
National Parent-Teachers Association
National Recreation and Park Association
National Safety Council
Society of State Directors of Health, Physical Education and Recreation
United States Office of Education
United States Public Health Service

At the state level, the state department of education will often provide consultants, in-service activities, conferences, clinics, and workshops. Many states also have a state course of study or curriculum guide. State education associations and state Associations of Health, Physical Education, Recreation and Dance can be of inestimable service.

The local chamber of commerce can provide information about the resources and makeup of the local community.

Professional Journals

The number of professional journals relating to physical education has increased dramatically in the last few years. Some that relate directly to curriculum and instruction are:

Adapted Physical Activity Quarterly
Alliance Update
American Corrective Therapy Journal
American Health
American Journal of Public Health
CAHPER Journal (Canadian)
Camping
Completed Research in Health, Physical Education, Recreation and Dance
Journal of Physical Education, Recreation and Dance
Journal of School Health
Journal of Teaching in Physical Education
Journal of the American Medical Association
Phi Delta Kappan
The Physical Educator
Quest
Research Quarterly for Exercise and Sport
Safety Education
School Safety
Sportsearch (an index to sport journals)
Strategies
Today's Education

Curriculum Guides

State departments of education and local school systems publish curriculum guides that detail the overall course of instruction for all schools and the specific requirements for specific subject areas, such as physical education. Curriculum guides serve as examples of how other schools, districts, and states have solved problems that may be similar in nature and can be used as a springboard for curriculum development. Curriculum guides generally include some or all of the following: (1) philosophy, goals, and objectives; (2) characteristics and needs of students; (3) program scope and sequence with suggested units of instruction for each grade level; (4) sample schedules; (5) administrative guidelines; (6) instructional activities; (7) evaluation techniques; and (8) resources for teachers. Teachers who are involved in writing curriculum guides find them more useful than those who are merely reading what someone else thinks is important. Curriculum guides should suggest specific, practical ideas that facilitate the teaching-learning process and provide usable resource materials. As school districts move away from traditional programs to more individualized instruction, curriculum guides become very useful to teachers. Curriculum guides enhance the articulation between programs at the different school levels and assure proper progression and development in the three domains of learning.

Commercial Publications

Textbooks and physical education equipment and media are available through various commercial companies. University libraries, salespeople, and school catalogs can be useful in locating these sources. Books on curriculum development can delineate principles and practices for effective curriculum design.

Media

Hardware catalogs are usually available at school district administrative offices or media centers. Information on software is available from AAHPERD, the NASPE Media Resource Center,[34] and commercial catalogs.

Questions and Suggested Activities

1. Visit a curriculum committee meeting in your college or university or in a local school district. Who was on the committee? What kind of input did each one give to the committee?
2. You have taught physical education in the local high school for one year and have been asked to chair a curriculum committee for upgrading the physical education program, K–12, in your local district. You are located in a small rural community district that includes one senior high school, one junior high school, and two small elementary schools. How will you go about selecting your curriculum committee? What characteristics will you look for in each member of your team? What goals would you want your group to reach?
3. Talk to a number of girls and boys from a junior or senior high school that is considered to have a good program of physical education. Ask them what they like or dislike about the program and whether they have any input into curriculum considerations.
4. Examine several older and more recent curriculum guides to determine what, if any, changes have been made to meet the changing social forces of our time. What changes would you suggest?

5. Conduct a survey of your community in terms of the factors listed in the chapter. What does the data suggest about an appropriate curriculum for a school in your community?

6. Discuss the relationship of the physical education curriculum to the total school curriculum.

7. How do the growth and development patterns of children and adolescents affect the curriculum?

8. Visit a school (or study a curriculum guide) and try to determine what kinds of learning are occurring in the cognitive, psychomotor, and affective domains. What kinds are omitted? Suggest ways in which all three domains could be included in the curriculum.

9. Discuss the implications of the "animal school" on the curriculum (see Epilogue).

10. Would a national curriculum model in physical education fulfill the purposes of education in the United States?

11. Visit a school board meeting and discuss what occurs there.

12. You have just been hired to teach physical education at a brand new school in Saudi Arabia. The school is for grades seven to nine and has approximately 250 students. There is no school district, just a superintendent and board of directors. What factors will you consider before designing the new curriculum?

13. Describe the curriculum patterns that best reflect your philosophies of education and of physical education.

14. Visit a school or study the program described in a curriculum guide. Try to determine the dominant curriculum pattern of the program. What changes would you suggest to make the program most effective?

15. Interview several teachers of physical education or peruse physical education literature to determine current trends and innovations in public education and physical education.

16. Describe the ideal physical education program in your mind. What was your program like? Was your program a success? What contributed to its success? (Jewett and Bain: 102)

Suggested Readings

Gillam, G. McKenzie. "Back to the 'Basics' of Physical Education." *The Physical Educator* 42 (Fall 1985):129–33.

Grieve, Andrew. "Try It—You'll Like It: An Effective Format for the Physical Education Curriculum Guide." *Journal of Health, Physical Education and Recreation* 43 (May 1972):34–35.

Harrington, Wilma M. "Making It Happen: Connecting Theory and Practice." *Journal of Physical Education, Recreation and Dance* 55 (August 1984):32–33.

Haywood, Kathleen M., and Thomas J. Loughrey. "Growth and Development Implications for Teaching." *Journal of Physical Education and Recreation* 52 (March 1981):57–58.

Heitmann, Helen M. "Integrating Concepts into Curricular Models." *Journal of Physical Education and Recreation* 52 (February 1981):42–45.

Jewett, Ann E., and Linda L. Bain. *The Curriculum Process in Physical Education.* Dubuque, Iowa: Wm. C. Brown Company Publishers, 1985.

Kneer, Marian E., ed. "Curriculum: Theory into Practice." *Journal of Physical Education and Recreation* 49 (March 1978):24–37.

Mancuso, Jo, ed. "Quality Secondary School Physical Education." *Journal of Physical Education and Recreation* 49 (January 1978):42–52.

Melograno, Vincent, ed. "Physical Education Curriculum for the 1980s." *Journal of Physical Education and Recreation* 51 (September 1980):39–54.

Meredith, Marilu. "Expand Your Program—Step Off Campus." *Journal of Physical Education and Recreation* 50 (January 1979):21–22.

Mullen, Marlowe R. "Lifting the Curtain of Tradition." *The Physical Educator* 39 (May 1982):78–82.

National Association for Sport and Physical Education. *Basic Stuff Series.* Reston, Virginia: American Alliance for Health, Physical Education, Recreation and Dance, 1981 and 1987.

Ornstein, Allan C. "Curriculum Contrasts: A Historical Overview." *Phi Delta Kappan* 63 (February 1982):404–8.

Pate, Russell, and Charles Corbin. "Implications for Curriculum." *Journal of Physical Education and Recreation* 52 (January 1981):36–38.

Peddiwell, J. Abner. *The Sabertooth Curriculum.* New York: McGraw-Hill Book Company, 1939.

Placek, Judith H. "A Conceptually-Based Physical Education Program." *Journal of Physical Education, Recreation and Dance* 54 (September 1983):27–28.

Riley, Marie. "Title X: A Proposal for a Law to Guarantee Equal Opportunity for Nonathletes." *Journal of Physical Education and Recreation* 46 (June 1975):31.

Seiter, Margaret M., Maripat Goggin, and Barbara Kres Beach. *Shaping the Body Politic: Legislative Training for the Physical Educator.* Reston, Virginia: AAHPERD, n.d.

Shephard, Roy J., et al. "Curricular Time for Physical Education? A Controlled Experiment in French Canada Asks How Much Curricular Time Should Be Spent on Physical Education." *Journal of Physical Education, Recreation and Dance* 53 (November–December 1982):19–20.

Tyler, Ralph W. *Basic Principles of Curriculum and Instruction.* Chicago: University of Chicago Press, 1949.

References

1. Linda Bain, "Status of Curriculum Theory in Physical Education," *Journal of Physical Education and Recreation* 49 (March 1978), pp. 25–26.
2. Robberta Mesenbrink, et al., "New Forms and Substances in Physical Education," in *Curriculum Report,* National Association of Secondary School Principals 4 (December 1974).
3. Ann E. Jewett and Linda L. Bain, *The Curriculum Process in Physical Education* (Dubuque, Iowa: Wm. C. Brown Company Publishers, 1985), pp. 25–29.
4. Alvin Toffler, *The Schoolhouse in the City* (New York: Praeger Publishers, in cooperation with Educational Facilities Laboratories, 1968), pp. 367–69.
5. Abraham H. Maslow, "A Theory of Human Personality," *Psychological Review* 50 (1943), pp. 370–96.
6. Glen Hass, *Curriculum Planning: A New Approach,* 2d ed. (Boston: Allyn & Bacon, Inc., 1977), p. 234.
7. Maslow, "A Theory of Human Personality," pp. 370–96.
8. Larry Kehres, "Maslow's Hierarchy of Needs Applied to Physical Education and Athletics," *The Physical Educator* 30 (March 1973), pp. 24–25.
9. Ibid., p. 25.
10. Ibid.
11. George Leonard, *The Ultimate Athlete* (New York: The Hearst Corporation, 1975).
12. Hass, *Curriculum Planning: A New Approach,* p. 234.
13. Alvin Toffler, *Future Shock* (New York: Bantam Books, 1970), p. 420.
14. Margaret M. Seiter, Maripat Goggin, and Barbara Kres Beach, *Shaping the Body Politic: Legislative Training for the Physical Educator* (Reston, Virginia: AAHPERD, n.d.).
15. William Geiger and David Kizer, "Developing a Teaching Awareness," *The Physical Educator* 36 (March 1979), pp. 25–26.
16. David Pratt, *Curriculum: Design and Development* (New York: Harcourt Brace Jovanovich, 1980), pp. 183–87.
17. Hass, *Curriculum Planning: A New Approach,* p. 233.

18. John Kudlas, "Outdoor/Environment Programs," in Patricia E. Barry, ed. *Ideas for Secondary School Physical Education* (Reston, Virginia: AAHPERD Publications, 1976).

19. Daryl Siedentop, *Physical Education: Introductory Analysis* (Dubuque, Iowa: Wm. C. Brown Company Publishers, 1972), p. 185.

20. Daryl Siedentop, Charles Mand, and Andrew Taggart, *Physical Education: Teaching and Curriculum Strategies for Grades 5–12* (Palo Alto, California: Mayfield Publishing Company, 1986), pp. 185–202.

21. Ibid., pp. 203–28.

22. Rudolf von Laban, *Modern Educational Dance,* 2d ed., revised by Lisa Ullman (New York: Frederick A. Praeger, 1963).

23. George Graham, Shirley Ann Holt/Hale, Tim McEwen, and Melissa Parker, *Children Moving: A Reflective Approach to Teaching Physical Education* (Palo Alto, California: Mayfield Publishing Company, 1980).

24. American Alliance for Health, Physical Education, Recreation and Dance, *Basic Stuff Series.*

25. Hal A. Lawson and Judith H. Placek, *Physical Education in the Secondary Schools: Curricular Alternatives* (Boston: Allyn & Bacon, Inc., 1981), pp. 210–26.

26. Philip E. Allsen, Joyce M. Harrison, and Barbara Vance, *Fitness for Life: An Individualized Approach,* 3d ed. (Dubuque, Iowa: Wm. C. Brown Company Publishers, 1984).

27. Charles B. Corbin and Ruth Lindsey, *Fitness for Life: Physical Education Concepts* (Glenview, Illinois: Scott, Foresman and Company, 1977).

28. Mary A. Steinhardt and Patricia M. Stueck, "Personal Fitness: A Curriculum Model," *Journal of Physical Education, Recreation and Dance* 57 (September 1986), pp. 23–29.

29. Donald R. Hellison, *Goals and Strategies for Teaching Physical Education* (Champaign, Illinois: Human Kinetics Publishers, 1985).

30. Helen M. Heitmann and Marian E. Kneer, *Physical Education Instructional Techniques: An Individualized Humanistic Approach* (Englewood Cliffs, New Jersey: Prentice-Hall, 1976).

31. Ann E. Jewett and Marie R. Mullan, *Curriculum Design: Purposes and Processes in Physical Education Teaching-Learning* (Washington, D.C.: American Association of Health, Physical Education and Recreation, 1977).

32. Anthony A. Annarino, Charles C. Cowell, and Helen W. Hazleton, *Curriculum Theory & Design in Physical Education,* 2d ed. (Prospect Heights, Illinois: Waveland Press, 1986), p. 220.

33. Siedentop, Mand, and Taggart, *Physical Education: Teaching and Curriculum Strategies for Grades 5–12,* p. 141.

34. The NASPE Media Resource Center, Department of Physical Education, University of South Carolina, Columbia, South Carolina 29208.

Scope and Sequence in the Physical Education Program

Study Stimulators

1. Explain what is included in a balanced curriculum.
2. Identify the methods that should be used in selecting content for a specific curriculum.
3. Should physical education credit be awarded for nonphysical education activities?
4. Describe how sequence relates to teaching activity skills or content.
5. Describe appropriate objectives and activities for each grade level.

The content selected for the curriculum and the order in which it is organized for presentation are called scope and sequence.

Scope

Scope refers to the content of the curriculum at each grade level. It includes *what* should be taught to meet the needs of the students and the objectives of physical education. Many schools have an inadequate curriculum with a narrow scope that focuses only on a few sports in physical education classes plus an athletic program. In contrast, the curriculum should be broad in scope, encompassing a variety of rich and guided experiences in instructional, intramural, recreational, and athletic situations, in order to meet the wide diversity of physical, intellectual, emotional, and social needs of children and youth. Too many experiences, however, could dilute the effectiveness of the content that is included.

Program Balance

A balanced program is one that contains an emphasis on the various aspects of the program consistent with the program objectives and the needs of students. Without balance, the goals and objectives of the curriculum cannot be achieved. Balance can be achieved in a number of ways. First, curriculum goals and objectives must consider the needs and interests of the learners, the needs of society, and the subject matter to be learned. The curriculum pattern chosen should provide a logical structure for organizing learning activities. A balance among the goals or objectives of physical education can be maintained by allocating time to each objective in terms of the value placed on that objective. These objectives include knowledge, physical skills, physical fitness, social skills, and attitudes and appreciations. Curricula in which only sports are taught are not balanced, nor are curricula that exclude instruction in fitness or knowledge. Social skills such as teamwork and sportsmanship are often cited in the objectives, but hard to find in the instructional program. The proposed curriculum and the actual curriculum should be the same so that a "hidden curriculum" does not result. The amount of time allocated to each area of the curriculum will depend on the context for which the curriculum is developed and the philosophy of the curriculum committee.

Time allotted to class instruction, intramurals, and extramurals must also be balanced. Commitment should be first to class instruction, second to an intramural program, and last to an extramural program, although in excellent programs distinguishing between in-class and extra-class programs is often hard. Sport education and adventure education programs use time before and after school and on weekends to apply skills learned in physical education classes.

Intramural and related programs provide an opportunity for students to use and refine skills learned in class instruction and to learn skills not available in class time (due to the inaccessibility of facilities during school hours), such as bowling, skiing, skating, hiking, and rock climbing.

Extramural or interscholastic athletics provide competition for highly skilled students. To meet educational objectives, athletic programs must be carefully designed and managed by dedicated professionals. Although the direction of athletics is an administrative responsibility, the duty of the curriculum committee is to ensure that the program is carried out so that the planned educational values are being achieved. Legislation requires equal opportunities for boys, girls, and the handicapped to participate in extra-class programs.

Methods for the Selection of Content

Since far more activities and experiences exist than can possibly be included in the curriculum, only the most appropriate should be selected for inclusion in the program. Many programs try to do everything and therefore they do nothing well. Students repeat activities and content year after year, but spend so little time on each that they master none of them. The selection of learning experiences should depend on the needs and interests of the students, the needs of the society, and the expressed philosophy and objectives of the program. Learning experiences should be selected that actually result in the objectives stated, without producing undesired side effects.

The selection of activities has sometimes been based on the teachers' interests and abilities or the coaches' desire to develop the skills involved in the athletic program. This kind of program usually results in an unbalanced program based primarily on team sports.

In many programs, very little curriculum time is allotted to lifetime sports. Parents and participants suggest the need for adding to the curriculum such activities as golf, swimming, tennis, bowling, dance, boating, camping, and fitness. Outdoor adventure and initiative activities are also increasing in popularity. Increased interest in physical fitness and self-help suggest a need for more emphasis on cognitive involvement in physical education. Content should be selected by a curriculum committee composed of educators, parents, and students, using a system of analyzing and selecting those experiences that meet the needs of students and the objectives of the program. The following steps are suggested for selecting the activities for the curriculum:

Step 1. Determine broad activity or concept categories.
Step 2. List possible activities.
Step 3. Establish a systematic method for selecting curricular experiences.
Step 4. Assign weight values to criteria.
Step 5. Evaluate experiences by awarding points for each criterion.
Step 6. Arrange experiences by rank.
Step 7. Evaluate experiences by relative value.

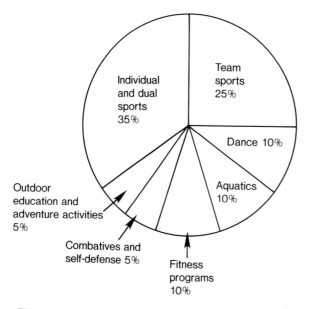

Figure 16.1 A scope chart for high school physical education.

Step 1—Determine Broad Activity or Concept Categories
Categories should agree with the curriculum pattern selected in the preceding chapter. Examples of activity categories that might be included are:

Aquatics
Team sports
Gymnastics
Individual sports
Rhythms and dance
Physical fitness
Outdoor education and adventure activities

Concept areas that might be included are:

Exercise physiology
Kinesiology
Motor development
Motor learning
Social and psychological aspects of movement
Movement in the humanities

    A scope chart should be prepared that shows the percentage of the total program to be spent in each broad activity or concept area. These percentages should reflect the philosophies of the curriculum committee, the school district, and the teachers in the program. They should provide a balanced program of experiences relating to students' needs and developmental levels. An example of a scope chart is shown in figure 16.1.

Step 2—List Possible Activities

Within each category, list all possible activities. Literally hundreds of activities *could* be included. A sample list of activities is shown in figure 16.2. The other columns will be explained in succeeding steps. For purposes of the example, an activity-centered curriculum pattern has been used. If concept categories have been chosen, activities should be selected that help students understand the concepts to be studied.

Step 3—Establish a Systematic Method for Selecting Curricular Experiences

Since school time is obviously limited and only the most appropriate experiences for a given situation can be considered, a systematic method for selecting relevant curricular experiences will need to be established. List criteria that are considered to be essential for including an activity in the curriculum. Keep criteria few in number and stated as realistically as possible. The following criteria are generally considered to be essential:

1. Is the experience consistent with each of the stated objectives of physical education and education?
2. Is the experience consistent with the present and future growth and developmental needs of students?
3. Is the activity relatively free of hazards?
4. Is the activity feasible under local considerations? Some possible criteria for determining which activities are most suitable for a particular area include:
   a. Is the activity acceptable to the community? (For example, in some areas of the country, dancing may be prohibited by certain religious groups.)
   b. Is the activity of interest to students? (Regional interests and inner-city factors, for example, may influence the interests of students and possible carryover values. For example, the cost of participating in golf would be prohibitive to most inner-city youth.)
   c. Are the necessary resources available in the school or community, including facilities, equipment, finances, expertise of faculty members or resource persons, time constraints, transportation, and climate?

Step 4—Assign Weight Values to Criteria

Several possible ways exist for assigning weights to each criterion. One way is to weigh all criteria equally with each one counting a set number of points. A more realistic way is to weigh each criterion differently based on its importance to the selection process. This can be done by assigning a different number of points to each criterion as shown in figure 16.2. These weights should be based on the rank order of importance given to the objectives of physical education. Individual factors such as safety and feasibility may be considered separately.

Step 5—Evaluate Experiences by Awarding Points for Each Criterion

Make up a chart with the criteria across the top and the experiences down the side as shown in figure 16.2. Give a copy to each member of your curriculum committee and have them evaluate each experience by awarding points according to the plan decided on in step 4. Then, average the points from all members of the committee.

| ACTIVITY | OBJECTIVES | | | | Total 100 | Rank | Safety High-Med.-Low | Student Needs and Interests | Rank | Locally Feasible Yes/No |
	Fitness 30	Skills 40	Knowl-edge 20	Social 10						
AQUATICS										
Lifesaving	16.5	28	17	6.5	68	1	Med.	15.2%	3	Yes
Swimming (Beg.)	19.5	28	12	5	64.5	3	Med.	25.4%	1	Yes
Swimming (Int.)	22.5	28	12	5	67.5	2	Med.	17.2%	2	Yes
DANCE										
Aerobic Dance	29	29	10.5	7.5	76	5	High	51.0%	1	Yes
Ballet	24	37	16	7.5	84.5	1	High	13.2%	6	Yes
Folk and Square Dance	22	30.5	16	8	76.5	4	High	24.9%	4	Yes
Jazz Dance	25	32	14.5	7.5	79	3	High	32.1%	2	Yes
Modern Dance	25	32	15	7.5	79.5	2	High	22.3%	5	Yes
Social Dance	18	30.5	13	8	69.5	6	High	31.5%	3	Yes
PHYSICAL FITNESS										
Jogging	30	20	10	5.5	65.5	1	High	59.0%	1	Yes
Weight Training	21	20	10	5	56	2	Low	45.3%	2	Yes
TEAM SPORTS										
Basketball	19	38.5	10	6	73.5	5	Med.	31.6%	3	Yes
Flag Football	19	37	12	6.5	74.5	4	Med.	26.0%	5	Yes
Field Hockey	23	35	13	6.5	77.5	2	Med.	18.4%	6	Yes
Soccer	27	36	14.5	8	85.5	1	Med.	29.9%	4	Yes
Softball	17	35	11	7	70	7	Med.	37.6%	1	Yes
Speedball	23	35	12	7	77	3	Med.	5.0%	7	Yes
Volleyball	17	34	13.5	7	71.5	6	Med.	33.0%	2	Yes

INDIVIDUAL SPORTS									
Archery	7	34	15	4.5	60.5	9	Low	11.0%	9	Yes
Badminton	18	34	12	5.5	69.5	7	Med.	25.3%	6	Yes
Bowling	6	30	11	5	52	10	High	42.1%	3	Yes
Cycling	24	27	14	5	70	6	Med.	45.0%	2	Yes
Fencing	16	34.5	16	5	71.5	5	Med.	10.8%	0	Yes
Golf	8.5	33.5	14	6	62	8	Med.	28.8%	5	Yes
Gymnastics	25	38.5	16	6	85.5	1	Low	21.2%	8	No
Racketball/Handball	22	33	13	5.5	73.5	4	Med.	42.0%	4	No
Tennis	22	35	11.5	6	74.5	3	Med.	59.0%	1	Yes
Track and Field	28	37	14	6.5	85.5	1	Med.	24.1%	7	Yes
OUTDOOR EDUCATION-ADVENTURE									
Camping	15	20	15	9	59	9	Low	25.1%	6	Yes
Backpacking	28	27	15	7	77	1		34.3%	3	Yes
Hiking	26	20	12	7	65	7		31.8%	4	Yes
Orienteering	24	20	13	10	67	6		25.6%	5	Yes
Initiative Activities	20	25	17	10	72	3		35.2%	2	Yes
Scuba Diving	22	26	15	8	71	4		15.1%	9	No
Small Crafts	22	25	15	7	69	5		12.8%	7	Yes
Canoeing	22	22	12	7	63	8		10.3%	8	Yes
Skiing	22	34.5	12	5.5	74	2	→	41.0%	1	No

Figure 16.2 A list of possible activities with assigned weights and ranks within categories.

Step 6—Arrange Experiences by Rank

Based on the average points for each activity, arrange the experiences by rank within each category. Eliminate experiences that do not meet the criteria selected in step 3. Experiences that best meet the objectives for the program and the needs of the students should be given priority. Some activities will satisfy the physical fitness objective but be of little value for social skills. Others may contribute to the leisure-time interests of students but be of little value for physical fitness. By ranking the experiences within the broader categories selected in step 1, the committee can determine which of the experiences within each category best meet the selected criteria.

Step 7—Evaluate Experiences by Relative Value

When a number of desirable experiences meet all of the criteria for inclusion in the curriculum, but because of time all cannot be included, two possibilities exist. First, experiences can be eliminated on the basis of local criteria. For example, of the field sports—football, soccer, speedball, and speed-a-way—soccer appears to command such an interest in the community as a leisure-time activity that the committee feels students need specific instruction in it. Canoeing may be discarded due to inadequate facilities within reach of the school. Second, experiences can be organized into categories with specified amounts of time devoted to each area. Heitmann suggested several patterns for broadening curricular scope to meet the needs of individual students while at the same time achieving curricular objectives. She stated:

> Explore the feasibility of the various *curricular patterns*. The basic pattern begins with the various objectives of the physical education program. Establish these global goals as areas into which the various activities will fall. Courses that can be accommodated can be placed into these areas.
>
> Once courses are organized according to the basic categories you can then decide if some courses are essential which you would require and if some could be enrichment.[1]

Figure 16.3 shows examples of how Heitmann's organizational patterns might be used in a physical education curriculum. For example, in the figure, area 1 includes health- and fitness-related courses; area 2, aquatics; area 3, dance; area 4, individual sports, and area 5, team sports.

Programs are often planned so that every student is required to experience a minimal exposure to (1) team sports, (2) individual and dual sports, (3) rhythms and dance, (4) aquatics, and (5) fitness activities. Although a minimum exposure requirement exists, students are encouraged to explore activities beyond the minimum exposure in areas of their greatest interest.

Extra-class Activities

Extra-class activities such as intramurals, sportsdays, playdays, and club activities should be chosen in a manner similar to the steps listed above. Student interest is a major factor in the selection of these activities. By using gymnasiums when athletic teams are outdoors and community facilities such as bowling centers, golf courses, skating rinks, swimming pools, and tennis courts, a wide variety of activities can be scheduled, including some that would not be possible during class time. Intramurals can be scheduled before or after school, during the noon hour, or during a scheduled activity period.

Pattern 1

Core Required

Fitness	Aquatics	Dance	Individual Sports and Combatives	Team Sports
Fitness for Life	Beginning Swimming	Introduction to dance forms	Self-Defense	Biomechanical concepts of sport

---

Select One from Each Area

Weight Training	Intermediate Swimming	Folk	Archery	Basketball
Jogging	Lifesaving	Square	Badminton	Flag Football
Aerobic Dance	Water games	Modern	Bowling	Field Hockey
		Jazz	Cycling	Lacrosse
		Ballet	Fencing	Soccer
		Social	Golf	Softball
			Gymnastics	Speedball
			Racquetball	Volleyball
			Skiing	
			Tennis	
			Track and Field	
			Wrestling	
			Martial Arts	

Pattern II

Core Required

Fitness	Aquatics	Dance	Individual Sports and Combatives	Team Sports
Fitness for Life	Beginning Swimming	Introduction to dance forms	Self-Defense	Biomechanical concepts of sport

---

Select Any Four from Any Area or from Three of the Five Areas

Weight Training	Intermediate Swimming	Folk	Archery	Basketball
Jogging	Lifesaving	Square	Badminton	Flag Football
Aerobic Dance	Water games	Modern	Bowling	Field Hockey
		Jazz	Cycling	Lacrosse
		Ballet	Fencing	Soccer
		Social	Golf	Softball
			Gymnastics	Speedball
			Racquetball	Volleyball
			Skiing	
			Tennis	
			Track and Field	
			Wrestling	
			Martial Arts	

Figure 16.3 Examples of suggested organizational patterns.
Based on information from Heitmann, Helen M. "Curricular Organizational Patterns for Physical Education," presented to the NASPE Curriculum Academy Working Symposium, St. Louis, Missouri, November 4–6, 1978.

Pattern III

Core—Select one from each area

Weight Training	Swimming	Folk	Archery	Basketball
Jogging	Lifesaving	Square	Badminton	Flag Football
Aerobic Dance	Water games	Modern	Bowling	Field Hockey
		Jazz	Cycling	Lacrosse
		Ballet	Fencing	Soccer
		Social	Golf	Softball
			Gymnastics	Speedball
			Racquetball	Volleyball
			Skiing	
			Tennis	
			Track and Field	
			Wrestling	
			Martial Arts	

Pattern IV

Select one track

Track 1	Track 2	Track 3
Fitness for Life	Fitness for Life	Fitness for Life
Swimming	Swimming	Swimming
Folk and Square Dance	Social Dance	Modern Dance
Archery/Badminton	Tennis/Bowling	Golf/Racquetball

Figure 16.3 (Continued)

Interscholastic activities are generally specified by state high school activities associations, and regulations are sent to the schools prescribing seasons and game schedules. Additional activities can be added by working directly with the state association.

Should Substitute Activities Be Allowed Physical Education Credit?

In many schools and colleges, physical education credit is awarded for participation in marching band, ROTC, or varsity athletics. The question often arises as to whether this credit is justifiable. To answer this question, each activity should be evaluated in the same way every other experience in the curriculum was evaluated—by evaluating its ability to help students achieve the objectives of physical education. The goals of physical education, as specified in AAHPERD's *Guidelines for Secondary School Physical Education,* include the development of movement skills, personal health and fitness, a knowledge of the scientific principles related to activity, exercise, and health, and an understanding of the role of physical activity and sport in society.[2] District goals may, by law, specify more specific outcomes to be achieved. If an activity makes a contribution to the development of the student for the goals of physical education, it might be considered as a portion of the physical education requirement. If the activity does not meet these criteria, then physical education credit should be denied. Consideration should also be given to the many experiences that might be missed through continued participation in one of these substitute activities. When students are excused from physical education for four years or more, that says to the students and the public that physical education programs are not particularly beneficial. The President's Council on Physical Fitness and Sports recommends that "no substitution of band, ROTC, athletic programs or other extra-class activities for physical education class work" be allowed.[3]

Two recent AAHPERD publications, *Physical Activity & Well-being* and the condensed version, *The Value of Physical Activity,* have been prepared by the National Association for Sport and Physical Education to help physical educators summarize the benefits of physical education for students, parents, school administrators, and boards of education, and to point out the relationship between activity and academic achievement.[4]

Sequence

Sequence refers to the order in which curriculum components should be taught. Appropriate sequencing depends on the achievement of basic movement patterns such as throwing, catching, and using space prior to engagement in game skills such as fielding and guarding. Failure to provide a graduated sequence of instruction in knowledge and skills has probably been the biggest stumbling block to quality programs in physical education. For example, the same basketball unit has often been taught to the same students year after year with no new or progressive learning occurring. This would be equivalent to teaching students "2 + 2" or similar arithmetic skills from grades K through 12. No matter what is written down in the curriculum, if students do not achieve the prerequisites, sequence is hampered.

The physical education program needs to be organized into a continuous flow of experiences through a carefully planned and graduated sequence of ideas and skills from preschool through college. This sequence should be developed in the light of student needs and interests and built progressively toward the attainment of a single set of physical education objectives.

Preschool programs should stress self-care skills and developmental tasks. Elementary school students should acquire proficiency in fundamental motor patterns. Proficiency in motor skills used in active team games should be stressed in the middle or junior high school because of the physical and social needs of the students. Lifetime activities should be added during the high-school years.

Planning must be coordinated at all grade levels to ensure sufficient breadth to the activities, provide for the development of skills that will be required for later activities, and avoid unnecessary overlap, omissions, or undue repetition of instruction. Students, therefore, will be able to progress toward an increasingly mature utilization of their knowledge and skills to solve complex problems related to themselves and to society. A scope and sequence chart for activities in grades K through 12 is shown in figure 16.4.

Students do not learn all there is to know or develop skill proficiency in an activity in a single encounter. Teachers are often frustrated when students absorb only the smallest part of a unit of instruction. Often teachers try to do too much and so nothing is learned well. Willgoose summed this up very well when he said:

> The chief problem facing most physical education teachers is not what to teach, but
> how far one should go at specific grade levels. One way to get around this dilemma is to
> think less in terms of stereotyped grade levels and more in terms of *skill levels.* For

SCOPE AND SEQUENCE CHART

Scope						*Sequence*								
Activity	K	1	2	3	4	5	6	7	8	9	10	11	12
Gymnastics: Educational	o	o	o	o	o	o	o						
Olympic								o	o	o	o	o	o
Rhythmic								o	o	o	o	o	o
Dance: Folk		o	o	o	o	o	o	o	o	o	o	o	o
Round		o	o	o	o	o	o	o	o	o	o	o	o
Square					o	o	o	o	o	o	o	o	o
Ballroom								o	o	o	o	o	o
Modern								o	o	o	o	o	o
Jazz								o	o	o	o	o	o
Creative	o	o	o	o	o	o	o	o	o	o	o	o	o
Aquatics: Swimming	o	o	o	o	o	o	o	o	o	o	o	o	o
Water Games					o	o	o	o	o	o	o	o	o
Diving								o	o	o	o	o	o
Sailing or Canoeing								o	o	o	o	o	o
Lifesaving											o	o	o
Water Safety	o	o	o	o	o	o	o	o	o	o	o	o	o
Track and Field: Sprint	o	o	o	o	o	o	o	o	o	o	o	o	o
Hurdles	o	o	o	o	o	o	o	o	o	o	o	o	o
Relays	o	o	o	o	o	o	o	o	o	o	o	o	o
Mid-distance					o	o	o	o	o	o	o	o	o
Cross-country								o	o	o	o	o	o
High Jump	o	o	o	o	o	o	o	o	o	o	o	o	o
Long Jump	o	o	o	o	o	o	o	o	o	o	o	o	o
Pole Vault											o	o	o
Discus								o	o	o	o	o	o
Shotput								o	o	o	o	o	o

Figure 16.4 A scope and sequence chart.

Scope						Sequence							
Activity	K	1	2	3	4	5	6	7	8	9	10	11	12
Outdoor Pursuits: Camping					o	o	o	o	o	o	o	o	o
Backpacking											o	o	o
Skating (Ice or Roller)								o	o	o	o	o	o
Skiing								o	o	o	o	o	o
Hiking	o	o	o	o	o	o	o	o	o	o	o	o	o
Orienteering					o	o	o	o	o	o	o	o	o
Cycling					o	o	o	o	o	o	o	o	o
Survival Skills					o	o	o	o	o	o	o	o	o
Manipulative Skills with Objects	o	o	o	o	o	o	o						
Tag Games	o	o	o	o	o	o	o						
Relay Games	o	o	o	o	o	o	o						
Low Organization Games			o	o	o	o	o	o	o	o	o	o	o
Hand, Paddle, Racquet Games: Handball				o	o	o	o	o	o	o	o	o	o
Two or Four Square	o	o	o	o	o	o	o						
Tetherball	o	o	o	o	o	o	o						
Paddle Tennis					o	o	o						
Table Tennis					o	o	o	o	o	o	o	o	o
Badminton								o	o	o	o	o	o
Racquetball										o	o	o	o
Tennis										o	o	o	o
Target Games: Shuffleboard	o	o	o	o	o	o	o						
Archery								o	o	o	o	o	o
Golf										o	o	o	o
Bowling										o	o	o	o

Figure 16.4 *(continued)*

SCOPE AND SEQUENCE CHART

Scope	Sequence												
Activity	K	1	2	3	4	5	6	7	8	9	10	11	12
Team Games: Basketball					x	x	x	o	o	o	o	o	o
European Handball								o	o	o	o	o	o
Field Hockey								o	o	o	o	o	o
Floor Hockey				x	x	x	x	o	o	o	o	o	o
Football-type				x	x	x	x	o	o	o	o	o	o
Soccer				x	x	x	x	o	o	o	o	o	o
Softball				x	x	x	o	o	o	o	o	o	o
Speedball								o	o	o	o			
Volleyball				x	x	x	o	o	o	o	o	o	o
Combatives: Combative Games				o	o	o	o	o	o	o	o	o	o
Wrestling								o	o	o	o	o	o
Fitness: Testing	o	o	o	o	o	o	o	o	o	o	o	o	o
Circuit Training						o	o	o	o	o	o	o	o
Calisthenics						o	o	o	o	o	o	o	o
Isometrics								o	o	o	o	o	o
Weight Training								o	o	o	o	o	o
Aerobics	o	o	o	o	o	o	o	o	o	o	o	o	o
Fitness Knowledge	o	o	o	o	o	o	o	o	o	o	o	o	o
Leadership: Instructional Assistants	o	o	o	o	o	o	o	o	o	o	o	o	o
Officiating						o	o	o	o	o	o	o	o
Athletic Training											o	o	o

Lead-up activities are indicated with x's.

Figure 16.4 *(continued)*

Table 16.1 An example of skill order sequence in volleyball

Beginning	Intermediate	Advanced
I. Skills: Overhead pass Dig Underhand serve Teamwork	I. Review: Overhead pass Dig Underhand serve Teach: Overhand serve Spike Block Team strategy	I. Review: All skills Teach: Rolls Emphasize: Advanced strategy and team play
II. Concepts: Basic rules Scoring Basic strategy	II. Official rules Offensive strategy Defensive strategy	II. Official rules Officiating Offensive strategy Defensive strategy
III. Lead-up games to learn skills, brief introduction to official game	III. Official game, including tournament play	III. Official game, with advanced strategy and tournament play

example, in a middle school or junior high school, it would be more efficient to build a sequence of skills and knowledge in an activity through at least three levels of expectation.[5]

Table 16.1 shows an example of beginning, intermediate, and advanced levels of volleyball.

Graham and his associates suggested using a spiral curriculum in which the student progresses to a higher level of skill each time the activity is introduced.[6] An example of skill sequencing for throwing is shown in figure 6.1 on page 152. In the spiral curriculum, activities are presented several times in the curriculum, with students engaging in the activity at a higher level each time it is encountered.

Turkington and Carre suggested several techniques for sequencing instruction.[7]

1. Students select a specific physical education class from the school schedule based on interest and ability level.
2. Students are randomly assigned to physical education class periods, but select an activity at the appropriate level from the activities offered that period.
3. Students are randomly assigned to physical education class periods, but each teacher provides an opportunity for each student to work at the appropriate level in whatever activity is offered.
4. Students are randomly assigned to physical education classes with a teacher-selected activity. Several teachers teach the same activity and divide students into ability groupings.

Determining Sequence

Considerations for determining skill sequence or grade placement include student characteristics, the subject matter, and safety. The physical, mental, and social development of students, along with previous fitness, knowledge, and skill competencies, will be the primary considerations in placing activities into grade levels. Student interests should also be considered.

An attempt should be made to match the subject matter with student characteristics. In doing this, consider the complexity and amount of information to be presented and the difficulty of skills to be learned. Proper sequencing will result in safe, effective learning and successful student participation.

Curricular Scope and Sequences for Various School Levels

Determining the scope and sequence of the curriculum from preschool through college is a complex and significant task requiring a careful consideration of the correct emphasis at the different stages of child and adolescent development. Following is an overview of recommended program emphases at the different school levels. Because of the way activities are categorized into groups, a scope chart for one school system may or may not fit the curriculum for a different school system. Categories and percentages must be determined by following the steps presented earlier in the chapter.

Preschool and Kindergarten (Ages Three through Five)

The orientation of the program is toward the child as a unique individual. The curriculum emphasis should be on: (1) the development of perceptual-motor skills, such as balance, eye-hand coordination, and laterality; (2) the development of gross motor skills, such as running, walking, crawling, climbing, and pushing; and (3) the development of self-awareness and expression through movement. Activities should emphasize spontaneous, vigorous, large-muscle movement in an environment that provides freedom and opportunity for the children to explore and create their own movement patterns.

Primary Grades (Ages Six through Eight)

The orientation of the program continues to be on the individual child as a unique person. The curricular emphasis should be on: (1) perceptual-motor development; (2) the development of fundamental or basic movement patterns, such as skipping, walking backwards, and rolling; (3) the development of self-awareness and an awareness of what the body can do within its environment, including force, space, and time relationships; (4) an improvement in muscular strength, endurance, flexibility, and agility; (5) basic safety; (6) the development of simple concepts about physical activity; and (7) the development of positive attitudes toward activity.

Activities should concentrate on large-muscle and creative movement. Rhythmic activities (singing games, creative movement, and simple folk and aerobic dance movements), gymnastic skills (stunts, tumbling, self-testing activities, and apparatus), fundamental skills, low-organized games, and educational movement (throwing, catching, dribbling, striking) are often combined into a movement-exploration method of teaching that emphasizes the child's progress in relation to himself or herself rather than as compared with other students in the group. Aquatics should be included where facilities permit. Physical fitness should be maintained by participation in a variety of activities within the program. A possible scope chart for the primary grades is shown in figure 16.5.

Intermediate Grades (Ages Nine through Eleven)

The orientation at this level is to the individual child as a member of a group of peers. The curricular emphasis is on: (1) the development and refinement of specific motor skills, (2) the development of a high level of physical fitness, (3) the development of social skills through

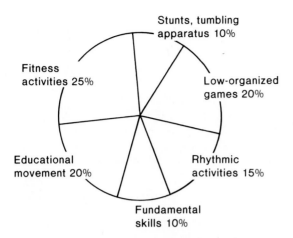

Figure 16.5 A possible scope chart for the primary grades.

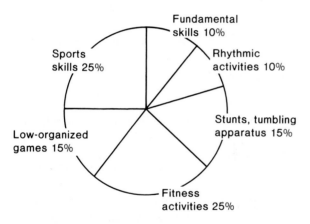

Figure 16.6 A possible scope chart for the intermediate grades.

more highly organized activities, (4) the development of self-esteem through successful participation in peer groups, and (5) the development of basic activity-related concepts such as rules and strategies in games.

Activities should include rhythmic activities, gymnastic skills, fundamental skills, simple games and relays, and sports lead-up games. Aquatics and outdoor adventure activities should also be provided as facilities and instructor expertise permit. Physical fitness should be an essential component of all activities within the program. A possible scope chart for this level is shown in figure 16.6.

Activities should be carefully planned to meet
the needs of the students at each age level.

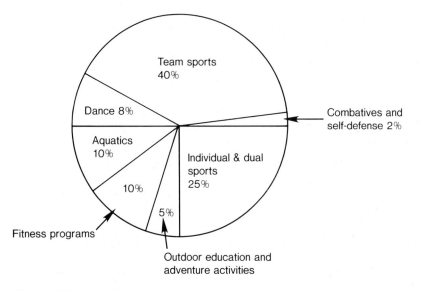

Figure 16.7 A possible scope chart for junior high school.

Middle and Junior High School

The orientation at this level is on the individual student as an emerging adult with a need for a broad exposure to the challenges facing the individual in society and strategies for coping with those challenges. The curricular emphasis is on: (1) the development and maintenance of physical fitness; (2) the development of a wide variety of specific activity skills; (3) a basic understanding and appreciation of a broad variety of activity and fitness concepts that will facilitate intelligent choices regarding out-of-school and future participation; (4) the development of self-awareness and self-confidence—physically, emotionally, and socially, and (5) the development of social skills leading to increased concern for others.

A variety of activities should be included so that students can make an intelligent selection of those they wish to pursue for future participation. In view of the physiological and emotional characteristics of these adolescents, activities should be selected in which students can feel successful and that progress toward higher levels of skill proficiency. A minimum level of competence should be achieved in activities so that students will be able to use the skills for personal enjoyment. Team sports are important because of the social interaction they provide. In addition, the curriculum should include individual and dual sports, dance, aquatics, and fitness activities. Combatives, self-defense, and adventure activities should also be provided. A possible scope chart for junior high school is shown in figure 16.7.

Senior High School

The orientation is on the individual as a capable, intelligent pursuer of activities appropriate for one's own needs and interests when given guidelines and options for doing so. The curricular emphasis is on: (1) the development of competencies in and appreciation for participation in selected lifetime activities; (2) the development of knowledge and understanding

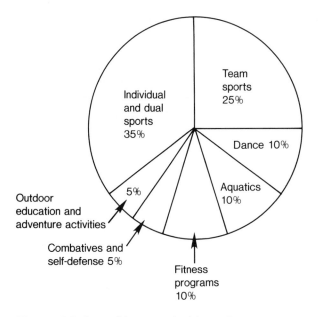

Figure 16.8 A possible scope chart for senior high school.

essential to provide insight and motivation for a lifetime of vigorous physical activity; (3) the development and maintenance of personal physical fitness; and (4) the development of self-confidence, individual initiative, and responsibility to self and society.

The activities should include a wide variety of activities from which to choose. The following should be provided: individual and dual sports, dance, aquatics, team sports, physical fitness, combatives and self-defense, outdoor pursuits, and opportunities for service and leadership development. A possible scope chart for senior high school is shown in figure 16.8.

College

The orientation is on the individual student's adaptation to current and future life conditions. The curricular emphasis is on preparing the student for a lifetime of vigorous physical activity by developing: (1) skills and interests in selected activities; (2) a desire for maintaining physical fitness; and (3) a knowledge and understanding of physical education and its contribution to the complete life.

A broad spectrum of activities should be included that encourage lifetime participation, with several levels of entry for beginning, intermediate, and advanced students. Most of the activities will be the same as those found at the high-school level, but with increased opportunities for developing advanced levels of skill. Physical fitness courses should emphasize the underlying concepts and develop the ability to design lifetime individualized fitness programs.

Questions and Suggested Activities

1. Review curriculum guides to determine what activities are normally taught at each grade level.
2. Obtain a list of activities included in the physical education programs at different schools. Evaluate their appropriateness for inclusion in the program based on the criteria discussed in this chapter.
3. You are hired to teach physical education and be the coach at a new high school in Alberta, Canada. The school has twelve seniors, thirty juniors, forty-seven sophomores, and thirty-eight freshmen. The nearest high school is eighty-five miles away. Due to the weather conditions, you are indoors for seven of the nine school months. The principal tells you to set up a program that will keep all the students active and interested during the school year. What will you do?
4. You have just been assigned as department chairperson of a school in your district. The school has been teaching the same sports year-in and year-out. The sports that have been taught are football and soccer in the fall, basketball and wrestling in the winter, and softball and track and field in the spring. What changes would you suggest to your faculty for broadening the scope of the curriculum?
5. Identify the procedures you would use to select the activities listed above that will meet the objectives or competencies you have identified.
6. Use the procedures identified in the above question to rank the activities you have listed in order of their contribution to the objectives you have identified for your program. Which activities did you eliminate? Why?
7. Visit several schools at the elementary and secondary levels. Discuss the curriculum at each level with teachers to determine what is being taught. Are students progressing in skill development?
8. Select an activity for a particular school level. List the concepts and skills to be covered and arrange them in order of difficulty from easiest to most difficult.

Suggested Readings

Bain, Linda L. "Socialization into the Role of Participant: Physical Education's Ultimate Goal." *Journal of Physical Education and Recreation* 51 (September 1980):48–50.

Benson, Joseph A. "An Alternative Direction for Middle School Physical Education." *The Physical Educator* 39 (May 1982):75–77.

Lewis, George T. "A Strategy for Reducing the Gap Between Theory and Practice in Physical Education." *The Physical Educator* 35 (October 1978):132–33.

Melograno, Vincent. "The Balanced Curriculum: Where Is It? What Is It?" *Journal of Physical Education, Recreation and Dance* 55 (August 1984):21–24, and (November–December 1984):70–72.

Munson, Coralee, and Elba Stafford. "Middle Schools: A Variety of Approaches to Physical Education." *Journal of Health, Physical Education and Recreation* 45 (February 1974):29–31.

Pangrazi, Robert, Paul Darst, Steve Fedorchek, and Ken Coyle. "The Needed Link—A Physical Education Curriculum Designed Exclusively for Junior High Students." *The Physical Educator* 39 (May 1982):71–74.

Ramsby, C. Ted, and Sam Reuschlein. "Use of Cooperative Education in Secondary School Physical Education." *The Physical Educator* 39 (May 1982):83–85.

Seefeldt, Vern. "Middle Schools: Issues and Future Directions in Physical Education." *Journal of Health, Physical Education and Recreation* 45 (February 1974):32–34.

Stafford, Elba. "Middle Schools: Status of Physical Education Programs." *Journal of Health, Physical Education and Recreation* 45 (February 1974):25–28.

Vickers, Joan N. "The Role of Expert Knowledge Structures in an Instructional Design Model for Physical Education." *Journal of Teaching in Physical Education* 2 (Spring 1983):17–32.

References

1. Helen M. Heitmann, "Curricular Organizational Patterns for Physical Education," paper presented to the NASPE Curriculum Academy Working Symposium, St. Louis, Missouri, November 4–6, 1978.
2. National Association for Sport and Physical Education, *Guidelines for Secondary School Physical Education* (Reston, Virginia: AAHPERD, 1986).
3. President's Council on Physical Fitness and Sports, *Youth Physical Fitness: Suggestions for School Programs* (Washington, D.C.: U.S. Government Printing Office, 1983), p. 76.
4. Vern Seefeldt, ed., *Physical Activity & Well-being* (Reston, Virginia: AAHPERD, 1986); and Vern Seefeldt and Paul Vogel, eds., *The Value of Physical Activity* (Reston, Virginia: AAHPERD, 1986).
5. Carl E. Willgoose, *The Curriculum in Physical Education,* 4th ed. (Englewood Cliffs, New Jersey: Prentice-Hall, 1984), pp. 147–50.
6. George Graham, Shirley Ann Holt/Hale, Tim McEwen, and Melissa Parker, *Children Moving: A Reflective Approach to Teaching Physical Education* (Palo Alto, California: Mayfield Publishing Company, 1980).
7. H. David Turkington and F. Alex Carre, "Individualized Physical Education: The British Columbia Approach," *Journal of Physical Education, Recreation and Dance* 56 (February 1985), pp. 36–38, 48.

17

Scheduling and Administrative Organization

Study Stimulators

1. Describe the following scheduling innovations:
   a. Time utilization patterns
   b. Student grouping patterns
   c. Staff utilization patterns
2. Describe each of the steps in the scheduling process.
3. Tell why scheduling is so difficult to do.

Scheduling is the process of adapting the physical education program, including classes and extracurricular activities, to the individual school and its community, staff, students, facilities, and time restraints. It is a time-consuming but essential job.

Physical educators should work with local school administrators to achieve the best possible scheduling arrangement for physical education within the master schedule. To do this, physical educators need to be aware of the many trends in scheduling. The introduction of the computer into education vastly increases scheduling possibilities based on student need and subject-matter requirements. Technology has provided loop films, videotape recording and playback, and programmed learning modules that can release the student from the teacher at certain times in the instructional program. Coeducational classes provide new possibilities for reorganizing staff and facilities creatively to meet student needs.

Scheduling Innovations in Education

Innovations in education are probably most obvious in the area of scheduling. They will be presented here briefly to help you become familiar with the various possibilities. For ease of discussion, they are broken into the following groups: (1) time utilization patterns, (2) student grouping patterns, and (3) staff utilization patterns.

Time Utilization Patterns

Time utilization patterns generally include traditional scheduling, modular scheduling, or flexible scheduling.

Traditional Scheduling

Traditional scheduling involves assigning a specified number of students to an instructor for a given time period each school day. Each subject is allowed an equal amount of time each day. One teacher teaches a class for the entire semester. A student schedule in a traditional program might look like this:

Daily Classes

8:00– 8:55	English
9:00– 9:55	math
10:00–10:55	industrial arts
11:00–11:55	social studies
12:00–12:55	lunch
1:00– 1:55	physical education
2:00– 2:55	science

A recent variation of the traditional schedule is an eight-period schedule, divided into a two-day cycle with periods 1 through 4 (A schedule) on the first day and periods 5 through 8 (B schedule) on the second day. A two-week cycle would look like this:

A   B   A   B   A   /   B   A   B   A   B

Some advantages attributed to the traditional schedule include ease of scheduling and time for establishing student-teacher rapport. Disadvantages include high teacher-student ratios; heterogeneous classification of students in classes; and time wasted repeating lectures, films, and other activities that could be handled better in one large group. Excellent programs of physical education have been and will continue to be conducted with traditional methods of scheduling.

Modular and Flexible Scheduling

Although modular and flexible scheduling are often used synonymously, some slight differences exist between the two. Both patterns involve variations in the number and length of class meetings for a given subject each week. Class sizes may also vary. In each case, the school day is divided into short periods of time called modules (or mods), usually ten to thirty minutes, with twenty minutes being the most popular. Modules can be combined in almost any arrangement to provide appropriate lengths of time for different instructional purposes. Classes may vary in length from day to day and from subject to subject. An example of a schedule for one day is shown in figure 17.1.

In modular scheduling, students and teachers have a different schedule each day for a five- or six-day cycle. Once established, the cycle remains the same throughout the term. The modular schedule is much like many college schedules in which some classes are one and one-half hours twice a week, some one hour three times a week, and others three hours once a week.

In flexible scheduling, instructors request class lengths and frequency of class meetings each week. A computer then revises the schedule, and at the beginning of each cycle, the teachers and students pick up their new schedules.

Advantages of modular or flexible scheduling are greater opportunities for large-group presentations, small-group practice sessions, and individualized instruction; increased student responsibility for learning; and increased use of facilities. Disadvantages include the difficulties of scheduling, the need for increased supervision of students, and the insecurity of some teachers and students within the constantly changing environment.

Time	Day 1	Day 2	Day 3	Day 4	Day 5
8:00	Industrial arts	Industrial arts	Industrial arts	Industrial arts	Typing
8:30	Math	Industrial arts	Math	Industrial arts	Typing
9:00	Math	Industrial arts	Math	Industrial arts	Typing
9:30	Independent study	Industrial arts	Social studies	Industrial arts	Math
10:00	Social studies	Social studies	Social studies	Social studies	Math
10:30	Social studies	Physical education	Social studies	Social studies	Physical education
11:00	Physical education	Physical education	Physical education	Independent study	Physical education
11:30	Physical education	Physical education	Physical education	English	Physical education
12:00	L	U	N	C	H
12:30	English	English	English	English	English
1:00	English	Math	English	Math	English
1:30	Chorus	Career education	Chorus	Independent study	Boys' chorus
2:00	Independent study	Independent study	English	Independent study	Independent study
2:30	Independent study	Independent study	Independent study	Independent study	Independent study

Figure 17.1 An example of a student modular or flexible schedule.

Year-Round Schools

Year-round schooling began as an economy move to save money for construction costs and has proved to be advantageous in other ways as well. Most students are under the 45–15 schedule, in which they attend classes for forty-five days and then have fifteen days off. Some advantages include savings in per-pupil expenditures because of increased use of facilities, opportunities for individualized instruction and tutoring, decreased absenteeism and vandalism, and increased motivation. Year-round schooling is currently more prevalent at the elementary and middle school levels because of the difficulties involved in scheduling athletics, choir, debate, and other performing and extra-class activities at the secondary level.

Student Grouping Patterns

Student grouping patterns are methods of grouping students into or within classes for instruction. They include homogeneous and heterogeneous groupings. Homogeneous grouping refers to putting students who are similar together in the same group. Heterogeneous grouping implies that students in the same group are different from one another. The assignment of students to classes and learning groups should be made based on individual learning needs. The ideal grouping arrangement would take into consideration all of the factors affecting learning—intelligence, capacity, maturity, knowledge, skill, fitness, interests, and so on. However, the inability to scientifically measure such factors has served as a deterrent to homogeneous grouping.

On the secondary level, the most feasible procedure is the organization of subgroups within the physical education program. For example, where a number of teaching stations and teachers are available, ability grouping may be accomplished by sending a large number of students to physical education at one time. The physical education staff then divides them into homogeneous groups according to objective skills test results or interests. Groupings should vary as activities change, since students have different interests and skill levels in different activities. Grouping persons with similar interests and skills enhances success and, therefore, the social and emotional development of students. The mainstreaming of handicapped students and coeducational programs have considerably increased the range of abilities in physical education classes. A wide range of student abilities can be frustrating to teachers and might result in recreational rather than instructional programs.

On the other hand, the beneficial aspects of heterogeneous grouping include highly skilled students acting as role models and peer tutors for their less-skilled classmates, thereby increasing motivation and social interaction. Instruction should be provided for students with physical limitations including those with inadequate skill development and the physically underdeveloped. Physical performance tests can be used to identify physically underdeveloped students and to appraise the motor aspects of physical fitness. Students should be placed in the least restrictive environment in which an appropriate learning situation can be provided.

Teaching styles can facilitate dealing with individual differences. Peer (reciprocal) tutoring, inclusion, task, and problem-solving activities are particularly useful when dealing with heterogeneous groups. Activities that emphasize cooperation rather than competition can also be effective with heterogeneous groups of students.

Students benefit from the additional help
provided by team teachers.

Staff Utilization Patterns
Alternative staff utilization patterns include team teaching and differentiated staffing.

Team Teaching
Team teaching is an arrangement in which two or more teachers share the responsibility for planning, instructing, and evaluating one or more class groups for improving instruction. It is a means of organizing personnel to provide a program more effective and efficient than each could provide separately. It capitalizes on the talents and interests of each team member. One common type of team teaching is *turn teaching* in which teachers divide a large group of students into smaller groups that rotate from teacher to teacher. Each teacher teaches a different topic, activity, skill level, or portion of the activity. An example of this is the American Red Cross progressive beginner course, in which ten stations are set up and children are moved from one station to another as each skill is learned in the crawl stroke progression.

A second variation of team teaching occurs when a master teacher, who is chosen on the basis of expertise, directs the entire activity and supporting teachers assist with materials, equipment, discipline, and individual help as shown in figure 17.2. Master teachers often change from activity to activity on the basis of their competencies in the various activities.

Some advantages of team teaching are the utilization of individual interests and competencies of teachers and the ability to group and regroup students in varying teacher-pupil ratios in terms of facilities, student abilities, or type of activity.

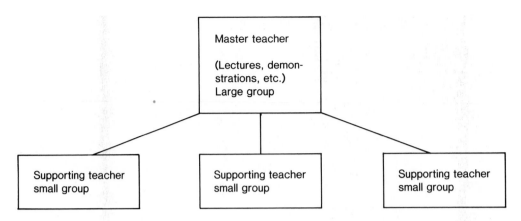

Figure 17.2 A possible team-teaching arrangement.

Differentiated Staffing

Differentiated staffing is a staffing pattern in which staff members play different roles in the educational process because of different skills, interests, and career goals. Although many different approaches have been developed, a team generally consists of a master teacher, two or more experienced or inexperienced teachers, student teachers, paraprofessional aids, and secretarial help as shown in table 17.1.

Many districts are implementing various methods of differentiated staffing under the name of career ladders. The Holmes,[1] Carnegie,[2] and other recent educational reports recommend various methods of differentiated staffing.

Paraprofessional aids can be undergraduate or graduate students, community volunteers, or paid part- or full-time staff. Each paraprofessional is assigned duties commensurate with his or her ability and training. In some states, however, paraprofessionals cannot assume the responsibility for instructing students.

Since differentiated staffing provides for a variety of salaries dependent on the differing responsibilities of staff, it rewards those who develop additional competencies in teaching, thereby allowing talented teachers to stay in teaching rather than move to the more lucrative areas of administration or business. At the same time, it discourages "endurance pay," which is based on years in teaching regardless of expertise or contribution.

Disadvantages are the modification of the entire school program needed to implement the system, the reduction of student contact hours by the most experienced teachers, and the threat of being replaced by lower-paid interns.

Scheduling Procedures

The following steps are suggested as a guide toward the achievement of a workable schedule:

Step 1. Identify the most desirable grouping pattern for class assignments.
Step 2. Determine class size.
Step 3. Determine appropriate time allotments for daily, weekly, and unit instruction.
Step 4. Determine staffing patterns and teacher loads, and assign teachers.
Step 5. Identify teaching stations and equipment.
Step 6. Develop a schedule.

Table 17.1 An example of differentiated staffing

Title	Degree	Responsibilities
Master teacher; twelve-month contract	M.S. or Ed.D	Design programs Evaluate instruction Supervise other staff Provide in-service opportunities Plan and implement budget Teach Serve as liaison with other school personnel and with the community
Teacher; ten-to-twelve-month contract (tenured)	B.S. or M.S.	Teach and evaluate students Meet with parents
Associate teacher or Intern; ten-month contract (nontenured)	B.S.	Teach in areas of specialty Give individual tutorial assistance
Student teachers	Degree in progress	Teach with supervision Provide individual tutorial help Prepare teaching materials
Paraprofessional aids	None	Set up and care for equipment Call roll Keep records Supervise class or locker room Reproduce, administer, and grade tests Lead warm-up exercises Referee games Assist with practice drills Prepare learning materials Set up and operate media hardware Prepare bulletin board displays

Step 1—Identify the Most Desirable Grouping Pattern for Class Assignments

Students can be grouped homogeneously or heterogeneously for physical education classes. In most schools, students are assigned to physical education classes according to the period they have free in the schedule. In middle and junior high schools, students are usually assigned by grade level in school. Senior high school students are often scheduled into classes in tenth through twelfth or eleventh and twelfth grade groupings, with freshmen or freshmen and sophomores scheduled by grade level. When students of more than one grade level are scheduled together into classes, assignments are more often based on student interest. Within these arrangements, teachers are generally free to rearrange students into homogeneous groups by students' interests, abilities, and needs.

Step 2—Determine Class Size

Identify the appropriate class size for each learning group, task, and instructional method. Class size may range from very large to only one student, depending on the aim of the instruction. For example, a film could be shown to a large group, skills need to be practiced

in smaller groups, and individual help or contract learning may be on a one-to-one basis. Team sport classes usually lend themselves to larger class sizes to accommodate competitive situations.

Ideally, class size should be consistent with the requirements of good instruction and safety in the activity to be taught. The class size should ensure that the student can receive adequate teacher assistance and individual practice or study. For example, a tennis unit with four courts available would best be limited to sixteen students if the course objectives are to be met. Since scheduling sixteen students in a traditional class each period would be impossible, a suitable alternative is to schedule a reasonable "average" class size (i.e., the same pupil-teacher ratio as for other subject areas in the school),[3] and then to adjust class sizes among the physical education teachers in terms of the units to be taught. The average class size for secondary school physical education can be determined by the following formula:

Average class size =

$$\frac{\text{Total students in school}}{\text{Number of teachers} \times \text{Number of periods/day taught by each teacher}}$$

The average class size recommended is usually thirty-five.[4] Adapted physical education classes should have no more than twenty. Physical education needs to demonstrate the sound instructional techniques that justify reasonable class sizes and avoid "throw-out-the-ball" type programs.

Step 3—Determine Appropriate Time Allotments for Daily, Weekly, and Unit Instruction

In 1986, the U.S. Senate passed a resolution supporting daily physical education for all students (see figure 2.1 on page 39). However, the individual states prescribe the minimum instructional time allotment per day or per week (either by law or by suggestion).

The American Alliance for Health, Physical Education, Recreation and Dance (AAHPERD),[5] the Society of State Directors of Health, Physical Education, and Recreation,[6] and the President's Council on Physical Fitness and Sports[7] recommend a daily instructional period for elementary school pupils of thirty minutes, or a total of 150 minutes per week. At the secondary school level, they recommend a minimum of one standard class period daily or equivalent class time.

One of the biggest areas of concern in curriculum planning is the failure to provide long enough periods of time in instructional units for students to develop the skill and knowledge needed for participation in a given activity. Units of two, three, and four weeks are inadequate for skill development with most skills. Research substantiates that the beginning-level learner often experiences frustration in so short a period of time. Bain indicates that the curriculum should provide "in-depth instruction in those activities of particular interest to students. Units of instruction need to be of sufficient length to develop levels of skill in the activity required to enjoy participation in it (usually a minimum of ten to twelve weeks)."[8] This is especially true when students participate in physical education classes for only two or three days per week.

Scope charts with percentages of times for each area can be translated into units by multiplying the percentage by the number of weeks (or periods) in the year to get the weekly (or period) allotment for each category. Time can be allotted to specific activities or to areas for student choice within the category time allotment. However, care should be taken to limit the number of activities so that each unit will have adequate time for learning to occur.

Cycle 1

1983
1986

	Orientation	Flag football	Tennis	Folk and square dance	Archery	Swimming	Closing and testing
Weeks	½	7	7	7	7	7	½

Sophomores

Cycle 2

1984

	Orientation	Basketball	Golf	Social dance	Gymnastics and apparatus	Swimming	Closing
Weeks	½	7	7	7	7	7	½

Juniors

Cycle 3

1985

	Orientation	Soccer	Track and field	Wrestling and self-defense	Weight training and jogging	Volleyball	Closing
Weeks	½	7	7	7	7	7	½

Seniors

Figure 17.3 An example of cycle scheduling.

Yearly schedules should include (1) the sequence and length of time of physical education activity units within a school year, (2) the sequence of physical education activities over a span of several years, and (3) the relationships of class instruction, intramurals, and extramurals. Two types of yearly plans for class instruction have emerged: the cycle and the modified cycle.

In the *cycle* plan, the course of study changes for the whole school each year, as shown in figure 17.3. This means that all students are participating in the same activity at the same time. Activities are usually different each year. The advantages of this system are (1) that teachers have to prepare for only one class at a time and equipment can be left set up all day; (2) that motivation is increased by reducing the repetition of activities; and (3) that the length of time for each activity is increased, thus facilitating greater learning.

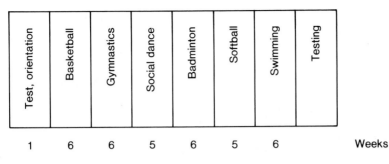

Test, orientation	Basketball	Gymnastics	Social dance	Badminton	Softball	Swimming	Testing
1	6	6	5	6	5	6	Weeks

Figure 17.4 An example of the block system.

The disadvantages of the cycle plan are that students fail to progress from lower to higher levels of skill in each activity and that teachers become bored when they teach the same activity all day long. This system works well in small schools where teachers and facilities are limited.

The second type of yearly plan is a *modified cycle,* in which all of the cycles are taught each year but to different classes. For example, the sophomores receive cycle 1; the juniors, cycle 2; and the seniors, cycle 3. Advantages are that progressions in specific activities can be built into the program and since teachers generally teach more than one grade level, boredom is reduced. A disadvantage may creep in, however, if too many activities are taught and the program is spread so thin that students fail to learn any activity well.

Two methods of scheduling activities within the yearly plans are the block system and the alternating system. The *block* system, which is shown in figure 17.4, involves instructional units in which the same activity is scheduled each class period for several consecutive weeks before another activity is scheduled. Blocks should usually be six or more weeks in length. Proponents argue that massed practice favors skill learning and retention and that facility scheduling is easier, especially in off-campus facilities. Opponents point out that many schools teach the same sports year after year. The greatest danger is in trying to compress activities into very short units.

A modification of the block is teaching two activities (one week each) and then allowing students to choose which activity to devote their time to for the remainder of the block or teaching one unit until some students have mastered the material and then starting a new activity. In both of these variations, a teacher would be teaching two activities simultaneously.

In the *alternating* system, students receive instruction in more than one activity each week. For example, on Mondays, Wednesdays, and Fridays, basketball is taught; on Tuesdays and Thursdays, instruction is in golf. A modification of the alternating system is the *finger* system, usually used at the elementary school level. In it a different activity is taught on each day of the week as shown in figure 17.5.

The major advantage of the alternating system is that variety increases motivation for some students. The disadvantages are the lack of continuity in each activity and the failure to provide long enough units for skill development.

When determining the length of time for lessons and units, consideration should be given to the age and ability of the students and the task to be learned. Younger students and beginners have shorter attention spans and fatigue sooner, so shorter lessons distributed daily

Days   M   T   W   T   F

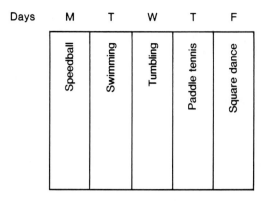

Figure 17.5 An example of the finger system.

are more appropriate. Older and more advanced students can benefit from longer periods of time occurring less often. Simple skills can be taught in a shorter length of time than more complex skills.

Units should be long enough so the objectives of the unit can be achieved, yet short enough to prevent boredom with the activity. Some units at the junior high school level may be devoted to learning basic skills so that students are introduced to activities from which they will be allowed to choose later on in the curriculum.

Step 4—Determine Staffing Patterns and Teacher Loads, and Assign Teachers

Analyze staffing requirements and existing staff strengths and assign teachers to classes on the basis of the competencies (skills and knowledge) needed to teach the activity. Teachers of potentially hazardous activities such as aquatics, gymnastics, skiing, and adventure education should have specialized training to the extent that they are recognized and certified by the national agencies associated with these activities. Special qualifications, including the ability to work with students at various skill levels, or with particular phases of the instructional program, and preferences about classes, times for planning, and related matters should also be considered.

Elementary School Staffing Patterns

Four methods of staffing physical education classes have emerged at the elementary school level. In the first, a physical education specialist is employed to teach all physical education classes in a given school. The advantage of this method is that the specialist has a knowledge of motor learning and teaching methods specific to physical education. The disadvantage is the cost of an additional salary for a specialist in each school.

In the second method, a rotating specialist assists classroom teachers by team teaching with them at least once a week and by providing leadership in program development. This system combines the specialist's knowledge of physical education with the classroom teacher's knowledge of the students. The specialist can present master lessons and in-service workshops and develop effective learning programs, but if the classroom teacher does not follow through, the program will be a once-a-week learning experience. Another problem is that specialists must often travel to several schools and may lack the time needed for effective planning as well as the rapport with teachers and students in each school.

The third method of staffing in elementary school programs is for classroom teachers to trade assignments. One teacher teaches physical education for another, who in turn teaches art or music for the first teacher. In this way, teachers can teach in their areas of preference and expertise. The disadvantage is that they may not get to know the students as well in other than their own classes.

The fourth method is for classroom teachers to teach physical education to their own classes. Classroom teachers are generally more familiar with the children because they see them in a variety of subject areas. They can also integrate physical education with other classroom subjects. The disadvantage of this method is the teachers' lack of knowledge in physical education, which usually results in the least-effective instruction in physical education.

Secondary School Staffing

Secondary schools may be staffed by "generalists" or "specialists" within the field of physical education. A specialist has an in-depth knowledge and skill in a few areas, such as aquatics or dance, and can usually assist learners to achieve higher levels of skill by anticipating and resolving potential learning problems with the subject matter. A generalist has an adequate level of skill in most curriculum offerings. The generalist sees the student in a variety of activities and can anticipate the learning needs of individual students.

Teacher Loads

Consideration of the teaching load is essential to high-quality instruction. At the elementary school level, AAHPERD recommends not more than nine thirty-minute periods per day. Time is needed between classes for preparation just as in secondary schools.[9] At the secondary school level, the recommendation is that class instruction per teacher not exceed five class periods or hours per day or more than two hundred students per teacher.[10]

Most physical education instructors are scheduled for after-school work such as coaching athletic teams, conducting intramural programs, coaching cheerleaders, and advising various clubs. Two prevalent methods used by school districts to compensate teachers for these extra duties include giving the teacher additional salary for the extra work (usually not commensurate with the responsibility and time involved) or reducing the teacher's instructional load. Many physical education authorities prefer a reduced instructional load on the basis that no person, no matter how well paid, can work productively and efficiently for an excessive number of hours.

Step 5—Identify Teaching Stations and Equipment

A teaching station is an area assigned to a teacher for a class, preferably with some physical or visual barrier between two classes to cushion sound from one to another. Distance may serve as a barrier between classes. The following method can be used to calculate the number of teaching stations and teachers needed for an *elementary school* physical education program:

1. Count the classes in the school (e.g., one class each of six grades + two kindergartens = eight classes)
2. Decide on the periods per week per pupil (five)
3. Decide on the number and length of each period (ten thirty-minute periods per day)

4. Teaching stations $= \dfrac{\text{Classes} \times \text{periods/week}}{\text{Number of periods/day} \times \text{days/week}} =$

$\dfrac{8 \times 5}{10 \times 5} = .8$, rounded off to 1.

One teacher and one teaching station are needed.

The method used to calculate the number of teaching stations and teachers needed for a *secondary school* physical education program is as follows:

1. Number of sections to be offered $= \dfrac{\text{Total number of students}}{\text{Class size}}$

2. Number of teaching stations (classes per period) =
$\dfrac{\text{Total number of students}}{\text{Class size} \times \text{number of periods/day}}$
Round off to the next higher whole number.

3. Number of teachers needed $= \dfrac{\text{Number of sections}}{\text{Number of periods taught/day/teacher}}$

An example is shown in the following chart.

Total Number Students	Class Size	Periods Per Day	Periods Per Week	Sections Offered	Teaching Stations	Teachers Needed
1,500	30	6	5	50	10	10.0
1,500	35	6	5	43	9	8.6
1,500	40	6	5	38	8	7.6

(Note: Each teacher teaches five periods. Fractions equal a part-time teacher in physical education.)

Program flexibility is increased when large numbers of students are assigned to a physical education program in which there are multiple teaching stations. Few schools possess all the facilities they need. Sometimes multipurpose rooms, hallways, auditorium stages, little theaters, and leftover classrooms can provide needed facilities for physical education.

Community resources should be used to supplement school facilities. For example, bowling alleys, skating rinks, swimming pools, ski resorts, equestrian facilities, and adventure courses can be rented by requesting students to pay a small fee. The use of community resources can help education bridge the gap between school and community. Transportation may cause legal problems, and should be discussed with the principal for approval before adopting any off-campus program. Elective programs can help to resolve problems with fees and transportation, since the class is not required of those who cannot afford the fees or transportation. Teachers should retain control of classes taught in off-campus facilities even when an outside professional is teaching. Courses offered before or after the normal school day can take advantage of facilities out of transportation range during regular class time.

Excellent programs take advantage of
community resources.

Equipment

For equipment, AAHPERD recommends:

> Facilities, supplies and equipment should be provided for the instructional program in
> accordance with the needs, interests and number of students to be served. . . .
> The physical education program should have enough equipment to provide each
> student with an opportunity to actively participate throughout the entire class period.[11]

Equipment can sometimes be built by industrial arts classes, parents, or teachers, or purchased by parent-teacher associations. Good teaching also requires provision of appropriate books, periodicals, media, and other teaching aids.

Step 6—Develop a Schedule

Work out a schedule that coordinates time, teachers, and facilities. Outdoor facility use depends on the weather, so plan outdoor units accordingly. A possible scheduling chart is shown in figure 17.6.

Although scheduling is essentially an administrative function, the success of the program is based on its implementation by the various faculty members involved. Teachers must avoid a curriculum that attempts to do a little bit of everything with nothing done well.

An Example of Scheduling

Given: Eight hundred students, four teachers, a six-period day, five days per week

Step 1

The committee decides to implement a required program in grade nine and a selective program (required, but with student selection of activities) in grades ten through twelve. The major advantage of the selective system is that students can develop expertise in activities in which they will participate throughout their adult lives. A second advantage is the ability to meet student needs and interests within a traditional school system.

Students will be assigned to a specific teacher who can diagnose strengths and weaknesses and provide assistance in making choices tailored to their individual needs. Because of the introduction to a variety of activities in earlier grades, students will more easily be able to make appropriate choices. They will be required to select a specified number of activities in each category during each school year, as shown in this example:

Class	Team Sports	Individual	Fitness	Aquatics
Sophomore	3	1	1	1
Junior	2	3	1	
Senior	1	4	1	

Another way to balance the program might be to require a certain number of specified activities to be taken anytime prior to graduation.

Organization and record-keeping duties for the selective program will be distributed among teachers by assigning a different teacher each period as the *master teacher*. The master teacher is responsible for all of the students for that period. This includes distributing class rolls, accumulating grades, and distributing and collecting lockers and towels.

On the first day of each unit, students all meet to select the next activity. Students will be told the activities and the teacher who is teaching each activity. Seniors choose first, then juniors, followed by sophomores. When the class enrollment for an activity is reached, the class will be closed for that block. A card will be issued to each student on which the activity is marked for that block. The cards will be collected and processed by hand or by computer. Roll sheets for each teacher are made from the cards. A sample record card is shown in figure 17.7.

Use of a selective program can also facilitate the adaptation of class sizes to the facilities available for instruction. Thus, instruction can be effective in areas such as tennis or racquetball where facilities are often limited.

One ninth-grade class will be offered each hour, and the remainder of the students will be scheduled into the period best fitting their schedules. All classes will be coeducational.

Step 2

The average class size is forty.

$$\frac{800 \text{ students}}{4 \text{ teachers} \times 5 \text{ periods/teacher}} = 40$$

Since approximately one-fourth of the students are ninth graders (two hundred), the number of sections of freshmen will be five: (200 / 40 = 5). The remainder of the sections will have

	BLOCK 1		BLOCK 2		BLOCK 3	
Jones Garcia Lungo Platero	Golf Tennis Flag football Prep.	g f g	Aerobic dance Volleyball Swimming (beg.) Prep.	b a e	Gymnastics Basketball Wrestling Prep.	b a h
Jones Garcia Platero Lungo	Social dance Prep. Flag football Archery/ Tennis	a g d,f	Cycling Prep. Soccer Fitness	i g b	Aerobic dance Prep. Swimming (beg.) Basketball	b e a
Jones Platero Lungo Garcia	Rec. dance Soccer Prep. Archery/ Tennis	a g d,f	Bowling Swimming (beg.) Prep. Fitness	i e b	Aerobic dance Volleyball Prep. Basketball	c b a
Jones Platero Lungo Garcia	Prep. Flag football Rec. dance Archery/ Tennis	 g a d,f	Prep. Tennis Swimming (beg.) Fitness	 f e b	Prep. Aerobic dance Volleyball Basketball	 c a b
Jones Garcia Lungo Platero	Rec. dance Tennis Soccer Badminton/ Bowling	a f g b	Bowling Aerobic dance Swimming (beg.) Fitness	i c e b	Jazz dance Outdoor pursuits Basketball Volleyball	c i a b
Jones Lungo Platero Garcia	Golf/Softball Archery Tennis Cycling	g d f i	Fitness Basketball Bowling Flag football	b a c g	Basketball Volleyball Swimming Aerobic dance	b a e c

a--Gym A	d--Track	g--Field
b--Gym B	e--Pool	h--Wrestling room
c--Dance studio	f--Tennis	i--Community facility

Figure 17.6 A possible schedule.

approximately forty students per section, but all tenth- through twelfth-grade students will be placed on one roll. The schedule begins to look like this:

	Ninth Graders		Tenth through Twelfth Graders	
Period 1	0 classes =	0	3 classes =	120
Period 2	1 class =	40	2 classes =	80
Period 3	1 class =	40	2 classes =	80
Period 4	1 class =	40	2 classes =	80
Period 5	1 class =	40	3 classes =	120
Period 6	1 class =	40	3 classes =	120
		200 +		600 = 800

BLOCK 4	BLOCK 5	BLOCK 6
Bowling i Badminton a Swimming (int.) e Prep.	Cycling i Soccer g Track and field d Prep.	Archery d Tennis f Softball g Prep.
Badminton b Prep. Swimming (int.) e Volleyball a	Gymnastics b Prep. Basketball a Golf/Softball g	Golf g Prep. Tennis f Badminton/ Bowling a
Gymnastics h Basketball a Prep. Volleyball b	Badminton b Swimming (int.) e Prep. Golf/Softball g	Cycling i Archery d Prep. Badminton/ Bowling a
Prep. Bowling i Basketball a Volleyball b	Prep. Softball g Swimming (int.) e Badminton/ Bowling a	Prep. Badminton a Track and field d Golf/Softball g
Modern dance c Volleyball a Swimming (int.) e Basketball b	Ballet c Badminton b Golf g Archery/ Tennis d,f	Social dance c Tennis f Track and field d Golf/Softball g
Volleyball b Wrestling h Swimming (int.) e Basketball a	Tennis/ Archery d,f Track and field d Badminton b Soccer g	Badminton/ Bowling a Softball m Tennis f Golf g

Ninth-grade ac-
tivities are
underlined.

Figure 17.6 (continued)

Once the students are scheduled by period, the tenth through twelfth graders will divide up into selected activities. Class enrollments may vary according to the activity.

Step 3

Our committee voted to have six six-week blocks per year. This fits in nicely with our thirty-six-week school year. This will give students enough time to learn the activities, but not so much time that they get bored. Ninth-grade units will vary according to subject matter. Team sport units will be longer, since students are expected to have basic skills before advancing to the selective program. Other units are introductory to give students a basis for choosing activities later on and are, therefore, shorter.

```
┌─────────────────────────────────────────────────────────────────────┐
│                                                                       │
│  Name _____    Sex: M/F Period _____     │
│                                                                       │
│    First Block          Second Block          Third Block             │
│    Tennis               Swimming              Wrestling               │
│    Soccer               Fitness               Volleyball              │
│    Flag football        Aerobic dance         Badminton               │
│    Social dance         Soccer                Jazz dance              │
│    Archery              Basketball            Basketball              │
│    Fencing              Volleyball            Aerobic dance           │
│                                               Swimming                 │
│                                                                       │
│    Fourth Block         Fifth Block           Sixth Block             │
│    Basketball           Fencing               Aerobic dance           │
│    Swimming             Fitness               Softball                │
│    Fencing              Swimming              Tennis                  │
│    Modern dance         Ballet                Track and field         │
│    Volleyball           Outdoor pursuits      Social dance            │
│    Gymnastics           Basketball            Modern dance            │
│    Wrestling            Track and field       Cycling                 │
│    Outdoor pursuits     Social dance          Golf                    │
│                                               Fitness                  │
│                                                                       │
└─────────────────────────────────────────────────────────────────────┘
```

Figure 17.7 A sample record card.

Step 4

Teachers will be assigned to classes based on expertise, personal preference, and special qualification. All swimming instructors are certified Red Cross Water Safety instructors. The archery teacher is a certified National Archery Association instructor. All teachers can teach team sports and will rotate teaching those classes. Teachers will also teach at least one ninth-grade class each. Competencies are as follows:

Teacher	Expertise
Mrs. Platero	WSI, individual sports
Mr. Lungo	WSI, bowling, wrestling, track
Miss Jones	gymnastics, dance, individual sports
Mr. Garcia	tennis, golf, badminton

Step 5

Teaching stations include the following:

Gym A	Tennis courts
Gym B	Bowling lanes (community)
Dance studio	Golf course (community)
Pool	Field space, for three classes
Balcony	Wrestling/gymnastics room
Weight room	

Equipment is available for each student in the class sizes taught.

Step 6

Our schedule might look like the one in figure 17.6. Staff schedules are such that teachers with the competencies to teach activities scheduled for certain periods are available to teach them during the periods in question.

Questions and Suggested Activities

1. Locate and read articles or books on flexible or modular scheduling, team teaching, or differentiated staffing. Visit a school using one of these innovations. Do you favor or oppose the innovation?
2. Describe how differentiated staffing could be used advantageously in a physical education program.
3. Read several articles or books on alternative or nontraditional schools. Could physical education be taught in such settings?
4. Joe teaches physical education at Savannah High School. In the past ten years, the school has used a traditional time utilization method. The teachers have convinced the administration to try a modular approach on a trial basis. Outline a presentation to the parent-teacher association on the advantages and disadvantages of the modular program in physical education.
5. The school day at Younowhere Junior High is divided into six fifty-minute periods with five minutes between classes. The students complain that they never have enough time to finish activities that they start in class, and the teachers are frustrated by not having enough time to cover the materials in a class period. What creative scheduling methods could be used to help the teachers and students have more flexibility with their time?
6. Mr. Smith teaches cycling in the fall. His largest class is twenty with several classes having only twelve to fifteen students. Because of his small classes, you have ninety students in flag football. Should his class be dropped for lack of interest?
7. You have been hired to teach physical education and be the coach at a new high school in Alberta, Canada. The school has twelve seniors, thirty juniors, forty-seven sophomores, and thirty-eight freshmen. The nearest high school is eighty-five miles away. Due to the weather conditions, you are indoors for seven of the nine school months. The principal tells you to set up a program that will keep all the students active and interested during the school year. What will you do?

Suggested Readings

American Association for Health, Physical Education and Recreation. *Organizational Patterns for Instruction in Physical Education.* Washington, D.C.: AAHPER, 1971.

Hausdorf, Walter F., and Julian R. Covell. "Expanding Programs with Limited Resources." *Journal of Physical Education and Recreation* 52 (February 1981):50–51.

Klappholz, Lowell A., ed. "Building and Maintaining Physical Fitness through Selectives." *Physical Education Newsletter* no. 124 (March 1981).

Klappholz, Lowell A., ed. "Tips on Utilizing Teacher Aides in Physical Education." *Physical Education Newsletter* no. 132 (December 1981).

Kneer, Marian E. "Ability Grouping in Physical Education." *Journal of Physical Education, Recreation and Dance* 53 (November–December 1982):10–13, 68.

Moore, C. A. "Handy Gadget Simplifies Scheduling." *Journal of Physical Education and Recreation* 48 (June 1977):18.

Sanders, Harry J. "Harford County's Selective Program." *Journal of Physical Education, Recreation and Dance* 52 (September 1981):66–67.

Sharp, George, and Karen Hanzawa. "Flexibility and Variety in Elective Physical Education." *Journal of Physical Education, Recreation and Dance* 52 (September 1981):90–91.

Spasoff, Thomas C. "Maintaining Student Interest in Elective Physical Education." *Journal of Physical Education and Recreation* 48 (June 1977):19.

Stein, Julian U. "Physical Education Selective Activities: Computerizing Choices." *Journal of Physical Education, Recreation and Dance* 58 (January 1987):64–66.

References

1. Holmes Group, *Tomorrow's Teachers: A Report of the Holmes Group* (East Lansing: The Holmes Group, Inc., 1986).

2. Task Force on Teaching as a Profession, *A Nation Prepared: Teachers for the 21st Century* (New York: Carnegie Forum on Education and the Economy, 1986).

3. National Association for Sport and Physical Education, *Guidelines for Middle School Physical Education and Guidelines for Secondary School Physical Education* (Reston, Virginia: AAHPERD, 1986).

4. President's Council on Physical Fitness and Sports, *Youth Physical Fitness: Suggestions for School Programs* (Washington, D.C.: U.S. Government Printing Office, 1983), p. 76.

5. National Association for Sport and Physical Education, *Essentials of a Quality Elementary School Physical Education Program, Guidelines for Middle School Physical Education,* and *Guidelines for Secondary School Physical Education* (Reston, Virginia: AAHPERD, 1981, 1986, 1986).

6. Society of State Directors of Health, Physical Education, and Recreation, *A Statement of Basic Beliefs About the School Programs in Health, Physical Education and Recreation* (Kensington, Maryland, 1985), p. 8.

7. President's Council on Physical Fitness and Sports, *Youth Physical Fitness: Suggestions for School Programs,* p. 76.

8. Linda L. Bain, "Socialization into the Role of Participant: Physical Education's Ultimate Goal," *Journal of Physical Education and Recreation* 51 (September 1980), pp. 48–50.

9. National Association for Sport and Physical Education, *Essentials of a Quality Elementary School Physical Education Program.*

10. President's Council on Physical Fitness and Sports, *Youth Physical Fitness: Suggestions for School Programs,* p. 76.

11. National Association for Sport and Physical Education, *Guidelines for Secondary School Physical Education.*

18

Evaluating and Revising the Instructional Program

Study Stimulators

1. Define formative and summative evaluation. What are the purposes of each?
2. Describe the process for evaluating a program in physical education.
3. Describe several kinds of data-gathering instruments and tell the advantages or disadvantages of each.

As resources diminish and academic standards receive renewed emphasis, physical education programs are cut or threatened. When programs do not produce observable results, parents and school administrators are not hesitant to use the time and resources in other ways. Rog proposed ten questions to use in measuring the vulnerability of physical education programs:

1. Does your building principal hold high expectation[s] of student achievement in physical education?
2. Do you hold high expectations of student achievement in your physical education classes?
3. Is your physical education program and its goals clearly understood by others in the school and community?
4. Are the students in your physical education program evaluated primarily on their skill performance?
5. Does your program have frequent monitoring of student progress using criterion-referenced testing based on identified objectives of student achievement?
6. Do students in all of your schools have physical education programs available to them at least 150 minutes per week?
7. Does your state require that physical education programs be made available to all students in order for your school to receive state aid?
8. Are all of your physical education classes being taught by physical education specialists or specific skill specialists?
9. If your school system's athletic program were cut, would your physical education program survive?
10. Do you have evaluation data on the achievements of your students in physical education which would demonstrate to your school committee the value of keeping your program?[1]

Evaluation is one of the ways available to provide information to the public about the success of physical education programs. If physical educators can describe results, they are more likely to get the support needed for effective physical education programs in the schools.

Several years ago, Cassidy proposed a curriculum merry-go-round on which one could climb at any point in the process of curriculum design and ride around until one's purposes were accomplished. The advantage of this concept is that curriculum design is then perceived as the continuous process it ought to be.[2] One of the most important steps in this process is the evaluation of whether the objectives of the program have been achieved. The evaluation provides new information with which to begin the cycle all over again. Objectives must be reevaluated to see if they are desirable within the constantly changing environment. Curriculum patterns and teaching-learning strategies must be revised so that student achievement more nearly approximates the objectives that have been established.

An extensive review of the entire curriculum is often impractical on a continuous basis. Therefore, departments of physical education should select a specific portion of the curriculum to evaluate each year. Through constant appraisal and revision, the curriculum can be gradually improved to meet the purposes for which it was established.

Program evaluation involves both measurement (quantitative) and judgment (qualitative) appraisals. For example, fitness tests can be used to measure physical fitness. Knowledge tests measure concept acquisition. Questionnaires and inventories assess the extent to which students have positive feelings about physical fitness. The scores are then evaluated to determine whether the students achieved the objectives specified in the program.

With the increased concern for accountability in education, evaluation provides empirical data for reporting to students, parents, administrators, boards of education, state departments of education, public media, accrediting agencies, and sponsors of educational research regarding the successes or failures of programs.

Since the curriculum is, in essence, a body of experiences that lie between the objectives and the teaching methods of a school, an outstanding curriculum can be developed only to discover that students fail to achieve the desired learning outcomes because of failure to translate curriculum development into methods of teaching. Evaluation can help determine whether the program works and how its effectiveness can be increased. The two major purposes of program evaluation are (1) to provide information for program improvement during the instructional process—formative evaluation, and (2) to assess the validity and effectiveness (or success) of the curriculum—summative evaluation. Both formative and summative evaluation provide feedback for improving physical education programs.

Formative Evaluation

Formative evaluation is feedback to teachers and program designers throughout the program or activity. It is used to evaluate whether students are achieving the instructional objectives and to revise the program *while* it is being developed. Since most programs are only 60 percent effective the first time, they can only be improved if evaluation points out what is working or is not working and where changes can be made to improve the program. For example, if students are having difficulty learning badminton skills, waiting until the results of the posttest reveal that the students did not learn would be useless. Self-testing activities conducted each day or week could expose the specific learning problems of students. Perhaps the difficulty is a lack of eye-hand coordination by the student or an instructional pace that is too fast. Once the cause is known, instruction can be redesigned to resolve the problems and increase student learning. Formative evaluation discloses whether the content is relevant or useless, practical or impractical. It reveals whether the instruction is too fast or too slow, too difficult or too easy. Student interest and motivation can also be checked.

Although formal evaluation techniques may be used, formative evaluation generally uses informal, criterion-referenced evaluation techniques, such as those reviewed in chapter 8, to point out strengths and weaknesses of individual lessons or short units. Informal evaluation techniques vary in quality depending on the skills of the person constructing the instruments. However, when carefully constructed, these instruments can be valid for evaluating local programs. They provide data that can help to determine the effectiveness of the instruction and the feasibility in terms of cost, teacher time, and student and teacher attitudes toward instruction. When teaching strategies are discovered to be impractical or ineffective, changes can be made at once to revise, add, or subtract lesson content or to change methods to achieve the desired results.

Summative Evaluation

Summative evaluation is evaluation of the final product. It is used to determine the overall effectiveness of a unit or program. It takes place at the end of a unit or program and provides feedback necessary to improve the program by revealing how well students have achieved specific objectives or whether a specific educational program is worth more than an alternative approach. Unexpected outcomes, such as negative attitudes produced or excessive costs, should also be analyzed. Although summative evaluation may use informal evaluation techniques, it tends to rely on formal evaluation methods, such as standardized tests and inventories that are norm-referenced. Often an external evaluator is called in to evaluate a program. Accreditation teams serve this function by evaluating the overall school program to determine whether the school curriculum meets the goals established by the accrediting association and the school. If the program is adequate, the school is accredited for a period of time, usually five to ten years.

Procedures for Program Evaluation

The following steps are suggested for evaluating curricular programs:

Step 1. Describe the program to be evaluated.
Step 2. Identify the purposes of the evaluation.
Step 3. Establish criteria for judging quality and making decisions.
Step 4. Describe the information needed to make the decisions.
Step 5. Obtain, record, and analyze information.
Step 6. Interpret data in terms of standards.
Step 7. Make decisions and formulate recommendations.

Following a description of all of the steps, an example of the process will be presented.

Step 1—Describe the Program to Be Evaluated

A description of the program helps to avoid overlooking aspects that should be evaluated. The description should include the following:

1. A statement of the philosophy behind the program.
2. The people involved—students, their families, faculty, and administrators.
3. Performance objectives—cognitive, psychomotor, and affective—including entry behaviors and intended and unintended outcomes arranged in a hierarchy from general to specific.
4. Subject matter content.
5. Instructional elements such as scheduling patterns, learning activities, student-student and student-teacher interactions, use of media, motivation, and evaluation and grading techniques.
6. Facilities and equipment.
7. Costs.
8. Administrative conditions.

Periodic program evaluation helps
administrators, teachers, and students to reach
program goals.

Step 2—Identify the Purposes of the Evaluation

Identify areas of concern about the program and anticipate decisions that will need to be made by asking questions such as: Are goals and objectives appropriate?, Are students achieving the objectives?, What problems exist?, What are the reactions of various audiences to the program?, and What unanticipated outcomes are there? Decisions that might need to be made could include adopting a new program, discontinuing a program, changing student grouping patterns, increasing the budget, changing the staff, using community facilities, or implementing different instructional strategies. Possible alternatives should be identified in each instance.

Persons responsible for making the decisions should be identified. These may include students, teachers, administrators, or the board of education. A date should be specified for making the decisions, along with policies within which the evaluation must occur.

Step 3—Establish Criteria for Judging Quality and Making Decisions

Two types of standards can be used for judging the quality of programs—absolute standards and relative standards. *Absolute standards* are those established by personal or professional judgment. These criteria are established in the same way that performance objectives are created.

The problem with using absolute standards lies in selecting the level that is indicative of success in the program. Standards can be derived from criteria achieved in similar programs in other schools, in former programs in the same schools, or by guesstimates by administrators, teachers, parents, students, and community members working together.

Preassessment scores of current students provide guidelines for developing standards. When students fail to achieve the standards, the program can be revised to produce the desired achievement, the objectives can be changed, or the program can be thrown out and a new one created.

Relative standards are those reflected by various alternative programs. In other words, the program is compared with other programs to determine which one has the best outcomes. National norms for fitness and skill are published by the American Alliance for Health, Physical Education, Recreation and Dance. These norms tell how students compare with other students nationally. Locally constructed norms can be used to evaluate how students compare with students previously completing the programs.

Standards that should be considered in all evaluation studies include (1) validity—the extent to which the evaluation provides the information it is supposed to provide; (2) reliability—the degree to which the data collected would be the same on different trials of the test; (3) objectivity—the extent to which the data are the same regardless of who administers the test; (4) cost effectiveness in terms of the time, energy, and money invested; and (5) timeliness—in time to make a decision.

Step 4—Describe the Information Needed to Make the Decisions

Prior to evaluating student achievement of program objectives, the objectives should be analyzed to determine whether they are worthwhile and will produce the intended outcomes. Empirical analysis should include information from other groups or specialists to determine the objectives considered to be essential. However, agreement with the objectives or methods used in other curricula does not mean that the objectives are worthwhile. In chapter 15, a list of guidelines for evaluating curricular goals and objectives was included (see page 507). Evaluators should review these guidelines to determine whether the goals and objectives need revision.

Information on achievement of the objectives can be gained from students, teachers, parents, and outside observers. Both formal and informal evaluation techniques can be used. Some commonly used techniques include (1) controlled research, (2) structured external evaluation, (3) standardized tests, (4) teacher-constructed evaluation techniques, (5) subjective judgment, and (6) informal analysis.

Controlled research involves the use of randomization to assign control and experimental groups, and then the construction and testing of hypotheses. In this way the program results can be compared with a different or preceding program or the posttest results can be compared with the pretest results to see if they are statistically significant.

Structured external evaluation was one of the earliest methods used for evaluating the total physical education program. The first scorecard was developed by William Ralph LaPorte in the 1930s. Since that time a number of scorecards have been developed by various state departments of education. They are often used by evaluation teams from accrediting associations. *The Assessment Guide for Secondary School Physical Education Programs,*[3] created by AAHPERD, provides a set of standards for evaluating the physical education program in the areas of (1) administration, (2) the instructional program, (3) the intramural program, and (4) the athletic program. A sample of the criteria in the areas of administration and the instructional program is shown in figures 18.1 and 18.2.

Criteria	Response (Circle)			Notes
	Instruc-tional Pro-gram	Intramural Program	Athletic Program	
16. Written department policies are available concerning standard operating procedures involving:				
A. Uniforms, lockers, towels, locks, lost and found.	Yes No	Yes No	Yes No	
B. Emergencies and location of first aid supplies.	Yes No	Yes No	Yes No	
C. Facility problems or hazardous conditions.	Yes No	Yes No	Yes No	
D. Teacher evaluation.	Yes No	Yes No	Yes No	
E. Absences, excuses and attendance.	Yes No	Yes No	Yes No	
F. Legal responsibilities of personnel.	Yes No	Yes No	Yes No	
G. Scheduling.	Yes No	Yes No	Yes No	
H. Facility supervision.	Yes No	Yes No	Yes No	
I. Purchase of equipment and supplies.	Yes No	Yes No	Yes No	
J. Maintenance and management of facilities, equipment, and supplies.	Yes No	Yes No	Yes No	
17. Secretarial and support personnel are available to meet program needs.	Yes No	Yes No	Yes No	
18. Allotment of time and facilities for all programs are equitable and meet program needs.	Yes	Yes No	Yes No	
19. Number of available indoor and outdoor teaching stations meet all programs needs. They:				
A. Are conducive to quality instruction.	Yes No	Yes No	Yes No	
B. Are adequate to handle peak hour loads.	Yes No	Yes No	Yes No	
C. Contain adequate office space.	Yes No	Yes No	Yes No	
20. Community facilities are utilized to avoid costly duplication, to expand program offerings, and to make use of superior facilities.	Yes No	Yes No	Yes No	

Figure 18.1 A sample of the evaluative criteria for administration.
Source: From the Assessment Guide for Secondary School Physical Education Programs, developed by the National Association for Sport and Physical Education of the American Alliance for Health, Physical Education, Recreation and Dance, 1977.

Standardized tests have been developed by AAHPERD to evaluate psychomotor skills and physical fitness. Several problems exist when using standardized tests for program evaluation. One is the selection of inappropriate instruments for the program being evaluated. Tests must have content validity; that is, they must test the objectives specified in the program. Since most standardized tests are directed toward lower-level cognitive and psychomotor skills, other instruments may be needed in addition to standardized tests if the program is to be evaluated fairly. Validity, reliability, and appropriate norms for the group to be tested must also be assessed prior to adoption. Teaching to the test is another common problem with standardized tests. When evaluating a new program, the teacher should never see the test before it is given. With regard to standardized tests, Worthen and Sanders pointed out that "in all the history of evaluation in education it has proven exceedingly difficult to demonstrate the superiority of *any* procedure in terms of test performance."[4]

Teacher-constructed evaluation techniques were discussed in detail in chapter 8. In addition to student achievement, they can be used to disclose such items as student participation in extra-class or leisure-time activities, attendance, tardiness, discipline, dropouts, awards, assignments completed, library books checked out on a given subject, and choices made in selective activities. Parent and community involvement through attendance at parent-teacher association meetings, back-to-school nights, parent-teacher conferences, board of education meetings, and school visits can also be recorded.

Subjective judgment by teachers, administrators, parents, students, and community members can provide valuable information. Annual interviews or meetings to discuss goals and objectives, assess achievement of objectives, and predict needs and problems should deal with such questions as: Are goals and objectives appropriate?, Should anything be added to or deleted from the program?, Why or why not?, What is not going well?, and How could it be improved?

Informal analysis by teachers and administrators should assess the effects of the program on faculty and staff. Adverse effects can result in physical and emotional deterioration resulting in a less-effective program for teachers and students. Chapter 14 discussed a number of techniques for informal analysis.

In any evaluation program, a variety of evaluation instruments should be used. Failure to do so can result in a biased interpretation of program effectiveness. The selection of each technique should be based on the objective and the group to be evaluated.

A schedule or work plan should be formulated to keep the evaluation proceeding on time. The plan should include a description of who will do what, with what instruments, using what population sample, and by what date. A suggested format appears in figure 18.3.

Step 5—Obtain, Record, and Analyze Information

Obtain and record the information specified in step 4, including such areas as student experiences, student gains and losses, unintended outcomes, and program costs in terms of time, money, and other resources. Determine a format for classifying and recording the information. Analyze the information by using appropriate statistical methods.

Criteria	Response (Circle)		Notes
6. Instructional program areas that are designed to meet objectives focusing on the organization, development, and refinement of skillful movement include the following units in *prescribed elective* courses:			
A. Sport, dance, and exercise activities offered at progressive skill levels.	Yes	No	
B. Students grouped for instruction according to grade level or ability.	Yes	No	
C. Formal instruction (coeducational whenever possible) provided in team sports, individual and dual sports, aquatics, dance, and lifetime / leisure time activities.	Yes	No	
D. Adapted program that is an integral part of the regular program that provides instruction compatible with physical disabilities (goal to successfully integrate students into regular classes).	Yes	No	
7. Instructional program areas that are designed to meet objectives focusing on knowledge of the basic theoretical concepts of human movement behavior as they relate to sport, dance, and exercise include the following areas in *required* theoretical course work and / or cognitive unit objectives within activity coursework:			

Figure 18.2 A sample of the evaluative criteria for instruction.
Source: From the Assessment Guide for Secondary School Physical Education Programs, developed by the National Association for Sport and Physical Education of the American Alliance for Health, Physical Education, Recreation and Dance, 1977.

Step 6—Interpret Data in Terms of Standards

The purpose of program evaluation is to determine the worth or value of the program. Thus, after all of the data have been collected, a judgment must be made as to whether the program has been successful. As in the other phases of curriculum design, many people should be involved in making these judgments, including students, parents, faculty, administrators, the board of education, and community and professional leaders. Conclusions should be drawn concerning the effectiveness of the program and the progress of the students involved.

Criteria	Response (Circle)		Notes
A. Biomechanical and kinesiological concepts.	Yes	No	
B. Psychological concepts related to motor performance.	Yes	No	
C. Exercise physiology.	Yes	No	
D. Philosophy of human movement.	Yes	No	
E. Sports, medicine / athletic injury.	Yes	No	
F. Historical development of sport, dance, and exercise forms.	Yes	No	
G. Rules and strategies of sport forms.	Yes	No	
H. Motor learning principles.	Yes	No	
I. Motor development.	Yes	No	
J. Sport sociology.	Yes	No	
K. Humanities and sciences subject matter relationships to movement forms.	Yes	No	
8. Written course outlines are followed by instructors and available to students. These outlines include:	Yes	No	
A. Rationale for inclusion in instructional program	Yes	No	
B. Behavioral objectives.	Yes	No	
C. Prescribed evaluation procedures based upon stated behavioral objectives.	Yes	No	
D. Sequential skill progressions.	Yes	No	

Figure 18.2 *(continued)*

Two questions should be answered in the interpretation of the information collected: (1) were the objectives achieved? and (2) was there a logical connection between entry behaviors, learning activities, and desired outcomes? Achievement of the program objectives is determined by comparing the data with the standards specified in step 3.

To interpret the relationship among entry behaviors, learning activities, and desired outcomes, the pretest and posttest data must be analyzed. If students score high on the pretest, whether the learning was or was not effective is not known, since students already could achieve the standard for proficiency. This indicates that the instruction was unnecessary and can be eliminated. When students score low on the pretest and low on the posttest, the instruction was inadequate. It needs to be revised or an alternative program adopted. Low pretest scores accompanied by high posttest scores demonstrate that sound instruction has occurred and students are learning as planned.

OBJECTIVE	ACTION BY	METHOD	POPULATION	DEADLINE
1. Pass five mastery tests.	Mr. Ames	Mastery tests.	All students in the school.	January and June
2. Complete contract.	Miss Jones	Count of completed contracts, analyze uncompleted contracts for problem areas.	All students in the school.	January and June
3. Take fitness appraisal.	Mr. Sims	Fitness appraisals recorded on class record sheets.	All students in the school.	January and June
4. Increase fitness.	Mrs. Garcia	Computer analysis of fitness appraisals.	All students in the school.	January and June
5. Positive feelings of students toward the unit; toward fitness.	Mr. Platt	Inventory of student feelings.	Random samples of 100 students.	January and June
6. Comparison with current program.	Mrs. Garcia	Computer analysis of fitness appraisals.	Test random sample of students in regular program and statistics from Step 4.	January and June

Figure 18.3 An evaluation work plan for Fitness for Life.

Step 7—Make Decisions and Formulate Recommendations

Once the data have been evaluated, decisions must be made concerning whether to retain or discontinue the program, adopt a new program, or change various facets of the program such as the budget, staff, facilities, or instructional strategies. The persons identified in step 2 as those responsible for the program must evaluate the data in terms of the criteria listed in step 3. If the standards have all been met, the decision will be easy—to retain the program as is. If none of the standards have been met, the program will undoubtedly be replaced. However, when some of the criteria have been met and others have not been met, decisions will need to be made concerning whether the objectives are valid, whether the program can be changed in some way to achieve the objectives, or whether to adopt a new approach.

Recommendations provide a basis for administrative action such as further implementation, modification, or revision. The results of the evaluation with accompanying recommendations should be communicated to the faculty, administration, students, parents, and other interested community members.

An Example of Program Evaluation

Step 1

The Fitness for Life program is an individualized program designed to help students write and apply their own fitness programs during school and throughout their lives. Students contract with an instructor to do the following:

1. Pass five mastery tests on (a) how to write programs for cardiovascular endurance, weight control, and strength and flexibility; (b) how to measure cardiovascular endurance, strength, and flexibility; and (c) fitness concepts.
2. Complete a nine-week contract for cardiovascular endurance according to the specifications on the course handout.
3. Take a fitness appraisal before and after completion of the contract and show progress.

Students complete the contract on their own time and check with the instructor for assistance as needed or to take mastery checks. A fourth outcome desired in the program is that students will have positive feelings about fitness activities and about the unit.

Step 2

Some concerns about the Fitness for Life program included:

1. Did students actually increase physical fitness during the nine-week contract?
2. Did students have positive feelings about physical fitness and about the unit?
3. Were the instructors satisfied with the program?
4. Was the new program better than the existing program?
5. What administrative problems existed?

Step 3

The following absolute standards in the form of objectives were selected at the beginning of the Fitness for Life program. Eighty percent of the students will

1. Achieve good or excellent on the 1.5-mile run.
2. Achieve a percent body fat of 20 percent or below for girls and 15 percent or below for boys.
3. Obtain a score of 80 percent or better on all five tests of fitness concepts.
4. Complete a fitness contract for nine weeks at the contracted level of exercise.
5. Have positive attitudes toward participation in physical fitness activities.

Objective 2 was later revised due to the incidence of anorexia among girls.

For relative standards, a comparison with the AAHPERD norms revealed that students in the Fitness for Life program were below the national average prior to participating in the program.

Step 4

The following measures were considered to provide the information needed to evaluate the program. The Cooper 1.5-mile run and percent fat measured by skinfold calipers were used to evaluate fitness. Students in Fitness for Life classes were tested and found to improve significantly more in physical fitness than students who were enrolled in regular physical education classes at the same time. Therefore, it was concluded that the Fitness for Life program was better than the regular program for achieving fitness.

An attitude inventory was constructed to assess attitudes toward fitness. A questionnaire measured continued participation in fitness programs several years later. Another questionnaire requested feedback on preferred methods of instruction.

An external evaluation team was invited to assess the effectiveness of the program. They interviewed teachers, obtained questionnaire responses from students, and interviewed students who dropped out of the class.

Students in the fitness program were required to log in each time they requested individual help. Dates on which tests were taken were recorded. A contract was required on which students recorded their weekly participation in selected activities.

A continuous dialog between teachers and students in the program helped to provide feedback on what was or was not working. Teachers met weekly to discuss the progress of the program.

In the Fitness for Life program, teachers were frustrated by the procrastination of students in taking written tests. Students also complained about the need to log in each week.

Step 5

The faculty decided that a coordinator would be assigned to take responsibility for getting each portion of the data collected. The final evaluation would take place by the entire faculty one month prior to the end of the school year.

Figure 18.4 shows the results of the data collected during the evaluation of the Fitness for Life program. Only a sample of the total students participating in the program took the pretest on the mastery tests and completed the attitude inventory and instructional methods questionnaires. This was done by randomly assigning a few students in each class to each section of the inventory or questionnaire rather than by having all students complete all of the sections. This conserved student time and resulted in students being more attentive than they might have been to a long evaluation instrument. Since the fitness tests were used as a basis for the individual contracts, almost all of the students took them. The number of students achieving the 80 percent criterion on the mastery tests and the percentage achieving mastery are shown in the figure.

Step 6

An analysis of the data in figure 18.4 revealed that 80 percent of the students achieved the three unit objectives with one exception. In test 3, only 75 percent of the students achieved mastery. Data from the questionnaire revealed that some of the test questions were confusing to students. An analysis of the test showed that questions 6 and 10 were consistently missed. Perhaps the solution is better instruction in the area of planning the weight-control program. Another solution might be to clarify the questions on the test.

The data showed that students in the Fitness for Life program achieved significant increases in all four components of physical fitness. The differences in fitness between students in the regular program and the fitness program were also significant. Students appeared to be positive toward the instruction and toward physical fitness, with the exceptions noted. Some revisions in the program could resolve these problems.

Step 7

In the Fitness for Life program, the following recommendations were made:

1. The program should be retained.
2. The grading system should be changed to an "A-pass-fail" system in which students can get an "A" grade or a "pass grade" (B or C equivalent) or a "fail" to provide more challenge to students to excel.
3. The test and the handout on weight control should be rewritten.
4. Students in the "good" or above categories must log in only every other week. This will provide more time for students needing help.
5. Test deadlines for each test will be posted to reduce procrastination.
6. A meeting should be held in December to evaluate the changes.

Questions and Suggested Activities

1. Obtain copies of various scorecards and evaluate them. Choose the one best suited to your program level and evaluate a program of your choice. Discuss the findings with your class.
2. Using a curriculum for a junior or senior high school in your area, establish a plan for continuous and periodic evaluation of the curriculum in terms of the achievement of stated curricular objectives.

OBJECTIVE	PRETEST DATA		
	Number of Students	Number Achieving Criterion	%
1. Pass five mastery tests.			
Test 1	20	2	10%
Test 2	20	1	5%
Test 3	20	0	0%
Test 4	20	1	5%
Test 5	20	3	15%
Total			
2. Complete contract.			
3. Take fitness appraisals.	200	200	100%

4. Increase fitness.	PRETEST MEAN Girls	PRETEST MEAN Boys
percent fat.	19.43	15.10
1.5-mile run.	14:38	13:24

5. Positive feelings of students.	FAVORABLE	UNFAVORABLE
Orientation session.	TH TH I	IIII
Mastery tests.	TH TH II	III
Contract.	TH TH	IIII
Fitness appraisals.	TH TH IIII	I
Grading system.	IIII	TH TH I
Instructor assistance.	TH I	IIII
Toward fitness.	TH TH TH	

6. Comparison with current program.	CURRENT PROGRAM		
	Number of Students	Number Achieving Criterion	%
Concept tests.	800	111	13.9
percent fat.	800	500	62.5
1.5-mile run.	800	436	54.5

Figure 18.4 A recording form for the Fitness for Life program data.

| POSTTEST DATA | | | CRITERION MET | |
Number of Students	Number Achieving Criterion	%	Yes	No
200	180	90.0%	X	
200	185	92.5%	X	
200	150	75.0%		X
200	190	95.0%	X	
200	195	97.5%	X	
200	165	82.5%	X	
200	192	96.0%	X	

POSTTEST MEAN Girls	POSTTEST MEAN Boys	SIGNIFICANT Yes	No
16.7	12.28	X	
13:27	12:11	X	

COMMENTS

Great!

Too easy, except Test 3, which had confusing questions.

Want ABC system.
Too busy to talk, too many log-ins.

| FITNESS FOR LIFE PROGRAM | | | CRITERION MET | |
Number of Students	Number Achieving Criterion	%	Yes	No
200	150	75	X	
200	152	76	X	
200	181	90.5	X	

Figure 18.4 *(continued)*

3. Evaluate the curriculum in several junior or senior high schools. Compare the programs in terms of such factors as seasonal content, variety of activities, preparation for adult life, and elective or required programs.
4. Define accountability. Why is evaluation essential to achieve accountability in physical education?
5. Some parents are concerned that their children are losing interest in the school's physical education program and are not acquiring any useful skills. They feel that the physical education classes are simply "glorified play times," that balls are merely handed out each period, and that students participate in the same activities from year to year. If you were head of the department, how would you improve the program?
6. You have been assigned to evaluate the physical education program at your school because the students scored below the fiftieth percentile on national fitness and knowledge test scores. What will you do?

Suggested Readings

Aten, Rosemary. "Formative and Summative Evaluation in the Instructional Process." *Journal of Physical Education and Recreation* 51 (September 1980):68–69.
Bennett, John P. "Quality Control of Secondary Physical Education Programs." In Ronald P. Carlson, ed., *IDEAS II for Secondary School Physical Education*. Reston, Virginia: American Alliance for Health, Physical Education, Recreation and Dance, 1984, pp. 26–28.
Heitmann, Helen. "Curriculum Evaluation." *Journal of Physical Education and Recreation* 49 (March 1978):36–37.
Swanson, James R. "Developing and Implementing Objectives in Physical Education." *Journal of Physical Education and Recreation* 50 (March 1979):68–69.

References

1. James A. Rog, "Will (Should) Your Physical Education Program Survive?" *NASPE News* 6 (October 1982).
2. Rosalind Cassidy, *Curriculum Development in Physical Education* (New York: Harper & Row, Publishers, 1954).
3. American Alliance for Health, Physical Education, and Recreation, *Assessment Guide for Secondary School Physical Education Programs* (Washington, D.C.: AAHPER, 1977).
4. Blaine R. Worthen and James R. Sanders, *Educational Evaluation: Theory and Practice* (Worthington, Ohio: Charles A. Jones Publishing Company, 1973).

Epilogue

Fable of the Activity Curriculum
or
The Difference in Individual Differencies

By Dr. G. H. Reavis,
Asst. Supt. Cincinnati Public Schools

Illustrations by W. A. Ownbey,
Supervisor, State College, Cape Girardeau

Once upon a time, the animals decided they must do something heroic to meet the problems of "a new world," so they organized a school. They adopted an activity curriculum consisting of running, climbing, swimming, and flying and, to make it easier to administer, all the animals took all the subjects.

The duck was excellent in swimming, better in fact than his instructor, and made passing grades in flying, but he was very poor in running. Since he was slow in running, he had to stay after school and also drop swimming to practice running. This was kept up until his web feet were badly worn and he was only average in swimming. But average was acceptable in school, so nobody worried about that except the duck.

The rabbit started at the top of the class in running, but had a nervous breakdown because of so much makeup work in swimming.

The squirrel was excellent in climbing until he developed frustration in the flying class where his teacher made him start from the ground-up instead of from the tree-top-down. He also developed charlie horses from overexertion and then got C in climbing and D in running.

The eagle was a problem child and was disciplined severely. In the climbing class he beat all the others to the top of the tree, but insisted on using his own way to get there.

At the end of the year, an abnormal eel that could swim exceedingly well, and also run, climb, and fly a little had the highest average and was valedictorian.

The prairie dogs stayed out of school and fought the tax levy because the administration would not add digging and burrowing to the curriculum. They apprenticed their child to a badger and later joined the groundhogs and gophers to start a successful private school.

Does this fable have a moral?

*Before revised curriculum
*After revised curriculum

Photo Credits